Social Research Methods

Edward Bell
Alan Bryman
Steven Kleinknecht

Sixth Canadian Edition

OXFORD
UNIVERSITY PRESS

OXFORD
UNIVERSITY PRESS

Oxford University Press is a department of the University of Oxford.
It furthers the University's objective of excellence in research, scholarship,
and education by publishing worldwide. Oxford is a registered trade mark of
Oxford University Press in the UK and in certain other countries.

Published in Canada by
Oxford University Press
8 Sampson Mews, Suite 204,
Don Mills, Ontario M3C 0H5 Canada

www.oupcanada.com

First Edition published in 2005

Library and Archives Canada Cataloguing in Publication

Title: Social research methods / Edward Bell, Alan Bryman, Steven Kleinknecht.
Names: Bryman, Alan, author. | Bell, Edward, 1955- author. | Kleinknecht, Steven W. (Steven William), author.
Description: Sixth Canadian edition. | Includes bibliographical references and index.
Identifiers: Canadiana (print) 20210320427 | Canadiana (ebook) 20210320451 | ISBN 9780190165789 (spiral bound) | ISBN 9780190165796 (softcover) | ISBN 9780190165772 (EPUB)
Subjects: LCSH: Social sciences—Research—Textbooks. | LCSH: Social sciences—Methodology—Textbooks. | LCGFT: Textbooks.
Classification: LCC H62 .B78 2022 | DDC 300.72—dc23

Cover image: Alexander Spatari/Getty Images
Cover design: Laurie McGregor
Interior design: Laurie McGregor

Oxford University Press is committed to our environment.
This book is printed on Forest Stewardship Council® certified paper
and comes from responsible sources.

FSC
www.fsc.org
MIX
Paper from
responsible sources
FSC® C103567

Printed in Canada

1 2 3 4 — 23 22 21 20

Dedication

To my teachers, who continue to shape me.
Edward Bell

To my mom and dad, for always being in the stands cheering me on.
Steven Kleinknecht

Brief Contents

Contents

Guide to the Book

Who would benefit from reading this book?

This book was written for undergraduate students taking a research methods course in social science disciplines such as sociology, criminology, social work, politics, history, and education. It covers a wide range of methods, approaches to research, and ways of carrying out data analysis.

Research methods are not tied to any particular nation, and the principles underlying them transcend national boundaries. The same is true of this book. The original text by Alan Bryman was written with the needs of UK post-secondary students in mind, but it was widely adopted in Europe and Canada as well. Feedback from adopters and reviewers suggested that the book could be made even more useful for Canadian instructors and students through the addition of Canadian and, more broadly, North American examples, sources, and research studies. Edward Bell's adaptations have preserved the qualities that contributed to the book's initial success—its clarity, comprehensiveness, and presentation of social research methods in an international context—while expanding on those strengths by incorporating elements that are integral to North American, and especially Canadian, courses in the social sciences. *Social Research Methods* has always offered comprehensive coverage of qualitative, quantitative, and mixed methods. The sixth Canadian edition offers more in-depth coverage of qualitative research through the contributions and expertise of its new co-author, Steven Kleinknecht.

Structure of the book

In social research, an important distinction is made between the quantitative and qualitative approaches to inquiry. This distinction lies behind the structure of the book and the way it approaches issues and methods. Since both perspectives are crucial in developing an understanding of social phenomena, both receive full-blown treatment and analysis.

The Preface that begins this new edition has two purposes: to provide an entrée into the world of social research methods, and to make the case that research methods are something to get excited about. The rest of the text is divided into four parts, which are followed by an appendix.

PART I comprises two scene-setting chapters that deal with basic ideas about the nature of social research, and a chapter on research ethics. It also includes an appendix that outlines the stages of research.

- Chapter 1 examines issues such as the nature of the relationship between theory and research and the degree to which a natural science approach is an appropriate framework for the study of society. It's here that the distinction between quantitative and qualitative research is first encountered: the two are presented as different *research orientations* with different ways of conceptualizing how people and society should be studied. This chapter also includes a discussion of *research questions*: what they are, why they are important, and how they are formulated.
- Chapter 2 introduces the idea of a *research design*, along with the basic frameworks within which social research is carried out (experimental, cross-sectional, longitudinal, and case study designs).
- Chapter 3 deals with research ethics for all types of social research.
- The Appendix to Part I outlines the stages of research in an ideal scenario (with the caveat that real-world research is never quite so

straightforward). These first three chapters and appendix provide the basic building blocks for the rest of the book.

PART II consists of five chapters concerned with quantitative research.

- Chapter 4 presents the fundamentals of quantitative research and provides the context for later chapters.
- Chapter 5 focuses on structured interviewing and the design of questionnaires. It delves into how to write questions for both questionnaires and interviews. It also discusses how to compose a self-completion questionnaire, using data from already-completed questionnaires and interviews.
- Chapter 6 covers structured observation, a method developed for the systematic observation of behaviour.
- Chapter 7 deals with quantitative sampling: how to select a sample and the considerations involved in assessing what can be inferred from different kinds of samples.
- Chapter 8 presents a range of basic non-technical tools for quantitative data analysis. The emphasis is on how to choose a method of analysis and how to interpret findings. In order to keep the focus on methodological concepts and interpretations, formulae are not discussed.

PART III presents five chapters on aspects of qualitative research.

- Chapter 9 plays the same role for Part III that Chapter 3 does for Part II. It provides an overview of the nature of qualitative research and hence the context for the other chapters in this part.
- Chapter 10 discusses ethnography and participant observation. The two terms are often used interchangeably to refer to the immersion of the researcher in a social setting, a technique that is the source of some of the best-known studies in social research.
- Chapter 11 examines the kinds of interview that qualitative researchers conduct (typically semi-structured or unstructured) and focus groups, in which groups of individuals are interviewed on a specific topic.
- Chapter 12 applies qualitative approaches to content analysis, a method used in the study of "documents" ranging from books, letters, and newspapers to movies, chat lines, and television shows. It also examines two ways to analyze language: conversation analysis and discourse analysis.
- Chapter 13 explores some approaches to the analysis of qualitative data, including grounded theory and coding.

PART IV moves beyond the quantitative/qualitative division to explore what the two approaches have in common, how they may complement each other, and how they may be combined in the same research project.

- Chapter 14 proposes that the distinction between quantitative and qualitative research may be less fixed than is sometimes supposed, and presents some ways in which they can be combined to produce multi-strategy research.
- Chapter 15 offers advice on conducting a research project, taking readers through the main steps involved, and provides guidance on writing up research, an often-neglected area in the teaching of the research process.

Finally, the *Appendix* presents an easy-to-access resource for successful research.

- The appendix explains how to use **IBM SPSS Statistics software** (SPSS) and **QSR NVivo** software to perform, respectively, the quantitative data analyses described in Chapter 8 and the qualitative data analyses discussed in Chapter 13.

Special Features of the Book

Several features make this sixth Canadian edition especially helpful to students:

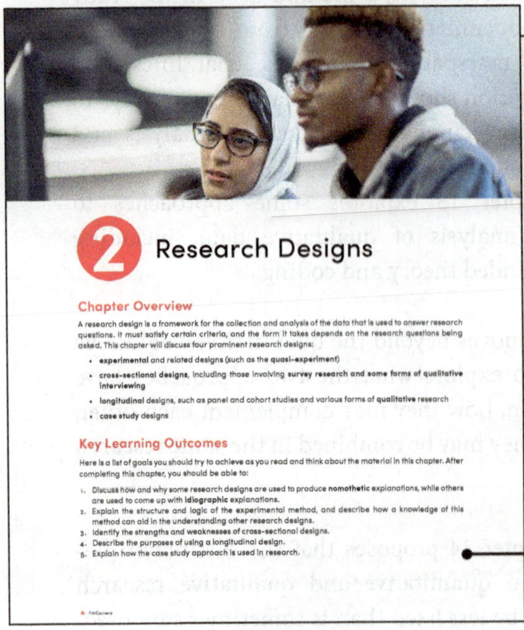

2 Research Designs

Chapter Overview

A research design is a framework for the collection and analysis of the data that is used to answer research questions. It must satisfy certain criteria, and the form it takes depends on the research questions being asked. This chapter will discuss four prominent research designs:

- **experimental** and related designs (such as the **quasi-experiment**)
- **cross-sectional designs**, including those involving **survey research and some forms of qualitative interviewing**
- **longitudinal** designs, such as panel and cohort studies and various forms of **qualitative research**
- **case study designs**

Key Learning Outcomes

Here is a list of goals you should try to achieve as you read and think about the material in this chapter. After completing this chapter, you should be able to:

1. Discuss how and why some research designs are used to produce **nomothetic** explanations, while others are used to come up with **idiographic** explanations.
2. Explain the structure and logic of the experimental method, and describe how a knowledge of this method can aid in the understanding other research designs.
3. Identify the strengths and weaknesses of cross-sectional designs.
4. Describe the purposes of using a longitudinal design.
5. Explain how the case study approach is used in research.

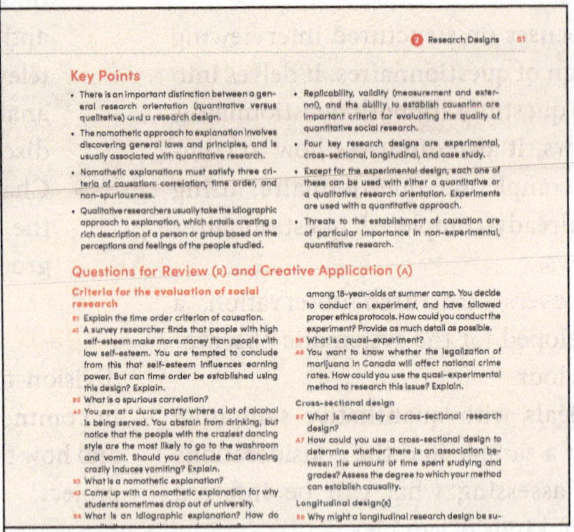

2 Research Designs 61

Key Points

- There is an important distinction between a general research orientation (quantitative versus qualitative) and a research design.
- The nomothetic approach to explanation involves discovering general laws and principles, and is usually associated with quantitative research.
- Nomothetic explanations must satisfy three criteria of causation: correlation, time order, and non-spuriousness.
- Qualitative researchers usually take the idiographic approach to explanation, which entails creating a rich description of a person or group based on the perceptions and feelings of the people studied.
- Replicability, validity (measurement and external), and the ability to establish causation are important criteria for evaluating the quality of quantitative social research.
- Four key research designs are experimental, cross-sectional, longitudinal, and case study.
- Except for the experimental design, each one of these can be used with either a quantitative or a qualitative research orientation. Experiments are used with a quantitative approach.
- Threats to the establishment of causation are of particular importance in non-experimental, quantitative research.

Questions for Review (R) and Creative Application (A)

Criteria for the evaluation of social research

R1 Explain the time order criterion of causation.

A1 A survey researcher finds that people with high self-esteem make more money than people with low self-esteem. You are tempted to conclude from this that self-esteem influences earning power. But can time order be established using this design? Explain.

R2 What is a spurious correlation?

A2 You are at a dance party where a lot of alcohol is being served. You abstain from drinking, but notice that the people with the craziest dancing style are the most likely to go to the washroom and vomit. Should you conclude that dancing crazily induces vomiting? Explain.

R3 What is a nomothetic explanation?

A3 Come up with a nomothetic explanation for why students sometimes drop out of university.

R4 What is an idiographic explanation? How do ...

among 18-year-olds at summer camp. You decide to conduct an experiment, and have followed proper ethics protocols. How could you conduct the experiment? Provide as much detail as possible.

R5 What is a quasi-experiment?

A6 You want to know whether the legalization of marijuana in Canada will affect national crime rates. How could you use the quasi-experimental method to research this issue? Explain.

Cross-sectional design

R7 What is meant by a cross-sectional research design?

A7 How could you use a cross-sectional design to determine whether there is an association between the amount of time spent studying and grades? Assess the degree to which your method can establish causality.

Longitudinal design(s)

R8 Why might a longitudinal research design be su-...

NEW! List of numbered learning outcomes. Learning outcomes aligned with main headings and end-of-chapter key points to guide students' reading.

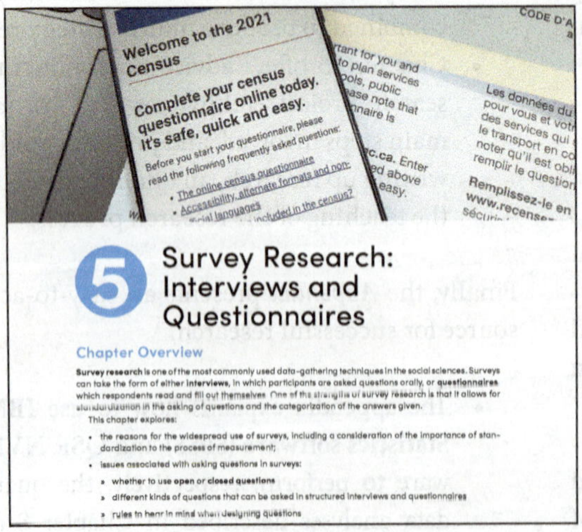

5 Survey Research: Interviews and Questionnaires

Chapter Overview

Survey research is one of the most commonly used data-gathering techniques in the social sciences. Surveys can take the form of either **interviews**, in which participants are asked questions orally, or **questionnaires**, which respondents read and fill out themselves. One of the strengths of survey research is that it allows for standardization in the asking of questions and the categorization of the answers given.

This chapter explores:

- the reasons for the widespread use of surveys, including a consideration of the importance of standardization to the process of measurement;
- issues associated with asking questions in surveys:
  - whether to use **open** or **closed questions**
  - different kinds of questions that can be asked in structured interviews and questionnaires
  - rules to bear in mind when designing questions

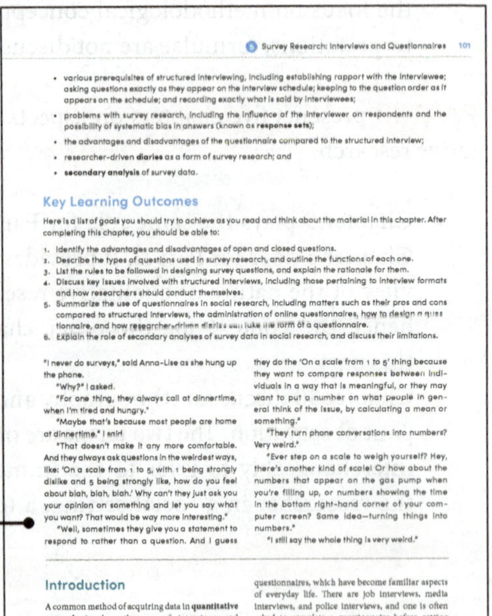

5 Survey Research: Interviews and Questionnaires 101

- various prerequisites of structured interviewing, including establishing rapport with the interviewee; asking questions exactly as they appear on the interview schedule; keeping to the question order as it appears on the schedule; and recording exactly what is said by interviewees;
- problems with survey research, including the influence of the interviewer on respondents and the possibility of systematic bias in answers (known as **response sets**);
- the advantages and disadvantages of the questionnaire compared to the structured interview;
- researcher-driven **diaries** as a form of survey research; and
- **secondary analysis** of survey data.

Key Learning Outcomes

Here is a list of goals you should try to achieve as you read and think about the material in this chapter. After completing this chapter, you should be able to:

1. Identify the advantages and disadvantages of open and closed questions.
2. Describe the types of questions used in survey research, and outline the functions of each one.
3. List the rules to be followed in designing survey questions, and explain the rationale for them.
4. Discuss key issues involved with structured interviews, including those pertaining to interview formats and how researchers should conduct themselves.
5. Summarize the use of questionnaires in social research, including matters such as their pros and cons compared to structured interviews, the administration of online questionnaires, how to design a questionnaire, and how researcher-driven diaries can take the form of a questionnaire.
6. Explain the role of secondary analyses of survey data in social research, and discuss their limitations.

"I never do surveys," said Anna-Lise as she hung up the phone.

"Why?" I asked.

"For one thing, they always call at dinnertime, when I'm tired and hungry."

"Maybe that's because most people are home at dinnertime," I said.

"That doesn't make it any more comfortable. And they always ask questions in the weirdest ways, like: 'On a scale from 1 to 5, with 1 being strongly dislike and 5 being strongly like, how do you feel about blah, blah, blah.' Why can't they just ask you your opinion on something and let you say what you want? That would be way more interesting."

"Well, sometimes they give you a statement to respond to rather than a question. And I guess they do the 'On a scale from 1 to 5' thing because they want to compare responses between individuals in a way that is meaningful, or they may want to put a number on what people in general think of the issue, by calculating a mean or something."

"They turn phone conversations into numbers? Very weird."

"Ever step on a scale to weigh yourself? Hey, there's another kind of scale! Or how about the numbers that appear on the gas pump when you're filling up, or numbers showing the time in the bottom right-hand corner of your computer screen? Same idea—turning things into numbers."

"I still say the whole thing is very weird."

Introduction

A common method of acquiring data in **quantitative research** involves the use of interviews and questionnaires, which have become familiar aspects of everyday life. There are job interviews, media interviews, and police interviews, and one is often asked to complete a questionnaire before getting

Chapter-opening vignettes. At the beginning of each chapter, the topics to be addressed are introduced in an informal and provocative way to help students grasp the real-world relevance of key issues.

10 Ethnography and Participant Observation

Chapter Overview

Ethnography and **participant observation** require extended involvement in the activities of the people under study. This chapter explores:

- the problems of gaining access to different settings and ways of overcoming them;
- whether **covert research** is practicable and acceptable;
- the role of **key informants**;
- the different roles that ethnographers can assume in the course of their fieldwork;
- the function of **field notes** and the forms they can take;
- the role of visual materials in ethnography; and,
- bringing an ethnographic study to an end.

Key Learning Outcomes

Here is a list of goals you should try to achieve as you read and think about the material in this chapter. After completing this chapter, you should be able to:

1. Describe the methodological and ethical issues involved in gaining and maintaining access to field sites and participants, conducting overt and covert research in open and closed research settings, and working with key informants.
2. Identify the different roles ethnographers can take on while collecting data, including *complete participant*, *participant-as-observer*, *observer-as-participant*, and *complete observer*, as well as how active or passive they will be in these roles.
3. Discuss strategies for writing different types of field notes and analytic memos while conducting ethnographic research.

Chapter overviews. Each chapter opener includes an overview that serves as a route map, alerting readers to what they can expect to learn.

Examples. In general, undergraduates lack both the time and the resources required to carry out a full-scale research project. This makes it all the more important to include examples of how professional researchers have done their work and the lessons they have learned in the process. Most of the major topics discussed in the text are illustrated with several examples from published research, both in-text and in numbered boxes throughout each chapter.

Oral History Consent Form

Consent to Participate in an oral history interview being conducted by students enrolled in [course] at ____________ University. This is to state that I agree to participate in a program of research being conducted by 45 students under the supervision of Dr. ________ of the Department of ________________ University ([telephone number], email: [email address]).

PURPOSE: I have been informed that the purpose of the project is to explore the history of those parts of the _________ area that have been demolished or otherwise "lost" to us due to urban change. Students have formed into teams of 3 to 5 and will be exploring specific sites of memory such as ________, stories of immigration and displacement, and the former [site]. We will be working closely with [organization] and the [organization] which are developing exhibitions on the [site] and [topic] in [year], based in part on these student projects.

PROCEDURES: The interview will be conducted at participants' homes, at facilities provided by ________ University or at another appropriate place. Interviewers will record participants' life stories using video, or audio depending on the preference of the interviewee. Participants can choose to discuss any aspect of their lives and they may refuse to answer any questions. Interviews normally take about 1.5 hours, but participants may take as long as they would like and are free to stop at any time.

RISKS AND BENEFITS: Describing difficult experiences can be upsetting and emotionally difficult. As the student projects will contribute to two exhibitions, as well as a website, with your permission, your story will be heard.

CONDITIONS OF PARTICIPATION: Please review the following conditions and options with the interviewer. Feel free to ask questions if they appear unclear.

___I understand that I am free to withdraw my consent at any time during the interview and discontinue from that point forward.

In terms of **identification and reproduction of my interview**, I agree to (please choose one):

___**Open public access**: My identity may be revealed in any publications or presentations that may result from this interview.

___I agree to the possible broadcasting and reproduction of sound and images of my interview by any method and in any media by participants of this research project. I consent that my interview, or portions of it, be made available on the Internet through Web pages and/or online databases of the project.

___I agree that transcripts and/or recordings of my interview will be stored at a local archive for long-term ... ing it at the Centre for

... e instructor; others will ... erviewee. Once the stu- ... destroyed by the student

... the student project only.

... use in their assignment ... to let future researchers

... MENT. I FREELY AND

it comes to informed consent because researchers want the participants to behave naturally and authentically. If participants were to be fully informed regarding the purpose of the experiment, it would be difficult to avoid the **reactive effects** that occur when people know they are being observed. For this reason, experiments usually involve some deception.

For example, Milgram (1963) designed a series of studies in an effort to understand the brutality that occurred in Nazi concentration camps during the Second World War. In particular, he wanted to know how a person could be led to cause extreme harm to an innocent human being, and whether being ordered to do so by an authority figure had anything to do with it. Milgram devised a laboratory experiment in which a supposedly reputable researcher (the authority figure) asked participants to act as "teachers" who would punish "learners" by giving them increasingly severe electric shocks whenever they gave incorrect answers to questions. Neither the shocks nor the howls of pain coming from the "learners" were real, but the "teachers"/participants did not know this. Some of them were further disadvantaged in that they could not see the "learners": they could only hear the shrieks of pain supposedly coming from them.

In all instances, the "teachers" were told that the shocks were part of the study and would not cause any permanent harm, despite the increasingly shrill ... everyday people were willing to inflict serious harm on innocent others if ordered to do so by an authority figure—a finding that may have important implications for the understanding of human atrocities and ultimately their prevention, although that interpretation of his findings has come into question (Perry, 2012). Nonetheless, the fact remains that the study involved a number of ethically questionable elements. For one thing, the "teachers"/participants themselves suffered at least short-term harm; most felt very uncomfortable administering what they believed to be powerful shocks, and while the experiment was in progress many participants came to doubt the experimenter's claim that the "learners" were not suffering any serious harm. Some were apparently traumatized by the experience, and expressed serious misgivings about taking part in the study decades later (Perry, 2012).

Another issue was the deception that the participants experienced: they were told that the experiment was investigating how people learn, not how people come to commit cruel acts, and they were led to believe that the shocks were real. Thus to the extent that the participants were not fully informed about the purpose of the experiment, they were lied to, although once it was over they were *debriefed* (given previously withheld information about the study) in that they were informed by the "learner" that the shocks had not really been as painful as he

Boxes. Special feature boxes provide in-depth examples of how the various research methods discussed in the book have been used in real research situations. The boxes also list the advantages and disadvantages of a particular method, summarize important points, discuss methodological controversies, and offer practical advice.

Box 2.3 | Evaluation research

Adam Melnyk/Shutterstock

feasible or ethical to randomly assign research participants to the two groups, such studies are usually quasi-experimental. For instance, data gathered from people before a change may be compared with data acquired after; the "before" people become the control group, the "after" people the experimental group. This approach has the added advantage that the two groups are

Box 4.2 | A multiple-indicator measure of another concept

In Hay's (2014) study of secularization (see Box 1.3), religious pluralism was measured using a single, five-point Likert item that formed part of an extensive survey of Canadians' value systems. However, secularization (the dependent variable in Hay's analysis) was measured with several different indicators in order to tap into different dimensions of the concept. One dimension, religiosity, was measured by averaging the responses to three 10-point items indicating the importance respondents placed on: (a) "believing in God;" (b) "obeying God, doing what he wishes;" and (c) "relating to God in a personal way." A second dimension, relating to frequency of religious attendance, was measured with the question, "Do you currently attend church temple or mosque?" Respondents who answered "yes" were then asked: "How often?" The response choices were: "once a week or more" (given a code of 5 after reverse-coding), "monthly" (4), "every few months" (3), "once or twice a year" (2), and "never" (1). A third dimension, concerned with the participants' belief in the religion of their parents, had the response categories "believe all of it" (4), "-believe most of it but not all" (3), "believe some parts but disbelieve others" (2), and "don't believe any of it" (1).

Methods in Motion | Applications to Canadian Society

Why are some Canadians politically conservative and others liberal?

Bell, Aitken Schermer, & Vernon (2009) did a behavioural genetic study of political attitudes and behaviours that addressed the issue of why some Canadians tend to have conservative or right-leaning attitudes, while others are more liberal or left oriented in their political views. The methodology used in the study (the details of which go beyond the scope of this book) was a kind of natural experiment comparing monozygotic (identical) twins, who are essentially genetic clones of each other, with dizygotic (fraternal) twins, who share only about 50 per cent of the genetic material that varies between human beings. The researchers examined how similar the identical twins were in their political attitudes, and compared that with how similar the fraternal twins were on that score. If identical twins are more similar on the characteristic under examination than the fraternal twins, that would indicate that genetic factors or other biological influences have some impact on the trait in question. The results of the study showed that the identical twins were in fact much more similar in their political attitudes than the fraternal twins, which suggests that genetic factors play a role in the formation of these attitudes. The study also found evidence that social factors (such as educational influences and media effects) affected political orientations, although it did not test for specific social influences. Taken as a whole, the results indicate that "nature" and "nurture" *interact* in the formation of political attitudes.

These sorts of studies are uncommon in sociology, political science, or anthropology, although they are conducted more frequently in psychology and the health sciences. They have far-reaching implications for the social sciences, in particular for disciplines in which biological influences are seldom examined. The standard paradigm in the latter fields of study assumes that some combination of socialization, culture, and situational factors can explain the origins of most attitudes and behaviours. Researchers using behaviour genetic methods, on the other hand, acknowledge that those sorts of influences are crucial, but argue that a more complete understanding of the human condition can be achieved by considering both social and biological factors.

If behaviour genetics and other approaches that consider both social and biological influences were to be more widely adopted in the social sciences, that could have a major impact on the theoretical perspectives that are developed and rise to prominence in academe. For example, a blend of sociological conflict theories with Darwinian evolutionary theory is one possibility (e.g., Sanderson, 2001). Such approaches have the potential to promote *consilience* or the unity of knowledge (Bell & Kandler, 2017).

Methods in Motion: Applications to Canadian Society. These boxes highlight recent Canadian research that illustrates how the methods discussed in the chapter have been used to study Canadian society.

Research in the News

The effect of social trust on Canada's reaction to the COVID-19 pandemic

rookiephoto/Shutterstock

As a researcher choosing between structured observation and survey-based measures of behaviour, which method would help you better understand the intentions behind participants' social distancing behaviours?

Public health during the COVID-19 pandemic may depend on things that go beyond discoveries in medical science such as treatment protocols and vaccines. According to Cary Wu, a York University sociologist, and Eric Kennedy, a historian at York, social trust must also be present for a nation to cope with the global epidemic. "If people do not trust, it's very difficult to promote collective action," Wu explained in a CBC interview (Weber, 2020). In a pandemic, trust in fellow citizens, politicians, the health-care system, and perceived outsiders could be affected, he maintained. Without a high level of social trust, it's hard to get people to conform to public health directives such as those regarding physical distancing and mask wearing.

Both Wu and Kennedy are embarking on social research programs involving surveys in an effort to determine what effect the pandemic has had on social trust in Canada. So far, their results suggest that levels of social trust have remained high during the crisis. "By and large, Canadians are reporting taking a lot of the steps that they've been called upon to take," Kennedy explained. He also reported that Canadians are more trusting of public officials than is the case in other countries. "Canadians are more likely to follow social distancing requirements. People perform better in terms of complying with policy matters," he said (Weber, 2020). Both Wu and Kennedy are hoping that their research will help those in charge of promoting public health in Canada to enhance levels of social trust as the pandemic wears on.

Methods in Motion | Applications to Canadian Society

Systematic social observation of the police

Schulenberg (2014) describes her experiences in using systematic social observation (SSO) to study decision-making processes and the use of discretion among members of a Canadian re- and the personal characteristics of the people observed affect the phenomenon of interest. Since SSO is a method that yields both quantitative and qualitative data it has the potential to pro-

Research in the News. These boxes outline a research story that has appeared in a major media outlet, illustrating how social research can have real impacts on our everyday lives.

Practical tips. Most chapters include at least one set of practical tips on how to approach regular tasks or avoid common mistakes.

Disagree _____
Strongly disagree _____

The advantage of the vignette over this kind of attitude item is that it anchors the choice in a more realistic situation and thus reduces the risk of an unreflective reply. Finch (1987) also argued that on a sensitive topic like this, some respondents may feel uncomfortable or fear that they will be judged on their replies. The fact that the vignette is about other people (and imaginary ones at that) creates a certain distance between the questioning and the respondent, and hence the chance for a more candid answer. One obvious requirement of the vignette technique is that scenarios must be believable.

Finch also pointed to some limitations with this style of questioning, however. It may be impossible to establish what assumptions are being made by the respondents about the characters in the scenario (such as their age, ethnicity, and number of children at home) and the significance of those assumptions for the validity and comparability of people's replies. It is also difficult to establish how far respondents' answers reflect their own normative views or indeed how they themselves would act when confronted with the kinds

more difficult than we would imagine.

Run a pilot study

It is always desirable to conduct a pilot study before collecting data from respondents: not just to ensure that individual questions operate well but also to ensure that the research instrument as a whole is appropriate. Pilot studies may be particularly crucial in research using questionnaires, since there will be no interviewer present to clear up any confusion.

Here are some specific uses of pilot studies in survey research:

- If the study is going to employ mainly closed questions, a researcher can pose open questions in pilot qualitative interviews and then use them to generate the fixed-choice answers.
- Piloting an interview schedule can give interviewers some experience in using it and help them develop confidence.
- If everyone (or virtually everyone) who answers a question gives the same answer, the resulting data are not likely to be useful. A pilot study gives you an opportunity to identify

Practical Tip | Getting help in designing questions

When designing questions, be empathetic: put yourself in the position of the people who will be answering them. This can be difficult, because the questions may not always apply to the person producing them—for example, to a young student doing a survey of retired people. Even so, you need to think about how you would reply. This means concentrating not just on the questions themselves but also on the links between the questions. For example, do filter questions work in the expected way?

Then try out the questions on some friends or classmates, as in a pilot study (see the next section). Ask them to be critical and to consider how well the questions connect to each other. Also, look at some questionnaires and structured interview schedules designed by experienced researchers. Those researchers may not have asked questions on your particular topic, but the way they have asked their questions should give you an idea of what to do and what to avoid.

End-of-chapter questions. Questions designed to test understanding of key concepts have been expanded to include both review and application questions. These different question types have been indicated with **R** and **A** icons, and are grouped under headings that mirror the structure of the chapter.

Key Points

- Figure 4.1 depicts quantitative research as a linear series of steps moving from theory to conclusions, although this is an ideal from which there are many departures.
- Examining the reliability and validity of measures is important for assessing their quality.
- Quantitative research has the following key goals: measurement, the establishment of causality, generalization, and replication.
- Quantitative research has been criticized by qualitative researchers. These criticisms tend to revolve around rejecting the view that a natural science model is appropriate for studying the social world.

Questions for Review (R) and Creative Application (A)

The main steps in quantitative research

R1 What are the main steps in quantitative research?

A1 Assume you are conducting a study to determine which variables influence poverty. Name one variable that might have an impact on the chances that a person will live in poverty, and use it to derive a specific hypothesis that can be tested with survey data.

Concepts and their measurement

R2 Why may multiple indicators of a concept be preferable to using a single indicator?

A2 Describe three different ways to measure the concept "homophobia."

Reliability and validity

R3 Name and define four different kinds of measurement validity, providing an illustration of each one.

A3 How might a researcher measure the concept "satisfaction with university student housing"? How could the test-retest method be used to establish reliability? What drawbacks might there be to the use of this method in the example you have provided?

The main goals of quantitative researchers

R4 Outline the main goals of quantitative researchers. What is to be gained by achieving them?

A4 Assume you have to design a study that will examine why some people vote in national elections while others do not. Name two independent variables that would be appropriate to use in this study. What steps can be taken to ensure that your findings will be applicable to some larger population, i.e., to people who will not be participating in your study?

The critique of quantitative research

R5 Explain how the techniques used by quantitative researchers may produce findings that are not applicable to everyday life.

A5 You are using surveys to conduct research on alcohol consumption among stay-at-home moms. Might there be a gap between stated and actual behaviour on this topic? Why? What could you do to reduce or eliminate the gap?

Interactive Classroom Activities

1. Divide the class into groups of seven or more. Each group is to do the following:
   a. Come up with a causal statement that involves two variables, for example, "Being a victim of racism affects one's self-esteem."
   b. Provide a nominal and an operational definition for each variable (in this example, "racist victimization" and "self-esteem").
   c. Explain how each operational definition has face validity.
   d. Explain, giving concrete examples, how concurrent, construct, and convergent validity could be established for both of the operationalizations proposed in point b.
   e. Explain, giving concrete examples, how the operationalizations could be tested for reliability.

---

information on the case that is relevant to the findings of the qualitative investigator.

Visit our online resource center for free assessment: https://learninglink.oup.com/

Interactive Classroom Activities

1. This activity involves some friendly competition. Divide the class into small groups. Each group is given 15 minutes to come up with as many examples of spurious correlations as they can (e.g., the correlation between the number of fire trucks at a fire and the amount of fire damage). Examples given in this chapter or in previous classes are not allowed. After the time is up, a spokesperson from each group presents the group's spurious correlations to the rest of the class, and the instructor judges whether each one is in fact an example of a spurious correlation. The instructor also keeps a record of all groups' accepted correlations. The group with the most accepted correlations wins.

   Once that has been done, the class examines each correlation individually. The instructor asks for volunteers to name an antecedent third factor that might be causing the two variables to vary together (e.g., it would be the severity of the fire for the fire trucks and damage example given above).
2. Divide the class into small groups. Each group is to
   a. pick a social phenomenon or experience of interest (e.g., sex work, homelessness);
   b. provide a *nomothetic* explanation for it; and
   c. provide an *idiographic* explanation for it.

   The groups are to go into as much detail as possible. When that is completed, each group is paired with another group (A and B, C and D, E and F, etc.) such that Group A presents its results to the rest of the class, while Group B has the task of providing a critical evaluation (enumerating both strengths and weaknesses) of Group A's arguments. Then the reverse: Group B presents and Group A critiques. Repeat for Groups C and D, E and F, and so on.

Relevant Websites

The *National Longitudinal Survey of Children and Youth* site provides information on an ongoing, longitudinal study in Canada.
www12.statcan.gc.ca/census-recensement/2011/ref/92-135/surveys-enquetes/nationalchildren-nationaleenfants-eng.cfm

The *Online Dictionary of the Social Sciences* site, maintained by Athabasca University, "has 1000 entries covering the disciplines of sociology, criminology, political science and women's study with a commitment to Canadian examples and events and names."
http://bitbucket.icaap.org/dict.pl

The *Research Methods Knowledge Base* provides a detailed discussion of various types of experimental design.
www.socialresearchmethods.net/kb/desexper.php

The *Human Genome Project* site offers some basic information on this 13-year project and its implications for understanding human behaviour.
https://web.ornl.gov/sci/techresources/Human_Genome/index.shtml

The *Behavior Genetics Association*, an international organization, provides a forum for the dissemination of behavioural genetic research and offers methodological workshops.
www.bga.org

(Websites accessed 4 September 2021)

OXFORD learning link More resources are available on Oxford Learning Link. Visit *https://learninglink.oup.com/* for:

- Student Study Guide
- Student self-quiz
- Flash cards
- Audio clips
- Videos
- Web links
- Activities

Interactive classroom activities. Appearing at the end of each chapter, these offer students and instructors the perfect opportunity to put the concepts learned in each chapter into practice in the classroom.

Key Points

- There is an important distinction between a general research orientation (quantitative versus qualitative) and a research design.
- The nomothetic approach to explanation involves discovering general laws and principles, and is usually associated with quantitative research.
- Nomothetic explanations must satisfy three criteria of causation: correlation, time order, and non-spuriousness.
- Qualitative researchers usually take the idiographic approach to explanation, which entails creating a rich description of a person or group based on the perceptions and feelings of the people studied.
- Replicability, validity (measurement and ex nal), and the ability to establish causation important criteria for evaluating the qualit quantitative social research.
- Four key research designs are experime cross-sectional, longitudinal, and case study
- Except for the experimental design, each o these can be used with either a quantitativ a qualitative research orientation. Experim are used with a quantitative approach.
- Threats to the establishment of causation of particular importance in non-experime quantitative research.

Questions for Review (R) and Creative Application (A

Criteria for the evaluation of social research

R1 Explain the time order criterion of causation.

A1 A survey researcher finds that people with high self-esteem make more money than people with low self-esteem. You are tempted to conclude from this that self-esteem influences earning power. But can time order be established using this design? Explain.

R2 What is a spurious correlation?

A2 You are at a dance party where a lot of alcohol is being served. You abstain from drinking, but

among 15-year-olds at sum to conduct an experimen proper ethics protocols. How experiment? Provide as mu

R6 What is a quasi-experimen

A6 You want to know wheth marijuana in Canada will rates. How could you use t tal method to research this

Cross-sectional design

R7 What is meant by a cros

Key points. Each chapter concludes with a summary of its most significant points. **Relevant websites.** A list of websites offering further information or elaboration is provided at the end of each chapter.

Relevant Websites

This *Canadian Election Study* site provides access to structured interviews and questionnaires and the numerical data derived from them for the Canadian elections of 2011, 2015, and 2019.

http://ces-eec.arts.ubc.ca/

This YouTube video explains how to make an online survey using Google Docs.

www.youtube.com/watch?v=DEhD0m1fhAQ

In the *General Social Survey on Time Use, 2015 Questionnaire*, you can find an example of a research diary that forms part of a larger structured interview.

https://www23.statcan.gc.ca/imdb/p3Instr.pl?Function=assembleInstr&lang=en&Item_Id=217656#qb218258

The *General Social Survey—Canadians' Safety, 2019*, contains the questionnaires used by Statistics Canada to assess perceptions of our criminal justice system and experiences of criminal victimization in Canada.

https://www23.statcan.gc.ca/imdb/p2SV.pl?Function=getSurvey&SDDS=4504

The *General Social Survey—Social Identity, 2020*, provides the questionnaires used by Statistics Canada to examine how Canadians identify with their social and cultural environments.

https://www23.statcan.gc.ca/imdb/p2SV.pl?Function=getSurvey&SDDS=5024

The *Inter-University Consortium for Political and Social Research* is an international association of about 700 academic institutions and research organizations that "provides leadership and training in data access, curation, and methods of analysis for the social science research community." Click on "Find Data" to access over 500,000 digital files for examples of questions used in a wide variety of social research projects.

www.icpsr.umich.edu/icpsrweb/ICPSR

The *UK Data Service* provides a searchable databank of questions used on social surveys in the UK.

http://ukdataservice.ac.uk

(Websites accessed 4 September 2021.)

Glossary. Learning a new subject usually involves learning some new terminology, or at least new meanings for familiar words and phrases. To help you keep track of new terms and concepts, key terms are **bolded** the first time they appear in each chapter and are defined in the glossary near the end of the book.

Glossary

Terms in *italic* type are defined elsewhere in the Glossary.

action research Same as participatory action research.

adjacency pair Two kinds of talk activity that are linked together, such as an invitation and a response.

analytic induction An approach to the analysis of qualitative data in which the collection of data continues and the hypothesis is modified until no cases inconsistent with it are found.

arithmetic mean What everyday language refers to as the "average": the sum of all the scores divided by the number of scores. Also known simply as the **mean**.

biographical method See *life history method*.

bivariate analysis Examination of the relationship between two variables, as in *contingency tables*; *correlation*.

CAQDAS An abbreviation of "computer-assisted (or computer-aided) qualitative data analysis software."

case study A *research design* that entails detailed and intensive analysis of either a single case or (for comparative purposes) a small number of cases.

causality A connection between *variables* in which one variable changes as a result of a change in another, as opposed to a mere *correlation* between them.

cells The areas in a table where the rows and columns intersect and data are inserted.

census A count of an entire *population*; by contrast, a *sample* counts only some units of a population.

chi-square test Chi-square (χ^2) is a test of *statistical significance* used to establish confidence that a finding displayed in a *contingency table* can be generalized from a *probability sample* to the *population* from which it is drawn.

closed, closed-ended question A question in an *interview schedule* or *questionnaire* that presents the respondent with a fixed set of possible answers to choose from; also called a **fixed-choice question**.

cluster sampling A procedure in which the researcher first samples sets of cases ("clusters") and then samples units within them, usually using a *probability sampling* method.

code, coding In *quantitative research*, codes are the tags used to assign the data on each *variable* to a category of the variable in question. Numbers are usually assigned to each category to allow easier computer processing. In *qualitative research*, coding is the process in which data are broken down into component parts, which are then assigned names.

coding frame or coding manual A list of the codes to be used in the analysis of a particular set of data. For answers to a structured interview schedule or questionnaire, the coding frame delineates the categories used for each *open question*. With *closed questions*, the coding frame is essentially incorporated into the fixed answers from which respondents must choose; hence the term "pre-coded question."

concept A general or abstract idea; a category that serves to organize observations and ideas about some aspect of the social world.

concurrent validity A type of validity that is tested by relating a measure to an existing criterion or a different indicator of the concept to see if one predicts the other; one of the main forms of *measurement validity*.

connotation A term used in *semiotics* to refer to the meanings of a *sign* associated with the social context within which it operates: a sign's connotations are supplementary to its *denotation* and less immediately apparent.

constant An attribute on which cases do not differ; compare with *variable*.

constructionism, constructionist An *ontological* position (the antithesis of *objectivism*) according to which social phenomena and their meanings are continually being created by social actors; also known as **constructivism**.

construct validity (1) Same as *measurement validity*; (2) a type of measurement validity that is established by determining whether the concepts being measured relate empirically in a manner that would be predicted by relevant theories.

content analysis An approach to the analysis of documents and texts that seeks to quantify content in terms of predetermined categories in a systematic

Online resources

Textbooks today do not stand on their own: they are only the central elements in a complete learning and teaching package. *Social Research Methods* is no exception. This sixth Canadian edition is supported by an outstanding array of ancillary materials for both students and instructors, including an enhanced e-book with integrated videos, self-grading quizzes, and additional resources.

Additional Materials

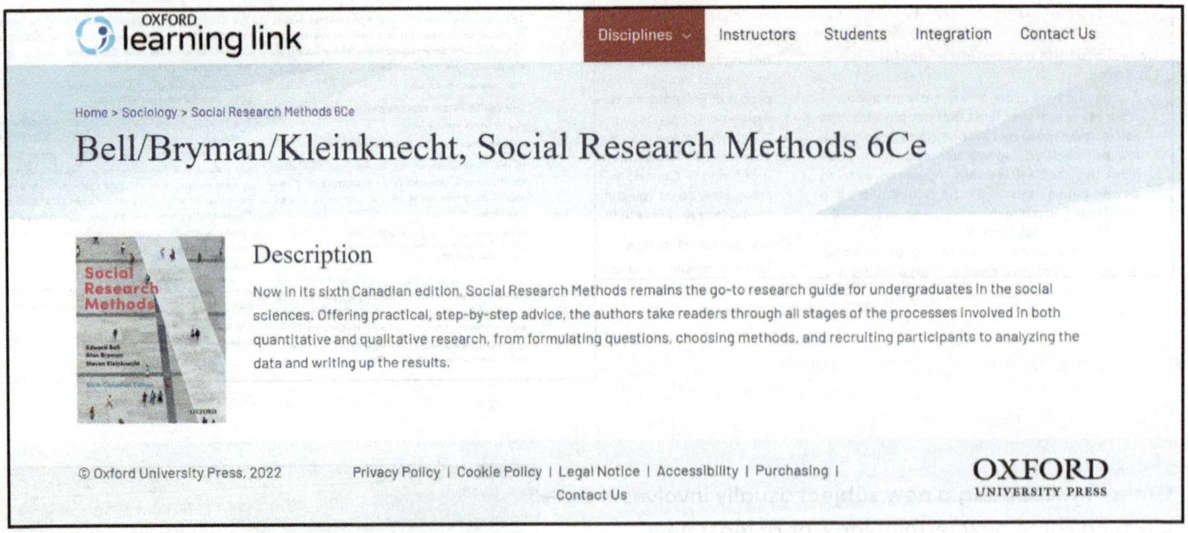

For Students

(Available at www.oup.com/he/SocialResearch6Ce)

In addition to the enhanced e-book, OUP Canada offers these resources free to everyone using the textbook:

- Interactive flash cards for students
- Self-grading quizzes for students
- Printable checklists
- Researcher's Toolkit
  - FAQs for each part of the research process
  - List of "Dos and Don'ts" of research
  - Set of vignettes highlighting potential problems when conducting research
  - Examples of research projects
- Audio clips
- Activities
- Videos
- Web links

OXFORD learning link

At the end of each chapter, you may notice the logo along with a list of materials; this will let you know what additional material on this topic is available on Oxford Learning Link.

For Instructors

Online Instructor's Manual

This revised online resource includes comprehensive outlines of the text's chapters, additional assignments, classroom activities designed to encourage student engagement, and teaching aids that will enhance the learning experience.

PowerPoint Slides

Hundreds of slides for classroom presentation—newly updated and enhanced for this edition—summarize key points from each chapter and can be edited to suit individual instructors' needs.

Online Test Bank

A comprehensive electronic test bank that gives instructors a wide array of options for sorting, editing, importing, and distributing questions—provides approximately 1500 questions in multiple-choice, short-answer, and true/false formats.

How to use this book

Social Research Methods can be used in many ways. Some instructors, for reasons of time or preference, may not want to include all chapters or all sections of a specific chapter. Following is an overview of the major topic areas and the parts of the book where they are addressed:

- **Wider philosophical and methodological issues** are discussed at some length in Chapter 1. Instructors who do not wish to use this contextual material can largely ignore the chapter, except for the section on formulating a research question. Those who do want to emphasize issues of context should also see Chapter 14.
- **Practical issues involved in doing quantitative research** are the subject of Part II. Chapter 2 is a useful introduction to this topic because it maps out the main research designs used in both quantitative and qualitative research.
- **Practical issues involved in doing qualitative research** are the subject of Part III. Again, Chapter 2 outlines the most common designs.
- **Data analysis** is covered in Chapters 8 (quantitative) and 13 (qualitative), and a guide to the use of computer software for these purposes can be found in the Appendix. Even if the module is taught without actual computer applications, exposure to them will reinforce the textual material and may be useful for later work.
- **The quantitative/qualitative distinction** is used in two ways: to organize the discussion of research methods and data analysis, and to introduce some wider philosophical issues that have a bearing on social research. Chapter 1 reviews the main areas of difference between quantitative and qualitative research, while Chapter 14 explores ways of integrating the two. If time is a concern, the latter chapter can be skimmed.
- **Writing up research** is as much a part of the research process as data collection and analysis. Chapter 15 discusses a variety of issues related to writing and should be drawn to students' attention even if it is not discussed in class.
- **Specific advice on doing a research project.** As we have already noted, the whole book is relevant to student projects, but Chapter 15 addresses this subject directly. If time is a factor, the Appendix to Part I briefly overviews the stages of research for students.

Acknowledgments

The previous edition of this book was written shortly after the death of Alan Bryman, who created the original version for a UK readership several years ago. Alan was, probably unknowingly, a mentor to me. Working with him had a major influence on my approach to social research methods and to the social sciences in general, and he opened my eyes to many important issues in the philosophy of science. His DNA is still all over this book. James Teevan produced the first Canadian edition, and his efforts are greatly appreciated.

This sixth edition of the book introduces Steven Kleinknecht as a co-author. Steve's expertise includes a wealth of knowledge and experience in doing qualitative research, and he is no stranger to the world of quantitative research methods. Steve's many contributions allowed us to probe more deeply and thoroughly into a broad range of topics. It was a pleasure exchanging chapter drafts with him for mutual feedback as we went through the process of creating this latest edition of the book together.

Amy Gordon did a stellar job launching the project as Developmental Editor, and was a valuable sounding board as we presented our ideas for the new edition. Mariah Fleetham took over in that role after the project was underway, and was a resourceful and encouraging presence as she oversaw the completion of the book. Tara Tovell was an efficient and effective copyeditor, with a keen eye for style, detail, and contemporary usage. Senior Acquisitions Editor Ian Nussbaum always seemed to be in our corner when we needed him, providing unflagging support in tough times.

Many thanks go to the academic reviewers who provided valuable comments and criticisms, and who filled us in on how their students typically react to the content and features presented in the book. Your detailed assessments have allowed us to make many improvements and have saved us from going down the wrong path on more than one occasion. Thank you to Kevin Gosine, Brock University; Alicia Horton, University of the Fraser Valley; Oral Robinson, University of British Columbia; Meridith Burles, University of Saskatchewan; Heather Mair, University of Waterloo; Efe Peker, University of Ottawa; Deidre Rose, University of Guelph; Rochelle Tucker, Simon Fraser University; Sarah Knudson, St. Thomas More College at the University of Saskatchewan; Neda Maghbouleh, University of Toronto Mississauga; and several anonymous reviewers.

I'd also like to thank my students, who over the course of many years have been the source of much inspiration and influence on how I see the world, both as a researcher and as a fellow human being.

Producing this book would not have been possible without the love and devotion of my family. To my wife Jennifer, children Ted and Angelica, and soon to be daughter-in-law Brooke: thanks for everything.

Edward Bell

My respect and gratitude go out to those I've worked with on this text and those who have informed my understanding of research methods. Given Alan Bryman's passing in 2017, I did not have the privilege of working with him on this project. I value his strong understanding of the art and science of research which are clearly on display in his writing. I am thankful that my friend and colleague, Ed Bell, invited me to join him on this project. I've learned much from Ed in working with him at Brescia and now as co-authors. When we began contemplating ideas for the sixth edition, little did we know the world was headed for a pandemic. Amidst much social upheaval, we wrote. We are fortunate, though, to have completed this task with considerably less disruption to our everyday lives than so many others who have experienced significant hardships over the last several months. I am thankful for the frontline workers and health-care professionals whose dedication and sacrifice allowed people like Ed and me to continue to do our jobs in relative safety. I am also thankful for having learned the craft of qualitative research from great mentors like Billy Shaffir, Dorothy Pawluch, and Bob Prus. In 2001, they introduced me to the professional side of academia by way of the Canadian Qualitative Analysis Conference. My life and career have benefited immensely from participating in and co-organizing the conference with wonderful colleagues like Tony Puddephatt, Carrie Sanders, Lisa-Jo and Jeff van den Scott, and Deana Simonetto. Planning, laughing, and problem-solving alongside people I enjoy working with has been a great gift. I've applied many of the lessons learned through the conference to my writing in this text. Thank you to those who participate in our studies. The time you share not only teaches us about society, it also provides us with a practical understanding of the research process. These insights have been invaluable in my writing and teaching. Thank you to my students, who inspire me with their energy, enthusiasm, and curiosity for learning about the social world. A special thank you to my wife, Mandy, and our children, Lincoln, Lauren, and Darren. Your love and support mean the world to me.

Steven Kleinknecht

Preface

Why Study Research Methods?

At this point in your life you probably haven't devoted much thought to social research methods. In all likelihood you are reading this book in conjunction with the first methods course you have ever taken. That means you are about to experience something new. Since you are going to expend considerable time and effort doing something you've never done before, it would make sense to pause for a moment and ask yourself the following existential questions: Why am I here? Why should I read this book? Why should I study social research methods? What's the point of it all? Pondering those questions will make what is to come much more meaningful for you.

So why are you here? When we ask our students that question (usually on the first day of classes) they often tell us that a solid background in social research methods is indispensable if they are to develop a sophisticated understanding of the topics they are passionate about.

What are you passionate about? Does it matter to you that just under half the world's population struggles to survive on less than $5.50 per day (World Bank, 2018), while others are so wealthy that they can't relate to ordinary people? Do you have an interest in gender equity, environmental sustainability, crime, single parenthood, ethnic tension, cyber bullying, racism, the living conditions of Indigenous people, changing notions of the family, sexual mores? In order to come up with informed, thoughtful analyses of these and other social issues, and to be capable of evaluating the claims made by others on these topics, it is crucial to be familiar with the various research methodologies used in the social sciences to investigate these subjects. Just as learning how clothes are made can help you tell the difference between a good pair of jeans and a shoddy pair, understanding where social knowledge comes from will help you distinguish between valid claims and fatuous ones.

There are some answers to the "Why are you here?" question that we seldom get from students. Consider the following. The acquisition of knowledge through research always goes beyond coming up with new ideas or getting more information or developing novel ways of looking at society, however important those things may be. To produce or acquire knowledge is a political act. It is tied in with the exercise of power. Social research always has political ramifications, because it always implies, subtly or not so subtly, that some ways of organizing society are better than others. Some researchers are happy to leave their political involvement at that level: an implication in their work that certain social structures or practices should change or be preserved. Others go so far as to engage in advocacy, taking part in public campaigns to persuade governments and the public at large that some sort of action should be taken. Whichever position the researcher takes, the politics of research cannot be avoided. What varies is how loudly the trumpet is sounded, which is a matter for the individual researcher to decide. Debates about the wisdom of social researchers becoming advocates are part of the storied history of the social sciences, some of which will be told in this book.

We often hear that "knowledge is power," and in many ways that is true. Dictators know this best; they all try to limit access to knowledge in order to preserve their control over others. In fact, the powerful in any society may try to inhibit free inquiry and the flow of ideas. But the "knowledge is power" maxim leaves several questions unanswered. What is knowledge? How can it be acquired? How are we to tell the difference between a sound idea and one that should be ignored? How can we gather information that will help us understand our subject matter, and what sorts of information should we seek? How should that information be analyzed and evaluated? Are there some things that we will never fully understand, regardless of how hard we try?

This book explores a variety of answers to those questions, which will make it somewhat different from your other readings and textbooks. In most courses in the social sciences, students spend their time absorbing, and sometimes challenging, claims made about the social world. For example, you may learn that men are more likely to commit violent crimes than women. You may come to understand what it feels like to be homeless. Or perhaps you'll encounter a theory explaining why some countries are rich and powerful while others are not. That sort of endeavour—learning about and reflecting on claims to knowledge—is clearly worthwhile, but it will not be our central concern. Instead, we will focus on how those types of claims are generated and how they gain acceptance as knowledge. In other words, instead of exploring the body of facts, concepts, theories, and interpretations that social scientists use to make sense of the world, we'll look at how all those things are acquired or created. One of the most profound questions that can be asked of someone making a claim to knowledge is, "How do you know that?" That simple question is at the heart of this book. And like so many simple questions, it has no simple answer.

To produce knowledge, we need a methodology—a way to get it. And if you accept the premise that knowledge is power, then learning about research methods means learning about how to become powerful, or at least more powerful. You could even say that "methodology is power," and you wouldn't be far off the mark.

How could methodology be power? For one thing, if you know how knowledge is generated, you won't be fooled as easily as someone who doesn't know. Another way to put this is that learning about research methodologies is an excellent way to enhance your critical thinking skills—skills that are essential in any situation where power is exercised, which is everywhere.

Another way in which methodology can be power is that it can help to make you a producer of ideas. Start thinking of yourself not only as someone who takes in ideas and evaluates them, but also as someone who projects ideas onto the world. Start thinking of yourself as a researcher: someone who has the potential to examine the human condition and contribute to our understanding of it. That's far more interesting and impactful than just reading other people's work, although reading is an essential part of the process.

When can you start being a researcher? At various points in your university career you will probably be called on to do some small research projects. The knowledge you will gain by learning about social research methods can put you at an advantage with that sort of assignment, and it could even be an entrée to more sophisticated work if you decide to go on and develop your research capabilities in graduate school or in some other way.

Although it is important to acknowledge that social research and its attendant methodologies have political ramifications, we shouldn't lose sight of the fact that it is the height of folly to pursue one's political goals with bad social science. To reduce suffering and promote human flourishing we need rigorous social research, which is dependent on sound research methods. Learning how to take good field notes, getting instruction on how to construct effective survey questions, using appropriate sampling procedures, and a host of other methodological issues are not trivial matters. In fact, doing those sorts of things properly are prerequisites to acquiring the knowledge needed to achieve one's broader social goals. Without good methodologies we have very little to offer that is not available elsewhere.

If you want to learn about how knowledge is created in the social sciences, or if you aspire to make an impact on the world by doing social research yourself, reading this book is a good way to start. We hope it will at least pique your interest in how social researchers do what they do, and what the implications of social research are. To paraphrase Gore Vidal: the more one learns, the more interesting consciousness becomes.

PART I

Fundamental Issues in Social Research

The first two chapters of this book will acquaint you with a number of fundamental methodological concepts that feature prominently in the social sciences, in particular the notion of a *general research orientation* and the idea of a *research design*. In Chapter 1, two general orientations are identified—the quantitative and qualitative approaches—along with a variety of considerations that affect the practice of social research as a whole. Chapter 2 presents various kinds of research design and identifies some criteria used to evaluate social research. Together these chapters provide the basic conceptual building blocks that will be drawn upon throughout the book. Chapter 3 features a discussion of research ethics, which are a primary concern for every kind of social research and affect every stage of the research process. Part I concludes with an appendix that offers an overview of how social research is done.

1 General Research Orientations

Chapter Overview

The aim of this chapter is to examine the fundamental assumptions upon which social research is based. An important distinction commonly drawn by practitioners of social research—between the **quantitative** and **qualitative** approaches—is explored in relation to those considerations. We will consider:

- the relationship between theory and research—in particular, whether theories and the hypotheses derived from them are tested by gathering data (the **deductive** approach) or whether data gathering is used as a means to *create* theory (the **inductive** approach);
- **epistemological** issues, such as whether a natural science model like the one used in physics or biology is suitable for the study of the social world;
- **ontological** issues, such as whether the social world should be regarded as a reality external to individuals over which they have little or no control, or as something that social actors may fashion into their personal realities;
- how *values* and *practical issues* impinge on the research process; and
- how these issues relate to both quantitative and qualitative research; a preliminary discussion, followed up in Chapter 14, suggests that although the quantitative and qualitative orientations are different, they complement each other.

Key Learning Outcomes

Here is a list of goals you should try to achieve as you read and think about the material in this chapter. After completing this chapter, you should be able to:

1. Explain the relationship between theory in the broad sense and data gathering; in particular, you should be able to recognize that the purpose of collecting data may be to *test* theories or to *create* theories.

▲ LeonWang/Shutterstock

2. Discuss the positivist, interpretivist, and critical approaches to social science, including their key assumptions regarding the purposes of social research and how it should be conducted.
3. Describe the distinctions between qualitative and quantitative research.
4. Identify how different factors, including values, politics, and issues related to the research question(s) may influence social research.

Soon-Yi wants to find out why Indigenous people in Canada are more likely to live in poverty than other Canadians, but doesn't know where to begin. Should she start by examining the history of colonialism and conflict between Indigenous peoples and settler-colonizers, familiarizing herself with issues such as disputes over land claims and treaties, residential schools, or anti-Indigenous prejudice? Or how about gathering aggregate data on present conditions like residence patterns, economic activities, the age structure, or educational trajectories? The list of topics she could investigate seems endless.

Maybe rather than beginning her study by accumulating information, it would be better to start out with some hunches and then gather data to see whether they are supported by evidence. For example, perhaps the discrepancy in economic conditions is a manifestation of a centuries-old world system of dominance and exploitation. Similarly, it could have arisen through a clash of values and cultures. Then there is the question of how to gather the information to address those theories. Should she consult mainly historical sources? How about living in an Indigenous community for a while and recording her interactions and observations? Or would it be better to stay where she is and select a few Indigenous individuals for interviews in which they could share their life stories? Or maybe she should design a detailed questionnaire on prejudice and send it out to large random samples of Indigenous and non-Indigenous people?

Soon-Yi wonders about the ethical implications of each of these approaches. She also puzzles over what she should do if it turns out that Indigenous people take positions on her research topic that differ significantly from her own. Should she try to determine whose perspective is more realistic, and if so, how could she do that? Can those sorts of issues ever be resolved? Are there "right" and "wrong" answers on such matters? As she ponders these issues, she begins to reflect on the nature of social reality itself. Is it, as many social researchers put it, "out there," independent of the person who perceives it, or is it socially constructed?

Then there are the more practical questions: What, if anything, can be done about the issue of poverty among Indigenous Canadians? Can society be changed so that Indigenous poverty is eliminated, or at least reduced? Considering the matter more broadly, are the social forces that affect our lives so strong that we have no choice but to conform to them, like leaves in a windstorm?

A great many social thinkers and researchers have confronted the same issues that Soon-Yi is contemplating. In fact, there are a number of rich intellectual traditions that can be drawn on to make sense of these matters and to assist people in making the kinds of methodological and practical decisions that she has to make. In this chapter you will be introduced to that body of ideas and the debates surrounding them.

Introduction

This book is about social research. It would be easy to "cut to the chase" and get on with explaining what the various research procedures are, when each is appropriate, and how to use them. But the practice of social research does not exist in a vacuum, sealed off from philosophical and political debates and contested assumptions. As we will see, the explanations of social phenomena that scholars offer and their choice of research methods often depend on the positions they take on those issues.

The way in which social research is done may also be affected by what is motivating the researcher to conduct the study. A variety of motives can come into play. Quite often the goal is to assess the adequacy of a particular social theory, such as Ellis et al.'s (2020) use of minority threat theory to make sense of Black Muslim immigrants' interactions with police forces in Minneapolis, Boston and Toronto. The study found, consistent with the theory, that Somali immigrants perceived the negative treatment they received from the police to be related to their "racial," religious, and ethnic status rather than to their actions. In other cases, the aim is to gather information to create theories; for example, a researcher may pose as a street person to find out how the homeless are treated by the public, as Orwell did in Paris and London in the 1920s (Orwell, 1933). Sometimes simple "fact-finding" or exploratory work is carried out. For instance, Milgram's (1963) famous study of obedience was done partly to see how far participants would go in obeying an authority figure's commands, and the results were astounding—many people appeared to be willing to inflict severe pain on innocent others. Similarly, Bell's (2007) study of the western Canadian separatist movement was motivated in part by a desire to know how much public support the movement had, and it produced evidence that the movement was more popular than previously thought.

In other instances, research is driven by what is seen as a pressing social problem. In fact, the discipline of sociology came into being in the eighteenth and nineteenth centuries partly as a way of understanding the social crises and societal upheavals of the day, and that tradition has continued to the present time. Nagra and Maurutto (2016), for example, investigated the difficulties young Canadian Muslims experience at border crossings and airports, while Lyon and Frohard-Dourlent (2015) explored how same-sex partners in common-law relationships in Canada experience the relatively new socio-legal environment in which formal marriage is an option. Yet another stimulus for research is personal experience (Lofland & Lofland, 1995). Sugiman (2004), who is a "sansei" or third-generation Japanese, examined Japanese-Canadian women's experiences of internment during the Second World War after hearing about the personal histories of her family and friends.

Regardless of the motivation for doing research, the data gathered are usually viewed in relation to theories of some kind. That's because theories are an attempt to "make sense of it all," to find order and meaning in a seemingly infinite mass of information. How is that done?

Theory and research

The connection between theory and research is not straightforward. There are several issues at stake here, but two stand out: first, the form of the theory; and second, the relationship between data and theory.

Degree of abstraction

The term "theory" is used in a variety of ways, but its most common meaning is *an explanation of observed regularities or patterns*. For example, one could try to come up with a theory to explain why schizophrenia is more common in the working class than in the middle class, or why more men than women are alcoholics. Theories are composed of interrelated and usually verifiable statements or propositions. The statements and propositions come in varying forms, and different types may be combined in the same theory. Here are three common components of a theory:

1. *Definitions* specify what the key terms in the theory mean; for example, "Attachments are stable bonds between people who are fond of each other."
2. *Descriptions* outline the characteristics of the phenomena of interest; for example, "Attachments to parents and other family members tend to decline in adolescence. Later, often after age 25, new attachments develop as a person marries or lives with a romantic partner, becomes a parent, or gets a steady job."

3. *Relational statements* connect two or more **variables**, so that knowing the value of one variable conveys information about the other; for example, "As the proportion of people aged 15–25 decreases, the crime rate also decreases." Relational statements come in two forms:
   a. *deterministic*, which means the two variables always go together in a particular way; for example, "as the number of people aged 15–25 decreases by 1 per cent, the crime rate also shrinks by 1 per cent." If research uncovers an instance in which the variables are not related in this way, the relational statement must be modified.
   b. *probabilistic*, which means the two variables go together with some degree of regularity, but the relationship is not inevitable; for example, "regions of the country where the number of people aged 15–25 is decreasing are more likely to experience a decline in the crime rate than regions in which the number of people in that age category is increasing." Here, finding a case that does not fit the pattern does not mean that the theory must be modified; this could simply be one of the times when the variables are not related in the usual way.

There are different types of theories. One distinction that is sometimes made is between *theories of the middle range* (Merton, 1967) and *grand theories*. The former are more limited in scope, and can be tested directly by gathering empirical evidence. For instance, Durkheim's (1897/1952) theory of suicide, which maintains that suicide is a function of the level of social integration, is a theory of the middle range. One way to test it would be to compare suicide rates for married people with those for single, divorced, or widowed individuals. Merton's (1938) anomie theory, which suggests that crime is more common when a society instills a desire for wealth in everyone but provides insufficient means for all to achieve it, is another theory of the middle range. Such theories represent attempts to understand and explain a limited aspect of social life.

Grand theories, by contrast, are general and abstract. They include theories such as structural-functionalism, symbolic interactionism, critical theory, post-structuralism, feminism, and so on. Grand theories generally offer few direct indications of how to collect evidence to test them, but they provide ways of looking at the world that can be the inspiration for a wide variety of research programs. For example, *standpoint theory* was developed by Dorothy Smith (2004; 2005) and others from a general feminist perspective. This theory maintains that the way we view the world and make our way in it is largely determined by our placement in various hierarchies of status and power. One offshoot of standpoint theory has been an increased willingness to examine the views and perceptions of poor or marginalized groups in society. Similarly, Box 1.1 shows how an abstract theory like Giddens's structuration theory (1984) can be applied to a specific issue and yield some important insights.

Box 1.1 | Grand theory and social research

Giddens's (1984) structuration theory attempts to bridge the gulf between notions of social structure, which is said to shape or constrain human activities, and agency, which refers to freedom of action in social life. This theoretical issue is explored in empirical research by Neves, Waycott, & Malta (2018), who examined the use of digital technologies among older adults (65+) in Canada and Australia. The authors were trying to determine whether there was any validity to the common

(Continued)

idea that older people are averse to the use of digital technologies, and whether adopting these technologies could enhance seniors' connectedness with friends and relatives and in so doing help to reduce loneliness and feelings of isolation.

The researchers used a mixed-methods design (see Chapter 14) that included **semi-structured interviews**, focus groups, attitude scales and field observations. The participants were frail institutionalized older adults (Canadian sample) and similarly indisposed older adults living with assistance in the community (Australian sample). Each participant was given a portable electronic device and was encouraged to use a communications app that was installed in it. The results indicated that the common idea of an age-based digital divide did not adequately describe the social complexity surrounding the use of technology among people in this age group. While many participants required assistance to learn how to use the app, most did use it, although with varying degrees of sophistication and creativity. A major motivator was that in many cases it proved successful in reducing participants' loneliness and boredom, which led to a desire to keep using the app beyond the period of the study.

The social structures that had an impact on the use of digital technology in some cases facilitated its adoption but in other cases hindered it. The willingness of relatives to assist in the learning process was an important factor in making it possible for people in the study to use the technology. Some non-institutionalized participants stated that geographical isolation from their close relatives prompted them to use the app, while one resident in a care home limited her use of the app when other residents were around because of feelings of distrust and alienation towards them. In keeping with structuration theory, agency was described as taking place within the context of these sorts of social structures, and as evolving through a complex interplay between personal perceptions and desires on the one hand, and the social context on the other.

Although theory plays a crucial role in the social sciences, not all studies make reference to it. For example, some qualitative writers focus on providing a rich description of the experiences of a group of people without trying to come up with a comprehensive theory that would explain those experiences. Nonetheless, as Box 1.2 shows, social scientists are often under pressure from their peers to relate their work to theories of some kind.

As Box 1.2 indicates, some social scientists will reject research that has no direct connection to theory in either the grand or the middle-range sense of the term. However, non-theoretical work can provide insights that are useful or revealing in their own right. McKeganey and Barnard's (1996) research on British sex workers and their clients is a case in point. The authors related their research findings to investigations of people in the sex industry in several other countries, and what they describe offers good illustrations of ideas that form an important part of the sociologist's conceptual toolkit. Although it is not possible to tell whether the authors had the **concept** in mind when they collected their data, their book offers real-life examples of Goffman's (1963) notion of "stigma" and the way stigmatized individuals, in this case sex workers and their clients, manage a spoiled identity. Their analysis also sheds light on Hochschild's (1983) concept of "emotional labour," a term she coined to refer to what flight attendants do when they feign friendliness in order to deal with difficult passengers. Similarly, several other non-theoretical studies provide data that could eventually be used to evaluate or devise a theory.

Our discussion of what theory is and its importance invites consideration of another question: What is the relationship between theory and research? Up to this point we have focused primarily on how theory can guide research, in particular on how the collection and analysis of data can be used to test theories. But this notion of research as essentially "theory testing" does not provide a complete picture of what social scientists do. Theory may also

Box 1.2 | The need for theory

sunflowerey/123RF

Teevan and Dryburgh (2000) collected data from 57 Canadian male adolescents concerning their participation in deviant activities, such as truancy, theft, vandalism, and fighting, and asked them why they acted the way they did. Then the boys were read specially adapted sociological explanations of such behaviour and asked what they thought of them. In effect, they were asked to evaluate the sociologists' theories as if they were sociologists themselves. The idea was to give marginalized people a voice and to see the issue in question from the point of view of those studied—two common approaches in qualitative research. Some journal reviewers liked the idea but thought that the findings' relevance for sociological theory needed to be explored. Eventually the authors brought a variety of social theories to bear on the data they had gathered, and in doing so provided a critical assessment of existing explanations for delinquency and conformity.

A young person painting graffiti on a wall. Some call this behaviour vandalism, while others consider it art. What social theories might you invoke to explain what this person is doing? How might the young person explain it? Do you think his explanation would have anything in common with your social theories?

follow upon or *arise from* the collection and analysis of data. Here we begin to see two different ways to go about acquiring knowledge: the *deductive* and *inductive* approaches.

Deductive and inductive approaches

The deductive method is the most common approach to social research, although by no means the only one. The sequence of steps taken in deductive research is depicted in Figure 1.1. Note that the researcher starts by coming up with a theory that seeks to explain a particular phenomenon, and then deduces specific hypotheses from it that are tested with empirical data (see Box 1.3 for a concrete example) and then are either confirmed or rejected. In the case of the research described in Box 1.3, which examined several theories simultaneously, some hypotheses were supported while others were not. If the data gathered do not support the researchers' hypotheses, the theory may have to be revised or rejected.

It is also important to bear in mind that when the deductive approach is put into operation, the researcher does not necessarily follow the exact linear sequence shown in Figure 1.1. For example, a new hypothesis may come to mind during the data-gathering stage; or the relevance of the data for a *second* theory may become apparent *after* the data have been collected. Although the sequence outlined in Figure 1.1 is a common one, it is only a general model, one that is not strictly followed in all cases.

In fact, some research makes no attempt to follow the sequence outlined in Figure 1.1. Some investigators prefer an *inductive* approach in which theories and interpretations are the *outcome* of research. In inductive social science, the researcher begins not by coming up with a theory to be tested, but by *gathering or examining data* relevant to the phenomenon being investigated; see Figure 1.2, which illustrates the difference between induction and deduction. The Research in the News box on page 10 provides an example: Bikos (2017) offered her interpretations and conclusions regarding police culture *after* she had gathered qualitative information on the topic.

When the inductive method is used, data are gathered not to test a theory, but to come up with the information required to *construct* a theory or interpretation. That's why with induction, data gathering

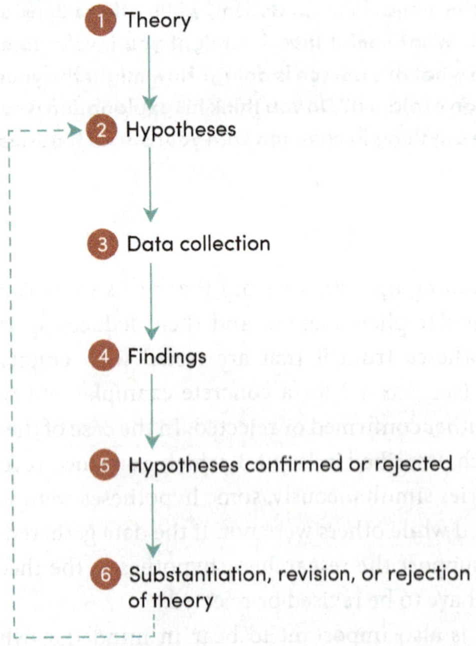

FIGURE 1.1 The process of deduction

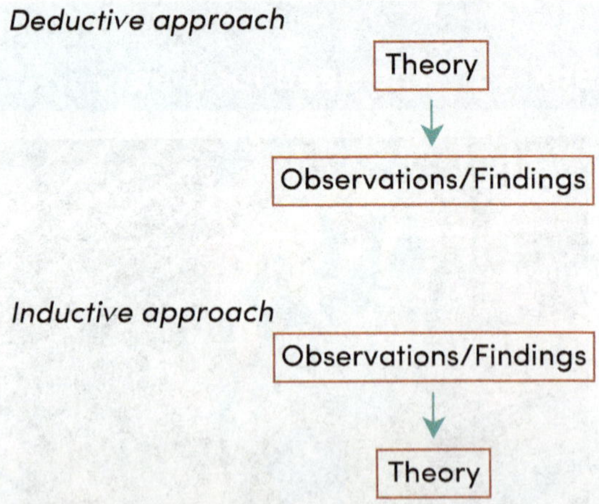

FIGURE 1.2 Deductive and inductive approaches to the relationship between theory and research

comes first, and the effort to create concepts and theories out of it comes later. After some theoretical reflection a researcher may decide to collect more data to establish the conditions under which the newly developed theory does or does not hold. This strategy of moving back and forth between data and theory is often described as *iterative*. The practice of deriving theories from qualitative data is sometimes referred to as **grounded theory**, discussed in Chapters 9 and 13.

In actual research situations it is impossible to conduct a study that is purely deductive or purely inductive. Just as deduction always entails an element of induction (theories do not emerge from a pristine mind unaware of previous findings) so the inductive process always entails a modicum of deduction (no researcher will be totally unaware of theories and perspectives that might be applicable to the phenomenon he or she is observing). Often some combination of both can be found in the same research.

Although some researchers using induction undoubtedly try to develop theories, sometimes the results of their research are little more than empirical **generalizations**, however useful they may be. An example is a Statistics Canada finding that the number of people in same-sex marriages in this country increased from 42,030 in 2011 to 48,740 in 2016 (Statistics Canada, 2017), which a researcher

Box 1.3 | A deductive study

Guenter Guni/iStockphoto

Women wearing headscarves in Iran, a society that has experienced far less secularization than many Western countries. Do you think that some of the theories examined in Hay's (2014) research can help to explain the high levels of religiosity found in Iran? For example, could the acceptance of religious beliefs and practices there be related to cultural factors that favour societal cohesion over personal autonomy? Could low levels of religious pluralism be a factor?

For millennia, religion has been the basis for beliefs about our place in the cosmic order, what it means to be human, how we should treat each other, and whether anything exists beyond the material, physical universe. However, in many Western countries a process of *secularization* has occurred in which fewer and fewer people embrace religious beliefs and practices, a process that became especially marked after the middle of the twentieth century. To be sure, religion has not disappeared in Western countries, including Canada. In fact, about 26 per cent of Canadians attend religious services once a month or more frequently (Statistics Canada, 2013), and 29 per cent say religion is very important to them (Pew Research Center, 2019). Nonetheless, several indicators suggest that the proportion of Canadians who are firmly religious is considerably lower than it was several decades ago. What can account for this profound social change?

Hay (2014) has taken a deductive approach to this issue. As in all deductive research, his goal was "theory testing." He started by proposing some theories, derived testable hypotheses from them, and then set out to determine which, if any, of the hypotheses were supported by the data. He reviewed seven well-known theories of secularization, and deduced specific hypotheses from each one. For instance, the deprivation-compensation theory holds that the existential security that affluent people in developed societies enjoy through health care and education, long life expectancy, and the absence of military conflict shields many of us from the traumas that draw people toward religion. The hypothesis he derived from this theory was that people who have experienced real tragedy in their lives are more likely to be religious than people who have no direct exposure to such things. Hay then analyzed contemporary survey data that included measures of religious beliefs and practices, as well as a number of variables that provided indicators of factors that were relevant to each of the theories.

There was limited support for deprivation-compensation theory, but there was strong support for three other theoretical positions. One theory that gained support involves the idea that a growing acceptance of personal autonomy in spiritual and moral matters has led to increased levels of secularization. A second position that was consistent with the results holds that the religious pluralism found in wealthy countries creates a situation in which it is very difficult for a particular faith group to make the claim that it is the "one true religion," which casts doubt on all religious doctrines and so increases levels of secularization. A third theory that was substantiated by the data maintains that increasing acceptance of human evolution and the belief that observable phenomena are purely material or physical in nature has reduced levels of religiosity in Canada.

Research in the News

Police culture: An inductive study

Police forces have faced severe criticism recently for their workplace culture and practices, some of which have sparked protest movements around the globe. The Civilian Review and Complaints Commission for the RCMP and the national Auditor General's Office have published damning reports on sexual harassment and other forms of abuse that officers themselves have endured on the job. In an article that appeared in the *Globe and Mail,* Lesley Bikos (2017), a former member of the London, Ontario, police service, described her research into noxious aspects of police culture across a variety of police organizations.

Bikos conducted in-depth interviews with officers from 23 different police services. Her research was inductive in that her goal was not to test a pre-existing theory. As a former officer she had some familiarity with the subject matter before she began her study, but her interpretations and conclusion largely took shape after she had collected some rich, detailed interview data, which she used to make sense of the social context in which police culture evolves.

Her interviews with officers unearthed many accounts of sexual assault and intimidation in the workplace, along with racism, homophobia, and sexism. Police culture in general was commonly described by her informants as being characterized by a "high-school mentality." She determined that the toxic work environment that the police find themselves in "damages many of its officers physically, mentally, and spiritually."

Bikos concluded that a crucial factor that perpetuates the toxic work environment in police departments is a lack of protection for officers who want to speak out against the infractions that they have experienced or witnessed. The "small percentage of bad-apple officers" who wreak havoc in the workplace would not be such a problem if better mechanisms for reporting and investigating objectionable behaviours were in place. Other factors that she identified that could contribute to a change in police culture included greater training and professionalization in the force, civilian involvement in promotional decisions and internal investigations, and better communication across ranks.

could use in the context of a discussion of the changing forms of the family in Canada.

The next section examines some epistemological issues that affect the conduct of social research.

Epistemological considerations

Those who do social research base their work on a number of epistemological assumptions—notions of what can be known and how knowledge can be acquired. A related epistemological issue pertains to the question of what should be regarded as acceptable knowledge. A fundamental debate in this context is whether the social sciences should follow the same principles and procedures as the natural sciences. Three broad positions on these matters have emerged: the positivist, interpretivist, and critical approaches to social science.

Positivism

One epistemological position that affirms the importance of following the natural sciences is **positivism**. Although definitions of the term vary, positivism is generally taken to entail the following:

1. Only phenomena confirmed by the senses (sight, hearing, etc.) can be accepted as

knowledge: this is the principle of **empiricism**. Ideas must be subjected to the rigours of empirical testing before they can be considered knowledge.

2. A key purpose of theory is to generate hypotheses that can be tested and thereby allow explanations of observed laws and principles to be assessed (*deduction*).
3. Knowledge can also be arrived at through the gathering of facts that provide the basis for generalizations or laws (*induction*).
4. Science must (and presumably can) be "value-free." That is, it must be conducted in such a way that different researchers, given the same data, will always reach the same conclusions, no matter how different their values might be. In the past this "value-free" quality was called "objectivity"; today it is more likely to be called **intersubjectivity**.
5. There is a clear distinction between scientific statements, which describe how and why certain social phenomena operate the way they do, and normative statements, which outline whether certain acts or social conditions are morally acceptable. Only scientific statements have a place in the domain of science; normative statements belong in the realm of philosophy or religion. This idea is implied by point 1 above, because the truth of moral claims cannot be confirmed by the senses.

It is possible to see in these five points a link with some of the issues already raised about the relationship between theory and research. Positivism assumes a fairly sharp distinction between theory and research and includes elements of both deduction and induction. One role of research is to test theories and gather the information necessary for the development of scientific laws. Positivism also implies that it is possible to collect observations without any reference to pre-existing theories, and to develop new theories purely on the basis of those observations. Finally, theories and propositions not directly testable through empirical observation are often not considered to be genuinely scientific.

A common mistake is to treat positivism as synonymous with science and the scientific. In fact, philosophers of science and social science differ quite sharply over how best to characterize scientific practice, and since the early 1960s positivism has acquired some negative connotations. One reason for dissatisfaction was the fact that in the past, certain researchers in the positivist tradition ignored some fundamental differences between human beings and the often inanimate or not fully conscious entities studied by natural scientists. Unlike subatomic particles or plants, for example, we humans have thoughts, feelings, and values—perhaps even some capacity for volition. Those aspects of human behaviour were often not addressed in the leading positivistic theories of the day. The positivist idea that science can or should be value-free was also a source of dissatisfaction. Critics pointed out that "neutral" social scientists often took moral positions on social issues, at least implicitly. For example, theories implying that social equilibrium or harmony is normal seemed to suggest that social change was not needed or not desirable. Critical social science, discussed below, claims that it is the duty of the researcher to help bring about social change in order to create a better world.

Interpretivism

Interpretivism to some extent grew out of the epistemological critique of positivism, and provides an alternative to the sort of social science typically done by positivists. Interpretive researchers maintain that it is the role of social scientists to grasp the subjective *meanings* of people's actions. They make the point that people act on the basis of the meanings that they attribute to their acts and to the acts of others. Individuals use their own common-sense constructs to interpret the reality of their daily lives, and it is those interpretations that motivate their behaviour.

Interpretivists claim that it is the job of the social scientist to gain access to the "common-sense thinking" of the people they study and hence to understand people's actions and their social world *from the point of view of the actors*. Thus, any thoughts constructed by the social scientist to grasp this social reality must be founded on the perceptions and lived experience of those they study: people living their daily lives within their own social world (Schutz, 1962, p. 59). In order to gain access to other people's perspectives, interpretivists commonly immerse themselves in the social environments frequented by the people they study, or at least conduct lengthy interviews with them. The insights gained by the researcher commonly follow from the information derived in this way, so the process used tends to be inductive.

Many interpretive social scientists argue that the subject matter of the social sciences—people, groups, and institutions—is fundamentally different from that of the natural sciences. For them it follows that the study of the social world requires a different logic and research procedure, one that reflects what they see as the distinctiveness of humans as against other living things or inanimate objects. This clash reflects a division between the positivist emphasis on the *explanation* of human behaviour and society, and the interpretivist preference for an *empathetic understanding* and *interpretation* of human existence. This division, which precedes the emergence of modern social science, finds expression in Max Weber's (1864–1920) notion of *Verstehen* (which means "empathetic understanding"). Weber described sociology as a "science which attempts the interpretive understanding of social action in order to arrive at a causal explanation of its course and effects" (1947, p. 88). Weber's definition seems to embrace both explanation *and* understanding, but the crucial point is that the task of "causal explanation" is undertaken with reference to the "interpretive understanding of social action." This is a different emphasis from a more Durkheimian view in which the external forces that affect behaviour may not be perceived by those involved, or at least may have no meaning for them.

Symbolic interactionism is an example of a sociological perspective that falls under the heading of interpretivism. The ideas of the founders of symbolic interactionism—in particular George Herbert Mead (1863–1931), who maintained that the individual's *self-concept* emerges through an appreciation of the perceptions of others—have been hotly debated. Symbolic interactionists argue that interaction takes place in such a way that individuals are continually interpreting the symbolic meaning of their environment (including the actions of others) and acting on the basis of that imputed meaning (cf. Collins, 1994). In research terms, according to Blumer (1962, p. 188), "the position of symbolic interaction requires the student to catch the process of interpretation through which [actors] construct their actions."

Taking an interpretative stance can result in surprising findings, or at least findings that appear surprising if the researcher's or reader's everyday experience does not include the particular social context being studied. Box 1.4 provides an interesting example.

Of course, as the example in Box 1.4 suggests, when social scientists adopt an interpretive stance, they are not simply revealing how members of a social group interpret the world around them. The social scientist almost certainly aims to place those interpretations into a social scientific framework. Thus, there is a double interpretation going on: the researcher is interpreting others' interpretations. Indeed, there is even a third level of interpretation, because the researcher's interpretations have to be further interpreted in terms of the concepts, theories, and literature of the social sciences. Thus, in Box 1.4 the idea that Riverside was not perceived as a high-crime area by residents was Foster's interpretation of the residents' interpretations. She then had the additional job of placing her findings into a social scientific framework, which she accomplished by relating them to existing concepts and discussions in criminology: concepts such as informal social control, neighbourhood watch schemes, and the role of housing style as a possible influence on criminal activity.

Critical approaches to social science

Like interpretivism, critical social science developed in part as a reaction to positivism. Social scientists who adopt a critical approach use a diversity of research methods, including those used by positivists and interpretivists, and may use a deductive or inductive approach. But they disagree with the positivist notion that researchers should take a value-neutral stance regarding their subject matter. In fact, they maintain that research and knowledge

Box 1.4 | Interpretivism in practice

Foster (1995) conducted **ethnographic** research using **participant observation** and semi-structured interviews in a housing estate in East London, UK, referred to as Riverside, a residential complex experiencing a high level of crime according to **official statistics**. However, she found that residents did not perceive the estate to be a high-crime area; nor were they overly anxious about becoming victims of crime. Those perceptions could be attributed to a number of factors, but a particularly important one was "informal social control," which was used in conjunction with more formal methods such as policing. People expected a certain level of crime, but felt fairly secure because informal social control worked to keep the level of crime contained.

Informal social control has several aspects. One is that neighbours often look out for each other. In the words of one of Foster's interviewees: "If I hear a bang or shouting I go out. If there's aggravation I come in and ring the police. I don't stand for it" (Foster, 1995, p. 575). Another aspect of informal social control is that people often feel secure because they know each other. A second respondent said: "I don't feel nervous . . . because people do generally know each other. We keep an eye on each other's properties. . . . I feel quite safe because you know your neighbours and you know they're there . . . they look out for you" (Foster, 1995, p. 575).

should not be considered as ends in themselves, but as means to be used to rid the world of suffering and oppression (Neuman, 2003).

Marxists, for example, argue that those who own the means of production deceive, constrain, and exploit the weak. The masses could be free if social scientists, by asking embarrassing questions and making pointed arguments, would uncover exploitation, expose hypocrisy, and reveal to the general populace the nature and extent of their oppression. This would transform the masses from what Marx called a *Klasse an sich* (a class in itself, an objective reality) into a *Klasse für sich* (a class for itself, one with an awareness of its exploitation).

Critical social scientists also believe that research should be action oriented. It should involve *praxis*: putting one's theoretical and academic positions into practice. The idea of praxis is contained in Marx's famous dictum that "philosophers have only *interpreted* the world in various ways; the point, however, is to *change* it [emphasis in original]" (Marx, 1845/1998, p. 574). This exhortation applies not only to positivism, but also to interpretive perspectives on social life.

A critical perspective has been adopted by a wide variety of scholars, including those engaged in feminist, post-colonial, anti-poverty, anti-racism, and queer studies. Another example is participatory action research, which is discussed in the section below and examined again in later chapters. Institutional ethnography and critical discourse analysis, examined in Chapters 10 and 12, respectively, are further examples of critical social science.

Participatory action research (PAR)

Of all the approaches to social science, PAR is the one most closely associated with social and political activism. The origins of participatory action research (sometimes referred to as "action research," "emancipatory research," or "participatory research") can be found in the immediate post–Second World War era in the work of Lewin (1946) and others who sought to bring social science to bear directly on specific social problems. Lewin is said to be the originator of the adages, "no research without action, no action without research," and "nothing is so practical as a good theory" (Ring, 1967, p.114).

In the early 1970s, PAR began to take on a more explicitly activist orientation when people in Latin America, Africa, Asia, and elsewhere became disillusioned with the ability of conventional social science to improve social conditions in their countries. These individuals expanded the methodology of PAR such that local people affected by the issue at hand acted as partners and co-equals with professional social scientists and government officials. All three groups worked together to devise research questions, choose research methods, gather and analyze data, and undertake a course of action to ameliorate the problem (Frisby et al., 1997; Smith, 1997).

Now, working for social justice is built into the methodology of PAR itself. Participants (including community partners) first reflect on a social problem and how it might be studied and rectified, and then use the results of that process as the basis for social action. Once action has been taken, participants discuss the consequences of the action and how those consequences might be used to generate more knowledge and inform further action. In this way a social problem is dealt with by the people directly affected by it, in collaboration with others.

The PAR process has the potential to transform the participants personally, intellectually, and even spiritually. Debbink and Ornelas (1997), for instance, describe how some Alberta dairy farmers worked together with Mexican *campesinos* (low-income farmers) and an activist intellectual to bring donated Alberta cattle to an impoverished, rural Mexican community. Similarly, Frisby, Crawford, & Dorer (1997) outline how some low-income women in British Columbia teamed up with social scientists and local recreation directors to help women with limited means gain access to physical activity services. In both cases, people directly affected by a problem and researchers from outside the community interacted as equals to produce knowledge and address a social issue.

PAR has a special relevance for Indigenous people in Canada. Peltier (2018, p. 1) lays out in rather stark terms the shortcomings of conventional research methods:

> In the past, people who have had limited knowledge about Indigenous peoples, worldviews, or communities have conducted *research on* Indigenous peoples. These researchers often employed a 'helicopter approach' where they would arrive in communities, collect data, and rarely, if ever, return. … In elementary school, I became one of many *subjects* in IQ and achievement *research on* Indigenous children. It remains uncertain what these researchers did with the data they collected, how it was interpreted, and, more importantly, how it may have contributed to *mis*information about my community.

As a corrective, Peltier (2018) advocates an approach that combines PAR with Indigenous methodologies through what is called "two-eyed seeing," a way of knowing in which both Indigenous epistemologies and Western approaches to knowledge are valued. In her study of Indigenous access to plural systems of health care, which comprise Indigenous healing and Western medicine, she first sought community sanction for the research by consulting local Elders and participating in spiritual ceremonies. She then reached out to health directors in three Indigenous communities to determine whether her topic was of relevance to those communities, which allowed her to develop her social relationships with the groups she would study. She then ensured that her project adhered to both national and local research ethics protocols.

A local advisory committee was set up to ensure accountability to the community. It directed the hiring of an Indigenous research assistant and the recruitment of participants, and helped to develop the research instruments, thus contributing to the co-creation of knowledge. Participants were asked to recount their personal experiences of how cancer had an effect on their emotional and spiritual lives and on their relationships with family and their community. Part of the narrative involved a description of how Indigenous healing or Western medicine, or some combination thereof, was part of their lived experience. Each participant had an opportunity to read and reflect on a copy of the story that came out of the interaction with the researcher. All the stories gathered were used to create a collective, teaching story, which was developed cooperatively using qualitative data coding (see Chapter 13). The final results of the study were shared with the participants and with members of other Indigenous communities, and were disseminated at academic conferences and through academic publications.

Summary

The aim of this section has been to outline how epistemological considerations are related to research practice. As noted, a key concern is whether a natural science or positivist approach can supply legitimate knowledge of the social world. We've seen that positivists often use the deductive method, although they concede that it is possible to generate theories using induction. By contrast, we've discerned that interpretive researchers typically adopt an inductive strategy, and that critical social scientists may use either one. Another important issue involves the purpose of social research, in particular whether social scientists, in both their academic work and their roles as citizens, should be actively engaged in issues of social justice.

It is important not to overstate the connections between epistemological issues and research practice: they represent tendencies only. Particular epistemological principles and research practices do not necessarily go hand in hand in a neat, unambiguous manner. Often hybrid approaches are taken, which combine different positions and approaches. This point will be made again on several occasions.

Ontological considerations

There are two ontological debates that are of particular interest to social scientists. The first is concerned with the following questions: Do social phenomena have an objective reality, independent of our perceptions? Or is what passes for reality a set of mental constructions? If you answer "yes" to the first question, you are in the **objectivist** camp. People on this side of the debate maintain that there is such a thing as social reality, and that it is the job of social scientists to discover what that reality is. An affirmative answer to the second question means that you agree with the **constructionist** position. People holding this view are in sympathy with Nietzsche's famous aphorism that there are no facts, only interpretations (1883/1968, p. 267). Such people maintain that there is no objective social reality against which our conceptions and views of the world may be tested. A middle-ground or "soft constructionist" position is also possible, and is held by many. It maintains that there may be an objective social reality, but that many of our ideas do not reflect it: instead, those ideas are constructed to justify or rationalize various forms of domination. Box 1.5 provides two illustrations of the less stringent form of constructionism.

A second debate revolves around these questions: Is social reality akin to the physical world as most people see it—largely fixed and "out there," something that individuals and groups have to confront but over which they have little or no control, like a snowstorm? Or is social reality not necessarily pre-existing and fixed, but rather created through our actions? A "yes" to the first question indicates support for a variant of objectivism, while a "yes" to the second affirms a kind of constructionism. In this chapter we'll focus mainly on this second debate: whether social reality can be created.

Some social scientists suggest that social phenomena confront individuals as external facts beyond their reach or influence. For example, an organization has rules and regulations and adopts standardized procedures for getting things done. A division of labour assigns people to different jobs. There is a hierarchy of authority, a mission statement, and so on. Objectivists see any organization as possessing a reality external to any of the specific individuals who inhabit it; they may leave, but it will stay. Moreover, the organization represents a social order in that it exerts pressure on individuals to conform to organizational requirements. People learn and apply the rules and regulations and follow the standardized procedures. They do the jobs to which they are appointed. If they do not do these things, they may be reprimanded or even fired. The organization is therefore a constraining force that acts on and inhibits its members. To a large extent, this is the "classic" way of conceptualizing an organization.

An alternative ontological position challenges the suggestion that things such as organizations are external realities confronting social actors who have limited power to influence or change them.

Box 1.5 | Constructionism in action

Lantz and Booth (1998) examined media treatment of the apparent rise in the incidence of breast cancer that began in the early 1980s and found that its depiction as epidemic can be treated as a social construction. They analyzed a variety of popular magazines and noted that many of the articles drew attention to the lifestyles of modern women, such as delaying first births and having careers. The authors also argued that the articles ascribe blame: "Women are portrayed as victims of an insidious disease, but also as victims of their own behaviours, many of which are related to the control of their own fertility" (1998, p. 915).

This article concludes that, as a social category, the breast cancer epidemic was represented in popular magazines in a particular way—one that blamed the victims and their lifestyles, particularly in the case of young women. Yet, in fact, fewer than 20 per cent of cases of breast cancer were in women under the age of 50. Lantz and Booth's study is fairly representative of a constructionist ontology in suggesting that the idea that young women's lifestyles cause breast cancer was constructed as a social fact by popular-magazine writers.

Similarly, Hallgrimsdottir, Phillips, & Benoit (2006, p. 266) argue that the media "contributes to constructing, reproducing and deepening the social stigmas associated with working in the sex industry." The authors compared media depictions of sex-trade workers in Victoria, British Columbia, from 1980 to 2004 with accounts provided by street sex workers, escorts, and others in this sector. Whereas the media portrayed such people as wicked and blameworthy in the earlier years, and as exploited, trapped, and innocent girls more recently, the sex workers themselves interpreted their work lives very differently. Although there was considerable heterogeneity in their experiences and attitudes toward their trade, many saw sex work as a largely mundane matter of earning a living. Because they are marginalized and stigmatized, however, their voices are seldom heard; most people have their ideas about the sex trade constructed for them by the media.

Strauss, Schatzman, Ehrich, Bucher, & Sabshin (1973), for example, carried out research in a psychiatric hospital and proposed that its organization was best conceptualized as one of "negotiated order." Instead of viewing order as a pre-existing characteristic, they argued that it is worked at and created to some extent, and that the rules are far less extensive and less rigorously imposed than might be supposed from an objectivist account of organizations.

Indeed, Strauss and colleagues saw rules more as general understandings than as commands (1973, p. 308). Precisely because relatively little of the activity of doctors, nurses, and other personnel is specifically set down or prescribed, the social order of a hospital is an outcome of agreed-upon patterns of action that are themselves the products of negotiations among the different parties involved. For instance, the official rules may say that only a doctor can increase medication; however, some nurses are routinely given this power, even though this is never actually stated in the regulations. The social order is in a constant state of change because the hospital is "a place where numerous agreements are continually being terminated or forgotten, but also are continually being established, renewed, reviewed, revoked, [and] revised. . . . In any pragmatic sense, this is the hospital *at the moment* [emphasis added]: this is its social order" (Strauss et al., 1973, pp. 316–317). The authors argued that a preoccupation with the formal properties of organizations (rules, organizational charts, regulations, and roles) makes it hard to recognize the degree to which order in organizations has to be *established* in everyday interaction. This *informal* organization arises because there cannot be rules for every possible contingency, and because the existing rules are sometimes problematic. However, this is not to say that the formal properties of organizations have *no* effect on individual action.

Although Strauss and colleagues stressed the active role of individuals in the social construction of reality, they did not push the argument to an extreme. For example, they did not claim that nurses can negotiate their roles to the point where they are allowed to operate on patients. But not all writers adopting a constructionist position are similarly prepared to acknowledge the existence or importance of an objective reality. It is precisely this split between seeing the social world as an objective reality and seeing it as a subjective reality in a continuous state of flux that Giddens sought to straddle in formulating his idea of structuration (recall Box 1.1).

The constructionist perspective that maintains that social reality can be negotiated also suggests that the concepts people employ to help them understand the natural and social world are social products whose meaning is constructed in and through social interaction. For example, a concept such as "masculinity" is treated as a social construction. This implies that masculinity is not a distinct, timeless, and universal entity, but something whose meaning is built up through interaction. That meaning is likely to be ephemeral, in that it will vary over time and place. The construction of one's masculinity may even have to be "recuperated" from time to time, such as when Canadian politicians endeavour to restore their public gender identities (Maiolino, 2015). This sort of social construction can be seen particularly well in **discourse analysis**, examined in Chapter 12. As Potter (1996, p. 98) observed: "The world . . . is *constituted* [emphasis in original] in one way or another as people talk it, write it, and argue it." This sense of constructionism frequently sparks an interest in how social phenomena are represented.

Relationship to social research

Questions of social ontology cannot be divorced from issues concerning the conduct of social research. Ontological assumptions and commitments affect both the way research questions are formulated and the way the research is carried out. For example, a researcher who sees organizations as objective social entities that act on individuals is likely to emphasize their formal properties. Alternatively, a researcher who is interested in the negotiated, changing nature of organizations is likely to focus on the active involvement of people in reality construction. In each case, a different research design is required.

General orientations: Quantitative and qualitative research

Many writers on methodological issues distinguish between quantitative and qualitative research. We have done so above without explicitly describing the difference between the two. The most basic difference is that quantitative research uses numbers and statistics in the collection and analysis of data, while qualitative research relies mainly on words and other non-numerical symbols. Some writers see the distinction between the two types of research as fundamental; others believe it to be no longer useful or even "false" (Layder, 1993, p. 110). Although this issue has been vigorously debated, we're convinced that there is a meaningful difference between quantitative and qualitative research. That difference will be a recurring theme in this book, both because it is a useful way of classifying various research methods and because it is a helpful reference point for a range of issues in the practice of social research.

On the surface, it seems that the main difference between quantitative and qualitative research is that quantitative researchers rely more on formal and mathematical measurement and analysis techniques than qualitative researchers do. But many sociologists and others suggest that the differences are deeper than merely the amount of quantification. For many writers, quantitative and qualitative research differ in their epistemological foundations and in other respects too. Indeed, when we look at the areas that were the focus of the last three sections—the relationship between theory and research, epistemological considerations, and ontological issues—we can see quantitative and qualitative research as forming two distinctive *general orientations* to the conduct of

TABLE 1.1 Fundamental differences between quantitative and qualitative research strategies

	Quantitative	Qualitative
Role of theory in research	Mainly deductive; testing of theory	Mainly inductive; generation of theory
Epistemological orientation	Natural science model; positivism	Interpretivism
Ontological orientation	Objectivism	Constructionism

social research. Table 1.1 outlines the differences between quantitative and qualitative research in terms of the three areas.

Thus, quantitative research:

- usually entails a deductive approach to the relationship between theory and research in which theory testing is a prime objective;
- incorporates the practices and norms of the natural science model and of positivism in particular; and
- generally embodies a view of society as an external, objective reality.

By contrast, qualitative research:

- takes a predominantly inductive approach to the relationship between theory and research, in which the generation of theories and interpretations is the main goal;
- rejects the use of the natural science and positivist models in social research and replaces them with methodologies that seek to determine how individuals interpret their social world; and
- embodies a view of social reality as a constantly shifting and emergent property of individuals' creations.

There is even more to the quantitative/qualitative distinction than this contrast suggests. The nature of quantitative and qualitative research respectively will be outlined in greater detail in Chapters 4 and 9. Then in Chapter 14 their contrasting features will be further explored as we examine the effects of the commitment to a positivist epistemology in quantitative research and the rejection of that epistemology by qualitative researchers.

Although it is useful to contrast the two general orientations, it is important not to hammer a wedge between them. For example, although quantitative research tends to be deductive and qualitative work inductive, there are notable exceptions to that general rule. It may seem perverse to introduce a basic set of distinctions and then suggest that they are problematic, but a recurring theme of this book is that discussing the nature of social research is just as complex as conducting research itself. We can outline the typical philosophical assumptions and research practices of the two general orientations, but the full reality is messier than those neat categories would suggest. Issues become more complicated the deeper we delve into them.

For example, we've seen that qualitative research is typically described as being more concerned with generating theories than testing them. However, there are many studies in which qualitative research is used to test rather than generate theories. Ellis et al.'s (2020) study of interactions between Black Muslim immigrants and the police, discussed above, used a qualitative approach, but an important goal of the research was to determine whether a pre-existing theory—minority group threat theory—was supported by the qualitative data that was gathered. Another example is Hier's (2002) investigation of Toronto rave scenes, with their all-night dancing and amphetamine use. Hier wanted to show that the regulation of raves was a contest between a city that feared increased drug use and rave supporters, who eventually won the day by arguing that banning raves would drive the drugs underground with even worse consequences. Similarly, although Wilson's (2002) study of the same topic is broadly interpretivist, with its examination of how ravers view their social situation, it includes some objectivist overtones. For example, in exploring the effects of technology, including the Internet, on the scene, he was describing a world that is "out there" and as having a formal, objective quality. And, of course, there are quantitative studies that incorporate elements of the qualitative orientation, such as studies of social attitudes that explore people's perceptions of societal issues in considerable depth (e.g., Kandler, Bell, & Riemann, 2016).

The point here is that, in general, quantitative and qualitative research represent different research orientations, and that the two approaches may be quite different in terms of the role of theory, epistemological issues, and ontological concerns, but the distinction is not hard and fast. Also, it is becoming more commonplace for research projects to combine both within a single research project, as we will see in Chapter 14.

Finally, lest there be any doubt about it, the position taken in this book is that both general orientations—the quantitative and the qualitative—are invaluable in the quest for knowledge and understanding. And both have profound social and political importance.

Influences on the conduct of social research

You can now see how social research is influenced by a variety of factors. Figure 1.3 summarizes the influences examined so far, but adds three more: the impact of *values*, *politics*, and *issues related to the research question*.

Values

How might the values, personal beliefs, and feelings of researchers affect their work? Perhaps one would expect social scientists to be completely value-free and objective in their studies. Research that simply reflects the personal views of its practitioners would be biased and invalid, and thus unscientific. Durkheim (1858–1917) wrote that *social facts* are objects whose study requires that all "preconceptions must be eradicated" (1938, p. 31). Since values are a form of preconception, his point implies that they should be suppressed when conducting research. But is that humanly possible? Social researchers never work in a moral or evaluative vacuum: they are always influenced by value presuppositions that have implications for the conduct of social research. This view is increasingly accepted among social researchers. Indeed, it is now recognized that values can play a role at any or all points in the process of social research, including the following:

- choice of research area
- formulation of the research question
- choice of method
- formulation of the research design and data collection techniques
- data collection
- analysis of data
- interpretation of data
- conclusions

This can have both positive and negative consequences. Values can help us act ethically and may motivate us to be a positive influence in the world. At the same time, they may shade off into ideological bias or observational blind spots if they lead us to ignore theoretical perspectives we don't like or evidence that does not match our expectations. Similarly, problems can arise if researchers become too emotionally involved with the people they study.

One way of dealing with the problem of values and bias is to recognize that research cannot be value-free, and to try to ensure that values in the research process are acknowledged and made explicit. This is part of a larger process of **reflexivity** or self-reflection that researchers are encouraged to carry out. As Turnbull (1973, p. 13) put it at the beginning of his book on an African society known as the Ik:

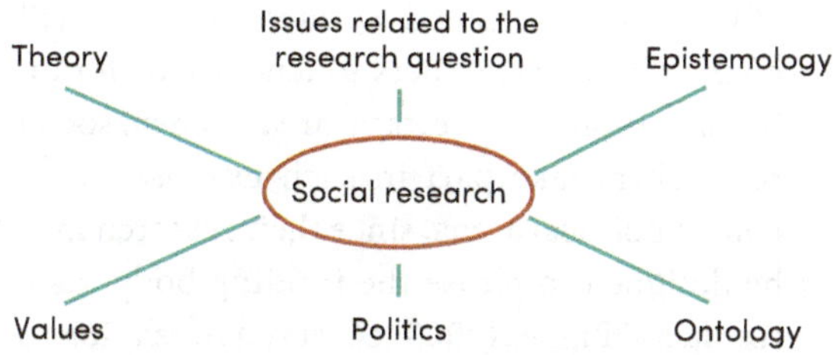

FIGURE 1.3 Influences on social research

> The reader is entitled to know something of the aims, expectations, hopes, and attitudes that the writer brought to the field [in his case, Western values about the family], for these will surely influence not only how [the writer] sees things but even what [the writer] sees.

Researchers are increasingly prepared to forewarn readers of their biases and assumptions and to explain how these may have influenced their findings. Since the mid-1970s many researchers have published "insider" accounts of what doing research is really like, as opposed to the generalities presented in social research methods textbooks (like this one). These accounts frequently function as "confessions" of personal biases and reveal the pride that researchers take in telling readers how open they are in revealing them.

Still another approach is to argue for consciously value-laden research. Some writers on social research celebrate what Mies (1993, p. 68) called a "conscious partiality." For example, Tastsoglou and Miedema (2003) clearly adopted a feminist, anti-racist approach in studying immigrant women in the Maritimes. A similar perspective allowed Pratt and Valverde (2002) to describe a large Canadian newspaper as a "notorious tabloid," "obsessed" with what it called bogus refugees. It is also exemplified in Hallgrimsdottir et al.'s (2006) condemnation of the media's role in stigmatizing sex workers in British Columbia. In fact, some feminist researchers would consider it inappropriate (as well as difficult) to do research on women in an objective, value-neutral way because that would be incompatible with their values. Instead, many feminist researchers argue for research that exposes the conditions of women's disadvantage in a male-dominated society, as Demaiter and Adams (2009) did in their study of women in the IT sector, featured in the Methods in Motion box on page 21. Some feminist writers argue that only research on women intended *for* women is consistent with women's wider political needs.

There are, then, different positions that can be taken in relation to values and value-free research. Few writers today believe it is possible to be truly objective. There is a greater awareness of the limits of objectivity, and some of the more categorical pronouncements on the subject, such as Durkheim's, have fallen into disfavour. At the same time, giving free rein to one's political beliefs and value positions can be problematic. Researchers today still have to fight the all-too-human propensity to demonize those whose values are different from their own, and they still struggle with the temptation to summarily reject research findings when the researcher's ideological or moral positions are not compatible with their own.

Politics in social research

At various places in this book we take the position that social research has political implications. Here are some examples of the ways in which social research may be political:

- Social researchers often *take sides*. There are many ways this can happen. To consider just a few: feminist researchers may focus on the disadvantages that women face and the possibilities for improving the position of women in society; some social scientists may favour increased government intervention in economic affairs, while others defend the free market; sociologists and political scientists in Quebec may be split between sovereigntists and federalists.
- A related issue involves research *funding*. Much social research is funded by organizations such as private firms or government departments that may have a vested interest in the outcomes of the research. The very fact that these organizations fund some research projects but not others opens the door to political influence. Such organizations may seek to invest in studies that will be useful to them or supportive of their operations and world views. They will often call for researchers to tender bids for an investigation in a certain area. When social researchers take part in such exercises, they enter a political arena, since their research may be designed to please the funding body. As a result, as Hughes (2000) observed in relation to research in the field of crime, an investigation

Methods in Motion | Applications to Canadian Society

Women in male-dominated occupations: How do they fare?

Demaiter and Adams (2009) did a qualitative study of how Canadian women cope in the male-dominated world of information technology (IT) workplaces. As is typical of qualitative research, the study involved only a relatively small number of people: interviews were conducted with 11 successful women in eight IT organizations located in four different provinces. The authors acknowledge that the "small sample size and the uniqueness of study participants prevent generalization" (Demaiter & Adams, p. 39), which is commonly the case with this sort of research. However, as we will see in later chapters, it is not necessarily the goal of qualitative research to come up with findings that can be generalized to some larger population. Instead, qualitative researchers seek to find out how the people in the study perceive their world by allowing them to speak for themselves. The sorts of insights that can be derived from research of this kind are difficult to attain in quantitative research, which normally requires research participants to choose from a fixed set of responses.

For the interviews, Demaiter and Adams used a semi-structured format that included open-ended questions. The interviews were conducted in three different ways: eight by telephone, two in person, and one by email. Here again the authors were open about the limitations of their methods: "We acknowledge the fact that the mixed format [for interviews] . . . is not ideal" (Demaiter & Adams, p. 40). The authors are not alone in having to settle for a methodology that wasn't exactly what they would have preferred. In fact, virtually all studies in the social sciences involve methodological compromises of one sort or another, partly because the resources available to do the research are always limited. Nevertheless, the results can still be highly informative if wise methodological decisions are made.

The authors found that, by and large, the women they interviewed did not perceive their gender to be a barrier to their career advancement. One database analyst, for example, stated: "Yes, I've never felt that I was at a disadvantage (or an advantage) because I am a woman" (Demaiter & Adams, p. 41). Yet when asked to elaborate on their experiences, many of the women suggested that gender was in fact an issue in their workplace. For example, one interviewee said, "I mean you have to be super smart, super intelligent, like way above average to go beyond a certain level because the glass ceiling is definitely there" (Demaiter & Adams, p. 43). Demaiter and Adams concluded that the women in their study may have been successful in their careers partly because they were, to a certain extent, oblivious to the gendered nature of their workplace—they forged ahead undaunted by the gender barriers they faced.

In addition to providing a window from which to view women's experiences in male-dominated occupations, this study illustrates a point raised in the Preface to this book, namely that issues of power and politics inevitably enter the picture whenever social interaction takes place. What differs from study to study is the extent to which the political implications are made explicit. In the case of this project, the political elements of the study are never far from the surface. For instance, the authors write that the women's "tendency to downplay the significance of gender" in their career histories may serve to "prevent meaningful change" (Demaiter & Adams, p. 31), which suggests that the researchers see their work as informing a larger discussion on gender relations in Canadian society, an issue that has important political dimensions. Again, virtually all research in the social sciences is to some degree relevant to politics in the larger sense of the word.

of gun crimes among the "underclass" is more likely to receive funding than one concerned with wrongdoing committed by agents of the state. Morgan (2000) pointed out that research funded by government is typically empirical and quantitative; it tends to be concerned with the short-term costs and benefits of a particular policy or innovation; and it is generally uncritical in the sense that the underlying government policies are not questioned: all the government wants to know about is the effectiveness of their implementation. Political issues often arise when the funding agency itself is trying to secure a continuous stream of government funding.

- Gaining *access* to research participants can also be a political process, especially in the case of organizations. Access to organizations is usually mediated by **gatekeepers** concerned not only about the researcher's motives but also about what the organization stands to gain from the investigation, what it will lose by participating in terms of staff time and other costs, and the potential risks to its image. Often, gatekeepers seek to influence how the investigation will take place: what kinds of questions can be asked; who can and cannot be a focus of study; the amount of time to be spent with each research participant; the interpretation of the findings; and the form the reports will take, even to the point of asking to approve drafts.
- Public institutions, such as police departments, schools, and hospitals, as well as most commercial firms, are concerned with how they are going to be represented in publications. Consequently, gaining access is almost always a matter of *negotiation* and as such inevitably turns into a political process. The product of such negotiations is often referred to as "the research bargain," and in many cases there is more than one bargain that has to be struck. Once in the organization, researchers often discover layers of gatekeepers. For example, let's say a provincial government grants a research team permission to talk to the boys in a group home. Before the research can begin, the head of the home has to be brought onside, then the staff, and then the actual adolescents. Frequently, one of the staff is then given the responsibility of dealing with the fieldworkers. A suspicion that the researchers are really working for management then has to be overcome. And it is unwise to assume that simply because gatekeepers have granted access, a smooth passage will ensue in subsequent dealings with the people to be studied. Perhaps the most powerful of the boys will turn out to be the key gatekeeper. Researchers may find themselves used as pawns if subgroups attempt to enlist them in advancing a particular goal. Research participants who doubt the utility of social research may even try to obstruct the research process. For example, in Beagan's (2001) study of "everyday inequalities" among Canadian medical students, some of the students refused to complete a survey when they heard she was asking about the treatment of gays and lesbians, and one student who did participate nevertheless reported annoyance with being asked about sexual orientation.
- There may be pressure to restrict the *publication* of findings. Hughes (2000) cited a study of plea bargaining in the British criminal justice system as a case in point. The researchers had uncovered what were deemed at the time to be disconcerting levels of informal plea bargaining, and they concluded that the formal judicial process was being weakened. The English legal establishment sought to thwart the dissemination of the findings and was persuaded to allow publication only when a panel of academics confirmed the **validity** of the findings. Similarly, the editors of academic journals may refuse to publish pieces that do not conform to their own ideological or political preferences.

This is just a small handful of the ways in which politics intrudes in the research process.

Issues related to the research question

Some important determinants of how research is conducted follow from the research question one is trying to answer. Specifically, the choice of research orientation, design, or method has to match the specific research question being investigated. For instance, if a researcher is interested in measuring the impact of various possible causes of a social phenomenon, a quantitative strategy is probably appropriate. Alternatively, if the focus is on the world views of members of a certain social group and how those views develop, a qualitative research strategy—one sensitive to the way participants interpret their social world—may be the way to go. If a researcher is interested in a topic on which little or no research has been done, a quantitative strategy may be difficult to employ because there is little prior literature from which to draw leads about possible causes. A more qualitative, exploratory approach may be preferable because that type of investigation is typically associated with the generation of theory rather than theory testing (see Table 1.1) and with a relatively unstructured approach to the research process.

A related dimension that has important implications for how the research will be conducted involves the nature of the topic and of the people being investigated. A researcher who wants to study individuals involved in illicit activities—for example, price fixing, shoplifting, or drug dealing—may find it difficult to develop the rapport with them that is needed to conduct a social survey. It is not surprising, therefore, that researchers in these areas tend to use a qualitative strategy. On the other hand, it's unlikely that the hypotheses in Box 1.3 on secularization could have been tested using a qualitative approach.

Formulating a research question

Creating a research question is like picking a destination for a hike: where you will start out, the route you will take, and what you will experience along the way are largely determined by the endpoint you are trying to reach. What you stand to accomplish with a particular research study and how you will accomplish it are profoundly affected by the goal you have in mind, which is expressed in your research question.

A research question states the purpose of the study in the form of a question. This is useful because a question can often be more evocative and stimulating than a simple declarative statement. A question arouses curiosity and challenges the researcher to find ways to answer it. Here are some examples of research questions taken from a quantitative study of voluntary associations in Canada: "Does individual income level affect whether an individual is a voluntary association member? Does this effect differ between neighbourhoods?" (Duncan, 2010, p. 578). Here are two research questions taken from a qualitative study of older immigrant women in Quebec: "What does it mean to older women to grow old in a land of immigration? What are the effects of immigration on their living conditions, especially when they have immigrated after 50?" (Charpentier & Quéniart, 2017, p. 437).

The process of formulating and assessing research questions is something of an art, but here are some general thoughts. As you may have noticed in the research questions quoted above, the form the question takes may differ depending on whether the study is quantitative or qualitative in orientation. Quantitative questions usually ask whether a particular variable or set of variables has an influence on the phenomenon of interest. Duncan's (2010) question, for example, reveals that her study was designed to inquire into whether personal income affects the likelihood that one will join a voluntary association, and if so, whether that relationship varies depending on the neighbourhood in which one lives. Implied in her questions is a certain causal model that may apply to some larger population, one that extends beyond the people studied. This is the deductive method at work.

Qualitative research questions tend to be less specific, and are generally not designed to evaluate causal models of this kind. They tend to be "open-ended, evolving, and non-directional" (Creswell, 2013, p. 138). The reason for this is that qualitative researchers usually want to allow multiple interpretations and perspectives to emerge from the people and settings they are examining. Also, since qualitative social scientists often use the inductive method, they don't have a fully preconceived notion of what they expect to find, making it pointless to ask a specific question at the beginning of a study. Flexibility in exploring whatever one encounters in the course of doing the research is essential if one is to uncover the meanings and interpretations held by the people studied, and the processes by which they develop. For instance, Charpentier and Quéniart's (2017) research question, "What does it mean to older women to grow old in a land of immigration?" was purposely open-ended because their goal was to give the women they studied a voice, not to march them through specific topics and issues that they as researchers may have considered to be important. The data they collected allowed them to discern certain themes and patterns of response offered up by the participants in their study, which is the goal of the inductive method.

Quantitative research may start with the choice of a general area of interest: for example, male homosexuality. At this stage, a very general research question might be "How do people in general feel about gays?" This broad research area would have to be narrowed down: for example, to "How does the Canadian adult population react to the portrayal of gays in television dramas?" But even that is too broad, so the next level of specification might be something like "Do young straight men react differently than young straight women to the portrayal of gay male romance on television program X? If so, do those differences reflect a more fluid sexual identity on the part of young women as compared to young men?" Such questions could be linked to larger theories of sex roles, sexual orientation acquisition, socialization, and the tolerance of difference in society.

Research questions in qualitative inquiries may become more specific over time too, but that usually occurs primarily after the researcher has started to gather data. A general research question may be retained throughout the study, but more specific sub-questions normally evolve as the research unfolds. For example, ethnographic research may begin with a general question such as "What is going on here?" (Wolcott, 2008, p. 73), but as the researcher learns more about the people to be analyzed, more specific questions usually come to mind. These questions could be something like the following: "How do the people under study deal with those who violate group norms? In cases where people are punished for their violations, how do the offenders make sense of the punishment they receive, and how does it affect how they feel about the other members of the group?"

No single study can answer all the research questions that will occur to the researcher. Only a small number of them can be selected. The need to narrow the topic is not only a matter of the time available and the cost of doing research. It is also a reflection of the need for a clear focus.

As suggested above, the research questions may change as the study progresses, for a number of reasons. The discovery of a new data source may change the focus a bit, as might some of the initial findings. For instance, if in the study of male homosexuality the researchers find that having a gay relative in the immediate family makes a large difference in people's attitudes, the research question and the attendant methodology and theoretical orientation may be revised. The research question may also change because of limitations in time and other resources available to the researcher. Box 1.6 offers some tips on developing research questions.

Research questions set realistic boundaries for research. A poorly formulated research question can result in unfocused and substandard research. No matter how well designed a questionnaire is or how skilled qualitative interviewers are, clear research questions are required to avoid going off in unnecessary directions and tangents. Research questions are crucial because they guide:

- the literature search;
- decisions about the kind of research design to employ;
- decisions about what data to collect and from whom;
- the analysis of the data; and
- the writing up of the findings and conclusions.

Box 1.6 | Considerations when developing research questions

A good research question will:

- be as clear as possible so that it will be understandable to others;
- be researchable: it must allow for the development of a research design and the collection of data; this means that extremely abstract terms may not be suitable;
- relate in some way to existing studies that suggest how your question may be approached. Even with a topic that has not been widely researched, there will probably be some relevant literature (for example, on related or parallel topics). Establishing connections with existing studies will help to show how your research can make a contribution to the existing knowledge on the topic;
- be linked to the other research questions in the study, so that you can develop a single argument or at least a set of related arguments; this is hard to do with unrelated research questions; and
- be neither too broad (no research project can do justice to all aspects of a topic) nor too narrow (unable to make a meaningful contribution to an area of study).

If you are unsure about how to formulate research questions (or about other aspects of research), look at journal articles or research monographs to see how other researchers have handled them.

Key Points

- Theory can either precede research and data gathering (the deductive method) or emerge out of it (induction).
- Epistemological considerations loom large in the choice of a research strategy. To a great extent, the issues revolve around the advantages and disadvantages associated with the positivist, interpretivist, and critical approaches to science.
- Quantitative and qualitative research constitute different approaches to social investigation and carry with them important epistemological and ontological assumptions.
- Ontological considerations, such as objectivism versus constructionism, also constitute important dimensions of the quantitative/qualitative contrast.
- Values can impinge on the research process in various ways; as a consequence, research often has political dimensions.
- The political dimensions of research relate to the exercise of power at different stages of an investigation.
- Issues related to the research question can also affect decisions about research methods. Clear research questions improve the chances of success.

Questions for Review (R) and Creative Application (A)

Theory and research

R1 What is a "theory," as the term is used in this chapter?

A1 Name a social regularity or pattern (e.g., women are more likely to suffer from eating disorders than men), then provide a social theory that might explain it. Be sure to comment on how the theory would explain the phenomenon.

R2 What is the purpose of gathering data if the deductive method is used?

A2 Name one specific hypothesis that can be derived from the theory you mentioned to address the previous bullet. Provide an example of a hypothetical research finding that would support the hypothesis.

R3 What is the inductive method, and how can it be used to come up with theories or interpretations of social phenomena?

A3 How could you use induction to analyze in-class interactions between professors and students? What sorts of theories or interpretations might you come up with if you were to use induction in that setting?

Epistemological considerations

R4 What is meant by the terms "positivism," "interpretivism," and "critical social science"?

A4 How could you use each of these three approaches to social science to do a study on how social media usage shapes a person's self-image?

Ontological considerations

R5 What do the terms "objectivism" and "constructionism" mean?

A5 Provide an objectivist account of why women are more likely to pursue a career in nursing than men. Then compare and contrast it with a constructionist view of this issue.

General research orientations: Quantitative and qualitative research

R6 Outline the main differences between quantitative and qualitative research in terms of the relationship between theory and data, epistemological considerations, and ontological issues.

A6 Illustrate your answer by describing how quantitative and qualitative researchers could conduct a study on academic achievement among trans high school students.

Influences on the conduct of social research

R7 How might someone's personal values influence the topics they choose to research?

A7 Explain how values might have affected Demaiter and Adams's (2009) decision to do research on women in the information technology sector (see the Methods in Motion box on page 21).

Research questions

R8 What are the main characteristics of a good research question?

A8 Imagine that you are curious about the connection between growing up in an economically poor neighbourhood and joining a street gang. Produce a research question that would be appropriate for a quantitative study on this topic. Then construct a research question that a qualitative researcher might use.

Visit our online resource center for free assessment: https://learninglink.oup.com/

Interactive Classroom Activities

1. Divide the class into small groups of students. Each group is to select a social phenomenon, human behaviour, or experience that they think is especially interesting or important to understand. The groups then come up with a research question or questions that could be used as a focal point for research. For example, "What causes eating disorders?" Or, "What is it like to be a victim of domestic violence?" The students can pick any topic they like.

   Each group then explains how they would *research* the topic they have chosen. They are to do that by answering the following questions, drawing on the knowledge they've gained in class and from reading this chapter:

   a. Have your social or cultural *values* influenced your choice of subject matter? Explain.
   b. Can your topic be researched *scientifically*? Explain. (Hint: Think of the different ways in which social researchers define "science.")
   c. Explain how a *positivist*, an *interpretive researcher*, and a *critical social scientist* would conduct research on the topic you've chosen. Provide as much detail as possible.

d. Make up some results that researchers in each of the three approaches to science might produce. In other words, pretend that you did the research in each of the three ways and came up with some findings. *You may have a different set of findings for each of the three approaches.* Use your imagined findings to generate three answers to your research question(s), one for each of the three approaches to science.

Once those tasks have been completed, each group is to select a spokesperson(s) to report their group's work to the rest of the class. Those listening are to ask questions and offer a critique of the group's presentation.

2. The class is divided into three groups in order to conduct a debate. The first group must make the case for position "a" below; the second group argues in favour of position "b"; and the third group can choose either "a" or "b." Each group is given 20 minutes to prepare its case.

a. The social researcher's most important duty is to *explain* the social world, not to change it. The search for practical applications such as positive social change is best left to other people because it may create political bias on the part of the researcher, such as when findings are ignored or rejected simply because they come from people who do not share the researcher's political views.

b. The social researcher's most important duty is to *make the world a better place* by ridding society of things such as racism, economic inequality, and sexism. Research that does not have positive social change as its primary goal is not worth doing.

After all groups have made their arguments, each one is allowed time for rebuttal. When that is finished, the class votes to decide which group made the strongest case.

Relevant Websites

A good way to become familiar with how research is done is to read articles published in academic journals. You may not be able to fully understand the methodologies and data analyses at this stage of your academic career, but reading articles will help you become familiar with formal research presentations. Below are the Web addresses for some leading Canadian and international social science journals. You may not be able to access articles in a particular journal directly; it may be necessary to sign on to your institution's library server first.

Canadian Journal of Sociology

http://ejournals.library.ualberta.ca/index.php/CJS/index

Canadian Review of Sociology

www.csa-scs.ca/canadian-review/

Canadian Political Science Review

http://ojs.unbc.ca/index.php/cpsr

Canadian Journal of Political Science

www.cambridge.org/core/journals/canadian-journal-of-political-science-revue-canadienne-de-science-politique

Canadian Social Work Review

https://caswe-acfts.ca/cswr-journal/

Native Social Work Journal

https://zone.biblio.laurentian.ca/handle/10219/378

Canadian Journal of Education

https://cje-rce.ca/#

American Journal of Sociology

www.journals.uchicago.edu/toc/ajs/current

American Sociological Review

http://journals.sagepub.com/home/asr

Social Forces

http://sf.oxfordjournals.org

Qualitative Sociology

www.springer.com/social+sciences/journal/11133

British Journal of Sociology

https://onlinelibrary.wiley.com/journal/14684446

Sociology

https://journals.sagepub.com/home/soc

International Journal of Sociology

www.tandfonline.com/loi/mijs20#.VVtagvlVhBc

Here are some websites you can visit to learn more about participatory action research:

International Institute for Environment and Development

www.iied.org/participatory-learning-action-pla

Community-Based Research Canada

http://communityresearchcanada.ca/home

The Tavistock Institute

www.tavinstitute.org

The websites below offer information and guidance on Indigenous research methods:

National Indigenous Research and Knowledges Network

https://www.nirakn.edu.au/

Indigenous Research Methodologies

https://guides.library.ubc.ca/IndigResearch

Indigenous Research Resources, compiled by Lakehead University

https://www.lakeheadu.ca/research-and-innovation/research-services/resources/indigenous

FAQ on Doing Indigenous Research in a Good Way, offered by Memorial University

https://www.mun.ca/research/Indigenous/faq.php

(Websites accessed 4 September 2021.)

OXFORD learning link

More resources are available on Oxford Learning Link. Visit https://learninglink.oup.com/ for:

- Student self-quiz
- Flash cards
- Audio clips
- Videos
- Activities

2 Research Designs

Chapter Overview

A research design is a framework for the collection and analysis of the data that is used to answer research questions. It must satisfy certain criteria, and the form it takes depends on the research questions being asked. This chapter will discuss four prominent research designs:

- **experimental** and related designs (such as the **quasi-experiment**)
- **cross-sectional designs**, including those involving **survey research and some forms of qualitative interviewing**
- **longitudinal** designs, such as panel and cohort studies and various forms of **qualitative** research
- **case study** designs

Key Learning Outcomes

Here is a list of goals you should try to achieve as you read and think about the material in this chapter. After completing this chapter, you should be able to:

1. Discuss how and why some research designs are used to produce **nomothetic** explanations, while others are used to come up with **idiographic** explanations.
2. Explain the structure and logic of the experimental method, and describe how a knowledge of this method can aid in the understanding other research designs.
3. Identify the strengths and weaknesses of cross-sectional designs.
4. Describe the purposes of using a longitudinal design.
5. Explain how the case study approach is used in research.

▲ FatCamera

"Would you tell me, please, which way I ought to go from here?"

"That depends a good deal on where you want to get to," said the Cat.

"I don't much care where—" said Alice.

"Then it doesn't matter which way you go," said the Cat.

"—so long as I get *somewhere*," Alice added as an explanation.

"Oh, you're sure to do that," said the Cat, "if you only walk long enough."

Alice's Adventures in Wonderland
(Carroll, 1865/2009, p. 56)

It's not hard to feel a little like Alice when you start out on the journey that is a research project, especially if the voyage is one you are somewhat reluctant to undertake (this is not at all uncommon). Where should I be going with this study? How can I get there? How can I tell if I'm on the right track? Such questions flood the mind at the beginning of the trip. As Alice learned, finding the right way starts with knowing where you want to end up. In research, a lot depends on what you want to accomplish with the project, which in turn depends on the sort of research question you have posed. In this chapter we'll explore what kinds of destination are possible, some ways of getting to them, and some techniques for determining whether you are on the right path.

Introduction

Once a general research orientation has been chosen, the next step is to select a **research design**. A research design is a broad structure that guides the collection and analysis of data. Choosing a research design involves decisions about what you want to accomplish with the study. Is one of your goals to describe possible causal connections between **variables**? Will you explore how a social phenomenon changes over time, and how it may be linked to other events and situations? Will it be important to search out the meanings that the research participants attach to certain things, and how they act on those meanings? Do you want to be able to generalize your findings to people and groups that were not part of the study? How these questions are answered will affect your choice of research design.

Another important consideration in choosing a research design is the kind of explanation you would like to develop. Quantitative researchers often explain a phenomenon in terms of proposed causes and effects that are expressed in *laws* and *principles*. Such laws and principles are usually fairly general, and are meant to apply to people who were not part of the study. For example, a study that finds that men are more likely than women to approve of pornography may explain that result with a neo-Darwinian theory of erotic attraction and sexual disgust. This sort of explanation is supposed to apply to humanity in general, not just to the people who participated in the study. This approach to explanation is called *nomothetic*.

Nomothetic explanations have to satisfy *three criteria of causation*. In other words, three conditions have to be satisfied before the explanation is considered acceptable. Suppose you are trying to explain why some people are more violent than others, and your explanation involves the idea that the propensity to be violent is influenced by watching violent movies. For this to be accepted as a causal explanation, it would have to meet the following criteria:

1. *Correlation*. The proposed cause and the proposed effect have to vary together. In our example, as the number of violent movies watched changes, the level of violence would have to change as well. You would have to observe that, in general, the greater the number of violent movies watched, the higher the level of violence.
2. *Time order*. The proposed cause must precede the effect in time. Assume that you do find a correlation between watching violent movies

and real violence. You would also have to show that the increase in the watching of violent movies came *before* the increase in violence. If you found that the increase in the watching of violent movies occurred after the level of violence went up, your explanation would have to be rejected.

3. *Non-spuriousness.* Alternative explanations for the correlation observed have to be ruled out. "Spurious" literally means false or illegitimate. A common source of spuriousness is a variable that influences both the proposed cause and the effect. Suppose our data reveal that people who are violent tend to watch a lot of violent movies, and that people who reject violence watch very few violent films, i.e., that the two variables are correlated. Can we conclude from this that watching violent movies *causes* people to be more violent? In order to answer that question, we would try to determine whether some third factor is the cause of the correlation between the number of violent movies watched and the level of violence. For instance, could it be that people with low impulse control are drawn to violent movies and tend to commit acts of violence? If so, then the level of impulse control affects both the watching of violent movies (the original proposed cause) and the level of violence (the effect). If that is the case, the correlation between watching violent movies and the level of real violence is spurious, and your explanation does not hold up. As a further illustration of spuriousness, imagine that you live in a summer resort community where there is ample opportunity for swimming. Throughout the calendar year, there is probably a correlation between the number of ice-cream cones sold on a particular day and the number of people swimming: as one increases the other also increases. But does purchasing ice-cream cones *cause* people to go swimming? Of course not. Those two things are influenced by a third factor: warm weather.

Quantitative researchers choose research designs that help to satisfy these three criteria. Qualitative researchers, on the other hand, aim for different kinds of explanations. They usually seek to produce a rich description of a person or group based on the perceptions and feelings of the people studied, rather than to discover general laws and principles. They may also try to get a sense of how those phenomena develop over time and how they can result from interpersonal interactions or one's position in a power hierarchy. These sorts of accounts are called *idiographic* explanations, and they usually involve a detailed "story" or description of the people studied that is based on *empathetic understanding*. Bowen (2015), for instance, used this approach to determine how off-street sex workers in Vancouver viewed the experience of transitioning from the sex industry into "square" (non-sex) occupations and lifestyles. On the basis of the insights gained from the study, she revealed that people who are in the process of leaving the industry or who are contemplating leaving are often stigmatized and humiliated for their past behaviours, and that the voices of such people must be heard if government transition programs are to be effective. Qualitative researchers will choose research designs that will produce these sorts of idiographic explanations.

Once a design has been selected, a specific method for collecting data has to be chosen. There are many different ways of gathering data. One way is to use a preset instrument, such as a self-completion **questionnaire** or a structured **interview schedule**. Another is to utilize a less formalized method like **participant observation** or **ethnography** in which the researcher takes part in the activities of a group of people, sometimes even living among them for a time.

Consider one of the research designs to be covered in this chapter: the case study. It entails a detailed exploration of a specific case, which could be a community, an organization, a person, or an event. Once you've selected a case to investigate, how will you get data on it? Do you use participant observation? Do you observe from the sidelines? Do you conduct interviews? Do you examine documents? Do you administer questionnaires? Any or all of these methods can be used.

Research designs

Experimental design

When people hear the word "research," the use of experiments often comes to mind. However, true experiments are fairly rare in sociology, though they can be found in areas such as social psychology and studies of organizations. Researchers in social policy may also use them to assess the impact of reforms or new policies. The main reason for discussing experiments here is that a true experiment involves a systematic comparison of what happens when one set of participants has a particular experience or treatment while another does not, a logic that can also be found in other research designs. The greatest strength of experiments is that they can in some instances be effective in establishing causation (sometimes referred to as **internal validity**), especially when they are used to isolate the effects of a small number of factors. This does not mean that the experimental method is necessarily superior to the others. As we shall see below, experiments, like other methodological approaches, have their strengths and weaknesses when they are used in social research, and are better suited to some research topics than others.

Manipulation

If experiments may be strong in establishing causation, why do social researchers not make more use of them? The reason is simple: to conduct a true experiment, it is necessary to do something to people and observe the effects. To put the matter more formally, an experiment *manipulates* an **independent variable** (a proposed cause of some phenomenon) to determine its influence on a **dependent variable** (the proposed effect). Typically, some people are allocated to a "treatment" group in which the independent variable is changed or manipulated, while others are placed in a "control" group where no manipulation takes place. The dependent variable is then observed and measured. The problem is that many of the independent variables of concern to social researchers cannot be manipulated. For example, some sociologists maintain that a country's national character is affected by whether the country came into existence through revolution (for example, Lipset, 1990). In order to test this idea experimentally, revolution would have to be induced in some randomly selected areas to produce new countries, while in others no revolution would be fomented. The researcher would then compare the national characters of the revolutionary countries with the non-revolutionary ones. Needless to say, such experimental manipulations would usually be impossible to carry out.

This example also illustrates a second reason why experiments are so rare in sociology: ethical concerns often preclude them. Suppose you are interested in the effect of poverty-induced poor nutrition on children's academic performance. In order to examine this issue experimentally, you could select a number of six-year-olds and randomly assign them to one of two groups. Those in the first group would be underfed for six months, while those in the second would be given ample, nutritious diets. Then you would test the two groups to see if they differed in academic achievement. Although sound from a purely methodological standpoint, such a study would be hideous from an ethical perspective. (If conducting such a study sounds farfetched, Chapter 3 examines Canadian experimental research from the 1940s and 1950s in which serious malnutrition among Indigenous people was allowed to continue for two years in order to establish baseline measurements for a study on the effectiveness of various dietary interventions.) In fact, as we will see in Chapter 3, ethical issues may arise even when the experimental manipulation appears to be innocuous and is of very short duration.

Another reason why experiments are uncommon in sociology is that many of the things of interest to sociologists—gender roles, political preferences, the formation of social movements, and so on—have complex, long-term causes that cannot be easily simulated in experiments. Could the experimental method be used to explain the rise of second-wave feminism in the 1960s? Unfortunately not: experiments are generally limited to relatively simple, short-term manipulations of independent variables (see Brannigan, 2004). A further reason is that even where social scientists are successful in using experiments to identify causal variables, the perceptions and feelings of the participants—which provide information vital to a full understanding of the phenomenon in question—are usually not examined in depth (Dobash & Dobash, 2000).

Before moving to a more complete discussion of experimental designs, it is important to introduce a basic distinction between *laboratory* and **field experiments**. The former take place in artificial settings, whereas the latter occur in real-life surroundings such as classrooms and factories. The Rosenthal and Jacobson (1968) study described below is a well-known example of a field experiment.

Classic experimental design

Rosenthal and Jacobson (1968) tried to determine what effect teachers' expectations had on their students' academic performance. In addition to illustrating the classical experimental design, their study is a good example of research that gets a lot of attention, is then subject to intense methodological scrutiny (see Brannigan, 2004, pp. 80–89 for critiques), and ultimately provides the impetus for further research designed to improve on the original.

The research was conducted in a US school where many poor and minority-group children were enrolled. In the spring all the students were given a test and told it was designed to identify "spurters"—that is, students who were likely to experience a sudden improvement in their academic performance. At the beginning of the following academic year, the teachers were given the names of the spurters in their classes. But this was a ruse: the students identified as spurters were simply selected at random; they were not chosen on the basis of their test performance. The test was re-administered eight months after the original one, allowing the authors to compare the so-called spurters with the other students on things such as IQ scores, reading ability, and intellectual curiosity. Since Rosenthal and Jacobson believed that there was no initial difference in ability between the spurters and the others, any improvements were attributed to the fact that the teachers had been led to expect the spurters to perform better. The authors report that the teachers' expectations that the spurters would show superior academic performance actually caused those students to do better than the others, presumably because they received differential treatment from the teachers. But here again, ethical issues arise. Was the study fair to the students designated as non-spurters? Should their teachers have been given false information indicating that they were not especially gifted students? Did their participation in the study impede their academic development?

The Rosenthal and Jacobson study includes most of the essential features of what is known as the classical experimental design. The people in the study (in this case, students) are randomly assigned to two groups. The experimental manipulation (different levels of the independent variable, here heightened teacher expectations) is carried out on the **experimental group** or *treatment group* (the spurters). The other group is not given the treatment and thus forms a **control group**. The dependent variable—academic performance—is measured before the experimental manipulation to make sure that the two groups really are, on average, equal at the start (see Figure 2.1). If they are equal, and because of **random assignment** they should be, the researchers can feel confident that any differences in student performance found between the two groups *after* the manipulation were due to the treatment. Everything else about the two groups is presumed to be the same, leaving differences in teacher expectations as the only possible explanation for any differences that are found between the spurters and non-spurters.

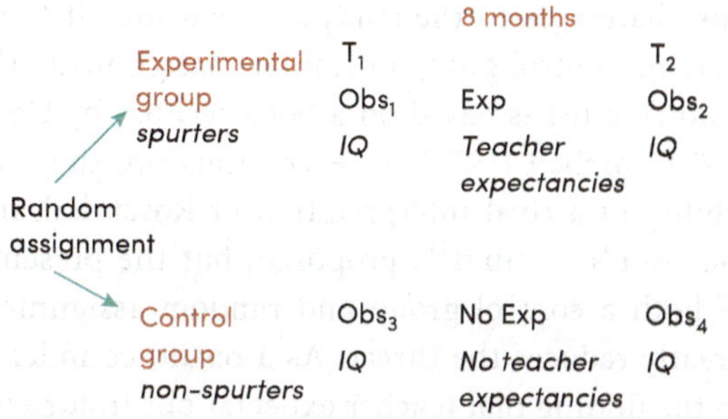

FIGURE 2.1 Classical experimental design

To capture the essence of the classical experimental design, the following simple notation is used:

- **Obs**: an **obs**ervation made of the dependent variable. There may be more than two observations but, to simplify, the design shows the most common configuration: pre-test and post-test; here, IQ test scores before the experimental manipulation and after.
- **Exp**: the **exp**erimental treatment (independent variable); here, the creation of teacher expectancies. **No Exp** refers to the absence of an experimental treatment and represents the experience of the control group.
- **T**: the **t**iming of the observations made in relation to the dependent variable; here, the time when an IQ test is administered

What is the purpose of the control group? Surely it is what happens to the spurters (the experimental group) that really matters. For this study to be a true experiment, however, it must control for (in other words, eliminate) rival explanations of its causal findings, leaving teacher expectations as the only factor that could have created any differences in performance between the two groups. Of course, student performance is a complex phenomenon, with many causes, but the present study wanted to examine only one of those causes (teacher expectations). The presence of a control group *and* the random assignment of participants to the experimental and control groups help to eliminate rival explanations for differences in academic performance, which in this case are any explanations other than different teacher expectations. To see this, consider some threats that would pose serious challenges to the study's conclusions if there were *no* control group or random assignment. The following list is based on a book written by Cook and Campbell (1979). In each situation, the possibility of a rival interpretation of Rosenthal and Jacobson's findings is proposed, but the presence of both a control group and random assignment greatly reduces the threat. As a result, confidence in the finding that teacher expectations influenced student performance is enhanced.

- *History.* This refers to events other than the manipulation of teacher expectations that might have caused the spurters' scores to rise. For example, suppose that the school's principal had taken steps to raise standards in the school. Without a control group, we could not be sure whether it was the teachers' expectations or the principal's action that produced the increase in spurters' grades. With a control group, we can say that the principal's action should have had an effect on the people in that group too, and therefore that the differences between the experimental and control groups can be attributed to the effect of teacher expectations alone.
- *Testing.* This threat refers to the possibility that participants may become more experienced at taking a test or sensitized to the aims of the experiment as a result of the pre-test. The presence of a control group, which presumably would also experience the same things, diminishes this possibility.
- *Instrumentation.* This threat refers to the possibility that changes in the way a test is administered can account for an increase (or decrease) in scores between a pre-test and post-test; for example, perhaps the teachers know their students better or are more friendly the second time they give the test. Again, if there is a control group, the people in that group should be affected as well.
- *Mortality.* A particular problem for studies that span a long period of time is the risk that some people will leave the experiment before it is over: for example, some students might move to a different school, or experience a long-term illness. Since this problem is likely to affect the control group too, it may not make a difference to the results. However, experimenters should try to determine whether mortality has affected the experimental and control groups differently.
- *Maturation.* Quite simply, people change over time and the ways in which they change may have implications for the dependent variable. The spurters might have improved anyway as

they got older, regardless of the effect of teacher expectancies. But the control group would also mature, so maturation effects cannot explain the differences between it and the experimental group.

- *Selection.* When participants are not assigned randomly to the experimental and control groups, variations between them in the post-test may be due to pre-existing differences between the two groups. For example, if all the best students were given the spurter label, it might have been their pre-existing academic ability rather than teacher expectations that caused them to do better. However, since a random selection process was employed here, the "selection" risk is greatly reduced. With random assignment, the top students would make up roughly the same proportion of the spurter group as the non-spurter group, cancelling out the effect of pre-existing academic ability. However, even with the use of random assignment, if the number of people in each group is relatively small, there is still a risk of pre-existing differences between the experimental and control groups.

Even if all these threats have been overcome, further issues may arise. First there is the question of whether the variables used in the study have been adequately measured. This refers to the matter of **measurement validity**, a topic addressed in detail in Chapter 4. In the case of the Rosenthal and Jacobson (1968) study, there are potentially two aspects to this question. First, has academic performance been adequately measured? Reading scores seem to correspond to what they are supposed to be measuring. However, given the controversy surrounding IQ tests and what they measure, we may feel unsure that gains in IQ test scores can be regarded as strongly indicative of academic performance. Similarly, to take another of the authors' measures, is intellectual curiosity a valid measure of academic performance? Does it really measure what it is supposed to measure?

Another question is whether the experimental manipulation really worked. In other words, was the identification of some schoolchildren as spurters enough to create the conditions needed for the hypothesis about teacher expectations to be tested? The study depended on the teachers' remembering the "information" they were given about the spurters for the duration of the experiment, but it is possible that as time went on some of them came to doubt or forget it; in that case, the manipulation would have been contaminated.

A second set of issues concerns the generalizability of a study's findings. In other words, do the study's conclusions apply to other people, settings, or time periods? These matters pertain to the study's **external validity**. Cook and Campbell (1979) identified five major threats to the external validity and hence the generalizability of findings derived from an experiment:

- *The representativeness of the study participants.* To what social and psychological groups can a finding be generalized? Can it be generalized to a wide variety of individuals who differ in ethnicity, social class, religion, gender, and type of personality? In the Rosenthal and Jacobson study, the students were largely from poorer groups and a large proportion from ethnic minorities. This may limit the generalizability of the findings.
- *The effects of the setting.* Can the results of a study be applied to other settings (in Rosenthal and Jacobson's case, to other schools)? There is also the wider issue of whether expectation effects can also be discerned in non-educational settings.
- *History effects.* This threat raises the question of whether the findings can be generalized to the past and into the future. The Rosenthal and Jacobson research was conducted more than 50 years ago. Would the findings still apply today? Also, their investigation was conducted at a particular juncture in the school year. Would the same results have been obtained if the research had been conducted at different points in the year?
- *The effects of pre-testing.* As a result of being pretested, people in an experiment may become

sensitized to the experimental treatment, with the result that their responses are affected as they become more test-wise. Consequently, the findings may not be generalizable to groups that have not been pre-tested, and, of course, in the real world people are rarely pre-tested. This may have occurred in the Rosenthal and Jacobson research, since all students were pre-tested at the end of the previous academic year, so the students new to the school in the fall (when the teachers were told about spurters) presumably were not pre-tested.

- **Reactive effects** *produced by the experimental arrangements.* People are frequently, if not invariably, aware of the fact that they are participating in an experiment. Their awareness may influence how they respond to the experimental treatment; for example, they may react by behaving in a socially acceptable manner rather than sincerely and spontaneously, which could affect the generalizability of the findings. Since Rosenthal and Jacobson's study participants do not appear to have been aware that they were in an experiment, this problem is unlikely to have been significant. The issue of **reactivity** and its potentially damaging effects is a recurring theme in many types of social research.

Then there is the question of **replicability**. A study is replicable if others are able to repeat it and get the same results. Sometimes replications are conducted to make sure that the original research was carried out properly; this is especially important if a study's results do not match prior findings on the topic. For replication to be possible, the initial researcher must spell out all the research procedures in great detail.

Rosenthal and Jacobson laid out their procedures and measures in detail, and anyone carrying out a replication could obtain further information from them. Consequently, their research is replicable, although there has never been an exact replication. Clairborn (1969) conducted one of the earliest replications and followed a procedure very similar to Rosenthal and Jacobson's, although the study was carried out in three middle-class suburban schools, and the timing of the creation of teacher expectancies was different from the original study. Clairborn failed to replicate Rosenthal and Jacobson's findings, casting doubt on the external validity of the original research and suggesting that the first two threats to external validity referred to earlier in this chapter may have limited the applicability of the findings.

Virtually all experiments in the social sciences involve deception of some kind. In the Rosenthal and Jacobson study, for example, the experimenters told the teachers that certain students were spurters, which simply was not true. But could the experiment have been carried out without any deception? For example, could the experimenters have told the teachers that they were testing the effects of teacher expectations on student achievement? Could they have given the teachers a list of students and said, "Pretend that these students are gifted, although they are not any more gifted, on average, than the students not on the list. We want to see whether you would treat such children differently, and whether differential treatment affects their academic performance." Surely, that sort of approach would not have produced authentic behaviour on the part of the teachers, and the teachers might well have refused to participate under those conditions for ethical and practical reasons. Clearly, some form of deception was necessary for the experiment to work.

But, as suggested above, deception raises ethical concerns—it is basically a form of lying. Chapter 3 will discuss the ethical implications of using deception in social research, as well as other sorts of ethical dilemmas facing researchers in the social sciences.

The laboratory experiment

One of the main advantages of laboratory over field experiments is the researcher's greater control over the research environment. In particular, it is easier to randomly assign participants to different experimental conditions in the laboratory than in a real-life situation, which enhances the researcher's ability to establish nomothetic causation. For example, Walsh, Hickey, & Duffy (1999) were able to tell some randomly assigned university students in Eastern Canada that previous results on the mathematics test they were about to take showed that women perform less well than men on such tests. Other students, also randomly assigned, were not told this. The data showed that women scored lower than men when informed of this "fact." When told that the test was to compare Canadians and Americans, there was no gender difference. Without the chance to randomly assign participants, there would always be some doubt that the treatment (being told that women score lower than men on the test) rather than a pre-existing difference between the two sets of participants actually caused the women to do less well than the men. Also, laboratory experiments are more easily replicated because they are less bound to a natural milieu that could be difficult to reproduce.

However, laboratory experiments also suffer from a number of limitations. Many of those shortcomings arise from low external validity. For instance, the experimental setting may not mirror real-world experiences and contexts, despite the fact that the participants are very involved in most experiments and take them very seriously. In addition, the treatment effects may be unique to the people in the study; others may not react the same way. In the case of Fisher and Ma's (2014) study described in Box 2.1, for example, the participants were drawn from an online panel and hence may not be representative of the general population, if only because their willingness to go online and their facility with the Internet may have made their responses to the experimental stimuli distinctive. They were also volunteers, who generally differ from non-volunteers (Rosnow & Rosenthal, 1997, ch. 5). In addition, the fact that they were given an incentive to participate (they were paid a small fee) might have further distinguished them from others since not everyone would be equally motivated to earn the reward given to those who participate. There was no effect of pre-testing because, as in many experiments, the participants described in Box 2.1 were not pre-tested. However, it is quite possible that reactive effects occurred: the people in the study knew they were in an experiment, and that may have affected their behaviour.

Quasi-experiments

Quasi-experiments have some characteristics of the experimental model but lack some of the features that help the researcher establish causation. Several different types of quasi-experiments have been identified (Cook & Campbell, 1979). Not all of them can be covered here, but a particularly interesting type are "natural experiments," in which experiment-like conditions are produced by naturally occurring phenomena or changes brought about by people not doing research. When that occurs, researchers can gather data in much the same way they do in experiments. For example, if an earthquake hit a particular city, but a city of comparable size and composition a short distance away was spared, the conditions for a natural experiment would be present. The effects of the natural disaster on civic pride or attitudes toward local political leaders could be measured by comparing the two cities on those variables. However, in natural experiments, it is usually impossible to randomly assign participants to experimental and control groups. The absence of random assignment casts doubt on any causal inferences, since the groups may not have been equivalent on all relevant characteristics before the independent variable was introduced. For instance, in the earthquake example, there may have been some pre-existing differences between the two cities before the earthquake struck that contributed to post-earthquake differences. So if the stricken city showed an increase in civic pride, perhaps that was not because of the earthquake, but because it had a more charismatic mayor than the neighbouring city. However, the results of such studies are still compelling because they are real rather than artificial interventions in social life, making them high in external validity.

St Helena in the South Atlantic provided a fascinating natural laboratory for the examination of various claims regarding the effect of television violence on children when TV was introduced to the island for the first time in the mid-1990s. The findings—from video footage showing young children at play during school breaks, from **diaries** kept by about 300 of the children, and from ratings by teachers—suggested that the introduction of television was not followed by an increase in the number of aggressive acts observed (Charlton, Coles, Panting, & Hannan, 1999; Charlton, Gunter, & Coles 1998). The researchers suggest that in environments such

Box 2.1 | A laboratory experiment

It is commonly recognized, both in scientific circles and in everyday life, that there are tangible benefits associated with being physically attractive. It is also well known that attractive people are thought to possess more positive attitudes and behavioural traits than the less attractive; hence the "beautiful is good" stereotype. Yet two researchers at the University of Alberta (Fisher & Ma, 2014) found that under certain experimental conditions, participants felt less empathy toward an "attractive" child.

The researchers wanted to know whether the attractiveness of children in need affects the empathy that non-relatives feel toward them. In one version of the study, the perceived attractiveness of a young girl was manipulated by showing one group of participants a picture of her that had not been altered. A second group was shown a version of the picture that had been digitally modified to make the girl appear less attractive. A "high severity" of need condition was created by telling some participants that the child in the picture was from a village in Africa that had just been struck by a mudslide, making her a homeless orphan. People experiencing the "low severity" manipulation were told of the mudslide, but were informed that the young girl's home and parents were not harmed by it. The results indicated that participants in the low severity condition who were presented with the "attractive" version of the girl's photograph showed lower levels of empathy toward her than those shown the less attractive image: the opposite of the "beautiful is good" stereotype. In the high severity condition, physical attractiveness had no effect on the level of empathy. The researchers reasoned that when severe harm is not imminent, people perceive attractive children to be more socially competent and hence more capable of taking care of themselves. But when children are in grave danger or distress, those superficial considerations are overridden by strong feelings of compassion and a desire to help, regardless of how attractive the child may be.

as St Helena, where children are closely watched by the community and are expected to avoid violence or aggression, television may have little effect on their behaviour.

Another type of natural experiment can be found in *twin studies*, which are commonly used in *behavioural genetic* research. Monozygotic (popularly known as "identical") twins share 100 per cent of their genetic structure, whereas dizygotic ("fraternal") twins have in common only about 50 per cent of the genes that vary between human beings. This natural difference allows researchers to estimate the strength of environmental and genetic influences on a variety of attitudes and behaviours (Knopik, Neiderhiser, DeFries, & Plomin, 2017). The presence of greater behavioural or attitudinal similarities among monozygotic than dizygotic twins suggests a genetic influence. For example, recent behavioural genetic studies indicate that social and political attitudes are affected not only by societal and situational factors, but also by genes (Alford, Funk, & Hibbing, 2005; Bell, Kandler, & Riemann, 2018). Additional examples of opportunities for quasi-experiments are presented in Box 2.2.

Quasi-experimental designs have been particularly prominent in **evaluation research** studies, which examine the effects of organizational innovations such as a longer school day or greater worker autonomy in a plant (see Box 2.3). Sometimes the results are surprising. A quasi-experimental investigation on the effect of support for people who take care of the elderly (Demers, 1996) showed that the extra support made caregivers feel less depressed, but *more* burdened. Demers was not sure why, although she speculated that perhaps the help was seen as something else to be coordinated and managed.

Box 2.2 | Quasi-experiments

A common type of quasi-experiment compares data collected before and after a policy shift by government or industry. For example, the numbers of car accidents before and after the lowering of a speed limit can be compared. If the number goes down after the speed limit has been lowered, the policy would appear to be a success, but one cannot be sure because there is no control group not experiencing the change. Perhaps the change was caused by something other than the reduction in the speed limit, such as increased media coverage of car accidents.

Another example might involve the installation of cameras to detect speeding. If the cameras are placed only in randomly selected places and not in others, the research changes from a quasi-experiment to a real one, since the locations without cameras would constitute a control group. Governments find it difficult, however, to subject some people to one condition and others to another. The prison system, schools, and other institutions controlled by governments are part of the real social world, and as such have to meet goals that are very different from those of experimental research. That makes it next to impossible for governments to randomly assign people to different conditions. Therefore, they usually have to make do with quasi-experimental evaluations of policy changes. A criminologist may want to randomly assign criminals to jail or home custody and then compare the two forms of detention, but the potential for some of the at-homes to reoffend would be seen as too great a risk. Because minor criminals are more likely to get home custody than are more serious criminals, a fair test is not possible without random assignment. Similarly, when Canada abolished the death penalty, it was not for the purpose of conducting an experiment: abolition was a policy decision. But data could be examined as if the change were part of a quasi-experiment, for example, by comparing the murder rate before and after capital punishment was abolished, even though the legislation was not intended for that purpose.

The situation that Demers found herself in—not being sure how to interpret her findings—is actually quite common. It's one thing to come up with a set of findings, but another to explain them. The solution usually involves doing more research.

Quasi-experiments are also used to evaluate the effectiveness of institutional policies. For example, Hanson, Broom, & Stephenson (2004) wanted to know whether treating sex offenders after they are released from prison has any effect on their chances of reoffending. A total of 724 convicted male sex offenders were divided into two groups: those who underwent mandatory treatment after release to community supervision, and those who were released prior to the implementation of the mandatory treatment program. (Some of the latter group had received treatment during or prior to incarceration, although the extent of that treatment was not known.) This division was not perfect, since the men in the first group may have differed in some relevant way from those in the second; the fact that some in the latter category received treatment is also an issue. In any case, the results showed that, after an average 12-year follow-up period, there were equal rates of reoffending in both groups: about 20 per cent for sex crimes, which was not very encouraging for the professionals who treat offenders.

A major challenge in evaluation research, particularly in Canada, is finding appropriate ways to assess government programs and services that affect Indigenous people. As noted in Chapter 1, research involving Indigenous participants has been fraught with exploitation and cultural insensitivity, and the residential schools system in Canada is an example of a program that illustrates in a very tragic way what can go wrong if Indigenous perspectives

Box 2.3 | Evaluation research

Adam Melnyk/Shutterstock

As a researcher studying the effects of a music program, what questions would you ask participants before and after the program in order to gauge its impact on their health? Would you focus on their objective health indicators, or the subjective perception of their own health? What might be the benefit of doing both?

A key question asked in evaluation research is whether a new policy initiative or organizational change achieved its goals. Ideally, to answer that question the design would have one group that is exposed to the treatment—the new initiative—and a control group that is not. Since it is often not feasible or ethical to randomly assign research participants to the two groups, such studies are usually quasi-experimental. For instance, data gathered from people before a change may be compared with data acquired after; the "before" people become the control group, the "after" people the experimental group. This approach has the added advantage that the two groups are basically the same, making random assignment unnecessary.

Such a design was used to evaluate the effect of a community arts program on the well-being of older adults in the Vancouver area (Phinney, Moody, & Small, 2014). Over three years, four groups of participants took part in the collective creation of a physical work of art or a performance that was presented to the public. Baseline quantitative measures of well-being were taken in the first year of the program, with the same measures administered again at its completion. The researchers also did a qualitative analysis of the project by conducting five focus groups at the conclusion of the program. The quantitative results indicated that the participants had higher levels of perceived overall health and sense of community,

are ignored (Truth and Reconciliation Commission of Canada, 2015). Evaluation research is only beginning to come to terms with these sorts of issues. Increasing attention is now being paid to the larger structures of power, both historic and contemporary, that give rise to various program designs, and it is increasingly recognized that Indigenous ontologies and epistemologies must be respected (Shepherd & Graham, 2020).

Significance of experimental design

Although, as noted at the outset of this section, true experiments are rare in sociology for a variety of reasons, it is important to draw attention to a significant general lesson that an examination of experiments reveals. At the heart of the experimental design is a *logic of comparison* which is used to isolate the causal influence of a particular variable—a goal to which researchers using other designs may also aspire. At the very least, an experiment allows the researcher to compare the results obtained from an experimental group with those from a control group. In the case of the Fisher and Ma (2014) experiment in Box 2.1, the research compared the effects of different levels of a child's physical attractiveness and distress on the level of empathy felt by an observer. The advantage of such comparisons is that they permit a better understanding of the phenomenon in question than would be possible if it were examined under one condition alone. The argument and lower levels of physical pain, when the program was over. The themes that emerged from the focus groups included the conclusions that the program provided the seniors with structure and discipline, facilitated coping, required hard work and effort, brought out their artistic side, promoted social involvement, and made a positive contribution to the community.

Quantitative quasi-experimental designs in evaluation research go back a long way, but as the Phinney et al. (2014) study indicates, evaluations based on qualitative research have also emerged. Although there are differences of opinion about how qualitative evaluation should be carried out, there is consensus on the importance of, first, understanding the context in which an intervention occurs and, second, hearing the diverse viewpoints of the stakeholders (Greene, 2000). For example, Pawson and Tilley (1997) advocate a pluralistic methodology that examines not only the context but also the mechanisms that allow programs to work. Tilley (2000) provided an example of the approach in an evaluation of the use of closed-circuit television (CCTV) in parking lots. He observed that there are several ways in which CCTV deters car crime. For instance, it serves as a direct deterrent to offenders (fewer people are willing to commit crimes if they think they will be filmed and caught), which encourages greater usage of parking lots, which in turn increases personal surveillance, which itself deters crime. Examples of contexts relevant to the intervention include time (such as when the parking lot fills up and empties during rush-hour periods, or slow times during the day), and the availability of other nearby venues for offenders to commit car crimes. The kind of evaluation research advocated by Pawson and Tilley maps the different combinations of cause and context in relation to different outcomes.

Evaluation research is not limited to examining whether an initiative has achieved its stated goals. In fact, some approaches are "goal free" (Scriven, 1991) in that the people doing the evaluation are not told what the purpose of the program is. This allows evaluators to assess its overall impact, including unforeseen consequences, rather than limit their attention to how well it achieved specific, preconceived goals.

that in certain situations greater physical attractiveness in children evokes less empathy is much more persuasive when the empathy felt for attractive children can be compared with that elicited by those perceived to be less attractive.

That same logic of comparison is invoked in other research designs. For example, cross-sectional designs of the kind associated with survey research, discussed in the next section, compare groups of people that differ in certain ways, and can be used to evaluate causal hypotheses. For example, men and women may be compared in terms of their average incomes to assess the hypothesis that after taking other influences into account, gender affects economic inequality.

Cross-sectional design

Many people associate cross-sectional designs with questionnaires and **structured interviewing**. However, other data-gathering techniques may also be used in cross-sectional research, including **structured observation** and analysis of official statistics or diaries. These will be covered in later chapters, but we will outline the basic structure of the cross-sectional design here. In cross-sectional studies, observations are taken *at one point in time*—there are no before-and-after comparisons. Also, cross-sectional designs *do not involve any manipulation of the independent variable*: they are like snapshots taken of a group or phenomenon at one point in time.

A cross-sectional design entails the collection of data (usually quantitative) on more than one case. Researchers are interested in variation between different people, families, nation-states, and so on, and variation can be established only when more than one case is examined. Researchers employing this design usually select many cases, for at least two reasons. For one thing, a larger number makes it more likely that variation will be encountered in *all* the variables of interest. A second reason is that certain statistical techniques are likely to require large sample sizes (see Chapter 7).

In quantitative studies, data are collected on two or more variables, which are then examined to detect patterns of association. This approach sometimes makes it difficult to show cause and effect because the independent and dependent variables are measured simultaneously, making any demonstration of time order (showing that the cause actually precedes the effect in time) hard to prove. For example, there is a well-supported **negative relationship** between social class and serious forms of mental illness: poor people are more likely to be mentally ill than rich people. But there is also a debate about the nature of that relationship: Does being poor lead to stress and therefore to mental illness? Or does being mentally ill lead to difficulties in holding down a job and thus poverty? Or is it a bit of both? To take another example, a study of 1000 men found that those who had two or more orgasms a week exhibited a 50 per cent lower mortality risk compared with men who had on average less than one orgasm per week. It may be tempting to conclude that male orgasm leads to longer life expectancy, but it is also possible that the causal arrow points in the other direction: men who are ill (and thus at greater mortality risk) are less likely to be sexually active in the first place (Houghton, 1998, p. 14). This finding and the preceding one are similar, showing what Blaxter (1990) called "an ambiguity about the direction of causal influence." There is only an *association* between the two variables—no clear causal link. However, as will be shown below and in Chapter 8, there are a number of ways for researchers to draw cautious inferences about causality using cross-sectional designs.

Replicability, causal inferences, and external validity

How does cross-sectional research measure up in terms of replicability, the ability to establish causation, and external validity?

- Replicability characterizes most cross-sectional research, so long as the researcher spells out the procedures for selecting respondents, administering research instruments (structured interview or self-completion questionnaire, etc.), and the analysis of data.
- Establishing causality can be problematic. As was just suggested, it may be difficult to establish causal direction from the resulting data. Cross-sectional research designs can identify associations that are indicative of causation, but other designs may have to be employed to substantiate causal inferences.
- External validity is strong when the sample is a random one. When non-random methods of sampling are employed, external validity becomes questionable, an issue addressed in Chapter 7.

Variables that cannot be manipulated

As noted in the section on experimental design, in much (if not most) social research it is not possible to manipulate the variables of interest. This is a key reason why most quantitative social research employs a cross-sectional design rather than an experimental one. To more or less all intents and purposes, things like ethnicity, age, and socioeconomic status are "givens" and not really amenable to the kind of manipulation necessary for a true experimental design. Fictitious manipulations are possible, such as when an experimenter digitally alters photographs to produce different ages or ethnicities, perhaps to see the effects on job offers, but the manipulation is limited to the external signs of age and ethnicity, missing the more subjective and experiential aspects.

However, the very fact that certain variables are givens provides a clue as to how to make causal inferences in cross-sectional research. Many of the variables of interest can be assumed to be

Methods in Motion | Applications to Canadian Society

Why are some Canadians politically conservative and others liberal?

Bell, Aitken Schermer, & Vernon (2009) did a behavioural genetic study of political attitudes and behaviours that addressed the issue of why some Canadians tend to have conservative or right-leaning attitudes, while others are more liberal or left oriented in their political views. The methodology used in the study (the details of which go beyond the scope of this book) was a kind of natural experiment comparing monozygotic (identical) twins, who are essentially genetic clones of each other, with dizygotic (fraternal) twins, who share only about 50 per cent of the genetic material that varies between human beings. The researchers examined how similar the identical twins were in their political attitudes, and compared that with how similar the fraternal twins were on that score. If identical twins are more similar on the characteristic under examination than the fraternal twins, that would indicate that genetic factors or other biological influences have some impact on the trait in question. The results of the study showed that the identical twins were in fact much more similar in their political attitudes than the fraternal twins, which suggests that genetic factors play a role in the formation of these attitudes. The study also found evidence that social factors (such as educational influences and media effects) affected political orientations, although it did not test for specific social influences. Taken as a whole, the results indicate that "nature" and "nurture" *interact* in the formation of political attitudes.

These sorts of studies are uncommon in sociology, political science, or anthropology, although they are conducted more frequently in psychology and the health sciences. They have far-reaching implications for the social sciences, in particular for disciplines in which biological influences are seldom examined. The standard paradigm in the latter fields of study assumes that some combination of socialization, culture, and situational factors can explain the origins of most attitudes and behaviours. Researchers using behaviour genetic methods, on the other hand, acknowledge that those sorts of influences are crucial, but argue that a more complete understanding of the human condition can be achieved by considering both social and biological factors.

If behaviour genetics and other approaches that consider both social and biological influences were to be more widely adopted in the social sciences, that could have a major impact on the theoretical perspectives that are developed and rise to prominence in academe. For example, a blend of sociological conflict theories with neo-Darwinian evolutionary theory is one possibility (e.g., Sanderson, 2001). Such approaches have the potential to promote *consilience* or the unity of knowledge (Bell & Kandler, 2017).

temporally prior to other variables. For example, in a relationship between ethnic status and alcohol consumption, the latter cannot be the independent variable because it occurs after ethnicity. Ethnicity still cannot be said with certainty to be the cause, however: it is just a possible cause. Nonetheless, even though researchers are unable to manipulate things like ethnic status or gender, causal inferences can still be cautiously drawn from cross-sectional data.

The current discussion of the cross-sectional design places it firmly in the context of quantitative research. But qualitative research can also use a form of cross-sectional design. For example, Beardsworth and Keil (1992) carried out a study of the dietary beliefs and practices of vegetarians. They administered "relatively **unstructured interviews**," which were "guided by an inventory of issues," with 76 vegetarians and vegans (1992, p. 261). The interviews were taped and **transcribed**, yielding a large body of qualitative data. The research was not preoccupied with quantitative criteria such as establishing causation, external validity, replicability, measurement validity, and so on. Nonetheless, the conversational interview style made the study more externally valid than research using more formal instruments of data collection.

The study was concerned with the factors that influence food selection, like vegetarianism. The very notion of an "influence" carries a strong connotation of causality, suggesting that qualitative researchers can also be interested in the investigation of causes and effects, although they do not use the language of quantitative research with its talk of independent and dependent variables. As well, the emphasis was much more on understanding the experience of something like vegetarianism than is often the case with quantitative research.

This qualitative research bears many similarities to the cross-sectional design in quantitative research. It entailed interviewing quite a large number of people at a single point in time. And, as with many quantitative studies using a cross-sectional design, the examination of people's past and current eating habits was based on the participants' retrospective accounts of factors that affected their past and present behaviour.

Structure of cross-sectional designs

A cross-sectional design collects data on a series of variables (Obs_1, Obs_2, Obs_3, Obs_4, Obs_5, . . . Obs_n) for different cases (people, households, cities, nations, etc.) at a single point in time. The effect is to create a data set that comprises variables Obs_1 to Obs_n and cases $case_1$ to $case_n$, as in Figure 2.2. Each **cell** in the matrix has data in it.

	Obs_1	Obs_2	Obs_3	...	Obs_n
$Case_1$					
$Case_2$					
$Case_3$					
$Case_4$					
$Case_5$					
...					
$Case_n$					

FIGURE 2.2 The data rectangle in cross-sectional research

Longitudinal design(s)

With a longitudinal design, cases are examined at a particular time (T_1) and again at a later time or times (T_2, T_3, and so on), but without the manipulation of an independent variable that characterizes experiments (see Box 2.4). When used in quantitative research, it allows insight into the time order of variables and is better able to deal with the problem of "ambiguity about the direction of causal influence" that plagues cross-sectional designs. Because potential independent variables can be identified at T_1, the researcher is in a better, if not perfect, position to infer that the effects identified at T_2 or later occurred *after* changes occurred in the independent variables. In all other respects, the points made above about cross-sectional designs are the same as those for longitudinal designs. In spite of its heightened ability to show cause and effect, the longitudinal design is not frequently used in quantitative social research because of the additional time and cost involved.

Longitudinal studies can take different forms. For example, Goyder, Guppy, & Thompson (2003) examined how gender-influenced evaluations of occupational prestige had changed over 25 years. Some of the earlier male advantage had disappeared; indeed, some occupations showing a female incumbent were rated more highly than the same occupation with a male incumbent. Baer, Curtis, & Grabb (2001) did a 15-nation study examining whether membership in clubs and associations had changed over time. Kerr (2004) and Kerr and Michalski (2007) investigated hyperactivity in Canadian children as they grew older and its sources in poverty and family structure.

There are two basic types of longitudinal design: the *panel study* and the *cohort study*. With the former, the same people, households, or other groups are studied on at least two different occasions. A panel study, especially one at the household level, needs rules for handling new entrants (e.g., as a result of marriage or elderly relatives moving in) and exits

Box 2.4 | Longitudinal research and the case study

Case study research frequently includes a longitudinal element. The researcher can be a participant observer in an organization for an extended length of time, or may do ethnographic research with a community for many months or years, or may conduct structured or qualitative interviews with individuals over a prolonged period. Moreover, the researcher may be able to inject an additional longitudinal element by analyzing archival information and asking respondents to recall events that occurred before the study began, thus discovering some history.

A longitudinal element also occurs when a case that has been studied is returned to at a later time. A particularly interesting example of this occurred in "Middletown," a pseudonym for an American Midwest town first studied by Lynd and Lynd (1929) in 1924–5 and restudied in 1935 during the Depression to see what changes had occurred (Lynd & Lynd, 1937). In 1977, the community was again restudied, this time in a post-Vietnam War setting (Bahr, Caplow, & Chadwick, 1983), using the same research instruments but with minor changes.

(e.g., as a result of marital break-up or children leaving home).

One example of a panel study is the National Longitudinal Survey of Children and Youth (NLSCY), described in Box 2.5, in which the same Canadian children were studied in successive years. Another is a three-wave study of family structure and children's socioeconomic attainment in Canada conducted by Seabrook and Avison (2015), which found that mothers' education and family income were key to the children's success. The Research in the News box (page 46) provides an example of a panel study that had to be re-designed rather suddenly.

In a cohort study people sharing the same experience, such as being born in the same year or graduating from a particular school at the same time, are studied over time, but the same people may not be studied each time. For example, Walters (2004) used the 1982, 1986, 1992, and 1995 National Graduates Surveys to examine trends in the economic fortunes of Canadians graduating from post-secondary institutions. The same people were not selected for the sample each year, but the information was still useful in understanding each graduating cohort, as well as the similarities and differences between cohorts.

Panel and cohort studies share similar features. In social sciences such as sociology, social policy, and human geography, quantitative research using these designs usually takes the form of repeated survey research using a self-completion questionnaire or structured interview. Used in this way, panel and cohort studies can both illuminate social change and improve the understanding of causal influences.

Panel and cohort studies also share similar problems. First, there is the problem of sample attrition: some participants may die, some may move away, and some may simply choose to withdraw at later stages of the research. For instance, in a study by Dinovitzer, Hagan, & Parker (2003) on the educational attainment of Canadian immigrant youth, researchers were able to talk to only 65 per cent of those originally surveyed 19 years earlier. Comparing those who participated in the second round with those who were lost from the study, the authors found no significant differences. That sort of comparison is a common practice; when no difference is found, the losses are treated as random and thus acceptable to ignore. The main problem with attrition is that those who leave the study may differ in some important respects from those who remain, so that the latter do not form a representative group. However, there is some evidence from panel studies that attrition declines with time (Berthoud, 2000); in other words, those who do not drop out after the first wave or two of data collection tend to stay on the panel.

Box 2.5 | The National Longitudinal Survey of Children and Youth

This panel study involved a long-term effort to monitor Canadian children's development and well-being as they matured from infancy to adulthood. It began with a representative sample of children 11 years of age or younger in 1994–5 being interviewed, with follow-ups every two years. Statistics Canada collected the data, with direction provided by Human Resources Development Canada. The purpose of the study was to contribute to the development of policies that help children live healthy, active, and rewarding lives (see Michaud, 2001). The data for the final cycle (Cycle 8), which began in September 2008, were released in November 2010 (Statistics Canada, 2010).

Second, there are few guidelines for determining the best timing for further waves of data collection. Finally, there is evidence of a *panel conditioning* effect, whereby continued participation in a longitudinal study affects respondents' behaviour. Menard (1991) cited a study of family caregiving in which 52 per cent of respondents attributed a change in the way they cared for relatives to their participation in the research.

As suggested above, qualitative research may also incorporate elements of a longitudinal design. For example, it is used in ethnographic research

Research in the News

The effects of COVID-19 on physical and mental health, family life, and employment in Canada

Sociologist Scott Schieman, along with colleagues and students at the University of Toronto, had plans in the fall of 2019 to start a panel study of 2500 people that would examine the participants' employment and financial experiences each year for the next decade. But things changed when the pandemic struck a few months later. "We decided to change the design of the study," Schieman explained. "We realized that it was important to try to map and explain changes in people's experiences with employment, work and economic life as the pandemic was unfolding, especially given the sweeping shifts in the broader economy and social interaction" (Canadian Government News, 2020).

A decision was made to add an additional 2500 people to the study, and to analyze the larger sample's COVID-related experiences for the next five years. Online questionnaires along with qualitative interviews are being used to gather the data.

Some preliminary results have been surprising. The data indicate that for certain groups, work-life conflict actually decreased as the pandemic wore on. "We see the largest decrease, on average, among people who don't have any children," Schieman said. But others had different experiences. "[A]mong those with children, we find the largest increase in work-life conflict among those who have kids younger than six and between the ages of six to 12. This seems to have unfolded similarly for both men and women" (Canadian Government News, 2020). He emphasizes that over time, people's lives may be impacted by COVID-19 in ways that are still unknown, given that the pandemic has not yet run its course.

when the ethnographer is in a location for a lengthy period of time or when interviews are carried out on more than one occasion in order to examine change. In an example of the latter, Smith, Lister, & Middleton (2004) described a study of the experiences of citizenship for 110 young people. They were interviewed in depth in 1999 and then re-interviewed at two-year intervals to examine changes in their lifestyles, feelings, opinions, and ambitions in relation to citizenship issues. Only 64 people participated in all three waves of data collection, illustrating the high rate of sample attrition in this style of research.

Case study design

The basic case study design entails a detailed and intensive analysis of a single case. A case may be:

- a single community, as in Hughes's (1943) classic study of Drummondville, a textile town in Quebec; Chowdhury's (2018) work on Bangladeshi immigrants in Toronto; or Pratt and Valverde's (2002) research on Toronto's Somali community;
- a single family, as in Lewis's (1961) study of the Sánchez family in Mexico;
- a single organization, such as the automobile factory studied by Rinehart (1996), or a group within an organization, like the nurses in a Hamilton hospital researched by White (1990);
- a person, as in Nemni and Nemni's (2006) study of Pierre Trudeau or Foran's (2010) book on Mordecai Richler; such research is characterized by use of the **life history** or biographical approach (see Chapter 11);
- a single event, like the fight against locating a home for recovering addicts in a Richmond, British Columbia, neighbourhood (Huey, 2003), or the Alberta election analyzed by Bell, Jansen, & Young (2007);
- a state or province, as in Laplante's (2006) study of the rise of cohabitation in Quebec; or
- a sector of the economy, such as the seafood processing industry in rural New Brunswick examined in Knott's (2016) research on different types of mobile labour.

There is a tendency to associate case studies with qualitative research, such as Chowdhury's (2018) study of Bangladeshi immigrants in Toronto. Exponents of the case study design often favour methods like participant observation and unstructured interviewing, which are viewed as particularly helpful in generating an intensive, detailed examination of a case. However, case studies can also use quantitative methods, or some combination of quantitative and qualitative.

With a case study, the case is an object of interest *in its own right* and the researcher aims to provide an in-depth elucidation of it. Sometimes it is difficult to distinguish case studies from other research designs because almost any kind of research can be construed as a case study. Even research based on a national, **random sample** of Canadians could be considered a case study of Canada.

What distinguishes a true case study is the goal of finding and revealing the features of the case. Collecting in-depth, often qualitative data that may be unique to time and place is characteristic of this sort of research. Case studies are often idiographic in nature, seeking to provide a rich description of the subject matter, like Shalla's (2002) study of how Air Canada's customer sales and service agents became victims of airline restructuring.

When the predominant research orientation is qualitative, a case study tends to take an **inductive** approach to the relationship between theory and research. If a mainly quantitative strategy is adopted, the research is often **deductive**, guided by specific research questions derived from social theories.

Measurement validity, causal inference, external validity, and replicability of case studies

The question of how the case study fares on the research design criteria of measurement validity, establishing causation, external validity, and replicability depends in large part on whether the researcher feels these criteria are appropriate for their work. Writers of qualitative case study research tend to play down or ignore the salience of these factors (cf. Stake, 1995). Those influenced by the quantitative research tradition see them as more significant, and usually try to develop case studies that meet the criteria.

One question that has generated a great deal of discussion concerns the *external validity* or *generalizability* of case study research. How can a single case possibly be representative of other cases? For example, would the findings from a study of the Toronto police department be generalizable to all large urban police departments in Canada? The answer, of course, is that the findings probably cannot be applied to other police departments. Case study researchers do not usually delude themselves into thinking that it is possible to identify typical cases that can represent a class of objects, whether factories, mass media reporting, police services, or communities. In other words, they typically do not think that a case study is a sample of one.

Types of case

Yin (1984) distinguished three types of case, each of which relates to the issue of external validity:

- The *critical case*. Here the researcher has a clearly specified hypothesis, and a case is chosen on the grounds that it will allow a better understanding of the circumstances under which the hypothesis does or does not hold. The classic study by Festinger, Riecken, & Schachter (1956) of a doomsday/UFO cult is an example. The fact that, contrary to their dire predictions, the world did not end allowed the researchers to test propositions about how people respond to thwarted expectations. What did cult members do when, after quitting their jobs, leaving their homes, and waiting on a mountaintop, nothing happened? Did they sneak down and move to another town? No: they decided that their faith had saved humankind and that their new role was to tell others of that miracle so more people could be converted to their religion.
- The *extreme*, even *unique*, *case*; a common focus in clinical studies. Margaret Mead's (1928) well-known (albeit controversial) study of growing up in Samoa seems to have been motivated by her belief that it represented a unique case and thus could challenge the then popular nature-over-nurture hypothesis. She reported that, unlike adolescents in most other societies, Samoan youth did not suffer a period of anxiety and stress in their teenage years. She explained this by their culture's strong, consistently enforced standards of conduct and morality. These factors were of interest because many readers thought they might contain lessons for the West.
- The *revelatory case*. The basis for the revelatory case exists "when an investigator has an opportunity to observe and analyse a phenomenon previously inaccessible to scientific investigation" (Yin, 1984, p. 44). This can happen when previously unavailable evidence becomes accessible, as was the case with certain KGB files after the fall of the Soviet Union.

Cases may also be chosen for mundane reasons, such as convenience, and still provide an adequate context for answering certain research questions or examining key social processes. To take a concrete example, Russell and Tyler (2002) studied a Girl Heaven store in the UK (which caters to 3- to 13-year-old girls) not because it was a critical or unique case, or because it offered a context never before studied, but because of its capacity to illuminate the links between gender and consumption and the commodification of childhood in modern society. Indeed, often it is only at a very late stage in the research that the singularity and significance of the case becomes apparent (Radley & Chamberlain, 2001).

As we have mentioned, one of the standard criticisms of the case study is that its findings cannot be generalized. Case study researchers argue strenuously that this is not the purpose of their craft. A valid picture of one case may be more valuable than a potentially less valid picture of many. Their aim is to generate an intensive examination of a single case, which may or may not be used for theoretical analysis. Pratt and Valverde (2002) studied only Somalis and expressed a hope that others would study other immigrant groups in other places. Their central concern was the richness of the data and the quality of the theoretical reasoning that the case allowed. As we have noted, sometimes case studies are primarily inductive, used as information to generate theories. Other times they may be deductive in nature, providing the data required to assess theories.

Problems can arise when the research involves comparison of two or more cases. Dyer and Wilkins (1991), for example, argued that a multiple-case study approach means that less attention is paid to the specific details of a particular case, and more to the ways in which multiple cases can be contrasted. Furthermore, the need for comparison often leads the researcher to choose an explicit focus at the outset, when it might be advantageous to adopt a more open-ended approach. A preference for contextual insight and a less structured research approach is associated with a qualitative research strategy. As illustrated in Box 2.6, comparative case study work is often quantitative in orientation.

The strength of comparative designs is that they highlight the similarities and differences between cases, which can be used to assess or generate theories. They exhibit certain features similar to experiments and quasi-experiments, which also rely on the capacity to establish comparisons.

Bringing research orientation and design together

Finally, we can bring together the two general research orientations covered in Chapter 1 with the research designs outlined in this chapter. Table 2.1 shows the typical form associated with each

Box 2.6 | Comparative research: Cross-cultural studies

Phenomena such as voting behaviour or crime victimization in two or more countries can be compared using the same research instruments, seeking similarities and differences and a deeper understanding of social reality in different national contexts. At the very least such research supplies a replication.

Cross-cultural research is more expensive than other approaches. It also presents other problems. When using existing data such as official statistics or survey evidence, the researcher must ensure that the variable categories and data-collection methods are comparable. When new data are being collected, the researcher must check that data-collection instruments (for example, questionnaires and interview schedules) are translated properly. Even when translation is carried out competently, there may still be a problem with insensitivity to specific national and cultural milieus. For example, the London "tube," the Toronto "subway," and the Montreal "métro" differ in more than name: public transit experiences in the three cities may be very different in terms of ridership, safety, cleanliness, and so on.

A strength of cross-cultural research is that it helps to illustrate how social scientific findings may be culturally specific. For example, Wilson's (2002) examination of Ontario raves made frequent comparisons to the earlier rave scene in Britain. However, the UK scene was primarily an outgrowth of working-class struggles, whereas Canadian raves appealed more to middle-class, culturally alienated youths. Similarly, Baer et al. (2001) found that joining clubs and voluntary organizations increased toward the end of the last century in the US, West Germany, and the Netherlands, was stable in Canada and 10 other countries, but decreased in Spain. Finally, Young and Dugas (2012) compared Canadian print media coverage of climate change issues in English-language publications with those in written in French, and found that the different environmental and media cultures in the two language communities contributed to important differences in how climate change topics were narrated.

TABLE 2.1 Research strategy and research design

	GENERAL RESEARCH ORIENTATION	
Research design	**Quantitative**	**Qualitative**
Experimental	Typical form: Most experiments involve quantitative comparisons between experimental and control groups on the dependent variable. Example: the Rosenthal and Jacobson (1968) study discussed in this chapter.	Experiments are not used in qualitative research, although they may inspire or be inspired by qualitative findings. For example, a qualitative study of the teachers who participated in the Rosenthal and Jacobson (1968) study discussed in this chapter would be enlightening.
Cross-sectional	Typical form: Survey research and structured observation on a sample at a single point in time are two forms; content analysis of a sample of documents is another. Example: Box 1.3.	Typical form: Qualitative interviews or focus groups at a single point in time are two forms; qualitative content analysis of a set of documents relating to a single period is another. Example: the Beardsworth and Keil (1992) study of vegetarianism discussed in this chapter.
Longitudinal	Typical form: Survey research on a sample on more than one occasion, as in panel and cohort studies, is one form; content analysis of documents relating to different time periods is another. Example: Box 2.5.	Typical form: These include ethnographic research over a long period, qualitative interviewing on more than one occasion, or qualitative content analysis of documents relating to different time periods. Such research is longitudinal when the main purpose is to map change. Example: the Lynd and Lynd (1929; 1937) studies of "Middletown" discussed in this chapter.
Case study	Typical form: Survey research is conducted on a single case with a view to revealing important features about its nature. Example: the Bell et al. (2007) study of the 2004 Alberta provincial election.	Typical form: The intensive study done by qualitative interviewing of a single case, which may be an organization, person, family, or community. Example: Box 1.4.

combination of research orientation and research design, along with a number of examples.

The distinctions are not always perfect. In particular, in some qualitative research it is not obvious whether a study is an example of a longitudinal design or a case study design. Life history studies, research that concentrates on a specific issue over time, and ethnography, in which the researcher charts change in a single case, contain elements of both designs. Such studies are perhaps better conceptualized as longitudinal case studies rather than as belonging to one category or another. A further point is that there is no typical form in the qualitative research orientation/experimental research design cell. Qualitative research in the context of true experiments is very unusual; a quasi-experimental design is a more realistic alternative.

Key Points

- There is an important distinction between a general research orientation (quantitative versus qualitative) and a research design.
- The nomothetic approach to explanation involves discovering general laws and principles, and is usually associated with quantitative research.
- Nomothetic explanations must satisfy three criteria of causation: correlation, time order, and non-spuriousness.
- Qualitative researchers usually take the idiographic approach to explanation, which entails creating a rich description of a person or group based on the perceptions and feelings of the people studied.
- Replicability, validity (measurement and external), and the ability to establish causation are important criteria for evaluating the quality of quantitative social research.
- Four key research designs are experimental, cross-sectional, longitudinal, and case study.
- Except for the experimental design, each one of these can be used with either a quantitative or a qualitative research orientation. Experiments are used with a quantitative approach.
- Threats to the establishment of causation are of particular importance in non-experimental, quantitative research.

Questions for Review (R) and Creative Application (A)

Criteria for the evaluation of social research

R1 Explain the time order criterion of causation.

A1 A survey researcher finds that people with high self-esteem make more money than people with low self-esteem. You are tempted to conclude from this that self-esteem influences earning power. But can time order be established using this design? Explain.

R2 What is a spurious correlation?

A2 You are at a dance party where a lot of alcohol is being served. You abstain from drinking, but notice that the people with the craziest dancing style are the most likely to go to the washroom and vomit. Should you conclude that dancing crazily induces vomiting? Explain.

R3 What is a nomothetic explanation?

A3 Come up with a nomothetic explanation for why students sometimes drop out of university.

R4 What is an idiographic explanation? How do qualitative researchers produce them?

A4 Assume that your best friend just dropped out of university. Come up with an idiographic explanation of how that happened.

Research designs

Experimental design

R5 How are true experiments able to establish causal connections between variables? Explain.

A5 You want to know whether the amount of time spent on social media affects loneliness levels among 15-year-olds at summer camp. You decide to conduct an experiment, and have followed proper ethics protocols. How could you conduct the experiment? Provide as much detail as possible.

R6 What is a quasi-experiment?

A6 You want to know whether the legalization of marijuana in Canada will affect national crime rates. How could you use the quasi-experimental method to research this issue? Explain.

Cross-sectional design

R7 What is meant by a cross-sectional research design?

A7 How could you use a cross-sectional design to determine whether there is an association between the amount of time spent studying and grades? Assess the degree to which your method can establish causality.

Longitudinal design(s)

R8 Why might a longitudinal research design be superior to a cross-sectional one?

A8 How could a qualitative researcher use a longitudinal design to study people active in a local environmental movement?

Case study design

R9 What is a case study?

A9 Pick a particular case (it can be any person, group, or event) and explain how a qualitative researcher could study it. Then describe how a quantitative researcher could gather information on the case that is relevant to the findings of the qualitative investigator.

Visit our online resource center for free assessment: https://learninglink.oup.com/

Interactive Classroom Activities

1. This activity involves some friendly competition. Divide the class into small groups. Each group is given 15 minutes to come up with as many examples of spurious correlations as they can (e.g., the correlation between the number of fire trucks at a fire and the amount of fire damage). Examples given in this chapter or in previous classes are not allowed. After the time is up, a spokesperson from each group presents the group's spurious correlations to the rest of the class, and the instructor judges whether each one is in fact an example of a spurious correlation. The instructor also keeps a record of all groups' accepted correlations. The group with the most accepted correlations wins.

   Once that has been done, the class examines each correlation individually. The instructor asks for volunteers to name an antecedent third factor that might be causing the two variables to vary together (e.g., it would be the severity of the fire for the fire trucks and damage example given above).
2. Divide the class into small groups. Each group is to
   a. pick a social phenomenon or experience of interest (e.g., sex work, homelessness);
   b. provide a *nomothetic* explanation for it; and
   c. provide an *idiographic* explanation for it.

   The groups are to go into as much detail as possible. When that is completed, each group is paired with another group (A and B, C and D, E and F, etc.) such that Group A presents its results to the rest of the class, while Group B has the task of providing a critical evaluation (enumerating both strengths and weaknesses) of Group A's arguments. Then the reverse: Group B presents and Group A critiques. Repeat for Groups C and D, E and F, and so on.

Relevant Websites

The ***National Longitudinal Survey of Children and Youth*** site provides information on a longitudinal study in Canada.

www12.statcan.gc.ca/census-recensement/2011/ref/92-135/surveys-enquetes/nationalchildren-nationaleenfants-eng.cfm

The ***Online Dictionary of the Social Sciences*** site, maintained by Athabasca University, "has 1000 entries covering the disciplines of sociology, criminology, political science and women's study with a commitment to Canadian examples and events and names."

http://bitbucket.icaap.org/dict.pl

The ***Research Methods Knowledge Base*** provides a detailed discussion of various types of experimental design.

www.socialresearchmethods.net/kb/desexper.php

The ***Human Genome Project*** site offers some basic information on this 13-year project and its implications for understanding human behaviour.

https://web.ornl.gov/sci/techresources/Human_Genome/index.shtml

The ***Behavior Genetics Association***, an international organization, provides a forum for the dissemination of behavioural genetic research and offers methodological workshops.

www.bga.org

(Websites accessed 4 September 2021.)

OXFORD learning link More resources are available on Oxford Learning Link.
Visit https://learninglink.oup.com/ for:

- Student self-quiz
- Flash cards
- Audio clips
- Videos
- Activities

3 Research Ethics

Chapter Overview

Before research involving humans can begin, researchers in Canada and many other countries must demonstrate that what they are about to do is ethical. This is no small task, given that ethical considerations pertain to *all* research methods and come into play at *every stage* of research, from the recruitment of participants to the publishing of the results. This chapter examines some general ethical principles and their applications to real research situations. The backdrop for the discussion is the *Tri-Council Policy Statement: Ethical Conduct for Research Involving Humans (TCPS2)* (2018), which governs most research practices in Canada. The *TCPS2* was prepared by the Canadian Institutes of Health Research (CIHR), the Natural Sciences and Engineering Research Council of Canada (NSERC), and the Social Sciences and Humanities Research Council (SSHRC). It identifies three core principles, which are complementary and mutually reinforcing:

- *Respect for persons* stipulates that people's autonomy and their freedom to choose what will happen to them must be ensured. Research participants must therefore be made aware of what the study will entail, so that their consent is not only freely given but fully informed. Consent must also be ongoing; participants should be allowed to withdraw from the study at any time.
- *Concern for welfare* covers all aspects of a person's life as well as the welfare of groups and communities. This includes the physical, mental, emotional, spiritual, social, and economic facets of life. To protect the welfare of individuals and groups, the proper balance between the risks and benefits of research must be sought.
- *Justice* requires that people be treated fairly and equitably, so that no segment of the population bears an undue burden of risk associated with research, and no part of society is excluded from the benefits that research may bestow.

Each of these principles provides valuable guidance and can be used to identify research activities and practices that should be avoided for moral reasons.

▲ The Canadian Press/Nathan Denette

Key Learning Outcomes

Here is a list of goals you should try to achieve as you read and think about the material in this chapter. After completing this chapter, you should be able to:

1. Articulate why it is necessary to consider the ethical implications of all aspects of the research process.
2. Explain how the ethical principles of respect for persons, concern for welfare, and justice can be implemented in social research.
3. Review and assess the ethical dimensions of any research project.

You may be surprised to learn that there are stringent, formal policies in place to ensure that research in Canada is conducted in an ethical manner. But are such policies necessary? Surely researchers are decent people, not mad scientists who take pleasure in abusing the persons who participate in their studies. While it is true that those who do research are generally honourable individuals, every research situation has an ethical dimension to it, and sometimes the ethical implications of a procedure are not obvious. In fact, the history of the social sciences is riddled with studies in which well-meaning researchers harmed the people they studied in some way. In many cases the studies seemed to be quite acceptable when they were done, and it was only with the passage of time that the consequences for participants were recognized. And in some instances, what was done was later deemed to be not only unethical, but egregious. How is that possible? And why are ethical dilemmas still endemic to social research?

Introduction

As noted in Chapters 1 and 2, choosing a general research orientation and selecting a **research design** are matters that are normally dealt with very early in the research process. Another issue to be addressed in the initial stages of a study, and one that should be kept in mind in every phase of the project, is research ethics. How the ethics of a study are handled affects the integrity of the project as well as the reputation of the social sciences as a whole, so understanding research ethics is crucial. If you have read the first two chapters of this book you will have a basic understanding of how research is conducted and will be in a good position to grapple with the ethical dilemmas that researchers typically face.

The first priority of a social researcher should be to ensure that the people being studied are not harmed by their participation. This idea is similar to a fundamental precept among physicians and surgeons: "First do no harm." Notice the word "First": it means that the prevention of harm should override any other goal. The same principle lies at the heart of research ethics in the social sciences. What it means is that the welfare of research participants should take priority over everything else, *including the acquisition of knowledge*, even if that knowledge would expand our understanding of humanity or lead to improvements in the human condition. To some degree this principle conflicts with the concept of academic freedom. But minimizing the risks of participation and striking an appropriate balance between the risks and benefits of research is compatible with social scientists' freedom to choose the topics of their research and, within reasonable bounds, the methods to be used.

It may seem obvious that research participants should not be harmed by taking part in research activities, whether they be **experiments**, field research studies, or any other kind of social scientific investigation. As with many moral rules, however, knowing how to put this principle into practice is anything but simple. For example, defining "harm" and outlining its limits is more complicated than you might think. We all know that research participants should not be killed in the process of being studied, but is any and all harm unjustifiable? What about milder forms of harm, such as short-term anxiety or embarrassment? Is it morally acceptable to subject people to temporary discomfort if the research has the potential to improve our understanding of society or human behaviour in general? Similarly, most people would say that telling lies is generally not a good thing, in part because it may cause harm to the person who is lied to. But what about situations in which some temporary deception is necessary in order to create a research environment in which people feel free to behave in a natural or unguarded way? Typically, it is these sorts of "grey areas" that are debated in the discussion of research ethics, although very serious ethical violations have been known to occur.

Each method of social research comes with its own set of ethical issues. However, it's worth considering some general principles that pertain to all social scientific research. In Canada, most research must comply with the *TCPS2* (CIHR, NSERC, & SSHRC, 2018). Different academic organizations may also have their own ethical policies and procedures. For example, sociologists in Canada are encouraged to follow the *Code of Ethics* of the Canadian Sociological Association. Research in Canada is also subject to Canadian law, in particular the *Charter of Rights and Freedoms*. (See "Relevant Websites" at the end of this chapter.)

Before a research project involving humans begins—even before anyone is asked if they would like to participate in the study—a research ethics board (REB) must review and approve the project. REBs are normally made up of researchers from a variety of disciplines and usually include a community member from outside the institution under whose auspices the research will take place (which in the case of social research is usually a university). If the institution with which the researchers are affiliated administers research funds issued by any of the three agencies that created the *TCPS2* (CIHR, NSERC, & SSHRC), then its REB must abide by the *TCPS2* in making its judgments. What this means in practice is that REBs at virtually every university in Canada use the *TCPS2* in making their decisions and recommendations.

REBs may approve a research project, request modifications, or reject it outright. If the research is to be conducted over an extended period of time, the REB may also hold periodic reviews, or at least require that the researchers file an annual report. In addition, REB members themselves are required to follow procedures outlined in the *TCPS2*. For example, they must avoid any conflict of interest, such as having a financial stake in a project that is up for approval.

Van den Hoonaard (2001) has suggested that it may be more difficult to get ethics approval for **qualitative research** than for **quantitative** studies. Qualitative research is sometimes considered less scientific than the quantitative kind, and ethics committees may prefer the epistemology of the latter, with its derived hypotheses and specific plans. This can be a fatal problem, because if the REB rejects the research proposal, the work can neither receive funding nor be carried out. Also, whereas in quantitative research data are usually collected in one-on-one meetings, in qualitative research a whole group may be under observation, including some people who might not want the attention. One REB allowed a researcher to go ahead with her **ethnographic** work but required that she turn her head when someone who had not explicitly agreed to be part of the study entered her field of vision. This directive is an example of what some researchers would consider to be an overzealous attempt to prevent harm.

Another example of possible REB overreach involving ethnographic research occurred in Vancouver, where researchers sought permission to do observational fieldwork and in-depth interviews with intravenous drug users (Small, Maher, & Kerr, 2014; see Box 15.2). The ethnographers were told by their REB, which cited safety concerns, that they had to provide police with the names of the observers who would have contact with the drug users, a move that would have made it all but impossible to conduct the study.

Indeed, some researchers claim that the advent of REBs has had serious, deleterious consequences for the social sciences as a whole (e.g., van den Hoonaard

& Tolich, 2014). The fact that *TCPS2* acknowledges the right of researchers to appeal REB decisions is a tacit admission that at times they can be overly restrictive. In any event, a strong case can be made that REBs perform a valuable function in protecting the rights of research participants, as the discussion to follow will show.

General ethical principles

The first thing to note regarding general principles is that researchers themselves may disagree on the ethical acceptability of certain research practices. Indeed, there are disputes from the 1960s and 1970s that are still being rehashed today, as we shall see. Also, although the *TCPS2*'s codes and guidelines provide some direction, they often allow for a degree of flexibility. Nonetheless, there is little disagreement that recognizing the ethical implications of doing social research is crucial if informed decisions are to be made.

The *TCPS2* outlines three core principles for the conduct of research involving human participants: respect for persons, concern for welfare, and justice. Although they are listed separately, there is considerable overlap between them.

Respect for persons

The principle of respect for persons maintains that humans should not be treated as mere "objects" or as a means to an end. Even if the end is a worthy one, it cannot justify the use of unethical means. As we noted above, even if the knowledge a researcher is seeking will be of benefit to all humankind, the welfare of the individuals and groups under study is of paramount importance. Researchers must recognize that people have rights, including the right to be treated with dignity by social researchers. Respect for persons is arguably the most fundamental of all the principles considered here.

The starting point of respect for persons in research is the stipulation that the people being studied must give free, informed, and ongoing consent to participate in the research. Most researchers now adhere to the principle that potential participants should not only be asked for their permission before they are placed in a study, but should also be informed of all the risks and benefits to which they would be exposed. To assess those risks and benefits, prospective participants need a basic idea of what the study will entail. Special arrangements for consent have to be made if the person being considered for inclusion is not able to exercise sound judgment due to their young age, cognitive impairment, mental health, or physical infirmity. In such cases a trusted, authorized third party is required to make the decision on their behalf.

In most quantitative studies and in some forms of qualitative research, people who are weighing the pros and cons of participation are given an *information sheet* or *letter of information* outlining what the research is about, how it will be conducted, and what the risks and benefits of participation are. The document normally includes the names of the people in charge of the research, their institutional affiliation, and contact information. It also typically contains assurances of confidentiality along with a description of how the data will be stored and the form in which the results are to be published. A sample from a research study in which one of the authors of this book participated is shown in Figure 3.1.

Prospective participants should be encouraged to think about the project; they should also be given a chance to ask questions and seek clarification if necessary. If they have all the information required and are willing to participate, a *consent form* is sometimes provided for them to sign. This form may include a brief synopsis of the study and state explicitly that research volunteers are free to leave the study at any time without penalty. Consent must be freely given and cannot be coerced. Sometimes the consent form and the information document are merged into one, as illustrated in Figure 3.1. A consent form taken from a Canadian study involving qualitative interviews conducted by university students is shown in Figure 3.2.

In some forms of qualitative research, such as ethnography and participant observation, providing information sheets and consent forms may be impractical; in some cases, it might even defeat the purposes of the study. In cases where a formal agreement between the researchers and the informants

Letter of Information: A study of personality in adult twins

Dear _________:

You recently participated in a research project conducted by Dr. _________ at the University of _________, in which you completed a number of questionnaires. We are very grateful for your participation in our research. At this time, we would like to in invite you to take part in a further research study examining relationships between different measures of personality.

If you agree to participate in this study, you will be asked to complete the following questionnaires: the Toronto Alexithymia Scale, the Deadly Sins Scale, the AQ-9 (a measure of attitudes toward mental illness), the Moral Foundations Questionnaire, the Political Issues Questionnaire, and the Self-Report Altruism Scale. Each of these is a paper-and-pencil personality questionnaire, and each will take between approximately 5 to 15 minutes to complete.

Most of the items in the questionnaires require you to indicate the extent to which different statements are descriptive of you or your twin. Please feel free to complete the items at your own pace, in your own home. It is not necessary to fill out all of the questionnaires in one sitting. We do, however, ask that you fill out the questionnaires by yourself rather than with your twin, as we are interested in your unique responses.

There are no known risks involved in participating in this study. Participation in this study is voluntary. You may refuse to participate, and to not answer any questions that you do not feel comfortable addressing. You may withdraw from the study at any time.

Once you have completed as many of the questionnaires as you wish to complete, please mail them back to us in the provided self-addressed stamped envelope. The questionnaires will then be stored in a locked cabinet in Dr. _________'s office until they have been scored. At that point, they will be shredded. Only Dr. _________ and his research assistant will have access to the questionnaires and to the response sheets. Your name will never be given out nor will it appear in any written report about the study. All of your responses will be kept completely confidential.

Once we have processed your questionnaires, you will be sent $25.00 and your name will be entered into a draw for a chance to win one of ten $100.00 prizes. At the completion of the study, we will send you a summary of the study's findings, if you so request.

If you have questions regarding any aspect of this study, you are welcome to contact Dr. _________ by telephone (xxx-xxx-xxxx) or by email (xxxxxx@xxx.ca). If you have any further questions about the manner in which this study is being conducted or about your rights as a research participant, you may contact the Director of the Office of Research Ethics at the University of _________ by telephone (xxx-xxx-xxxx) or via email (xxxxxx@xxx.ca).

Completion and return of the questionnaires indicates your consent to participate in the study.

Thank you for your interest in this study. This letter is yours to keep for future reference.

Dr. _________, Professor of _________, University of _________

FIGURE 3.1 A Letter of Information

might signal a lack of trust, less formal approaches such as verbal assurances and ad hoc explanations may be employed. Whichever method they choose, researchers must provide REBs with documentation outlining how **informed consent** will be obtained.

The principle of free and informed consent seems straightforward, but putting it into practice can be difficult and usually involves some ethical trade-offs. Homan (1991, p. 73) observed that abiding by this principle "is easier said than done." At least two major points stand out here:

- It's extremely difficult to give prospective participants absolutely all the information required to make an informed decision about their involvement. Relatively minor transgressions of the principle of informed consent are pervasive in social research: for example, not giving all the details about the study for fear of contaminating people's answers to questions.
- In ethnographic research, the researcher is likely to come into contact with a wide spectrum of people, and ensuring that absolutely everyone has the opportunity to give informed consent is not practicable. Even when all participants in a certain setting are aware that they are being observed, it's unlikely that all of them will have been similarly (let alone identically) informed about the nature of the research.

Oral History Consent Form

Consent to Participate in an oral history interview being conducted by students enrolled in [course] at ____________ University. This is to state that I agree to participate in a program of research being conducted by 45 students under the supervision of Dr. ________ of the Department of ____________ University ([telephone number], email: [email address]).

PURPOSE: I have been informed that the purpose of the project is to explore the history of those parts of the _________ area that have been demolished or otherwise "lost" to us due to urban change. Students have formed into teams of 3 to 5 and will be exploring specific sites of memory such as ________, stories of immigration and displacement, and the former [site]. We will be working closely with [organization] and the [organization] which are developing exhibitions on the [site] and [topic] in [year], based in part on these student projects.

PROCEDURES: The interview will be conducted at participants' homes, at facilities provided by ________ University or at another appropriate place. Interviewers will record participants' life stories using video, or audio depending on the preference of the interviewee. Participants can choose to discuss any aspect of their lives and they may refuse to answer any questions. Interviews normally take about 1.5 hours, but participants may take as long as they would like and are free to stop at any time.

RISKS AND BENEFITS: Describing difficult experiences can be upsetting and emotionally difficult. As the student projects will contribute to two exhibitions, as well as a website, with your permission, your story will be heard.

CONDITIONS OF PARTICIPATION: Please review the following conditions and options with the interviewer. Feel free to ask questions if they appear unclear.

___I understand that I am free to withdraw my consent at any time during the interview and discontinue from that point forward.

In terms of **identification and reproduction of my interview**, I agree to (please choose one):

___**Open public access**: My identity may be revealed in any publications or presentations that may result from this interview.

___I agree to the possible broadcasting and reproduction of sound and images of my interview by any method and in any media by participants of this research project. I consent that my interview, or portions of it, be made available on the Internet through Web pages and/or online databases of the project.

___I agree that transcripts and/or recordings of my interview will be stored at a local archive for long-term preservation. Your interview may be accessed by researchers and the public by viewing it at the Centre for _______ and/or at a local ________-area archive holding the preservation copy.

OR

___ **Anonymity**: My identity will be known only to the interviewer and the course instructor; others will not gain access to my identity unless they gain special permission from me, the interviewee. Once the student project is completed in [month/year], the audio and/or video recording will be destroyed by the student (though a copy of the interview may be given to you).

In cases where family photographs or documents are scanned or photographed:

___ I agree to let the student researcher copy family photographs and documents for use in the student project only.

OR

___ I agree to let the student researcher copy family photographs and documents for use in their assignment and for their being archived with the interview recording. I likewise give permission to let future researchers use these images in their publications.

I HAVE CAREFULLY STUDIED THE ABOVE AND UNDERSTAND THIS AGREEMENT. I FREELY AND VOLUNTARILY AGREE TO PARTICIPATE IN THIS STUDY.

INTERVIEWEE:

NAME (please print) ______________________________

SIGNATURE ______________________________

Date and Birthplace (optional) ______________________________

INTERVIEWER:

NAME (please print) ______________________________

SIGNATURE ______________________________

DATE:

If at any time you have questions about your rights as a research participant, please contact _________, Chair of the Research Ethics Committee, Department of _______, _______ University at [phone number] or by email at [email address].

FIGURE 3.2 A Consent Form

Adapted from consent form from Concordia University: http://storytelling.concordia.ca/sites/default/files/Oral%20History%20consent%20form%20Urban%20Change%20model.pdf

Experiments are particularly problematic when it comes to informed consent because researchers want the participants to behave naturally and authentically. If participants were to be fully informed regarding the purpose of the experiment, it would be difficult to avoid the **reactive effects** that occur when people know they are being observed. For this reason, experiments usually involve some deception.

For example, Milgram (1963) designed a series of studies in an effort to understand the brutality that occurred in Nazi concentration camps during the Second World War. In particular, he wanted to know how a person could be led to cause extreme harm to an innocent human being, and whether being ordered to do so by an authority figure had anything to do with it. Milgram devised a laboratory experiment in which a supposedly reputable researcher (the authority figure) asked participants to act as "teachers" who would punish "learners" by giving them increasingly severe electric shocks whenever they gave incorrect answers to questions. Neither the shocks nor the howls of pain coming from the "learners" were real, but the "teachers"/participants did not know this. Some of them were further disadvantaged in that they could not see the "learners": they could only hear the shrieks of pain supposedly coming from them.

In all instances, the "teachers" were told that the shocks were part of the study and would not cause any permanent harm, despite the increasingly shrill cries of pain. The experiment continued until the "teacher"/participant refused to administer more shocks. In the version of the study in which the "teachers" could not see the "learners," a substantial majority (62 per cent) of the former administered the strongest shocks possible. Further, in one variant of the experiment, the research volunteers were given the option of ordering another person (actually an accomplice of Milgram's) to administer the shocks; in this situation, more than 90 per cent of them ordered the greatest shocks possible. Many of the participants were visibly upset as they carried out the experimenter's orders, but they still did what the authority figure told them to do.

Milgram saw these results as shedding light on the circumstances that led to the horrors of the Nazi concentration camps. It appeared that ordinary, everyday people were willing to inflict serious harm on innocent others if ordered to do so by an authority figure—a finding that may have important implications for the understanding of human atrocities and ultimately their prevention, although that interpretation of his findings has come into question (Perry, 2012). Nonetheless, the fact remains that the study involved a number of ethically questionable elements. For one thing, the "teachers"/participants themselves suffered at least short-term harm; most felt very uncomfortable administering what they believed to be powerful shocks, and while the experiment was in progress many participants came to doubt the experimenter's claim that the "learners" were not suffering any serious harm. Some were apparently traumatized by the experience, and expressed serious misgivings about taking part in the study decades later (Perry, 2012).

Another issue was the deception that the participants experienced: they were told that the experiment was investigating how people learn, not how people come to commit cruel acts, and they were led to believe that the shocks were real. Thus, to the extent that the participants were not fully informed about the purpose of the experiment, they were lied to, although once it was over they were *debriefed* (given previously withheld information about the study) in that they were informed by the "learner" that the shocks had not really been as painful as he had let on, and that he had not been harmed by them. However, in keeping with the procedural norms of the era, the debriefing provided was rather cursory and did not fully disclose the deception involved in the study. In most cases the participant left the lab without being told that the shock machine was not real and that the "learner" was an accomplice of the experimenter rather than a research participant. In some cases, participants were not given a full explanation of how the experiment was conducted until almost a year later (Perry, 2012).

Most people would agree that in everyday life, lying and deception should be avoided. On the other hand, the experiment would not have worked had the volunteers known the truth from the outset. Imagine the outcome if participants had been told,

"We're going to see whether you are willing to inflict severe pain on an innocent person, and by the way, the 'shocks' you will be asked to give will not be real." But does the need for unguarded behaviour justify the deception? Was the knowledge gained worth the psychological distress the participants experienced when they believed they were causing innocent persons to suffer? This is the sort of question that researchers and REB members must ponder.

It must be emphasized that Milgram is not alone in his use of deception: in fact, most social research experiments involve some kind of pretense, although the level of deception used in his day is now viewed by many as excessive—it is unlikely that an REB in North America would allow a similar study to proceed today. For that reason, Milgram's experiment has rarely been replicated, except in parts of the world where research ethics codes are less stringent.

As you think about the ethics of Milgram's study, keep in mind that REBs are not infallible and that REB members sometimes disagree among themselves about the ethics of a particular study. As a student, you need to make up your own mind about ethical issues. Don't feel obliged to accept the ethical claims of more experienced social researchers; history has shown that empirical, theoretical, or technological expertise is no guarantee of moral wisdom. But do listen carefully to the arguments of experienced researchers. It is incumbent on you to consider what is at stake in any research situation, especially the probable harms and benefits to the research participants, and to think about the effects—both good and bad—that the knowledge produced by the study would generate for the world at large.

Deception can be a controversial issue in qualitative research as well. Punch (1994, p. 91), for example, observed that "some dissimulation is intrinsic to social life and, therefore, to fieldwork." He quoted Gans (1962, p. 44) in support: "If the researcher is completely honest with people about his activities, they will try to hide actions and attitudes they consider undesirable, and so will be dishonest. Consequently, the researcher must be dishonest to get honest data."

Goode (1996) argued that judgments about deception should be considered on a case-by-case basis. Some writers argue that if all ruses were disallowed, a great deal of useful information—about terrorists, cults, drug gangs, white-collar criminals, and so on—would be inaccessible, because finding out about their activities often requires some kind of disguised observation. Some social reformers might add that exposing the sins of the powerful would also justify the use of deception, but that argument opens the door to its use in other situations. Would it be acceptable to use deception to examine the transgressions of the underclass and the less powerful? Is lying to a priest to uncover pedophilia more acceptable than lying to an animal rights activist to reveal a plan to destroy a mink coat factory?

Sometimes it may be beyond the power of a qualitative researcher to obtain informed consent. For example, Van Maanen (1991) used his experience as a ride operator in Disneyland as the basis for a study he produced many years after he had been employed there during school vacations. He never went back and asked permission from the people he described in his work; to do so would have been close to impossible. Is the absence of consent acceptable in such a situation? Is it a form of deception?

Although the use of deception can be controversial in both quantitative and qualitative research, there is consensus on a number of criteria regarding its use. First, deception should be used only as a last resort. Second, if deception is used, that use should be as sparing as possible. Finally, where feasible, anyone deceived should be fully debriefed as quickly as possible; specifically, the researcher must reveal the deception and explain why it was used. Milgram's research illustrates the potential for harm to participants if the debriefing is not comprehensive and done in a timely manner.

Another issue regarding informed consent is whether the researcher is obliged to reveal the names of all those who have sponsored the project, whether individuals or organizations. At one Ontario university, ethical rules prohibit any reference to the names of research sponsors on the information sheet. This rule reflects the possibility that some people might feel pressured or coerced if they knew that the research was sponsored by (for example) the Canadian Cancer Society. But another university considers it unethical *not* to supply that information, on the grounds that it is necessary to enable the participant to give informed consent. For instance, some people might not want the government to know anything about them, so if a department such as National Defence were funding the study, they would want to be informed so they could decide not to participate. Yet even if the sponsor's name is revealed, participants' ability to give informed consent may not be guaranteed, since the name may be virtually unknown to the general public. Ethical issues are never simple.

As noted above, only people competent to make a decision about participating in a research study should be asked to give their consent. That category normally includes most adults, although for reasons of illness, other incapacitation, or language difficulties some adults may not be capable of making an informed decision and must have a competent person make the decision on their behalf. Similarly, young children are not ordinarily considered capable of giving informed consent. Parents or legal guardians are usually given the information sheet as well as an opportunity to ask questions and seek clarifications about the research before signing the consent form for their child. Quite often a parent or guardian is required to be present when the child interacts with the researcher, especially if the study involves children who are very young. Exceptions include situations in which older children fill out questionnaires that the parents or guardians have seen and approved.

Concern for welfare

"Welfare" in this context covers all aspects of the well-being of the person, group, or community affected by the research, including physical, mental, emotional, spiritual, social, and economic well-being. A very basic "welfare" concern in social research involves respect for privacy and confidentiality. REBs normally require that the identities and records of the people being studied remain confidential to prevent any embarrassment or harm, especially harm to their reputations or personal relationships. This injunction means that the research participants should not be identifiable when the findings are published, although exceptions may occasionally be made in the case of historical work or of studies dealing with public figures. In quantitative research, participants are usually identified by code numbers rather than names when the data are processed; their actual identities are stored in a secure location. In such studies research participants are normally told on the information sheet that the data they provide will form part of a statistical aggregate (as in "50 per cent of respondents expressed some dissatisfaction with their romantic partner's listening skills") and therefore they will not be personally identifiable.

Researchers have to be especially resourceful in situations where participants prefer to remain anonymous. One method that is sometimes employed is the *randomized response technique*, which was originally designed for interview situations in which the respondent is asked about controversial or illegal activities. One reason for developing this technique was to protect researchers as well as respondents from the risk that police would examine the data and then bring the researchers into court as witnesses. (Can some harm be anticipated here, as when the still-free criminals repeat their crimes?)

The random response process begins with respondents flipping a coin but not revealing the results. About half of them should get heads, half tails. All respondents are then instructed: "For the following question, if you have heads you must say yes, regardless of whether it is true or not. With tails you should answer the question truthfully." Then comes the question: "Have you ever used cocaine?" Even if no one had in fact used it, roughly 50 per cent should say yes because they got heads.

Assume that 60 per cent of respondents say yes. The excess over the 50 per cent (heads who had to say yes) can be used to calculate how many people used cocaine. Here the excess is 10 per cent, presumably representing people who got tails and have used the drug. Then, since one would expect roughly the same number of cocaine users in the heads group, that figure must be doubled to get the percentage of the total sample who had used cocaine.

One of the authors of this book did this as a class exercise and had students raise their hands to say yes or no. When the behaviour in question was shoplifting after the age of 16, 80 per cent answered

Box 3.1 | What about research using the Internet?

Michael Simons/123RF

As a researcher, consider how you could conduct online research in an ethical way. What kinds of steps would you need to take to secure the informed consent of your participants and to protect your data?

A great deal of research is now done online (see Chapters 5, 7, 8, 10, 11, and 12). All the ethics guidelines discussed in this chapter apply to online research, with a handful of exceptions. One exception involves material that is publicly available and protected by law, such as Statistics Canada public-use files or data in public archives. In such cases the researcher is not required to obtain informed consent, although he or she must obey the relevant laws and regulations. Another exception applies to online information that is publicly accessible and does not involve any expectation of privacy. Such material would include films, newspaper materials, official publications, third-party interviews, and any other online research that does not entail direct interaction with research participants.

Any situation that does involve direct contact with research participants, including online surveys and interviews, is subject to the same ethics protocols as in-person research. The same goes for gaining access to online materials in situations where there is a reasonable expectation of privacy, as in the case of social media that may limit access to materials unless the creator's permission is granted, such as Facebook, Instagram, and LinkedIn. Internet chat room discussions, email, and the postings of organizations having restricted memberships, such as self-help groups, fall into this category as well. In these sorts of situations, both researchers and research participants have to be especially vigilant, since it is relatively easy to conduct **covert research** online. It would be quite easy, for example, for a researcher to pose as a regular participant in a self-help chat room for sex addicts, and use the material as data for a qualitative study. But doing so would be equivalent to joining an in-person discussion group and not revealing one's identity as a researcher. (The ethical implications of covert research will be discussed later in this chapter.)

Sending research data over the Internet is another concern. If data containing identifiable information are to be transferred via the Internet, the data should be encrypted to ensure the security of the information. Even when sensitive data are merely stored on a computer that is connected to the Internet, encryption should be considered.

"yes," meaning a 60 per cent (30 per cent plus another 30 per cent) shoplifting rate. When the topic was post-puberty homosexual behaviour, however, "yes" responses came out at only 50 per cent. Here there are several possibilities: no one had engaged in the activity; a few had, but because heads and tails rarely come out exactly 50–50, they were concealed in the difference; some "heads" students were afraid their classmates would think a raised hand was an admission; or perhaps some "tails" students who had engaged in the activity did not want to give any indication that they had, fearing that a "yes" response would be interpreted as an admission. In any case, although randomized response techniques have not been used extensively in social research, there is evidence that they can be effective in studying sensitive topics (Blair, Imai, & Zhou, 2015).

In qualitative research, dealing with privacy and confidentiality issues is quite different, especially if the study involves in-depth analysis of a small number of people. Pseudonyms are typically used to protect people's identities, but quite often the detailed description of the physical and social setting, which qualitative researchers usually include to provide the needed context for the study, can offer enough clues to identify some of the participants. The study of an American town that Vidich and Bensman (1968) called "Springdale" (not its real name) is instructive in this regard. Their book was uncomplimentary about the town and several of its leaders, and many people felt that its tone was patronizing. To make matters worse, it was possible to identify individuals in the published account. The town's inhabitants responded with a Fourth of July parade in which people wore badges citing their book pseudonyms, and an effigy of Vidich was set up so that it was peering into manure. The townspeople also announced their refusal to cooperate in any more social research; they were clearly upset by the publication, and to that extent were harmed by it.

Another area of controversy surrounding privacy and confidentiality in qualitative studies pertains to covert research: investigations in which the people being observed are not informed that they are part of a study. In spite of the widespread insistence on informed consent and privacy rights, and the recognition that covert observation is especially prone to violations of those principles, covert studies still appear from time to time. The defence is usually that the benefits of the research outweigh any harm that may come to the people being studied. Virtually all codes of ethics allow covert research as a last resort, but most state that it should be avoided "as far as possible." Those who use this method argue that it is necessary to prevent research participants from changing their behaviour because they know they are being studied. Still, where informed consent has not been obtained prior to the commencement of the research, permission to use the data gathered should be obtained post hoc whenever possible. That is a general rule, but it is often broken in dealing with dangerous people such as pimps and other criminals. Where such permission has not been obtained, it is absolutely crucial to maintain the anonymity of the people observed.

One difficulty with the arguments justifying the use of covert methods is the assumption that it is impossible to obtain the data using other means. Covert observers sometimes base their judgments on the *anticipated* difficulty of gaining access to a setting rather than the actual experience of being denied entry. For example, Homan justified his use of covert participant observation of a religious sect on the grounds that sociologists were viewed very negatively by group members; hence "It seemed probable that the prevalence of such a perception would prejudice the effectiveness of a fieldworker declaring an identity as sociologist" (Homan & Bulmer 1982, p. 107).

One of the most famous and controversial cases of covert research can be found in Humphreys's *Tearoom Trade* (1970), a study that Desroches (1990) partially replicated in Canada using less contentious methods. The researchers (Humphreys himself and police acting for Desroches) observed homosexual encounters in public washrooms ("tearooms"), taking the roles of "watch queens"—people who watch out for possible intruders while other men meet and engage in sexual activity. Such "voyeurism" was offensive to some critics.

As part of his research, Humphreys recorded some of the participants' car licence numbers. He was then able to track down their names and addresses, thus further compromising their privacy, and ended up with a sample of 100 active tearoom-trade participants. To reduce the risk of being recognized, Humphreys waited a year before contacting the respondents whose licence numbers he had written down, and also changed his hairstyle. After this deception, he then conducted an interview (Desroches did not do this) with a sample of the men about their health issues (a ruse), including some questions about marital sex. He did not tell them he knew about their activity, nor did he debrief them when the study was finished. Humphreys learned that many of the men he observed were actually married, respected members of the community—a finding that allowed him to challenge a popular stereotype of the day.

Was his research ethical? Those who say "yes" argue that he had no choice but to do covert research because very few people engaging in gay sex in those days were willing to talk about it; in fact, sexual acts between men were against the law and the people committing them were subject to prison sentences. Humphreys's supporters also maintain that the knowledge his studies produced led to a better understanding of human sexuality and the treatment of stigmatized individuals. His detractors argue that the knowledge gained did not justify the deception and invasion of privacy that his research participants experienced. The debate continues to this day.

Regardless of one's position on the ethics of Humphreys's work, the public reaction when it was first published illustrates what can happen to the reputation of social researchers as a whole if there is a perception that one of their kind has committed serious ethical violations. The following is an excerpt from an article written in the *Washington Post* in 1970, shortly after the controversy erupted:

> We're so preoccupied with defending our privacy against insurance investigators, dope sleuths, counterespionage men, divorce detectives and credit checkers, that we overlook the social scientists behind the hunting blinds who're also peeping into what we thought were our most private and secret lives. But they are there, studying us, taking notes, getting to know us, as indifferent as everybody else to the feeling that to be a complete human involves having an aspect of ourselves that's unknown. (Von Hoffman, 1970)

The ethical quandaries surrounding privacy and confidentiality inherent in qualitative research are also illustrated in the work of O'Connell Davidson and Layder (1994). These researchers conducted a small-scale ethnographic project on a sex worker, whom they called Desiree, and her clients and assistants. While Desiree and the women who served as her receptionists were fully aware of O'Connell Davidson's status, the clients were not. Both researchers admitted their invasion of client privacy and failure to obtain consent from them, but were "untroubled" by the intrusion because the clients were anonymous to O'Connell Davidson and she was not "in a position to secure, store or disclose information that could harm them" (O'Connell Davidson & Layder, 1994, p. 214). The fact that there was no harm to participants was regarded as the litmus test of the ethical status of the research. They offered a further defence by saying that ethical transgression is pervasive: "Virtually all social research is intrusive and exploitative to some degree" (O'Connell Davidson & Layder, 1994, p. 215). There was an acknowledged commitment to attend to the concerns of Desiree and her receptionists, as well as considerable sympathy for them, but these sentiments did not extend to her clients:

> I have . . . no personal liking and no real sympathy for them. I have a professional obligation to preserve their anonymity and to ensure that they are not harmed by my research, but I feel no qualms about being less than frank with them, and no obligation to allow them to choose whether or not their actions are recorded. (O'Connell Davidson & Layder, 1994, p. 215)

Although an effort was made to follow ethics protocols, it appears that not all the participants received the same level of ethical protection, and that the researchers believed that not all research participants *deserved* the complete range of ethics coverage. This sort of arrangement is more common than one might think and has far-reaching implications. It also illustrates how difficult it can be to resolve ethical dilemmas in social research. Do sex-trade clients have a right to choose to be excluded from research studies? What if they are abusing the sex workers? What if they are not? Does it matter whether such studies contribute to a better understanding of the sex industry—for instance, by revealing the physical risks that people in the sex trade take? Such questions must be weighed carefully and are not easily answered.

Sometimes a researcher may feel obliged to disregard concerns about privacy and confidentiality if the research uncovers evidence of serious harm or criminal activity. In his ethnographic research,

Totten (2001) wanted to know how youth gang members interpreted the violence they perpetrated against their girlfriends, and how they accounted for their racist and homophobic activities. One underlying factor he observed was their mental construction of masculinity, which included the belief that such activities are acceptable for men. Most had lived on the street, were themselves victims of severe child abuse and neglect, and had witnessed their mothers being beaten. They saw their own violence as affirming their masculinity.

That was the sociology, but what about the welfare of the people concerned? Here the researcher was in some instances compelled to act. By law, he had to report any abuse suffered by children under the age of 16, regardless of whether they were gang members or their victims. Second, those deemed at risk of suicide had to be referred to mental health–care providers. Finally, some of the gang members were on probation or living in treatment facilities, so the relevant authorities also had to be informed. Totten handled the confidentiality issue by studying only the boys who agreed to those limitations on confidentiality.

Legal issues can affect confidentiality for other reasons. When Marie-Ève Maillé was a graduate student in Quebec in 2010, she interviewed 93 people affected by a large wind farm in the province that was operated by a private company. When she conducted the interviews, she followed good research practice by telling the interviewees that their identities would remain private. The data collection was particularly sensitive because many people in the area surrounding the wind project were bothered by its construction and operation, and a few years later filed a class action lawsuit against the company.

Maillé volunteered to act as an expert witness for the people who launched the lawsuit. But as the legal proceedings unfolded, she was ordered by a judge to provide the company that owned the wind farm with the raw data from her study, declaring it to be evidence relevant to the case. To protest the judge's order, over 200 Quebec researchers signed an open letter published in *Le Devoir* stating that if Maillé had to turn over her confidential data, that would set a precedent that would seriously impede scientific inquiry in the province (*Le Devoir*, 2016). Ultimately, in 2017, the Superior Court of Quebec ruled that she would not have to give up her data to the court. The decision was hailed as a victory for research participants, the researchers who rely on them, and the general public that benefits from open inquiry and scientific discovery (Kondro, 2016; Castonguay, 2017).

Another aspect of the "concern for welfare" criterion, one that can affect the larger community or even the society as a whole, involves sponsored research. Most social research in Canada is funded either by SSHRC or by the university with which the researcher is affiliated, but other government agencies, private individuals, corporations, unions, and non-profit organizations can also sponsor research. Ethical issues arise if the sponsor places conditions on the methodology to be used or the publication of the results, or has certain expectations regarding the findings. In the United States, a social researcher was asked by the owner of an apartment building to do a study of the behaviour of tenants in "singles" apartments after neighbours complained about bad behaviour (Bailey, 1994). The sponsor in this case made it clear that the research was expected to show that the tenants were in fact good people and desirable neighbours. Perhaps the most famous Canadian case of a sponsor trying to influence the research process involved Dr Nancy Olivieri, who took part in research on a drug designed to treat thalassaemia, a blood disease. She claimed that the drug was not effective and had harmful effects, and wanted to inform the research participants. A controversy arose when the pharmaceutical company that sponsored the research denied her claims and cited a confidentiality agreement that she had signed that would be violated if she were to contact the participants. Another famous case involved three Canadian scientists who claimed that their supervisors at Health Canada had tried to coerce them into approving certain drugs for use on cows and pigs even though the scientists objected that the drugs could have harmful effects on humans; the scientists were subsequently fired, although one was later reinstated. In 2010, the head of Statistics Canada resigned over the federal government's decision to discontinue the mandatory long-form **census** and replace it with a voluntary version, which in his view would not be adequate to fulfill Statistics Canada's mandate. (The decision was reversed by a later government.)

People conducting social research should be mindful of the perils of sponsored research. The *TCPS2* states that financial considerations do not reduce the need to abide by the principles that underlie its policies, and that the scientific integrity of the research process must be upheld. Any conflict of interest, including a financial conflict of interest involving a relationship with a sponsor, must be reported to the appropriate REB. Most fundamentally, the public good, in particular the welfare of the research participants, "takes precedence over the interests of researchers, institutions, and sponsors" (CIHR, NSERC, & SSHRC, 2018, p. 143).

Methods in Motion | Applications to Canadian Society

The effect of ethics reviews on qualitative research

Did the implementation of formal ethics reviews stifle social research in Canada? Van den Hoonaard and Connolly (2006) examined this issue by gathering information on Canadian master's theses completed in anthropology in the 10 years from 1995 to 2004. The mid-point in that time span—2001—marked the year that the first edition of the *Tri-Council Policy Statement on Ethics in Human Research (TCPS)* (CIHR, NSERC, & SSHRCC, 1998) was implemented on a national basis. The authors chose anthropology theses in part because a large portion of the research done in that discipline is qualitative, and qualitative researchers have been the most vocal about the negative consequences that stringent ethics policies may have on social research.

One of the major complaints of qualitative researchers is that ethics policies in Canada and elsewhere have been designed according to a bio-medical model that calls for standard research protocols, signed consent forms, and other elements that are not compatible with qualitative and especially ethnographic studies. In qualitative research, topics and even methodologies may emerge out of the research process itself, so information sheets on the goals of the research, consent forms outlining the risks and benefits of participation, and other features of the bio-medical model can in many cases seriously interfere with the research: imagine how members of an outlaw motorcycle gang would respond to a researcher who handed them information sheets and consent forms to sign. Such difficulties are often not addressed in national ethics regulations. Indeed, the authors point out that the original *TCPS* (1998) contained 476 paragraphs, of which only four pertained to "natural observation research."

Van den Hoonaard and Connolly (2006) found, contrary to expectation, that the number of anthropology master's theses actually increased in the 10-year period under investigation, and that the number of research projects involving research participants (as opposed to archival documents, secondary data sources, and so on) also increased. This suggested that ethics reviews did not put a brake on anthropological research, although the authors noted that the data did not include cases in which research was abandoned because ethics rules were too strict. More ominously, however, they noted that the proportion of theses involving only qualitative interviewing rather than full-blown ethnography had increased since 2001. They suggested that this trend might be a consequence of overly stringent ethics regulations on ethnographic research.

More recent versions of the *Tri-Council Policy Statement* were created with substantial input from qualitative researchers. The current version, the *TCPS2* (CIHR, NSERC, & SSHRC, 2018), has an entire chapter on qualitative research, and the new guidelines recognize that requiring formal consent documents and other elements of the bio-medical model may not be appropriate in all research situations.

Justice

Justice in the context of research ethics includes the idea that the burdens and benefits of research should be spread evenly across society. No person or group should be exploited in the research process or systematically excluded from its benefits. This is a major concern in health research, in which care has to be taken that vulnerable people are not treated as guinea pigs for the benefit of others, whether some interest group or the larger society. Unfortunately, there is a history of this sort of abuse in Canada, such as what happened in Indigenous communities and residential schools in the 1940s and 1950s. Nutritional experiments were conducted, apparently without informed consent, on children and adults who were found to be suffering from serious malnourishment. In one study, rather than provide emergency food aid, the researchers set up experimental and control groups to test the effectiveness of vitamin and other dietary supplements; those in the control group continued with their meagre diets. In some cases, Indigenous children were prevented from receiving dental care for extended periods of time on the grounds that it would interfere with an assessment of their nutritional status, and experimenters in some cases prolonged the existence of inadequate diets for two years in order to establish baseline measurements. Moreover, the experimenters were aware of the link between malnutrition and the high disease and mortality rates found among Indigenous people (Mosby, 2013). At the same time, medical researchers should not arbitrarily exclude from their studies certain categories of people (such as members of specific ethnic, gender, or age groups), especially if such people stand to benefit from experimental drugs or other treatments.

With regard to social research, inclusiveness is usually not a pressing issue, partly because social scientific studies lack the immediate life-and-death consequences that are common in medical research, and also because vulnerable and exploited groups are often sought out for study, particularly by sociologists and anthropologists. However, there is always a risk that members of disadvantaged groups will be abused, mistreated, or disrespected by the researchers who study them. For example, some street people might resent an ethnographer's implication, however subtle, that they need "help" of some kind, or the assumption that the researcher has a superior sort of wisdom or political insight. Some Western anthropologists have been barred from re-entering the countries where they did their fieldwork because the locals found them to be intrusive and disrespectful.

Justice in a research context also includes the principle of minimizing harm to participants. As we suggested above, it is a rule of thumb when harm is expected that it must not outweigh the potential benefits of the research. But as the examples discussed earlier have shown, harms and benefits can be difficult to judge correctly, and assessments of them ultimately involve value judgments as well as scientific decisions. Most social scientists are not curing cancer or ending racism. How much suffering or harm, if any, can be justified in social scientific research? That is a key ethical question facing both researchers and the REBs that oversee their work.

Research likely to harm participants is regarded by almost everyone as unacceptable. But what is "harm"? Harm can mean a number of things, including physical harm, loss of self-esteem, stress, or even a mild sense of shame. And what does "likely" mean: a 1 per cent chance? 10 per cent? 50 per cent?

Researchers should do their best to anticipate and guard against consequences for research participants that are expected to be harmful or disturbing. But it's not always easy to know where to draw the line. For example, in the Rosenthal and Jacobson (1968) study of teacher expectations discussed in Chapter 2, it is at least possible that the pupils not identified as "spurters" (students expected to excel quickly) were adversely affected in their intellectual development by the increased attention given to the "spurters." After all, teachers have limited time and energy, and time spent with the "spurters" meant time away from everyone else. Was that a violation of research ethics? Was the harm suffered by the "non-spurters" outweighed by the knowledge gained by the researchers? Similarly, in Festinger, Riecken, & Schachter's (1956) study of a doomsday/UFO cult, the researchers joined the group at a crucial time (close to the projected end of the world), thereby deluding group members into thinking that they had succeeded in winning new converts. Was that ethical? Was the harm to the cult members less important than the understanding of cults gained through this research project?

One of the problems with trying to balance harms and benefits is that it is not possible to identify all the circumstances in which harm is likely—although that fact should not be taken to mean that there's no point in seeking to protect research participants. Kimmel (1988) noted this in connection with the 1939 Cambridge–Summerville Youth Study: an experiment conducted on 506 boys aged 5 to 13 who were identified either as likely to become delinquent or as having an average likelihood in that regard. The boys were randomly assigned either to an experimental group in which they would receive preventive counselling, or to a no-treatment control group. In the mid-1970s the boys (by then men) were examined and the results were quite shocking:

> Treated subjects were more likely than controls to evidence signs of alcoholism and serious mental illness, died at a younger age, suffered from more stress-related diseases, tended to be employed in lower-prestige occupations, and were more likely to commit second crimes. (Kimmel, 1988, p. 19)

In other words, the treatment itself may have had unintended negative consequences, although given the complex and long-term nature of the forces that cause delinquency it seems likely that non-experimental factors contributed to the results. Nonetheless, the findings do illustrate the difficulty of anticipating harm to participants. Might a questionnaire on marital happiness lead a respondent to question and eventually leave a marriage? Could asking a grade eight boy in gym class about steroid use encourage him to experiment with a drug that until then was unknown to him? Some interviewees may be uncomfortable answering any question; some may find the cut and thrust of a focus group discussion stressful, especially if they inadvertently reveal more than they had intended. Does it follow that such studies should not be conducted? Is the risk of harm, even mild harm, worth the potential increase in knowledge that this kind of research may make possible? That is the crux of the issue when a researcher seeks a proper balance between harms and benefits. Most ethical codes maintain that if there is any prospect of harm to participants, and if the risks of the research are greater than the risks of everyday life, informed consent is a minimum requirement.

Clearly, the principle of justice in social research is closely tied in with the precepts discussed earlier, in particular the notions of informed consent, privacy, and confidentiality. People are certainly less likely to be harmed if they know what to expect in a research situation, and if they know that their participation is voluntary. Thus, it is particularly important to inform participants of their *right to withdraw from the study at any time*—and to honour that right.

A good illustration of what can go wrong when research participants are pressured into remaining in a study can be found in the Stanford mock prison study (Haney, Banks, & Zimbardo, 1973). In this experiment, psychologically healthy male university students were randomly selected to be either "guards" or "prisoners" in a simulated prison set up in the basement of a university building. "Guards" were given uniforms, wooden batons, and reflective sunglasses (to avoid eye contact with the "prisoners" and thus to dehumanize them), and were told to instill fear in the "prisoners." The "prisoners" were given humiliating smocks and headgear to wear, and had to address the "guards" in a respectful manner regardless of how they were being treated. The aim of the study was to see whether taking on the role of "guard" would create feelings of omnipotence and lead to belligerent behaviour, and whether being treated like a prisoner would produce feelings of subservience, self-alienation, resentment, and hostility. In short, the aim of the study was to see whether placing ordinary people in these roles would lead to stereotypical prison behaviour.

The study was designed to last two weeks. Zimbardo describes what happened:

> At the end of only six days we had to close down our mock prison because what we saw was frightening. It was no longer apparent to us or most of the subjects where they ended and their roles began. The majority had indeed become "prisoners" or "guards" no longer able to clearly differentiate between role-playing and self. There were dramatic changes in virtually every aspect of their behavior, thinking and feeling; human values were suspended, self-concepts were

> challenged, and the ugliest, most base, pathological side of human nature surfaced. We were horrified because we saw some boys ("guards") treat other boys as if they were despicable animals, taking pleasure in cruelty, while other boys ("prisoners") became servile, dehumanized robots *who thought only of escape*, of their own individual survival, and their mounting hatred of the guards. (Zimbardo, 1971; quoted in Aronson, 1992, pp. 10–11; emphasis added)

A whole host of ethical issues come into play in this experiment, but let's focus on the right to leave a study at any time. Many of the "prisoners" wanted to leave long before the study was terminated. Yet they were given every indication that they had no choice but to stay in the study, and were convinced that for all practical purposes they were in a prison. A few were allowed to leave early, but only after showing signs of extreme stress and even hysteria. It's hard to see how this was not a violation of research ethics. Looking back on what he had created, Zimbardo himself was appalled.

Another point this experiment illustrates is the need for close oversight of ethical issues on the part of REBs. Like the Milgram (1963) study, Zimbardo's research was conducted before the era of stringent ethics reviews. REB oversight is absolutely necessary because even well-meaning researchers like Zimbardo and Milgram may be completely unaware that their work raises ethical problems—even if those problems seem quite obvious to others. For example, it simply did not occur to Zimbardo that his experiment was causing his research participants significant harm. It was not until a student research assistant told him she thought the treatment of the "prisoners" was awful that he relented and brought the study to an end. Presumably, a strict REB review would have spared the "prisoners" considerable agony.

In recent years, the Stanford prison study has also been criticized on methodological grounds. Some of these criticisms are discussed in the Research in the News box on pages 70–71, where it is apparent that methodological controversies can spill over into the realm of research ethics, an idea that is explored in more detail below.

Another issue related to harm to participants concerns payment for participation. In general, it is considered unethical to offer payment if that would lead volunteers to take risks they would not otherwise accept. Similarly, payment should not put undue pressure on people to take part or remain in a study, and for that reason should not exceed the sorts of benefits to which the participants are accustomed.

The participants in a study of suburban Toronto immigrants conducted by Dinovitzer, Hagan, & Parker (2003) were offered $5 to participate. It seems unlikely that anyone answered the questionnaire they were sent simply for the small amount of money involved. Still, some REBs do not allow the people being studied to be paid for their participation, except to cover the costs of taking part (parking, etc.). The purpose of this rule is to prevent poor people from "selling themselves" to researchers. Few would be critical of Beagan's (2001) offer to Canadian medical students of a chance at a $200 draw (which technically got around the payment rule) for taking part in her study of discrimination. But would offering $10,000 for testing a promising drug with potentially dangerous side effects be acceptable? What about selling a kidney for research purposes? Fortunately, the risk of harm to participants in social scientific research is usually not as severe as the risks associated with medical research, so those sorts of questions rarely have to be considered.

Benefit in the social sciences is typically indirect; in most cases it follows from an increase in knowledge. However, direct benefits can accrue, for instance in cases where research findings inspire positive social reform or contribute to valuable societal conservation. One way to maximize the benefit derived from social research is to conduct it in a methodologically sound manner. It is considered unethical to put research volunteers through the rigours of participation if the study is not designed or conducted properly and therefore is of little or no value. As you will learn as you make your way through this book, researchers can disagree over what constitutes a sound methodology. Nonetheless, each methodological perspective assumes that there are optimal ways of doing the research, and if these are ignored it's doubtful that anyone, including the researcher, will get the maximal benefit from it. Maximizing benefit is also related to the inclusiveness principle discussed above: no group or individual should be arbitrarily excluded from research.

Finally, justice in the conduct of social research includes fairness in the adjudication of research proposals by REBs. The procedures and protocols that REBs use have to be reasonable and equitable, and their decisions unbiased. In order to achieve those ends, REBs must be independent of the institutions in which they function. This means, for example, that universities cannot overturn the decisions of their REBs.

As we noted above, sometimes REBs can be overcautious in trying to protect the interests of research participants. This is often a concern in survey research, which normally involves minimal risk to participants. J. Paul Grayson, a sociologist at York University, conducted a study in which he found evidence that the excessively formal and legalistic letters of introduction that some universities require researchers to send to prospective participants lowers participation rates (Charbonneau, 2005). Low response rates may result in sample sizes that are too small for analysis and can lead to additional expenses for follow-up.

Conclusions

These ethical principles, and the larger discussion of research ethics contained in the *TCPS2* (CIHR, NSERC, & SSHRC, 2018), provide an invaluable guide for the conduct of social research. Their implementation can

Research in the News

Methodological controversies in the Stanford prison experiment

Zimbardo's Stanford prison experiment is one of the most famous studies ever done by a social scientist, and as such has garnered a lot of media attention in the half-century since it was conducted. The ethics of the study have long been debated, but more recently it is the methodology that has come under fire, even in the popular media. An investigation into the study published in *Medium GEN* by Ben Blum (2018) has revealed some serious shortcomings in the study (see also Le Texier, 2019).

Blum questions the general narrative taken by Zimbardo that psychologically "normal" people can be transformed into either abusive, sadistic guards or cowering, deeply disturbed prisoners by simply assigning them these roles randomly and letting the power of the prison situation spontaneously run its course. A crucial methodological flaw revealed by Blum is that the "guards" were given extensive, explicit instructions on how to treat the "prisoners," in particular how to break them down psychologically. An undergraduate research assistant told the "guards" the day before they came in contact with the "prisoners" that the latter were to address each other by number only, that they were not allowed to refer to their situation as an experiment or a simulation, and that failure to abide by these sorts of rules could result in punishment. "I was given the responsibility of trying to elicit 'tough-guard behaviour,'" the research assistant explained.

This created *demand characteristics*, which are cues picked up by research participants that lead them to act in certain ways in order to avoid "ruining" the study or to otherwise please the researcher. Often participants believe that it is their responsibility to exhibit the sorts of behaviours that the researcher is expecting to find, and so do not behave in a genuine and authentic way. Demand characteristics can be unintentional and subtle, but in the case of the Stanford prison study they were quite explicit. One of the "guards," who had studied acting, even faked a southern accent in order to appear more intimidating to the "prisoners." "I took it as a kind of improv exercise," he said. The "prisoners" also appear to have been affected by demand characteristics. One of them, who during the study appeared to have a hysterical emotional breakdown, told Blum: "Anyone who is a clinician would know that I was faking." The participant stated that he staged the breakdown in order to be released from the study.

These are serious methodological flaws that cast doubt on the study's main conclusions, and have received only scant attention and discussion by Zimbardo over the years. The reluctance to fully address these issues also brings to light an ethical dimension of the study that had not been widely considered before—namely, the duty of the researchers to provide a candid and comprehensive account of how the research was conducted.

be challenging, however, especially when acquiring informed consent might lead participants to behave less naturally than they otherwise would. Balancing risks and potential benefits can also be problematic. But be that as it may, wherever the procedures outlined above are not followed, the onus is on the researcher to convince the REB that it would be appropriate to go ahead with the study.

Another kind of challenge arises when professional researchers disagree on the ethical status of a particular practice, such as the covert methods used by Humphreys (1970) in his *Tearoom Trade* study. There is no simple answer to these ethical dilemmas, especially if there is no way to measure harms and benefits directly. However, it is incumbent on researchers to be vigilant in protecting the rights of research participants, and to maximize the benefits and minimize the harm that is created by their research.

Key Points

The *TCPS2* outlines three core principles for the ethical conduct of research:

- *Respect for persons* demands that research participants be asked for their free, informed, and ongoing consent.
- *Concern for welfare* includes all aspects of the well-being of individuals, groups, and communities affected by the research.
- *Justice* covers all dimensions of fairness in the treatment of research participants and the researchers themselves.

Most social research in Canada has to abide by those principles. In most cases, before social research can be conducted it has to be approved by a Research Ethics Board (REB) that uses the *TCPS2* to guide its decisions. It may be difficult to measure harms and benefits in social research, so the implementation of these principles is rarely simple and straightforward.

Researchers may disagree on how the three core principles are to be implemented, but they still must do everything they can to comply with them.

Questions for Review (R) and Creative Application (A)

R1 Explain what is meant by "harm to participants." Does it refer to physical harm alone?

A1 What harm might be suffered by a person completing an online questionnaire on the topic of illegal drug use? Would the harm be so severe that the study should not be conducted? Explain.

A2 What harm may be suffered by a person participating in qualitative interviews on the topic of lived racism? Would the harm be so severe that the study should not be conducted? Explain.

R2 What are some of the difficulties involved in implementing the principle of informed consent when doing ethnographic research?

A3 Assume you are doing ethnographic research at a homeless shelter. Is it necessary to get informed consent from every person you interact with or observe? Explain.

R3 Can deception in social research ever be justified? Explain.

A4 Assume you are participating in survey research that seeks to determine the degree to which participants possess sexist attitudes. Would some deception regarding the purposes of the research be justified? Explain.

R4 What is meant by "balancing risks and potential benefits"?

A5 List the risks and potential benefits of Milgram's (1963) "electric-shock" experiments. Did the potential benefits outweigh the risks? Explain.

A6 List the risks and potential benefits of Humphreys's (1970) *Tearoom Trade* study. Did the potential benefits outweigh the risks? Explain.

Interactive Classroom Activities

1. After reviewing the three core principles for ethical research with the class, the instructor will show one of two films: Milgram's *Obedience* or Zimbardo's *Quiet Rage: The Stanford Prison Experiment*. Before viewing the film, students are given the following questions to think about as they watch it:
   a. What scientific knowledge did this study produce? In other words, what can we conclude from this study?
   b. Can the knowledge generated by this study be used to explain real-life situations?
   c. Was this study ethical?

   After the film has been shown, an open class discussion is held to address the first two questions. Once that is completed, the instructor informs the class that a debate will be held to answer the third question, and divides the class into three groups. Group 1 must argue that the study was ethical; Group 2 must argue that the study was not ethical; and Group 3 can choose either of these positions. All groups are to justify their positions as best they can, and are encouraged to allude to the material discussed in this chapter. Once all three groups have argued their case, a vote is held to determine how the class as a whole views the ethics of the study, i.e., whether, on balance, they find it to be ethical or not.
2. Using the classroom screen, the instructor can walk the class through the *TCPS2* tutorial available at https://ethics.gc.ca/eng/education_tutorial-didacticiel.html (accessed 4 September 2021). It includes multidisciplinary examples, some interactive features, audio and video downloads, and a quiz.

Relevant Websites

The ***TCPS2*** (CIHR, NSERC, & SSHRC, 2018) is available online.

https://ethics.gc.ca/eng/policy-politique_tcps2-eptc2_2018.html

This ***TCPS2*** tutorial, which provides an excellent introduction to the document and gives users the opportunity to apply ethical principles to case studies, is available at

https://ethics.gc.ca/eng/education_tutorial-didacticiel.html

Visit the ***Canadian Sociological Association*** website to read its *Code of Ethics*.

www.csa-scs.ca/code-of-ethics

This link leads to the Canadian ***Charter of Rights and Freedoms***.

https://laws-lois.justice.gc.ca/eng/Const/page-15.html

Quiet Rage is a documentary film about the Stanford mock prison study that can be found at

https://www.youtube.com/watch?v=hIUlBrvqyyo

(Websites accessed 4 September 2021.)

OXFORD learning link

More resources are available on Oxford Learning Link. Visit **https://learninglink.oup.com/** for:

- Student self-quiz
- Flash cards
- Audio clips
- Videos
- Activities

APPENDIX TO PART I
An Overview of the Research Process

You now have some notion of how and why social research is done. Before moving on to the rest of the book, which expands on many of the points raised in the previous three chapters, let's step back and take a look at the big picture.

What follows could be described as the "ideal" stages of research. They are ideal not because they represent the best way to do things, but rather to indicate that they are an abstraction, a simplification of a more complex reality. There is no single best way to do research, any more than there is a single best way to build a house or paint a portrait. Sometimes the order of the tasks presented in the overview of the research process on page 74 can be rearranged. Also, it's not uncommon to go from one step to the next and then backtrack to adjust something in a previous step. Nonetheless, some general points and observations can be made that outline how research may progress from its initial stages to its completion.

In the beginning: Motivation

Where does research begin?

Sometimes research begins with a sense of wonder, a feeling of amazement with the social world that is accompanied by a strong desire to understand and explain it. Sometimes it begins with a sense of crisis, as when a society is strained to the breaking point and scholars are looking for solutions. This motivation has been around since the beginnings of social science in the eighteenth century. Since then, the challenges posed by urbanization, industrialization, ethnic conflict, and gender inequality (to name only a few) have provided the impetus for countless research projects. In other cases, the process of inquiry may begin with simple curiosity about what's out there: as one wag put it, if you walk by a house with its curtains closed and wonder what goes on inside, you'd probably make a good social scientist. With these sorts of motivations, researchers may be inspired to test a theory or interpretation of some social phenomenon, or to develop a new theory or interpretation.

Not all research begins with lofty motivations. In fact, the reasons for conducting a study are often quite mundane. For example, research may be done to enhance the career of the researcher, especially if it is supported by substantial funding. Sometimes researchers compete with one another to see who can produce the most publications or get the most attention for their work. More generally, research may be motivated by "sheer egoism," a reason that topped the list of motivations for writing drawn up by George Orwell (1946/2004). Graduate students (and some undergraduates) may do research simply to fulfill degree requirements. In most instances, the motivations for doing research are some combination of the exalted and the mundane.

The research question(s)

Once the decision has been made to do research in a particular area, the first task is to come up with a research question, or a set of research questions, that will give the study a focus or goal. A good research question should allow you to contribute to the existing knowledge of the topic, if only in a modest way. As we have mentioned earlier, research questions in quantitative studies tend to be more precise and explicit than those found in qualitative research,

An Overview of the Research Process

Motivation

↓

Research question(s)

↓

Literature review

↓

Choose general orientation

↕ ↕

Quantitative (choose design)

↓

Experiments
Surveys
– Structured interviews
– Questionnaires
Structured observation
Case studies

↓

Ethics review

↓

Gather data

↓

Analyze data

↓

Findings

↓

Conclusions
– Do the findings support the hypotheses?
– Implications for existing theories?
– New hypotheses, concepts, or theories generated?
– Implications for further research?
– Relevance to public policy?

Qualititative (choose design)

↓

Ethnography
Participant observation
Unstructured interviews
Semi-structured interviews
Life history
Oral history
Narrative analysis
Focus groups
Content analysis
– Ethnographic
– Semiotics
– Hermeneutics
– Conversation analysis
– Discourse analysis

↓

Ethics review

↓

Gather data

↕

Analyze data

↓

Findings

↓

Conclusions
– Do the findings provide a new interpretation of a person, group, setting, event, or text?
– Implications for existing theories?
– New hypotheses, concepts, or theories generated?
– Implications for further research?
– Do the findings illustrate group processes or social conflict in a new way?
– Relevance to public policy?

although qualitative researchers must have at least a general idea of what they are trying to accomplish. With both types of inquiry, it's fairly common to revise research questions as the project proceeds, especially in the early stages.

Literature review

Chances are you won't be the first person to investigate your topic or to use the methodology you have in mind. Reading up on what others have done will help you understand your subject matter more fully and will prevent you from venturing into territory that has already been thoroughly explored. A good knowledge of the literature may also reveal contradictions or gaps in the existing understanding of your topic, which can form the basis of your project. Sometimes a review of the literature can lead to substantial revisions in research questions; for example, if you encounter a finding that lacks a compelling explanation and decide to make it the focus of your inquiry. Reviewing the literature may also spark ideas about how various methodologies could be applied to your area of interest.

Choosing a general research orientation: Quantitative and/or qualitative

Once you've come up with your research question(s) and reviewed the existing literature in the area, you can decide on your general research orientation. However, it's not uncommon to decide on a particular orientation even before reviewing the literature or formulating any questions. For example, researchers specializing in qualitative studies are likely to start with the assumption that their research will be qualitative rather than quantitative in nature. Likewise, a researcher who has done a number of quantitative survey projects may start by designing a study with such surveys in mind, and may not even review the pros and cons of approaching their topic with a qualitative orientation.

Of course it's also possible to combine quantitative and qualitative approaches in a single study, as the arrows below "Choose general orientation" in the figure suggest. In practice, however, most studies are predominantly of one sort or the other.

Picking a research design from the ones available within a general research orientation

Once your research orientation has been decided, a number of research designs are available for consideration. Some of the designs listed in the figure were not discussed in the first three chapters of the book, but will be described later. Consult the Glossary for brief descriptions of any designs you are not familiar with.

The choice of the research design depends on a number of things, but your first concern should be to find a design that's *appropriate for your research questions*. For example, if you've chosen to explore political attitudes using quantitative methods and want to be able to apply your findings to some larger population, a survey design would be appropriate. Similarly, if you want to do a qualitative study of how professional jazz dancers cope with the pressures of auditions, then unstructured or semi-structured interviews would be a reasonable choice of design. Another consideration is whether a cross-sectional or longitudinal design would be most appropriate to answer the research questions.

Other factors that affect the choice of design include things like the availability of resources such as funding and time. If you can't afford to select a large probability sample, a full-blown survey analysis will be out of reach. Likewise, ethnography might be your design of choice, but time and travel constraints could rule that out. In most cases, some sort of compromise has to be made between the best possible research design and what is feasible under the circumstances.

Ethics review

As we emphasized at various points in Part I of this book, ethics are an important consideration at every stage of a research project, including the writing up of results. Once a research design has been picked, researchers in most cases have to present an ethics committee with a proposal that outlines how ethical considerations will be handled in each phase of the study. Note that this step can usually be skipped if the research does not involve human or animal participants; for instance, if the goal is to offer a new interpretation of a body of theoretical work without gathering empirical data.

Gather data

Data gathering can begin as soon as the ethics committee grants its approval. Sometimes a pilot study is conducted to determine whether the chosen method of data collection needs any refinement. For example, a pilot study can be used to find out whether the questions prepared for use in a survey are clear enough for respondents to understand, or whether potential participants in a qualitative study react strongly to the presence of the observer.

Analyze data

In quantitative studies, data analysis usually begins after all the data have been gathered. In qualitative research, by contrast, the process is often iterative, with preliminary data analysis leading to a change in either the kind of information to be sought or the way it is to be gathered. That is why there is a two-headed arrow between "Gather data" and "Analyze data" in the qualitative section of the figure. At this stage software may be used (for example, SPSS for quantitative analysis or NVivo for qualitative).

Findings

The findings are the results of the data analysis. For instance, a quantitative researcher might find that support for a particular government policy is strongly associated with age and ethnicity. Or a qualitative study of heroin addicts in Vancouver's downtown east side might find that they resent the people from whom they purchase their drugs.

Conclusions

Finally, what does it all mean? At this point an effort is usually made to relate the findings of the study to existing theories, knowledge, or interpretations of the topic. This is where you enter the debate about the subject matter with other scholars.

Quantitative social scientists will discuss whether their findings support their hypotheses (if they had specific hypotheses to begin with—not all of them do). Support for a hypothesis could provide substantiation for a particular theory. For instance, findings indicating that economic development leads to greater similarity in gender roles would support a version of modernization theory. If the hypotheses are not supported or if the findings are not consistent with the theory, a case can be made that the theory has to be revised or abandoned. Sometimes the findings will generate new hypotheses, concepts, or theories. In virtually all cases, the researcher will be able to suggest ways in which further research could be beneficial—perhaps different variables should be examined, or maybe the key variables need to be measured differently.

Qualitative researchers will discuss whether their findings suggest a new interpretation or conceptualization of the subject matter, or whether they provide a new illustration of group processes or social conflict. For example, findings derived from qualitative interviews with 16-year-old mothers might reveal something new about how young people view their sexuality and their relationships with their peers, which may be quite different from what is currently believed. Similarly, qualitative researchers can usually outline the ways in which further research would be desirable; for instance, by expanding the study of 16-year-old mothers to include 16-year-old fathers. And both quantitative and qualitative studies may include discussions of how their conclusions may be relevant to issues of public policy, such as public funding for daycare.

PART II

Quantitative Research

Part II of this book is concerned with quantitative research. Chapter 4 sets the scene by exploring its main features. Chapter 5 focuses on structured interviews and questionnaires—two of the most widely used data-gathering techniques in quantitative research—and includes guidelines on how to ask questions using those instruments. Chapter 6 discusses structured observation, a method that takes a systematic approach to the study of people in their natural surroundings. Quantitative sampling—the selection of people or other units of analysis to be included in the sorts of study discussed in Part II—is the topic of Chapter 7, and an overview of quantitative data analysis is provided in Chapter 8. These chapters describe the essential tools for doing quantitative research, from basic methodological principles to practical applications.

4 The Nature of Quantitative Research

Chapter Overview

This chapter is concerned with **quantitative research**, one of the two principal investigative orientations taken in the social sciences. The emphasis here is on what quantitative research typically entails, though departures from this ideal type will be outlined later on. This chapter explores:

- the main steps of quantitative research, presented as a linear succession of stages;
- the importance of measurement in quantitative research, and the ways in which measures are devised for **concepts**;
- procedures for checking the **reliability** and **validity** of those measures;
- the primary goals of quantitative researchers: measurement, establishing **causality** (sometimes referred to as **internal validity**), **generalization**, and **replication**; and
- some criticisms of quantitative research.

Key Learning Outcomes

Here is a list of goals you should try to achieve as you read and think about the material in this chapter. After completing this chapter, you should be able to:

1. Identify the main steps taken in quantitative research.
2. Explain the importance of concepts and their measurement.
3. Describe what is meant by reliability and measurement validity, and explain why researchers go to considerable lengths to achieve them.
4. Discuss the key goals of quantitative research.
5. Outline some shortcomings of quantitative research.

▲ Anna Kraynova/Shutterstock

For his class project, Mario wants to ask some fellow students questions about a topic that's always fascinated him: drug and alcohol use, and how it might affect a person's self-image. But how will he get the information he needs? He quickly jots down a few notes, but soon realizes that coming up with effective questions is more difficult than he imagined. His first question reads: "Do you take drugs?"; but he quickly realizes that "drugs" is too vague, since for some people that would include things like Aspirin and cough medicine. And what about alcohol? Isn't alcohol a kind of drug too? Now he begins to think about other potential problems. What if some people refuse to say what their level of drug and alcohol consumption is? Would some people be offended by the question? And when they do answer, how will he know if they're telling the truth? Is there a second method he could use, such as observing people in a local pub, to see if their behaviour is consistent with the survey data? And once he's asked the basic questions about consumption, how will he approach the self-image part of his research? What exactly should he be asking about? Should the information be recorded in numeric form? If so, how do you do that? When he has finished analyzing the data, will he be able to say that his findings apply to some larger population, such as all university students? In this chapter we will explore how researchers deal with the kinds of issues that Mario is facing.

Introduction

In Chapter 1, quantitative research was outlined as a distinctive research strategy involving particular **epistemological** and **ontological** assumptions. It should be clear by now that much more than the presence of numbers distinguishes a quantitative from a qualitative research orientation. In very broad terms, quantitative research entails the collection of numerical data, a **deductive** relationship between theory and research, a preference for the natural science approach to inquiry (**positivism** in particular), and an **objectivist** conception of social reality. This chapter spells out the main steps in quantitative research, and outlines how some of its main concerns, such as **measurement validity**, are addressed.

The main steps in quantitative research

Figure 4.1 outlines the main steps in quantitative research. The steps and the order in which they appear are very much an ideal account of the process: research is rarely as linear or straightforward as the figure implies. However, it represents a useful starting point for coming to grips with the main facets of quantitative methods.

The fact that the model starts off with a theory signifies a broadly deductive approach to the relationship between theory and research. That a hypothesis

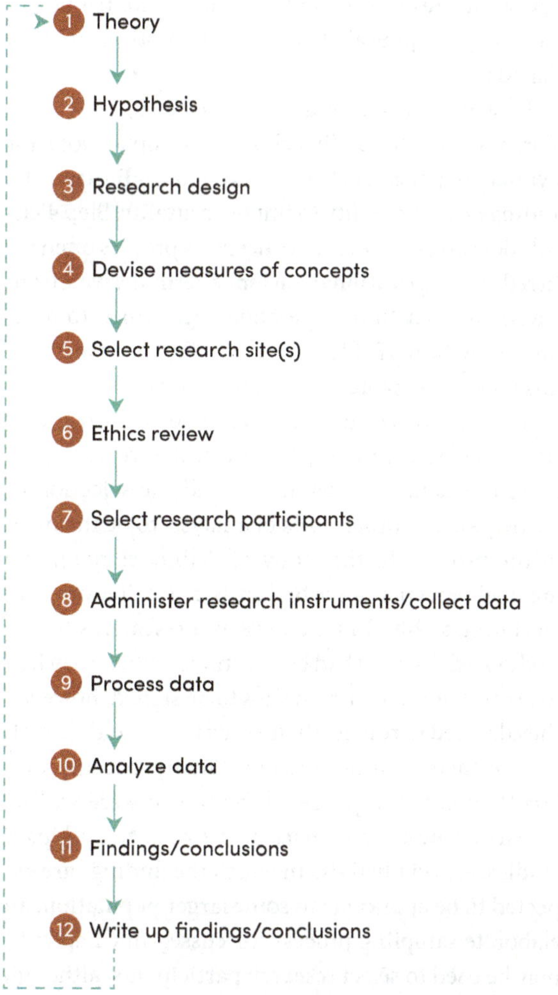

FIGURE 4.1 The process of quantitative research

is derived from the theory and then tested is also indicative of the deductive method. This approach was used by Logie, Lys, Okumu, & Fujioka (2019) in a study of sexually transmitted infection (STI) prevention strategies adopted by Indigenous and non-Indigenous youth in the Northwest Territories. The research showed that depression, resilience, and food insecurity were related to STI prevention practices. The authors first presented a theoretical framework and then several hypotheses that followed from it, which were tested using survey data. However, a great deal of quantitative research does not specify a hypothesis beforehand; instead, there may simply be a loosely defined set of concerns in relation to which the social researcher collects data. This was the case for Gazso-Windlej and McMullin's (2003) study of how time, resources, and patriarchy contribute to the unequal spousal sharing of domestic labour in Canada.

In step 3 a research design is selected, a topic explored in Chapter 2. This choice has implications for a variety of issues, such as the **external validity** of the findings and the ability to impute causality. Step 4 entails devising measures of concepts, a process often referred to as **operationalization**, a term derived from physics to refer to the operations performed to measure something (Bridgman, 1927). Further aspects of this issue are explored later in this chapter.

The next three steps involve choosing a research site or sites, arranging for an ethics review (discussed in detail in Chapter 3), and the selection of participants or other units of analysis to be included in the project. In the study of delinquency among male adolescents described in Box 1.2, Teevan and Dryburgh's (2000) first choice as a research site was a school where they had connections. When they had to arrange for permission slips to be signed, however, they decided to restrict their study to boys old enough to give their own permission. Finally, because of a less-than-eager response, all boys who were willing to participate became part of the project. In bigger studies, especially those in which the findings are expected to be applicable to some larger population, an elaborate sampling process (discussed in Chapter 7) may be used to select research participants, although this approach is rare in experimental research.

Step 8 is the administration of the research instruments. In **experimental** research, this usually means pre-testing participants, manipulating the **independent variable** for the experimental group only, and post-testing. In cross-sectional research using survey research instruments, it involves interviewing the members of the **sample** with a structured **interview schedule** (a list of questions or statements to which the person being interviewed responds) or distributing a self-completion **questionnaire**. In research using **structured observation**, this step involves watching the setting of interest and the people in it, and then recording the types of behaviours observed.

Step 9 simply refers to the fact that the information collected must be systematically recorded so that it can be analyzed. With some information this can be done in a relatively straightforward way. For example, for information relating to matters such as people's ages, incomes, and the number of years they spent at school, the information does not have to be transformed: the scores can simply be recorded in a computer file. For other **variables**, processing the data entails **coding** the information—that is, transforming it into numbers to facilitate quantitative data analysis. This consideration leads into step 10: analysis of the data. In this step, the researcher chooses among various statistical techniques to test for relationships between variables, tries to determine whether the measures are reliable, and so on.

Next, in step 11, the researcher must interpret the results of the analysis; it is at this stage that the "findings" emerge. Here the researcher must consider the reasons why the research was done in the first place, in particular how the results may be used to answer the research question(s). If a hypothesis was presented prior to the collection of data, was it supported? What are the implications of the findings for the theoretical ideas that were the background to the research? Do the findings support the theory? If not, should the theory be revised? Should it be abandoned entirely?

Then the research must be written up in step 12. Until it enters the public domain in some way, as a paper to be presented at a conference, a report to the agency that funded the research, or as a book or journal article to be read by other researchers or students, it cannot have an impact beyond satisfying the researcher's personal curiosity. In writing up their findings and conclusions, researchers must do more than simply relay their results to others: they must convince readers that the research conclusions are important and the findings robust. A significant part of doing research is convincing others of the relevance and validity of one's findings.

Once the findings have been published, they become part of the stock of knowledge in their domain. Thus, there is a feedback loop from step 12 back to step 1. The presence of both an element of deduction (steps 1 and 2) and **induction** (the feedback loop) is indicative of the **positivist** foundations of quantitative research. The emphasis on the translation of concepts into measures (step 4) is also a feature of positivism, and it is to that important phase of the research that we now turn. As we will see, certain considerations follow from the need for measurement in quantitative research—in particular, finding valid and reliable ways to measure concepts.

Concepts and their measurement

What is a concept?

Concepts are ideas or mental representations of things. They are the building blocks of theory and represent the points around which social research is conducted. Just think of the numerous concepts that have already been mentioned so far in this book:

> emotional labour, secularization, hyperactivity, academic achievement, teacher expectations, crime, research ethics, gatekeepers, drug and alcohol use, and self-image

Each represents a label given to elements of the social world that seem to be significant and to have common features. As Bulmer (1984) succinctly puts it, concepts "are categories for the organization of ideas and observations" (p. 43). One item mentioned in Chapter 2, but missing from the list above is IQ. It has been omitted because it is not, strictly speaking, a concept. It is a *measure* of the concept of intelligence. This is a rare case for social science, a measure so well known that the measure and the concept are almost synonymous.

A concept can be either an independent or a **dependent variable**. In other words, a concept can be presented as a possible cause of a certain aspect of the social world (independent), or it can represent something needing an explanation (dependent). Often the same concept will be an independent variable in one context and a dependent variable in another. The concept "social mobility," for example, can be used in either capacity: as a possible explanation of certain attitudes (are there differences between the downwardly mobile and others in their political attitudes?) or as something to be explained (why are some people upwardly mobile and others not?). Equally, concepts may be used for descriptive or comparative purposes. For instance, a researcher might be interested in changes in the amount of social mobility in Canada over time, or in variations among nations in their levels of social mobility.

Why measure?

There are three main reasons for the attention given to measurement in quantitative research:

- Measurement can allow for the delineation of *fine differences* between people in terms of the characteristic in question. This is very useful since, although it is often easy to distinguish between people in terms of extreme categories, finer distinctions are much more difficult to recognize. Clear variations in levels of job satisfaction—people who love their jobs and people who hate their jobs—are easy to see, but small differences are much more difficult to detect.
- Measurement can provide a *consistent device* or yardstick for gauging such distinctions. This consistency relates both to the time at which the measure is administered and to the people who are administering it. A measure's dependability should not be affected by either of those things. With regard to time, this rule means that the measure should generate consistent results *unless* the phenomenon or characteristic being measured has changed. For example, measures of worker morale administered at different times should indicate the same level of morale unless the morale itself has changed. Similarly, the data

produced by the measure should be the same regardless of who did the measuring. Whether a measure actually possesses this consistency pertains to the issue of *reliability*, which will be examined later in this chapter.
- Measurement provides the basis for *estimates of the nature and strength of the relationship between variables* (for example, through **correlation** analysis, which will be examined in Chapter 8).

Indicators

Concepts used in quantitative research are given two types of definition. One is a *nominal* definition, which describes in words what the concept means, much as a dictionary definition does. For example, a nominal definition of "crime" might be: "any violation of the *Criminal Code of Canada*." By contrast, a concept's **operational definition** (from the idea of operationalization, discussed above) spells out the operations the researcher will perform to measure the concept. For example, one way to measure the incidence of crime is to use statistics provided by police forces; another is to ask a sample of people whether they have been victims of certain crimes.

To measure a concept it is necessary to have an indicator or indicators that stand for or represent the concept. Sometimes the term **indicator** simply refers to a measure in the ordinary sense: for example, the total income reported on a tax return is an indicator of a person's wealth. However, sometimes it refers to an indirect measure of a concept that cannot be tapped easily or directly. For example, absenteeism may be used as an indirect measure of employee morale. Income declared for tax purposes may be a direct measure of personal income, but if used as an indicator of social class, it becomes an indirect measure.

There are a number of ways to devise indicators; for example:

- through questions that are part of a structured interview schedule or self-completion questionnaire. The questions can be concerned with the respondents' attitudes (e.g., toward a social issue like immigration), their personal experiences (e.g., stress), their behaviours (e.g., leisure pursuits), and so on;
- by developing criteria for classifying observed behaviour (e.g., pupil behaviour in a classroom);
- through the use of official statistics (e.g., those from Statistics Canada); and
- by developing classification schemes to analyze the content of written material (e.g., Sobel's [2015] assessment of Canadian citizenship guides issued between 1947 and 2012 as indicators of how the federal government defined what it means to be a Canadian and how naturalized citizens were expected to behave).

Indicators can be derived from a wide variety of sources and methods. Very often a researcher has to consider whether one indicator of a concept suffices. Instead of relying on a single indicator, the researcher may use several to tap a concept. One way to do that is to combine a number of **Likert items** (see Box 4.1).

Using multiple-item measures in survey research

The main advantage in using a **multiple-indicator measure** of a concept is that there are potential problems in relying on just a single indicator:

- A single indicator may misclassify some individuals if the wording of the question leads to a misunderstanding of its meaning. If there are several indicators, however, it is possible that the other items will allow proper classification of the person.
- A single broad, general indicator may not capture all the meaning in the underlying concept. If you were to ask people how satisfied they are with their work, for instance, you might miss the complexity of the situation. People who answer "not satisfied" may like some parts of their work, just as those who claim to be "satisfied" may dislike specific aspects of their work.
- Alternatively, a more specific question may cover only one **dimension** of a particular concept. For example, to measure job satisfaction, is it sufficient to ask people how satisfied they are with their pay? Almost certainly the answer is "no," because for most people there is more to job satisfaction than just satisfaction with pay. In this case, a single indicator will miss things like satisfaction with benefits, with the work itself, and with other

aspects of the work environment. By asking a number of questions, the researcher can get access to a wider range of issues covered by the concept.

- Multiple indicators of a concept allow for sophisticated data analyses, such as **factor analysis** and *cluster analysis*. Factor analysis provides an indication of the extent to which (a) multiple measures really are measuring a single concept as opposed to more than one concept; and (b) individual items are measuring the concept in question. Bell, Aitken Schermer, & Vernon (2009), for example, used factor analysis to develop measures of political attitudes. Cluster analysis allows researchers to determine whether people or other units of study can be grouped together on the basis of shared characteristics. Kennedy, Krogman, & Krahn (2013), for instance, identified four clusters of Edmonton residents based on the sustainable consumption behaviours in which they engaged (see Box 4.1).

Box 4.1 | Likert items

The investigation of attitudes is a prominent area in survey research. One of the most common techniques for investigating attitudes is the Likert **scale**. Named after Rensis Likert, who developed the method, it is typically a multiple-indicator measure of the intensity of feelings about a particular topic. In its most common format, it comprises a series of statements (known as "items") on an issue or theme. Usually, each respondent is asked to indicate his or her level of agreement with the statement. The format for indicating level of agreement is normally a five-point scale from "strongly agree" to "strongly disagree," but seven-point and other formats are used as well. There is usually a middle position of "neither agree nor disagree" or "undecided" indicating neutrality on the issue. A respondent's reply on each item is scored and then the scores are aggregated to form an overall score.

Variations on the typical format of agreement are scales referring to evaluation (for example, "very poor" to "very good") and frequency. Kennedy et al. (2013) used the latter in a study of sustainable consumption that was conducted in Edmonton. Respondents were presented with several items such as "Leave vehicle at home to avoid driving," "Buy local food," and "Actively encourage others to reduce their consumption," 12 of which were selected for analysis. Participants in the study chose either "Never," "Rarely," "Sometimes," "Often," or "Always" as their response.

There are several points to remember in combining Likert items. The following are particularly important:

- The items must be statements, not questions.
- The items must all relate to the same topic (in the example above, sustainable consumption).
- The items that make up the scale should be interrelated.
- It is useful to vary the phrasing so that some items imply a positive view of the phenomenon of interest and others a negative one. For example, in the 2007 Alberta Survey conducted by the Population Research Laboratory at the University of Alberta, attitudes toward body checking in minor hockey were measured using five-point Likert items. One item read: "Body checking is the main cause of injuries for children in organized minor hockey." A second was: "Body checking is an essential part of the game of organized minor hockey." The first implies a negative view of body checking, the second a more positive one. Under these conditions, it would be logically inconsistent to answer every question the same way, so if someone has done that it indicates that **response set** may be a problem. A respondent who either agreed or disagreed with all the items could not be answering truthfully, and might have to be excluded from the study.

- Multiple indicators can help to weed out **response sets** (see Chapter 5), which can occur if, for a variety of reasons, a person's response does not reflect his or her real position on the matter examined. For example, someone may "agree" with an item or set of items just to appear cooperative or friendly. Multiple indicators can be used to test for this. For instance, if on a particular item someone agrees that unemployment is the most important problem facing Canadians today, but later also agrees that Canada has bigger problems than unemployment, that's an indication of response set. In such situations the researcher may chose to exclude the person's responses from the data set.

Dimensions of concepts

As was suggested earlier, the concept of interest may have multiple facets or dimensions, which are often revealed in the theories and research associated with it. In developing a measure for a concept, its different aspects or components should be considered. Bryman and Cramer (2001) demonstrated this approach with reference to the concept of "professionalism." The idea is that people scoring high on one dimension of the concept (e.g., respecting confidentiality) may not necessarily score high on other dimensions (e.g., fiscal honesty or continuing education), so that for each respondent one can have a multidimensional "profile."

However, in much quantitative research, there is a tendency to rely on a single indicator for each concept. This is quite adequate for some purposes, in particular when one is measuring an uncomplicated variable such as age. Some studies, like Hay's (2014) research on secularization in Canada (see Box 4.2), employ both single- and multiple-indicator measures of concepts. What is crucial is that the measures be reliable and valid representations of the concepts they are supposed to be gauging.

Coding unstructured data

Many forms of social science data are essentially unstructured and unorganized, including answers to open questions in interviews and questionnaires, and the content of newspaper articles. To make sense of the information, researchers must go through it all, deriving themes or categories of behaviour to

Box 4.2 | A multiple-indicator measure of another concept

In Hay's (2014) study of secularization (see Box 1.3), religious pluralism was measured using a single, five-point Likert item that formed part of an extensive survey of Canadians' value systems. However, secularization (the dependent variable in Hay's analysis) was measured with several different indicators in order to tap into different dimensions of the concept. One dimension, religiosity, was measured by averaging the responses to three 10-point items indicating the importance respondents placed on: (a) "believing in God;" (b) "obeying God, doing what he wishes;" and (c) "relating to God in a personal way." A second dimension, relating to frequency of religious attendance, was measured with the question, "Do you currently attend church temple or mosque?" Respondents who answered "yes" were then asked: "How often?" The response choices were: "once a week or more" (given a code of 5 after reverse-coding), "monthly" (4), "every few months" (3), "once or twice a year" (2), and "never" (1). A third dimension, concerned with the participants' belief in the religion of their parents, had the response categories "believe all of it" (4), "believe most of it but not all" (3), "believe some parts but disbelieve others" (2), and "don't believe any of it" (1).

form the basis for **codes** (the labels or titles given to the themes or categories): for example, "hostile to outsiders," or "not hostile to outsiders." Next, the researcher usually assigns numbers to the codes. This may be a largely arbitrary process in the sense that the numbers are simply tags to allow the material to be stored quantitatively. Then it is necessary to go through the information again to look for incidences of the theme or category, and to record the appropriate numbers on a computer spreadsheet. This approach is sometimes called *post-coding*. Post-coding can be an unreliable procedure because there may be inconsistencies in the judgments of different coders, which leads to both measurement error and lack of validity. Box 4.3 provides an example of this kind of coding.

When Schuman and Presser (1981; see Box 5.1) asked an open question about the features of a job that people like, the answers were to be grouped into 11 codes: pay; feeling of accomplishment; control of work; pleasant work; security; opportunity for promotion; short hours; working conditions; benefits; satisfaction; other responses. Each of these 11 categories was assigned a number: 1 for pay; 2 for feeling of accomplishment; 3 for control of work; 4 for pleasant work, and so on.

Murphy and Fedoroff (2013) used a combination of fixed-response and open-ended questions to explore how 30 registered sex offenders viewed their experiences with either the Ontario or the National Sex Offender Registry. People on these registries have to report annually to their local police and receive a yearly visit from the police at their residence, but unlike in the United States, the registries themselves are not available for public viewing. The responses to the open-ended questions were analyzed to discern whether there was consensus or disagreement among participants and to identify recurrent themes. About two-thirds of the offenders who commented on the matter stated that being on a sex offender registry was not a great burden or even an intrusive experience, and about half said that having to register was "fair," given the crimes they had committed. However, some offenders objected to the manner in which the police conducted their annual visits.

When coding, you should observe three basic principles (Bryman & Cramer, 2001):

- The categories must not overlap. If they do, the numbers assigned to them will not denote distinct behaviours or types of responses.
- The list of categories must be exhaustive, covering all possibilities. If it does not, some material cannot be coded. That is why many classification schemes, such as those used to code open questions, include the category "other."

Box 4.3 | Coding an open question

Foddy (1993) asked a small sample of his students to state their fathers' occupations; then he requested three details: nature of business, size of business, and whether their father was the owner or an employee. The replies to the "size of business" question were particularly varied, including "big," "small," "very large," "3000 acres," "family," "multinational," "200 people," and "Philips." The problem here is obvious: these categories do not provide a useful measure of size. The problem has only partly to do with the difficulty of coding an open question; it is also due to a lack of specificity in the question. If Foddy had asked, "How many employees are (were) there in your father's place of employment?" a more meaningful set of answers would have been forthcoming. Whether his students would have known this information is, of course, yet another issue. However, his experience illustrates some potential problems with asking an open question, particularly one that lacks a clear reference point.

- There should be clear rules about how codes are to be applied, with examples of the kinds of answers that may be subsumed under a particular category. Such rules are meant to promote a coder's consistency over time in how the material is assigned to categories and, if more than one person is coding, that the various coders are consistent with each other.

Coding is also used in qualitative research, but its role and significance there are somewhat different (see Chapter 13).

Reliability and measurement validity

Reliability

Reliability is concerned with the *consistency* of measures. The term has at least three different meanings.

Stability over time

"Stability" refers to whether the results of a measure fluctuate as time progresses, assuming that what is being measured is not changing. This means that if one administers a measure to a group and then re-administers it perhaps an hour later, there should be little variation in the results. Most thermometers have this kind of reliability.

The most obvious way of testing for the stability of a measure is the *test–retest* method. This involves administering a test or measure on one occasion and then re-administering it to the same sample on another occasion, that is:

$$\begin{array}{cc} T_1 & T_2 \\ Obs_1 & Obs_2 \end{array}$$

One would expect to find a high correlation between Obs_1 and Obs_2. For example, those who score high on the first observation should also score high on the second, and those who score low on the first should score low on the second. Imagine a multiple-indicator measure that is supposed to tap a concept called "designerism" (a preference for buying goods and especially clothing with "designer" labels). The measure would be administered to a sample of respondents and then later re-administered. If the correlation between Obs_1 and Obs_2 is low, the measure is unstable, implying that it cannot be relied upon.

However, there are a number of problems with this approach to evaluating reliability. Respondents' answers at T_1 may influence how they reply at T_2: for instance, perhaps answering a question on designer goods increases some respondents' interest in them. Yet giving an answer at T1 is not supposed to affect later measurements. Second, events may intervene between T_1 and T_2 that influence the degree of consistency. For example, if a long span of time is involved, changes in the economy or in respondents' personal financial circumstances can influence their views about designer goods and their predilection for them.

There are no clear solutions to these problems, other than introducing a complex research design and so turning the investigation of reliability into a major project in its own right. Perhaps for these reasons, many, if not most, research projects do not include tests of stability over time.

When such tests are done, they may indicate that there is no problem, even when a substantial amount of time has elapsed. Berthoud (2000), for example, was pleased that an index of illness achieved high test–retest reliability even though the tests were conducted a year apart.

Internal reliability (or internal consistency)

The key issue here is whether multiple measures that are administered in one sitting are consistent—in other words, whether respondents' scores on any one indicator tend to be related to their scores on the other indicators. For example, on a scale created to measure attitudes toward liberal democracy, people who agree with the statement that voting is an important right should also agree that freedom of speech is an important right. Cronbach's alpha coefficient is a commonly used test of internal reliability. Its value varies from 1 (denoting perfect internal reliability) to 0 (denoting none). The value .80 is typically employed to mark the minimum acceptable level of internal reliability, though many writers work with a lower value. Berthoud (2000, p. 169), for instance, wrote that a minimum level of .60 is "good." In the case of George and Chaze's (2014) battery of items to measure discrimination against foreign trained engineers in Canada, alpha was .92 for both the international and locally trained subsamples. In a study of environmental values among Chinese- and Anglo-Canadians by Deng, Walker, & Swinnerton (2006), the alphas ranged from .50 to .89 for various variables. The study of domestic labour by Gazso-Windlej and McMullin (2003) could only achieve alphas averaging .50 for its Likert-style items measuring gender ideology, although the study was only exploratory. The use of Cronbach's alpha has grown as a result of its incorporation into computer software for quantitative data analysis.

Another way of testing for internal reliability is the split-half method. Take the Likert items used by Kennedy et al. (2013) in their study of sustainable consumption (see Box 4.1). The 12 indicators would be divided into two halves of 6, allocated on a random or an odd-numbered item/even-numbered item basis. The degree of correlation between the scores on the two halves for all respondents would then be calculated. If the 12 items are consistent, a respondent's score on the two groups of indicators should be similar, perhaps high on both, or low on both. A perfect positive correlation and therefore complete internal consistency would yield a correlation coefficient of 1; no correlation and therefore no internal consistency would produce a coefficient of 0. The meaning of correlation and correlation coefficients will be explored in much greater detail later on. The chief point at this stage is that the correlation coefficient establishes how closely respondents' scores on the two groups of indicators are related.

Inter-observer consistency

When more than one researcher is taking part in an activity involving subjective judgment, such as the recording of observations or the translation of data into categories, their judgments may differ. This problem can arise in a number of contexts: for example, if answers to open-ended questions have to be categorized, or in structured observation when observers have to decide how to classify participants' behaviour. Is the person under observation "afraid," "concerned," or "just thinking" when reading about the spread of COVID-19? Problems arise if all observers do not classify a particular behaviour in the same way. Cramer (1998, ch. 14) provides a very detailed treatment of inter-observer consistency and the techniques that can be used to maximize it.

Measurement validity

As we noted in Chapter 2, measurement validity refers to whether an indicator (or set of indicators) devised to gauge a concept really does so. When people argue about whether an IQ score really measures or reflects someone's level of intelligence, they are raising questions about the measurement validity of the IQ test in relation to the concept of intelligence. Whenever students and their teachers debate whether multiple-choice examinations provide an accurate measure of academic ability, they too are raising questions about measurement validity. Establishing face validity, concurrent validity, construct validity, and convergent validity provides evidence that you have measured what you wanted to measure.

Face validity

At the very minimum, a researcher who develops a new measure should establish that it has face validity—that is, that it appears to reflect the content of the concept in question. Face validity can be established by asking those with expertise in a field to act as judges to determine whether, on the face of it, the measure seems to reflect the concept concerned. Alternatively, researchers can assess their own measures for face validity, as Kennedy et al. (2013) did in their study of sustainable consumption (see Box 4.1). Establishing this sort of validity is essentially an intuitive process.

Concurrent validity

The researcher can also seek to gauge the concurrent validity of the measure by examining a criterion relevant to the concept in question at about the same time as the measure of interest is administered. Assuming that as job satisfaction goes down, absenteeism goes up, a researcher seeking to establish the concurrent validity of a new measure of job satisfaction might look to see if people who, according to the new measure, are satisfied with their jobs are less likely to be absent from work than those who are not satisfied. If there is no difference in absenteeism between those who are satisfied and those who are not, doubt is cast on whether the new measure is really gauging job satisfaction.

Construct validity

Some writers advocate that researchers estimate the construct validity of a measure, which involves seeing whether the concepts used in the research relate to each other in a way that is consistent with what their theories would predict. For example, suppose that a researcher wants to establish the construct validity of the new measure of job satisfaction. Drawing on a theory maintaining that job satisfaction is influenced by the stimulation that comes from performing several different activities, he or she may anticipate that people who do routine jobs are less satisfied with their jobs than those who have greater opportunities for variety, complexity, and creativity. If these variables correlate in the expected way, then the measure in question has construct validity. On the other hand, some caution is required if the relationship is weak or non-existent—for example, if those who do routine jobs are just as satisfied as those with jobs involving a lot of variety. If so, the measures used may be invalid, or the deduction that is made from the theory may be misguided, or the theory itself may be in need of revision. Whatever the problem may be, it's probably best to seek another measure and try again.

Convergent validity

In the view of some methodologists, the validity of a measure ought to be gauged by comparing it to measures of the same concept developed through other methods. For example, if a questionnaire asks managers how much time they spend on various activities (attending meetings, touring their organization, informal discussions, and so on), its validity may be determined by directly observing the managers to see how much time they actually spend on those activities.

An interesting instance of convergent invalidity is described in Box 4.4. Crime surveys were consciously devised to serve as a check on official police

Box 4.4 | A case of convergent invalidity: Crime statistics

Steve Jolicoeur/Shutterstock

Police gathering evidence at a crime scene. The crime will definitely be entered into the official crime statistics. Why will it become part of the official record while other crimes might not?

Official police reports and national crime victimization studies often provide very different indications of the amount of crime in society. As part of the General Social Survey (GSS), Canadians are asked about their victimization experiences. It is widely known that the victimization data show more crime than the official police reports because many Canadians do not report their experiences with crime to the police, for a variety of reasons (inconvenience, embarrassment, etc.). To take one example, for robbery the victimization rate reported in the surveys is almost three times the official rate. But for auto theft, the police data show 50 per cent more thefts, because the GSS does not gather data on the theft of company cars or cars taken from car dealerships (Silverman et al., 2000, p. 58). So there will probably always be a discrepancy between police statistics and victimization surveys on the amount of crime that exists. Another illustration of a lack of concurrence between two methods of data gathering pertains to murder rates. The police report 15 per cent more homicides in Canada than does the Mortality Database drawn from death certificates (Gabor, Hung, Mihorean, & St-Onge, 2002); some officials in charge of the latter may be reluctant to classify certain deaths as homicides because doing so might upset the relatives of the victims.

statistics. The two sets of data are collected in quite different ways: official crime statistics are collected as part of the bureaucratic processing of offenders in the criminal justice system, whereas crime victimization surveys provide data from interviews with members of the general public. In the case reported in Box 4.4, a lack of convergent validity was found. This illustrates a problem with the convergent approach to testing validity: it's not easy to establish which of the two measures provides the more accurate picture. In the case of crime statistics, the two methods are really measuring somewhat different things. Victimization surveys measure the crimes that people experience, as well as some things that may not be crimes; they also omit certain crimes (for example, when a stolen item is presumed to be "lost") and rely on respondent memory, which can be faulty (see Chapter 5). Police statistics, on the other hand, measure the crimes that people are willing to call the police about, plus the crimes the police themselves discover; therefore, not all crimes end up in official police statistics. Figure 4.2 illustrates some of the problems associated with crime rates that are based on police statistics. At any step along Figure 4.2, some potential crimes drop away. For example, if a criminal act goes unnoticed, or is noticed but not recognized as criminal, or is noticed and recognized as criminal but is not reported to the police, it does not enter the official statistics. As you can see, a substantial amount of crime—often referred to as "the dark figure"—is not included in crime statistics (Silverman, Sacco, & Teevan, 2000). The "true" volume of crime at any one time is almost always a contested notion (Reiner, 2000).

Reflections on reliability and validity

There are, then, a number of ways to investigate the merit of measures devised to represent social scientific concepts. However, the discussion of reliability and validity is potentially misleading because not all new measures of concepts are submitted to the rigours just described. In fact, the reliability and validity of many measures are never tested. When a new multiple-indicator measure is devised, there may be an examination of face validity and a test for internal reliability, but in many cases no further testing takes place.

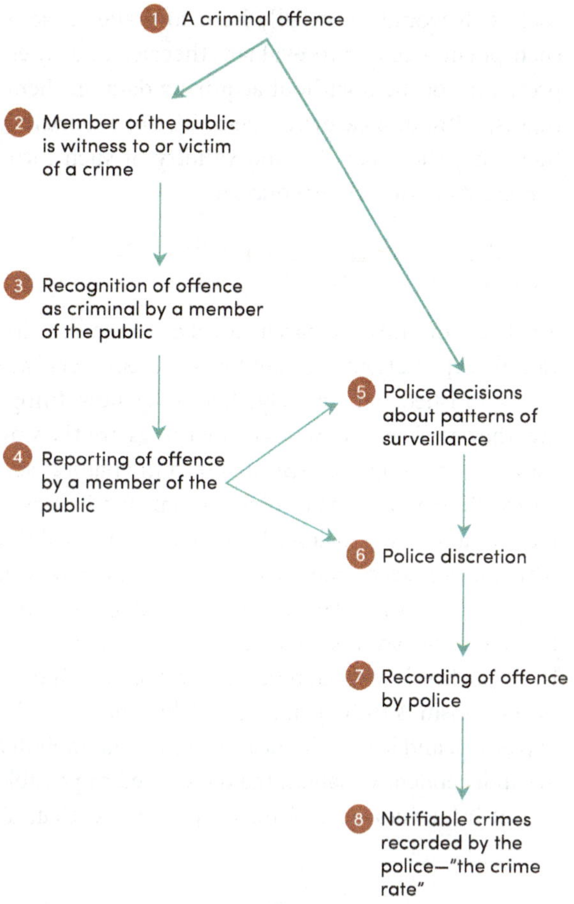

FIGURE 4.2 The social construction of crime statistics: Eight steps

Source: Adapted from a figure in Beardsworth, Bryman, Ford, & Keil (n.d.).

It should also be remembered that, although reliability and validity are analytically distinguishable, they are related: if a measure is not reliable, it cannot be valid. For example, a multiple-indicator measure lacking internal reliability is probably measuring two or more different things and therefore is not a valid indicator of the single concept it is supposed to be measuring.

The main goals of quantitative researchers

Measurement

To understand the social order one must be able to go into the world and measure things like prejudice, the incidence of homelessness, attitudes toward the federal government, or the distribution of wealth in society. It would be awfully hard to make sense of such phenomena or to evaluate theories and interpretations of them without acquiring data on them: that is, without measuring them. It's not surprising, then, that the reliability and validity of such measurement are matters of concern.

Establishment of causality (internal validity)

Most quantitative research involves a search for causal explanations. Quantitative researchers are rarely satisfied with merely describing how things are: they are keen to find out why things are the way they are—an emphasis also found in the natural sciences. Researchers examining racism, for instance, may want not only to describe it but also to explain it, which means searching for its causes. They may seek to explain racism in terms of personal characteristics (such as a low level of education) or social characteristics (such as low social mobility). In the resulting reports, racism is the dependent variable, the one to be explained, and levels of education and social mobility are independent variables, the ones tested as possible causal influences on racism. Keep in mind that, as suggested in Chapter 2, establishing causality in the social sciences is very difficult, and that correlation alone is not sufficient to demonstrate causation.

When an experimental design is employed, the independent variable is the one that is manipulated, and there is little ambiguity about the direction of any causal influence. However, with cross-sectional designs of the kind used in most social survey research, there is often ambiguity about the direction of the purported causal influence because the data on all variables are collected simultaneously: this means that in many instances we cannot say with full confidence that a particular independent variable preceded the dependent one in time, one of the three criteria of nomothetic causation mentioned in Chapter 2. To refer to independent and dependent variables in the context of cross-sectional designs, we must infer the temporal sequence of variables based on common sense or prior theory, as in the example concerning level of education and racism in the previous paragraph. However, there is always the risk that the inference is wrong, that the variable presumed to be the cause did not precede the dependent variable in time (see Box 4.5).

Box 4.5 | The case of displayed emotions in convenience stores

Following a review of the literature, Sutton and Rafaeli (1988) hypothesized a **positive relationship** between the display of positive emotions by staff to retail shoppers (smiling, friendly greeting, eye contact) and the level of retail sales. In other words, when retail staff are friendly and give time to shoppers, higher sales follow. Sutton and Rafaeli had data from 576 convenience stores in a US national retail chain. Structured observation of the retail workers provided data on the display of positive emotions, and quantitative sales data provided information for the other variable.

The hypothesis was not supported; indeed, stores in which retail workers were less inclined to smile, be friendly, and so on, had better sales. Sutton and Rafaeli (1992, p. 124) considered restating their hypothesis to make it seem that they had found what they had expected (which would have raised ethical concerns) but fortunately resisted the temptation. Instead, they conducted a qualitative investigation of four stores in order to understand what was happening. They used several methods: unstructured observation of interactions between staff and customers; semi-structured interviews with store managers; casual conversations with store managers, supervisors, executives, and others; and data gathered through posing as a customer. The qualitative investigation suggested that the relationship between the display of positive emotions and sales was indeed negative, but that sales were likely to be a cause rather than a consequence of the display of emotions. In stores with high levels of sales, staff were under greater pressure and encountered longer lineups at checkouts. Therefore, they had less time and inclination for the pleasantries associated with the display of positive emotions.

Thus, the causal sequence was not

More displayed positive emotions → More retail sales

but

More retail sales → Fewer displayed positive emotions

This study illustrates the difficulty associated with inferring causal direction when using a cross-sectional research design.

Good quantitative research inspires confidence in the researcher's causal inferences. Research of the more experimental type is often better able to establish causality than cross-sectional research because with the former it is easier to demonstrate the direction of causal influence and to control for other independent variables. However, as we saw in Chapter 2, experiments are not appropriate for many of the topics of interest to social scientists. Instead, quantitative researchers who employ cross-sectional designs often use techniques that allow them to make at least tentative causal inferences, such as statistical controls (see Chapter 8). The rise of **longitudinal research** almost certainly reflects a desire on the part of quantitative researchers to improve their ability to generate findings that permit a causal interpretation.

Generalization of findings

In quantitative research, researchers usually want to generalize their findings beyond the people who participate in the study and the particular context in which the research is conducted. These concerns pertain to external validity, an issue introduced in Chapter 2.

A particularly important matter in this regard is whether a study's findings are applicable in settings outside the research environment—in particular, everyday or natural social settings. Sometimes the research setting is so artificial or so different from real life that we may question whether the results actually tell us anything about the sorts of things that people normally experience. The more the social scientist intervenes in natural settings or creates unnatural ones, such as a laboratory (or even just a special room for interviews), the greater the chance that the findings will be externally invalid. Measurement validity and plausible evidence of causation cannot guarantee this form of external validity.

A second concern with external validity is whether the results of a study can be generalized beyond the people or cases analyzed by the researcher. The researchers conducting the study in Box 1.2 asked 57 adolescent male volunteers about their delinquency and examined whether any of the currently popular sociological theories of delinquency could explain their behaviour. How far can the findings of this study be generalized? To other male adolescents who attended the same school? To all Canadian male adolescents? If the findings are fully externally valid, they can be applied to any population of interest. If they possess no external validity, the findings apply only to the 57 boys studied and to no one else. Usually, external validity falls somewhere between these extremes, and it is in this context that how people are selected to participate in research becomes crucial. If a **representative sample** of people is selected (see Chapter 7), the researcher can be confident that the results of the study may be applied to the population from which the sample was drawn. The goal of arriving at generalizable findings in this way can be seen as a parallel to the goal of developing scientific "laws" in the natural sciences.

Probability sampling, explored in Chapter 7, is normally the first choice among researchers seeking a representative sample. This procedure largely eliminates bias by using a random selection process. Random selection does not guarantee a representative sample, but it does improve the chances of getting one. Here it is important to emphasize that even a perfectly representative sample would be representative only of the population from which it was selected: strictly speaking, therefore, results obtained from that sample cannot be generalized beyond that population. This means that, if the population from which a sample is taken is all inhabitants of a particular town, city, or province, generalizations should be made only to the inhabitants of that town, city, or province. It may be very tempting to see the findings as having a wider applicability, so that results from a sample representing a city such as Vancouver or Toronto could be considered relevant to similar cities. Even so, no inferences should be made beyond the population from which the sample is selected.

The concern with the generalizability of research findings is particularly strong among quantitative researchers using cross-sectional and longitudinal designs. Experimental researchers are concerned about generalizability too, as the discussion of external validity in Chapter 2 suggested, but people doing experiments usually give greater attention to establishing causation than to external validity.

Replication

The natural sciences are often depicted as seeking to reduce to a bare minimum the contaminating influence of the scientist's biases, values, characteristics, and expectations. Were those influences allowed to affect research, the claims of the natural sciences to provide a definitive picture of the world would be seriously undermined. Scientists also try to minimize if not eliminate routine errors in the conduct of their research. To guard against such problems, scientists believe that they should be able to replicate one another's research. If a certain finding cannot be reproduced after repeated tries, serious questions are raised about its validity. Likewise, researchers in the social sciences often regard the ability to replicate as an important criterion for judging research. It's easy to see why: the risk that the researcher's values will affect his or her findings would appear to be all the greater in the case of the social world, and routine errors are always possible. Consequently, researchers usually take care to spell out all research procedures so that others can replicate them.

Methods in Motion | Applications to Canadian Society

How the "field" may influence men's bodies, their self-acceptance, and their views on cosmetic surgery

Ricciardelli and Clow (2009) examined two rarely studied topics: men's attitudes toward their physical appearance and their views on whether it is appropriate for men to have cosmetic surgery. The purpose of the study was to determine whether men's self-confidence, self-deprecation (feelings of low self-esteem), and levels of comfort regarding their bodies affected their assessment of their physical appearance and their acceptance of cosmetic surgery. The people participating in the research were 103 Canadian men who lived in the greater Toronto area. Although the sample was small in size and not selected at random (which meant that the results could not be generalized to any larger population; see Chapter 7), the findings were informative nonetheless.

One of the strengths of the study was that it combined quantitative and qualitative methods. For the former, the authors used 18 Likert items (see Box 4.1 for examples of these sorts of measures) administered online. The items were used to gauge the men's perceptions of their physical appearance, their satisfaction with their bodies, how others judged their bodies, and their views on cosmetic surgery. The items were analyzed using multiple regression (a topic discussed in Chapter 8). The qualitative element of the study was a single, open-ended question that asked the men to "please describe your feelings towards cosmetic surgery." The answers were analyzed with the intention of identifying common themes.

The quantitative findings indicated that the men expressing high self-confidence were less likely to believe that their physical appearance made other people think they were lazy, and that men with higher levels of self-deprecation were more likely to believe that their appearance decreased their self-confidence. The results also showed that the men with high scores on the self-deprecation measure were more likely to dislike and be embarrassed by their bodies, while lower self-confidence was associated with a higher willingness to have cosmetic surgery. In the open-ended responses, those who were in favour of cosmetic surgery often used the third person to describe their feelings: for example, "if surgery could boost their esteem they should do it" (Ricciardelli & Clow, 2009, p. 123). The authors speculated that such men were distancing themselves from the notion of cosmetic surgery because the culture around them deemed such body modifications to be appropriate for women but not for men. By using the third person, the authors suggest, the men were seeking to protect their male gender identity.

Following Bourdieu (1987), the authors saw their results as illustrating the impact of the "field"—the totality of the individual's social networks as well as the society at large—on self-evaluation, in this case on judgments about the acceptability of one's body and physical appearance. They also suggest that their study shows social and self acceptability to be closely associated with the body, and the field as influencing the value and meaning given to certain physical attributes. They also conclude that it is a mistake to think that only women are highly conscious of their bodies and feel judged on the basis of their physical characteristics; men too face negative consequences if they have the "wrong" kind of physical features.

Unfortunately, replication tends to be considered pedestrian and uninspiring, although that is beginning to change, at least in disciplines such as psychology (Ritchie, 2020). Until recently, it has not been considered a high-status activity in either the natural or social sciences, and standard replications are the exception rather than the rule in most academic journals. A further reason for the low incidence of published replications in the social sciences is the difficulty of ensuring that the conditions are precisely the same as those in the original study. If there is room for doubt on that score, any differences in findings may be attributed to the design of the replication rather than to a deficiency in the original study. Nonetheless, it is crucial that the methods used to generate findings are made explicit, so that replication is at least possible. Providing all the information needed to conduct a replication is often regarded as an important quality of quantitative research.

An example of the benefits of replication can be found in Goyder, Guppy, & Thompson's (2003) study of occupational prestige conducted in the Kitchener–Waterloo area of Ontario. The authors replicated research done 25 years earlier (Guppy & Siltanen, 1977), taking great pains to ensure that the methodologies of the two studies were as similar as possible. The replication not only provided a check for biases and routine errors; given that a quarter-century had passed since the original study, it also provided a measure of how much attitudes had changed with regard to occupational prestige and gender. As reported in Chapter 2, the authors concluded that the earlier male advantage in occupational prestige had disappeared by the time the replication was done; in fact, women in people-oriented jobs enjoyed higher prestige than men did in the more recent study. If the authors had not taken care to ensure accurate replication of the original study, it would have been impossible to know whether the differences in the findings represented actual social change or were simply a by-product of using different methodologies.

Critiques of quantitative research

Every approach to research has its strengths and weaknesses. Over the years quantitative research, along with its epistemological and ontological foundations, has been the focus of criticism, particularly from exponents of qualitative research. The criticisms pertain to quantitative research as a general research strategy, and to specific methods and research designs with which quantitative research is associated.

Six criticisms of quantitative research

To give a flavour of the critique of quantitative research, six criticisms are covered briefly here:

- Quantitative researchers fail to distinguish people and social institutions from "the world of nature." Some critics object to the idea of treating the social world as if it were no different from the natural order. They argue that because people interpret the world around them, their actions and experiences cannot be studied using the methods employed in the natural sciences. They claim that science is applicable only to entities and processes lacking this sort of self-reflection, such as chemical elements, photosynthesis, and the circulation of blood. But many quantitative researchers maintain that humans (and other animals) really are part of the world of nature, and that it is simply wrong to think that our existence cannot be usefully analyzed using science. For instance, they would claim that consciousness itself is amenable to the scientific method, as are emotions, decision-making processes, and so on. Similarly, they hold that quantitative research is indispensable in understanding social problems. For example, to understand poverty it is important to know about things like mean and median incomes, as well as how to analyze various social categories that may be statistically associated with poverty, such as gender, sexual identity, ethnicity, and so on. The debate continues.
- The measurement process produces an artificial and false sense of precision and accuracy. For example, quantitative research presumes that different individuals responding to the same question on a survey are interpreting its key terms in the same way. Yet a question such as "What is your social class?" can be interpreted in at least two ways: as a reference to current wealth, or as a reference to ancestry going back generations. Many methodologists find significant variations in respondents' interpretations of such terms. Researchers often attempt to solve this problem by using questions with fixed-choice answers—"Are you upper class, middle class, working class?" and so on—but this approach provides "a solution to the problem of meaning by simply ignoring it" (Cicourel, 1964, p. 108). Quantitative social researchers counter that there are ways to test for shared meanings, although they would concede that this issue deserves more attention than it usually gets.
- The reliance on instruments and procedures produces a disjuncture between research and everyday life. This issue relates to the question of external validity. For example, many methods of quantitative research rely heavily on research instruments such as structured interviews and self-completion questionnaires. As Cicourel (1982) pointed out, researchers tend to assume that survey respondents have both the knowledge they need to answer the questions and a sense that the topic matters in their everyday lives. Can researchers who pose a set of questions designed to measure attitudes toward federal–provincial relations, for example, be sure that respondents have sufficient knowledge and interest in the topic to produce meaningful responses? Quantitative researchers would respond that the judicious use of filter questions (see Chapter 5) can address this problem. Similarly, there may be an important difference between what people say to researchers and what they actually do in real life (see Box 4.6). Another criticism, introduced in Chapter 2, is directed at experimental research that relies on controlling situations

Box 4.6 | Gap between stated and actual behaviour

A study of racial prejudice conducted many years ago by LaPiere (1934) illustrates that there may be a difference between what people say and what they actually do. LaPiere spent two years travelling with a young Chinese student and his wife, observing from a distance to see if they were refused entry at hotels and restaurants. Of 66 hotels approached, only one turned the couple away; of 184 restaurants and diners, none refused entry.

LaPiere then allowed six months to elapse before sending questionnaires to the hotels and restaurants visited. One question asked: "Will you accept members of the Chinese race as guests in your establishment?" Of the establishments that replied, 92 per cent of restaurants and 91 per cent of hotels said no. LaPiere's simple though striking study clearly illustrated a gap between reports of behaviour and actual behaviour. The fact that the question asked was somewhat unclear is not usually noted in connection with this widely cited study. "Will you ...?" can be interpreted in two ways: as a question about the future or as a question about current policy. Why the more obvious formulation "Do you ...?" was not used is not clear, though it is unlikely that this point had a significant bearing on the findings and their implications for survey research. On the other hand, the results might have been just another example of the widespread difference between holding a prejudiced attitude and engaging in a discriminatory act. An experimental study of prejudice among college students (Frazer & Wiersma, 2001) showed that in hypothetical situations, students would hire Black and White applicants of varying abilities equally, but a week later recalled the Black applicants as less intelligent than the Whites even though the two groups were presented as having the same qualifications and offered identical answers to job interview questions. In the real world, peer pressure can make an unprejudiced person discriminate, to "go along," while a prejudiced person may not discriminate for fear of social condemnation or a lawsuit.

The gap is usually worst when predictions of future behaviour are involved. In 2004 the Canadian Blood Services reported that 28 per cent of Canadians said they intended to give blood in the next year, but only 3.7 per cent actually did. And in any election many people say that they intend to vote—and even reveal their preferences to pollsters—but then do not follow through.

to determine causal connections. According to Brannigan (2004), such research can produce only small, short-term manipulations of independent variables; yet much of everyday life is affected by long-term, ongoing social processes.

- The analysis of relationships between variables promotes a view of social life that is remote from everyday experience. Blumer (1956) argues that studies designed to bring out the relationships between variables omit "the process of interpretation or definition that goes on in human groups" (p. 685). This **symbolic interactionist** assessment incorporates the first and third criticisms above, that the meaning of events to individuals is ignored and that the connection to everyday contexts is missing. Quantitative researchers recognize those risks, but claim that their research does not preclude a search for how people interpret their everyday existence. For example, quantitative sociologists sometimes ask respondents what they think about social inequality, and try to link the responses with variables such as age, gender, class, and ethnicity. Nonetheless, more thorough and research participant–centred inquiries into questions of meaning are usually undertaken by qualitative sociologists.
- Explanations for findings in quantitative studies may be provided without examining the

perceptions of the people to whom the findings purportedly pertain. A related issue arises when valid quantitative findings are achieved, but the explanation for them is not informed by an empathetic understanding of the people involved. For example, it's empirically true that in many developed countries today much larger proportions of children are born to unwed parents than was the case in previous decades. Many researchers conclude from this that marriage is losing its popularity in certain sectors of society, such as among the poor in inner-city areas. However, in-depth field research conducted by Edin and Kefalas (2005) suggests that among the poor single mothers they studied in Philadelphia, marriage is in fact highly valued, but is expected to happen later in life, after the children have been born. "What is striking about the body of social science evidence," they write, "is how little of it is based on the perspectives and life experiences of the women who are its subjects. ... [S]urveys, though they have meticulously tabulated the trend, have led us to a dead end when it comes to fully understanding the forces behind it" (Edin & Kefalas, 2005, p. 5).

- Quantitative researchers tend to assume an objectivist ontology. As we saw in Chapter 1, quantitative researchers often assume that a reality exists that may be independent of the observer or of individual consciousness. They may also see the social order as fixed or given—at least at a particular point in history—rather than created by individuals through negotiation, although the latter view is not universal among quantitative researchers. People who do quantitative work maintain that it is not a mistake to assume that some things may exist and have certain social effects regardless of whether or how we perceive them. Again, the debate is ongoing.

Research in the News

COVID-19 deaths in Ontario long-term care homes related to their profit status

It is well known that residents of long-term care homes in Canada have been devastated by COVID-19. As with many medical issues, socio-political factors can help to explain how the pandemic ran its course in Canada.

In Ontario, the fate of the residents of these homes may have been affected by whether the home was privately owned and operated. The *Toronto Star* (Saba, 2020) has highlighted a study published in the *Canadian Medical Association Journal* (Stall, Jones, Brown, Rochon, & Costa, 2020) that used quantitative data analysis techniques that showed that both the extent of a COVID-19 outbreak in a long-term care home as well as the number of resident deaths were related to the profit status of the home. Among care homes with an outbreak of COVID-19, for-profit homes had more extensive virus outbreaks and more deaths than homes run on a non-profit basis (e.g., by a charity) or those run by the local municipality. The researchers also provided evidence that older design standards, which were more common in the for-profit group, as well as chain ownership among that group largely accounted for these differences.

According to Nathan Stall, the lead author of the study, care homes built according to older, pre-1998 provincial standards were more likely to have smaller rooms that were shared by up to four residents, as well as shared washrooms and crowded common areas, all of which are risk factors for the spread of the virus. Stall also explained that privately owned homes tended to offer lower levels of care due to lower staffing levels (Saba, 2020). The authors of the study state that their findings will help to inform debates concerning how care homes should be financed, operated, and regulated.

Key Points

- Figure 4.1 depicts quantitative research as a linear series of steps moving from theory to conclusions, although this is an ideal from which there are many departures.
- Examining the reliability and validity of measures is important for assessing their quality.
- Quantitative research has the following key goals: measurement, the establishment of causality, generalization, and replication.
- Quantitative research has been criticized by qualitative researchers. These criticisms tend to revolve around rejecting the view that a natural science model is appropriate for studying the social world.

Questions for Review (R) and Creative Application (A)

The main steps in quantitative research

R1 What are the main steps in quantitative research?

A1 Assume you are conducting a study to determine which variables influence poverty. Name one variable that might have an impact on the chances that a person will live in poverty, and use it to derive a specific hypothesis that can be tested with survey data.

Concepts and their measurement

R2 Why may multiple indicators of a concept be preferable to using a single indicator?

A2 Describe three different ways to measure the concept "homophobia."

Reliability and validity

R3 Name and define four different kinds of measurement validity, providing an illustration of each one.

A3 How might a researcher measure the concept "satisfaction with university student housing"? How could the test–retest method be used to establish reliability? What drawbacks might there be to the use of this method in the example you have provided?

The main goals of quantitative researchers

R4 Outline the main goals of quantitative researchers. What is to be gained by achieving them?

A4 Assume you have to design a study that will examine why some people vote in national elections while others do not. Name two independent variables that would be appropriate to use in this study. What steps can be taken to ensure that your findings will be applicable to some larger population, i.e., to people who will not be participating in your study?

The critique of quantitative research

R5 Explain how the techniques used by quantitative researchers may produce findings that are not applicable to everyday life.

A5 You are using surveys to conduct research on alcohol consumption among stay-at-home moms. Might there be a gap between stated and actual behaviour on this topic? Why? What could you do to reduce or eliminate the gap?

Interactive Classroom Activities

1. Divide the class into groups of seven or more. Each group is to do the following:
   a. Come up with a causal statement that involves two variables, for example, "Being a victim of racism affects one's self-esteem."
   b. Provide a nominal and an operational definition for each variable (in this example, "racist victimization" and "self-esteem").
   c. Explain how each operational definition has face validity.
   d. Explain, giving concrete examples, how concurrent, construct, and convergent validity could be established for both of the operationalizations proposed in point b.
   e. Explain, giving concrete examples, how the operationalizations could be tested for reliability.

f. Describe a methodologically sound way in which participants could be selected for the study.
g. Describe the extent to which the study would have external validity, and in particular the extent to which the findings could be generalized to people who were not studied.

Once these steps are done, each group presents its work to the rest of the class. A different person in the group is to speak to each of the seven points mentioned above. After speaking to each point, group members should pause to allow the rest of the class to comment on what was just presented, with both strengths and weaknesses to be discussed.

2. The instructor engages the class as a whole in a discussion of measurement validity by:
   a. Asking for a nominal definition of the psychological concept of "depression." Student feedback is sought until a working definition of depression is achieved.
   b. Assessing the measurement validity of a depression scale used by Statistics Canada in the Canadian Community Health Survey—2020 (available at https://www23.statcan.gc.ca/imdb/p3Instr.pl?Function=assembleInstr&lang=en&Item_Id=1,262,397#qb1263385, accessed 27 July 2020.) The scale is made up of the 10 items (variables dep_Q005 through dep_Q050) given below:

   Over the last two weeks, how often have you

   i. had little interest or pleasure in doing things?
   ii. felt down, depressed, or hopeless?
   iii. had trouble falling or staying asleep, or sleeping too much?
   iv. felt tired or had little energy?
   v. had poor appetite or overate?
   vi. felt bad about yourself, or that you are a failure or have let yourself or your family down?
   vii. had trouble concentrating on things, such as reading the newspaper or watching television?
   viii. been moving or speaking so slowly that other people could have noticed? Or the opposite, being so fidgety or restless that you have been moving around a lot more than usual?
   ix. had thoughts that you would be better off dead, or of hurting yourself?

   The fixed responses for these questions are: (1) Not at all; (2) Several days; (3) More than half the days; (4) Nearly every day.

   The final question is:

   x. How difficult have these problems made it for you to do your work, take care of things at home, or get along with other people?

   Its response categories are: (1) Not difficult at all; (2) Somewhat difficult; (3) Very difficult; (4) Extremely difficult.

   The measurement validity of each individual item is to be assessed by the class. The class is asked to come up with at least one strength and one weakness for each item.
   c. Asking the class whether this list of items covers all aspects (dimensions) of depression contained in the class's nominal definition. If it does not, the class is to construct additional items that would rectify the problem.

Relevant Websites

The ***Statistics Canada*** site provides access to a wide variety of quantitative information about Canada. It also offers up-to-date figures on things such as the inflation rate, the level of unemployment, and Canada's population.

www.statcan.gc.ca/start-debut-eng.html

The *Canadian Research Institute for Social Policy (CRISP)*, at the University of New Brunswick, conducts policy research on Canadian children and youth, fosters training in quantitative research methods, and helps economically developing nations enhance their research output on child development.

www.unb.ca/research/institutes/crisp/

The *Web Center for Social Research Methods* provides an illustration of how to create a Likert scale.

www.socialresearchmethods.net/kb/scallik.php

(Websites accessed 4 September 2021.)

OXFORD learning link More resources are available on Oxford Learning Link. Visit https://learninglink.oup.com/ for:

- Student self-quiz
- Flash cards
- Audio clips
- Videos
- Activities

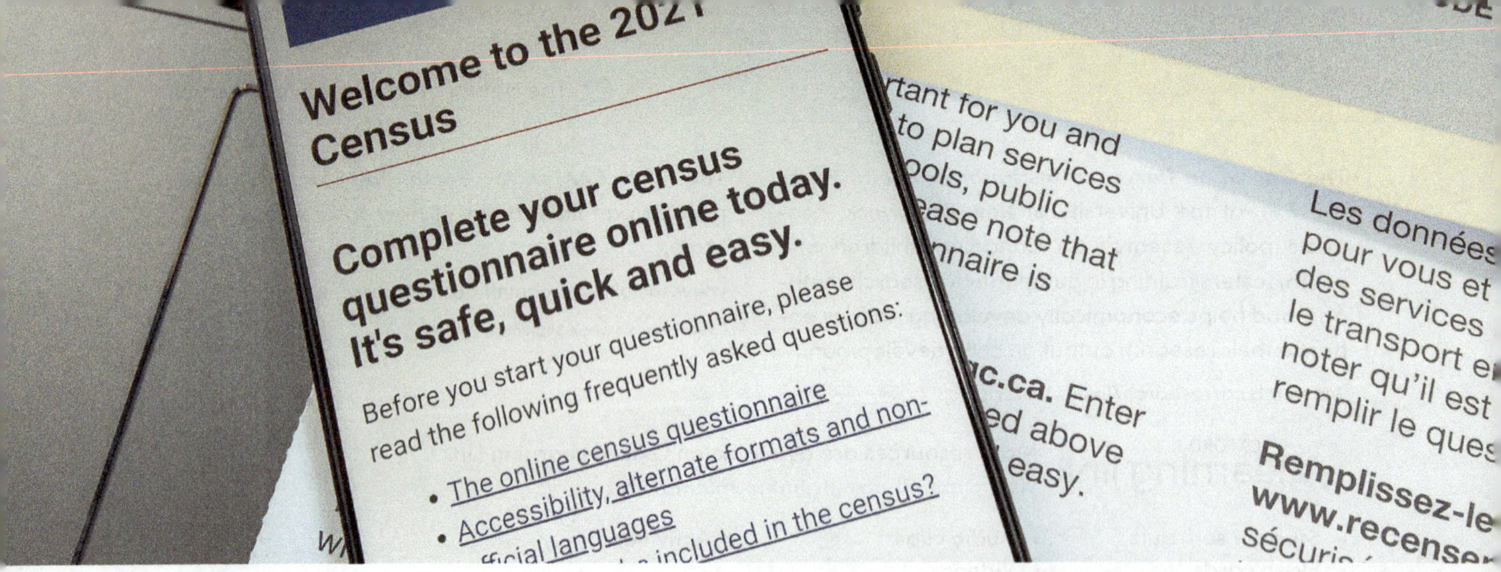

5 Survey Research: Interviews and Questionnaires

Chapter Overview

Survey research is one of the most commonly used data-gathering techniques in the social sciences. Surveys can take the form of either **interviews**, in which participants are asked questions orally, or **questionnaires**, which respondents read and fill out themselves. One of the strengths of survey research is that it allows for standardization in the asking of questions and the categorization of the answers given.

This chapter explores:

- the reasons for the widespread use of surveys, including a consideration of the importance of standardization to the process of measurement;
- issues associated with asking questions in surveys:
  - » whether to use **open** or **closed questions**
  - » different kinds of questions that can be asked in structured interviews and questionnaires
  - » rules to bear in mind when designing questions
  - » optimal question order
  - » how questionnaires can be designed to minimize error and make answering easier for respondents
  - » projection or **vignette** questions in which respondents are asked to reflect on a hypothetical scenario presented to them
  - » the importance of pre-testing questions
  - » the use of questions taken from previous research
- the different ways to do survey research, such as using more than one interviewer, conducting interviews by telephone, or using the Internet or email to administer questionnaires;

▲ JHVEPhoto/Shutterstock

- various prerequisites of structured interviewing, including establishing rapport with the interviewee; asking questions exactly as they appear on the interview schedule; keeping to the question order as it appears on the schedule; and recording exactly what is said by interviewees;
- problems with survey research, including the influence of the interviewer on respondents and the possibility of systematic bias in answers (known as **response sets**);
- the advantages and disadvantages of the questionnaire compared to the structured interview;
- researcher-driven **diaries** as a form of survey research; and
- **secondary analysis** of survey data.

Key Learning Outcomes

Here is a list of goals you should try to achieve as you read and think about the material in this chapter. After completing this chapter, you should be able to:

1. Identify the advantages and disadvantages of open and closed questions.
2. Describe the types of questions used in survey research, and outline the functions of each one.
3. List the rules to be followed in designing survey questions, and explain the rationale for them.
4. Discuss key issues involved with structured interviews, including those pertaining to interview formats and how researchers should conduct themselves.
5. Summarize the use of questionnaires in social research, including matters such as their pros and cons compared to structured interviews, the administration of online questionnaires, how to design a questionnaire, and how researcher-driven diaries can take the form of a questionnaire.
6. Explain the role of secondary analyses of survey data in social research, and discuss their limitations.

"I never do surveys," said Anna-Lise as she hung up the phone.

"Why?" I asked.

"For one thing, they always call at dinnertime, when I'm tired and hungry."

"Maybe that's because most people are home at dinnertime," I said.

"That doesn't make it any more comfortable. And they always ask questions in the weirdest ways, like: 'On a scale from 1 to 5, with 1 being strongly dislike and 5 being strongly like, how do you feel about blah, blah, blah.' Why can't they just ask you your opinion on something and let you say what you want? That would be way more interesting."

"Well, sometimes they give you a statement to respond to rather than a question. And I guess they do the 'On a scale from 1 to 5' thing because they want to compare responses between individuals in a way that is meaningful, or they may want to put a number on what people in general think of the issue, by calculating a mean or something."

"They turn phone conversations into numbers? Very weird."

"Ever step on a scale to weigh yourself? Hey, there's another kind of scale! Or how about the numbers that appear on the gas pump when you're filling up, or numbers showing the time in the bottom right-hand corner of your computer screen? Same idea—turning things into numbers."

"I still say the whole thing is very weird."

Introduction

A common method of acquiring data in **quantitative research** involves the use of interviews and questionnaires, which have become familiar aspects of everyday life. There are job interviews, media interviews, and police interviews, and one is often asked to complete a questionnaire before getting medical treatment or after using a service of some kind. Research interviews and questionnaires share some common features with the everyday variety, although greater care is usually taken to elicit information that is valid and reliable. The information gathered often pertains to matters such as behaviour, attitudes, norms, beliefs, and values.

Open or closed questions?

One of the most significant considerations in survey research is whether to ask a question in an "open" or "closed" format. With an open question, respondents can reply however they wish. With a closed question, they are presented with a set of fixed alternatives from which they have to choose an appropriate answer (see Boxes 4.1 and 4.2 in the previous chapter for examples of closed questions, including **Likert scale** items). What, then, are some of the advantages and limitations of the two formats?

Open questions

Open questions present both advantages and disadvantages to a survey researcher. By and large, however, problems associated with the processing of answers tend to limit their use, especially in quantitative research.

Advantages

Open questions, by allowing respondents to answer in their own terms, have certain advantages over closed ones:

- They allow for replies that the survey researcher might not have contemplated and therefore might not have offered as fixed-choice options. This makes them useful for exploring new or changing areas.
- They make it possible to tap the participants' unprompted knowledge and understanding of issues.
- The salience of particular issues for respondents can also be examined.
- They can generate fixed-choice format answers (a point we will return to later in this chapter).

Disadvantages

Open questions also present problems for a survey researcher:

- It's more time-consuming to record the answers in an open interview.
- The answers have to be **coded** (see Chapter 4), which can also take a lot of time and effort.
- Many prospective questionnaire respondents may be put off by the need to compose an answer, because of the bother and inconvenience.
- Because of the difficulty of writing down exactly what respondents say in an interview, there may be more inaccuracies in the recording of answers. One obvious solution is to use a recording device such as a digital audio recorder, but this can make some respondents nervous, and **transcribing** recorded answers takes a long time. (Issues with transcription will be discussed in Chapter 11.)
- They run the risk of *intra-interviewer variability*, whereby an interviewer is not consistent in asking questions or recording answers, either with different respondents or with the same respondent.
- They also face *inter-interviewer variability*, which may occur when there is more than one interviewer (the usual case). If interviewers are not consistent with each other in the ways they ask questions and/or record answers, measurement error can occur.

Needless to say, these sources of error are not mutually exclusive; they can coexist, compounding the problem even further. Closed questions reduce the incidence of these problems.

Closed questions

The advantages and disadvantages of closed questions are in many respects implied in the considerations relating to open questions.

Advantages

Closed questions offer the following advantages:

- They minimize intra-interviewer variability and inter-interviewer variability.
- Some respondents may not understand what a question is getting at; the available answers may provide some clarification.
- Because interviewers and respondents are not expected to write or speak extensively and instead are to select an answer from a range of possible responses, closed questions can be answered quickly and easily, reducing response rate issues. They are also are easier to process.

All of the above points illustrate how closed questions promote *standardization* in both the asking of questions and the recording of answers. Standardization means that variations in replies are due to "true" or "real" variations in the characteristic being measured rather than extraneous factors. Still, there is always a chance that some responses to closed questions will be inaccurately measured, and there are a number of reasons for this. Some prominent sources of error in survey research are:

1. poorly worded questions;
2. interviewer error in asking a question;
3. misunderstanding on the part of the interviewee;
4. interviewee lapses in memory;
5. interviewer error in recording information;
6. mistakes in entering the data into a computer file; and
7. biases related to the characteristics (such as gender or "race") of the interviewers and/or the interviewees.

To take a simple illustration, a closed question on alcohol consumption among students will show that students vary in the amount of alcohol they consume. Most measurement will contain an element of error, so it is helpful to think of the measured variation in alcohol consumption as made up of two components: true variation and error. In other words:

measured variation = true variation + variation due to error

The aim is to keep the error portion to a minimum (see Figure 5.1), since error reduces the validity of a measure. Standardization in interviews and questionnaires means that two sources of variation due to error—items 2 and 5 in the preceding list—are likely to be less pronounced.

Variation due to error can come from several other sources.

Disadvantages

Closed questions also present certain disadvantages, however:

- Respondents' answers may lack spontaneity and authenticity. It is also possible that the answers provided do not cover all the potential replies. One solution is to use an open question to generate the categories (see Box 5.1). Another is to include "other" as a response option and category and then invite respondents who choose it to elaborate on their choice. Closed questions may irritate respondents who are unable to find an answer category that they feel applies to them. In theory, all possible answers should be provided.
- Respondents may differ in their interpretation of the questions or the answers provided; for example, the understanding of the word "soon" in a question can vary widely from person to person.
- In interviews, a large number of closed questions reduces conversation and gives the interview an impersonal feeling, reducing rapport.

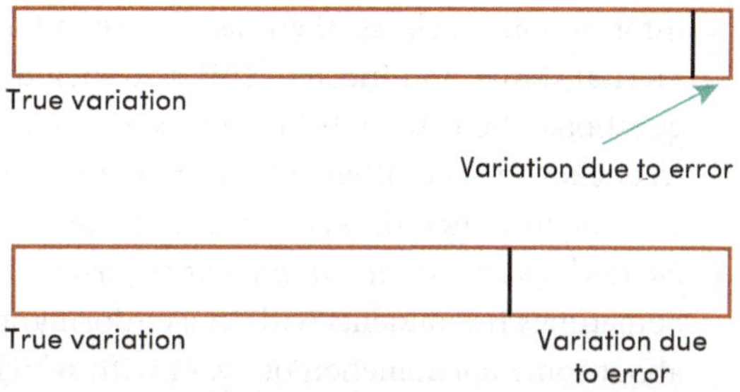

FIGURE 5.1 A measure with little error and one with considerable error

TABLE 5.1 Open questions and closed questions: Advantages and disadvantages

OPEN QUESTIONS	
Advantages	*Disadvantages*
» May produce responses researcher did not anticipate.	» More time consuming than closed questions.
» Can provide knowledge that is unprompted by the researcher.	» Answers must be coded.
» Offer an indication of the salience of the topic to the participant.	» Participants may be perturbed with having to compose an answer.
» Are a source of information for creating fixed-choice questions.	» Possible inaccuracies in recording answers.
	» Risk of intra- and inter-interviewer variability in recording answers.
CLOSED QUESTIONS	
Advantages	*Disadvantages*
» Answers do not have to be coded.	» Answers may lack spontaneity and authenticity.
» Minimize intra- and inter-interviewer variability in recording answers.	» Answers provided may not cover all possible replies.
» Answers provided may clarify, for respondents, what the question is asking.	» Respondents may differ in their interpretation of the questions asked and the answers provided.
» Easier for respondents to provide answers to questions, which may boost response rate.	» Can recreate an impersonal atmosphere, reducing rapport.
» Easier to process responses.	

Types of questions

Structured interviews and questionnaires generally contain several different types of question. There are various ways of classifying them, but here are the main forms:

- *Personal, factual questions.* These are questions that ask respondents to provide personal information, such as their age, occupation, marital status, and income. This also includes questions about their behaviour, such as the frequency of their attendance at religious services or how often they go out to a movie.
- *Factual questions about an entity or event.* Sometimes respondents will act as informants about some phenomenon or event with which they are familiar, particularly when information is not readily available from other sources. Asking people about what they witnessed at a riot—how many people were there, the approximate ages of people engaged in looting—is an example. This sort of question can lead to problems because in everyday life most people are not careful, systematic observers, and they may have biases that affect their perceptions and recollections.
- *Questions about attitudes.* A five-point Likert scale is one of the most common formats for measuring attitudes. Often the responses to a number of Likert items are aggregated to form a composite measure of an attitude.
- *Questions about beliefs.* For example, in Hay's (2014) study of secularization in Canada (see Box 1.3), one item used to measure moral autonomy pertained to the belief that "it is up to the individual to decide what is right and wrong." The response categories were: "Agree

Box 5.1 | A comparison of results for closed and open questions

Schuman and Presser (1981) conducted an experiment to determine whether responses to closed questions could be improved by asking the questions first in open-ended format and then developing categories of reply from respondents' answers. They asked a question in both open and closed formats about what people look for in a job, using different samples for each. They found considerable disparities between the two sets of answers. They then revised the closed categories to reflect the answers they had received to the open-ended question, and re-administered the questions to two large samples. The questions were: "This next question is on the subject of work. People look for different things in a job. Which one of the following five things do you most prefer in a job? [closed question] What would you most prefer in a job? [open question]" The answers they received were as follows:

CLOSED FORMAT		OPEN FORMAT	
Answer	**%**	**Answer**	**%**
Work that pays well	13.2	Pay	16.7
Work that gives a feeling of accomplishment	31.0	Feeling of accomplishment	14.5
Work where there is not too much supervision and you make most decisions yourself	11.7	Control of work	4.6
Work that is pleasant and people who are nice to work with	19.8	Pleasant work	14.5
Work that is steady with little chance of being laid off	20.3	Security	7.6
	96% of sample		57.9% of sample
		Opportunity for promotion	1.0
		Short hours/lots of free time	1.6
		Working conditions	3.1
		Benefits	2.3
		Satisfaction/liking a job	15.6
Other/dk/na	4.0	Other responses	18.3
	100%		100%

With this revised form of the closed question, Schuman and Presser found that a much higher proportion of the answers to the open question corresponded to the closed categories. They argued that the new closed question was superior to its predecessor and also superior to the open question. However, it was still disconcerting to find that only 58 per cent of the answers given to the open question matched the categories offered in the closed one. Also, the distributions were somewhat different: for example, twice as many respondents cited a feeling of accomplishment with the closed format as with the open one. Nonetheless, the experiment demonstrated the desirability of generating forced-choice answers from open questions.

strongly" (5), "Agree somewhat" (4), "Neither agree nor disagree" (3), "Disagree somewhat" (2), and "Disagree strongly" (1).

- *Questions about knowledge.* Sometimes questions are designed to "test" respondents' knowledge in a certain area. For example, a poll sponsored by Historica Canada in 2020 estimated that almost half of Canadians knew that Canadian scientists contributed to the development of the polio vaccine, but only about 29% were familiar with Viola Desmond and her achievements (she appears on Canada's $10 bill) (Historica Canada, 2020).
- *Questions about others.* It's usually better to interview the person directly than to rely on the second-hand accounts of others, because respondents' knowledge of others' behaviour may be distorted or inaccurate (Beardsworth & Keil, 1997). However, if the researcher is interested in the respondent's own perceptions of how someone else acts or feels, questions pertaining to such matters are appropriate. Responses to this sort of question can be used as a check on the validity of self-reports, or may be relied on if the person in question is unable or unwilling to describe their own thoughts or behaviours.

Rules for designing questions

Over the years, numerous rules have been devised in connection with the dos and don'ts of asking questions. Yet mistakes persist. So here are three simple rules of thumb, followed by some more specific guidelines.

General rules of thumb

Keep the research questions in mind

The questions you ask in a questionnaire or structured interview should be designed specifically to answer your research questions. Focusing on the research questions will help protect you against the pain of realizing too late that a particular research question was not addressed in your study. It will also reduce the risk of pursuing issues that are irrelevant, which would be a waste of your time as well as that of your respondents.

What exactly do you want to know?

Rule of thumb number two relates to the first one. It's important to focus on exactly what you want to know. Consider this seemingly harmless question:

> Do you have a car?

What is this question seeking to tap? Car ownership? Access to a household car? Use of a company car? The ambiguity of the word "have" means that a "yes" answer could signify any of the three. If you want to find out whether a respondent owns a car, you need to ask specifically about ownership. Be as specific as possible.

How would you answer it?

Rule of thumb number three is to put yourself in the position of the respondent. Ask yourself the question and try to work out a reply. If you do this, there is at least a chance that the ambiguities inherent in a question like "Do you have a car?" will become evident. For example, you may remember that you have access to a car that you don't actually own. Putting yourself in the position of the respondent can reveal the difficulty of answering poorly constructed questions.

Specific rules when designing questions

Avoid ambiguous terms in questions

If possible, avoid terms such as "often" and "regularly" as measures of frequency. They are ambiguous, and different respondents will take them to mean different things. It may not always be possible to get a specific number from respondents, but that should be your goal. Consider a question asked of people who have said that they own a cellphone:

> How often do you use your cellphone to place a call?
>
> Very often ____
> Quite often ____
> Not very often ____
> Not at all ____

The problem with this question is that, with the exception of "not at all," all the terms in the response categories are ambiguous. Instead, ask about actual frequency, such as:

> How often do you use your cellphone to place a call?
>
> *(Please tick whichever category comes closest to the number of times you use your cellphone.)*
>
> More than 10 times per day _____
> 5–9 times per day _____
> 1–4 times per day _____
> A few times a week _____
> A few times a month _____
> Almost never _____

Alternatively, you could simply ask respondents to estimate the number of times per day they use their cellphone to make a call.

It's also important to bear in mind that certain common words, such as "dinner," mean different things to different people. For some, dinner is a light midday meal, whereas for others it is a substantial evening meal. In such cases it is necessary to clearly define the terms that are being used.

Avoid long questions

Most methodologists agree that long questions are undesirable. Interviewees can lose track of long questions, and respondents completing a questionnaire may be tempted to skim or even skip over them. However, Sudman and Bradburn (1982) suggested that this advice is more applicable to attitude questions than to those asking about behaviour. They argued that when the focus is on behaviour, longer questions can have certain positive features in interviews: for example, they are more likely to provide memory cues and facilitate recall because of the time it takes to ask them. By and large, however, it's best to keep questions short.

Avoid double-barrelled questions

> How satisfied are you with your pay and working conditions?

The problem here is obvious: people may be satisfied with one but not the other. Not only will the respondent be unclear about how to reply, but the answer provided may pertain to pay, to conditions, or to both.

The same rule applies to fixed-choice answers. In Box 5.1, one of Schuman and Presser's (1981) answers is:

> Work that is pleasant and people who are nice to work with.

While there may well be symmetry between the two ideas in this answer—pleasant work and nice people—there is no *necessary* correspondence between them. Pleasant work may be important for people who are indifferent to their co-workers. For examples of triple- and quadruple-barrelled questions, see Box 5.2.

Avoid very general questions

It may be tempting to ask a very general question when what is needed is a response to a specific issue. A question such as

> How satisfied are you with your job?

seems harmless, but it lacks specificity. Does it refer to pay, working conditions, the nature of the work, or all of these? Respondents are likely to vary in their interpretation of the question, and this will be a source of error. A favourite general question comes from Karl Marx's *Enquête ouvrière*, a questionnaire sent to 25,000 French socialists and others (whether any were returned is unknown). The final question (the one-hundredth!) reads:

> What is the general, physical, intellectual, and moral condition of men and women employed in your trade? (Bottomore & Rubel, 1963, p. 218)

If you find it difficult to come up with precise questions to replace very broad, general ones, you might take inspiration from Blauner (1964), who provides a very detailed and nuanced description of job satisfaction among American factory workers based on some 80 specific questions.

Box 5.2 | Matching questions and answers in closed questions

A publisher inserted a feedback questionnaire into copies of a novel, including a series of Likert-style items regarding the book's quality. In each case, readers were asked to indicate whether a particular attribute was "poor," "acceptable," "average," "good," or "excellent." However, the items were presented as questions that, strictly speaking, demanded "yes" or "no" answers. For example:

> Was the writing elegant, seamless, imaginative?

None of the response options provided by the publisher could be considered logical answers to the questions that were posed. The questions would have been better presented as statements, for example:

> Please indicate the quality of the writing in each of the following categories:

Elegance:

Very Poor	Poor	Average	Good	Excellent

Seamlessness:

Very Poor	Poor	Average	Good	Excellent

Imaginativeness:

Very Poor	Poor	Average	Good	Excellent

This approach would also solve the additional problem of the "triple-barrelled" question that asks about three distinct aspects of the writing, leaving the reader unable to express differing opinions of each.

It could be argued that readers would understand that they were being asked to rate the book in terms of each attribute. The problem is that the impact of a disjunction between question and answer is simply not known—which means that any conclusions drawn by the publisher might well be wrong.

Avoid leading questions

Leading or loaded questions push respondents in a particular direction; for example:

> Would you agree to cutting taxes, even though welfare payments for the neediest sections of the population might be reduced?

Phrasing the question in this way is likely to make it difficult for some people to agree, even if they do feel that taxes are too high.

Mismatched questions and answers, and requesting a single response for a question that covers more than one issue, are not limited to publishers' inserts in novels. They also appear in questionnaires that academic reviewers are asked to complete as part of their evaluation of manuscripts that have been submitted for publication in leading social science journals. Reviewers for one journal are asked to rate the "Importance of topic for public opinion scholars," using response categories on a seven-point scale "where 1= very poor and 7 = excellent." Reviewers providing evaluations for another prominent journal are asked, "Does the paper address novel questions and provides [*sic*] novel insight? Does it explore important but overlooked phenomena, a creative approach to a topic, new or seldom used designs and methods, or understudied samples?" Reviewers are to give a single response to this set of questions, using the categories "inadequate," "marginal," "good," and "not applicable."

Avoid questions that actually ask two (or more) questions

Some of the questions cited above clearly transgress this rule, but there are also more subtle versions of the problem. A question such as

> Which party did you vote for in the 2019 federal election?

provides an illustration. What if the respondent did not vote in that election? The question is really two questions, which should be asked separately:

> Did you vote in the 2019 federal election?
>
> Yes
>
> No
>
> If YES, for which political party did you vote?

Avoid questions that include negatives

The problem with questions that include negative terms such as "not" is that some respondents may miss the negative and give answers opposite to what they intended. There may be situations when it's impossible to avoid using a negative, but questions like the following should be avoided as far as possible:

> Do you agree with the view that university students should not have to take out loans to finance their education?

Instead, the question should be asked in a positive form; for example: "Do you find it acceptable that some university students have to take out loans to finance their education?" Questions with double negatives are never appropriate, because it's impossible to be sure that respondents have interpreted them correctly. The following provides an example:

> Would you rather not drink non-alcoholic beer?

Minimize technical terms

Use simple, plain language and avoid jargon. Don't ask a question like this:

> Do you sometimes feel alienated from your work?

The problem here is that many respondents may not be familiar with the term "alienated," and even if they are, they may not understand it in the same way. The same goes for acronyms and abbreviations: avoid them whenever possible.

Ensure that respondents have the requisite knowledge

There is little point in asking about matters unfamiliar to respondents. For example, it's doubtful that meaningful data regarding opinions on foreign affairs can be gained from people who do not follow international political issues.

Ensure that the answers provided for a closed question are balanced

It's important that the range of answers provided for a closed question be properly balanced between positive and negative options. A set of responses like this

> Excellent _____
> Good _____
> Borderline _____
> Poor _____

is weighted toward a favourable response. "Excellent" and "Good" are both positive; "Borderline" is a neutral or middle position; and "Poor" is a negative response. A second negative response choice, such as "Very poor" is needed.

Ensure answers provided for a closed question do not overlap

Care must be taken to ensure that answers to closed questions are mutually exclusive. For example, a question on the respondent's age with a set of responses like this

> 20–30 _____
> 30–40 _____
> 40–50 _____
> 50–60 _____

would confuse anyone with an age of 30, 40, or 50, as these answers each fit into two of the supplied options.

Don't overstretch people's memories

It might be useful to know exactly how many times respondents have used their cellphones in the previous month, but few people will be able to give you an accurate answer for such an extended period of time. For this reason, it's important to choose a suitable time frame, such as per day in the case of cellphone use.

Carefully consider using "Don't know" as a closed answer option

One area of controversy regarding closed questions is whether the answer set should include a "don't know" or "no opinion" option when asking questions concerning attitudes. The main argument for including a "don't know" option is to ensure that respondents will not be forced to express views that they don't actually hold. Many recommend offering the "don't know" option in the form of a *filter question* to remove those respondents who have no opinion on the topic. Filter questions are used to determine whether it is appropriate to ask certain questions of a particular respondent. The interviewer could ask the filter question, "Do you have an opinion on this issue?" of everyone and then ask the second question only of those who say that they do have an opinion.

The alternative argument in connection with the "don't know" option is that it offers an easy way out for respondents. A series of experiments conducted in the US found that many respondents who claim to have no opinion on a topic do in fact hold one (Krosnick et al., 2002). Respondents with lower levels of education are especially likely to select the "don't know" option; and later questions in a questionnaire (see the next section for question-order effects) are the most likely to elicit a "don't know" response. The researchers concluded that data quality is not enhanced by the inclusion of a "don't know" option and that it may prevent some respondents from expressing an opinion that they do actually hold.

Pay close attention to question order

Quite a lot of research has been directed at finding out how responses are affected by asking questions at different points in an interview schedule. Results have varied and few if any consistent effects have been found. Mayhew (2000) tells an interesting anecdote on question order in a crime survey. By mistake, half of the respondents were asked the question "Taking everything into account, would you say the police in this area do a good job or a poor job?" twice: once early on, and once again later, in the context of questions on contact with the police. Almost a quarter (22 per cent) of those respondents gave a more positive rating the second time. Mayhew suggests that as the interview wore on, respondents became more sensitized to crime-related issues and more sympathetic to the pressures on the police. As appealing as this explanation sounds, it cannot account for the 13 per cent who gave a lower rating the second time around. That is quite a reliability issue. (See also Box 5.3.)

It's hard to draw any general lessons from question-order research, at least in part because experiments do not always reveal clear-cut effects, even in cases where effects might legitimately have been expected. Nonetheless, two general lessons have emerged:

- Unless the study is designed to test question-order effects, all respondents should receive questions in the same order.
- Researchers should be sensitive to the possible effects that a question could have on subsequent questions.

In addition, the following rules about question order are sometimes proposed:

- Early questions should be directly related to the announced research topic. This removes the risk that respondents will be put off by apparently irrelevant questions asked at an early stage in the interview. It also means that personal questions about age, social background, and so on should *not* be asked at the beginning of an interview.
- Questions likely to be important or meaningful to respondents should be asked early in the interview, to stimulate their interest and attention. This suggestion may conflict with the previous one if questions about the research topic are not of interest to respondents.
- If possible, questions that may cause embarrassment or anxiety should be left for later in the schedule—although not to the very end. Respondents should not leave the interview (or

complete the questionnaire) with misgivings or negative feelings about the research.

- With a long schedule or questionnaire, questions should be grouped logically in related sections, and should not jump back and forth from one topic to another.
- Within each group of questions, general questions should precede specific ones. If a specific question comes first, the aspect of the general question that it highlights may be discounted by respondents who feel they have already covered it. For example, if a question asking how people feel about their salary precedes a general question about job satisfaction, some respondents may discount the issue of pay when responding to the job satisfaction question, since they have already addressed it.
- It is sometimes recommended that questions dealing with opinions and attitudes precede questions about behaviour and knowledge. This is because questions that tap opinions and attitudes may be affected by the latter sorts of questions. For instance, if a husband reports that he does only 20 per cent of the housework, making that statement can affect how he responds when asked if housework should be shared equally between spouses.
- If a respondent provides an answer to a question that is to be asked later in the interview, the question should still be asked later on, when the interviewer arrives at the scheduled point. A different answer may be offered at the latter juncture because of question-order effects.

Box 5.3 | About question order

Imagine that there are two pollsters: one who favours the federal New Democratic Party and another who favours the Conservatives. The key question in both their surveys is: "If an election were held today, for which party would you vote?" That question would be followed by an alphabetical list of the main political parties. Look at the two sets of Likert items that follow (assume there are five response options ranging from "Strongly agree" to "Strongly disagree"), and imagine that the items immediately *preceded* the voting question. Try to determine whether these items would influence responses to the voting question and, if so, how.

Set One:

1. Canada must do more to reduce global warming.
2. The environment should be the federal government's top priority.
3. Corporate taxes should be increased to pay for social assistance for Canada's poorest families.
4. Canada must do more to protect Indigenous rights.

Set Two:

1. The Canada–United States–Mexico free trade deal will help create jobs in Canada.
2. Canada's mounting debt is mortgaging the future of its children.
3. Lower taxes would benefit everyone, especially hard-working Canadian families.
4. Our laws should protect law-abiding citizens, not criminals.

For those who do not follow politics closely, the first set would probably increase the number of respondents saying they would vote NDP, while the second would likely do the same for the number declaring their intention to vote Conservative. Although most pollsters avoid such blatant biases, sometimes more subtle influences on respondents go unnoticed. In any event, this is an interesting exercise because it illustrates the importance of question order in survey research: if it is necessary to use these items, they ought to be presented *after* the voting question.

Avoid provoking response sets

This issue (see also Chapter 4) is especially relevant to multiple-indicator measures, where respondents reply to a battery of related questions or items. A response set exists if responses are motivated by something other than the person's actual feeling about the items. They can result from psychological predispositions like acquiescence (a desire to be "cooperative" or to please the researcher) or laziness, and in such cases are evident when someone responds to a series of items in the same way, regardless of the content of the items. To avoid acquiescence, researchers using multiple-item measures may include some items that logically call for opposite positions, so that if respondents are consistent in their attitudes, they can neither agree with all the items nor disagree with all of them. This also requires the respondent to carefully read each question. Similar procedures may be used to avoid the effects of laziness or boredom. For example, when visiting a doctor's office for the first time, patients usually have to fill out a form containing a long list of diseases, indicating whether they have ever suffered from them. Someone may begin carefully, reading the list and checking off "No, No, No, ...," but eventually tire of the task and just tick "No" for the remaining items without reading them closely. Those who persist in choosing the same answer regardless of the question may have to be removed from the study. Response sets may also stem from a desire to be liked or respected by the interviewer, so instructing interviewers to avoid both becoming overly friendly with respondents and appearing judgmental about their replies can help. Using vignettes can also help reduce answers motivated by **social desirability**.

Practical Tip | Common mistakes when asking questions

Over the years, the authors of this book have read many projects and dissertations based on structured interviews and questionnaires. A number of mistakes recur regularly, among them the following:

- ***Excessive use of open questions.*** While resistance to closed questions is understandable, open questions are likely to reduce the response rate and cause analysis problems. Keep them to a minimum.
- ***Excessive use of yes/no questions.*** Sometimes students include lots of questions that call for a yes/no response (usually a sign of inadequate thinking and preparation). The world rarely fits into this kind of response. Take a question like:

  Are you satisfied with the opportunities for promotion in your firm?

  Yes ________ No ________

  Attitudes are complex, and most respondents will not be simply "satisfied" or "not satisfied." For one thing, people's feelings about such things vary in intensity. An improvement would be to rephrase the item as:

  How satisfied are you with opportunities for promotion in your firm?

  Very satisfied ____
  Satisfied ____
  Neither satisfied nor dissatisfied ____
  Dissatisfied ____
  Very dissatisfied ____

  This sort of format also makes it possible to calculate some widely used statistics that are discussed in Chapter 8.

- ***Too many questions that allow respondents to choose more than one answer.*** Although there are times when such questions are unavoidable, the replies they produce are often difficult to analyze.

Consider using vignette questions when appropriate

Closed questions that are used to examine ethical standards and beliefs may be employed in conjunction with the **vignette technique**. It involves presenting respondents with one or more scenarios and asking them how they would respond if confronted with the circumstances depicted in the scenario. For example, Kingsbury and Coplan (2012) used vignettes to examine how some Ontario mothers of preschool children reacted to hypothetical accounts of their child's shyness and aggression. The researchers hypothesized that mothers would look more favourably on gender-congruent behaviours (such as shyness in girls) than gender-incongruent ones (physical aggression in girls), especially if they held more traditional attitudes toward sex roles. The findings provided some support for the hypotheses, although the results were mixed.

Box 5.4 outlines a vignette designed to tease out respondents' norms concerning several aspects of family obligations, including the nature of the assistance required (direct involvement or simple provision of resources); geographical considerations; the choice between paid work and unpaid care; and among heterosexual couples, the gender question (should it be the man or the woman who gives up paid work for unpaid care?). The specificity of the situation facing Jim and Margaret increases as the vignette develops. The first question (a) does not say whether they are prepared to move; the second (b) says that they are; and in the last question (d) they have in fact moved and are facing a new dilemma.

Many aspects of the issues tapped by the questions in Box 5.4 can be accessed through attitude items. For example:

> When two heterosexual working spouses decide that one of them should quit work to

Box 5.4 | A vignette to establish family obligations

Jim and Margaret Robinson are a married couple in their early forties. Jim's parents, who live several hundred kilometres away, have had a serious car accident and they need long-term daily help. Jim is their only son. He and his wife both could get transfers to work nearer his parents.

a. What should Jim and Margaret do?
   - move to live near Jim's parents
   - have Jim's parents move to live with them
   - give Jim's parents money to help them pay for daily care
   - let Jim's parents make their own arrangements
   - do something else (specify)
   - don't know

b. In fact, Jim and Margaret are prepared to move and live near Jim's parents, but teachers at their children's school say that moving right now could have a bad effect on their children's education.

   What should Jim and Margaret do? Should they move or should they stay?
   - move
   - stay

c. Why do you think they should move/stay?

d. Jim and Margaret do go to live near Jim's parents. A year later Jim's mother dies and his father's condition worsens to the point where he needs full-time care.

   Should one of either Jim or Margaret take an extended leave from work to take care of Jim's father? IF YES, who should: Jim or Margaret?
   - Yes, Jim should give up his job.
   - Yes, Margaret should give up her job.
   - No, neither should give up their job.
   - don't know/depends

Source: Adapted from Finch (1987, p. 108).

care for ailing parents, the wife should be the one to give up her job.

Strongly agree _____
Agree _____
Undecided _____
Disagree _____
Strongly disagree _____

The advantage of the vignette over this kind of attitude item is that it anchors the choice in a more realistic situation and thus reduces the risk of an unreflective reply. Finch (1987) also argued that on a sensitive topic like this, some respondents may feel uncomfortable or fear that they will be judged on their replies. The fact that the vignette is about other people (and imaginary ones at that) creates a certain distance between the questioning and the respondent, and hence the chance for a more candid answer. One obvious requirement of the vignette technique is that scenarios must be believable.

Finch also pointed to some limitations with this style of questioning, however. It may be impossible to establish what assumptions are being made by the respondents about the characters in the scenario (such as their age, ethnicity, and number of children at home) and the significance of those assumptions for the validity and comparability of people's replies. It is also difficult to establish how far respondents' answers reflect their own normative views or indeed how they themselves would act when confronted with the kinds of choices outlined in the scenarios. Often what people say they would do in a particular situation turns out to be very different from what they actually do. People are not necessarily being dishonest—predicting behaviour, whether our own or someone else's, is often more difficult than we would imagine.

Run a pilot study

It is always desirable to conduct a pilot study before collecting data from respondents: not just to ensure that individual questions operate well but also to ensure that the research instrument as a whole is appropriate. Pilot studies may be particularly crucial in research using questionnaires, since there will be no interviewer present to clear up any confusion.

Here are some specific uses of pilot studies in survey research:

- If the study is going to employ mainly closed questions, a researcher can pose open questions in pilot qualitative interviews and then use them to generate the fixed-choice answers.
- Piloting an interview schedule can give interviewers some experience in using it and help them develop confidence.
- If everyone (or virtually everyone) who answers a question gives the same answer, the resulting data are not likely to be useful. A pilot study gives you an opportunity to identify

Practical Tip | Getting help in designing questions

When designing questions, be empathetic: put yourself in the position of the people who will be answering them. This can be difficult, because the questions may not always apply to the person producing them—for example, to a young student doing a survey of retired people. Even so, you need to think about how you would reply. This means concentrating not just on the questions themselves but also on the links between the questions. For example, do filter questions work in the expected way?

Then try out the questions on some friends or classmates, as in a pilot study. Ask them to be critical and to consider how well the questions connect to each other. Also, look at some questionnaires and structured interview schedules designed by experienced researchers. Those researchers may not have asked questions on your particular topic, but the way they have asked their questions should give you an idea of what to do and what to avoid.

such questions and modify them as necessary to elicit more varied answers.

- In survey interviews, it may be possible to identify questions that make respondents feel uncomfortable and to detect any junctures where interest tends to flag.
- Questions that respondents tend to skip or have difficulty understanding (more easily recognizable in an interview than in a questionnaire context) should become apparent. If certain questions are frequently skipped, it may be because of unclear or threatening phrasing, poorly worded instructions, or confusing positioning in the interview schedule or questionnaire (see Box 5.5). Whatever the cause, missing data are undesirable and a pilot study may be very helpful in identifying problems.
- A pilot study may also offer an opportunity to consider the overall structure of the study. If the questions do not flow well, it may be necessary to move some of them around.

The pilot should not be carried out on people who may become members of the sample in the full study, since participation in the pilot could affect their responses in the study proper. If the population you are investigating is small, you don't want to be forced to exclude certain people, since that could affect the representativeness of

Box 5.5 | A bad questionnaire

How would you fix this questionnaire?

"Hello. I am taking a sociology course on research methods and would like to ask you some questions. Would that be ok?"

1. Were you ever scared that you were HIV-positive?
   Yes ______ No ______

For questions 2 to 6, please answer Agree or Disagree.

2. As a religious person, I feel sorry for AIDS victims.
3. I think victims of any disease deserve compassion.
4. I think the new legislation will be a boon to AIDS victims.
5. The government should not allocate more money to AIDS research.
6. People with AIDS and other sexual diseases should be quarantined.

If you agree, has your viewpoint changed since the 1980s when AIDS first widely emerged?

Yes ______ No ______

Now there are just a few more questions.

7. If one were planned, would you fight having an AIDS hospice on your street?
   Yes ______ No ______
8. How does your spouse feel about AIDS victims?
   Compassionate ______ Sympathetic ______
   Concerned ______ Angry ______ Don't know ______
9. Elizabeth Taylor has raised much money for AIDS research. Should people be doing more fundraising in this area?
   Yes ______ No ______
10. Do you know any AIDS victims?
    Yes ______ No ______

Finally, I need a few facts for comparison purposes.

11. How old are you? ______
12. Did you graduate from high school?
    Yes ______ No ______
13. Did you ever have yourself tested for AIDS?
    Yes ______ No ______

Thank you for your cooperation.

the sample. If this is an issue, do the pilot study on respondents from a different but similar population. Beagan (2001) did this in her study of medical students.

Consider using existing questions

Finally, it is sometimes possible to use questions that have been employed by other researchers for at least part of the questionnaire or interview schedule. This may seem like stealing, but it is a legitimate research practice so long as the original source is cited. One advantage of using existing questions is that they may have already been piloted and tested for their reliability and validity. Robinson, Shaver, & Wrightsman (1999), for example, provide an extensive set of survey questions that have been used to measure political attitudes, along with measures of their reliability and validity.

A further advantage is that existing questions allow for comparisons with other research. For instance, in psychology it is quite common to use standardized personality and intelligence tests; these permit comparisons between different samples and allow different researchers to make consistent measurements. Similarly, some of the questions used in Bell, Aitken Schermer, & Vernon's (2009) study of the heritability of political orientations were taken from earlier studies. They were either used verbatim or slightly revised to make them suitable for the sample to which they were administered. Walklate (2000, p. 194) described how in developing a survey instrument for victims of crime, she and her colleagues used "tried and tested questions taken from pre-existing criminal victimization surveys amended to take account of our own more localized concerns." Existing questions can also be used to investigate whether change has occurred over time by comparing current results with those arrived at in earlier time periods. At the very least, examining questions used by others may provide ideas about how best to approach your own questions, even if you eventually decide to modify those used by other researchers.

Issues related to conducting interviews

In addition to crafting good questions, there are other issues to be considered when doing research using structured interviews and questionnaires. These are addressed below.

Interview formats

In a traditional interview, an interviewer stands or sits in front of the respondent, asks a series of questions, and writes down or keys in the answers. However, there are several possible departures from this pattern.

More than one interviewer or interviewee

Multiple interviewers are rare in social research because of the considerable cost involved in dispatching more than one person to conduct an interview. In the case of **focus groups** it is more common, but in that instance there is more than one interviewee as well, and to administer a structured interview to a focus group would be very unusual. In most survey research a specific individual is the object of questioning by one interviewer. Indeed, it is usually advisable to *discourage* as far as possible the presence or intrusion of others during the interview. Studies in which more than one person is being interviewed tend to be conducted by qualitative researchers, although that is not always the case. For example, Pahl's (1990) study of patterns in the control of money among couples employed structured interviewing first of the couples and then of husbands and wives separately.

Alternatives to in-person interviews

It is customary in academic social research not involving national samples to use face-to-face interviews. However, telephone interviewing is the norm in fields such as market or government research. Telephone interviews have several advantages over the face-to-face variety:

- They are far cheaper and quicker to administer than in-person interviews, which may require the interviewers to spend a great deal of time travelling to meet with respondents; this is a particular problem when a sample is geographically dispersed.

- Telephone interviews are easier to supervise than the personal kind. This is a particular advantage when several interviewers are calling from the same location at the same time, since supervisors may be able to detect interviewer errors, such as rephrasing questions or probing inappropriately. Face-to-face interviews can be recorded for the purpose of assessing data quality, but the recording of interviews raises issues of confidentiality and so must be treated with caution.
- Telephone interviewing can also reduce bias arising from the characteristics of the interviewers or interviewees (for example, gender, class, and ethnicity). The remoteness of the interviewer in telephone interviewing removes this potential source of bias to a significant extent, since the interviewers' "race" and general appearance cannot be seen, although their gender is usually apparent.

On the other hand, telephone interviewing suffers from certain limitations when compared to the personal interview:

- People who do not have a telephone or otherwise cannot be contacted by phone cannot be part of the study. Since lack of a phone is most likely to be a feature of poorer households, the potential for sampling bias exists. Also, many people choose to be ex-directory (they pay to have their telephone numbers *not* listed in a telephone book) or they use only cellphones and for that reason are not listed. This presents a problem if the researcher is using a directory to select respondents. A solution to the latter problem is *random-digit dialling*. With this technique (used, for example, in the General Social Survey administered by Statistics Canada), a computer randomly selects telephone numbers within a predefined geographical area. This method can give you access to ex-directory households, though it's important to note that in some areas it is prohibited by law to contact cellphones in this way.
- Respondents with hearing impairments are likely to find telephone interviews more difficult than personal interviews.
- A telephone interview is unlikely to be sustainable beyond 20 to 25 minutes, whereas personal interviews can be conducted for longer periods of time (Frey, 2004).
- There is some evidence that telephone interviews fare less well than personal interviews in obtaining data on sensitive issues such as drug and alcohol use, income, tax payments, and health. The evidence is not entirely consistent on this point, but when many questions of this kind are to be asked, a personal interview may be superior (Shuy, 2002).
- Telephone interviewers cannot see the respondents and therefore cannot respond to signs of puzzlement or unease on their faces. In a personal interview, the interviewer may respond to such signs by restating the question or attempting to clarify its meaning, though this has to be handled in a standardized way as much as possible. A further issue is that interviewers may be able to collect subsidiary information, such as whether the home in which the interview was conducted is in need of repair. That sort of information cannot be acquired over the telephone.
- Frequently, the target of the research is a specific individual in a household or firm: for example, the person in a certain role or position, or someone with particular characteristics. It is probably more difficult to ascertain by telephone interview whether the correct person is replying.
- The telephone interviewer cannot employ visual aids such as "show cards" from which respondents select their replies (see Box 5.6). Similarly, diagrams or photographs cannot be used.

There is some evidence that the quality of the data gathered through telephone interviews is inferior to that produced by face-to-face interviews. According to

Box 5.6 | Two show cards

Card 4 (age)	Card 6 (for various items)
a. Less than 20	1. Strongly agree
b. 20–29	2. Agree
c. 30–39	3. Undecided
d. 40–49	4. Disagree
e. 50–59	5. Strongly disagree
f. 60–69	
g. 70 and over	

Holbrook, Green, & Krosnick (2003), a series of experiments in the US using long lists of questions found that respondents interviewed by telephone were more likely to express no opinion or give "don't know" as an answer; give the same answer to a series of linked questions; express socially desirable opinions; be apprehensive about the interview; and be dissatisfied with the time taken by the interviews (even though they were shorter than the face-to-face kind). Also, telephone interviewees tend to be less engaged in the interview process.

Computer-assisted interviewing

Today it is common to use computers in the interview process. There are two main formats for such interviews: computer-assisted personal interviewing (CAPI) and computer-assisted telephone interviewing (CATI). The use of CAPI has been growing lately, mainly because of the increased portability and affordability of laptop computers and other electronic devices, and the availability of quality software packages.

With computer-assisted interviewing, the questions in the interview schedule appear on the screen, the interviewer keys in the reply, and the computer shows the next question. This approach is especially useful when filter questions are asked. In the 2015 Canadian Election Study (funded by Elections Canada), respondents were asked the filter question, "The federal election was held on Monday, October 19. In any election, some people are not able to vote because they are sick or busy, or for some other reason. Others do not want to vote. Did you vote in the recent federal election?" Only those who said yes were then asked, "Which party did you vote for?" Once the response to the filter question has been keyed in, the computer will automatically go to the next relevant question, eliminating inappropriate items where necessary. This removes the possibility of interviewers inadvertently asking meaningless questions or failing to ask some that should be asked. In this way, computer-assisted interviewing improves standardization in the asking and recording of questions.

Computer-assisted interviewing makes it easier to perform other tasks as well. For example, sometimes it is beneficial to randomize the order in which certain items are presented to the respondent in order to determine whether the responses given depend on the order in which the items are listed. Automatic randomization was used in the Goyder, Guppy, & Thompson (2003) study of occupational prestige done in southwestern Ontario. As the authors put it: "The deck was electronically shuffled for each new respondent." Another advantage of computer-assisted interviews is that if interviewers are out in the field all day, the data can be sent to the research office electronically.

Using online (email) personal interviews

Online interviews run a higher risk of respondent dropout than other forms do. However, Mann and Stewart (2000, pp. 138–139) have suggested that it is possible to develop a relationship of mutual trust when using them. This can be accomplished by regularly sending messages to respondents assuring them that their responses are helpful and significant, especially since online interviewing is still an unfamiliar experience for most people and takes longer than other forms. It is worth the trouble because online interviews make it relatively easy for the researcher to go back to interviewees for further information or reflections—something difficult to do with face-to-face interviews.

A further issue for the online personal interviewer is whether to send all the questions at once or to conduct the interview on a question-followed-by-reply basis. The problem with sending all at once is that respondents may read through them and reply only to the most interesting ones. Bampton and Cowton (2002) reported that conducting email interviews by sending questions in small batches takes the pressure off interviewees to make a quick reply, gives them the opportunity to provide considered replies (although there can be a loss of spontaneity), and gives the interviewers greater opportunity to respond to interviewee answers.

There is evidence that prospective online interviewees are more likely to agree to participate if agreement is solicited prior to sending the actual questions. Another way to encourage respondents to participate is for the researcher to use some form of self-disclosure, such as directions to a website that contains detailed contact information. It also helps to provide personal material about the researcher (such as a photo), as well as information relevant to the research topic (Curasi, 2001; O'Connor & Madge, 2001, 2003). Such steps are necessary because unsolicited emails ("spam") are often seen as a nuisance and can result in an immediate refusal to take the message seriously.

Curasi (2001) conducted a comparison in which 24 interviews carried out through email correspondence were contrasted with 24 parallel face-to-face interviews. The interviews were concerned with shopping online. She found that:

- face-to-face is better than online for maintaining rapport with respondents;
- because greater commitment and motivation are required to complete an online interview, replies are often more detailed than in face-to-face interviews; and
- online interviewees' answers tend to be more considered and grammatically correct because they have more time to ponder and tidy up answers. Whether this is a positive feature is debatable. There is the obvious advantage of a "clean" transcript, but there may be some loss of spontaneity.

On the other hand, Curasi found that some online responses were short on detail, perhaps because replies had to be typed, not just spoken. The full significance of the difference between email and face-to-face interviewing is still being explored by researchers.

Webcam technologies like Skype and Zoom may offer further possibilities for online personal interviews, making the online interview similar to the telephone version and quite comparable to an in-person interview because those involved in the exchange can see each other. However, one of the main advantages of the email interview is lost: respondents' answers need to be transcribed.

Conducting interviews

Know the interview schedule

Before interviewing anybody, an interviewer should have a thorough knowledge of the interview schedule. Interviewing can be stressful, and it is possible that under strain standard interview procedures can cause interviewers to get flustered and leave questions out or ask the wrong questions. All interviewers need to be fully trained to reduce interviewer variability in asking questions, a potential source of error. Fowler (1993) cited evidence to suggest that a training period shorter than one full day is rarely sufficient.

Introducing the research

Prospective respondents have to be offered a credible rationale for participating in the research, in particular for giving up their valuable time. This aspect of conducting interviews is of special significance at a time when survey response rates appear to be declining. The introductory rationale may be either spoken by the interviewer or printed for the respondent to read. It is usually spoken if interviewers "cold call" potential respondents at their homes, either in person or by telephone. A written rationale is common to alert respondents that someone will be contacting them to request an interview. In many cases, respondents may be presented with both modes—for example, researchers will send respondents a letter inviting them to participate in a study and then call or speak to them in person.

Rapport

As suggested earlier, interviewers need to establish a *rapport* with respondents. A relationship must be forged fairly quickly to encourage respondents to participate in and persist with the interview. While this injunction essentially invites the interviewer to be friendly with respondents and put them at ease, it is important not

Methods in Motion | Applications to Canadian Society

Father involvement in parenting in Canada: The role of mental health

There is considerable evidence that the degree to which fathers are involved in raising their children has important, long-lasting effects on their children's well-being. However, relatively little research has been conducted on what might enable or impede fathers' participation in bringing up their children, especially in the Canadian context. Shafer and Renick (2020) focus on one possible factor: the fathers' mental health—specifically, the degree to which fathers exhibit symptoms of depression. The effect of paternal mental health on childrearing in Canada has to date received very little attention from social researchers.

To conduct their study, the authors used a **quota sample** (see Chapter 7) drawn from an *online opt-in survey panel*, which is made up of people who have joined a centralized database of respondents willing to participate in surveys, often for small amounts of money or other rewards. The sample included biological fathers, social fathers, and stepfathers in Canada whose children were from 1 to 18 years of age. A number of data quality checks were performed, but given the nature of the sampling process, Shafer and Renick cautioned that their findings may not be applicable to Canadian society as a whole.

The results indicated that by and large, the fathers in the study had fairly high levels of involvement with their children, with scores on various involvement scales clustering at the high end of the spectrum. On the whole, Canadian fathers seem to be good parents, offering responsible and affectionate support for their kids. Paternal depression levels were, on average, comparatively low.

With regard to the association between depressive symptoms and fathers' involvement in childrearing, higher levels of depression were related to lower levels of father-child relationship quality, after accounting for various socio-demographic factors. One of the key findings of the study was an association between high levels of depression and the use of harsh disciplinary techniques, which according to previous research tends to create dysfunctional relationships between fathers and their children and are often accompanied by physical and mental health difficulties on the part of the children. Nonetheless, depressed fathers generally fulfilled the basic responsibilities of providing the necessities of life for their children about as well as the fathers who were not depressed.

to take it too far. Too much rapport can result in the interview going on too long and can also lead respondents to tailor their answers to please the interviewer. Thus, achieving the appropriate rapport between interviewer and respondent is a delicate balancing act.

Topics and issues to include in an introductory statement

In an introductory statement to a prospective interviewee:

- Clearly identify yourself.
- Identify the auspices under which the research is being conducted (for example, a university, a government agency).
- If you are a student doing research for a thesis, make that fact clear.
- Indicate what the research is about in broad terms and why it is important, and give an indication of the kind of information to be collected.
- Indicate how the respondent has been selected (for example, by a random process, by convenience, because of special characteristics).
- Provide reassurance about the confidentiality of any information given by the respondent.
- Explain that participation is voluntary.
- Reassure respondents that they will not be identified or identifiable. This can usually be achieved by pointing out that when the

data are aggregated or analyzed at the group level, individual participants cannot be identified.

- Give the respondent the opportunity to ask questions; be sure to provide a contact telephone number or email address. If in person, simply ask if the respondent has any questions.

These suggestions are also relevant to the covering letter that should accompany online and mailed questionnaires. The latter should also include a stamped, pre-addressed return envelope.

Probing

A highly problematic area for researchers employing a structured interview method is probing respondents who need help with their answers. This may occur if respondents do not understand the question and then struggle to provide an adequate answer, or if they do not provide a complete answer and have to be probed for more information. For example, in the 2013 Alberta Survey, respondents were asked "What is your religion, if any?" If they answered "Christian," the probe available for all interviewers was: "Any particular denomination?"

A potential problem with some probes is that some interviewers may be more inclined to use it than other interviewers, and the probe itself may affect the response given, which could lead to reliability problems. A bigger problem arises if different interviewers use different probes, although proper organization and training should preclude that.

Some general tactics with regard to probes are as follows:

- If further information is required, usually in the context of an open-ended question, standardized probes should be employed, such as "Can you say a little more about that?" or "Are there any other reasons why you think that?"
- If, with a closed question, the respondent replies in a way that does not match one of the pre-designed answers, the interviewer should repeat the fixed-choice alternatives and make it clear that the answer must be chosen from those provided.
- When the interviewer needs to know about something that requires quantification, such as the number of visits made to a doctor in the last four weeks or the number of banks in which the respondent has accounts, but the respondent answers in general terms ("quite often" or "I have several"), the interviewer needs to persist for a more precise answer. With fixed-response surveys, this will usually entail repeating the response options. The interviewer should not suggest an answer on the basis of the respondent's reply since the respondent may not be comfortable with the idea of disagreeing with the interviewer.

In a face-to-face interview, the interviewer may use "show cards" (see Box 5.6) instead of reading out a series of fixed-choice alternatives. Sometimes called "flash cards," they display all the answers from which the respondent is to choose and are handed to the respondent at different points in the interview. There are several situations in which it may be beneficial to use show cards:

- Sometimes there is a very long list of possible answers; for example, respondents may be asked about which social media sites they use most frequently. To read out a list of sites would be tedious and it is probably better to hand the respondent a list from which to choose.
- Some people are not keen to divulge personal details such as their age or income. One way of reducing the impact of such questioning is to present respondents with age or income ranges with a letter or number attached to each (see Box 5.6). A similar approach may be used with other sensitive topics such as sexual practices. However, this procedure will obviously not be appropriate if the research requires *exact* figures pertaining to sensitive topics.
- Sometimes, during the course of an interview, respondents will be presented with a series of statements or questions to which the same possible responses apply—for example: "strongly agree, agree, neutral, disagree, and strongly disagree." It would be time-consuming and off-putting to read out all five possible

answers over and over again, but it might also be expecting too much of respondents to ask them to keep all the possible answers in their heads for the entire batch of questions to which they apply. Providing a show card listing the possible responses is an obvious solution.

Prompting

Prompting occurs when the interviewer suggests a specific answer to a particular interviewee. It is very rare and should be used only as a last resort. An example of unacceptable prompting would be to ask an open-ended question and then suggest a possible answer to a respondent who appears to be struggling to think of an appropriate reply. In all situations, interviewers should do what they can to allow respondents to come up with their own replies. Otherwise, the data gathered will not be authentic—they may also reveal more about the interviewer than the interviewee.

Assessing interviewers

Researchers use various ways to determine whether an interviewer has been trained properly, including:

- checking individual interviewers' response rates;
- recording a sample of interviews;
- examining completed schedules to determine whether any questions are being left out and ensure that they are being completed properly; and
- making call-backs on a sample of respondents (usually about 10 per cent) to make sure they were interviewed and to ask about the interviewer's conduct.

Questionnaires

A questionnaire is essentially a structured interview without an interviewer. Questionnaires can be delivered and retrieved in several different ways. One way is by mail. That is how Anderson et al. (2006) studied family physicians in southwestern Ontario, and how Bell et al. (2009) distributed questionnaires to twins in their research on the heritability of political attitudes. Sometimes respondents will be asked to deposit their completed questionnaires at a specified location: for a study conducted in a business organization, for instance, the location might be their supervisor's office. Researchers may hand out questionnaires to students in a class and collect them there as well, as Smith and McVie (2003) did in their longitudinal cohort study on crime. And, of course, questionnaires can also be filled out online, which was an option for the 2016 Canadian census. Online platforms like Amazon's Mechanical Turk and software such as Survey Monkey are becoming increasingly popular among social researchers.

In many ways the questionnaire and structured interview are very similar. The obvious difference is that with questionnaires, respondents must read the questions themselves and record their own answers. Because there is no interviewer to administer it, the research instrument has to be especially easy to follow and the questions particularly easy to answer. As a result, questionnaires tend to differ from structured interviews in the following ways:

- They have fewer open questions because closed questions are easier to answer.
- They have easy-to-follow designs to minimize the risk that a respondent will inadvertently miss a question or part of one.
- They are shorter to reduce the risk of "respondent fatigue" (it's much easier for a tired respondent facing a long questionnaire to abandon it than it is for a tired interviewee to ask an interviewer to leave).

Advantages of the questionnaire over the structured interview

Cheaper, quicker, more convenient to administer

Interviewing in person is expensive and time-consuming. The cost is obviously less with telephone and email interviews, but even there the questionnaire enjoys cost advantages. A class of 400 students can fill out questionnaires in one class period, and the number of people accessing a questionnaire online is virtually unlimited. Even with a team of telephone interviewers, it takes a long time to conduct personal interviews with such large sample sizes. However, it is important to remember that questionnaires may not be filled out immediately (respondents usually complete them at *their* convenience). In many situations it is necessary to send out follow-up letters and/or duplicate questionnaires to those who fail to complete them in a timely manner.

Absence of interviewer effects

We have already noted that interviewer characteristics may affect respondent answers. Obviously, those sorts of effects are not an issue with questionnaires, since there is no interviewer present. Similarly, with a questionnaire, no one is there to read the questions to the subject in the wrong order, to present them in different ways to different respondents, or to state the items with varying emphases from person to person; the problems those practices can cause are precluded.

Probably of greater importance is the tendency for people to exhibit a social desirability bias when an interviewer is present, giving "politically correct" rather than genuine responses. Research summarized by Tourangeau and Smith (1996) strongly suggests that respondents tend to report more drug use and alcohol consumption and higher numbers of sexual partners and abortions when responding to questionnaires than in structured interviews.

Disadvantages of questionnaires versus structured interviews

Cannot explain the question

It's always important to ensure that the questions asked are clear and unambiguous, but this is especially true with questionnaires, since there is no interviewer to help respondents with questions they cannot understand.

Greater risk of missing data

Incomplete questionnaires are more common. It is also easier for respondents to decide not to answer a question when they are on their own than when they are with an interviewer; questions that respondents find boring or irrelevant are especially likely to be skipped, although some software programs can be set up in such a way that participants cannot skip certain questions. Questionnaire respondents are more likely than interview participants to become tired of answering questions that are not fully salient to them, and to abandon the project entirely. Put positively, when a research issue is important to the respondent, a high response rate is possible. This means that when the questions are highly relevant, a questionnaire may be a good choice, especially because of its much lower cost.

Cannot probe

There is no opportunity to probe respondents to elaborate on an answer. However, this problem mainly applies to open questions, which are not widely used in questionnaire research.

Difficult to ask a lot of questions

Long questionnaires are rarely feasible because of the risk of respondent fatigue. They may also discourage prospective respondents from participating at all.

Difficult to ask other kinds of questions

Long or complex questions should be avoided as far as possible, since some respondents find them difficult to follow.

Questionnaire can be read as a whole

When respondents are able to read the whole questionnaire even before answering the first question, none of the questions asked is truly independent of the others. It also means that the researcher cannot be sure that questions have been answered in the correct order, raising the possibility of question-order effects, although some software packages can minimize this problem.

Not appropriate for some kinds of respondents

Respondents whose literacy is limited or whose facility with the language used is restricted may not be able to answer a questionnaire. The second of these difficulties cannot be entirely overcome with an interview, but the difficulties are likely to be greater with a questionnaire.

One last problem: Who filled out the questionnaire?

With mailed or online questionnaires, the researcher can never be sure whether the questions were answered by the designated respondent or someone else. It is also impossible to prevent other members of a household (for example) from helping the respondent answer the questions.

Online social surveys

As mentioned, the number of surveys being administered online has grown considerably. There are both pros and cons with online surveys as compared to mailed questionnaires (see Box 5.7). There is also a crucial distinction between surveys administered by email (email surveys) and surveys administered via the Web (Web surveys). In the case of the former, the questionnaire is sent via email to a respondent, whereas with a Web survey, the respondent is directed to a website in order to answer it.

Email surveys

With email surveys it is important to distinguish between embedded and attached questionnaires. When the questions are embedded in the body of the email, there may be an introduction to the questionnaire followed by a graphic that partitions the introduction from the questionnaire itself. Respondents may be asked either to indicate their replies using simple notation, such as an "X," or to delete alternatives that do not apply to them. If a question is open, they are asked to type in an answer. When finished, they simply hit the reply button to return the completed questionnaire.

An attached questionnaire arrives as an attachment to an email that introduces it. As with the embedded questionnaire, respondents must select and/or type their answers. To return the questionnaire, it must be attached to a reply email.

The chief advantage of the embedded questionnaire is that it requires less computer expertise. Knowing how to read and then return an attachment requires a certain facility with online communication that is still not universally possessed. Also, the recipients' operating systems or software may not be able to handle attachments, or respondents may refuse to open them because of concerns about viruses. On the other hand, since most email software allows only limited formatting, the appearance of embedded questionnaires tends to be rather dull and featureless, although this situation is rapidly changing. Furthermore, it is slightly easier for respondents to type answers into an attachment that uses well-known software such as Microsoft Word because if the questionnaire is embedded in an email the alignment of questions and answers may be lost.

Web surveys

Web surveys invite prospective respondents to visit a website where the questionnaire can be found and completed online. The Web survey has an important advantage over the email survey in that it can use a much wider variety of embellishments, such as "radio buttons" and pull-down menus of possible answers. With open questions, the respondent is invited to type directly into a boxed area.

However, the advantages of the Web survey go beyond appearance and format. As with interview software, questionnaires can be designed so that when there is a filter question, it skips automatically to the next appropriate question. The questionnaire can also be programmed either to show only one question at a time or to allow the respondent to scroll down and look at all the questions in advance. If a question is missed, the software may provide a prompt telling the respondent that it was not answered and that a response is needed. Finally, respondents' answers can be automatically programmed to download into a database, eliminating the daunting task of coding a large number of questionnaires. Software packages designed to produce questionnaires with all the features just described are now widely available.

Web surveys are also advantageous in that they may give researchers access to unique populations, such as people who share a particular interest. Web surveys are particularly useful for reaching

Box 5.7 | Advantages and disadvantages of online surveys compared to mailed questionnaires

This box summarizes the main advantages and disadvantages of online surveys, both email and Web varieties, compared to mailed questionnaires. Note that all three share one disadvantage relative to personal and telephone interviews: namely, that the researcher can never be certain of who is actually answering the questions.

Advantages

- *Low cost.* Even though mailed questionnaires are inexpensive to administer, online surveys cost even less.
- *Faster response and processing.* Online surveys can be returned considerably faster than mailed questionnaires. Researchers also appreciate the automatic skipping of irrelevant questions that is possible when they use filter questions, as well as the opportunity for immediate downloading of replies into a database.
- *Fewer unanswered questions.* There is evidence that online questionnaires are completed with fewer unanswered questions than mailed questionnaires.
- *Better response to open questions.* Open questions are more likely to be answered online, and online replies are usually more detailed.

Disadvantages

- *Low response rate.* Typically, response rates for online surveys are lower than those for comparable mailed questionnaires.
- *Restricted to online populations.* This restriction should ease over time, but since the online population still differs in significant ways from the non-online population, it remains a difficulty.
- *Confidentiality and anonymity issues.* It is standard practice for survey researchers to indicate that replies will be kept anonymous. However, with email surveys the addresses of the respondents are known, which may make it difficult for people to believe that their identity really will be protected.
- *Multiple replies.* With Web surveys, there is a risk that some people may complete the questionnaire more than once, although software is available that can reduce that possibility. There is much less risk of this with email surveys.

cnythzl/iStockphoto

Have you ever participated in an online survey, either through email or via the Web? If so, were you concerned about a possible lack of anonymity? Did this affect how you answered the questions?

Sources: Adapted from Cobanoglu, Ward, & Moreo (2001); Kent & Lee (1999); Schaeffer & Dillman (1998); Sheehan & Hoy (1999); Sinclair, O'Toole, Malawaraarachchi, & Leder (2012); Tse (1998).

stigmatized populations who are difficult to reach offline, such as people with eating disorders or extreme political views (Wright, 2005).

Potential respondents need to be directed to the website containing the questionnaire. One way to do this is to email them, as Andrews, Smith, Henzi, & Demps (2007) did in their study of academic integrity (i.e., cheating and plagiarism) in Canadian and American dental schools. It may be most efficient to send the email invitation to someone who can forward it to large numbers of potential participants. In the Andrews et al. study the invitation was sent to academic deans who then forwarded it to faculty members and students. For surveys in which participation must be restricted, it may be necessary to set up a password system to filter out people for whom the questionnaire is not appropriate.

Designing the questionnaire

No matter the medium of delivery, there are important considerations that must go into a questionnaire's visual design. These are discussed below.

Clear presentation

Make sure that the layout is easy on the eye and that it facilitates answering all the questions applicable to the respondent. Using a variety of styles (different fonts and print sizes, boldface, italics, capitals, etc.) can enhance the questionnaire's appearance *so long as they are used consistently.* Thus, all general instructions should appear in one style, all headings in a second, all specific instructions (e.g., "Go to question 7") in a third, and so on. Mixing print styles or uses (e.g., using a particular style for both general instructions and specific questions) may confuse respondents.

Vertical or horizontal closed answers?

Bearing in mind that most questions in a questionnaire are likely to be closed, you will need to decide whether to arrange the fixed answers vertically or horizontally. Usually, a vertical arrangement is used unless respondents are asked to choose their answer from a row of numbers or abbreviations, as is often done with Likert scales. Many writers prefer a vertical format because it reduces the risk of confusion. With a horizontal format there is a significant risk, especially if the respondent is in a hurry, that the required tick or circle will be put in the wrong place (for an example, see Box 5.8). Also, a vertical format more clearly distinguishes questions from answers. A further advantage of the vertical format is that it may facilitate the manual recording of answers, especially when pre-codes appear on the questionnaire.

Clear instructions about how to respond

On questionnaires in which the selection of responses is not automated, always be clear about how respondents should indicate their replies to closed questions. Are they supposed to place a tick by the appropriate answer, or are they to underline it? Should they circle it? Is it acceptable to choose more than one answer? If not, this should be indicated in the instructions, for example:

> *(Please choose the ONE answer that best represents your views by placing a tick in the appropriate box.)*

If this is not made clear and some respondents choose more than one answer, their replies cannot be counted and will have to be treated as if they were missing. If choosing more than one category is acceptable, this too must be made clear, for example:

> *(Please choose ALL answers that represent your views by placing a tick in the appropriate boxes. You may tick more than one box for each question—choose as many as apply to you.)*

It is a common error for such instructions to be omitted and for respondents to be unsure about how to reply.

Box 5.8 | Should a closed question have a vertical or a horizontal format?

The following question is taken from the 2015 Canadian Election Study—Mailback Survey:

Which party do you feel closest to?

Conservative Party	1
Liberal Party	2
NDP	3
Bloc Québécois	4
Green Party	5
Other (*specify*) ________	6

And this is the same question in a horizontal format:

Which party do you feel closest to?

Conservative 1 Liberal 2
NDP 3 Bloc Québécois 4
Green Party 5
Other (*specify*) ________6

Source: Fournier, Cutler, Soroka, & Stolle, D. (2015), accessed 8 August 2020.

Keep question and answers together

This simple rule may seem obvious, but it is often transgressed: a question, or the question and the answers that accompany it, should not be split between two separate pages. A common error is for a question to appear at the bottom of a page and the responses on the next page. The danger here is that the respondent will either (a) fail to answer the question or (b) pay insufficient attention to the question and give a superficial answer (this problem is especially likely when a series of questions with a common answer format is being used, as with a Likert scale).

Researcher-driven diaries as a form of questionnaire

When the researcher is interested in precise accounts of behaviour, what Elliott (1997) called the *researcher-driven diary* can be used as a kind of questionnaire. The researcher asks participants to record their perceptions, feelings, or actions with regard to certain experiences shortly after they occur. Laurenceau and Bolger (2005) used the diary method to study marital and family processes. Hessler et al. (2003) used researcher-driven diaries in an email study of adolescent risk behaviour that produced rich narratives of the participants' everyday lives. Sometimes this method is supplemented by a personal interview in which the researcher will follow up on points raised in the diary: for example, by asking the diarist what he or she meant by certain remarks. Diary data may also be used in conjunction with information derived from surveys, as in Robinson and Lee's (2014) examination of the effect of new information technologies on people's social lives and mass media use.

Corti (1993) distinguished between "structured diaries" and "free-text diaries." Either can be employed by quantitative as well as qualitative researchers. Structured diaries, such as those used by O'Sullivan, Udell, & Patel (2006) to examine sexual practices among college students, have the general appearance of a questionnaire with largely closed questions. At the end of each day the students in the study indicated whether they had engaged in sexual activity that day, and if they had, they used a checklist to mark which sexual activity had been performed, whether they used a condom, how safe from HIV infection they felt during the sexual encounter, and so on.

Sullivan's (1996) research on the domestic division of labour provides another illustration of a structured diary. The kind of diary Sullivan used is often described as a "time-use" diary because it is designed for recording, more or less at the time of the actual behaviour, how long people engage in activities such as food preparation, child care, or eating. Sullivan also asked couples to record on a five-point scale the amount of enjoyment they derived from those kinds of activities.

Recording events as they happen is often considered a more accurate approach than recording them at the end of the day, largely because there is less risk of forgetting. However, it is more intrusive than end-of-day reporting or answering a questionnaire because it is a constant interruption and may even change people's behaviour. For example, one can become preoccupied with the behaviours under study and thus engage in them in a more thoughtful or premeditated way.

Sometimes diaries can be constructed as part of a larger structured interview. This was the approach taken in the 2015 Time Use study, which was part of the General Social Survey conducted for Statistics Canada. A 24-hour diary was produced by asking people what they were doing on a certain day, starting at 4:00 a.m. The first question was: "Last [day of the week] at [4:00 a.m.], what were you doing?" (Most people say "sleeping," and are later asked how much time they spent sleeping, and what time they went to sleep.) Sometimes questions such as "Where were you?" or "Who was with you?" are asked as well.

An example of a free-text diary is provided in Crook and Light's (2002) study in which university students were asked to keep a diary for a week, divided into 15-minute intervals, of the different kinds of study and learning activity in which they engaged, where the activity took place, and the study resources used (for example, the library). The various activities were grouped into three types: classes, private study, and social study (that is, study with a peer). They were able to show the very different amounts and patterns of study typically undertaken during a day.

Using free-text recording of behaviour carries the same kinds of coding problems as those associated with open-ended survey questions—namely, the time-consuming nature of the exercise and the risk of introducing error while coding answers. However, the free-text approach is less likely to be problematic when, as in the case of Crook and Light's (2002) research, diarists are given instructions about what is required and the behaviours of interest are specific and concrete. It would be much more difficult to code free-text entries relating to more general behaviours such as the domestic activities studied by Sullivan (1996).

Corti (1993) recommended that people doing research involving diaries should:

- provide explicit instructions for diarists;
- be clear about the time periods in which the behaviour of interest is to be assessed (for example, daytime, certain 24-hour periods, particular weeks), and indicate that in the diary template;
- supply a model of a completed section of a diary; and
- provide brief checklists of "items, events, or behaviour" to jog the memory.

Advantages and disadvantages of the diary as a method of data collection

The studies illustrating the use of diaries discussed above suggest potential advantages:

- When fairly precise estimates regarding frequency and/or amount of time spent in different forms of behaviour are required, the diary may provide more valid and reliable data than questionnaires.
- When information about the sequencing of different types of behaviour is required, it is likely to perform better than questionnaires or interviews.
- A diary is useful for collecting data on behaviour that is personally sensitive, such as sexual activity.

On the other hand, the diary method may present the following problems:

- Diaries tend to be more expensive than personal interviews because of costs related to recruiting diarists and ensuring that they are using their diaries properly.
- There is a risk of attrition as diarists tire of the task, which raises reliability issues.
- Failure to record details quickly enough can result in errors or omissions.

However, diary researchers such as Sullivan argue that the information collected through diaries is more accurate than that collected through interviews or questionnaires on the same topic.

Secondary analysis of survey data

Survey research, including questionnaires, can be extremely time-consuming and expensive to conduct, and is usually well beyond the means of most students. This is where *secondary analysis* comes in. Large amounts of quantitative data already exist, collected by individual social scientists and by organizations such as government departments and university-affiliated research centres (see Box 5.9). The latter include the Institute for Social Research at York University, and the Institute of Urban Studies at the University of Winnipeg. Sources such as these make raw statistical data available on topics such as income, fertility, crime, and unemployment, as well as a host of other social and political issues. Using secondary data rather than collecting your own has the additional advantage of sparing an already over-surveyed public yet another round of questions. For this reason, secondary analysis should be considered not just by students but by all social researchers. Indeed, some granting agencies require applicants proposing to collect new data to demonstrate that relevant data are not already available in an archive.

Box 5.9 | Existing data sets

Many important studies have been conducted through secondary analysis of existing data. Among the high-quality data sets used by researchers in Canada are the following:

1. The National Longitudinal Survey of Children and Youth, which contains data on young people up to age 25; used by Brannigan, Gemmell, Pevalin, & Wade (2002), Kerr (2004), Beran, Hughes, & Lupart (2008), Ames, Rawana, Gentile, & Morgan (2015), and Comeau, Duncan, Georgiades, Wang, & Boyle (2020).
2. The National Population Health Survey, begun in 1994–5 with data gathered every two years until 2011; it examines health and health care in Canada; used by Légaré, Décarie, & Bélanger (2014) and Friedenreich et al. (2019).
3. National Graduates Surveys, which ask graduates about their employment two years after finishing their post-secondary education; used by Walters (2004) and Marin & Hayes (2017).
4. The Longitudinal Immigration Database (IMDB) developed by Citizenship and Immigration Canada and Statistics Canada to provide data for the study of immigrants' long-term earnings; used by Li (2003) and Mata & Pendakur (2017).
5. The Canadian Election Studies, which provide data for all federal elections from 1965 to the present; they are available through the Inter-University Consortium for Political and Social Research; scores of publications have been produced using these surveys, for example, Gidengil, Everitt, Blais, Fournier, & Nevitte (2006), Goodyear-Grant & Croskill (2011), Kevins & Soroka (2018), & Anderson and McGregor (2020).

These are only a few of the available data sets.

Advantages of secondary analysis

There are several reasons for considering secondary analysis a serious alternative to collecting new data. Its advantages have been enumerated by Dale, Arber, & Proctor (1988):

- *Cost and time.* As we noted above, secondary analysis often offers good-quality data for a tiny fraction of the cost involved in collecting new data.
- *High-quality data.* Most of the data sets employed for secondary analysis are of extremely high quality. First, the sampling procedures have often been rigorous, in many cases producing samples that are as close to **representative** as is reasonably possible. Although those responsible for these studies face the same problems of **non-response** as anyone else, well-established procedures are usually in place for following up with non-respondents and thus keeping this problem to a minimum. Second, the samples are frequently national in scope, or at least cover a wide variety of regions, which is a highly desirable—and costly—feature. Third, many data sets have been generated by highly experienced researchers and, in the case of some of the large data sets, gathered by social research organizations with strong control procedures to check on data quality.
- *Opportunity for longitudinal analysis.* Another valuable feature of secondary analysis is that it can provide an opportunity for **longitudinal research**. Sometimes, as with the General Social Survey (GSS; see Box 5.10), a panel format (in which the same participants are

Box 5.10 | General Social Survey features

Introduction

In 1985, Statistics Canada introduced the General Social Survey (GSS), which covers major topics such as the health of Canadians and their levels of social support. The GSS has two principal objectives: first, to gather data regularly on Canadian social trends; and second, to provide information on specific policy issues of current interest. The GSS is a continuing research project that operates on an annual cycle. Each annual survey classifies participants by age, sex, education, and income. Core content areas, however, cannot be treated adequately every year. Therefore, they are usually covered every five years. The content by cycle is as follows:

Cycle	Year	Topics
1	1985	Health, Social Support
2	1986	Time Use, Social Mobility, Language
3	1988	Personal Risk, Victim Services
4	1989	Education and Work
5	1990	Family and Friends
6	1991	Health (Various Topics)
7	1992	Time Use, Culture, Sport and Unpaid Activities
8	1993	Personal Risk, Alcohol and Drug Use
9	1994	Education, Work, Transition into Retirement
10	1995	Family Effects of Tobacco Smoke
11	1996	Social Support, Tobacco Use
12	1998	Time Use
13	1999	Victimization, Spousal Violence, Senior Abuse, and Public Perceptions of Alternatives to Imprisonment
14	2000	Access to and Use of Information Communication Technology
15	2001	Family History
16	2002	Social Support and Aging
17	2003	Social Contact with Family, Friends, and Neighbours; Involvement in Formal Organizations; Political Activities and Volunteer Work; Values and Attitudes; Trust in Public Institutions
18	2004	Criminal Victimization
19	2005	Replication of Time-Use Study

examined at different times) is used to chart trends over time. Similarly, because certain interview questions are recycled and asked of different samples each year, shifting opinions or changes in behaviour can be identified.

- *Subgroup analysis.* When samples are large (as in the GSS) there is an opportunity to study subgroups. A sample of 100 people, for example, might include only three people over age 85. No quantitative researcher wants to talk

Cycle	Year	Topics
20	2006	Family Life in Canada
21	2007	Life transitions experienced by Canadians over the age of 45, such as those relating to employment, family composition, social networks and housing
22	2008	Social Networks, Social and Civic Participation
23	2009	Victimization
24	2010	Time-Stress and Well-Being
25	2011	Family
26	2012	Caregiving and Care Receiving
27	2013	Giving, Volunteering and Participating; Social Identity
28	2014	Canadians' Safety (Victimization)
29	2015–16	Time Use
30	2016	Canadians at Work and Home
31	2017	Family
32	2018	Caregiving and Care Receiving
33	2018	Giving, Volunteering and Participating
34	2019	Canadians' Safety (Victimization)
35	2020	Social Identity

Collection Methods

Telephone interviewing is the major form of data collection for three reasons: low cost, ease of monitoring interviewers, and data quality. The sample size for each cycle of the GSS is now approximately 25,000 households, generally one person per household.

Availability

GSS findings form the basis of a series of publications that present national and regional summary data, primarily in the form of tables and charts, along with initial analyses and findings. Public-use microdata files, together with supporting documentation, are available for secondary analyses. These files contain individual records, screened to ensure confidentiality.

Source: Statistics Canada (2019), accessed 8 August 2020.

about those three seniors, as in "only 33 per cent of the aged are in good health": that amounts to one person. With a national sample of 2000, the numbers are increased twenty-fold to 60. Even though this number is still small, it will allow a more meaningful estimate of seniors' health. It is impossible to reach such a number in a small study unless the group in question is the specific focus of the research.

- *Opportunity for cross-cultural (international) analysis.* It's easy to forget that many findings may not apply to countries other than the ones in which the research was conducted. Cross-cultural research can address that issue. A study of religiosity by Kelley and De Graaf (1997) is an example. The authors described the process as follows:

> Data are from the 1991 "Religion" module of the International Social Survey Programme (ISSP) … a module containing exactly the same questions, answer categories, and sequencing for all countries surveyed. … The samples are all large, representative national samples of adults. The most common procedure is to hold face-to-face interviews … followed by a leave-behind self-completion questionnaire containing the ISSP module … (1997, p. 642)

Kelley and De Graaf's results were based on a secondary analysis of data from 15 nations. Opportunities for such cross-cultural analysis appear to be increasing. For example, common core questions may be used in national surveys conducted in several countries. Both the US and Britain have the equivalent of our GSS. This allowed Grabb and Curtis (2004) to create a body of literature comparing the US and Canada, revealing cross-national regional differences where national differences were widely expected.

- *More time for data analysis.* Precisely because data collection is time-consuming, the analysis of the data may be rushed. It might seem that data collection would be the difficult phase and the analysis relatively straightforward, but this is not always the case. Working out what to make of the data requires considerable thought and, often, willingness to learn unfamiliar statistical techniques. Freedom from the task of collecting fresh data means that data analysis can be better planned and executed.
- *Reanalysis can offer new interpretations.* It's easy to think that once a set of data has been analyzed, the data have in some sense been used up. In fact, data can be analyzed in so many different ways that there is almost always additional insight to be gained from them. For example, a secondary analyst may look at relationships between variables that have not been previously considered, prompting a reconsideration of the data's relevance (see Box 5.11). Also, new methods of quantitative data analysis, with the potential of allowing different interpretations of the data, are continuously emerging. As

Box 5.11 | Secondary analysis and new research questions

Secondary analysis can involve topics that in all likelihood were not envisaged by those responsible for the data collection. In a secondary analysis of data on dietary choices, attitudes, and practices, Beardsworth, Keil, Goode, Haslam, & Lancashire (2002) added gender as a focus that had not been examined in previous analyses. The study showed that women were more likely than men to adopt a "virtuous" pattern of eating, one in keeping with Western ethical and nutritional principles. The article also showed that adherence to these principles had a negative side in that it may be related to feelings of guilt, irregular eating patterns, and concerns about body shape. Similarly, Bell and Kandler (2017) did a secondary analysis of American twin data that showed that political orientations, party identification, and interest in politics could not be fully explained by sociological factors, and that those political characteristics were still highly heritable after the sociological variables were taken into account. Both of these studies provide examples of profitable extensions of prior research using existing data.

awareness of such techniques spreads, and their potential relevance is recognized, researchers can apply them to existing data sets.

- *It fulfills the wider obligations of the social researcher.* For all types of social research, research participants give up some of their time, usually for no reward. It's not unreasonable that the public should expect the data they provide to be mined to the fullest. Making data available for secondary analysis enhances the chances that they will be put to maximal use.

Limitations of secondary analysis

The foregoing list of benefits sounds almost too good to be true. But there are some drawbacks to analyzing data gathered by others:

- *Lack of familiarity with the data.* With data collected by others, a period of familiarization is necessary to come to grips with a wide array of variables, the ways in which they were coded, and various aspects of their organization. With large data sets this period can be quite prolonged.
- *Complexity of the data.* Some of the best-known data sets employed for secondary analysis, such as the GSS, are very large both in the numbers of cases and in the numbers of variables they contain. Sometimes the sheer volume of data can present problems, and here too a period of acclimatization may be required. Also, some of the most prominent data sets employed for secondary analysis are *hierarchical*, meaning that the data are collected and presented at the level both of the household and of the individual (and sometimes at other levels as well). Different data may apply to each level. Thus, at the household level, data on variables such as the number of cars may be included, while at the individual level, data on income and occupation are found. The secondary analyst must decide which level of analysis to use; if the decision is to analyze individual-level data, the individual-level data must then be extracted from the data set.
- *The **ecological fallacy**.* This can be a problem if data gathered by region or neighbourhood (such as census data) are used to make statements about *individuals*. The term "ecological fallacy" comes from the common practice of acquiring data for a geographical area, such as the crime rate in a particular neighbourhood. Coleman and Moynihan (1996) provided an example of this fallacy as it relates to the relationship between ethnicity and crime. They observed that findings showing a higher incidence of crime in neighbourhoods with high concentrations of ethnic minorities had been used to imply that members of such minority groups were more likely than others to commit crimes. However, *individual* data are needed to examine this hypothesis, which may or may not be true. For example, it may not be the members of the minority groups who are responsible for the high levels of offending, but their non-minority neighbours. Similarly, people could be coming from adjoining neighbourhoods to commit crimes in a community they perceive as more vulnerable than their own. Group data cannot evaluate these possibilities. To avoid the ecological fallacy, the unit of analysis (individual, group, neighbourhood, etc.) of the data must be the same as the unit of analysis of the statement or hypothesis. For example, to test the hypothesis that people in group X are more likely to commit crimes than people not in group X, you would need data on *individuals*, not neighbourhoods or regions.
- *No control over data quality.* The point has been made on several occasions that secondary analysis offers researchers the opportunity to examine data of far higher quality than they could collect themselves. However, this point applies mainly to reputable data sets such as the GSS and others. With lesser-known data sets, more caution may be necessary with regard to data quality, although certain fundamental checks on quality are usually undertaken by the archives in which the data are deposited.

- *Absence of key variables.* Because secondary analysis entails the analysis of data collected by others for their own purposes, one or more of the secondary analysts' key variables may not be present, or may be measured differently in different years. Walters (2004) had this problem in a study of incomes earned by graduates of various kinds of post-secondary programs; therefore, he had to modify the original data. Similarly, an analyst might want to see if a known relationship between two variables holds even when other variables are taken into account, but might find that those other variables are not part of the data set. Considering more than one independent variable at a time is a form of *multivariate analysis*, a topic we will touch on in Chapter 8.

The need for survey data as a check and counterpoint to official statistics

Official government statistics are important sources of data for secondary analysis. Some of these sources, such as the census, are based on interviews and questionnaires conducted by state-run organizations. Others, such as the police data sometimes used to calculate the crime rate, are better understood as information gathered by state agencies to record what they have done in the process of conducting their duties. Here we explore potential deficiencies in the latter and how survey data may sometimes provide a needed correction to them.

To be sure, official statistics offer the social researcher certain advantages:

- The data are often based on whole populations rather than samples, making it possible to obtain a complete picture of the population in question.
- There is a greater prospect of analyzing the data both longitudinally and cross-culturally. Because the data are compiled over many years, it's possible to chart trends over time and perhaps to relate them to broader social changes. As well, official statistics from different nations can be compared for a specific area of activity. Durkheim's (1897/1952) famous study of suicide, for example, was the result of a comparative analysis of official statistics from several countries.

However, as mentioned in the previous chapter (see Box 4.4), some forms of official statistics can be very misleading if they record only those individuals who are processed by the agencies responsible for compiling the statistics, such as the police. Crime rates have been a particular focus of attention and concern among critics of the use of official statistics, but other official statistics suffer from the same problem. For example, official unemployment statistics may misrepresent the "real" level of unemployment. People who have given up trying to find work are often missed in the statistics, while those who work in the "underground or informal economy" (and thus are not actually unemployed) may be included in the unemployment statistics. In addition, the definition of "unemployment" used by those who compile official statistics may not be exactly the same as the ones used by social researchers.

Measurement problems may also arise if policies regarding the phenomenon to be counted vary over time. For example, if a local government decides to devote more police resources to monitoring activities such as drug use, the sex trade, or driving while intoxicated, official estimates of the incidence of those behaviours will almost certainly increase. Moreover, during such crackdowns police officers may be less likely than usual to let perpetrators off with a warning. Zero-tolerance programs have the same result. This illustrates how variations over time in official crime statistics may not be the result of variations in the frequencies of the activities tracked, but may simply reflect changes in the willingness to expend resources on surveillance or to proceed with prosecutions.

Problems with official statistics may also stem from factors related to "race," ethnicity, and class. For example, there may be variations in the likelihood that members of the public will report a crime when the perpetrator is a member of a particular ethnic group (Are Indigenous people more likely than others to be noticed and reported?), and for a variety of reasons police may be less inclined to investigate white-collar crime than street crime.

These deficiencies in official statistics may be offset by using other sources of data when performing secondary analysis, most notably those derived from interviews and questionnaires that are based on representative samples. A good example of this is the utilization of victimization surveys (such as the aforementioned GSS victimization studies) in criminology, which may be used in conjunction with official police statistics. Both types of data have their strengths and weaknesses, so a judicious use of both may be required to understand the full extent and consequences of criminal activity. Boivin and Leclerc (2016), for instance, point out that survey research indicates that only a small fraction of domestic violence cases is reported to the police, and seek to explain why by analyzing incident reports compiled by Quebec police officers.

Research in the News

The Gig Economy in Canada

Three Canadian sociologists—Paul Glavin, Alex Bierman, and Scott Schieman—have done research into the "gig economy" in Canada. Their investigation, done in conjunction with the 2019 Canadian Quality of Work and Economic Life Study, examines employment in jobs that are carried out on a per-task basis, such as those offered by companies like Uber and Skip the Dishes, and which are found in various freelance occupations.

In an op-ed piece in the newspaper *The Province* (Glavin, Bierman, & Schieman, 2019), the authors explain that life in the gig economy is often characterized by feelings of loneliness and powerlessness. They base their findings on online interviews conducted with a representative sample of the Canadian employed population. Gig workers, who comprise about one-fifth of the Canadian workforce, were roughly twice as likely to show signs of loneliness (such as expressing a lack of companionship, feeling left out, or feeling isolated from other people) compared to workers in other sectors. They also reported higher levels of anxiety and depression. Similarly, gig workers were 50 per cent more likely to experience feelings of helplessness and about 40 per cent more likely to report low levels of control over their lives. The authors conclude that "Canadians will soon need to grapple with the question of whether the ease and flexibility provided by the gig economy is worth these [psychological] costs."

Key Points

Survey research is one of the most widely used data-gathering techniques in the social sciences. Surveys include interviews, in which a researcher engages in a verbal discussion with the participant, and questionnaires, which respondents read and fill out on their own. This kind of research permits standardization in the asking of questions and the categorization of answers.

- While open questions undoubtedly have advantages in survey research, closed ones are typically preferable. They facilitate the asking of the questions, the recording of answers, and coding. This point applies especially to questionnaires.
- Open questions of the kind used in qualitative interviewing can play a useful role in formulating fixed-choice answers.
- Learning the rules of question asking will help you avoid some serious problems.

- Question order is very important and some general rules should be followed.
- Response sets are a potential problem in both structured interviews and questionnaires, but steps can be taken to lessen their impact.
- Always put yourself in the position of the respondent when devising questions.
- Ensure that the survey questions generate data appropriate to the research questions.
- A pilot study can identify problems in question formulation.
- Structured interviews can be administered in person, over the phone, or online.
- It is important for interviewers to keep to the wording and order of questions. Training in the asking of questions, the recording of answers, and how to establish rapport with respondents is essential.
- Questionnaires reduce some of the problems encountered in structured interviews, but they also have weaknesses.
- Online surveys take two major forms: Web surveys and email surveys.
- The researcher-driven diary is an alternative to using questionnaires and interviews, especially when the research questions are concerned with specific behaviours rather than attitudes or opinions.
- The visual presentation of closed questions and their general layout are important considerations in designing questionnaires.
- Secondary analyses allow researchers to conduct their inquiries without having to collect new data.
- Very often, secondary analysis involves high-quality data sets taken from large, representative samples.
- Secondary analysis presents a few disadvantages, such as the absence of theoretically important variables.
- Official statistics, especially those relating to crime, can be problematic for secondary analysis.
- The problems associated with official statistics may be offset by using survey data taken from representative samples.

Questions for Review (R) and Creative Application (A)

Open or closed questions?

R1 Why are closed questions generally preferred to open ones in survey research?

A1 Compose a closed question to measure people's attitudes toward recycling, then list possible shortcomings of the question.

Types of question

R2 What are the main types of question likely to be used in a structured interview or questionnaire?

A2 Compose a closed question to measure attitudes toward gun control, using a seven-point Likert scale.

Question order

R3 Explain why question order may significantly affect answers.

A3 Construct three survey questions to illustrate how question order may significantly affect answers. Place them in two different orders, and explain how placing them in a different order may make a difference in how people respond to them.

Response sets

R4 What are response sets and why is it important to know about them?

A4 Name and define three kinds of response set, providing an original example of each one.

Vignette questions

R5 In what circumstances are vignette questions especially appropriate?

A5 Make up a set of vignette questions to examine an addiction of your choice.

Pre-testing questions

R6 Why is it important to pre-test questions?

A6 Compose an open question that could be used in a pilot study to generate closed questions on the topic of what people find attractive in a romantic partner.

Using existing questions

R7 Why should researchers consider using questions devised by others?

A7 Assume you are doing a study on the frequency of tobacco smoking among university students, and that there are already widely used questions on this topic that have been administered to the general public. Would it be necessary to devise your own questions, or could you rely on the existing ones? Explain.

Interviews

R8 Why might a survey researcher prefer a structured interview to an unstructured one?

A8 In an interview study examining attitudes toward transgender people, would it be best to use only transgender interviewers, only non-transgender interviewers, or both? Explain.

Interview contexts

R9 In what circumstances is it preferable to conduct structured interviews with more than one interviewer?

A9 Assume you have unlimited time and money to do an interview study on gender differences in career aspirations. Would it be better to do in-person interviews or telephone interviews? Explain.

Questionnaires

R10 What advantages do questionnaires have over structured interviews? What disadvantages do they have compared to structured interviews?

A10 Assume your professor just asked you to fill out a questionnaire in class that will be used in a published research paper. What ethical issues are involved in this situation?

Online social surveys

R11 What advantages do online surveys have over traditional research methods for collecting data? What disadvantages do they have compared to traditional research methods?

A11 If you were asked to participate in an online survey concerning cheating on university exams, would you agree to do it? Explain why or why not, then explain how researchers could increase the response rate for the study.

The diary as a form of questionnaire

R12 In what circumstances is it preferable to use a diary approach rather than a conventional questionnaire?

A12 Construct five items that would be appropriate for a structured research diary designed to record people's food intake over a 24-hour period.

Other researchers' data

R13 What is secondary analysis? What are its advantages and disadvantages?

A13 Assume that you will be conducting a secondary analysis of survey data on the topic of gender differences in attitudes toward same-sex marriage. List three variables that may not be part of an existing data set on this topic, and explain why you think they may not be included in an existing data set.

Official statistics

R14 What are the drawbacks to using official police statistics to estimate crime rates?

A14 You are planning to do research on the personal and social factors that contribute to intimate partner violence. What problems would arise if you relied entirely on official police statistics for your data? Explain.

Interactive Classroom Activities

1. Students work in pairs for 15 minutes to design an opening statement to be given to prospective participants in a study on shoplifting committed by university students. All relevant details are to be included—e.g., how the potential respondents were selected, how confidentiality will be maintained, and so on. Students are then asked to write their statements on the board/screen, with the rest of the class commenting on the strengths and weaknesses of the statements.
2. Divide the class into an even number of small groups. Each group is to compose a 10-item structured interview schedule designed to address the following research question: "Does the recreational use of marijuana have an impact on university students' grades?" Each group is then paired with another group. A person in Group A verbally administers the survey to a person in Group B, and then another person in Group A administers it to a different person in Group B, and so on, until several people have been interviewed. After each person is interviewed, he or she comments on the experience—e.g., on whether the questions were clear, whether they felt embarrassed, whether the fixed responses adequately covered what came to their mind when they were asked the questions, and so on. The exercise is then repeated, with people in Group B interviewing people in Group A. Once all class groups are finished, the instructor leads an open discussion

that starts with the question "What did you learn from this exercise?"

3. The instructor reads each question, one at a time, from Box 5.5. After each question is read, the class is asked to point out its flaws. All members of the class are then given two minutes to come up with a revised version of the question. Individual students are called on to produce their revised versions, which are written on the board/screen. The class is then asked to comment on whether the revised versions solve all the problems contained in the original question, or if further revision would be appropriate.
4. The class is divided up into small groups. Each group is asked to come up with 10 survey questions designed to measure attitudes toward a controversial topic (e.g., assisted suicide, the removal of statues commemorating historical figures, animal rights, etc.) and to gather basic socio-demographic data. Once that has been done, each group puts its questions up on the board/screen, and the rest of the class provides a critique. Once all groups have had their turn, the groups get together again and revise their questions to address the concerns raised by their classmates. Each group presents its questions to the class a second time, with commentary on how the previous weaknesses have been corrected. The class again offers a critique to each group.

Relevant Websites

This ***Canadian Election Study*** site provides access to structured interviews and questionnaires and the numerical data derived from them for the Canadian elections of 2011, 2015, and 2019.

http://ces-eec.arts.ubc.ca/

This YouTube video explains how to make an online survey using Google Docs.

www.youtube.com/watch?v=DEhD0m1fhAQ

In the ***General Social Survey on Time Use, 2015 Questionnaire***, you can find an example of a research diary that forms part of a larger structured interview.

https://www23.statcan.gc.ca/imdb/p3Instr.pl?Function=assembleInstr&lang=en&Item_Id=217656#qb218258

The ***General Social Survey—Canadians' Safety, 2019***, contains the questionnaires used by Statistics Canada to assess perceptions of our criminal justice system and experiences of criminal victimization in Canada.

https://www23.statcan.gc.ca/imdb/p2SV.pl?Function=getSurvey&SDDS=4504

The ***General Social Survey—Social Identity, 2020***, provides the questionnaires used by Statistics Canada to examine how Canadians identify with their social and cultural environments.

https://www23.statcan.gc.ca/imdb/p2SV.pl?Function=getSurvey&SDDS=5024

The ***Inter-University Consortium for Political and Social Research*** is an international association of about 700 academic institutions and research organizations that "provides leadership and training in data access, curation, and methods of analysis for the social science research community." Click on "Find Data" to access over 500,000 digital files for examples of questions used in a wide variety of social research projects.

www.icpsr.umich.edu/icpsrweb/ICPSR

The ***UK Data Service*** provides a searchable databank of questions used on social surveys in the UK.

http://ukdataservice.ac.uk

(Websites accessed 4 September 2021.)

OXFORD learning link

More resources are available on Oxford Learning Link. Visit **https://learninglink.oup.com/** for:

- Student self-quiz
- Flash cards
- Audio clips
- Videos
- Activities

6 Structured Observation

Chapter Overview

Structured observation is a relatively underused method in social research. It entails the direct observation of behaviour, which is analyzed using categories that are devised before the observation begins. This chapter explores:

- the limitations of **survey research** for the study of behaviour;
- different forms of observation in social research;
- the potential of structured observation to contribute to our understanding of social behaviour;
- how to devise an **observation schedule**;
- different strategies for conducting structured observation;
- issues of **reliability** and **validity** in structured observation;
- field studies, in which a researcher intervenes in actual social life and records what happens as a consequence of the intervention;
- ethical issues in the above; and
- some criticisms of structured observation.

Key Learning Outcomes

Here is a list of goals you should try to achieve as you read and think about the material in this chapter. After completing this chapter, you should be able to:

1. Identify some problems with survey research that structured observation may rectify.
2. Describe the basic principles of structured observation.

▲ TommL/iStockphoto

3. List the key points to be considered when devising an observation schedule.
4. State some important strategies for observing behaviour.
5. Explain how the issues of reliability and validity apply to structured observation.
6. Discuss how field experiments may be a form of structured observation.
7. Outline some criticisms of structured observation.

Kate has just arrived at a "meet and greet" reception held by her university's social sciences division as part of Orientation Week. The invitation said that professors and even the dean would be in attendance. Laid out on a long table in the centre of the room are fruit and vegetable snacks, cheese and crackers, wine, beer, and fruit juices, as well as tea and coffee. Being naturally curious, Kate decides that instead of schmoozing she will take a glass of wine and make her way to a deserted part of the room.

She notices that the people who look middle-aged tend to be talking to other people who look middle-aged. Are they profs? A group has gathered around a middle-aged woman in a business suit who is holding forth about student grades in the social sciences compared to the humanities. Is she the dean? Kate also notices that in the past 10 minutes, the woman who might be the dean has talked to seven people who appear to be profs, but only two who look like students. The people who look like students seem far more likely to be talking to other students than to profs. Shifting her attention to the table in the centre of the room, Kate notices that the middle-agers who are drinking alcohol have almost all chosen wine rather than beer, and that the women prefer white to red by a factor of two to one. As a test of the latter observation, she sets the timer on her watch so she can do a formal count for 10 minutes. To her horror, the woman who appears to be the dean walks all the way across the room and asks her brusquely, "Are you doing some kind of study?"

Introduction

As illustrated in Chapter 5, in survey research, people's behaviour must be inferred from what they report on the survey. But as we have noted in previous chapters, such inferences can be problematic because what people say and what they do are not always the same thing. Structured observation offers a possible solution to that problem by observing behaviour directly. Explicitly formulated rules are used to make the observations and to record the information gathered.

Although structured observation may appear to be a logical alternative to survey research, it has not attracted a large following and tends to be used only in research settings such as classrooms, courts, and hospitals. One reason for this is that certain types of behaviour—such as criminal activity—are inherently difficult to observe. Another reason is that many social researchers want to generalize their findings, which means selecting large, random samples to provide information that can be extrapolated to some population of interest. Normally it is not feasible to adopt that sort of methodology in a structured observation study.

Problems with survey research

Chapter 5 dealt with several aspects of survey research, including the problems typically associated with it. Box 6.1 summarizes some of the main problems. Also recall that practitioners have developed, with varying degrees of success, ways of dealing with these shortcomings or at least of reducing their impact.

So why not just observe behaviour directly?

An obvious solution to the problems identified in Box 6.1 is not to rely on research instruments such as surveys, but to observe people's behaviour directly.

Box 6.1 | Problems with using survey research to investigate behaviour

- *Problems of meaning.* People may vary in their interpretations of key terms used in a question or in the answers provided. Does "watching television" include having it on in the background while you are making dinner?
- *Problems of memory.* Respondents may not remember certain aspects of their behaviour, or they may have false memories of it. For example, people may underestimate the number of alcoholic drinks they consume in a typical week.
- *Social desirability bias.* Perhaps the most important shortcoming of survey research is that respondents will often give answers that they think will reflect well on them; for example, overestimating donations to charity or under-reporting traffic tickets.
- *Threatening or embarrassing questions.* These may lead to replies that are not fully truthful. For example, men who recently underwent surgery for prostate cancer may not want to admit to any incontinence.
- *Gap between stated and actual behaviour.* How people say they would behave and how they actually behave is often inconsistent (see Box 4.6). Husbands, for example, traditionally overestimate how much time they devote to housework. Perrucci et al. (2000) found two quite different kinds of racial relations on a predominantly White university campus, behaviours they described as "front stage" and "back stage." The "back stage" behaviour, which showed less than full acceptance of racial minorities, did not become apparent until questionnaires were supplemented by direct observation.

Structured observation (sometimes called "systematic observation") is one way to do that. (See Box 6.2 for other types of observation research.) Using this method, the researcher formulates explicit rules outlining what behaviours are to be observed and how the observations are to be recorded. Each person in the study is observed for a predetermined period of time following rules set out in a document (similar to a structured **interview schedule**) that is usually called an *observation schedule*. The data collected in this way, like survey data, can then be treated as variables for analysis.

One of the classic schedules for the observation of small-group behaviour was developed by Bales (1951) (see Figure 6.1). Suppose you wanted to compare leaders and followers in terms of their behaviour: using Bales's observation schedule, it would be possible to examine the frequency with which each group asks questions and answers them, talks or keeps silent, and so forth. Similarly, age and gender differences could be explored in relation to Bales's categories 11 ("Shows tension") and 2 ("Tension release"). Or the same categories could be used to compare "authoritarian" and "shared" leadership styles. For example, is there less tension and thus less need for tension relief with an "authoritarian" leadership style, or with a "shared" one? A scheme like this could also be used to help leadership trainees improve their leadership skills.

If an observer coded what was happening in the group as a whole every 15 seconds, the coding for a 12-minute period might look something like Figure 6.2. Notice how often a question tends to be followed by an answer and a negative affect by a smoothing positive affect (Bales organized his categories so that the codes assigned to linked behaviours such as these add up to 13). In many cases, two types of leaders emerge: a task specialist and a socio-emotional leader who is more responsible for group members' feelings.

The observation schedule

Devising a schedule for recording observations is clearly a crucial step in a structured observation project. The considerations are very similar to those

1. Helps, rewards, affirms others
2. Tension release, jokes, shows satisfaction
3. Agrees, concurs, complies
4. Gives direction
5. Gives opinion, evaluation
6. Gives orientation, repeats, clarifies
7. Asks orientation, for repetition/clarification
8. Asks opinions
9. Asks for direction, possible ways of action
10. Disagrees, withholds help
11. Shows tension, withdraws
12. Shows antagonism, deflates, defends self

Sum of 13: Balancing task areas (neutral affect)

6 + 7 Communication

5 + 8 Evaluation

4 + 9 Decision

Sum of 13: Balancing socio-emotional reactions

(−) (+)

10 + 3 (Dis)agreement

11 + 2 Tension (reduction)

12 + 1 (Dis)integration

FIGURE 6.1 Small-group interaction process: Observation schedule for an imaginary study of small-group interaction

Source: Adapted from Bales (1951).

7	7	6	6	6	7	6	6	8	5	10	2
5	8	5	12	1	9	9	4	4	5	4	4
10	11	12	12	2	1	1	11	2	8	8	5
5	10	10	2	1	3	2	1	3	6	2	1

FIGURE 6.2 Coding sheet for imaginary study of small group

Note: Each cell represents a 15-second interval and each row represents 3 minutes.

involved in creating a structured interview schedule. For example:

- A clear focus is necessary, meaning that the research question needs to be clearly stated. The observer must know exactly who is to be observed and which specific behaviours are to be recorded.
- As with the production of a closed question for a structured interview schedule, the categories of behaviour must be both mutually exclusive (not overlapping) and exhaustive (everything must have a category). What if someone knocks on the door to ask about emptying the trash can while the study is underway? Perhaps the best approach is to have a category of behaviour coded "Other" or "Interruption." Pilot studies help to reveal possible problems associated with a lack of exhaustiveness.
- The classification scheme must be easy to use. Complex systems listing many types of behaviour may be unworkable. Much like interviewers using a structured interview schedule, observers need to be trained, but even a well-trained observer can become flustered or confused if faced with too many options.
- Problems can arise if the observation schedule requires too much interpretation on the part of the observer. For example, in Bales's scheme it can be difficult to distinguish between a category 10, "Withholds help," and a category 11, "Withdraws." If interpretation is needed, clear guidelines and considerable training and experience are required.

Strategies for observing behaviour

There are different ways to observe and record behaviours:

- Recording *incidents* means waiting for something to happen and then recording what follows from it. Essentially, this is what LaPiere (1934; see Box 4.6) did when he waited for a

Box 6.2 | Other types of observation research

- ***Participant observation.*** This is one of the best-known methods of social science research, especially in sociology and anthropology. It is primarily qualitative and entails the relatively prolonged immersion of the observer in a particular social setting (for example, a group, organization, or community). The main goal is usually to elicit the meanings that the people being observed attribute to their environment and behaviour. Participant observers vary considerably in how much they participate in the social settings in which they locate themselves. (For a more detailed discussion, see Chapter 10.)
- ***Non-participant observation.*** This term applies to situations in which the observer does not take part in what is going on in the social setting. Bell's (2007) study of western Canadian separatists is an example of this sort of observation. If the participants are not aware that they are being observed and analyzed, such research can be called **unobtrusive observation**. However, the people Bell observed knew that he was studying them. Non-participant observation may be either structured or unstructured (see below); Bell's approach was unstructured.
- ***Unstructured observation.*** As its name implies, unstructured observation does not follow formal rules for either making or recording observations. Instead, the observer records people's behaviour in as much detail as possible, and then develops a narrative account of that behaviour. Most participant observation is unstructured.

Chinese couple to negotiate entry to a hotel or restaurant and then noted whether they were allowed in or not.

- A wide variety of behaviours can be observed and recorded in either short or long periods of time. In research reported in Chapter 2, children in St Helena were videotaped over a two-week period during their morning, lunch, and afternoon breaks. The tapes were then coded using "the Playground Behaviour Observation Schedule, an instrument for recording the occurrence of 23 behaviours (e.g., games; fantasy play; character imitation; anti-social and pro-social behaviour) and their behaviour groupings (i.e., whether the behaviour was undertaken by an individual, a pair, by 3 to 5 children, or 6 or more). … A separate schedule was completed for each 30-second segment" (Charlton, Gunter, & Coles, 1998, p. 7).
- *Time sampling* is another approach to the observation of behaviour. Since it is usually not possible to observe a situation continuously for extended periods of time, researchers generally sample the times at which they make their observations. The times at which the observations are made are chosen in advance, either systematically or randomly. An example is a study of schools known as the ORACLE (Observational Research and Classroom Learning Evaluation) project (Galton, Simon, & Croll, 1980). In this research, eight children (four of each gender) and their teacher were observed at regular intervals. A mechanical device made a noise every 25 seconds, signalling the observer to record what the teachers or pupils were doing (in accordance with the observation schedule).

Issues of reliability and validity

Compared with interviews and questionnaires, structured observation "provides (*a*) more reliable information about events; (*b*) greater precision regarding their timing, duration, and frequency; (*c*) greater accuracy in the time ordering of variables;

and (*d*) more accurate and economical reconstruction of large-scale social episodes" (McCall, 1984, p. 277). This is a very strong endorsement, but there are issues of reliability and validity to consider. Some of them are similar to those faced by any researcher seeking to develop measures in social research (especially survey research), while others are specific to structured observation.

Reliability

One thing practitioners of structured observation have been concerned with is *inter-observer consistency*. Essentially, this entails considering how closely two or more observers of the same behaviour agree on how to code it (see Boxes 6.3 and 6.4).

A second consideration is *intra-observer consistency*: the degree of consistency in the application of the observation schedule by a single observer over time. Consistency is difficult to achieve because people tend to behave differently depending on the context. Reliability may also be threatened by factors such as observer fatigue and lapses in attention. However, observers can be trained to get highly reliable results using complex coding schedules. The procedures for assessing intra-observer reliability across all possibilities are broadly similar to those used to assess inter-observer consistency.

Validity

Faulty administration of any measure can obviously affect its validity. However, ensuring **measurement validity**—that is, ensuring that an indicator is measuring what it is supposed to measure—can be difficult even when the measure is administered properly.

The second point simply means that structured observation demands attention to the same kinds of issues (assessing **face validity**, **concurrent validity**, and so on) that interviews and questionnaires do.

Box 6.3 | Observing the effects of ADHD on childhood friendships

Normand and colleagues (2013) studied how attention deficit hyperactivity disorder (ADHD) may affect friendships among children aged 7–13. Children from the Ottawa–Gatineau region were recruited to participate, about two-thirds of whom had a diagnosis of ADHD. The recruited children were asked to invite their best friend to participate as well. The research was conducted at two different time periods, six months apart. One aspect of the study involved structured observation of the friendship pairs engaging in three dyadic activities: a rule-based car race in which each child controlled a toy vehicle; a sharing activity involving trading cards; and a game-choice task in which the friendship pair had to decide on which of several games offered they would play at the end of the session. During these interactions, observers counted various types of behaviour that correlate with childhood friendship quality and satisfaction, such as the number of rule violations committed in the first task, and the number of self-centred or insensitive negotiation tactics used in the other two.

The results indicated that children with ADHD committed a higher proportion of illegal manoeuvres in the car race, and that, unlike those without ADHD, increased the proportion of rule violations over time. Similarly, in the card-sharing task, ADHD children made a greater proportion of self-centred and insensitive proposals, and increased their level of insensitive proposals. When choosing games, children with ADHD made a higher proportion of insensitive proposals. All in all, it appeared that the ADHD children were at a marked disadvantage with regard to the behaviours associated with creating and sustaining healthy friendships.

Given the importance of high-quality friendships for personal well-being, the researchers recommended a number of interventions to help children with ADHD, including having parents coach their children on the importance of rule following, sensitivity to others, and compromise when interacting with friends or potential friends.

Box 6.4 | Cohen's kappa

Cohen's kappa is a measure of the level of agreement between two people's coding decisions that takes into consideration the possibility that agreement will occur by chance. It can be applied to any coding. Much like Cronbach's alpha (see Chapter 4), the coefficient varies from 0 to 1. The closer it is to 1, the higher the agreement and the better the inter-observer consistency. As a rough rule of thumb, a coefficient over .75 is considered "very good"; from .6 to .75, "good"; "fair" ranges from .4 to .59.

The first—error in implementation—relates to two matters in particular:

- Is the observation schedule being administered as directed? This is the equivalent of ensuring that structured interviewers follow instructions exactly. Variability between observers or over time makes the measure unreliable and therefore invalid. Observers should have a thorough understanding of how the observation schedule is to be implemented.
- Do people change their behaviour when they know they are being observed? If they do, that would constitute one of several kinds of "reactive effect" that can occur in various forms of research (see Box 6.5). If people adjust the way they behave because they know they are being observed (perhaps because they want to be seen in a favourable light by the observer), their behaviour would have to be considered atypical or not authentic. However, as McCall (1984) noted, there is evidence that participants become accustomed to being observed and that researchers tend to become less intrusive the longer they are in the field. However, these effects are likely to persist when the behaviour under observation involves sensitive issues such as sexuality or deviance.

Field experiments as a form of structured observation

A **field experiment** is a study in which a researcher directly intervenes in a natural setting to observe the consequences of that intervention. That's what LaPiere (1934) did when he arranged for a Chinese couple to seek entry to hotels and restaurants in order to observe the effects (although his study was an imperfect experiment because there was no control group of non-Chinese people). In a field experiment—unlike most types of structured observation—participants do not know that they are being studied.

Another famous field experiment was conducted by Rosenhan (1973). He was one of several people in the study who posed as patients and were admitted to mental hospitals in the US. Each pseudo-patient was instructed to claim that he or she was "hearing voices," and all except one of them were then diagnosed with schizophrenia. As soon as they were admitted, the pseudo-patients were instructed to cease exhibiting any symptoms. Even though they were all "sane," it took many of them quite a long time to be released. The length of hospitalization reportedly varied from 7 to 52 days, with an average of 19 days. Rosenhan noted that in four of the hospitals, pseudo-patients approached psychiatrists and nurses with a request for release and recorded the nature of the response: 71 per cent of psychiatrists moved on with their heads averted and 88 per cent of nurses did likewise. To Rosenhan this indicated that a mental patient can become powerless and depersonalized. Generally, in this sort of research, opportunities to employ an observation schedule are limited because excessive use will blow the observer's cover, although this did not appear to be a major obstacle in this case.

Rosenhan's study is highly controversial, in part because of its use of *deception*, the ethical

Box 6.5 | Reactive effects in social research

rawpixel/123rf

What sort of challenges might you face as a researcher who is observing this class? Might the class behave differently because of your presence?

Webb, Campbell, Schwartz, & Sechrest wrote about "reactive measurement effect" (1966, p. 13). It occurs when someone's awareness that they are participating in research leads to changes in their behaviour that confound the investigator's data. **Response sets**, social desirability bias, and political correctness can all cause **reactive effects**. If a respondent reacts to some characteristic of the interviewer (e.g., gender or ethnicity), that is another example of a reactive effect. Here are a few more:

- *The Hawthorne effect.* The classic studies illustrating this effect were done at the Hawthorne Works (located near Chicago) in the 1920s (see Roethlisberger & Dickson, 1939). A series of **quasi-experiments** showed that each time working conditions improved (e.g., through improved lighting), productivity went up, at least temporarily. But it also went up after working conditions deteriorated! It appeared that performance improved simply because the workers were aware of being observed and analyzed, not because of the experimental manipulation itself: this is known as the "Hawthorne effect." A well-known general problem in experimental studies is that some individuals will seek out cues about the aims of the research, and then adjust what they say and do to conform with what they believe to be the purpose of the study. That is a problem, even if such participants are mistaken about the aims of the research.
- *Role selection.* Webb et al. argued that participants may be tempted to adopt a particular kind of role in research. Some people with no strong opinion on a particular item may develop one when asked, in order to appear knowledgeable. Even telling them how important they are to the research can encourage some display of "expertise." Other, fairly opinionated individuals may back off a bit, scared by the audio recorder,

perhaps, or not wanting to come on too strong to a stranger.

- ***Researcher presence as a change agent.*** The simple fact that the researcher is present may change the situation that is being observed. For example, if an observer is sitting in a classroom, that means a chair is being occupied that otherwise might have been empty, which in turn may cause changes in space and privacy for those sitting nearby. When Whyte (1955), in his study of "Cornerville," joined one of the neighbourhood's bowling teams, he in effect removed one of his research participants from the team and turned that person into a rival on an opposing team.
- ***Trying to help or to be nice to the researcher.*** Although it is often assumed that research participants are always passive, this is not true, even in experiments. Some participants may try to please the researcher. An old saying holds that if you ask friends to do push-ups, they will ask "what?" or "why?" But people in an experiment (especially students, who are often asked to be participants) will ask "where?"! In fact, many participants will try to do what they think they are supposed to do, although a few may deliberately do the opposite. Some will even ask "Was I good?" at the end of the experiment. Such behaviour can be problematic if it affects the phenomenon being studied.
- ***Different researchers may elicit different reactions.*** Some may get the data they want by communicating, often unconsciously, their expectations. This is why experiments are supposed to be *double blind*, so that no one (not even the person administering the experiment) knows certain crucial details, such as which participants have received the treatment and which have not (*single blind* means that only the people being studied are kept in the dark). Here, hiring others to collect the data can help.

Reactive effects are likely to occur in any research in which participants know they are the focus of investigation. Webb et al. called for greater use of what they called **unobtrusive measures**: non-reactive methods that leave participants unaware that they are being studied. Records can be checked at hospitals and courts, for instance, removing the reactivity, but for ethical reasons permission must first be obtained, and getting such permission may be difficult or impossible.

Alternatively, the usual tools of social research can be used. A confidentiality guarantee backed up by reminders may help, as may anonymous questionnaires and telephone (rather than in-person) interviews, although these have their own downsides. It also helps to phrase questions so that they are as non-threatening and non-judgmental as possible; for example: "Many people did not have time to vote in the referendum or could not make up their minds. Did you vote?" If you want to allow more men to admit they fear being out late at night, don't ask how afraid they are. Use a vignette: "John does not like to walk alone at night in his neighbourhood. There is a lot of crime there, and police officers are rarely if ever seen. Is John almost a copy of you, a lot like you, a bit like you, not at all like you?"

Finally, although it is good to be aware of the shortcomings resulting from reactive effects, remember that no study is perfect, and that an imperfect study can still be an important source of knowledge. Also, maintain the same level of skepticism when the results you encounter please you as when they displease you. For example, research showing that university men are more violent than university women in heterosexual romantic relationships should be held to the same methodological standards as research showing no gender differences (for example, Katz, Kuffel, & Coblentz, 2002).

Research in the News

The effect of social trust on Canada's reaction to the COVID-19 pandemic

sockagphoto/Shutterstock

As a researcher choosing between structured observation and survey-based measures of behaviour, which method would help you better understand the intentions behind participants' social distancing behaviours?

Public health during the COVID-19 pandemic may depend on things that go beyond discoveries in medical science such as treatment protocols and vaccines. According to Cary Wu, a York University sociologist, and Eric Kennedy, a historian at York, social trust must also be present for a nation to cope with the global epidemic. "If people do not trust, it's very difficult to promote collective action," Wu explained in a CBC interview (Weber, 2020). In a pandemic, trust in fellow citizens, politicians, the health-care system, and perceived outsiders could be affected, he maintained. Without a high level of social trust, it's hard to get people to conform to public health directives such as those regarding physical distancing and mask wearing.

Both Wu and Kennedy are embarking on social research programs involving surveys in an effort to determine what effect the pandemic has had on social trust in Canada. So far, their results suggest that levels of social trust have remained high during the crisis. "By and large, Canadians are reporting taking a lot of the steps that they've been called upon to take," Kennedy explained. He also reported that Canadians are more trusting of public officials than is the case in other countries. "Canadians are more likely to follow social distancing requirements. People perform better in terms of complying with policy matters," he said (Weber, 2020). Both Wu and Kennedy are hoping that their research will help those in charge of promoting public health in Canada to enhance levels of social trust as the pandemic wears on.

Methods in Motion | Applications to Canadian Society

Systematic social observation of the police

Schulenberg (2014) describes her experiences in using systematic social observation (SSO) to study decision-making processes and the use of discretion among members of a Canadian regional police service. With this method, structured observation is employed to gather behavioural information on the people studied, while participant observation techniques are used to collect field notes and develop narratives that provide detailed descriptions of how situational factors and the personal characteristics of the people observed affect the phenomenon of interest. Since SSO is a method that yields both quantitative and qualitative data it has the potential to provide highly meaningful information on a topic, but it is rarely used because of the heavy burdens it places on the researcher.

In Schulenberg's case, she was interested in how police officers dealt with the anti-social and criminal behaviour they encountered while on patrol. To research her topic she went on 74 "ride-alongs" with officers, which allowed her to collect information on the 406 police–citizen interactions that took place in the 637 hours she spent in the field. A comprehensive observation schedule was used to record the behaviours she witnessed. For example, a number of codes were used to describe the role played by the citizens in the encounter: 1 indicated that a person was a complainant or victim; 2, that they were a suspect or person of interest; 3, that they were a disputant whose status as a victim or a suspect was unclear, and so on. Informal debriefing sessions with officers were used to create detailed descriptions of how the officers interpreted each citizen encounter and how they felt about it afterward. In addition, narratives were created that provided a thick description of the citizens' interactions with police. The narratives included information on things like whether the citizens had weapons or showed signs of mental illness, and how the police took action to deal with the situation.

The "SSO of police work," Schulenberg writes, "is not for the faint of heart. Beyond witnessing human nature, dead bodies, and citizens in crisis, SSO requires a high level of commitment, involvement, and personal sacrifice" (p. 308). She found herself immersed in police culture, and had to contend with a feeling that she may have become overly sympathetic to the police and their beliefs and values. At the same time, she found some aspects of what she experienced to be highly objectionable. Her status as a single woman made her the target of sexual propositioning and rude gestures, which she either ignored or deflected with choice comebacks of her own.

implications of which were discussed in Chapter 3. There have also been questions about the accuracy of Rosenhan's descriptions of how the pseudo-patients were treated, and about other critical details presented in his account of the study (see Cahalan, 2019).

Criticisms of structured observation

Some problems with structured observation have already been mentioned in our discussion of its reliability, validity, and generalizability. Other criticisms include the following:

- There is a risk of imposing an inappropriate observation schedule on the setting in question; this risk is especially great in settings about which little is known. This problem is similar to that of closed-question answer categories that do not fit the question format. One solution is to precede the structured observation with a period of unstructured observation, so that appropriate variables and categories can be identified in advance.
- Because it concentrates on directly observable behaviour, structured observation in itself cannot get at the *intentions* behind behaviour. When intentions are of interest, observers must impute them. Essentially, the problem is that structured observation cannot tell the observer very much about the *meanings* that people attach to their behaviours—information that according to Weber (1947) is crucial in understanding human thought and action. In a similar vein, contextual factors such as events in the larger world may be given insufficient attention as possible influences on the observed behaviour.
- There is a tendency for structured observation to generate many small bits of data. As a result, it can be difficult to find general themes that illustrate the bigger picture behind the scattered bits of data. This problem is compounded by the fact that observers may not know the meanings the actors attach to their behaviours.

On the other hand . . .

The previous section made it clear that there are limitations to structured observation. However, it's also important to remember that when overt behaviour is the focus of analysis and issues of meaning are less salient, structured observation is almost certainly more accurate and effective than asking people to report their behaviour in a survey. Structured observation may work best when accompanied by another method, especially one that can probe for the reasons behind people's behaviours. One such method is the *systematic social observation* approach described in the Methods in Motion box on pages 148–149.

Key Points

- Structured observation is an alternative to survey-based measures of behaviour.
- It involves explicit rules for recording behaviour.
- Structured observation has generally been applied to a narrow range of behaviours, such as that occurring in schools, courts, and hospitals.
- It shares with survey research many common problems concerning reliability, validity, and generalizability.
- Reactive effects must be taken into account, but should not be exaggerated.
- The field experiment is a form of structured observation, but can involve ethical challenges.
- Problems with structured observation include determining the meaning that people give to their behaviour and ensuring that the framework for recording the observations is valid.

Questions for Review (R) and Creative Application (A)

Observing behaviour

R1 Under what circumstances might structured observation be a better way to gather data than questionnaires or structured interviews? Explain.

A1 You want to observe children in an elementary school playground to examine the extent to which they exhibit aggressive behaviours and the conditions that may lead to aggression. Explain the pros and cons of using structured versus unstructured observation to conduct this research.

The observation schedule

R2 What goals and considerations should be kept in mind when constructing an observation schedule?

A2 Construct an observation schedule containing five items that could be used to observe fan behaviour at a hockey game, and a second schedule to be used for observing people attending a figure skating competition. Then explain how and why they are different.

Strategies for observing behaviour

R3 Discuss three different strategies for observing and recording behaviour in structured observation.

A3 Explain how time sampling could be used to make observations of people as they interact while parking their cars in a busy parking lot.

Issues of reliability and validity

R4 How do the considerations of reliability and validity in structured observation mirror those encountered in survey research?

A4 What are reactive effects? How might reactive effects be problematic in structured observation research that is used to examine how parents treat their children while they shop in a large department store?

Field experiments as a form of structured observation

R5 What are field experiments and what ethical concerns do they pose?

A5 What ethical issues should you consider if you do a field experiment that involves posing as a confused traveller who does not speak English or French at a busy Canadian airport?

Criticisms of structured observation

R6 Can structured observation ever reveal the intentions that lie behind the observed behaviour? Explain.

A6 Assume you are using structured observation to do a study of people participating in a protest march. Your observation schedule includes categories of behaviour that are peaceful in nature, and others that are violent. Explain why in this study it may be crucial to consider the intentions that lie behind the behaviours observed.

Interactive Classroom Activities

1. Divide the class into small groups. Each group is to come up with a detailed mock proposal for a structured observation study that involves gaining access to a specific location, group, or organization, for example, a mental hospital, school playground, casino, and so on. The proposal must include a discussion of the following:
   a. A specific research question that the study seeks to answer, a draft of which is to be produced.
   b. Whether the research will be overt or covert, and the ethical implications of that aspect of the study.
   c. How access to the location, group, or organization will be acquired.
   d. The formal observation schedule that is to be used, a draft of which is to be produced, along with an explanation of how it is to be administered and how issues of reliability and validity will be taken into account.
   e. What findings are expected from the study.

   Each group presents its mock proposal to the rest of the class for comment and critique.

2. The instructor gives a brief synopsis of the field experiment conducted by Rosenhan (1973). The class is then divided into three groups. Group 1 must argue (a) that the study was ethical and (b) that the methodology used was superior to any other methodology that could have been used to conduct the study, citing specific examples of other methodologies that would have been less effective. Group 2 must argue (a) that the study was not ethical and (b) that other methodologies would have worked equally well or better, citing specific examples of those alternative methodologies. Group 3 makes the case that there is no methodology that can be ethically applied to Rosenhan's topic, and that therefore no one should be allowed to conduct a study on it. After some time for preparation, group 1 presents its case to the rest of the class, followed by groups 2 and 3. Once all groups have presented, each group is given some time to meet to assess and critique the other groups. Each group then presents its critique to the rest of the class, with a general discussion to follow.

Relevant Websites

This is a short YouTube video of ***structured observation*** being done on children.

The ***Nature*** website offers a review of a book (Cahalan, 2019) that is critical of the Rosenhan experiment.

(Websites accessed 4 September 2021.)

OXFORD learning link

More resources are available on Oxford Learning Link.
Visit https://learninglink.oup.com/ for:

- Student self-quiz
- Flash cards
- Audio clips
- Videos
- Activities

7 Quantitative Sampling

Chapter Overview

Sampling principles are not exclusively the concern of **survey** and other **quantitative** researchers. The **qualitative** work you will read about in Part III also involves working with samples, but the nature of qualitative sampling is often rather different from the quantitative kind, so a discussion of the former has been placed in that part of the book. This chapter explores:

- the role of sampling in relation to the overall process of doing quantitative research;
- why **generalizable** findings (that is, findings that can be applied to some larger **population**) require a **representative sample**;
- the idea of a **probability sample**: one using a random selection process;
- the main types of probability sample: **simple random**, **systematic**, and **stratified random**, and the multi-stage **cluster sample**;
- the main issues involved in deciding **sample** size;
- different types of **non-probability sampling**, including **quota sampling**, which is widely used in market research;
- potential sources of **sampling error** in survey research;
- sampling in **structured observation** research, where times and contexts are sampled; and
- raising response rates.

Key Learning Outcomes

Here is a list of goals you should try to achieve as you read and think about the material in this chapter. After completing this chapter, you should be able to:

1. Define the key terms used in sampling.

▲ Creative Touch Imaging Ltd./Alamy Stock Photo

2. Identify three common sources of bias in sampling.
3. Explain how four types of probability sample (simple random, systematic, stratified random, and multi-stage cluster) are selected.
4. Outline the main characteristics of a probability sample.
5. Summarize the principal criteria used in deciding how large a sample should be.
6. Illustrate how three kinds non-probability sample (convenience, snowball, and quota) are used.
7. Cite some of the limitations involved in generalizing findings from both probability and non-probability samples to the population of interest.
8. Describe how sampling may be used in content analyses.
9. Enumerate some ways to increase response rates.

Do you like to spend more time and money than is actually necessary to accomplish something? Most people would say no, including social researchers, who inevitably face the prospect of doing their work with limited time and physical resources. Ideally, researchers would study huge populations, such as all women in Canada or all adults living in the Atlantic provinces, but the costs involved make that impossible. In other areas of life, reducing the time and money you devote to a project normally means a reduction in the quality of the final product—think of building a house on a limited budget. Fortunately, this is not necessarily the case with social research. With proper sampling techniques you can vastly reduce the time and resources needed to complete the research without seriously compromising the findings. You might think of sampling as "how to do a lot with relatively little." Under the right conditions, you can even calculate the probability that sample-based statistical findings are in error. This chapter introduces you to the techniques that make this possible.

Introduction

The term "sampling" refers to the selection of a subset of a population for research. Since only in very rare instances can an entire population be studied, sampling has an impact on virtually all the research discussed in this book. As we will see below, how the sampling is conducted determines what information is acquired and influences the researcher's interpretation of the results in important ways.

The key terms used in sampling are explained in Box 7.1. We'll begin with a discussion of sampling in studies involving **structured interviews** or **questionnaires**, and then consider the techniques used for other methods of quantitative research. Finally, ways to increase response rates are presented.

Suppose you are wondering about your fellow students' attitudes on certain matters, or perhaps about their behaviours or backgrounds. To examine any of these areas, either structured interviews or questionnaires would be appropriate. However, let's say that there are around 30,000 students at your university. It would be a huge undertaking for you to arrange for all of them to fill out a questionnaire, and the time and energy required to interview 30,000 people would be prohibitive. It's almost certain that a sample of students would have to suffice. In fact, the need to sample is almost universal in quantitative research.

But would any sample do? What if you gave questionnaires to everyone in your classes? Or if you stood in a busy location on campus and then interviewed anyone who agreed to speak with you?

If your goal is simply to get some experience in data gathering and analysis, or to conduct a pilot study, these samples would be fine. However, if the object is to get a representative sample, one that can be used to make inferences about all 30,000 students, these samples would not do. Why? There are various reasons, but the following stand out:

- If you distribute questionnaires in your classes, anyone not taking a course with you will be excluded. How many music or engineering majors take sociology?

Box 7.1 | Basic terms and concepts in sampling

- ***Element or unit:*** A single case in the population. In the social sciences that element or unit is usually a person, but many other things can be sampled as well: nations, cities, regions, schools, firms, and so on. Finch and Hayes (1994), for example, based part of their research on a random sample of wills of deceased people.
- ***Population:*** All the cases about which you are seeking knowledge, or all the cases to which your conclusions are meant to apply. For example, if you are studying voting behaviour, the population might be all the people in a particular jurisdiction who are eligible to vote. If the topic is hyperactivity among young children, the population might be all children aged 2 to 11. (Note that "population" in this context means something different from "population" in the everyday sense.)
- ***Sampling frame:*** The list of elements from which the sample will be selected.
- ***Sample:*** The elements selected for investigation, a subset of the population. The method of selection may involve probability or non-probability sampling (see next column).
- ***Representative sample:*** A sample that is a microcosm of the population, one that "represents" its essential characteristics. A sample such as this is most likely to be selected when a probability sampling process is used (see next).
- ***Probability sample:*** A sample selected using a random process such that each unit in the population has a known chance of being selected. The aim of probability sampling is to keep sampling error (see below) to a minimum.
- ***Non-probability sample:*** A sample selected using a non-random method. Essentially, this implies that some units in the population are more likely to be selected than others.
- ***Sampling error:*** An error of estimation that occurs if there is a difference between the characteristics of a sample and those of the population from which it was selected. Sampling error can occur even when a random method is used. For example, if valid measures indicate that 45 per cent of a national probability sample is in favour of more public funding for the arts, but the actual figure in the population is 49 per cent, the difference is caused by sampling error.
- ***Non-response:*** A situation that occurs whenever some unit selected for the sample refuses to participate in the study, cannot be contacted, or for some other reason does not supply the required data.
- ***Census:*** Data collected from all elements in the population rather than from a sample. The phrase "the census" typically refers to the enumeration of all (or nearly all) members of the population of a nation-state—that is, a national census.

- If you go out looking for people to interview, your sample will exclude anyone who happens to be somewhere else at that particular time. Some students will be at work, others will have skipped classes that day, and many will have a timetable different from yours. Some students may never need to go where you are.
- Your decisions about which people to approach may be influenced by your judgments about how friendly or cooperative they appear to be. Gender, "race," and age are only a few of the factors that could have an impact on your selection of prospective respondents.

The problem with these sampling methods is that they make the choice of possible participants dependent on non-universal criteria: availability in one case and personal judgment in the other. In the language of sampling, this means that the sample would be biased: it would not represent the population from which it was selected. It is extremely difficult to remove bias altogether and get a truly representative sample, but steps should be taken to keep it to a minimum.

Three sources of bias can be identified:

- Not using a random method to pick the sample. Essentially, a random method is one in which each element has the same chance of being selected, like numbers from a lottery cage (although in some circumstances that principle may be violated for technical reasons; for example, in order to get a sufficiently large number of people from a small subgroup into the sample). As we saw above, if a random method is not used, there is a risk that the selection process will be affected by human judgment, so that some members of the population are more likely to be selected than others. This source of bias is eliminated through the use of probability sampling, described later in this chapter.
- The sampling frame or list of potential participants is inadequate. If the sampling frame excludes some cases or is otherwise inaccurate, the sample derived from it may not represent the population, even if a **random sampling** method is employed to select participants from it.
- Some people in the sample refuse to participate or cannot be contacted—in other words, there is non-response. The problem with non-response is that those who agree to participate may differ from those who refuse or cannot be reached in ways relevant to the subject matter being investigated. If that is the case, the sample may not be representative. For example, if you are studying rates of criminal victimization and people who have been victims of violent crime decline to participate, that would skew the results.

If the data are available, a researcher can check to see how non-respondents differ from the population. It is often possible to do this in terms of characteristics such as gender or age, but these are not the only potentially relevant factors; in the case of a sample of university students, for example, you might want to find out whether non-respondents reflect the entire student body in terms of faculty of registration. However, it is usually impossible to check characteristics that go beyond basic demographic categories, such as attitudes toward separatism or patterns of smoking behaviour, because population data are generally not available on these topics.

Sampling error

To appreciate the significance of sampling error for achieving a representative sample, consider Figures 7.1 through 7.4. Imagine a population of 200 people and a sample of 50. Imagine as well that the topic is whether people watch reality TV programs, and that the population is divided equally between those who do (100) and those who do not (100). If the sample is representative, the sample of 50 should also be equally split in terms of this variable (see Figure 7.1). If there is a small amount of sampling error, so that the sample contains one person too many who does not watch reality TV and one too few who does, the distribution would look like Figure 7.2. Figure 7.3 shows a more serious over-representation in the sample of people who do not watch reality programs. This time there are three too many who do not watch them and three too few who do. Finally, Figure 7.4 shows a very serious over-representation of people

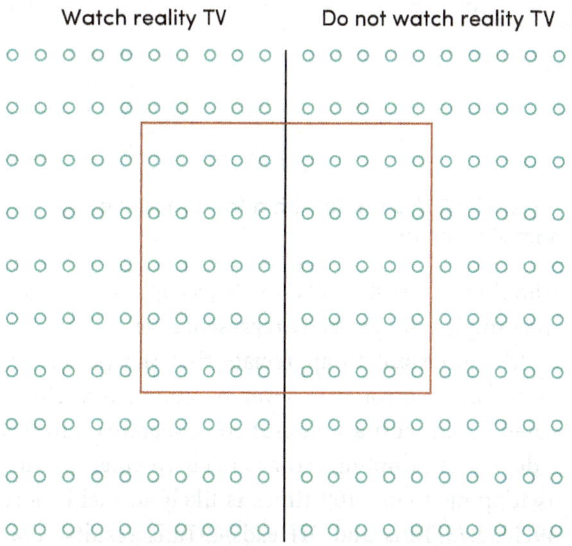

FIGURE 7.1 A sample with no sampling error

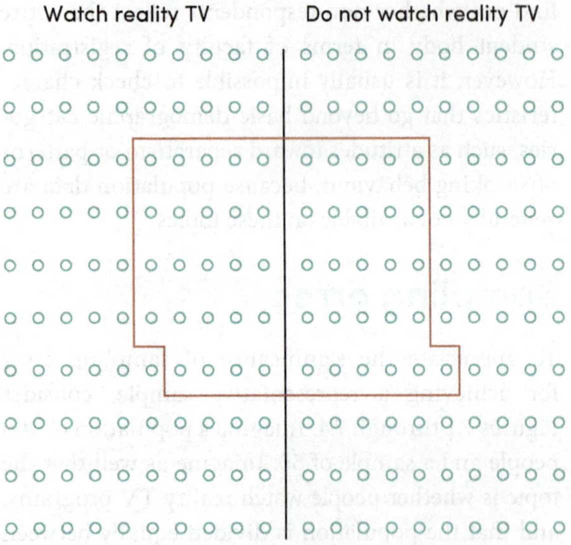

FIGURE 7.2 A sample with very little sampling error

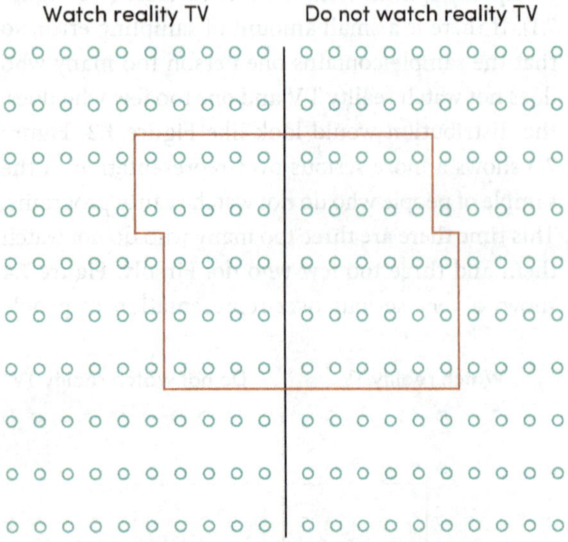

FIGURE 7.3 A sample with a fair amount of sampling error

who do not watch reality TV: 35, as opposed to 25 if the sample were perfectly representative.

It's important to appreciate that the possibility of sampling error can never be completely eliminated. Even with a well-crafted probability sample, a degree of sampling error is likely to creep in, just as flipping a coin 100 times is likely to yield more 49Heads/51Tails and 51Heads/49Tails results *combined* than 50Heads/50Tails outcomes, even though

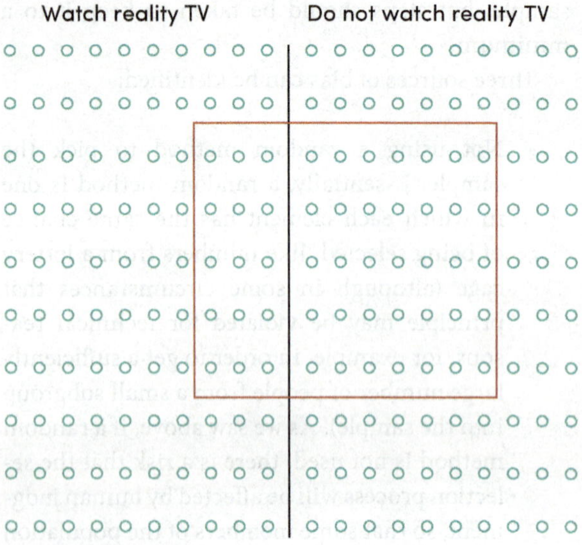

FIGURE 7.4 A sample with a lot of sampling error

the latter is the most probable single result. Ask your instructor to take a few minutes for an in-class experiment in which a coin is flipped 20 times, several times over, and you'll see the surprisingly large number of outcomes that are not 10Heads/10Tails. However, probability sampling stands a better chance than non-probability sampling of minimizing sampling error, so it's very unlikely that the sample will end up looking like Figure 7.4 when it is used. Moreover, probability sampling allows you to employ tests of statistical significance that will permit you to make inferences about the population from which the sample was selected, with a known probability of error. This topic will be addressed in Chapter 8.

Types of probability sample

Imagine a study on the social variables related to alcohol consumption, to be done at a university that has 9000 full-time students. This hypothetical example will be used in the illustrations that follow.

Simple random sample

The simple random sample is the most basic form of probability sample. With it, each unit of the population has an equal probability of inclusion in the sample. Suppose there is enough money to interview

450 students at the university. This means that the probability of inclusion in the sample is

$$\frac{450}{9000}, \text{ that is, 1 in 20}$$

This is known as the sampling ratio and is expressed as

$$\frac{n}{N}$$

where n is the sample size and N is the population size.

The key steps in devising a simple random sample are as follows:

1. Define the population. Here N is all full-time students at the university: 9000.
2. Select or devise a comprehensive **sampling frame**. In this case, let's assume that (a) the office that keeps student records has a list of all full-time students and (b) you have access to it (and all proper ethics protocols have been followed).
3. Decide on the sample size (n) you will use; here n is 450.
4. List all the students in the population and assign them consecutive numbers from 1 to N, here 1 to 9000.
5. Using a table of random numbers, or a computer program that can generate random numbers, select n (450) different random numbers from 1 to N (9000).
6. The students who match the n (450) random numbers constitute the sample. Two points are worth noting here. First, there is almost no opportunity for bias, since in this case the selection process is entirely random: students are not selected on the basis of subjective criteria such as whether or not they look friendly and approachable. Second, selection does not depend on availability: students do not have to walk by the interviewer in order to be included in the sample. The process of selection takes place without their knowledge, and they do not know they will be asked to be part of a social survey until they are contacted by someone associated with the study.

Step 5 mentions the possible use of a table of random numbers, found in the back of many statistics books or generated by computer software. Such tables are usually made up of columns of five-digit numbers; for example:

09188	08358
90045	28306
73189	53840
75768	91757
54016	87941

The first thing to notice is that, since these are five-digit numbers and the population size is just 9000 (a four-digit number), the only random numbers that might be appropriate are the two that begin with zeros, 09188 and 08358 (and the former is already larger than the largest possible case number for this study). To deal with this, drop one of the digits in each number—say the first digit. Using only the last four digits gives us the following:

9188	8358
0045	8306
3189	3840
5768	1757
4016	7941

Still, one of the resulting numbers—9188—exceeds 9000; no student has that case number. The solution is simple: ignore that number and go on to the next one. This means that the student assigned the number 45 will be the first to be included in the sample. Moving down the first column, the student assigned the number 3189 will be next; the student assigned 5768 next; and so on.

To avoid interviewing the same person twice, ignore any random number that appears more than once and continue down the list. This procedure produces what is called a simple random sample without replacement: no number is placed back in (replaced after having been selected) for a second chance at inclusion. Since virtually all simple random samples in social research are like this, the qualifier "without replacement" is usually omitted. Strictly speaking, "without replacement" means that the result is not a true simple random sample, as those chosen later have a greater chance of being selected than those selected earlier. (The first person chosen has one chance in 9000 of being selected; removing that person means person two has one chance in the remaining 8999. Thus, the 450th person chosen will have one chance out of the 8551 people remaining; a chance of one in 8551 is greater than a chance of one in 9000.) Researchers generally overlook this problem, since it is a small one compared with other sampling problems.

Systematic sample

A systematic sample is selected directly from the sampling frame, without using random numbers.

In the present case, 1 student in 20 is to be selected (450/9000). That "1 in 20" figure is called the *sampling interval*. A *random start* begins the process, which in this case can be achieved by selecting at random a number from 1 to 20, possibly by using the last two digits in a table of random numbers. With the 10 random numbers above, the first relevant one is 54016, since it is the first one where the last two digits yield a number in the desired range (1–20), namely 16. This means that the sixteenth student in the sampling frame is the first one to be included in the sample. Thereafter, take every twentieth student on the list; the sequence of case numbers would be: 16, 36, 56, 76, 96, 116, and so on. Who is the last person in the sample? Case number 8996.

In systematic sampling, it is important to ensure that there is no inherent ordering or pattern in the sampling frame, a feature called *periodicity*. For example, imagine that the sampling frame was set up such that case 1 was male, case 2 female, case 3 male, case 4 female, and so on for all cases. In the example above, that would yield a sample of 450 females and 0 males, in all likelihood a very unrepresentative sample. If there is any pattern to the list, arrange the cases in random order or choose a different sampling method.

Note that with systematic sampling, not every possible combination of cases has an equal chance of being selected. Once that first case number (here 16) is chosen, every case number in the sample must end in 6, and no even-numbered prefixes will qualify, such as 26, 86, or 166.

Stratified random sampling

In the imaginary study of university students discussed earlier, the student's discipline may be relevant to what you will be researching. Generating a simple random sample or a systematic sample may yield one in which, for example, the proportion of kinesiology students in the sample is the same as that in the student population, but usually it is not an exact match. Thus, if there are 1800 students majoring in kinesiology, a sampling ratio of 1 in 20 should produce 90 students in the sample from this faculty. But because of sampling error there might be, say, 85 or 93.

So long as data are available on each student's faculty of registration, it's possible to ensure that students are exactly represented in terms of their faculty membership by using **stratified random sampling**. In the language of sampling, this means stratifying the population (dividing it into subgroups) by a criterion (in this case faculty) and selecting either a simple random sample or a systematic sample from each of the resulting strata. In the present example, five faculties would mean five strata, with the sample in each stratum being one-twentieth of the total for each faculty, as in Table 7.1, which also shows a hypothetical outcome of a simple random or systematic sample, one that does not exactly mirror the population.

The advantage of stratified sampling is clear: it ensures that the sample is distributed in the same way as the population in terms of the stratifying criterion. Using a simple random or systematic sampling approach may result in a distribution exactly like that of the stratified sample, but it is unlikely. On the other hand, this strategy requires that the relevant criteria for stratification be known in advance of the research, which is not always the case.

Two more points are relevant here. Stratified sampling is feasible only when it is relatively easy to identify and allocate units to strata. Five strata based on physical activity level, from "competitive athletes" at one end to "couch potatoes" at the other, would be very hard to set up, because it would require an

TABLE 7.1 The advantages of stratified sampling

Faculty	Population	Stratified sample	Hypothetical simple random or systematic sample
Humanities	1800	90	85
Social sciences	1200	60	70
Natural sciences	2000	100	120
Business	1800	90	84
Engineering	2200	110	91
TOTAL	9000	450	450

initial study just to get the population data on activity level that you would need to create these strata. Second, more than one stratifying criterion can be used at the same time. In our example, we could stratify by faculty and gender, or faculty, gender, and whether students are undergraduates or postgraduates, and so on, as long as the criteria are easy to use and relevant to the research question. But this approach is practicable only when data on the relevant stratifying criteria are available for the population. Does your school have an accessible list of female undergraduate engineering students?

Multi-stage cluster sampling

In the previous example, the students to be interviewed all attend the same university. However, imagine a national sample of students. A major problem with large populations is the general lack of an adequate sampling frame. Is there a list somewhere of all students registered at Canadian universities? No. Without a sampling frame, it's impossible to select a simple random or systematic sample.

One way to deal with these problems is to employ cluster sampling. With cluster sampling, the primary sampling unit (the first stage of the sampling procedure) is not the individuals or units of the population to be studied, but an aggregate of them, known as a cluster. Imagine you want a nationally representative sample of 5000 students. One solution is to sample universities and then students from each of the sampled universities, with a probability sample at each stage. For example, you could randomly sample 10 universities from the entire population of universities, yielding 10 clusters, and then interview 500 randomly selected students at each of the 10 universities selected, to create a sample of 5000 students. (This would require "probability proportionate to size" sampling because each university has a different number of students, but that technique goes beyond the scope of our discussion here.)

Suppose the result of sampling 10 universities is the following:

- Alberta
- McGill
- Simon Fraser
- Winnipeg
- Dalhousie
- Guelph
- Brandon
- Western
- Nipissing
- Toronto

Note the absence of universities in Saskatchewan, Newfoundland and Labrador, New Brunswick, and Prince Edward Island. An alternative solution would be to select a *stratified cluster sample*, which combines the notion of stratified sampling discussed in the previous section with cluster sampling. In our example, we could first group all universities by region—for example, Atlantic Canada, Quebec, Ontario, the Prairies, and British Columbia—and then randomly sample two universities from each region. The next step would be to sample 500 students from each of the 10 universities, yielding a total sample size of 5000. (Again, technical adjustments would be required because the clusters are not of equal size.) These are the stages:

- Group the universities into five regions.
- Sample two universities from each region.
- Sample 500 students from each of the 10 universities.

Cluster sampling if done properly can be very effective. Its greatest merit is that it solves the problem of having no adequate sampling frame. The student study described above does not require a list of all university students in Canada, something that would be very hard to come by. With cluster sampling, no such list is ever required.

With large populations, cluster sampling is very economical compared to simple random or systematic sampling when doing in-person interviews because of reduced travel costs—research participants tend to cluster geographically. Using this technique for research based on telephone interviews has less of an economic advantage now than it once did because long-distance phone charges are so low, and of course if the research is to be done on the Internet, travel expenses are not an issue.

The advantages of multi-stage cluster sampling should be clear by now. However, as suggested above, even a very rigorous sampling strategy cannot eliminate all sampling error, as the example in Box 7.2 shows.

The qualities of a probability sample

Many researchers prefer probability samples because they allow one to make inferences from the sample to the population from which it was selected. In other words, with probability samples, the sample findings can be generalized to the population. This is not to say that the sample and population characteristics are exactly the same, but the first can be used to estimate the second with a known probability of error. In the example of alcohol consumption in the sample of 450 students (in the previous section), the mean number of units consumed by the sample ($\bar{X}$) can be used to estimate the population mean (μ) with a known margin of error. Greek letters are used to denote population characteristics; the Latin alphabet (the one used to write in English), for sample characteristics.

To expand on this point, it is necessary to use some basic statistical ideas. These are presented in Boxes 7.2 and 7.3, but they can be skipped if all you need is a broad idea of sampling procedures.

Sample size

"How large should a sample be?" "Is the sample big enough?" No issue in sampling raises more questions than sample size. Decisions about sample size are not straightforward, as we will see below. At the same time, the quest for the perfect sample is usually constrained by the practical considerations of cost and time.

Absolute and relative sample size

People unfamiliar with the field may be surprised to learn that it is the *absolute* size of a sample that is most important, not the proportion of the population that it makes up. This means that a national probability sample of 1000 Canadians has about as much validity as a national probability sample of 1000 Americans, even though the latter involves a much larger population.

Increasing the size of a sample increases the precision of the estimates derived from it; for instance, a larger sample size means that the 95 per cent confidence interval referred to in Box 7.2 is narrowed. However, a large sample cannot guarantee precision, so it might be better to say that increasing the size of a sample *probably* increases the precision of the estimates it can create. In other words, as sample size increases, sampling error tends to decrease. Common sample sizes are 100 (minimum) and then 400, 900, 1600, and 2500. These sample size increases cut the sampling error by half, then by one-third, then by one-fourth, and then by one-fifth respectively. (The reason has to do with the square roots involved in the denominator of the calculation; thus the original square root, 10, for a sample of 100 becomes 20, 30, 40, and 50 [the square

Box 7.2 | Generalizing from a random sample to the population

If an average of 9.7 units of alcohol is consumed in the previous seven days by respondents in a probability sample, would a similar figure be found in the population? The answer is complex but it is sketched out here and in Box 7.3. Assume for the sake of illustration that it would be possible to take an infinite number of random samples of the same size from a population. Not all the resulting sample means would be perfect estimates of the population mean. We can never know the population figure with 100 per cent certainty, but we can imagine another study with a sample mean of 9.6 units, another with 9.8, and so on. These outcomes, as long as there are enough of them and the sample size is sufficiently high, will take the form of a bell-shaped curve known as a normal distribution (see Figure 7.5) with the sample means clustering around the population mean. Of the sample means not exactly at the population mean, half will be below the population mean and half above it. Moving to the left or to the right (away from the population mean), the curve tails off, reflecting the smaller and smaller number of samples generating means that depart considerably from the population mean. The variation of sample means around the population mean is the sampling error and is measured using a statistic known as the **standard error of the mean**. This is an estimate of the amount by which a sample mean is likely to differ from the population mean. (Technically, it is the **standard deviation** of the sampling distribution of the mean; see Box 7.3). The standard deviation of a set of scores is a measure of how dispersed or spread out the scores are around the mean, and is calculated by taking each score, subtracting the mean, squaring that number, adding up all the resultant scores, dividing that sum by the number of scores, and then square rooting that number. (See Chapter 8 for more on standard deviation.)

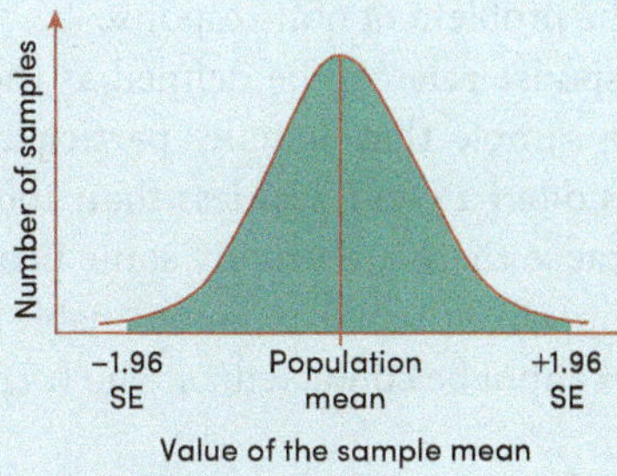

FIGURE 7.5 A distribution of sample means

Thinking about the amount by which a sample mean may differ from the population mean is an important consideration because sampling theory tells us that about 95 per cent of all sample means lie within (+ or −) 1.96 standard errors of the population mean (see Figure 7.5). In other words, we can be 95 per cent confident that our sample mean lies within 1.96 standard errors of the population mean.

To illustrate further, if a sample has been selected according to probability sampling principles, we can be 95 per cent certain that the population mean lies between

(a) [the sample mean] − [1.96 times the standard error of the mean]; and
(b) [the sample mean] + [1.96 times the standard error of the mean].

This is known as the 95 per cent confidence interval. If the mean level of alcohol consumption in the previous seven days in our sample of 450 students is 9.7 units and the standard error of the mean is 1.3, we can be 95 per cent certain that the population mean lies between

$$9.7-(1.96\times 1.3)$$

and

$$9.7+(1.96\times 1.3)$$

that is, between 7.152 and 12.248 units of alcohol.

Under certain conditions, the standard error of the mean in a stratified sample is smaller than in other probability samples. In other words, stratification may inject an extra increment of precision into the probability sampling process (for example, stratifying by university when levels of alcohol consumption vary widely between universities), since it eliminates a possible source of sampling error.

By contrast, a sample without stratification may exhibit a larger standard error of the mean than a comparable sample with stratification. This occurs because a possible source of variability between students is disregarded.

Box 7.3 | Sampling distributions

Assume a population of five cases (with scores = 6, 8, 10, 12, 14) from which a random sample of two cases is to be selected. The five scores sum to 50 and therefore the mean of the population is 50/5, or 10. Taking all possible random samples of two cases with replacement (meaning that after a case is chosen it goes back into the pool, so that two 6s or two 14s are possible), and calculating the mean of each sample of size two, the following set of means (or "sampling distribution of means") results:

		Value of first observation in sample				
		6	8	10	12	14
Value of second observation in sample	6	6	7	8	9	10
	8	7	8	9	10	11
	10	8	9	10	11	12
	12	9	10	11	12	13
	14	10	11	12	13	14

Thus, the 7, where 6 and 8 meet, is the mean of those two values, namely: [6 + 8]/2 = 7; the 13 appears where 12 and 14 meet: [12 + 14]/2 = 13.

Now count the number of the sample means in the table; there are 25. There is only one mean of 14, in the bottom right corner, but five means of 10, on the diagonal going from bottom left to top right. Thus, five of the 25 sample means, or 20 per cent of them, have a value of 10, the same as the population mean, which is what we are trying to estimate. Sample means of 9 and 11 are the next most frequent at 32 per cent (a combined total of 8 of 25 means). With 8 and 12, another 24 per cent (6 of 25) are now counted. So sample means of 8, 9, 10, 11, and 12 represent 76 per cent of all possible sample means. The sample means furthest from the population mean, the 6 and 14 (in each corner), are the rarest, at 4 per cent (1 of 25) each.

Those percentages are really probabilities. The probability of getting a sample mean of 7 is 2 chances in 25 or, as it is usually expressed, 8 chances in 100 or 8 per cent.

The logic of a confidence interval should now be more apparent. A researcher normally takes only one sample, but most random sample results stay close to the population value. In our

root of 2500], yielding the one-half, one-third, one-quarter, and one-fifth.) Notice that the increases in precision become less pronounced (going from 100 to 400 reduces sampling error by half, but 400 to 900 reduces it by only one-third) and thus the rate of reduction in the standard error of the mean declines. Sample size is likely to be profoundly affected by considerations of time and cost at such a juncture, since striving for smaller and smaller increments of precision becomes increasingly uneconomic as ever-larger samples become less and less cost efficient.

Fowler (1993) warned against simple acceptance of this size criterion and argued that it is not normal for researchers to be able to specify in advance "a desired level of precision" (p. 34). Moreover, since sampling error is only one component of any error entailed in an estimate, the notion of a desired level of precision is not realistic. Instead, to the extent that this notion affects decisions about sample size, it usually does so in a general rather than a calculated way. It is usually cost that ultimately determines sample size.

Non-response

Considerations about sampling error do not end with issues of sample size. It's also important to bear in mind the problem of non-response.

The response rate can be defined as the percentage of the sample that actually participates in the study. It is often a good deal less than 100 per cent, partly because there are usually some people in the sample who will either refuse or be unable to participate, who cannot be contacted, or who turn out to be example, 76 per cent of the sample means are within (±) 2 units of the population mean. When plotted, these results don't exactly take the shape of the bell curve shown in Figure 7.5, but you can see the broad outline. Including more and more cases in the sample shapes the lines into a normal curve.

With a real sample, an extension can be created on each side of the sample mean to make it more likely to be correct than if the sample mean by itself were used. The extension for a 95 per cent confidence interval is equal to 1.96 times the standard error of the mean. (In Box 7.2 the sample mean was 9.7, and the extensions were ± [1.96 × 1.3] or ± 2.548.). The extensions around the sample mean create what is called an interval. There is only a 5 per cent chance that the interval does not include the population mean for a 95 per cent confidence interval.

To illustrate, this is basically how athletes using banned substances are caught. They provide one bio-sample (actually two, but one is a backup), which the authorities then check against a more sophisticated version of the table below. For example, suppose that the population mean value for testosterone is 10 and athlete X comes in at 14. While that is a possible (non-drugged) outcome, it is rare. So if the doping committee is willing to be wrong 4 per cent of the time (the frequency with which an honest 14 occurs), the athlete can be accused. With a reputation at stake, however, a 4 per cent chance of error is too high. That is why the tests allow for only much less likely errors.

Mean	Sample Frequency	%
14	1	4
13	2	8
12	3	12
11	4	16
10	5	20
9	4	16
8	3	12
7	2	8
6	1	4
	25	100

unsuitable for the study. Others will be excluded if they leave a large number of questions unanswered, or if they do not take the interview or questionnaire seriously.

Unfortunately, survey response rates have been in "steep decline" for decades (Johnson & Wislar, 2012), with the added problem that there has been no consensus among researchers regarding how to define and calculate response rates. In their research on sustainable consumption in the Edmonton area, Kennedy, Krogman, & Krahn (2013) reported a response rate of 69 per cent. Schieman & Narisada (2014), who used a national sample of the Canadian workforce to examine people's sense of mastery over their lives, achieved a response rate of about 40 per cent. However, non-response bias (the extent to which people who are selected for the sample and participate in the study differ in relevant ways from those who are selected but do not participate) is increasingly considered to be more important than the response rate itself (Johnson & Wislar, 2012). Are the people who have been selected but cannot be contacted richer and on vacation? Are they ill and in hospital? Such differences may be important (depending on the research topic) and may have to be taken into account in the analysis. Researchers sometimes take steps to determine the level of non-response bias, as Schieman & Narisada (2014) did when they concluded that it was not an issue in their study.

Given that 100 per cent response rates are rare, sample size may have to be adjusted. For example, if the goal is a sample of 450 students and earlier surveys suggest that the response rate will be approximately 80 per cent, it may be advisable to sample 575 individuals, on the assumption that approximately 115 (20 per cent) will not participate, leaving 460 and still room for some additional refusals.

How far should researchers go to boost response rates? Smith (1995) showed that response rates are affected by things like the subject matter of the research, the type of respondent, and the effort expended on obtaining the cooperation of prospective respondents. Later in the chapter, a number of steps that can improve response rates to questionnaires (which are particularly prone to poor response rates) are discussed. However, boosting response rates can be expensive. Teitler, Reichman, & Sprachman (2003) discussed the steps taken to increase the response rate of a US sample that was hard to reach, namely both unwed parents of newborn children. They found that although increasing the sample from an initial 68 per cent to 80 per cent of all couples meant that the final sample more closely resembled the population from which it had been taken, diminishing returns set in. This does not mean that steps should not be taken to improve response rates, however. For example, following up on people who do not respond to a questionnaire usually results in an improved response rate, at little additional cost.

Heterogeneity of the population

Yet another consideration is the heterogeneity of the population from which the sample is to be taken. When a population is heterogeneous with regard to characteristics relevant to the topic under study, as a whole country or city normally is, the samples drawn are likely to be highly varied. When it is relatively homogeneous, such as a population of students or members of a particular occupation, the amount of variation is less. Generally, the greater the heterogeneity of a population, the larger a sample should be in order to maximize the chances that all groups will be adequately represented.

Kind of analysis

Finally, researchers should bear in mind the kind of analysis intended. An example is a **contingency table** showing the relationship between two variables. In a 2 × 2 table there are four cells into which the cases can fall, let's say, gender (M/F) × whether the person voted in the last election (Y/N). Suppose there were only 10 males and 10 females in the sample, and that 50 per cent of the men and 50 per cent of the women voted, showing no relationship between gender and voting. But suppose the sample by chance included one more woman who voted and one more man who did not. Now the figures show that 40 per cent of men voted versus 60 per cent of women—quite a difference. To prevent such a small change in the sample from having such a major impact on the estimate, a larger sample is required. You would probably want to have at least 50 males and 50 females. Because the population is approximately half male and half female, this is easy to achieve. But what if the variable is religion? Fifty Roman Catholics (or 50 Anglicans) are easy to find in any random sample of 1000 Canadians, but what about 50 Jehovah's Witnesses or 50 Hindus? One strategy to achieve statistically meaningful results is to randomly over-sample some of these small groups, as Dinovitzer, Hagan, & Parker (2003) did to guarantee sufficient social class variation in their study comparing educational attainment among immigrant and non-immigrant Canadian youth. Similarly, the Canadian Election Study usually over-samples the less populous provinces (such as Prince Edward Island) in order to make interprovincial comparisons. (A statistical adjustment can be made to compensate for the over-sampling when the data are used for purposes other than between-group comparisons.) This illustrates how sample size depends in part on the analysis to be conducted.

Types of non-probability sampling

Non-probability sampling includes all forms of sampling that are not conducted according to the canons of probability sampling outlined earlier. It covers a wide range of different types of sampling strategy, at least one of which—the quota sample—is claimed by some practitioners to be almost as good as a probability sample. This section covers three common non-probability samples: the convenience sample; the **snowball sample**; and the quota sample.

Convenience sampling

A convenience sample is one that is used simply because the elements are readily available to the researcher. Imagine a professor in a faculty of education who is interested in the qualities that teachers want in their principals, and who has several classes made up of teachers working part-time toward master's degrees. Now suppose that she decides to administer a questionnaire to those students—a sample of convenience. Chances are that she will receive all or almost all of the questionnaires back, thus achieving a high response rate. However, the use of the convenience sampling strategy makes it impossible to generalize the findings to teachers as a whole: the very fact that her students are taking this degree program marks them off as different from teachers in general. (In addition, of course, it's ethically questionable for a researcher to ask people who are dependent on them for a grade to take part in their research.)

This is not to suggest that convenience samples should always be avoided. In fact, they are used more often than you might think. Mairs & Bullock's (2013) research on sexually risky behaviour and HIV testing on the part of Canadian "snowbirds" in Florida was based on a convenience sample, as were MacKinnon & Luke's (2002) study of cultural change, and Beagan's (2001) analysis of medical students mentioned in earlier chapters. However, studies involving convenience samples should acknowledge that they are of limited use in estimating population characteristics.

Convenience samples are often utilized in pilot studies. Imagine that part of the education professor's research involves developing a battery of questions to measure the leadership preferences of teachers that she plans to use later, with a different sample. Since it is highly desirable to pre-test such a research instrument before actually using it, administering

Research in the News

The perils of polling

An article in the *Winnipeg Free Press* (Taniguchi, 2020) cites a 2020 poll conducted by a local survey research company indicating that a greater number of Manitobans believe that racism is a problem in the province than was the case five years earlier. A survey done by the company in 2015 suggested that 44 per cent of Manitobans thought that racism was a problem in their province, compared to 61 per cent in 2020.

However plausible these figures may be, the samples were not selected randomly, so there is no way to estimate how accurate the results were. To their credit, both the author of the newspaper article and the research firm on its website state that because of the sampling procedures used, "no error rate can be calculated." This is not to say that the results have no value—it's quite possible that more Manitobans *are* becoming aware of racism as a social problem. According to Lori Wilkinson, a sociologist at the University of Manitoba, "more people are seeing it [racism]. You ask people their opinions about anything, and it really depends on what's newsworthy or what's being discussed online" (Taniguchi, 2020). Wilkinson maintains that more people are becoming aware of racism because of recent worldwide anti-racism protests and the extensive media attention they have received.

Although representative sampling may not be feasible in a number of research situations, the results produced by non-probability sampling should be interpreted with caution. At a minimum, the researcher should, as was done here, state explicitly that there is no way to gauge their accuracy.

Box 7.4 | A convenience sample

Suppose you want to study university undergraduates to find out the extent of their part-time employment while at school. To save time and effort you decide to conduct the study at your own university. You could use probability sampling to get participants, but you think the research is not important enough to justify the cost. Instead, you choose five faculties, and within each, one or two of the specific degree programs it offers: anthropology, visual arts, chemistry, electrical engineering, French, kinesiology, media studies, and psychology. This choice of participants is designed to maximize variety in the types of degree programs represented while providing similar numbers of males and females (since in particular degree programs one gender frequently predominates). Questionnaires can then be given to students in first-, second-, third-, and fourth-year courses.

Together, these procedures represent a good attempt at generating a varied sample. It is a convenience sample, because the choices of university, faculty, degree program, and course are made purposively rather than randomly. Because of the way the questionnaires are administered (in class), there is a very high response rate. On the other hand, students who are absent from class do not get a chance to fill out a questionnaire. An important question is whether absence from class is connected in some way to part-time work, the latter variable being the focus of your study. In other words, is absence higher among students who work part-time, perhaps because they are working at the time of the class? Are some students too tired to go to class because of their part-time work? If so, you will probably underestimate the proportion of students who work part-time. Also, because you have selected a convenience sample, you must say so in your research report, acknowledging that the results cannot be generalized to Canadian students as a whole or even to the student population at your university.

it to a group that is not part of the main study is a legitimate way of exploring issues such as whether respondents will reply honestly to questions on sensitive topics, and whether the questions are clear and comprehensible. A convenience sample may also be used to test newly created scales for reliability and to generate ideas for further research. Box 7.4 contains another illustration of how a convenience sample may be used.

Snowball sampling

Snowball sampling is a form of convenience sampling, but worth distinguishing because it has attracted quite a lot of attention over the years. With this approach, the researcher makes initial contact with a small group of people who are relevant to the research topic and then uses them to establish contact with others. Tastsoglou and Miedema (2003) used this approach to create a sample of immigrant women in the Maritimes. Bowen (2015) used it to recruit informants for her study of people in the Vancouver area who either had experienced the transition from off-street sex work to "square" (non-sex) work, or were simultaneously employed in both. And Whalen and Schmidt (2016) chose snowball sampling to recruit participants for their study of Newfoundland women whose male partners were away from home, working in the Alberta oil industry. Box 7.5 describes the generation of a snowball sample of marijuana users for what is often regarded as a classic study of drug use.

Becker's comment on creating a snowball sample is interesting: "The sample is, of course, in no sense 'random'; [indeed] it would not be possible to draw a random sample, since no one knows the nature of the universe from which it would have to be drawn"

Box 7.5 | A snowball sample

Source: Irina274/iStockphoto

Multiple researchers have used snowball sampling to study issues around illegal drug use in the Downtown Eastside neighbourhood of Vancouver. Why might snowball sampling be useful in this scenario? What are some other research situations in which snowball sampling would be useful?

Becker reported on how he generated a sample of marijuana users:

> I had been a professional dance musician . . . and my first interviews were with people I had met in the music business. I asked them to put me in contact with other [marijuana] users who would be willing to discuss their experiences with me. ... Although in the end half of the fifty interviews were conducted with musicians, the other half covered a wide range of people, including labourers, machinists, and people in the professions. (1963, pp. 45–46)

(Becker, 1963, p. 46). What Becker is saying here is that there is no accessible sampling frame for the population from which the sample is to be taken. The difficulty of creating such a sampling frame means that a non-probability approach is the only feasible one. Moreover, even if it were possible to create a sampling frame of marijuana users or British visitors to Disney theme parks, it would almost certainly become obsolete very soon, because those populations are constantly changing. People become and cease being marijuana users all the time, while new theme park visitors arrive every minute.

The problem with snowball sampling is that it is very unlikely to be representative of the population, although, as Becker's experience suggests, the very notion of a population is problematic in some circumstances. However, snowball sampling is generally used not within a quantitative research strategy, but within a qualitative one: both Becker's work on marijuana users and Bryman's (1995, 1999) studies on theme parks used a qualitative research framework, and concerns about the ability to generalize do not loom large in qualitative research. Indeed, Tastsoglou and Miedema (2003) warned their readers not to generalize from their 40 women to all immigrant women in the Maritimes, much less to those in the rest of Canada. This is not to suggest that snowball sampling is entirely irrelevant to quantitative research: when the researcher needs to focus on relationships between people, tracing connections through snowball sampling can be a better approach than conventional probability sampling. Statistically small groups—gay francophone lawyers in New Brunswick, for example—are researchable with a snowball approach. Taking a random sample from that population would not be feasible.

Quota sampling

Quota sampling is not a predominant form of sample selection in academic social research, but it is widely used for commercial purposes in market research and in political opinion polling in some countries. However, the advent of the *online opt-in survey panel* has made quota sampling more common in academic research in recent years. Opt-in panels are made up of people who are willing to participate in online surveys, often in exchange for credit points or small amounts of money. Third parties who need participants for their research contact the people in charge of the panel and pay a fee to have their

Practical Tip | Sample size and probability sampling for students

For most quantitative researchers sample size does matter: the bigger the sample, the more representative it is likely to be (provided the sample is randomly selected), regardless of the size of the population from which it is drawn. However, students have to do their research with very limited resources, and a truly random sample may not be feasible for them. The crucial point is to be clear about your sampling decisions and to justify what you have done. Explain the difficulties that you would have encountered in generating a random sample. Explain why you could not increase your sample size. Above all, though, don't make claims about your sample that are not warranted. Never claim that your sample is representative, or randomly selected, unless that is true. Also, even if your sample is small, it may have some good features: the range of people included, a good response rate, high levels of honesty. Make sure to play up these positive features while being honest about the sample's limitations. This is what professional researchers do.

surveys administered to people on the panel. The advantages of using opt-in panels include fairly quick turnaround times and a relatively low cost.

The aim of quota sampling is to produce a sample that reflects a population in terms of the relative proportions of people in different categories (gender, ethnicity, age, socioeconomic status, region of residence, etc.), or in combinations of these categories. Unlike a stratified sample, however, a quota sample is not random, since the final selection of people in each category is left up to the researcher or the organization in charge of the opt-in panel. For Canadian studies, information about the stratification of the Canadian population or about certain regions can be obtained from sources such as the census and from surveys based on probability samples such as the General Social Survey, which can then be used to establish the proportion of the sample that is to be made up of people in the various categories.

Once the categories and the numbers of people to be surveyed within each one (the quotas) have been decided, the researchers or those contracted by them to select the sample try to pick people who fit those categories. The quotas are typically interrelated. As in stratified sampling, the population may be divided into strata covering several characteristics (for example, gender, employment, and age) all at once (see Table 7.2). For example, fifty 25- to 44-year-old unemployed females may be required to meet the quota. If necessary, statistical adjustments can be made to the sample data such that the relative sizes of the categories match those of the population.

A number of criticisms are frequently levelled at quota samples:

- The proponents of probability sampling argue that because the choice of respondent is left to the researcher or the organization collecting the data, a quota sample is not likely to be representative of the population. As noted earlier, if people are approached in person,

TABLE 7.2 Strata for gender, age, and employment

Older, female, unemployed (5%)	Younger, female, unemployed (4%)
Older, female, employed (17%)	Younger, female, employed (20%)
Older, female, other (7%)	Younger, female, other (1%)
Older, male, unemployed (3%)	Younger, male, unemployed (6%)
Older, male, employed (15%)	Younger, male, employed (15%)
Older, male, other (6%)	Younger, male, other (1%)

interviewers may be unduly influenced by their perceptions of friendliness or willingness to make eye contact (many people will look at the ground and shuffle past as quickly as possible, not wanting to be bothered). If people are recruited online, differences between people who have access to the Internet compared to those who do not can result in sample selection bias. For example, online populations tend to be younger, better educated, and have higher incomes than people without Internet access, which can affect the representativeness of the sample. And among people who do go online, there may be relevant differences between those who join opt-in panels—a form of self-selection—and those who do not.

- If prospective participants are approached in person, the characteristics of the people who are in the vicinity of the investigator when recruits are sought may not be typical of the population of interest. There is a risk, for example, that people not in full-time paid work may be over-represented, especially in locations such as malls, making the sample unrepresentative. Also, judgments about eligibility may sometimes be incorrect, for instance regarding the respondent's age, and even more so for social class. For example, someone who is actually young enough to be eligible but looks older may not be asked because the quota of the older group is filled. In such cases an element of bias is introduced.
- It is not appropriate to calculate a standard error term (such as the standard error of the mean) from a quota sample, so it is not possible to estimate the amount by which a sample characteristic is likely to differ from the population. In fact, most statistical estimates are problematic unless random sampling has been used.

Structured observation and sampling

Structured observation, like survey research, necessitates decisions about sampling. However, the issues that have to be considered are not limited to sampling people. Several other sampling issues may be involved:

- If the structured observation is to take place in public areas, there will be no sampling frames (lists of people who frequent those areas). It would be very difficult, for example, to get a complete list of people who walk along a particular street, or of men who frequent certain "tearooms." One can, however, choose the people by using a table of random numbers: for example, the third, then seventh, then eighteenth person seen in the public area. The same table can be used to establish random samples of time, place, or activity.
- Time sampling involves an observer recording whatever is happening at a particular time, for example, in a pub every 15 minutes after a random start time. This can be done on one person or on several individuals at once and the 15-minute figure can be varied using a table of random numbers. It may be necessary that individuals watched on more than one day not be observed at the same time of the day; the observation periods may have to be randomly selected. For example, it would be an error to observe a certain pupil in a school classroom always at the end of the day, when most students are tired, since tiredness could give a false impression of that pupil's behaviour.

Time sampling should be combined with the next strategy:

- Random sampling of specific places: for example, in a pub near the entrance, at the bar, by the pool table, outside where the smokers congregate, the washroom area, and the booths.
- "Behaviour sampling," whereby an entire group is watched and the observer records a particular kind of behaviour. Thus, in that same pub, the researcher can observe the *n*th pick-up (second, then fifth, etc.) after the previous one was observed, using a random number table to determine the *n*.

Considerations relating to probability sampling derive largely from concerns about **external validity**. For example, if a structured observation study is conducted over a relatively short span of time, questions are likely to arise concerning the stability or representativeness of the findings over longer periods. If the research is conducted in schools, for instance, observations conducted toward the end of the school year, when examinations are likely to loom large for both teachers and students, may produce different results than observations made at a different point in the academic year. Consequently, consideration has to be given to the timing of the observations. Furthermore, how are the sites in which structured observation is to take place selected? Are they representative? Using a random sampling procedure to select the schools would assuage any worries in this connection. However, gaining access to settings such as schools and business organizations is usually difficult; thus settings that are willing to grant access may not be representative.

Limits to generalization

An important point, often not fully appreciated, is that even when a sample is selected using probability sampling, any findings can be generalized only to the population from which the sample was taken. This is an obvious point, but it is easy to think that findings from any study have a broader applicability. If the study is based on a random sample of adult Calgarians, for example, its findings cannot be generalized to the whole province of Alberta, much less to other regions of Canada. The opinions of Calgarians may be very different from those of Edmontonians or people who live in Lethbridge, and even more different from the opinions of Montrealers or residents of St John's.

Methods in Motion | Applications to Canadian Society

The need for youth mental health services in Canada

Weins et al. (2020) used Statistics Canada's Canadian Community Health Survey (2011–2018) to examine trends in mental health among youth aged 12–24. The study was based on nationally representative samples that were gathered using stratified cluster sampling in which the strata were health regions, geographical areas within health regions, and dwellings within the latter.

The study found that the incidence of perceived poor/fair mental health, formally diagnosed mood and anxiety disorders, and the number of mental health consultations increased over the years covered by the study, especially among young adult women. Substance abuse disorders can be related to poor mental health, and the researchers report that cannabis use among adolescent males appeared to be decreasing in the period before the legalization of marijuana (2011–2017), but increased by 5.6 per cent in the first year of legalization (2018) compared to the previous year's levels.

The researchers conclude that these indicators point to a need for expanded mental health services for young people in Canada. They are cautious, however, in interpreting their findings in terms of an actual increase in the prevalence of mental illness. The pervasiveness of mental health problems may have expanded in the years covered by the study, but they also state that it is possible that the findings reflect changes in the ways mental and emotional disorders are diagnosed, greater awareness of mental health matters among members of the public, and greater acceptance of people who suffer from mental illness. Similarly, the apparent increase in cannabis use following legalization could reflect real differences in consumption levels, but it may also be related to less reluctance to admit to marijuana use following legalization. Wiens and colleagues conclude that regardless of the reasons for the higher percentages showing up in their data, the findings reflect a greater need for youth mental health services than was previously recognized.

One issue rarely discussed in this context, and almost impossible to assess, is whether there is a time limit on the findings generated. Quite aside from the fact that findings cannot (or at least should not) be generalized beyond the population sampled, is there a point at which one should say, "Well, those findings applied then, but do they apply now?" To take a simple example: no one should assume that the findings of a 1995 study of university students' budgeting and personal finance habits apply to today's students. Ever-increasing costs have changed the ways students finance their education, increasing their reliance on part-time work, parents, and loans. But even when there is no definable or recognizable source of relevant change, there is still the possibility (even the likelihood) that the findings are time specific. Changes over time are a major reason why it is important to conduct replications.

Content analysis sampling

There are several phases in the selection of a sample for content analysis. Applying content analysis to the mass media is explored here but the basic principles have broader applications.

Sampling media

Many studies of the mass media specify a research problem in the form of "examining the representation of X in the mass media." The X might be trade unions, women, food scares, crime, or drunk driving. But which mass medium to choose—newspapers, television, radio, chat rooms, social media? If newspapers, will the study focus on tabloids, broadsheets, or both? Will it include Sunday papers, or free newspapers? Will it examine feature articles and letters to the editor, or news stories only? Buchanan's (2014) study of the decline of local news coverage in two Ontario metropolitan newspapers analyzed every article of any kind contained in 19 randomly selected editions of each paper, yielding a total sample of 7129 articles.

Sampling dates

With an ongoing general phenomenon such as crime, probability sampling can be used to sample dates: for example, a systematic sample can be generated by randomly selecting one date and then selecting every *n*th date thereafter. Using a variation of this method, Collins (2014), in a study of how the gender of the offender and the victim may affect media portrayals of crime, randomly chose two numbers (two and seven) in order to select years to analyze articles published in the *Vancouver Sun*, *Saskatoon Star Phoenix*, *Winnipeg Free Press*, and *Toronto Star*. This produced the years 1982, 1987, 1992, 1997, 2002, and 2007. She then used a pseudo-random number generator (which uses an algorithm to produce a set of numbers that approximates a sequence of random numbers) to select twenty dates that would be used to search for relevant articles in each newspaper, which yielded a total of 1190 articles.

The time span analyzed in content analysis often depends on the research questions. Dumitrica and Bakardjieva (2018) wanted to examine how Canadian newspapers viewed the role of social media in grassroots political engagement and mobilization, but were unsure of what might constitute a good starting date. They speculated that because social media usage seemed to reach a critical phase around 2005, that would be a good year to use as the starting point. Their search for relevant articles published that year did not yield any that fit their criteria, but they found one released in 2006 and twenty-five published in 2007, with the latter year's total being typical of what was available for each of the next seven years. In the end they used articles published from 2006 through 2014 as the source of their data. Researchers often choose a time span that provides a good chance of producing the data needed to answer their research questions, and may adjust accordingly depending on what they find.

Reducing non-response

There is little consistent evidence on whether response rates are lower for interviews conducted over the telephone rather than face-to-face (see Table 7.3). However, there is a general belief that telephone interviews achieve slightly lower response rates than personal interviews (Shuy, 2002; Frey, 2004). Developments in telephone communications such

TABLE 7.3 Comparing the strengths of different ways of contacting members of the chosen sample

	MODE OF SURVEY ADMINISTRATION				
	Face-to-face interview	Telephone interview	Posted questionnaire	Email	Web
Resource issues					
Is the cost of the mode of administration relatively low?	✓	✓✓	✓✓✓	✓✓✓	✓✓✓
Is the speed of the mode of administration relatively fast?	✓	✓✓✓	✓✓✓	✓✓✓	✓✓✓
Is the cost of handling a dispersed sample relatively low?	✓(✓✓ if clustered)	✓✓✓	✓✓✓	✓✓✓	✓✓✓
Sampling-related issues					
Does the mode of administration tend to produce a good response rate?	✓✓✓	✓✓	✓	✓	✓
Is the researcher able to control who responds (that is, the person targeted is the one who answers)?	✓✓✓	✓✓✓	✓✓	✓✓	✓✓
Is the mode of administration accessible to all sample members?	✓✓✓	✓✓	✓✓✓	✓(because of need for respondents to be accessible online)	✓(because of need for respondents to be accessible online)
Is the mode of administration less likely to result in non-response to some questions?	✓✓✓	✓✓✓	✓✓	✓✓	✓✓

Notes: Number of ticks indicates the strength of the mode of administration of a survey in relation to each issue. More ticks correspond to more advantages in relation to each issue. A single tick implies that the mode of administering a questionnaire does not fare well in this area. Two ticks imply that it is acceptable and three ticks that it does very well. This table was influenced by Czaja and Blair (1996).

as the growing use of call screening and cellphones have certainly had an adverse effect on telephone survey responses.

Interviewers in both types of study play an important role in maximizing the response rate for a survey study. The following points should be borne in mind:

- Interviewers should be prepared to keep calling back if interviewees are unavailable. This requires taking into account people's likely work and leisure habits: there is no point in daytime calling for people who work during the day. People living alone may be reluctant to answer the door, especially after dark.
- Reassure people that you are not a salesperson. Because of the unethical tactics of organizations whose representatives falsely say they are doing market or social research, many people have become very suspicious of anyone who says they would "just like to ask a few questions."
- When conducting in-person interviews, dress in a way that is acceptable to a wide spectrum of people.
- Make it clear that you are happy to find an interview time to suit the respondent.

Practical Tip | Response rates

The lower the response rate, the more likely it is that questions will be raised about the representativeness of the sample. Mailed questionnaires in particular are often associated with low response rates, and as Mangione's classification, shown below, illustrates, some authorities consider a response rate below 50 per cent unacceptable. Then again, a great deal of published research achieves only a low response rate, so don't despair. The key point is to recognize and acknowledge the negative implications of a low rate.

Also, response rates are usually an issue only with randomly selected samples. Samples not selected using probability methods are not expected to be representative of a population even if all the people selected participate. But here again, it is necessary to acknowledge the limitations of the sample.

Improving response rates to mailed questionnaires

Mangione (1995, pp. 60–61) classified response rates to mailed questionnaires as follows:

Over 85%	excellent
70–85%	very good
60–69%	acceptable
50–59%	barely acceptable
Below 50%	not acceptable

Because of the tendency for mailed questionnaires to generate lower response rates than structured interviews (and the implications this has for the validity of findings), a great deal of thought and research has gone into improving response rates for the former. The following steps are frequently suggested:

- Write a good covering letter explaining the reasons for the research, why it is important, and why the recipient has been selected; provide guarantees of confidentiality.
- Make it personal by including the respondent's name and address in the covering letter, and by ensuring that each letter is individually signed. A cover letter addressed to "Occupant" will put most people off. The downside of the personal approach is that it may raise concerns: How did they know about me? Will my responses really be confidential? The researcher should try to deal with any potential fears in the letter.
- The mailed questionnaires should always be accompanied by a stamped return envelope or (at the very least) return postage.
- Don't allow the questionnaire to appear unnecessarily bulky. Some researchers reduce the size of the questionnaire to fit a booklet format. As with structured interviewing, begin with questions most likely to be of interest to the respondent.
- Follow up individuals who do not reply at first, possibly with two or three further mailings. The importance of reminders cannot be overstated—they do work. One approach is to send out a reminder letter to non-respondents two weeks after the initial mailing, reasserting the nature and aims of the survey and suggesting that the person contact a member of the research team to obtain a replacement copy of the questionnaire should the original one have been lost. Then, two weeks after that, those who still have not responded should be sent another letter along with a second copy of the questionnaire. These reminders have a demonstrable effect on the response rate. Some writers argue for even more than two mailings of reminder letters. If a response rate is worryingly low, further mailings are certainly desirable.
- Monetary incentives increase the response rate but can be deemed unethical. They are most effective if they arrive with the questionnaire

(as opposed to after its return). Apparently, most respondents will not take the money and discard the questionnaire. The evidence also suggests that quite small amounts of money have a positive impact on the response rate, but that larger amounts do not necessarily improve the rate any further.

Virtual sampling issues

A limitation of online surveys is that not everyone is online and has the technical ability to handle questionnaires in either email or Web formats, although fewer and fewer people lack these characteristics. Other factors that make such surveys problematic include the following:

- Many people have more than one email address, and the address known by the researcher may not be commonly used by the participant, making communication difficult.
- As mentioned earlier, Internet users are a biased sample of the population in that they tend to be better educated, wealthier, younger, etc. than non-users.
- Few sampling frames exist for the general online population, and most of these are likely to be either confidential or too expensive to acquire.

Such issues make it difficult to satisfy all the criteria for conducting probability sampling. The chief problem with virtual sampling strategies is that the representativeness of the sample is almost always in question. However, online opt-in survey panels are making it easier for social researchers to gain access to online participants, and one could argue that they provide better access to large populations and more diverse samples than other forms of non-probability sampling. Regardless of the type of sampling chosen, it is always necessary to discuss the limitations of the method used.

Key Points

- Probability sampling is a mechanism for reducing bias in sample selection.
- Key technical terms in sampling include representative sample, random sample, non-response, population, and sampling error.
- Randomly selected samples are important because they permit generalizations to the population of interest with a known probability of error.
- Sampling error generally decreases as sample size increases.
- Under certain circumstances, quota samples can be an alternative to random samples, but they have some deficiencies.
- Convenience samples can provide useful data, but have limited generalizability.
- Response rates vary by the medium of communication and most can be improved by persistent follow-up procedures.

Questions for Review (R) and Creative Application (A)

R1 What do each of the following terms mean: "population"; "probability sampling"; "sampling frame"; and "representative sample"?

A1 You have been asked to organize your high school reunion this year, and want to select a sample of your classmates to pick a venue for the event. How could you create a sampling frame and select a random sample of 50 people?

Probability sampling

R2 Why does probability sampling offer a greater chance of selecting a representative sample than non-probability sampling?

A2 A researcher positions herself on a street corner and asks every fifth person who walks by for an interview until she has a sample of 250. Would the results be generalizable to any specific population? Explain.

R3 What are the main types of probability sample? How is each one selected?

A3 You want to conduct an interview survey of 500 people in Winnipeg that would give you findings that are generalizable to all adults in the city. What type of sample should you select? Why?

Sample size

R4 Explain why non-response bias may be a more important consideration in sampling than the response rate.

A4 You are doing a study on the relationship between body acceptance and social media use among young women, and will use an online questionnaire to gather your data. Assume that you have chosen an appropriate method to generate a probability sample. What could you do to maximize the response rate? What characteristics of the sample should be the same as those of the population in order to get meaningful results (e.g., the ethnic breakdown)?

Non-probability samples

R5 What are the main kinds of non-probability sample, and how are they selected?

A5 Which form of non-probability sample is likely to be the least useful if your goal is to market a new type of cellphone? Which is likely the most useful? Explain.

Limits to generalization

R6 Besides selecting a probability sample of adequate size, what factors should be taken into consideration before generalizing the results of a study to a particular population?

A6 You just completed a study on racism in Canada using appropriate sampling techniques. For how long can you consider your results to be applicable to Canadian society? Explain.

Interactive Classroom Activities

The number of exercises chosen here will depend on the amount of class time available and the inclinations of the instructor. It may be advisable for the instructor to determine population and sample sizes in advance to simplify the calculations.

1. The instructor gives each student in the class (or a predetermined number of participants) an ID number, and asks them how many kilometres they have to travel to get to campus, which is recorded and then shown on the blackboard/screen, along with the gender of the student. The data are then treated as population data. (For very large classes, a subset of the class can be randomly selected for this using a "numbering off" procedure.) The instructor or a volunteer then adds up the total kilometres travelled for all participants, which is used to calculate the population mean. Each member of the class then uses a random number table to select simple random samples of increasing size, for example, $n = 1$, $n = 10$, $n = 20$, $n = 40$, and so on, which are used to calculate sample means. The class is then asked: How does the size of the sample affect its accuracy? Which sample size has the least amount of sampling error? Why?
2. Each member of the class then selects a systematic sample (every *n*th case, using a random start) the size of which matches that of the largest simple random sample selected in exercise 1. For example, if the population size was 80 and the largest simple random sample selected had a size of 40, every second case (80/40) would be selected for the systematic sample. The class is asked: How close is the mean of the systematic sample to that of the largest simple random sample? Why are the two sample means not always the same?
3. Each person in the class calculates the gender breakdown for each sample selected in exercise 1, and compares it to the overall gender breakdown of the population. The class is asked: How do these breakdowns differ by sample size? What does it mean to "stratify" a population by gender? Would stratifying be necessary in order to have the gender breakdown of the samples match that of the population?
4. The mean number of kilometres travelled by all females in the population is calculated, as is the

mean for all males. The means for women and men are then calculated for each sample selected in exercise 1. The class is asked: How is the accuracy of the means affected by sample size? Would it be appropriate to stratify by gender for this variable? Why or why not? How could a gender-stratified sample be selected to calculate the mean number of kilometres travelled to campus?

Relevant Websites

Statistics Canada provides a good general introduction to sampling. Both probability and non-probability sampling techniques are described here. Navigate the site by using the links on the left side of the page. Test your knowledge of sampling by doing the exercises provided.

www.statcan.gc.ca/edu/power-pouvoir/ch13/5214895-eng.htm

Statistics Canada provides the sampling techniques used for the 2018 General Social Survey—Giving, Volunteering and Participating here:

https://www23.statcan.gc.ca/imdb/p2SV.pl?Function=getSurvey&SDDS=4430#a2

This YouTube video illustrates how to select a ***simple random, convenience, systematic, cluster, and stratified sample***.

https://www.youtube.com/watch?v=be9e-Q-jC-0

(Websites accessed 4 September 2021.)

OXFORD learning link

More resources are available on Oxford Learning Link. Visit https://learninglink.oup.com/ for:

- Student self-quiz
- Flash cards
- Audio clips
- Videos
- Activities

8 Quantitative Data Analysis

Chapter Overview

This chapter presents some of the most basic and frequently used methods for analyzing quantitative data. To illustrate them, we'll use an imaginary data set on attendance at a gym—the kind of data set that could be generated from a small research project suitable for most undergraduates.

The chapter explores:

- the importance of anticipating questions of analysis early in the research process, before all the data have been collected;
- the different kinds of **variables** generated in quantitative research (knowing how to distinguish them is crucial in deciding which statistics to use);
- methods for analyzing a single variable (**univariate analysis**);
- methods for analyzing **relationships** between two variables (**bivariate analysis**); and
- analysis of relationships among three or more variables (**multivariate analysis**).

Key Learning Outcomes

Here is a list of goals you should try to achieve as you read and think about the material in this chapter. After completing this chapter, you should be able to:

1. Explain how to deal with **missing data**.
2. Differentiate between three types of variable: **nominal**, **ordinal**, and **interval/ratio**.
3. Interpret various forms of **univariate analyses**, including **frequency tables** and diagrams, **measures of central tendency**, and **measures of dispersion**.
4. Describe several kinds of **bivariate analyses**, including those involving **contingency tables**, **Pearson's *r***, scatter diagrams, **Kendall's tau-b**, **Cramér's *V***, **eta**, and the **chi-square test**.

▲ kan_chana/Shutterstock

5. Outline the purpose of inferential statistics and the meaning of the term "**statistical significance.**"
6. Discuss the goals of multivariate analyses, and how they can be used to test for **spuriousness, intervening variables**, and **statistical interactions.**

If you're like many students in the social sciences, the idea of learning about statistics doesn't fill you with joy. How about communing with nature? Yes, that would be much better—open fields, wild winds, the bright sky, a riot of colour provided by the plants and animals around you. On the other hand, it's often said that mathematics is the language that nature speaks, and statistics is a form of applied mathematics. Communing with nature via statistics can be just as invigorating as communing any other way, especially if you work at it for a while. Feel better now? If not, remember that the best way to learn a new language is to start with the basics. That's what we'll do in this chapter. In fact, we're not going to go beyond a basic level, and we won't even be using any formulas—we'll leave that for your statistics courses. What we will do is introduce the logic of statistics, which will give you the conceptual foundations you need to do quantitative data analysis. We'll also discuss some important ways of organizing quantitative data. Think of it as a new language class.

Introduction

Once a sample has been selected and the numerical data have been gathered, the next step is to analyze the information you have. Here we will discuss some basic ways to do that. We'll avoid the formulas that underpin those techniques, in order to keep the discussion focused on *interpreting* statistics and on methodological issues. One chapter could not do justice to the topic of numerical data analysis in any case; readers are advised to consult books that provide more detailed and advanced treatments (for example, Agresti & Finlay, 2009; Noack, 2018).

Before we begin, a warning is in order. The biggest mistake in quantitative research is to think that data analysis decisions can wait until after the data have been collected. Data analysis *is* carried out after that stage, but it's essential to be fully aware of what techniques will be used before data collection begins. **Interview schedules**, **questionnaires**, **observation schedules**, and **coding frames** should be designed with the data analysis in mind, for two main reasons:

- The statistical techniques that can be used depend on how a variable is measured. Inappropriate measurement may make it impossible to conduct certain types of data analysis.
- The size and nature of the sample also impose limitations on the kinds of techniques that are suitable for the data set.

A small research project

The discussion of quantitative data analysis provided here is based on an imaginary piece of research carried out by an undergraduate for her honours thesis on leisure in modern society. She chose that topic because of her enthusiasm for gyms and workout facilities, and her interest in how and why such venues are used. She had a hunch that they might be indicative of a "civilizing process" and used this theory as a framework for her findings (Rojek, 1995, pp. 50–56). She was also interested in issues relating to gender and body image, and suspected that men and women differ in their reasons for going to a gym as well as in their activities there.

She secured the permission of a gym close to her home to contact a sample of its members by mail. The gym had 1200 members and she decided to take a **simple random sample** of 10 per cent of them (that is, 120 members). She mailed questionnaires to members of the sample with a covering letter testifying to the gym's support for her research; the letter also included a Web address that allowed participants to fill out the questionnaire online. One thing she wanted to know was how much time people spent on each of the three main types of activity in the gym: cardiovascular workouts, weightlifting, and other activities (for example, stretching exercises). She defined each of these carefully in the covering letter and asked members of the sample to note down how long they typically spend on each of the three activities during a single visit to the gym. She ended up with 90 completed questionnaires out of the 120—a response rate of 75 per cent.

The entire questionnaire ran to four pages; 12 of the questions along with the responses of a fictional respondent are provided in Box 8.1. Questions 1, 3, 4, 5, 6, 7, 8, and 9 were **pre-coded**; the respondent simply had to circle the appropriate code. With the others, specific figures were requested, which were later transferred to the code column.

Missing data

The data for all 90 respondents are presented in Box 8.2. Each of the 12 questions is designated initially as a numbered variable (var00001, var00002, etc.); the number corresponds to the question number in Box 8.1 (var00001 is question 1, var00002 is question 2, etc.). An important issue in data analysis is how to handle the "missing data" generated when respondents do not reply to a question—whether because they accidentally skip it, because they do not want to answer it, or because it does not apply to them. For example, respondent 24 failed to answer question 2 on age. This was coded as 999, a number chosen because it cannot be mistaken for a person's age and is also easy to remember. Also, question 9 has a large number of 8s, because for this variable an 8 means "not applicable"—many people did not answer this question, having been filtered out by the previous one (that is, they do not have other sources of regular exercise). Everyone answered questions 10, 11, and 12, so there are no missing data for those variables; if there were, it would be necessary to code the missing data with another number that could not be mistaken for an actual number of minutes. The various missing data codes are stored in the information for each variable so they cannot be read by the computer as anything other than missing data.

Types of variables

Look at the different questions and notice that some of them call for answers in real numbers: questions 2 (***age***), and 10, 11, and 12. Question 8 has an either/or answer, which is called a **dichotomy** (only two possible responses). The rest of the questions take the form of lists of categories, but there are also differences among them. Some of the answers can be rank ordered: see questions 4, 5, and 6. Thus, for question 6 the category "every day" implies greater frequency than "4–6 days a week," which in turn is a greater frequency than "2 or 3 days a week," and so on. Compare this to questions 1, 3, 7, and 9 where the categories *can't* be rank ordered. In the case of question 3, for instance, "relaxation" is neither more nor less of something than "maintain or improve fitness" is.

In short, different types of variable can be generated in the course of research. The three main types are distinguished by looking at the relationship between the categories of the variable *as manifested by any one individual*. The three types, which pertain to different *levels of measurement*, are as follows:

- *Nominal variables.* These variables, also known as *categorical variables*, are composed of categories that have no relationship to one another except that they are *different*. In the case of religion, for example, the categories might be Roman Catholic, Protestant, Jewish, Muslim, Hindu, Other, and No Religion. Any two research participants will be either in the same category or in different categories: no other kind of comparison is possible. This means that the order of the categories is arbitrary: it could have begun with No Religion and ended with Roman Catholic. Switching the order has no implications for the way the data are interpreted.
- *Ordinal variables.* With these variables the different categories can be rank ordered. That means that "greater than" (>) and "less than" (<) statements can be made about the categories and the people in them. For example, in question 5 "always" indicates greater frequency

Box 8.1 | Part of a completed questionnaire on use of a gym

Questionnaire	Code
1. What is your gender? (please tick)	
Male ___✓___	①
Female ______	2
Other (please specify) ______________	3
2. How old are you?	
__21__ years	21
3. Which of the following best describes your main reason for going to the gym? (please circle one code only)	
Relaxation	1
Maintain or improve fitness ___✓___	②
Lose weight ______	3
Meet others ______	4
Build strength ______	5
Other (please specify) ______	6
4. When you go to the gym, how often do you use the cardiovascular equipment (treadmill, step machine, bike, elliptical, rower)? (please tick)	
Always ___✓___	①
Usually ______	2
Rarely ______	3
Never ______	4
5. When you go to the gym, how often do you use the weights? (please tick)	
Always ___✓___	①
Usually ______	2
Rarely ______	3
Never ______	4
6. Generally, how frequently do you go to the gym? (please tick)	
Every day ______	1
4–6 days a week ______	2
2 or 3 days a week ___✓___	③
Once a week ______	4
2 or 3 times a month ______	5
Once a month ______	6
Less than once a month ______	7
7. Do you usually go with someone else to the gym or usually on your own? (please circle one code only)	
On my own ___✓___	①
With a friend ______	2
With a partner/spouse ______	3
8. Do you have sources of regular exercise other than the gym?	
Yes ______ No ___✓___	1
If you have answered No to this question, please proceed to question 10.	②

Questionnaire	Code
9. If you have replied Yes to question 8, please indicate the main source of regular exercise in the last six months from this list. (please circle one code only)	
Casual or organized competitive sports ________	1
Recreational cycling ________	2
Jogging ________	3
Walking ________	4
Other (please specify) ________	5
10. During your last visit to the gym, how many minutes did you spend on the cardiovascular equipment (treadmill, step machine, bike, elliptical, rower)?	
__33__ minutes	33
11. During your last visit to the gym, how many minutes did you spend on weights?	
__17__ minutes	17
12. During your last visit to the gym, how many minutes did you spend on other activities (e.g., stretching exercises)?	
__5__ minutes	5

than "usually," which indicates greater frequency than "rarely," and so on. Note also that it would be illogical to re-order the categories as, say, "always, never, sometimes, usually."

The distance or amount of difference between the categories, however, may not be equal across the range. Thus, the difference between the categories "always" and "usually" is probably not the same as the difference between "usually" and "rarely," and so on. This is because no unit of measurement is used for this question. Ordinal variables are similar to words that have either a comparative "er" or a superlative "est" attached to them, as in "taller" and "tallest."

- *Interval/ratio variables.* These are variables for which a unit of measurement exists and thus the distances or amount of difference between the categories can be made identical across the range of categories. The values take the form of actual numbers (such as 1, 2, 7.5, etc.). In the case of variables var00010 to var00012, the unit is the minute and the difference between the categories is a one-minute interval. Thus, a person who spends 32 minutes on cardiovascular equipment is spending one minute more than someone who spends 31. That difference is the same as the difference between someone who spends 8 minutes and another who spends 9 minutes on the equipment. At the interval/ratio level of measurement, it is possible to say that two scores are equal or not equal (as at the nominal level), for example, $32 \neq 31$; that they have greater or lesser values (as at the ordinal level), for example, $32 > 31$, $8 < 9$; and that the distance or amount of difference between them can be specified, for example, $32 - 31 = 1$. This is the highest level of measurement, the one that allows the widest range of analysis techniques, including addition, subtraction, multiplication, and division.

Sometimes a distinction is made between interval and ratio variables. Ratio variables are interval variables with a fixed and non-arbitrary zero point (as in a wind speed of 0 kilometres per hour). Many social science variables exhibit this quality, for example, income, age, and years of school completed. In the discussions that follow we will use the more inclusive term "interval/ratio," but to understand, take two incomes: \$30K and \$45K. They are nominally unequal and the first is less than the second, in fact \$15K less. But with that real 0, one can also say that the first is 2/3 of the second (or the second is 1.5 times the first). The first income can also be said to stand in a 2:3 *ratio* to the second.

Box 8.2 | Gym survey data

Case	var00001	var00002	var00003	var00004	var00005	var00006	var00007	var00008	var00009	var00010	var00011	var00012
1	1	21	2	1	1	3	1	2	8	33	17	5
2	2	44	1	3	1	4	3	1	2	10	23	10
3	2	19	3	1	2	2	1	1	1	27	18	12
4	2	27	3	2	1	2	1	2	8	30	17	3
5	1	57	2	1	3	2	3	1	4	22	0	15
6	2	27	3	1	1	3	1	1	3	34	17	0
7	1	39	5	2	1	5	1	1	5	17	48	10
8	2	36	3	1	2	2	2	1	1	25	18	7
9	1	37	2	1	1	3	1	2	8	34	15	0
10	2	51	2	2	2	4	3	2	8	16	18	11
11	1	24	5	2	1	3	1	1	1	0	42	16
12	2	29	2	1	2	3	1	2	8	34	22	12
13	1	20	5	1	1	2	1	2	8	22	31	7
14	2	22	2	1	3	4	2	1	3	37	14	12
15	2	46	3	1	1	5	2	2	8	26	9	4
16	2	41	3	1	2	2	3	1	4	22	7	10
17	1	25	5	1	1	3	1	1	1	21	29	4
18	2	46	3	1	2	4	2	1	4	18	8	11
19	1	30	3	1	1	5	1	2	8	23	9	6
20	1	25	5	2	1	3	1	1	1	23	19	0
21	2	24	2	1	1	3	2	1	2	20	7	6
22	2	39	1	2	3	5	1	2	8	17	0	9
23	1	44	3	1	1	3	2	1	2	22	8	5
24	1	999	1	2	2	4	2	1	4	15	10	4
25	2	18	3	1	2	3	1	2	1	18	7	10
26	1	41	3	1	1	3	1	2	8	34	10	4
27	2	38	2	1	2	5	3	1	2	24	14	10
28	1	25	2	1	1	2	1	2	8	48	22	7
29	1	41	5	2	1	3	1	1	2	17	27	0
30	2	30	3	1	1	2	2	2	8	32	13	10
31	2	29	3	1	3	2	1	2	8	31	0	7
32	2	42	1	2	2	4	2	1	4	17	14	6
33	1	31	2	1	1	2	1	2	8	49	21	2
34	2	25	3	1	1	2	3	2	8	30	17	15
35	1	46	3	1	1	3	1	1	3	32	10	5
36	1	24	5	2	1	4	1	1	2	0	36	11
37	2	34	3	1	1	3	2	1	4	27	14	12
38	2	50	2	1	2	2	3	2	8	28	8	6
39	1	28	5	1	1	3	2	1	1	26	22	8
40	2	30	3	1	1	2	1	1	4	21	9	12
41	1	27	2	1	1	2	1	1	3	64	15	8
42	2	27	2	1	2	4	2	1	4	22	10	7
43	1	36	5	1	1	3	2	2	8	21	24	0
44	2	43	3	1	1	4	1	2	8	25	13	8

Case	var00001	var00002	var00003	var00004	var00005	var00006	var00007	var00008	var00009	var00010	var00011	var00012
45	1	34	2	1	1	3	2	1	1	45	15	6
46	2	27	3	1	1	2	1	1	4	33	10	9
47	2	38	2	1	3	4	2	2	8	23	0	16
48	1	28	2	1	1	3	3	1	2	38	13	5
49	1	44	5	1	1	2	1	2	8	27	19	7
50	2	31	3	1	2	3	2	2	8	32	11	5
51	2	23	2	1	1	4	2	1	1	33	18	8
52	1	45	3	1	1	3	1	1	2	26	10	7
53	2	34	3	1	2	2	3	2	8	36	8	12
54	1	27	3	1	1	2	3	1	3	42	13	6
55	2	40	3	1	1	2	2	1	4	26	9	10
56	2	24	2	1	1	2	1	1	2	22	10	9
57	1	37	2	1	1	5	2	2	8	21	11	0
58	1	22	5	1	1	4	1	1	1	23	17	6
59	2	31	3	1	2	3	1	1	4	40	16	12
60	1	37	2	1	1	2	3	2	8	54	12	3
61	2	33	1	2	2	4	2	2	8	17	10	5
62	1	23	5	1	1	3	1	1	1	41	27	8
63	1	28	3	1	1	3	3	2	8	27	11	8
64	2	29	2	1	2	5	2	1	2	24	9	9
65	2	43	3	1	1	2	1	2	8	36	17	12
66	1	28	5	1	1	3	1	1	1	22	15	4
67	1	48	2	1	1	5	1	1	4	25	11	7
68	2	32	2	2	2	4	2	2	8	27	13	11
69	1	28	5	1	1	2	2	2	8	15	23	7
70	2	23	2	1	1	5	1	1	4	14	11	5
71	2	43	2	1	2	5	1	2	8	18	7	3
72	1	28	2	1	1	4	3	1	2	34	18	8
73	2	23	3	1	1	2	1	2	8	37	17	17
74	2	36	1	2	2	4	2	1	4	18	12	4
75	1	50	2	1	1	3	1	1	2	28	14	3
76	1	37	3	1	1	2	2	2	8	26	14	9
77	2	41	3	1	1	2	1	1	4	24	11	4
78	1	26	5	2	1	5	1	1	1	23	19	8
79	2	28	3	1	1	4	1	2	8	27	12	4
80	2	35	2	1	1	3	1	1	1	28	14	0
81	1	28	5	1	1	2	1	1	2	20	24	12
82	2	36	2	1	1	3	2	2	8	26	9	14
83	2	29	3	1	1	4	1	1	4	23	13	4
84	1	34	1	2	2	4	2	1	8	24	12	3
85	1	53	2	1	1	3	3	1	1	32	17	6
86	2	30	3	1	1	4	1	2	8	24	10	9
87	1	43	2	1	1	2	1	1	2	24	14	10
88	2	26	5	2	1	4	1	1	1	16	23	7
89	2	44	1	1	1	4	2	2	8	27	18	6
90	1	45	1	2	2	3	3	2	8	20	14	5

TABLE 8.1 Types of variable

Type	Description	Examples in gym study	Variable name in SPSS
Nominal	Variables whose categories cannot be rank ordered; also known as categorical	var00001	gender
		var00003	reasons
		var00007	accomp
		var00008	othsourc
		var00009	exercise
Ordinal	Variables whose categories can be rank ordered but the distances between the categories are not equal across the range	var00004	carduse
		var00005	weiuse
		var00006	frequent
Interval/ratio	Variables where the distances between the categories are identical across the range	var00002	age
		var00010	cardmins
		var00011	weimins
		var00012	othmins

The three main types of variable and illustrations from the gym survey are provided in Table 8.1. Strictly speaking, items that have Likert-style response categories (see Box 4.1) produce ordinal variables. However, many writers argue that they can be treated as though they produce interval/ratio variables because of the relatively large number of categories they generate. For a brief discussion of this issue, see Bryman and Cramer (2001, pp. 58–59). Figure 8.1 provides guidance about how to identify variables of each type.

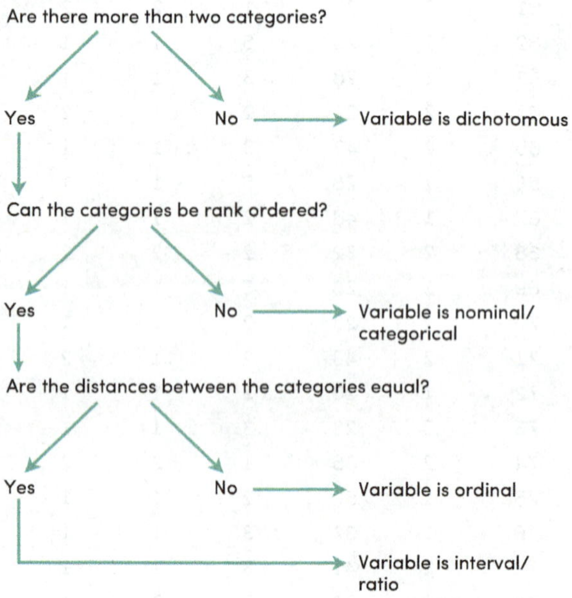

FIGURE 8.1 Deciding how to categorize a variable

Univariate analysis

Univariate analysis refers to the examination of one variable at a time. This section will outline several common approaches.

Frequency tables

A **frequency table** provides the number and percentage of people (or whatever else constitutes a case in the study) belonging to each of the categories of the variable in question and can be created for all three variable types. An example of a frequency table for a nominal variable is provided for var00003 (***reasons***) in Table 8.2. The table shows, for example, that 33 members of the sample go the gym to lose weight and that they represent 36.7 per cent (percentages are often rounded in frequency tables) of the entire sample.

Frequency tables are typically created using software. A very commonly used software program for

TABLE 8.2 Frequency table showing reasons for visiting the gym

REASONS FOR VISITING					
		Frequency	Per cent	Valid per cent	Cumulative per cent
Valid	Relaxation	9	10.0	10.0	10.0
	Fitness	31	34.4	34.4	44.4
	Lose weight	33	36.7	36.7	81.1
	Build strength	17	18.9	18.9	100.0
	Total	90	100.0	100.0	

statistical analysis is **IBM SPSS Statistics** (SPSS). In the Appendix at the end of this book you will find instructions for using SPSS to perform the data analyses discussed in this chapter.

When an interval/ratio variable (such as age) is put in frequency table format, some of the categories may be combined in some way: 20–29, 30–39, and so on. Be sure that the categories you create don't overlap (as in 20–30, 30–40, etc.): if they do, you're likely to end up with some 30-year-olds in the first group and some in the second. This would violate the *mutually exclusive rule*, discussed in Chapter 5, that no one should be able to fall into more than one category (required for telling whether two cases are equal or not equal). Also recall from Chapter 5 the *exhaustive rule*: every case must have a category into which it can be placed, even if it is only "missing data" or "not applicable."

Table 8.3 shows an example of a frequency table for an interval/ratio variable: var00002 (***age***). Not to group people in terms of age ranges would mean 40 different categories (one for each year from 18 to 57), which is too many to meaningfully describe. By creating five categories, you make the distribution of ages easier to comprehend. Notice that the sample totals 89 people, and that the "Valid per cent" column is based on a total of 89 rather than 90 because this variable contains one missing value (from respondent 24). Use the "Valid per cent" column to cite percentages because the "per cent" column includes missing values in the calculations.

Diagrams

Diagrams are sometimes used to display quantitative data. With nominal or ordinal variables, the *bar chart* and the *pie chart* are two of the easiest to use. A bar chart of the data in Table 8.2 is presented in Figure 8.2. The height of each bar represents the

TABLE 8.3 Frequency table showing ages of gym members

AGES OF GYM VISITORS					
		Frequency	Per cent	Valid per cent	Cumulative per cent
Valid	20 and below	3	3.3	3.4	3.4
	21–30	39	43.3	43.8	47.2
	31–40	23	25.6	25.8	73.0
	41–50	21	23.3	23.6	96.6
	51 and over	3	3.3	3.4	100.0
	Total	89	98.9	100.0	
Missing	User	1	1.1		
Total		90	100.0		

number of people in each category. Figures 8.2, 8.3, and 8.4 were produced with SPSS.

Another way of displaying the same data is in a pie chart (Figure 8.3). This type of diagram also shows the size of the different categories but more clearly brings out the size of each relative to the total sample. The percentage of the whole sample that each slice represents is also given in this diagram.

To display an interval/ratio variable such as var00002 (***age***), a *histogram* is often employed. Figure 8.4 uses the same data and categories as Table 8.3. As in a bar chart, the bars represent the relative size of each of the age bands, but there is no space between the bars. This is to distinguish histograms, which show interval/ratio variables, from bar charts, which are used with nominal and ordinal variables.

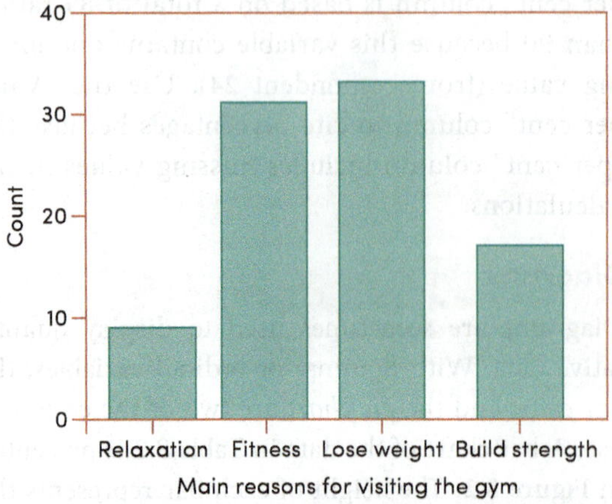

FIGURE 8.2 Bar chart showing main reasons for visiting the gym (SPSS output)

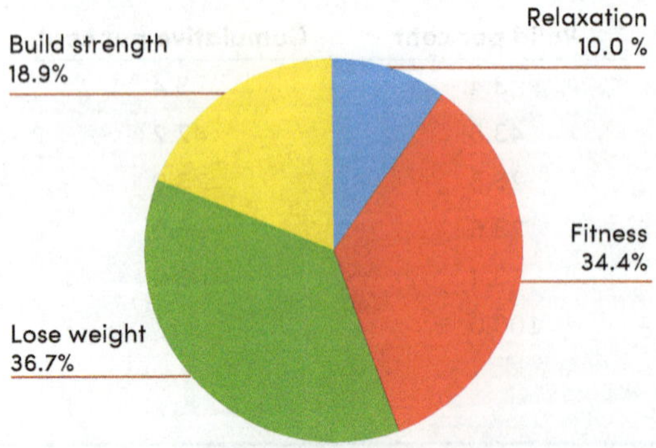

FIGURE 8.3 Pie chart showing main reasons for visiting the gym (SPSS output)

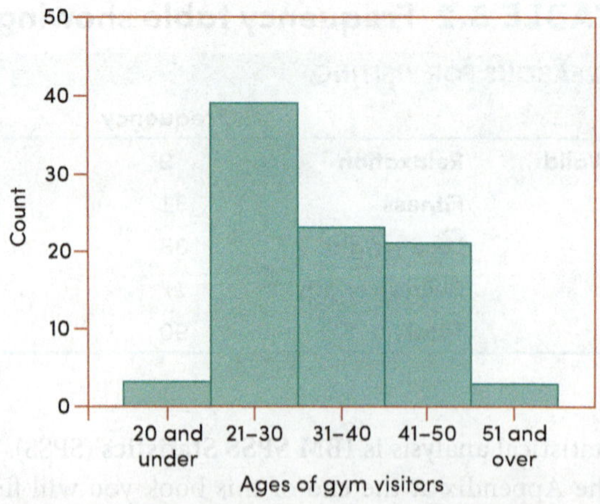

FIGURE 8.4 Histogram showing the ages of gym visitors (SPSS output)

More univariate analysis

Measures of central tendency

Measures of central tendency provide, in one number, a typical or "average" score for a distribution or group of scores. Three measures of central tendency are commonly used: the **mode**, the **median**, and the **mean**. Whether a particular one can be used depends on the level of measurement.

- *Mode*. This is the value that occurs most frequently in a distribution. The mode for var00002 (***age***) is 28, meaning that there are more 28s than any other score. The mode can be used with all types of variable but it is most applicable to nominal data.
- *Median*. This is the mid-point in a distribution of scores, derived by arraying all the scores in order (typically from the lowest to the highest) and then finding the middle one. If there is an even number of values, the median is calculated by taking the mean of the two middle numbers in the distribution. In the case of var00002, the median is 31. The median can be used with both interval/ratio and ordinal variables. It cannot be used with nominal data because those sorts of scores cannot be rank ordered.
- *Mean*. This is the average as it is understood in everyday use: that is, the sum of all numbers

in a distribution, divided by the number of scores. The mean for var00002 is 33.6, meaning that the average age in our sample of gym visitors is about 34. This is slightly higher than the median because a few considerably older members (especially respondents 5 and 10) inflate it. The mean is vulnerable to such **outliers** (extreme values at either end of the distribution), which exert considerable upward or downward pressure on the mean. In such instances the median is recommended, as it is not affected in this way. (Some researchers exclude outliers and then calculate the mean, noting the removal in the text.)

Measures of dispersion

The amount of variation in a sample—that is, its **dispersion**—can be just as important as its typical value. Two in-class tests can have the same mean of 60 per cent, but on one most people scored between 50 and 70, while on the other the grades are evenly dispersed from the low 20s to 100 per cent. (In the language of testing, the first test would be described as one that does not discriminate: the brightest and least bright students get fairly close marks.) In the gym study, is there more or less variability in the amount of time spent on cardiovascular equipment compared with weights?

The most obvious way of measuring dispersion is by calculating the **range**. This is simply the difference between the maximum and the minimum value in a distribution of interval/ratio scores. (Range can be applied to an ordinal variable too, but in that case it is more definitional than descriptive: for example, a range from "Working class" to "Upper class.") The range is 64 minutes for the cardiovascular machines and 48 minutes for the weights. This suggests that there is more variability in the amount of time spent on the former, probably because some people spend almost no time on cardiovascular equipment. However, like the mean, the range is influenced by outliers, such as respondent 41, who spent 64 minutes on the cardio equipment.

Another **measure of dispersion** is the **standard deviation**, which is a measure of variation around the mean. It is calculated by taking the difference between each value in a distribution and the mean, squaring it, dividing the total of these squared differences by the number of values, and then taking the square root. The standard deviation for var00010 (***cardmins***) is 9.9 minutes and for var00011 (***weimins***) it is 8.0 minutes. This indicates that not only is the average amount of time spent on the cardiovascular equipment (26.5 minutes) higher than for the weights (14.9 minutes), there is more deviation from the mean too. The standard deviation is also affected by outliers, which are sometimes excluded.

Bivariate analysis

Bivariate analysis examines whether there is a relationship between two variables. Several techniques are available for examining relationships, but their use depends on the level of measurement of the two variables being analyzed. Figure 8.5 details the main types of bivariate analysis to be discussed below, classified according to the type of variable involved.

Contingency tables

Contingency tables are probably the most flexible of all methods of analyzing relationships in that they can be employed in relation to any pair of variables, from nominal to interval/ratio. They are not the most efficient method, however, especially for interval/ratio data, which is the reason why the method is not recommended in all the cells in Figure 8.5. A contingency table is like a frequency table except that it allows two variables to be analyzed simultaneously, so that relationships between them can be examined. It is normal for contingency tables to include percentages, since they make the tables easier to interpret. Table 8.4 examines the relationship between gender and reasons for visiting the gym using our survey data. "Gender" is the **independent variable** (presumed cause) and for that reason becomes the column variable—a common preference among researchers. "Reasons" is the **dependent** variable (presumed effect) and is situated as the row variable (but see Box 8.3). In this case, gender is assumed to influence reasons for going to the gym; reasons for going to the gym cannot influence gender. The percentages are *column percentages*, representing *the independent*

	Nominal	Ordinal	Interval/ratio
Nominal	Contingency table + chi-square (χ^2) + Cramér's *V*	Contingency table + chi-square (χ^2) + Cramér's *V*	Contingency table + chi-square (χ^2) + Cramér's *V*. If the interval/ratio variable can be identified as the dependent variable, compare means with eta.
Ordinal	Contingency table + chi-square (χ^2) + Cramér's *V*	Kendall's tau-b	Kendall's tau-b
Interval/ratio	Contingency table + chi-square (χ^2) + Cramér's *V*. If the interval/ratio variable can be identified as the dependent variable, compare means with eta.	Kendall's tau-b	Pearson's *r*

FIGURE 8.5 Methods of bivariate analysis, level of measurement of one variable on top, that of the other variable on side

TABLE 8.4 Contingency table showing the relationship between gender and reasons for visiting the gym

	GENDER			
	Male		Female	
Reasons	No.	%	No.	%
Relaxation	3	7	6	13
Fitness	15	36	16	33
Lose weight	8	19	25	52
Build strength	16	38	1	2
Total	42	100	48	100

variable. The number in each cell is calculated as a percentage of the total number in its column. Thus, in the case of the top left-hand cell, the 3 men—of 42 in all—who go to the gym for relaxation represent 3/42 or 7 per cent of the men in the sample.

Contingency tables are generated to look for patterns of association. In this case, there are clear gender differences in reasons for visiting the gym. As our student anticipated, females are much more likely than males to go to the gym to lose weight. They are also somewhat more likely to go to the gym for relaxation. By contrast, men are much more likely to go to the gym to build strength. There is little gender difference in terms of fitness as a reason. In a real research situation, the investigator would take these results and interpret them in terms of some social theory.

Pearson's *r*

Pearson's *r* is a statistic used to examine relationships between two interval/ratio variables. Its chief features are as follows:

- The coefficient has values from 0 (which indicates that there is no linear relationship whatever between the two variables) to +1 or –1 (the first indicating a perfect positive relationship, the second a perfect negative).
- The closer a positive coefficient is to 1, the stronger the relationship; the closer it is to zero, the weaker the relationship.
- Similarly, the closer a negative coefficient is to –1, the stronger the relationship is; the closer it is to zero, the weaker the relationship.
- The sign of the coefficient (positive or negative) indicates the *direction* of a relationship. Negative means that as one variable is going up, the other is going down; it doesn't matter which is which. Positive means that the two are going in the same direction, either both up or both down.

For Pearson's *r* to be used, the relationship between the two variables must be broadly *linear*: when plotted on a scatter diagram, the values of the two variables will approximate a straight line (even though they may be scattered as in Figure 8.9), not a curve.

Box 8.3 | Relationships not causality

Analyzing associations between variables reveals *relationships* but not necessarily *causes* (although examining associations helps in the search for causes). Similarly, the *direction* of causation cannot be determined by merely establishing that a relationship exists between two variables. Indeed, in some cases what appears to be a causal influence working in one direction may actually work the other way round. An example of the problem of causal direction was presented in Chapter 4, where Sutton and Rafaeli (1988) expected to find that a display of positive emotions (for example, smiling or friendliness) by retail checkout staff caused increased sales. In fact, the relationship appeared to flow in the opposite direction: levels of retail sales seemed to exert a causal influence on the display of emotions. The more sales, the busier the staff, and the less time and inclination they had to smile!

At times one may feel confident in inferring a causal direction: the relationship between age and voting behaviour, for example. It is impossible for the way people vote to influence their age; so, if the two variables are related, age is the independent variable. It is not uncommon for researchers, when analyzing their data, to draw inferences about causal direction based on assumptions of this kind. However, some relationships may be *spurious* or non-causal: that is, the relationship between two variables may be caused by a third variable. For example, Rippeyoung (2013) examined whether the effects of breastfeeding can explain the gaps in cognitive ability between "non-poor," "near poor," and "poor" children in Canada (a purportedly causal relationship), or whether a third factor, a rich educational home environment, influences both breastfeeding and cognitive abilities. She found greater support for the spurious effect position, observing that there were no significant differences in breastfeeding rates between the three economic groups. Spurious relationships are discussed in more detail later in this chapter.

The old adage "practice makes perfect" suggests causality. Although this young woman regularly practises her painting technique, are there variables other than practice that could influence her success as a painter?

A scatter diagram should be created to test for linearity before Pearson's *r* values are used in a study.

Scatter diagrams

Scatter diagrams are shown in Figures 8.6 through 8.9. If one variable can be identified as likely to be the independent variable, it is by convention placed on the *X*-axis, the horizontal axis.

The scatter diagrams are based on the information in Box 8.4, which gives imaginary data for five interval/ratio variables. The scatter diagram for variables 1 and 2 is presented in Figure 8.6 and shows a perfect positive relationship, which yields a Pearson's *r* correlation of +1. This means that as one variable increases, the other variable increases as well, and the value of one variable perfectly predicts the value of the other. If the correlation is below 1, at least one other variable is affecting the relationship between them, possibly affecting variable 1 as well as variable 2.

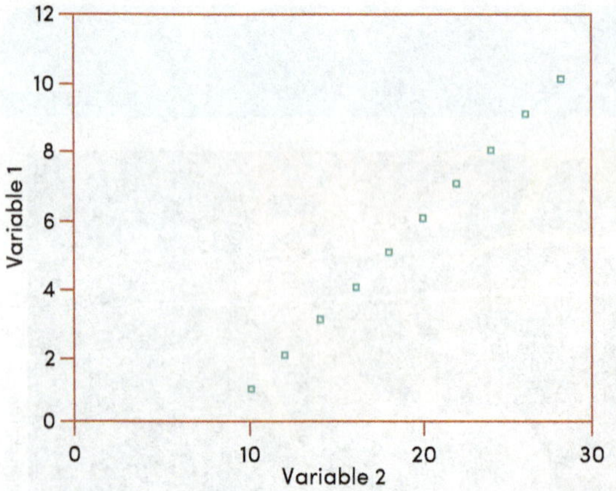

FIGURE 8.6 Scatter diagram showing a perfect positive relationship

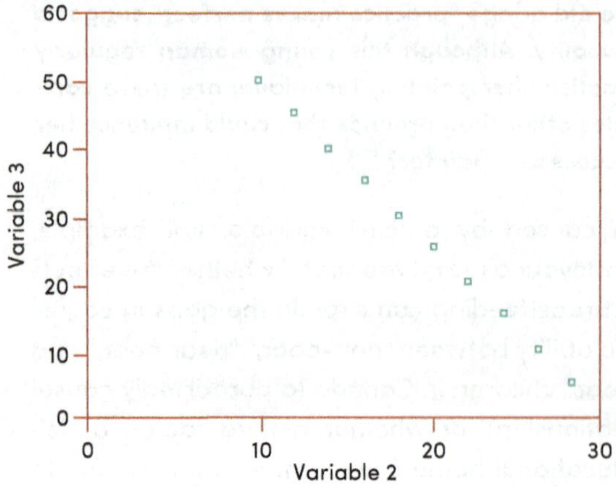

FIGURE 8.7 Scatter diagram showing a perfect negative relationship

The scatter diagram for variables 2 and 3 (Figure 8.7) shows a perfect negative relationship, which yields a Pearson's *r* correlation of –1. This means that as one variable increases, the other decreases, and that the values of one variable perfectly predict the values of the other. Here, as in the previous case, the line could be extended beyond the data to predict what would happen to either variable if the other moved beyond the range shown, although it is risky to go beyond what is known. Also, because social data usually include so many exceptions that few cases fall exactly on the line, predictions based on them tend to be general rather than specific.

Box 8.4 Imaginary data from five variables to show different types of relationship

Variables				
1	**2**	**3**	**4**	**5**
1	10	50	7	9
2	12	45	13	23
3	14	40	18	7
4	16	35	14	15
5	18	30	16	6
6	20	25	23	22
7	22	20	19	12
8	24	15	24	8
9	26	10	22	18
10	28	5	24	10

If, as in Figure 8.8, there is no apparent pattern in the scatter diagram, there is no or virtually no correlation between the variables. In the case of variables 2 and 5, the correlation is close to zero, at –.041. This means that the variation in the dependent variable is probably associated with variables other than the one used in this analysis.

If a relationship is strong, a clear pattern will be evident in the scatter diagram. This is the case with

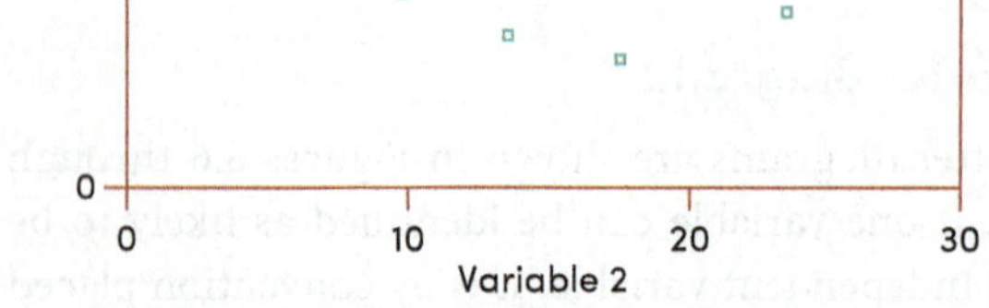

FIGURE 8.8 Scatter diagram showing two variables that are not related

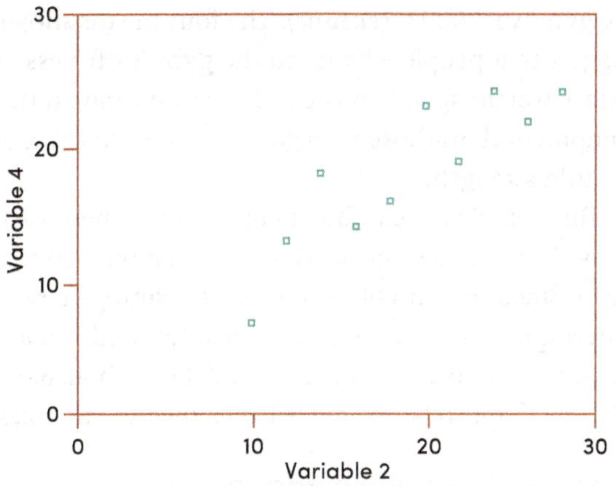

FIGURE 8.9 Scatter diagram showing a strong positive relationship

variables 2 and 4, whose scatter diagram appears in Figure 8.9. There is clearly a positive relationship; in fact, the Pearson's *r* is .88 (positive correlations are usually presented without the + sign). This means that the variation in the two variables is very closely connected, but that other variables also have some influence.

Going back to the gym survey, the correlation between ***age*** (var00002) and the time spent on weights, ***weimins*** (var00011), is –.27 (see Table 8.5): a weak negative relationship. This suggests that older people tend to spend less time on such equipment than younger ones, but that other variables also influence the time people spend there.

Kendall's tau-b

Kendall's tau-b is designed for pairs of ordinal variables, but is also used (as Figure 8.5 suggests) when one variable is ordinal and the other is interval/ratio. (Notice the general rule that data can be moved down a level, interval to ordinal, but not up.) It is exactly the same as Pearson's *r* in terms of possible outcomes in that the computed value of Kendall's tau-b can be positive or negative, and varies from 0 to ±1. In the gym study there are three ordinal variables: var00004 (***carduse***), var00005 (***weiuse***), and var00006 (***frequent***; see Table 8.1). Using Kendall's tau-b to calculate the correlation between the first two variables—frequency of use of the cardiovascular and weights equipment—it turns out to be very

TABLE 8.5 Correlations output for *age, weimins,* and *cardmins* (SPSS output)

Correlations of $p < 0.05$ are "flagged" with asterisks

CORRELATIONS		AGE	WEIMINS	CARDMINS
AGE	Pearson Correlation	1.000	–.273 **	–.109
	Sig. (2-tailed)	.	.010	.311
	N	89	89	89
WEIMINS	Pearson Correlation	–.273 **	1.000	–.161
	Sig. (2-tailed)	.010	.	.130
	N	89	90	90
CARDMINS	Pearson Correlation	–.109	–.161	1.000
	Sig. (2-tailed)	.311	.130	.
	N	89	90	90

**Correlation is significant at the 0.01 level (2-tailed).

Shows strength of relationship as indicated by Pearson's *r*

Shows number of cases, less any cases for which there are missing data for either or both variables

Shows level of statistical significance of computed value of Pearson's *r* low. A slightly stronger relationship is found between var00006 (frequency of going to the gym) and var00010 (***cardmins***, the amount of time spent on the cardiovascular equipment): close to .4. Another option for relating two ordinal variables is to use **Spearman's rho** (though it can only accommodate a small number of ties: that is, cases with the same rank on a variable). It ranges from −1, a perfect negative relationship, to +1, a perfect positive relationship. For example, look at the participation rank (A) and popularity rank (B) of a group of seven people.

Person	Mary	John	Bill	Sally	Kim	Susan	Joe
A	1	2	3	4	5	6	7
B	1	2	3	4	5	6	7

Spearman's rho is 1.0; knowing a person's participation rank perfectly predicts the popularity rank. It is called a rank correlation coefficient to remind you of its ordinal character and to distinguish it from Pearson's *r*.

Cramér's *V*

Cramér's *V* is suitable for examining the strength of a relationship between two nominal variables (see Figure 8.5). Its coefficient ranges from 0 to 1. It is always positive because nominal categories cannot be rank ordered; their values cannot go up or down.

The value of Cramér's *V* for the relationship between ***gender*** and reasons for going to the gym (var00003, ***reasons***) is .503, a moderate relationship. Cramér's *V* is usually reported with a contingency table and a chi-square test (see below). It is not normally presented on its own.

Comparing means and eta

There are many other bivariate statistics but we will present just one more. To examine the relationship between an interval/ratio variable and a nominal variable (if the latter can be construed as the independent variable), one can compare the means of the interval/ratio variable for each subgroup of the nominal variable. As an example, consider Table 8.6, which presents the mean number of minutes spent on cardiovascular equipment (var00010, ***cardmins***) for each of the four categories of reasons for going to the gym (var00003, ***reasons***). The four means shown suggest that people who go to the gym for fitness or to lose weight spend considerably more time on this equipment than those who go to the gym to relax or to build strength.

The statistic eta can be calculated with these variables; it expresses the level of association between them. Since one variable is nominal (meaning no rank ordering), its values are always positive; and it has a range from 0 to 1. The eta for the data in Table 8.6 is .48, a moderate relationship between the two variables.

Amount of explained variance

Squaring eta, Kendall's tau-b, Spearman's rho, and Pearson's *r* produces statistics that measure how much of the variation in one variable can be explained or predicted by the other variable. Thus, if *r* is −.27 (the correlation between ***weimins*** and ***age***), r^2 is .0729. This can be expressed as a percentage by multiplying r^2 by 100: thus 7.29 per cent of the variation in the time spent on weights can be predicted by age. This also shows that a strong correlation like .7 explains only 49 per cent of the variance. For nominal data, squaring Cramér's *V* (.503 for ***gender*** and ***reasons***) provides an approximation of the explained variance, so about 25 per cent of the variation in reasons for visiting the gym is attributable to gender.

Statistical significance and inferential statistics

One difficulty with working on sample data is a lingering worry about whether the findings can be generalized to the **population** from which the sample was drawn. As we saw in Chapter 7, there is always the possibility of **sampling error**, even when **probability sampling** procedures are followed (as in the gym survey). If this happens, the sample is to some degree unrepresentative of the wider population. To make matters worse, there is no practical way of finding out for sure how extensive the sampling error is, as no one can afford the time or money to study every case in the population—that's why a sample is used in the first place. This is where various tests of statistical significance come in.

What is a test of statistical significance? It provides an indication of the risk we are taking when we

TABLE 8.6 Comparing subgroup means: Time spent on cardiovascular equipment by reasons for going to the gym

	REASONS				
Time	Relaxation	Fitness	Lose weight	Build strength	Total
Mean number of minutes spent on cardiovascular equipment	18.33	30.55	28.36	19.65	26.47
N	9	31	33	17	90

use a particular sample statistic to estimate a population characteristic. For example, the mean age of the people in the gym sample is 33.6 years. Using the concept of the standard error of the mean, the 95 per cent confidence interval for the population mean extends from 31.72 to 35.47 years of age. The risk that this range does not contain the population mean is 5 per cent. Chapter 7 (see Box 7.2), in its discussion of the standard error of the mean, revealed some of the ideas behind statistical significance when estimating a population mean. The rest of this section looks at tests of significance for measures of bivariate association. All the tests have a common structure, illustrated in the following steps.

- *Set up a* **null hypothesis**. A null hypothesis is a hypothesis that is to be disproved; for example, that there is no association between two variables, or that two populations do not differ on some characteristic. In the context of our gym survey, a null hypothesis might state that there is no relationship between gender and reasons for visiting the gym. If your data lead to a rejection of the null hypothesis, you will have indirect support for the *research hypothesis* that there *is* a relationship in the population. But there is always a chance that a rejected null hypothesis is actually true. The amount of risk associated with rejecting a true null hypothesis is called the *level of statistical significance*.
- *Establish an acceptable level of statistical significance*. This is essentially the level of risk associated with rejecting the null hypothesis (implying that there *is* a relationship in the population) when in fact the null is correct (there is *no* relationship in the population). Levels of statistical significance are expressed as probability levels: that is, the probability of rejecting the null hypothesis when it is in fact true. The convention among most social researchers is that an acceptable level of statistical significance is $p \leq .05$ ("p" stands for probability), meaning that there are at most 5 chances in 100 that the sample shows a relationship not also found in the population. However, the maximum risk level the researcher is willing to accept may vary, depending on the circumstances. If more stringent tests of significance are desired, $p \leq .01$ or $p \leq .001$ may be used.
- *Determine the statistical significance of the findings*. The relevant statistical test depends on the measure of association involved, and is usually calculated with software, although statistics textbooks outline how significance tests can be calculated by hand with small data sets.
- *Decide whether to reject or not reject the null hypothesis*. The most common practice in the social sciences is to reject the null if the findings are statistically significant at the .05 level—that is, if the risk of error (i.e., getting a relationship as strong as the one that was found when in fact there is *no* relationship in the population), represented by the p-level, is no higher than 5 in 100. Such results are unlikely to have occurred by *chance* alone.

Two types of error are possible when inferring statistical significance (see Figure 8.10). A Type I error occurs when a null hypothesis that is actually true is rejected. This means that the results are the product of chance, and that the researcher was mistaken in concluding that there was a relationship in the

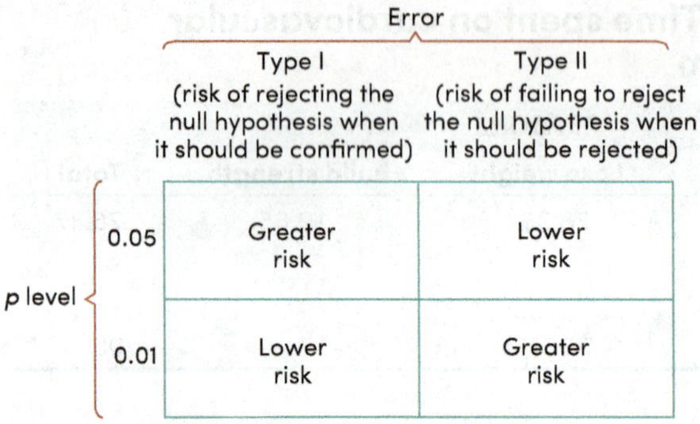

FIGURE 8.10 Type I and Type II errors

population. The level of significance is the probability of making a Type I error, so a $p = .05$ level of significance means a greater likelihood of making a Type I error than a $p = .01$ level of significance does.

The second type of error occurs when the null hypothesis should be rejected but is not. This is called a Type II error. These errors are more likely when the significance level is .01 than when it is .05, because using .01 makes it less likely that the null will be rejected. The two types of error cannot be minimized at the same time; if you decrease the chances of making a Type I error, you increase the chances of making a Type II error, and vice versa. Researchers usually make the conservative choice and seek to minimize Type I error; this makes it less likely that the null will be rejected in error, and hence less likely that the research hypothesis will be erroneously supported.

If an analysis reveals a statistically significant finding, this does not mean that the finding is important. It simply means that the results are probably not due to chance alone. For example, a study may find a correlation between time spent jogging per week and the amount of money spent on running shoes. Such a finding might be statistically significant, but is it important? Recall that statistical significance gets easier to achieve as sample size goes up. Also, it is important to appreciate that tests of statistical significance can be conducted only on probability samples.

Correlation and statistical significance

Examining the statistical significance of a correlation from a randomly selected sample provides information about the likelihood that the correlation exists in the population. For instance, with a Pearson's r of −.62 in the sample, what is the likelihood that there is no relationship between the two variables in the population? How likely is a −.62 to occur by chance alone, that is, because of sampling error?

Whether a correlation coefficient is statistically significant or not is affected by two factors:

- the size of the computed coefficient
- the size of the sample

This second factor may appear surprising, but it is true for all statistics. The larger a sample, the more likely it is that a given sample result is statistically significant. Thus, even though the correlation between age and the amount of time spent on weight machines in the gym survey is just −.27—a fairly weak relationship—it is statistically significant at the $p = .01$ level. This means that there is only one chance in 100 that there is no relationship between age and weights in the population. Because the statistical significance of a correlation coefficient depends so much on the sample size, it is important always to examine *both* the correlation coefficient *and* the significance level. This is true for any calculated statistic.

This treatment of correlation and statistical significance applies to both Pearson's r and Kendall's tau-b. A similar interpretation can also be applied to Cramér's V and the chi-square test.

The chi-square test

The chi-square (χ^2) test is applied to contingency tables like Table 8.4. It is a measure of the likelihood that a relationship between two variables in a sample would also be found in the population. The test works by calculating for each cell in the table an expected frequency—that is, one that would occur on the basis of chance alone. Think of the days of the week and crime: one might expect that 14.29 per cent (1/7) of all crimes would occur on each day of the week. That is what would be *expected* if there were no relationship between day of the week and crime. The data say otherwise; more crimes are committed on Friday and Saturday. The chi-square value, which for the

Research in the News

Big data in Canada

"Big data" is a term that lacks a specific definition. As the first word suggests, it refers to large data sets, some of which are so huge that conventional data processing systems are unable to handle them. The expression also pertains to large quantities of data gathered in ways that to date are not commonly used by social scientists. This would include largely electronic methods to acquire information on things like credit card use, cellphone use and location, email activity, bodily functions as recorded by monitors strapped to the body for prolonged periods, and above all Internet use. Big data sources also tend to be unstructured in that the data gathered must be put in some meaningful or systematic configuration before they can be used, which is often accomplished with complex algorithms.

If you've ever Googled a topic, say "cosmetics" or "lawnmowers," and then found advertisements for those products on the websites you visit, that means than someone or some organization has placed you in a big data set. That may be useful for you, or it may literally cause you grief. A pregnant graduate student in Charlottetown did an Internet search for topics relating to birth and babies, but unfortunately lost her pregnancy after 27 weeks. Yet Internet ads for things like baby clothes and breast pumps kept coming, which worsened her agony (Anderssen, 2014). The ethics surrounding big data become even murkier when the techniques are used by governments for surveillance purposes, a practice that is surprisingly common even in liberal democracies. What makes the matter ethically complex is that there can be clear social benefits to the use of big data, such as the contribution it can make to medical research, crime prevention, and national security.

According to *CTV News* (Jones, 2020), a Canadian company collected big data early in the COVID-19 pandemic that indicated the extent to which people were abiding by government recommendations to stay home. Ostensibly, the purpose of gathering the information was to assist government officials in reaching people who were not abiding by their recommendations so the officials could help them stay safe, although critics have raised privacy concerns. The data were gathered using location apps people downloaded onto their smartphones, although it's not clear that those who downloaded the apps knew the information could be provided to third parties. One pattern the data showed was that there appeared to be more people "out and about" in lower-income neighbourhoods and rural areas as opposed to more affluent localities. The company that gathered the information suggested that this may reflect the fact that people with lower incomes often work in occupations such as construction or in food, retail, or other service occupations that are not compatible with working from home. As with other frontline workers, for people in these jobs, obeying a stay-at-home recommendation would be considered "a luxury" (Jones, 2020).

data in Table 8.4 is 22.726, is calculated by taking the differences between the actual and expected values for each cell in the table and then summing those differences (the operation is slightly more complicated than this, but the details need not concern us here). The chi-square value means nothing by itself and can be meaningfully interpreted only in relation to its associated level of statistical significance, which in this case is $p < .0001$. This means that there is less than one chance in 10,000 of rejecting a true null hypothesis (that is, inferring that there *is* a relationship in the population when none exists). We can be extremely confident that there is a relationship between gender and reasons for visiting the gym among all gym members, since the chance of obtaining a sample that shows this chi-square value when there is no relationship among all gym members is less than 1 in 10,000.

But a chi-square value is also affected by the number of cases. You want a large chi-square to reject a null hypothesis, and a larger *n* makes this easier to achieve. This is why it is necessary to look at the data and not just at the final statistic. Examine Table 8.7, which shows the level of self-esteem for three categories of people (those who engage in contact sports, those who engage in non-contact sports, and those who do not engage in any sports). Because the independent variable is nominal, chi-square is more appropriate than Kendall's tau-b. Note the information in the bottom row of the table.

The first two parts of Table 8.7, A and B, show that just by doubling the size of the sample, the results change from being very likely due to chance in A (thus the null hypothesis of no relationship cannot be rejected) to less than 5 chances in 100 that they occurred by chance in B, and thus a rejection of the null. This is problematic because it suggests that one could collect more and more data until the null can be rejected. Now look at the last part of the table, C. Why was it included? When the data from B for high and low self-esteem are switched around in C, which in most instances should mean something, chi-square stays the same. This illustrates the point that statistical significance pertains only to whether the results may have resulted from chance alone, and says nothing about practical significance or importance. There is a big practical difference between a situation in which half the respondents at all levels of sports participation have low self-esteem and one in which half have high self-esteem, but that makes no difference to the level of statistical significance—it remains the same in each situation. The practical implications of a finding go beyond its level of statistical significance.

Comparing means and statistical significance

A test of statistical significance called *analysis of variance* can be applied to the comparison of means in Table 8.6. This procedure entails treating the total amount of variation in the dependent variable—amount of time spent on cardiovascular equipment—as made up of two types: variation *within* each of the four subgroups that make up the independent variable, and variation *between* them. The latter is often called the *explained variance* (explained by the group one is in) and the former the *error variance*. A test of statistical significance for the comparison of means entails relating the two types of variance to form what is known as an *F* statistic, which expresses the amount of explained variance in relation to the amount of error variance. In the case of the data in Table 8.6, the resulting *F* statistic is statistically significant at the $p < .001$ level. This finding suggests that there is less than one chance in 1000 that there is no relationship between the two variables among all gym members.

TABLE 8.7 How chi-square is affected by increasing the size of *n* and not affected by changes to column headings

	A			B			C		
Self-esteem	Contact sports	Non-contact sports	No sports	Contact sports	Non-contact sports	No sports	Contact sports	Non-contact sports	No sports
H	7	3	10	14	6	20	24	26	50
M	5	10	15	10	20	30	10	20	30
L	12	13	25	24	26	50	14	6	20
	$\chi^2 = 1.93$, not sig.			$\chi^2 = 5.08$, $p < .05$			$\chi^2 = 5.08$, $p < .05$		

Multivariate analysis

Multivariate analysis entails the simultaneous analysis of three or more variables, and can only be introduced here. It is sometimes called *elaboration* as it is more complicated and creates a more valuable picture than bivariate analysis: one rarely finds an adequate explanation of a particular phenomenon by looking at only one possible cause. (For more information on the techniques, consult a textbook on quantitative data analysis: for example, Agresti & Finlay, 2009; Noack, 2018.) There are three main contexts in which multivariate analysis is used. Each is explained below.

Is the relationship spurious?

To establish a relationship between two variables, not only must there be logical and temporal evidence of a relationship but the relationship must be shown to be non-spurious. A spurious relationship exists when there appears to be a relationship between two variables, but the relationship is not real: it is being produced because each variable is itself related to a third variable. Think about the positive relationship between the number of fire engines at a fire and the fire damage: the more engines, the greater the devastation. Does this positive association mean that the number of fire engines present *causes* the amount of fire damage? Of course not. The size of the fire accounts for both the number of engines responding and the damage. Variation in the two variables (number of fire engines and amount of damage) is caused by a third factor, the size of the fire.

Consider a social science example. Assume there is a positive relationship between income and voting behaviour such that the more income a person has, the more likely he or she is to vote for a conservative party. Does this mean that having more money *causes* people to move to the right? Or could this relationship be explained by age (see Figure 8.11)? The older one is, the more likely one is to have a higher salary; and the older one is, the more conservative one tends to be. If the apparent relationship between income and voting behaviour is in fact a function of age, that relationship is spurious. See Box 8.3 for another example.

FIGURE 8.11 A spurious relationship

Is there an intervening variable?

An intervening variable suggests that the relationship between the two original variables is not a direct one. Assume that there is a positive relationship between income and self-esteem—the higher one's income, the more positive one feels about oneself. But maybe there is more to it than that. Maybe income affects overall levels of physical vibrancy (richer people tend to be more physically fit and to smoke less than poorer people), which in turn affects self-esteem:

income → physical vibrancy → level of self-esteem

If this is true, what should happen to the relationship between income and self-esteem if physical vibrancy is controlled? (To control means to hold *constant*. Controlling in this instance might involve taking only people who had high levels of physical vibrancy, and seeing whether there is still a positive relationship between income and self-esteem among them.) If physical vibrancy were an intervening variable, that would weaken or eliminate the association between income and self-esteem. Also, notice the "control" word? Yes, the purpose of controls is to make **cross-sectional** research more like an experiment in which random assignment makes all other things equal or controlled.

Is there an interaction?

If the relationship between two variables holds for some groups or situations but not for others, an interaction exists. The word "interaction" is used in a statistical sense here, one that is different from its everyday meaning. In statistical terms, if the effect of one independent variable varies at different levels of a second independent variable, there is an interaction. In the gym study, for example, is the relationship between *age* and other sources of regular exercise (var00008, ***othsourc***) different for men and women? Table 8.8 shows the relationship between age and other sources of exercise and includes both men and women. (Age has been broken down into just three age bands to make the table easier to read.) The table suggests that the 31-to-40 age group is less likely to have other sources of regular exercise than the 30-and-under and 41-and-over age groups. However, Table 8.9, which breaks the relationship down by gender, suggests that the patterns for males and females are somewhat different. Among males, the pattern shown in Table 8.9 is very pronounced (the 31-to-40 age group is less likely to have other sources of exercise than the other two age groups), but for females the likelihood of having other sources of exercise declines with age. We can say that the relationship between age and having other sources of exercise is **moderated** by gender. Another way to put this is that there is an interaction between age and gender in predicting whether gym visitors have other sources of regular exercise.

Other uses for multivariate analysis

Multivariate analysis can also be used to determine how much of the variation in the dependent variable is explained or predicted by the independent variables. In addition, it provides a test to find out which, if any, of the independent variables are significant predictors after controlling for the others. These uses will be illustrated by examining *multiple linear regression*. Our brief discussion of this topic will also acquaint you with some key concepts in multivariate analysis.

Consider the variable ***weimins***, the number of minutes spent on weights. What might cause it to vary? One relevant factor might be ***age***. Perhaps the older people get, the less likely they are to work out using weights. To test this idea, we could perform a bivariate regression with ***weimins*** as the dependent variable and ***age*** as the independent variable.

The first part of Table 8.10 shows an R-square value of .074, which indicates that ***age*** by itself explains 7.4 per cent of the variation in ***weimins***—not

TABLE 8.8 Contingency table showing the relationship between age and whether gym visitors have other sources of regular exercise (percentages)

	AGE		
Other source of exercise	**30 and under**	**31–40**	**41 and over**
Other source	64	43	58
No other source	36	57	42
N	42	23	24

TABLE 8.9 Contingency table showing the relationship between age and whether gym visitors have other sources of regular exercise for males and females (percentages)

	GENDER					
	Male			Female		
Other source of exercise	**30 and under**	**31–40**	**41 and over**	**30 and under**	**31–40**	**41 and over**
Other source	70	33	75	59	50	42
No other source	30	67	25	41	50	58
N	20	9	12	22	14	12

TABLE 8.10 SPSS output showing results of bivariate regression

MODEL SUMMARY				
Model	**R**	**R-Square**	**Adjusted R-Square**	**Std. Error of the Estimate**
1	.273[a]	.074	.064	7.72123

[a]Predictors: (Constant), *age*

ANOVA[a]						
Model		**Sum of Squares**	**df**	**Mean Square**	**F**	**Sig.**
1	Regression	417.236	1	417.236	6.999	.010[b]
	Residual	5186.719	87	59.617		
	Total	5603.955	88			

[a]Dependent variable: *weimins*
[b]Predictors: (Constant), *age*

COEFFICIENTS[a]						
		Unstandardized Coefficients		**Standardized Coefficients**		
Model		**B**	**Std. Error**	**Beta**	**t**	**Sig.**
1	(Constant)	23.209	3.218		7.213	.000
	age	−.245	.093	−.273	−2.645	.010

[a]Dependent variable: *weimins*

very much. The value of R-square tends to be somewhat inflated, especially if the sample size is small (as in our example) or the number of independent variables is large (Agresti & Finlay, 2009, p. 366). A more realistic estimate is the adjusted R-square, which in our case has a value of .064 or 6.4 per cent.

The ANOVA section of the output indicates a significance or *p*-value of .010, which is the significance level of the model as a whole. Our model at this point consists of only one independent variable (***age***). The final section of the output, "Coefficients," has two subsections: "Unstandardized coefficients" and "Standardized coefficients." The unstandardized coefficient for ***age*** is −.245, which represents the estimated change in the dependent variable for each unit change in the independent variable. In our example, the model predicts that for each one-year increase in age, the time spent on weights decreases by .245 minutes. The standardized coefficient of −.273 indicates that for every standard deviation increase in age, the time spent on weights decreases by .273 standard deviation units. Standardized coefficients (sometimes called *beta weights*) are useful in comparing the effect of independent variables that may be measured in different units: the higher the standardized coefficient, the more important the independent variable is considered to be. Finally, the significance level for ***age*** is shown to be .010, indicating that the probability that the association between ***age*** and ***weimins*** is due to chance alone is 1 in 100: this suggests it's a pretty safe bet that there is a relationship between those two variables in the population.

As we have noted, a single cause or independent variable is rarely if ever enough to provide a good explanation for anything. Let's see what happens if we put a second independent variable—***gender***—into the model. Normally, the variables used in linear regression have to be at the interval/ratio level of measurement, but a special procedure allows us to use nominal variables like ***gender*** as well. Such variables have to be converted to indicator or "dummy" variables, a process that goes beyond the scope of our discussion here. Assume that the dummy variable we have created is called ***gender2***.

Table 8.11 shows the output generated after ***gender2*** was added to the model. The "Model

TABLE 8.11 Multiple regression output with *gender2* (gender dummy variable) in the model

MODEL SUMMARY				
Model	R	R-square	Adjusted R-square	Std. Error of the Estimate
1	.478[a]	.228	.210	7.09088

[a]Predictors: (Constant), *gender2*, *age*

ANOVA[a]						
Model		Sum of Squares	df	Mean Square	F	Sig.
1	Regression	1279.830	2	639.915	12.727	.000[b]
	Residual	4324.125	86	50.281		
	Total	5603.955	88			

[a]Dependent variable: *weimins*
[b]Predictors: (Constant), *gender2*, *age*

COEFFICIENTS[a]						
		Unstandardized Coefficients		Standardized Coefficients		
Model		B	Std. Error	Beta	t	Sig.
1	(Constant)	20.831	3.010		6.920	.000
	age	–.260	.085	–.289	–3.053	.003
	gender2	6.251	1.509	.393	4.142	.000

[a]Dependent variable: *weimins*

Summary" shows that the R-square value has increased to .228 (or that 22.8 per cent of the variation in ***weimins*** can be explained or predicted by the new model), and that the more conservative adjusted R-square has risen to .210 (or 21.0 per cent). This indicates that by adding ***gender2*** we have produced a much better model, although the majority of the variation in ***weimins*** is still unaccounted for. The ANOVA significance level is .000, which indicates that the findings for the new model as a whole (which includes both ***age*** and ***gender2*** as independent variables) have a probability of less than 1 in 1000 of being due to chance alone.

The "Coefficients" sections show an unstandardized coefficient of –.260 for ***age***, which means that, controlling for ***gender2***, for each one-year increase in age, the model predicts a decline of .260 minutes spent on weights. The standardized coefficient for ***age*** is –.289, indicating a decrease of .289 standard deviation units in ***weimins*** for each standard deviation increase in ***age*** (controlling for ***gender2***). The significance level for ***age*** is .003, which means that ***age*** remains significant even when ***gender2*** is held constant. Had the significance level exceeded .050, we would have had to consider dropping ***age*** from the model.

The "Coefficients" section shows an unstandardized coefficient of 6.251 for ***gender2***. Because of the way this dummy variable was coded, the coefficient means that, holding ***age*** constant, the model estimates that the average time men spend on weights is 6.251 minutes greater than that spent by women. The standardized coefficient of .393 tells us that according to the model, the average time men spend on weights is .393 standard deviation units higher than that of women (controlling for ***age***). Also, ***gender2*** has a *p*-value of .000, indicating that the association observed between it and ***weimins*** (after controlling for ***age***) has a probability of less than 1 in 1000 of being due to chance alone. Had the significance level been greater than .050, we would have had good reason to exclude ***gender2*** from the model. But with these results, it stays in.

Methods in Motion | Applications to Canadian Society

A multiple regression analysis of Indigenous people's attitudes toward the police

Indigenous people in Canada have substantially lower incomes than other Canadians, have higher incarceration rates, experience more racism than other ethnic groups, and are far more likely to be victims of homicide than non-Indigenous people (Cao, 2014). All these factors suggest that understanding the relationship Indigenous people have with the police is important in coming to terms with the larger issue of the plight of Indigenous people in Canada.

An important indicator of the status of Indigenous–police relations is the level of confidence Indigenous people have in the police, in particular how confident they are that they will receive fair treatment by police services in Canada. Cao (2014) examined this issue by performing a multiple regression analysis of Indigenous attitudes toward the police using the 2009 Victimization Study, which is part of Statistics Canada's General Social Survey and is based on a nationally representative sample (see Box 5.10).

To measure confidence in the police, the author created an index by combining the responses to six items that indicated how well, on average, participants believed their local police enforced laws, were responsive, were approachable, provided information to reduce crime, cared about neighbourhood safety, and treated people fairly. The results indicated that both Indigenous and non-Indigenous people were more likely to have favourable than unfavourable attitudes toward the police. However, Indigenous people had levels of confidence in the police that were lower than those for non-Indigenous people on all six measures, and all the differences were statistically significant. In the multivariate analyses, the association between being Indigenous and having lower levels of confidence in the police on the composite measure remained significant at $p < .05$ even after 13 relevant variables were controlled for, including visible minority status, social trust, contact with police, total criminal victimizations, and several socio-demographic variables. Cao suggests that "the differential confidence between Aboriginal and non-Aboriginal people found here is only the tip of the iceberg in the complicated relationship between the police and Aboriginal people" (p. 516), and that "the dominant mythology of Canada as a non-racist nation must be challenged" (p. 517).

☑ Checklist

Checklist for performing and writing up quantitative data analysis

- ☐ Have missing data codes been specified for all variables?
- ☐ Are the statistical techniques used appropriate for the level of measurement (that is, nominal, ordinal, or interval/ratio)?
- ☐ Are the most appropriate and powerful techniques for answering the research questions used?
- ☐ If the sample is not randomly selected, are inferences about a population avoided? If inferences are included, are their limitations outlined?
- ☐ If the data come from a cross-sectional design, have unsustainable inferences about causality been resisted?
- ☐ Does the analysis go beyond univariate to include bivariate and even multivariate analyses?
- ☐ Are the research questions answered, and only the analyses relevant to them presented?

Key Points

- Think about data analysis before designing your surveys and other research instruments; in particular, consider whether they are in a format that will permit you to answer your research questions in an optimal way.
- Know the difference between nominal, ordinal, and interval/ratio variables. Techniques of data analysis are applicable to some types of variable and not others.
- Become familiar with computer software such as SPSS, which is discussed in the Appendix.
- Don't confuse statistical significance with importance or practical significance.

Questions for Review (R) and Creative Application (A)

R1 What are missing data and how do they arise?

A1 You are using a variable that is measured with a five-point Likert scale. What codes could be used to designate missing data? Explain why they would be appropriate.

Types of variables

R2 Define each of the three types of variable outlined in this chapter (nominal, ordinal, and interval/ratio), and provide an example of each one.

A2 Identify the level of measurement (nominal, ordinal, or interval/ratio) associated with each of the following survey questions:

1. Do you enjoy talking about politics?
   Yes _____
   Unsure _____
   No _____
2. How many times have you talked about politics with friends or family in the last seven days? Please write the number here. _____
3. What is your main source for news about current political events? Please tick one only.
   Social media (Facebook, Twitter, Instagram, etc.) _____
   Television _____
   Radio _____
   Hard copy newspapers or magazines _____
   Other (please specify): _____
4. How important is it for you to be informed about political issues?
   Extremely important _____
   Very important _____
   Moderately important _____
   Slightly important _____
   Not at all important _____

Univariate analysis

R3 What is an outlier? How does the presence of an outlier affect the mean and the range?

A3 You have just gathered data that include a variable measuring the participants' ethnic identity. Which measure of central tendency would be most appropriate for this variable? Explain.

Bivariate analysis

R4 Can one infer causality from bivariate analysis? Explain.

A4 You have just found out that people who watch violent movies are more likely to commit a violent crime than people who do not watch those movies. Can you conclude from this that watching violent movies causes people to commit violent crimes? Explain.

R5 In what circumstances is each of the following used: Pearson's *r*, Kendall's tau-b, Cramér's *V*, Spearman's rho, eta?

A5 Your study indicates that the Pearson's *r* coefficient for the association between the variables "years of formal education" and "income" is 0.6. How much of the variation in income can be predicted by years of formal education?

Statistical significance

R6 What does "statistical significance" mean and how does it differ from "importance" or "practical significance"?

A6 What does it mean to say that an eta of .42 is statistically significant at $p < .05$?

R7 What does the chi-square test achieve?

A7 Your results indicate that the chi-square statistic for the variables "gender" and "highest level of education achieved" has a significance level of $p = .12$. What does that mean?

Multivariate analysis

R8 Define and provide an example of each of the following:

- a spurious relationship
- an intervening variable
- a statistical interaction

A8 The results from your multivariate model that uses "gender" and "father's occupation" to predict annual personal income has an adjusted R-square value of .44. What does that mean?

Interactive Classroom Activities

1. These activities require student access to SPSS, and may be facilitated by the instructor demonstrating the techniques to the class on the classroom screen, one at a time. Step-by-step instructions for each procedure are provided in the Appendix. Each student is to do the following:

   a. Enter the data for the gym study, provided in Box 8.2, into an SPSS file. Save the file to a flash drive or some other reliable storage device.
   b. Provide variable names, variable labels, and value labels for each variable, as appropriate. Then specify missing values for the age variable.
   c. Check that the data have been entered correctly by doing frequency distributions for each variable. Each student's frequency distributions should match those shown on the screen by the instructor.
   d. Recode the ***age*** variable following the instructions in the Appendix, then provide a variable label and value labels for the new variable. The instructor puts the frequency distribution for the new variable on the screen so students can check that they have created the variable properly. Save the file.
   e. Produce the bar chart, histogram, and pie chart shown in Figures 8.2 to 8.4. The class is asked to interpret each figure.
   f. Create the contingency table shown in Table 8.4, and include a chi-square test. The class is asked: What information is conveyed by the contingency table? What do the chi-square results indicate?
   g. Produce the correlation matrix shown in Table 8.5. The class is asked to interpret the correlation coefficient and significance level shown in each cell. Then they are asked: Why is there a diagonal of "1s" in the table? Why is some of the information in the table redundant?
   h. Produce the regression output shown in Table 8.10. The class is asked to interpret the R-square and adjusted R-square values, the significance level shown in the ANOVA table, the unstandardized and standardized coefficients for ***age***, and the significance level for ***age***.
   i. Introduce a second variable into the regression analysis by including the variable that measures the frequency with which patrons go to the gym (***frequent***). For the purposes of this exercise, disregard any level of measurement issues. The class is asked to interpret the R-square and adjusted R-square values, then compare them to what was found for the bivariate regression done in exercise h above, explaining any similarities or differences. The class is then asked to interpret the significance level shown in the ANOVA table, the unstandardized and standardized coefficients for ***age*** and ***frequent***, and the significance levels for ***age*** and ***frequent***.

2. This activity does not require access to SPSS. After presenting an overview of multivariate analysis, the instructor divides the class into small groups. Each group is to come up with a real or hypothetical example of:

   a. a spurious relationship;
   b. an intervening variable; and
   c. a statistical interaction.

   The examples must be original, i.e., they cannot be taken from the textbook or lecture materials.

   Each group must then explain, at least conceptually, how a researcher would go about testing for each one. That is, they are to explain how one can determine if a particular relationship is spurious, whether a certain variable is in fact an intervening variable, and whether an interaction exists, and illustrate that with the examples they just came up with. Once the groups have completed their work, they present their material to the rest of the class for comment and critique.

Relevant Websites

Statistics Canada offers a useful introduction to quantitative data gathering and analysis. Navigate the site using the tabs on the right.

https://www150.statcan.gc.ca/n1/edu/power-pouvoir/ch2/5214911-eng.htm

This YouTube video explains ***levels of measurement***.

www.youtube.com/watch?v=B0ABvLa_u88

This YouTube video illustrates the notion of correlation.

www.youtube.com/watch?v=SaSpZdf1oHU

If you'd like to do further work with SPSS software, the ***IBM*** site offers some free trial downloads.

www.ibm.com/products/spss-statistics

To learn more about big data, visit the ***Surveillance Studies Centre*** (Queen's University) website.

www.sscqueens.org/

(Websites accessed 4 September 2021.)

OXFORD learning link

More resources are available on Oxford Learning Link. Visit **https://learninglink.oup.com/** for:

- Student self-quiz
- Flash cards
- Audio clips
- Videos
- Activities

PART III

Qualitative Research

Part III of this book is concerned with qualitative research. Chapter 9 explores its main features, while Chapter 10 deals with ethnography and participant observation, two important ways of collecting qualitative data. Chapter 11 discusses qualitative interviewing and focus groups, which are also valuable ways to acquire qualitative information, while Chapter 12 looks at content analysis, a method of assessing texts (in the broad sense of the word) derived from a variety of sources. The final chapter in Part III, Chapter 13, illustrates the various ways in which data analysis is conducted in qualitative research. The discussion provided in these chapters gives you some important background knowledge that will help you understand qualitative social science research, as well as some practical instructions on how to conduct it.

9 The Nature of Qualitative Research

Chapter Overview

Qualitative analysis uses mainly words and images as data rather than numbers. Qualitative researchers tend to produce **inductive**, **constructionist**, and **interpretivist** studies, although they do not necessarily subscribe to all three of those perspectives. This chapter will consider:

- the main steps in qualitative research (although they are not followed as closely as the stages of **quantitative** research);
- the relationship between theory and research in qualitative studies;
- the role of **concepts** in qualitative research;
- criteria for evaluating qualitative research;
- the main goals of qualitative researchers: seeing through the eyes of research participants; rich description; presentation of context, including the presence of conflict; concepts and theories as the outcomes of research; and seeing social life and interaction as processes rather than static events;
- some common criticisms of qualitative research; and
- the main contrasts between qualitative and quantitative research.

Key Learning Outcomes

Here is a list of goals you should try to achieve as you read and think about the material in this chapter. After completing this chapter, you should be able to:

1. Describe the variety of methods qualitative researchers use to collect data and the general steps they follow as part of the research process.
2. Explain how qualitative researchers work towards developing theory and concepts iteratively as they emerge during data collection through an inductive process.

▲ The Canadian Press/Nathan Denette

3. Identify some of the different criteria that qualitative researchers use to assess the quality of their research findings, such as credibility, transferability, dependability, and confirmability.
4. Describe the main goals of qualitative research, including: seeing through the eyes of research participants; rich description; presentation of context, including the presence of conflict; concepts and theories as the outcomes of research; and seeing social life and interaction as processes rather than static events.
5. Discuss some of the critiques of qualitative research and the main ways qualitative and quantitative research differ.

Imagine that you are a non-Indigenous person participating in the National Inquiry into Missing and Murdered Indigenous Women and Girls. While some estimates maintain that the number of victims since 1980 is well into the thousands, you have been appointed to provide an in-depth study of one particular woman who was killed in northern Saskatchewan five years ago. Imagine as well that you're free to gather the "facts" of the crime—time of death, physical cause of death, the victim's whereabouts before the murder, and so on—but you feel that such information, although important, doesn't address the core issues involved. How important would it be for you, in order to reach a full understanding of this event, to find out what the murder meant to the victim's family and friends? What would be the most appropriate way to get the information you need to conduct the study? If it involves interviewing people who knew the victim, how could you get access to them? What sort of interview would you use? What would you talk about? Would it be useful to weave a historical account of colonialism in Canada into your analysis? How would you construct your research so as to not harm those who have already experienced hardship? Will consultation and community involvement improve the research? Finally, is it even possible for a non-Indigenous person to fully understand what happened? This chapter discusses how qualitative researchers deal with these sorts of questions as they conduct their analyses.

Introduction

As the opening vignette suggests, with qualitative research one moves beyond "the world of brute facts toward the realm of human meanings" (Bochner & Ellis, 2003, p. 509). This is accomplished with a focus on words and images rather than numbers, but there are other attributes of qualitative research you should know about. The following are also significant:

- It usually involves an *inductive* view of the relationship between theory and research: qualitative researchers usually start with field research and then develop theories and concepts from it.
- It is normally *interpretivist* in that it seeks to understand the social world through other people's interpretations of it.
- Qualitative writers are often *constructionist* in that they understand social life to be an outcome of the interactions and negotiations between individuals, rather than a fixed structure to which individuals must conform and adapt.
- Its approach is **naturalistic** in that qualitative researchers try to understand social life in its natural setting as people reflect on and go about their everyday lives.

Although all qualitative research tends to share these features, qualitative researchers can also differ significantly in both approach and subject matter. The following are different varieties of qualitative research:

- ***Ethnography/participant observation.*** These are two very similar approaches to qualitative data collection. In both cases, the researcher is immersed in a social setting for some time, observing and listening to people in order to gain an appreciation of their culture and experiences. It has been employed in such social research classics as Whyte's (1955) study of street corner life in a slum community and Gans's (1962) research on residents in the throes of urban redevelopment.

- *Qualitative interviewing.* This is a very broad term used to refer to in-depth, semi-structured or **unstructured interviewing**. Qualitative researchers conducting ethnographic or participant observation research typically also engage in a substantial amount of qualitative interviewing.
- ***Focus groups.*** Several people are interviewed together, often using a semi-structured format.
- Language-based approaches such as **discourse** and **conversation analysis**, including **critical discourse analysis**.
- *Qualitative analysis of **texts** and documents*, which falls under the general heading of **content analysis**.
- ***Participatory action research.*** As seen in Chapter 1, professional researchers and others collaborate with the people directly affected by a social problem to understand the issue and to take action to resolve it.

Each of these approaches will be examined in detail in later chapters. Quite often, qualitative studies will use a multi-method approach. For example, in addition to conducting qualitative interviews, an ethnographer may analyze texts and documents as well.

The main steps in qualitative research

The sequence of steps in the qualitative research process is outlined in Figure 9.1. These steps illustrate, in general terms, how research may progress from data gathering to conceptualization and theorization, a process that is examined in detail in Chapter 13. The work of Lyon and Frohard-Dourlent (2015) on how same-sex common-law partners view conventional notions of marriage will be used as an example of how this is done:

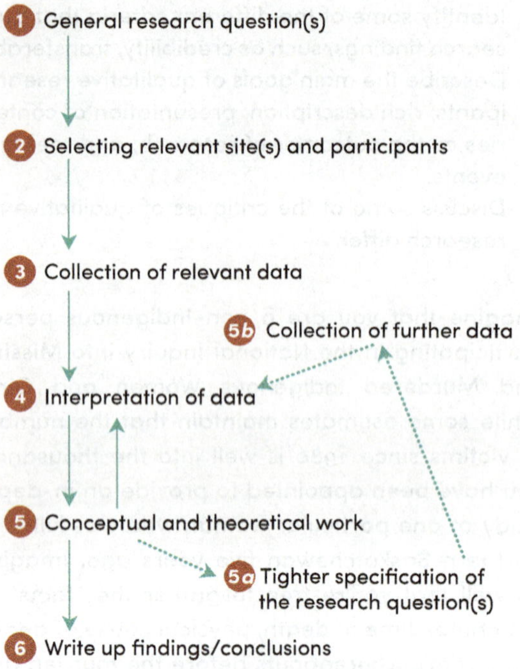

FIGURE 9.1 An outline of the main steps of qualitative research

- *Step 1: General research question(s).* Since 2005, all same-sex couples in Canada have had the right to get married. While some people in the LGBTQ community view the change in the law as a victory for marriage equality, others have reservations. For instance, the legal right to marry may bring with it conventional assumptions of what marriage is supposed to entail, such as the belief that child-rearing and monogamy are key features of the institution. Lyon and Frohard-Dourlent (2015) conducted qualitative interviews to explore how unmarried gay couples who cohabit deal with the tension that exists between the acceptance of marriage as a civil right and how having that right may impact the nature of LGBTQ relationships.
- *Step 2: Selecting relevant site(s) and participants.* Participants were recruited through blogs and websites (including the University of Toronto online announcements board), email lists, physical posters, and word of mouth. There were 22 people, 12 women and 10 men, chosen for the study, all of whom were

unmarried and living with their same-sex partner in the Greater Toronto Area.

- *Step 3: Collection of relevant data.* The authors conducted in-depth, open-ended interviews in which the participants were encouraged to talk about their current and former romantic relationships, their views on marriage, how their relationships were viewed by friends and relations, their levels of social support, and their future relationship goals. The interviews typically lasted from 90 to 120 minutes.
- *Step 4: Interpretation of data.* One of the key findings to emerge from the data analysis was that participants felt that their relationships were not viewed as having the same level of legitimacy as those of married same-sex couples. One participant stated that "if I were straight I might not be that into marriage. But for our queerness, I think for some of our families . . . it's necessary to take us seriously as a couple" (Lyon & Frohard-Dourlent, 2015, p. 413). The researchers also found that several of the people interviewed explained their qualms about marriage in personal rather than ideological terms. Instead of discussing the social or political implications of marriage, opposition to it often took the form of personal preferences. For example, one interviewee said that "it's nice that people ask [if we will get married], but I say 'No, we're not into it,'" (p. 417) and left it at that.
- *Step 5: Conceptual and theoretical work.* No new concepts emerged from Lyon and Frohard-Dourlent's work, but their article provided good illustrations of key terms used by researchers in this area, such as "heteronormative," "heterosexist," "homonormativity," and "queer-based meaning systems." In terms of theory, they proposed that the hard-fought political battle for marriage equality that was won by mainstream LGBTQ movements may have made people in same-sex relationships reluctant to criticize marriage as an institution, which in the long run could influence conceptualizations of what constitutes appropriate attitudes and behaviours for people in LGBTQ romantic relationships. (See also the Methods in Motion box.)
- *Step 5a: Tighter specification of the research question(s)*; and
- *Step 5b: Collection of further data.* Usually, the initial collection and interpretation of data lead to a sharpening of the research question(s), which is followed by additional data gathering to address the more specific concerns contained in the revised research questions. The authors' account of the trajectory of their research does not state explicitly that they collected additional data after starting to interpret the information that was gathered, but this may have taken place spontaneously in the process of interviewing. When this does occur, there can be an interplay between interpretation and theorizing on the one hand, and data collection on the other. For instance, once a particular interpretation has been made, further data may be collected to determine whether the interpretation is valid. This strategy is frequently described as *iterative*, and is a defining characteristic of **grounded theory**, discussed next and in Chapter 13.
- *Step 6: Writing up findings/conclusions.* In any form of research, an audience has to be convinced of both the credibility and the significance of the interpretations offered. Researchers are more than just conduits for what they see and hear. Lyon and Frohard-Dourlent made clear to their readers how the institution of marriage can both lend legitimacy to same-sex relationships and at the same time invoke social expectations for the people in those relationships that they may not accept. This may have led some research participants to feel ambivalent about marriage or even make contradictory statements about it as they tried to navigate a relatively new legal terrain and the multiple messages and meanings that surround it. Also, the authors used heterosexual marriage as a backdrop to their analyses of the same-sex variety, which allowed readers to reflect on the implications of the institution of marriage for society as a whole.

An important part of qualitative research concerns how the theory and concepts of the study relate to the research data. It is to that issue that our discussion now turns.

Theory and concepts in qualitative research

Most qualitative researchers treat theory as something that emerges out of the collection and analysis of data. Practitioners of grounded theory—a common approach to the analysis of qualitative data—stress the importance of using data to *develop* theoretical ideas. But some qualitative researchers argue that qualitative data can and should play a role in *testing* theories as well. Silverman (1993) maintains that there is no reason why qualitative research cannot be employed to test theories specified in advance of data collection. Besides, much qualitative research entails the testing of theories in the iterative process described above. Instead of seeking to test a theory from the outset, theoretical hunches or working hypotheses are more often constructed and tested in the midst of qualitative data collection. In Figure 9.1, the loop back from step 5a, "tighter specification of the research question(s)," to step 5b, "collection of further data," implies that a theoretical position may emerge in the course of research that spurs the collection of further data to test it. This oscillation between testing emerging theories and collecting data is a defining feature of grounded theory.

Blumer (1931) argues that a science without concepts would be analogous to "a carver without tools, a railroad without tracks, a mammal without bones, a love story without love" (p. 515): it would be impossible. It's not surprising, then, that concepts are significant in both quantitative and qualitative research. Unlike quantitative researchers, though, qualitative researchers do not make the *measurement* of concepts a central part of their work. For qualitative researchers, the emphasis is on conceptualizing "how human group life is accomplished in practice" and doing so "from participants' viewpoints in every instance" (Prus, 1997, p. 4). Concept development, as a feature of theory construction, often occurs "in a continuous dialogue with empirical data" (Becker, 1998, p. 109). The data inform the utility of the concept. If data indicate that the concept is not adequately summarizing the experiences and perspectives of participants, it is refined or discarded. This process begins during data collection, as researchers reflect on the fit between the concept and the observed reality of participants' life-worlds. The revision or rejection of one concept gives rise to another that better approximates the story told by the data.

Blumer's (1954) distinction between "definitive" and "**sensitizing" concepts** provides further insight into how qualitative researchers develop and employ concepts. Blumer argues that fine nuances in the form a concept can assume and alternative ways of viewing its manifestations may be lost in the process of operationalization. For that reason, Blumer recommends that social researchers regard their concepts not as "definitive" but as "sensitizing"—providing "a general sense of reference and guidance in approaching empirical instances" (1954, p. 7). For Blumer, concepts should provide a very general idea of what to look for, allowing the researcher to discover the variety of forms that the phenomenon identified by the concept can take.

But Blumer's distinction is not without problems. It is not clear how useful a very general formulation of a concept can be as a guide to empirical inquiry. If it is too general, it will fail to provide a useful starting point because its guidelines are too broad. If it is too narrow, it is likely to repeat some of the difficulties he identified with "definitive" concepts. However, his view is important in that it illustrates the value of beginning with a broad definition of a concept and then narrowing it down during the course of data collection (for an example, see Box 9.1).

Criteria for evaluating qualitative research

In Chapters 2 and 4 we noted that reliability and validity are important criteria for establishing and assessing the quality of quantitative research. But many qualitative writers argue that these criteria are not directly applicable to their work (Finlay, 2006). For example, since measurement is not a major

Methods in Motion | Applications to Canadian Society

The influence of same-sex marriage on social institutions and lesbian and gay relationships

What happens to the institution of marriage when the law changes to allow same-sex couples to marry? This is a research question posed by Green (2010), who used qualitative methods to examine three different predictions regarding same-sex marriage. Social conservatives maintain that gay marriage will contribute to further decline in the nuclear family, increase marital infidelity, and lead to less stable marriage bonds. Critical feminists and queer theorists argue that it will produce same-sex marriage institutions with the same problematic characteristics as those found in heterosexual marriage: obligatory monogamy, gender-specific social roles, and conventional expectations for child-rearing. Lesbian and gay assimilationists offer a similar prediction, but one that sees conventional marriage norms as largely positive: same-sex marriage will strengthen ties between gay couples, encourage monogamy, and help to stabilize queer families.

Green explored the various positions on gay marriage by conducting 30 semi-structured interviews with people from two Ontario cities who were in same-sex marriages; half the interviewees were lesbians and the other half gay men. Contrary to the social conservative position, many interviewees reported that their relationships with their spouses were strengthened after they exchanged marriage vows, and that they came to value stability and permanence in their relationship more after they were married. One gay man said: "I think it's just the sense of commitment that you feel. You've made a vow and, it's hard to describe, it definitely feels different than prior to [marriage]" (Green, 2010, p. 411). The people studied also mentioned that being married bestowed a sense of legitimacy on their relationship and on themselves as individuals. Extended family members, people at work, and society in general seemed more accepting of them after they were married. One lesbian remarked, "It was absolutely incredible, overwhelming, just, even my mother. . . . [P]eople we hadn't talked to in years would phone and ask if it was okay to come to the wedding. . . ." (Green, 2010, p. 413).

But contrary to both the critical feminist/queer theory position and the lesbian and gay assimilationist views, married same-sex couples did not completely buy into the conventional heterosexual idea of marriage. For one thing, there was more support for non-monogamous sexual relationships among those interviewed than in the public at large, although the support was more pronounced among the male interviewees. In fact, some couples were monogamous before marriage but not after. Said one gay man, "So, it sounds kind of backwards to the traditional model, but the fact that we're legally married to each other and permanently committed makes us both feel very secure about [having sexual relations outside of marriage]" (Green, 2010, p. 419). Green also found that the people in same-sex marriages claimed to have an egalitarian division of labour regarding household chores and yard work, and relatively equal power relationships within the marriage, although he emphasized that further research was needed to substantiate those claims. Green speculated about the future of same-sex marriage, in particular whether it can retain its unique characteristics if queer institutions continue to gain acceptance by the larger society and in the process lose their oppositional tenor. Like other predictions for social change, those regarding gay marriage can be tested only with the passage of time.

Box 9.1 | The emergence of a concept in qualitative research: The case of emotional labour

Sean Locke/iStockphoto

Is this woman's smile spontaneous and sincere, or is she just doing her job?

Hochschild's (1983) concept of emotional labour—labour that "requires one to induce or suppress feelings in order to sustain the outward countenance that produces the proper state of mind in others" (p. 7)—has become very influential in the sociology of work and in the developing area of the sociology of emotions. She gathered data on emotional labour by exploring how airline workers manage to keep smiling at truly obnoxious customers. Hochschild's initial conceptualization emerged from a questionnaire she had created on a related topic. To develop the idea of emotional labour she gained access to Delta Airlines, and in the course of her investigations she:

- watched training sessions for flight attendants and had many conversations with both trainees and experienced attendants;
- interviewed airline personnel such as managers and advertising agents;
- examined Delta advertisements spanning 30 years;
- observed the flight attendant recruitment process at Pan American Airways (because she had not been allowed to do this at Delta); and
- conducted "open-ended interviews lasting three to five hours each with thirty flight attendants in the San Francisco Bay Area" (Hochschild, 1983, p. 15).

For a contrasting occupational group also involved in emotional labour, she interviewed five debt collectors. Her book explored topics such as the human costs of emotional labour and the issue of gender in relation to it. It's clear that Hochschild's concept of emotional labour began with a somewhat imprecise idea that was gradually developed to address its wider significance. The concept has been picked up by other qualitative researchers in the sociology of work. For example, Leidner (1993) did an ethnographic study of a McDonald's restaurant and an insurance company to investigate how organizations seek to "routinize" emotional labour. See Box 9.3 for another adaptation of her work.

concern among qualitative researchers, measurement validity seems to have little bearing on their investigations.

One approach is to adopt most of the core ideas used to assess quantitative research without making any special adjustments. This is what Mason (2002) does, using terms such as "validity," "reliability," and "generalizability" (external validity) in much the same way that quantitative researchers do: for example, "If your research is valid, it means you are observing, identifying, or 'measuring' what you say you are" (2002, p. 39). Others have used terms similar to those employed in quantitative research but invested them with somewhat different meanings (e.g., Golafshani, 2003).

Many writers take a different approach, suggesting that qualitative studies should be judged or evaluated according to criteria quite different from those used in quantitative research. Lincoln and Guba (1985) and Guba and Lincoln (1994), for instance, argued that it is necessary to assess the quality of qualitative research in new ways, using new terms. They proposed two primary criteria for assessing a qualitative study: **trustworthiness** and *authenticity*. The latter in this context refers to the degree to which the research is transformative and emancipatory for the people studied and society at large. Here we will focus on trustworthiness, which is made up of four criteria:

- *credibility*
- *transferability*
- *dependability*
- *confirmability*

We'll consider each of these terms individually.

Credibility

The idea of credibility is tied to the notion that different people may interpret the social world in different ways. Since there can be several possible ways of experiencing or coming to terms with a particular social situation or event, the researcher has to ensure that the interpretations presented in the study ring true to the people observed. The establishment of credibility entails both following proper research procedures *and* submitting the findings to the people studied for confirmation that the account is consistent with the way they see their world. The researcher is, after all, describing their reality. This practice of getting feedback on the study from the participants involved is referred to as **respondent validation**, **member validation**, or *member reflection*.

The aim of respondent or member validation is to seek corroboration or criticism of the researcher's observations and interpretations. It can take several different forms:

- Each research participant may be provided with an account of what he or she said to the researcher or others. For example, in a study that explored issues of trust between mothers of children with disabilities and school principals, Shelden. Angell, Stoner, & Roseland (2010) gave all respondents a summary of the findings by either telephone or email. They also asked each participant if their views were represented in the findings, and whether verbatim quotes were accurate.
- Researchers may show pre-publication versions of their articles or books to their participants. They may also provide the study participants with an opportunity to ask questions about the methods and findings of the research and offer feedback and criticism. Taken further, Lassiter (2005, p. 15) makes a case for collaborative ethnography, which entails researchers and participants collaborating in all aspects of a study, "from project conceptualization, to fieldwork, and, especially, through the writing process."

In each case, the goal is to confirm that the researcher's findings and impressions are congruent with those of the people on whom the research was conducted and, if there are discrepancies, to find out why. However, the idea is not without practical difficulties:

- Respondent validation may lead some research participants to respond defensively and even demand censorship.
- Bloor (1997, p. 45) observed that research participants who develop relationships of "fondness and mutual regard" with the researcher may be reluctant to criticize the study.
- It's doubtful that research participants can validate all of a researcher's analysis, since it will be written for social scientists and will therefore include many specialized references, concepts, theories, and contextual issues unfamiliar to them. Skeggs (1994, p. 86), for example, reported that the "most common response" among her participants was "Can't understand a bloody word it says."

Transferability

Because qualitative research typically entails in-depth, intensive study of a small number of people, qualitative findings tend to flow out of the context in which the observations are made. As Lincoln and Guba (1985, p. 316) put it, whether the findings "hold in some other context, or even in the same context at some other time, is an empirical issue." Instead of trying to come up with findings that can definitely be applied to other times,

Research in the News

What's missing in media portrayals of violent crime

In 2017, a Canadian veteran of the war in Afghanistan shot and killed his wife, his mother, and his daughter, and then killed himself. Many of the media accounts of the tragedy focused on the perpetrator, in particular on the fact that he had suffered from post-traumatic stress disorder (PTSD) brought on by his combat experience. A common narrative in the media portrayals of the event involved the idea that Canadian soldiers suffering from PTSD and other combat-related ailments typically cannot get the help they need, despite the significant sacrifices they have made in Canada's military operations.

Lost from view in these media accounts was the fact that there were victims besides the person who committed the murder-suicide. The lives and circumstances of the other three people who died were largely overlooked and forgotten. Another thing that was missing was an acknowledgment that the murders were part of the larger societal issue of deadly violence against women (Renzetti, 2017). As Mount Allison University sociology professor Ardath Whynacht put it, "There were four victims that day and we're talking only about the services that could have helped him, and not, for example, services that might have helped his spouse be safer, in trying to leave that relationship and get space" (Renzetti, 2017).

places, and people, qualitative researchers are encouraged to produce what Geertz (1973) called **thick description**: rich, detailed accounts of a group's culture or people's experiences. Lincoln and Guba argued that thick description provides others with the database they need in order to assess the possible transferability of findings to other milieus.

Dependability

Lincoln and Guba proposed that to establish dependability, researchers should adopt an "auditing" approach. That is, they should keep complete records of all phases of the research process—problem formulation, selection of research participants, fieldwork notes, interview transcripts, data analysis decisions, and so on—and ensure that the records are accessible. Peers would then act as auditors, possibly during the course of the research and certainly at the end, to make sure that proper procedures have been followed and to assess the degree to which the study's interpretations and theoretical inferences can be justified.

Auditing has not, however, become a popular approach to enhancing the dependability of qualitative research. A rare example is a study of behaviour at an American "swap meet," where second-hand goods are bought and sold (Belk, Sherry, & Wallendorf, 1988). A team of three researchers collected data over four days through observation, interviews, photography, and video records. The researchers conducted several trustworthiness tests, including respondent validation. In addition, they submitted their draft manuscript and data set to three peers whose task it "was to criticize the project for lack of sufficient data for drawing its conclusions, if they saw such a void" (1988, p. 456). The same study highlighted some problems with this approach, among them the fact that, because qualitative research generates extremely large data sets, validation is very demanding for the auditors. That may be the major reason why auditing has not been widely used.

Confirmability

Objectivity is a difficult if not impossible standard to live up to in social research. For that reason, the confirmability criterion is designed to ensure that the researcher has acted in good faith. In other words, it should be apparent that personal values or theoretical inclinations did not blatantly and unduly sway either the conduct of the research or the findings derived from it. Lincoln and Guba suggest that establishing confirmability should be one of the objectives of auditors.

Overview of the criteria issue

There is a general recognition that quantitative researchers' notions of reliability and validity cannot be applied to qualitative research without some modification, although critics vary in their views on how much modification is necessary. To bolster their accounts, qualitative researchers may use some of the strategies advocated by Lincoln and Guba, such as thick description and respondent validation exercises.

The main goals of qualitative researchers

Seeing through the eyes of the people being studied

Many qualitative researchers try to view the social world through the eyes of the people they study. To accomplish this, Blumer (1969) advocates striving for a sense of "intimate familiarity" with research participants' everyday lives. Achieving a sense of intimate familiarity means "gaining an in-depth knowledge of the research participants, their setting or settings, and their situations and actions" (Charmaz, 2008, p. 53). This approach is in keeping with qualitative researchers' attempt to achieve *verstehen* (empathetic understanding) and their focus on studying the meanings people attribute to the social world in situ.

Qualitative researchers maintain that "(1) . . . face-to-face interaction is the fullest condition of participating in the mind of another human being, and (2) . . . you must participate in the mind of another human being (in sociological terms, 'take the role of the other') to acquire social knowledge" (Lofland & Lofland, 1995, p. 16). This tendency reveals itself in frequent references to seeking and privileging an insider perspective. Here are some examples:

- Armstrong (1993) carried out research on British soccer hooliganism through participant observation. He described his work as rooted in "*Verstehende* sociology—trying to think oneself into the situations of the people one is interested in . . . in this case the 'hooligan.' This approach involves recognizing social phenomena as due not to any single or simply identifiable cause and attempting to make sense from the [multi-causal] social actors' viewpoint" (Armstrong, 1993, pp. 5–6).
- For their research on teenaged girls and violence, Burman, Batchelor, & Brown (2001, p. 447) "sought to ground the study in young women's experiences of violence, hearing their accounts, and privileging their subjective views."

The goal of seeing through the eyes of the people under study is often accompanied by the closely related goal of probing beneath surface appearances. After all, by taking the position of those under study, researchers may be able to see things in a way that an outsider with little direct contact would not. This insight is revealed in:

- Hallgrimsdottir, Phillips, & Benoit (2006) study of sex-trade workers, which revealed that, contrary to media depictions, these workers often see their occupation in a mundane light (for example, as simply a way to make a living);
- Kleinknecht's (2011) research on computer hackers, which found that popular portrayals of hackers as "computer criminals" were often at odds with hackers' activities and how they defined themselves: those who take a passionate, creative approach towards problem-solving; and
- McDonough and Polzer's (2012) examination of the daily struggles of municipal employees following the creation of the "mega-city" of Toronto, which showed that rather than creating a leaner, more efficient workforce, the restructuring led many manual workers to question their commitment to excellence on the job, while white-collar employees felt they had to do extra work just to maintain professional standards of service.

On the other hand, sometimes qualitative research confirms popular notions of a particular group.

For example, Bell (2007) found that media depictions of the western Canadian separatist movement as decidedly right wing were essentially correct.

The empathetic effort to see the world through the eyes of their participants can present researchers with practical problems. For example: How far should one go to develop intimate familiarity and empathy? What if the research participant's experience includes illegal or dangerous activities? There is also the risk that the researcher will be able to see through the eyes of some of the people in a particular social scene but not those of others, such as people of another gender or culture. These and other practical difficulties will be addressed in later chapters.

Description and the emphasis on context

Qualitative researchers are much more inclined than their quantitative colleagues to include descriptive detail when reporting their research. However, they are not exclusively concerned with description. They also try to explain, and what they endeavour to explain may pertain to issues of power and exploitation. For example, Skeggs (1997, p. 22) tried to answer this question: "Why do women who are clearly not just victims of some ideological conspiracy, consent to a system of class and gender oppression which appears to offer few rewards and little benefit?"

Many qualitative studies do provide a detailed account of what goes on in the setting under investigation. On the surface, some of this detail may appear irrelevant; indeed, there is a risk of becoming too embroiled in descriptive detail. Lofland and Lofland (1995, pp. 164–165), for example, warned against what they called "descriptive excess" in qualitative research, whereby the amount of detail overwhelms or inhibits the analysis of the data.

But one of the main reasons for providing descriptive detail is that it permits a contextual understanding of social behaviour. This implies that we cannot understand the behaviour of members of a social group without some knowledge of the specific environment in which they operate. Behaviour that appears odd or irrational may make perfect sense when understood in the context within which it takes place. The emphasis on context in qualitative research goes back to the classic studies in social anthropology, many of which demonstrated how seemingly illogical practices (e.g., a magical ritual that accompanies the sowing of seeds) make sense when they are understood as part of the society's belief system. The provision of descriptive detail is also a manifestation of qualitative researchers' desire for naturalism: that is, their belief that researchers should study the social world as it actually is, rather than relying on contrived settings such as formal interviews or experiments.

Emphasis on process

Qualitative research tends to view social life in terms of processes. This tendency reveals itself in a number of ways, but the main one is the qualitative researcher's concern with showing how events and patterns unfold over time. Qualitative evidence often conveys a strong sense of change and flux. As Pettigrew (1997, p. 338) put it, process is "a sequence of individual and collective events, actions, and activities unfolding over time in context." Qualitative research using participant observation is particularly well suited to the study of process. Ethnographers are typically immersed in a social setting for a long time—in many cases, for years. Consequently, they are able to observe how events develop over time and how the different elements of a social system (such as values, beliefs, and behaviour) interconnect. Tracing interdependent streams of actions and events allows the researcher to present social life as a process (see Box 9.2).

A sense of process can also be developed through semi-structured and unstructured interviewing in which participants are asked to reflect on the activities leading up to or following an event. Shaffir and Kleinknecht (2005), for example, used informal interviews with 45 former Canadian politicians to explore how they coped with their involuntary exit from political life. The enormity of the loss was often described as being akin to a social death. A former Liberal parliamentarian described the process of coming to terms with the defeat as follows: "It's like the phases of death. You have loss, anger, sadness, and then you

Box 9.2 | Process in youth shelters

Karabanow (2002) described his experiences in two Canadian shelters for homeless and runaway youth. As a participant observer, he was able to monitor routine activities there and describe the shelter culture. In addition, he carried out in-depth interviews with three levels of shelter workers and used agency archival materials. The dramatic transformations in the shelters' external environment and internal operations that took place over a period of years provided the basis for an analysis of the evolution of their organizational processes. This example shows the development of a sense of process in at least two ways. First, observation of the shelters over time made it possible to bring out developments and interconnections between events. Second, connecting these events with historical and other data made it possible to show how the shelters were affected by the larger society.

come to accept it" (Shaffir & Kleinknecht, 2005, p. 714). The **life history** approach is another form of qualitative research that can be used to show process. One of the best-known studies of this kind is Lewis's (1961) classic study of a poor Mexican family, in which he conducted extended taped interviews with family members to reconstruct their life histories.

Flexibility and limited structure

Many qualitative researchers are disdainful of approaches that impose a predetermined set of assumptions on the social world. This position is closely related to the preference for seeing the world through the eyes of the people under study. After all, a structured method of data collection must be planned ahead of time on the basis of the *researcher's* prior ruminations and expectations regarding the nature of a social reality that they may never have encountered before. This structure limits the degree to which the researcher can genuinely adopt the world view of those being studied, and can lead to serious misunderstandings. Keeping structure to a minimum is supposed to enhance the likelihood that the research will reveal the perspectives of the people being observed. This approach allows aspects of people's social world that are particularly important to them to come to light—aspects that might never even cross the mind of a researcher using a more structured method. For that reason, qualitative research tries to avoid limiting areas of inquiry, and the research questions it asks tend be fairly general (see step 1 in Figure 9.1).

Ethnography, with its emphasis on participant observation, is particularly well suited to an unstructured approach. It allows researchers to immerse themselves in a social setting with a general research idea in mind and then gradually, through observation, narrow it down to a more specific topic.

Another advantage of the unstructured nature of most qualitative inquiry is that it offers the prospect of flexibility. The researcher can change the direction of the investigation much more easily than in quantitative research, which tends to have a built-in momentum once the data collection is underway. (If you send out hundreds of **postal questionnaires** and realize only after getting some back that you left out an important issue, it's not easy to rectify the situation.) **Structured interviewing** and **structured observation** can offer some flexibility, but it will be limited by the requirement that interviews be as comparable as possible. Having conducted ethnographic fieldwork in sites as disparate as a psychiatric institute in Quebec to a day shelter for individuals experiencing homelessness in Iceland, Dolson (2018) found that the fieldwork experience was often unpredictable and uncertain. To respond to these situations, he advocates fostering skills in adversity management: "attempting to be comfortable with the unexpected, and trying to make the best of ambiguous situations in which you have no idea what will happen next" (Dolson, 2018, p. 22). Qualitative researchers, especially ethnographers who confront some of the most precarious research situations, must remain open, flexible, and ready to improvise their research plans.

As noted previously, some qualitative researchers use sensitizing concepts as a starting point for their research. While this might be seen as removing some of the flexibility and unstructured character of qualitative research, Charmaz (2003) states, "We may use sensitizing concepts *only* as points of departure from which to study the data" (p. 259, emphasis in original). When used in this fashion, concepts offer tentative analytical direction to a project. Qualitative researchers believe it's important to remain receptive to new and alternative understandings as they emerge from the data. See Box 9.3 for an illustration of how a conceptual angle can help give direction to a study, while the unstructured data collection style of qualitative research can suggest alternative avenues of inquiry or ways of thinking.

Ultimate goals

The goals of qualitative research mentioned above—seeing through the eyes of others, bringing out a sense of process, and having a flexible and unstructured method of inquiry—are essentially immediate or proximate goals that are used as means of achieving a deep understanding of the people or groups being studied. But qualitative researchers' goals often go beyond simply understanding. They may also wish to do research in order to pursue social justice and bring about social change, as mentioned in our discussion of critical approaches to science in Chapter 1. Box 9.4 illustrates how people doing participatory action research can use qualitative methods to address a serious social problem. Indeed, qualitative studies have shed light on a wide range of societal injustices in Canada, including racism (Branker, 2017), homophobia (Abramovich, 2016), and poverty (Coloma & Pino, 2016).

Box 9.3 | Emerging concepts

In an update to Hochschild's (1983) work (discussed in Box 9.1), Canadian researchers Santin and Kelly (2017) used participant observation and informal interviews with flight attendants to revisit the concept of emotional labour following the 9/11 terrorist attacks. Consistent with Hochschild's findings, Santin and Kelly found that flight attendants continued to engage in "surface acting:" they would conceal their true emotions in order to please their employer or customers. However, they also discovered that changes to airline security protocols post-9/11 provided cabin crew with more discretionary power and emotional agency in responding to unruly passengers. The "9/11 effect" led to a shift in how emotional labour was carried out in the new pro-security context. It meant that cabin crew were not only providing a service to passengers, but also protecting them. Their new role as guardian partially shielded them from workplace repercussions that traditionally followed from not treating passengers in a passive, courteous manner. In line with Hochschild's findings, institutional norms continued to structure and constrain flight attendants' behaviour, but now new safety protocols offered them more control over their emotional labour. By exploring flight attendants' emotional labour post-9/11, Santin and Kelly expanded on Hochschild's ideas, adding three new concepts to our social science lexicon: the 9/11 effect, emotional agency, and role shields. Their study demonstrates how existing theoretical ideas can be used as sensitizing concepts in subsequent research and then built upon to develop new ways of understanding changing social contexts.

Box 9.4 | The use of qualitative methods in participatory action research

Type 2 diabetes among Indigenous children and youth is a growing problem, one with important implications for the quality of life among Indigenous people in Canada. Sharma, Reimer-Kirkham, & Meyerhoff (2011) sought to do something about it, but rather than approach the issue from the perspective of conventional social science, they used the methods of participatory action research (PAR) to address it. Instead of devising the methodology themselves and then seeking consent from prospective research participants, they first consulted members of the community where the research would take place to get their permission to do a study on the topic, and then asked for their views on what an appropriate methodology might be. After gaining permission to go ahead with the project from the band and chief of a rural Indigenous community in British Columbia, Sharma et al. held focus groups with several community groups, including Elders with diabetes, the Chief and Council, a health-care services team, and some Indigenous youths to determine how the study would be conducted. This was done in an attempt to neutralize the power differential between the researchers (who were non-Indigenous and had PhDs, secure middle-class incomes, and Western cultural outlooks) and the members of the community. It was especially important to recognize the potential for exploitation in this research, given the history of colonialism in Canada and the tendency of past researchers to marginalize Indigenous experiences and ways of knowing. The goal was to make the members of the community equal partners in the research, and in so doing allow them to bring their own issues and perspectives to bear on it.

The various participants decided collectively that the project would take the form of a short film to be created by five Indigenous youths aged 14–16. The film featured interviews with Elders suffering from diabetes, a description of what diabetes is, and some tips on healthy eating. The production of the film involved a constant negotiation of the relationship between the professional researchers and the youths. The former tried to stay in the background as much as possible, although they did end up editing the first version of the film. In order to enhance the collaborative nature of the project, the professional researchers then showed the edited version to the youths and removed any parts that the young people thought were inappropriate. This illustrates several aspects of PAR: explicit recognition of the power differentials that often characterize conventional research; an attempt to minimize those differentials in order to address the subject matter from the perspective of the people participating in the research; and full participation by the group that is the focus of the inquiry in order to produce knowledge and actions that are beneficial to them and not just to the professional researchers.

Critiques of qualitative research

Just as quantitative research has been criticized by people in the qualitative tradition, the latter has been taken to task by quantitative social scientists. Some of the more common criticisms of qualitative research are discussed below.

Too subjective

Quantitative researchers sometimes criticize qualitative research for being too impressionistic and subjective. By this they usually mean that qualitative findings depend too much on the researchers' values and opinions about what is significant. A related contention stems from the close personal relationships that many researchers strike up with the people they study, which can lead to bias. Also, because qualitative researchers often begin in a relatively open-ended way and then gradually narrow down their research questions or problems, they may not explain clearly at the outset why they came to focus on one area rather than another. In response to this critique, qualitative researchers argue that researchers who attempt to preserve their objectivity by remaining distant from the social world, risk the worst form of subjectivity: "the objective observer is likely to fill in the process of interpretation with [their] own surmises in place of catching the process as it occurs in the experience of the acting unit which uses it" (Blumer, 1969, p. 86). By not getting close to the social world and trying to see things from participants' points of view, we become prone to filling in gaps in our understanding with our own perspectives instead of the participants'.

Difficult to replicate

Some quantitative researchers argue that the problem of subjectivity is made worse by the difficulty of replicating a qualitative study, even though replication is uncommon in the social sciences, regardless of the research methods used. Because it is unstructured and relies on the researcher's ingenuity, and because it may examine processes and situations that are in flux, qualitative work is almost always impossible to replicate. What is observed and heard often depends on the researcher, as does the choice of what to concentrate on; different researchers may choose to observe different things and as a result they may come up with different findings. Also, the behaviour of the people being observed or interviewed is likely to be affected by the characteristics of the researcher (personality, age, gender, and so on). The difficulties that qualitative social scientists experience when they revisit ground previously covered by another researcher (often referred to as a "restudy") do not inspire confidence in the replicability of qualitative research (Bryman, 1994). Qualitative researchers answer that the replicability criterion is largely irrelevant to their research goals because it is not consistent with their epistemological and ontological positions. For example, they maintain that it is to be expected that different researchers will view a particular situation or event differently, and then take the study in different directions.

Issues of generalization

It is sometimes suggested that the scope of qualitative findings is restricted. Because research based on participant observation or unstructured interviews typically involves only a small number of individuals in a single organization or locality, it may be difficult to know whether the findings can be applied to other people or other settings. Can just one or two cases be representative of some larger population? Can Karabanow's (2002) study of two Canadian shelters for homeless youth (Box 9.2) be considered generalizable to all youth shelters in the country? In the case of research based on qualitative interviews rather than participation, are those who were interviewed representative of some larger population? Do the interview findings from sex-trade workers in Victoria (Hallgrimsdottir et al., 2006), for example, apply to sex workers in Toronto?

The answer to these questions in most qualitative research studies is "probably not." But a case study is not a sample of one drawn from a known population. The people interviewed in qualitative research are not necessarily meant to be representative of some larger group. In fact, with some social groups, such as workers in the sex trade, it may be impossible to enumerate the population in any precise manner, which makes the selection of a representative sample impracticable.

Moreover, in most cases it is not the purpose of qualitative research to produce generalizable knowledge. Such research normally stands on its own, providing in-depth analysis of a person or a small group of people—something that quantitative research rarely does. Also, qualitative research can contribute to the creation of generalizable knowledge insofar as it produces theories or concepts that can be assessed using other research methods. For instance, Williams (2000) argued that qualitative researchers are often in a position to produce generalizations regarding the people or events studied (a group of drug users or soccer hooligans, a strike) that "can be seen to be instances of a broader set of recognisable features" (2000, p. 215). In addition, Williams argued that a researcher studying the hooligans who follow a certain soccer club will often draw comparisons with the findings of other researchers who have studied comparable groups. He or she might also draw comparisons with followers of other professional sports teams, or with violent groups in contexts other than sport. Such generalizations will always be limited and somewhat more tentative, though no less useful, than the statistical generalizations produced by quantitative research.

Lack of transparency

Another criticism of qualitative research is that it may be less than transparent about what the researchers actually did and how they arrived at their conclusions. For example, qualitative research reports are sometimes unclear about how the participants were chosen for observation or interview. This contrasts with the tendency of quantitative researchers to include detailed accounts of sampling procedures in their reports. However, since qualitative research does not claim generalizability the way quantitative research does, sampling procedures are less relevant to their work.

Some contrasts between quantitative and qualitative research

Several writers have used tables to contrast quantitative and qualitative research (for example, Hammersley, 1992). Table 9.1 highlights the main differences. As with any summary of a large body of material, the table outlines general tendencies. The full picture is more nuanced: there are exceptions to these general points, as we will see in Chapter 14.

TABLE 9.1 Common contrasts between quantitative and qualitative research

Quantitative	Qualitative
Numbers	Words
Point of view of researcher	Points of view of research participants
Researcher distant	Researcher close
Theory testing	Theory development
Structured	Unstructured
Generalizable knowledge	Contextual understanding
Hard, reliable data	Rich, deep data
Macro	Micro
Behaviour	Meaning
Artificial settings	Natural settings

- *"Numbers" versus "Words."* Quantitative researchers set great store by precise, numerical measurements of social phenomena. They use those measurements to calculate statistics to understand social life, whereas qualitative researchers use mainly words in their analyses of society.
- *"Point of view of researcher" versus "Points of view of participants."* In quantitative research, investigators are in the driver's seat; their concerns structure the investigation. In qualitative research, the investigation is structured by the people being investigated: their perspective—what they see as important—provides the point of orientation.
- *"Researcher is distant" versus "Researcher is close."* In quantitative research, researchers tend to be less involved with their subjects and in some cases, as in research based on online or mailed questionnaires, they may have no direct contact at all. Quantitative researchers often consider this distance desirable, because they want to be as objective as possible and feel their objectivity would be compromised if they were to become too involved with the people they study. By contrast, qualitative researchers

seek involvement with the people they study in order to see the world through the eyes of their participants and promote a more equalitarian relationship.

- *"Theory and concepts tested in research" versus "Theory and concepts developed from data."* Before data collection begins, quantitative researchers typically have a theory in mind that they want to test. In qualitative research, concepts and theories develop as the data are collected.
- *"Structured" versus "Unstructured."* Quantitative research is typically highly structured to maximize validity and reliability; in qualitative research, the approach is less structured in order to allow the researcher to get a sense of the meanings people derive from their everyday lives, and to permit the development and elaboration of concepts and theories as the data are collected.
- *"Generalizable knowledge" versus "Contextual understanding."* Whereas quantitative researchers want their findings to be applicable to some larger population, qualitative researchers focus on understanding the behaviour, values, and beliefs of the people in their study. Qualitative findings usually develop out of the context these people find themselves in; hence the insights gained may or may not apply to other people.
- *"Hard, reliable data" versus "Rich, deep data."* Quantitative researchers often describe their data as "hard"—robust and unambiguous—because they strive for precision when devising their measurement techniques. Qualitative researchers, by contrast, claim that their contextual approach and often prolonged involvement in a setting mean that the information they collect is rich, nuanced, and very detailed.
- *"Macro" versus "Micro."* Quantitative researchers often seek to uncover large-scale social trends and connections between variables; as we noted above, their research is generally designed to be applicable to large populations. Qualitative researchers are usually concerned with in-depth analysis of small-scale aspects of social reality, such as personal interaction, although these may be linked to larger social and political issues.
- *"Behaviour" versus "Meaning."* It is sometimes suggested that quantitative researchers focus more on people's behaviour, and qualitative researchers more on the meaning of that behaviour for the actor.
- *"Artificial settings" versus "Natural settings."* Whereas quantitative research is often conducted in a contrived context, such as an experiment or a formal interview setting, qualitative researchers investigate people in their natural environments, such as social gatherings or workplaces.

Key Points

- Qualitative research does not lend itself to a clear set of linear steps. As a research strategy it tends to be more open-ended than is typically the case with quantitative research.
- In qualitative research, theories and concepts are outcomes of the research process.
- There is considerable unease about the direct application of reliability and validity criteria to qualitative research. Many writers prefer alternative criteria.
- Lincoln and Guba (1985; 1994) propose two key criteria to evaluate a qualitative study: trustworthiness and authenticity. Trustworthiness requires four conditions: credibility, transferability, dependability, and confirmability.
- Most qualitative researchers try to see the social world through the eyes of their research participants.
- Like all approaches to social research, qualitative methods have both strengths and weaknesses.

Their major strengths include the development of empathetic understanding, rich description of context, and emphasis on process. Weaknesses include a reliance on the researcher's own perspectives when making research decisions, difficulties in replication, limited generalization, and lack of transparency.

Questions for Review (R) and Creative Application (A)

R1 Do research questions have the same characteristics and significance in qualitative research as in quantitative research? Explain.

A1 Imagine that you want to do a qualitative research project on homelessness in your city. Come up with a general research question that could be the starting point for your inquiry.

R2 Is the approach to theory in qualitative research primarily inductive or deductive? Explain.

A2 Explain how a researcher could use grounded theory research to investigate how feelings of guilt arise among victims of childhood sexual abuse.

Evaluating qualitative research

R3 Why do qualitative researchers reject the notions of validity and reliability used in quantitative research?

A3 Explain how respondent validation might be used in a study of friendship networks among teenagers working at a fast-food restaurant, and what difficulties might arise in using this technique.

R4 What are the main goals of qualitative researchers? Explain.

A4 Why would it be important to provide a rich description of the context in which new immigrants to Canada find themselves in order to understand poverty in immigrant communities?

R5 What are some of the main criticisms of qualitative research? Are those criticisms valid? Explain.

A5 Sometimes qualitative studies are criticized because they are difficult to replicate. Explain why critics see replication as a problem, then make the case that this criticism reflects a misunderstanding of methods and purposes of qualitative research.

R6 "The difference between quantitative and qualitative research revolves entirely around the concern with numbers in the former and with words in the latter." To what extent is this statement accurate? Explain.

A6 The claim is sometimes made that quantitative research focuses on behaviour while qualitative work is primarily concerned with meaning. How might quantitative researchers investigate issues of meaning, and qualitative practitioners study behaviour?

Interactive Classroom Activities

1. Divide the class into small groups. Each group is to do the following:
   a. Come up with a topic that could be researched using qualitative methods.
   b. Produce a research question that could be used to investigate the topic.
   c. Select a hypothetical person or group to be studied.
   d. Describe some qualitative methods that could be used to study the topic.
   e. Explain what *verstehen* means, and how it could be achieved in their research project.
   f. Explain how the research will be able to examine the topic as a *process*.
   g. Make up some qualitative data; for example, imagine how the person or persons studied might interpret the phenomenon under study.

   Each group then presents a summary of their discussions to the rest of the class for comment and critique.

2. Divide the class into six groups. The groups are to marshal arguments making the following points:
   a. Group 1: Qualitative research is too subjective to be of any scientific value.
   b. Group 2: The idea that qualitative research is too subjective to be of any scientific value is

false and is based on a misunderstanding of the purposes of qualitative research.

c. Group 3: Qualitative research is difficult or impossible to replicate, so any conclusions based on it cannot be trusted.

d. Group 4: Qualitative research can be used to produce valid knowledge.

e. Group 5: Qualitative research produces knowledge that is of little of no value because the results of qualitative studies can rarely be applied to people or groups not studied.

f. Group 6: Qualitative research can produce knowledge of tremendous value regardless of whether the results can be generalized to other people or groups.

Each group presents its position to the class. General class discussions on the positions taken are held after Groups 2, 4, and 6 have made their case.

Relevant Websites

The *International Institute for Qualitative Methodology*, based at the University of Alberta in Edmonton, sponsors conferences and research training programs involving qualitative research methods. It also publishes the *International Journal of Qualitative Methods*, which is available free online.

www.ualberta.ca/international-institute-for-qualitative-methodology/index.html

Examples of qualitative studies can be found in the journal *Qualitative Research* and in the *Qualitative Sociology Review*; you may have to access these journals through your institution's library server.

http://qrj.sagepub.com

www.qualitativesociologyreview.org/ENG/index_eng.php

(Websites accessed 4 September 2021)

OXFORD learning link

More resources are available on Oxford Learning Link. Visit https://learninglink.oup.com/ for:

- Student self-quiz
- Flash cards
- Audio clips
- Videos
- Activities

10 Ethnography and Participant Observation

Chapter Overview

Ethnography and **participant observation** require extended involvement in the activities of the people under study. This chapter explores:

- the problems of gaining access to different settings and ways of overcoming them;
- whether **covert research** is practicable and acceptable;
- the role of **key informants**;
- the different roles that ethnographers can assume in the course of their fieldwork;
- the function of **field notes** and the forms they can take;
- the role of visual materials in ethnography; and,
- bringing an ethnographic study to an end.

Key Learning Outcomes

Here is a list of goals you should try to achieve as you read and think about the material in this chapter. After completing this chapter, you should be able to:

1. Describe the methodological and ethical issues involved in gaining and maintaining access to field sites and participants, conducting overt and covert research in open and closed research settings, and working with key informants.
2. Identify the different roles ethnographers can take on while collecting data, including *complete participant*, *participant-as-observer*, *observer-as-participant*, and *complete observer*, as well as how active or passive they will be in these roles.
3. Discuss strategies for writing different types of field notes and analytic memos while conducting ethnographic research.

▲ Chase Clausen/Shutterstock

4. Describe the use of visual ethnography as a way of incorporating and analyzing visual materials such as photographs in qualitative research.
5. Explain how institutional ethnography can be used to study the relationships between institutions and people's everyday lives.
6. Describe how ethnographers sample participants and field sites for inclusion in their studies and make decisions about how much data is sufficient.
7. Explain how ethnographers decide when to conclude their data collection and why they find it difficult to leave the field.

Do you like to travel to places you've never been to before? Have you ever observed a group of people you don't know very well and wondered what it would be like to be a member of their group? Have you ever witnessed profound human suffering and asked yourself how things ended up that way and how the people suffering managed to endure? Would you like to give such people a voice or expose the hardships that they face? If so, doing or at least reading about ethnography and participant observation should interest you.

Ethnography and participant observation involve placing yourself in a social environment that may be foreign to you, and staying there for an extended period of time. What kinds of groups or social settings intrigue you? Non-governmental organizations? Political movements? Sports teams? Criminal gangs? Hospital emergency rooms? Women's shelters? All of these can be subjects of ethnographic and participant observation research.

Introduction

Truly remarkable insights into the human condition have been achieved by researchers who have immersed themselves in a social setting for extended periods of time (sometimes for years). Different terms are used to describe this process. Discussions about *participant observation* have been fairly standard in textbooks on social research, but more recently writers on research methods have preferred the word *ethnography*. In both cases, researchers interact with the people they are studying, listening to what they say in conversation and asking them questions. Typically, participant observers and ethnographers gather further data through documents and interviews, especially on matters that are not directly observable, or about which they are unclear. Santin and Kelly (2017), for example, used participant observation as their primary method to study flight attendants' emotional labour, but they also conducted interviews with 15 flight attendants, a survey of 40 flight attendants, and a review of flight attendant training manuals.

The terms "participant observation" and "ethnography" are essentially synonymous, although here "ethnography" will be used in a broader sense, including participant observation; the latter will refer specifically to the observational component of ethnographic research.

This chapter outlines some of the main decisions that ethnographers must make, along with some of the many contingencies they face. However, given the diversity of the experiences that confront ethnographers and the variety of ways in which they deal with those experiences, it's difficult to generalize about this kind of research or to provide specific recommendations about it. The following comment makes this point well:

> Every field situation *is* different and initial luck in meeting good informants, being in the right place at the right time, and striking the right note in relationships may be just as important as skill in technique. Indeed . . . many unsuccessful episodes are due as much to bad luck as to bad judgement. (Sarsby, 1984, p. 96)

However, this statement should not be taken to mean that forethought and an awareness of alternative approaches are irrelevant. It is with those issues that the rest of this chapter is concerned. Issues involving the conduct of interviews by ethnographers are reserved for Chapter 11.

Access

One of the most important and yet most difficult steps in ethnography is gaining access to the social setting one wants to research. How to gain access depends on several things, one of which is whether the setting is relatively open (public) or closed (private or restricted) (see Lofland & Lofland, 1995). Closed settings generally include organizations of various kinds, such as firms, schools, cults, and social movements. Open settings are areas where anyone can gain access, such as libraries, parks, and sidewalks, but even there it can be quite difficult to make observations and talk to people. "Open" does not necessarily mean easy access to people.

Overt versus covert ethnography

One way to ease the access problem is to assume a *covert* role: in other words, to not disclose that you are a researcher. Getting access can be very problematic, and the adoption of a covert role removes some of the difficulties. These two distinctions—open versus closed setting, and overt versus covert role—suggest a fourfold distinction in forms of ethnography (see Figure 10.1); an example of Canadian research is given for each of the four types.

Three points should be noted about Figure 10.1. First, the "open versus closed setting" distinction is not hard and fast. Sometimes the process of gaining access in "open" settings can take on an almost formal quality; for instance, if you are talking to a gang leader in the street, you may have to answer some pointed questions about your goals. Also, "closed" organizations and social movements sometimes create contexts that have a public character, such as meetings arranged for members or prospective recruits. Bell (2007) attended many western Canadian separatist meetings and rallies that were open to the public, and was able to get a lot of information on the movement and its leaders that way.

Second, the "overt versus covert" distinction can vary from context to context even within the same research project. Although ethnographers may seek access through an overt route, many of the people with whom they come into contact may be unaware of their status as researchers. Atkinson (1981, p. 135) noted in connection with his research on the training of doctors in a medical school that although he was "an 'open' observer with regard to doctors and students," he was "a 'disguised' observer with regard to the patients." Also, some ethnographers move between the two roles (see Box 10.1).

Another interesting case is provided by Glucksmann (1994), who in the 1970s left her academic post for a job on a factory assembly line in an effort to find out why feminism appeared not to be relevant to working-class women. In a

Practical Tip | Micro-ethnography

In doing research for an undergraduate project or master's thesis, it's generally not feasible to conduct a full-scale ethnographic study, if only because of time limitations. Nevertheless, it may be possible to carry out a form of micro-ethnography (Wolcott, 1990), focusing on one specific aspect of a group. For example, if you were interested in call centres, you might focus on how staff members manage to interact and discuss work problems with one another despite continuous incoming calls and monitoring by supervisors. A shorter period of time (from a couple of weeks to a few months) can be spent in the organization—on either a full- or a part-time basis—to achieve this more limited goal.

	Open/public setting	Closed setting
Overt role	*Type 1* • Wilson's (2002) study of Toronto raves • Totten's (2001) study of youth gang members	*Type 2* • Karabanow's (2002) study of two Canadian youth shelters (Box 9.2) • Restoule et al.'s (2013) research on Indigenous students
Covert role	*Type 3* • Desroches's (1990) updates on homosexual activities in public washrooms	*Type 4* • Lauder's (2003) discussion of covert research on the Heritage Front

FIGURE 10.1 Four types of ethnography

Box 10.1 | Perils of covert observation: Field notes in the lavatory

Toronto Star Archives/Toronto Star via Getty Images

During her undercover stint at Fiera Foods, Sara Mojtehedzadeh worked on the croissant production line. What kinds of difficulties might researchers face when attempting to collect information without revealing their true identity and purpose?

Ditton's (1977) research in a bakery provides an interesting case study of the practical difficulties involved in taking notes during covert observation, as well as an illustration of an ethnographer who shifted positions from covert to overt observer at least in part because of those difficulties:

> Right from the start, I found it impossible to keep everything that I wanted to remember in my head until the end of the working day . . . and so had to take rough notes as I was going along. But I was stuck "on the line," and had nowhere to retire to privately to jot things down [except the washroom]. [Eventually] . . . my frequent requests for "time out" after interesting happenings or conversations in the bakehouse and the amount of time I was spending in the lavatory began to get noticed. I had to pacify some genuinely concerned work-mates . . . and "come out" as an observer—albeit in a limited way. I eventually began to scribble notes more openly, but still not in front of people when they were talking. When questioned about this, as I was occasionally, I coyly said that I was writing things down that occurred to me about "my studies" (Ditton, 1977, p. 5).

sense, she was a covert observer, but her motives for the research were primarily political, not academic. At the time she was undertaking the research she had no intention of writing the book, which was eventually published under a pseudonym. Was she an overt or a covert observer (or neither, or both)? Whichever description applies, this is an interesting case of what might be termed "retrospective ethnography": using observations that were gathered before the decision was made to conduct a study.

A third point with regard to Figure 10.1 is that the preferred choice is an overt role. There are several reasons for this. As Box 10.2 reveals, these reasons have to do with practical and especially ethical considerations. The ethics of covert research, which were addressed in depth in Chapter 3, involve issues of deception, lack of informed consent, and invasion of privacy, since the researcher has essentially fooled the participants into believing that they are not being observed for research purposes. Because of the ethical problems (and some of the practical difficulties) that beset covert research, the bulk of the following discussion of access issues focuses on overt research.

Access to closed settings

Gaining access to most organizations requires strategic planning, hard work, and sometimes luck. In selecting a case study for an ethnographic investigation, the researcher may employ several criteria, depending on the research area of interest. One may choose a certain case or setting because of its "fit" with the research questions, but there is no guarantee of access. Sometimes sheer perseverance pays off. Leidner (1993) was determined that McDonald's would be one of the organizations in which she conducted ethnographic research on the routinization of service work:

> The company was a pioneer and exemplar of routinized interaction, and since it was locally based, it seemed like the perfect place to start. McDonald's had other ideas, however, and

Box 10.2 | The covert role in ethnography

Advantages

- *Easier access.* Adopting a covert role can help with access problems; no special permission to gain entry to a social setting or organization may be needed.
- *Less reactivity.* Because participants do not know they are being observed by a researcher, they will speak and act more naturally than they would otherwise.

Disadvantages

- *The problem of taking notes.* It is difficult and sometimes impossible to take notes without revealing that you are conducting research. However, notes are very important to an ethnographer, and it's too risky to rely on memory alone.
- *The problem of not being able to use other methods.* If the researcher is in a covert role, steering conversations in a certain direction can increase the risk of detection, and it is essentially impossible to conduct interviews.
- *Anxiety.* Ethnography is frequently a stressful research method, and worries about detection only add to the anxiety. Moreover, if the ethnographer is found out, the whole research project may be jeopardized. In extreme cases, such as covert research on gangs, being found out could even put the researcher's life at risk.
- *Ethical problems.* Covert observation transgresses two important ethical tenets: deception of participants and failure to obtain informed consent (see Chapter 3). It can also involve a violation of privacy. Indeed, many writers think covert investigations can harm the practice of research in general, since innocent researchers may be tarred with the same brush as outed covert observers, who are considered snoops or voyeurs (or worse). On the other hand, covert participant observation may be justified in some situations, as Lauder (2003) concluded regarding his investigation of the neo-Nazi Heritage Front.

> only after tenacious pestering and persuasion did I overcome corporate employees' polite demurrals, couched in terms of protecting proprietary information and the company's image. (Leidner, 1993, pp. 234–235)

This kind of determination is necessary whenever the target is a specific organization or group (e.g., a particular religious sect or social movement). Rejection can mean having to find a completely different research topic.

On the other hand, for many research questions you are likely to find that several potential cases will be suitable. Organizational researchers have developed a range of tactics, some of which may seem rather unsystematic but are still worth considering:

- Use friends, contacts, and colleagues to help gain access; as long as the organization is relevant to the research question, the route should not matter.
- If possible, get someone in the organization to vouch for you and the value of your research. Such people are considered "sponsors." If permission is granted at a lower level of the hierarchy, you may still need clearance from top management or senior executives. People who must grant their permission for you to gain access are sometimes called **gatekeepers**.
- Offer something in return: for example, a *final* report (if you provide a working draft, people may ask you to make changes that you would not consider acceptable). However, this strategy carries a risk of making the researcher a cheap consultant. Some writers on research methodology do not recommend offering something in return, although it is commonplace among researchers on formal organizations.
- Provide a clear explanation of your aims and methods. Suggest a meeting to deal with the participants' concerns and explain what will happen in terms that people who are not familiar with social research can understand.
- Be prepared to negotiate; almost no one gets complete access.
- Be frank about the amount of people's time you are likely to need. Time is an important issue for commercial organizations, and for many non-profit groups too.

Access to open settings

Gaining access to people in open settings is similar in many ways. For instance, sometimes ethnographers have their paths smoothed by "sponsors" and "gatekeepers." In seeking access to a group of soccer hooligans, Giulianotti (1995) sought out someone who could play both roles for him. Later, he was able to call on existing acquaintances to ease his entrée into a second group. In seeking access to female intravenous drug users, Taylor (1993) contacted a drug counsellor who introduced her to some local users and accompanied her on her first few research visits. A "research bargain" (Becker, 1970) was struck in which Taylor agreed in return to see any of the counsellor's clients who preferred to discuss issues with a woman.

"Hanging around" is another common access strategy. An example of the difficulties that await the researcher using this approach can be found in one of Whyte's (1955) early field encounters in Boston's North End in his classic case study *Street Corner Society*. The following incident occurred in a hotel bar:

> I looked around me again and now noticed a threesome: one man and two women. It occurred to me that here was a maldistribution of females that I might be able to rectify. I approached the group and opened with something like this: "Pardon me. Would you mind if I join you?" There was a moment of silence while the man stared at me. He then offered to throw me downstairs. I assured him that this would not be necessary and demonstrated as much by walking right out of there without any assistance. (Whyte, 1955, p. 289)

Wolf (1991) used a hanging-around strategy to gain access to Canadian outlaw bikers. On one occasion he met a group of them at a motorcycle shop and expressed an interest in hanging out with them. But he tried to move too quickly in seeking information about them and was forced to abandon his plans. Eventually, Wolf's hanging-around strategy led to his being approached by the leader of a biker group (Rebels MC), who acted as his sponsor. To bring this off Wolf ensured that he was properly attired in biker garb, although this was not difficult for him as he had been a motorcyclist and had absorbed biker culture long before he started his research. Attention to dress and demeanour can be a very important consideration when seeking access to either public or closed settings.

Sometimes, researchers may gain access to a setting before they even think of doing a study there. Box 10.3 provides an example.

As these anecdotes suggest, gaining access to social settings is a crucial first step in ethnographic research. But it is also difficult and, in some cases, dangerous—for example, when the group in question is engaged in violent or criminal activities. Caution is essential when choosing an access strategy.

Ongoing access

Access problems do not end after initial contact and entrée to the group. Maintaining access is an ongoing activity and is likely to prove a persistent problem in closed contexts such as organizations.

- People will be suspicious, perhaps seeing the researcher as an instrument of top management (it's very common for members of organizations to believe that researchers have been put in place to check up on them). When conducting his research on the provision of care in a Canadian emergency shelter for homeless men, Ranasinghe (2017) was suspected by some of the shelter's clients of being a police officer.
- Group members will worry that what they say or do may get back to bosses or colleagues. Van Maanen (1991) noted that when conducting ethnographic research among police officers,

Box 10.3 | Access to Inuit: From friend to researcher

When Lisa-Jo van den Scott moved to Arviat, Nunavut, as the wife of a music teacher, she had no intention of researching Inuit culture. She had recently finished a master's degree in ancient Greek and did not envision getting caught up in conducting an ethnographic study. Taking to her new life in the remote northern hamlet, she began developing friendships, learning Inuktitut, volunteering at a drop-in centre, and working as an instructor at Nunavut Arctic College. With a genuine interest in becoming involved in the community, she often moved out of her comfort zone, trying new foods like *igunak* (raw, aged walrus meat), and taking part in throat singing. So complete was van den Scott's connection to the community, she was elected to the Elders' council as "the first non-Inuk, first non-Elder on the council" (L.K. van den Scott, 2018, p. 22). The relationships she developed were reciprocal, trust-based, and sincere.

As van den Scott became increasingly immersed in the day-to-day life of Arviat, her sociological curiosity about Inuit identity, space, and the built environment was piqued. In mentioning her research ideas to Inuk friends, she found that although they did not understand her sociological interests, they were eager to assist. Outside researchers do not always receive such a hospitable reception, but through honest demonstrations of commitment, van den Scott had become accepted as a friend and community member. Key to her ongoing access was an emphasis on *learning from* her participants rather than *studying* them. The difference is subtle but important. It involves a shift in the power dynamic, wherein the researcher becomes a student to the experts on a given way of life, the participants. It also encapsulates van den Scott's deep respect for the people that welcomed her into their lives and shared their stories with her. She writes that she was "committed to engaging with them with all the respect due to research participants as experts in their

(Continued)

own lives" (p. 24). Starting her research from the point of friendship also meant reminding herself that even if her friends did not always remember that she was a researcher, she could not lose sight of this. She strove to be **reflexive**, taking into account her position as a White researcher in a colonial setting, while also being a friend to her participants. She states, "That meant deciding what information made it into my field notes. Would being a friend affect my findings? Of course—but in which way? How much? What should I do?" (p. 26).

As van den Scott's experience reveals, entrée into a field site can happen unexpectedly as a result of chance life circumstances. A positive personal reputation and connection to participants can present opportunities for access, but it is also a balancing act as the ethnographer must take into account their roles as both friend and researcher. Fostering trust and rapport is often best achieved through an ongoing attentiveness to maintaining mutual respect between researcher and participants.

it's not unusual to observe activities that reflect badly on the police and may even be illegal. In such situations the researcher can establish credibility by using discretion.

- If the people being studied have concerns or suspicions about the researcher, they may appear to go along with the research but in fact sabotage it, engage in deception, provide misinformation, or not allow access to "back regions" (Goffman, 1956).

Here are three ways to smooth the path for ongoing access to closed settings:

- Be prepared to adapt how you present yourself. Sometimes it's helpful to play up your credentials: talk about your past work, your experience, your knowledge of the group, and your understanding of its problems. Other times it's more conducive to take on a student role, presenting yourself as someone who is interested in learning from the experts as van den Scott did in her research on Inuit (see Box 10.3).
- Don't give people a reason to dislike you: be non-judgmental when hearing about informal activities or about the organization; make sure that information given to you doesn't get back to others, whether bosses or peers.
- Help out occasionally with work, or offer advice without being critical.

Similar considerations apply to research in public settings:

- Make sure you have a plan for allaying people's suspicions. Ranasinghe (2017) "tried to ensure that while [he] was conspicuous, [he] was, nevertheless, not obtrusive or obstructive" (pp. 235–236). Over time he found that the emergency shelter's clients became less fearful and were more receptive to him.
- Be prepared for tests of either competence or credibility. When doing research on gang members in a poor community, Horowitz wrote that she was frequently told "confidential" stories (which turned out to be fictional) to see if she could keep a secret (Gerson & Horowitz, 2002).
- Be prepared for changes in circumstances. With an interest in how ultra-Orthodox Jews manage social change, Shaffir (2018) worked as a clerical assistant with the Tasher—a Hasidic Jewish sect—covertly observing their way of life in an enclave north of Montreal. When he told a couple members of the group that he had to reduce his workload so that he could focus on his master's thesis, they suggested he study their culture. By the next day they had changed their minds and asked him to leave his position due to a lack of funds. As an office clerk, though, he had made contacts within the community, which allowed him to remain in the field.

Key informants

Ethnographers rely heavily on informants, especially those who develop an understanding of the research and are able to identify situations, events, or people likely to be helpful to the investigation. Whyte (1955) again provides an extreme example, quoting a key informant named Doc:

> You tell me what you want to see, and we'll arrange it. When you want some information, I'll ask for it, and you listen. When you want to find out their philosophy of life, I'll start an argument and get it for you. If there's something else you want to get, I'll stage an act for you. (1955, p. 292)

Doc was also helpful in warning Whyte that he was asking too many questions, telling him to "go easy on that 'who,' 'what,' 'why,' 'when,' 'where' stuff" (1955, p. 303). Shaffir (2018) discusses his good fortune in finding his "Doc" in the Tasher ultra-Orthodox Jewish community:

> And when I established a favourable relationship with a Hasid whose role in the community was central—in effect, he came to serve as my "Doc," a key informant—my connections to Tasher increased exponentially. I could and would visit the enclave at will, meandering in the synagogues and shopping centre, and engaging Hasidim in friendly conversations. I had gained a measure of trust and was invited to establish a website featuring the community that included several of my publications about the community. (2018, p. 324)

Key informants can also provide support that helps with the stress of fieldwork. However, undue reliance on them can lead researchers to see social reality through their eyes only rather than viewing things from the perspectives of several group members or the group as a whole.

In addition, ethnographers encounter many other people who will act as informants whose accounts may or may not have been solicited. Some researchers prefer unsolicited information because of its spontaneity and naturalism. Very often, research participants develop a sense of the events or encounters that the ethnographer will want to see. However, as Hammersley and Atkinson (1995, pp. 130–131) observed, it's important to recognize that such offers may on occasion be staged for the ethnographer's benefit.

Solicited accounts can be obtained in two ways: by interviewing (see Chapter 11) or by casual questioning during conversations (though in ethnographic research the boundary between an interview and a conversation is by no means clear). When the ethnographer needs specific information on an issue that does not lend itself to direct observation or that is not cropping up during "natural" conversations, solicited accounts are likely to be the only way forward.

Roles for ethnographers

Related to the issue of ongoing access is the question of the role an ethnographer adopts in relation to the social setting and its members. Often the various roles in fieldwork are arrayed along a continuum from complete involvement to complete detachment (see Figure 10.2). It should also be noted that the full gamut of roles may be employed at different times in the course of a single ethnographic project, and for different purposes.

For example, the participant observer can be any of the following:

- *Complete participant.* The ethnographer is a fully functioning member of a social setting but one whose true identity is unknown to members: in other words, a covert observer. In such cases the ethnographer is engaged in regular interaction with people and participates in their daily lives but assumes the researcher's

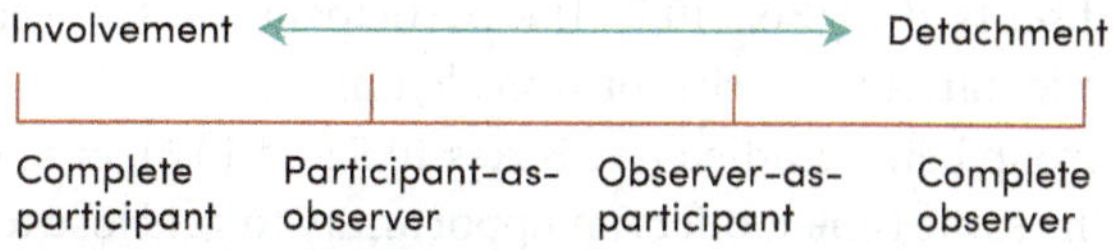

FIGURE 10.2 Classification of participant observer roles (Gold 1958)

role in private to write down notes once the situation has unfolded. This is what Humphreys (1970) did when he studied male homosexual encounters in public washrooms.

- *Participant-as-observer.* The ethnographer participates as described above, except that members of the social setting are aware that the ethnographer is studying them, such as in van den Scott's research (see Box 10.3).
- *Observer-as-participant.* The researcher is mainly an interviewer and observer, and participates only marginally in the group's activities. This was Bell's (2007) role in his study of western Canadian separatists. Ethnographic research on the police is often similar, since the opportunities for genuine participation are limited by legal and safety restrictions. Norris (1993) described how as an observer-as-participant, he concentrated on gathering two types of data: "naturally occurring inter-officer talk" and "detailed descriptions of how officers handled 'live' incidents" (1993, p. 126). For other examples of situations in which minimal participation may be appropriate, see Boxes 10.4 and 10.6.
- *Complete observer.* The final possibility is no interaction with the people observed. Most writers do not include this as a form of ethnography, since by definition there is little or no involvement or participation. There may be less risk of *reactivity* (participants behaving unnaturally because they know they are being observed) because the researcher is at a distance; but there is also greatly reduced potential for *understanding* because the researcher does not ask questions or try in any way to get into the heads of the people under study.

Each approach has advantages and disadvantages. In the case of covert ethnography, some of these are discussed in Box 10.2. The participant-as-observer role carries the risk of overidentification with the group being studied (see Boxes 10.5 and 10.6), but at the same time it offers an opportunity to get close to people. The observer-as-participant role carries the risk of not understanding the social setting and its people sufficiently and therefore making incorrect inferences. In an interesting variant of this problem, Hessler et al. (2003) cautioned observers (in a study of adolescent risk behaviour) against the temptation to act as counsellors to respondents.

Gans (1968) would add that even if it were possible, it is probably undesirable to adhere to a single role over the entire course of a project, since this would limit the ethnographer's flexibility in handling situations and people. In addition, the risks of either excessive involvement or excessive detachment would loom large.

Active or passive?

How active or passive should the ethnographer be? In most studies—even when the researcher is mainly an observer rather than a participant—involvement in the group's activities will be unavoidable from time to time. For example, Fine's (1996) research on the work of chefs in restaurants was carried out largely through semi-structured interviews. In spite of this limited participation, he sometimes found himself in the kitchen washing dishes to help out during busy periods. Similarly, in a study of bouncers, the participant observer will not have the luxury of deciding whether to become involved in fights, since involvement comes with the territory (Winlow, Hobbs, Lister, & Hadfield, 2001).

Sometimes ethnographers feel they have no choice about getting involved because a failure to participate might suggest a lack of commitment to the group. In such situations, standing back could lead to a loss of credibility in the eyes of the people studied. This situation can arise especially when the activities are illegal or dangerous. On the other hand, many writers counsel against active participation in criminal or dangerous activities. Both Armstrong (1993) and Giulianotti (1995) refused to fight while doing their research into soccer hooliganism. The latter wrote: "My own rules are that I will not get involved in fighting or become a go-between for the two gangs in organizing fights" (1995, p. 10). That is an illustration of why it is not a good idea to do covert research on criminals or those involved in dangerous actions: it is much more difficult for someone in such a role to decline to participate in group activities (see Box 10.5).

Box 10.4 | Virtual ethnography

sjenner13/123RF

What challenges might an ethnographer face when studying a virtual community as opposed to an offline community? Would these issues affect how active or passive the ethnographer must be?

Hallett and Barber (2014) argue that the study of online spaces should be included in ethnographic research because people's "natural habitat" now includes their "online habitat." Instagram, Facebook, Twitter, email, instant messaging, Skype, YouTube, blogs, and so forth are now predominant places for participating in social networks and acquiring information and interpretations of the world. Despite that fact, most ethnography is conducted offline; the authors themselves only ventured into cyberspace after their attempts to use solely in-person methods proved to be unworkable.

In researching an organization for undocumented college students in California, one of the authors began by researching the life history of a particular student, but found it difficult to keep in touch with him. The student didn't have a phone, and email messages often went unanswered. The researcher soon learned that the most dependable means of communication was Facebook, which the student checked many times a day. Facebook also proved to be an invaluable source of ethnographic information about the organization, how it established a sense of community, and how its members viewed the plight of undocumented students. The author states that he "had considered asking participants to journal about how they spent time and perceived the educational process. I soon realized that students were already 'journaling' on their Facebook pages, and these posts were more natural than I may have received if they had used paper and pencil to write at my request" (316).

Box 10.5 | Overidentification with the people one is studying

Sometimes, as a result of prolonged immersion in the lives of the people being observed, coupled with a commitment to seeing through their eyes, ethnographers become so wrapped up in the world of the people they are studying that they forget their role as researchers. Under such circumstances the ethnographer may find it difficult to maintain a social scientific perspective on the collection and analysis of data. For example, when Schulenberg (2014) conducted participant observation of Canadian police officers while doing "ride-alongs" with them, she had to contend with a feeling that she may have become overly accepting of the officers' beliefs and values. Similarly, Hobbs (1988, p. 6) wrote of his fieldwork that he "often had to remind himself that [he] was not in a pub to enjoy [himself] but to conduct an academic inquiry, and repeatedly woke up the following morning with an incredible hangover, facing the dilemma of whether to bring it up or write it up."

(Continued)

A related issue for Hobbs was involvement in illegal activity, which may be tempting if one becomes overly acculturated to a group in which criminal actions are known to occur:

> A refusal, or worse still an inquiry concerning the legal status of the "parcel," would provoke an abrupt conclusion to the relationship. Consequently, I was willing to skirt the boundaries of criminality on several occasions, and I considered it crucial to be willingly involved in "normal" business transactions, legal or otherwise. I was pursuing an interactive, inductive study of an entrepreneurial culture, and in order to do so I had to display entrepreneurial skills myself. . . . [My] status as an insider meant that I was afforded a great deal of trust by my informants, and I was allowed access to settings, detailed conversations, and information that might not otherwise have been available. (1988, pp. 7, 15)

Box 10.6 Annoyance or animosity toward the people one is observing

Overidentification with the people one is observing is not the only risk that participant observers face in relation to the social situations they study. Lee-Treweek (2000) carried out research on auxiliary caregivers in two homes for the elderly. In one of them she reacted in a way that was the opposite of overidentification. She disliked the home and found the staff unappealing because of their uncaring approach and lack of sympathy for the elderly residents. Nonetheless, she felt she "was gathering good data, despite [her] feelings of being an outsider" (2000, p. 120). Similarly, although Bell (2007) spent more than a year observing Western Canadian separatists, at no point was he ever tempted to join the group. The lesson here is that overidentification is not inevitable, and that researchers must be careful not to let either positive or negative feelings for the people they study distort their findings.

Field notes

Because of the frailties of human memory, ethnographers must jot down their observations. These should be fairly detailed summaries of events and behaviour, and the researcher's initial reflections on them. The notes need to specify the key dimensions of whatever is observed or heard. Here are some general principles:

- Write down notes, however brief, as soon as possible after seeing or hearing something interesting.
- Write up full field notes at the end of the day at the very latest, including details such as location, the people involved, what prompted the exchange or event, and date and time of day.
- You may also use an audio recorder to take notes from later, but you will have to allow plenty of time for transcription.
- Notes must be vivid, clear, and complete. If in doubt, write it down.

It's obviously best to take notes as soon as something significant happens. However, wandering around with a notebook and continually scribbling in it can make the people you are observing feel self-conscious. Thus, it may be necessary to take small amounts of time away from the group to write down your observations. In that case you must take care not to make the participants anxious or suspicious (see Box 10.1).

To some extent, strategies for taking field notes depend on how clearly delineated the research questions are. As we noted in Chapter 9, most qualitative research begins with general research questions, but there is considerable variation in their specificity. Obviously, when there is a clearly focused research question, the ethnographer's observations should be oriented to it. At the same time, it's important to maintain a fairly open mind, so that the study's flexibility with respect to the themes it explores—a strength of qualitative research—is not impaired.

In the context of her research on female drug users, Taylor (1993, p. 15) explained that in her early days in the field she tended to listen rather than talk because she "did not know what questions [she] wanted to ask." Armstrong (1993, p. 12) wrote in connection with his research on soccer hooliganism that his research "began without a focus" and that as a result "he decided to record everything." Therefore, a typical Saturday would mean 30 pages of handwritten notes. Such open-endedness usually cannot last long, because trying to record the details of absolutely everything is so tiring. Eventually the ethnographer begins to narrow down the focus of the research, sometimes by relating the emerging findings to the social scientific literature on the topic. This approach is implied by the sequence suggested in Figure 9.1.

For most ethnographers, the equipment needed for observation consists mainly of a notepad and pen (for example, Armstrong, 1993, p. 28). An audio recorder may be useful but, as we have noted, transcribing what you record will take time, and care must be taken to ensure the audio recordings are not disseminated, as they may unintentionally identify research participants. In addition, recording may be more obtrusive than writing notes. Although participants usually grow accustomed to the presence of the researcher over time, speaking into a recording device can rekindle fears about participating; and in some gatherings it may be difficult to use one because of extraneous noise. Photography can be an additional source of data, and pictures do help to stir the ethnographer's memory, but in some kinds of research (especially involving crime and deviance) photography may not be feasible.

Types of field notes

Some writers have found it useful to classify the types of field notes generated in the process of conducting ethnography. The following classification is based on categories suggested by Lofland and Lofland (1995) and Sanjek (1990):

Research in the News

An ethnographic study of bus-riding behaviour in Vancouver

As Lisa-Jo van den Scott's (2018) research on Inuit culture demonstrates (see Box 10.3), everyday happenstance can inspire research questions. This was the case for Dr. Amy Hanser, an Associate Professor of Sociology at the University of British Columbia (Plana, 2019). As a regular bus rider in Vancouver, she became curious about the unwritten rules of public transit. In an interview with the *Daily Hive* she stated, "The bus struck me as a great place to watch and see [mixing and diversity in the city] in action. In a way, there are two layers—there's the microcosms of individual behaviour and interactions, as well as the macrocosm of the city as a whole" (Plana, 2019). In the first part of her exploratory study, she rode the bus for three hours at a time and observed the passengers. She spent another two hours writing field notes and recording her observations. The next phase of her research will include additional observation as well as interviews with passengers and drivers.

- *Mental notes.* These are particularly useful when it is inappropriate to be seen taking written notes; however, they should be put into writing at the earliest opportunity.
- *Jotted notes (also called scratch or rough notes).* The researcher makes very brief notes to jog the memory about events that should be written up more fully later. Lofland and Lofland (1995, p. 90) described jotted notes as "little phrases, quotes, key words, and the like." Such notes need to be written inconspicuously, preferably out of sight, since writing in front of research participants may be off-putting for them.
- *Full field notes.* These are the main data source in ethnographic research. Full notes should be written as soon as possible, usually at the end of the day. Provide as much detail as possible about events, people, conversations, and so on. A particular comment from a participant or an account of an event that you witnessed may not seem very important at the time, but its significance may become apparent later on, once you have developed an interpretive structure. Without good notes, valuable data may be lost. Write down, in brackets, initial ideas about your interpretations, impressions, and feelings.

It's worth adding that in field notes the ethnographer's presence is frequently evident. This can be seen in Whyte's account (above) of almost being thrown down the stairs. However, in the finished work the ethnographer is sometimes written out of the picture. Field notes, except for brief passages, are primarily for the researcher's own use (Coffey, 1999), whereas the written report is for public consumption and has to be presented as a credible account of the social setting and culture in question. References to the ethnographer should be limited; otherwise, the report will look more like an account of his or her activities than those of the group purportedly under study.

Analytic memos

Most of the previous discussion focused on the mechanics of note taking. But content is even more important. Notes can be taken on the setting, the people, the methodological problems encountered, and so on. In addition, it's possible to create *analytic memos* recording some initial thoughts on what all those observations might mean. Analytic notes help to bridge the gap between the data and the concepts, interpretations, and theories that researchers develop to make sense of what they are observing. Such memos should be dated and reviewed regularly. They should also be kept separate from notes on actual observations because they are comments on data, not data themselves.

The rise of visual ethnography

The use of visual materials in social research is by no means new. Since the nineteenth century, cultural anthropologists have used photographs in their portrayals of traditional societies. However, books such as Pink's (2001) *Visual Ethnography* have marked a transition to a different way of using photos in social research.

In Chapter 12 we will discuss visual materials (primarily photographs) that were produced some time before the research began. Here we will consider visual materials that are produced more or less exclusively for research purposes: research-driven images, mainly photographs but also video recordings and other visual media. It's worth noting that although the term "visual ethnography" is increasingly popular, it does not always refer to the kind of sustained immersion in a social setting that is the subject of this chapter.

Qualitative researchers use visual materials in at least three ways:

- as memory aids in the course of fieldwork, where they essentially become components of the ethnographer's field notes
- as sources of data in their own right
- as prompts for discussion by research participants

Pink (2001) drew an important distinction between two positions on visual materials. The traditional framework is a **realist** one in which the material simply captures an event or setting that then becomes a "fact" for the ethnographer to

Methods in Motion | Applications to Canadian Society

Contemporary consequences of the historic relationship between Indigenous people and Euro-Canadian power structures

Browne (2007) used ethnographic methods and participant observation to examine how the historic political, social, and economic inequalities experienced by Indigenous women affected their interactions with nurses in a hospital in western Canada. She explored how socially constructed notions of culture, "race," and ethnicity can influence the quality of the health care that Indigenous women receive. Browne, who is both a nurse and a researcher, spent nine months conducting the study, which involved doing in-depth interviews with 14 registered nurses (four of whom were Indigenous) and 14 Indigenous female patients. She also shadowed the nurses as they worked with the Indigenous patients.

One thing Browne noted was that the nurses tended to ignore or downplay historically based power inequalities when they tried to make sense of their patients' demeanour, which was often passive, quiet, and introverted. A common interpretation was that the patients' behaviour stemmed from cultural factors. As one nurse put it, "[This patient] wouldn't look at me. She wouldn't answer anything. She would nod occasionally. . . . I mean, it's a cultural thing" (p. 2169). One of the patients explained things differently: ". . . a lot of native women, especially, don't want to say anything, don't talk. . . . I know my mom, for example, had a lot of fear in her from residential school" (p. 2170). Browne points out that these misunderstandings can have serious health consequences, as in the case of an Indigenous woman who did not mention that her intravenous needle had not been removed before she left the hospital. Her study shows how routine micro-level interactions, such as those between patients and nurses, may be influenced by larger, historically based relationships such as those between Indigenous people and the dominant Euro-Canadian society and state.

interpret along with other data. The image and what it represents are presented as unproblematic, as a window on reality. This has been the dominant framework within which visual resources have been produced and analyzed. By contrast, Pink also drew attention to a position that she described as *reflexive*. This entails an awareness of and sensitivity to the ways in which researchers themselves determine what the visuals reveal. This sensitivity requires a grasp of the ways in which researchers' personal characteristics—age, gender, social background, academic proclivities, and so on—may influence what images they choose to record, and how those images are presented.

This approach to the visual is frequently collaborative in the sense that research participants may be involved in decisions about what visuals should be recorded and how they should be interpreted. Further, it acknowledges that different people may interpret the images in different ways. In Pink's research on Spanish bullfighters, enthusiasts interpreted the images she took of bullfights in terms of bullfighter performance. Other viewers might see the same images in a different interpretive framework—for example, one centred on animal rights and cruelty.

Plate 10.1 presents an image called *The Bullfighter's Braid*, from Pink's research. Showing a female bullfighter, it appealed to many connoisseurs of the sport who saw in it various artistic and other meanings. For Pink, it held additional significance in terms of her interests in gender and the broader discipline of social anthropology (for more information on this photograph see Pink, 2001, p. 101, and http://www.brooklynsoc.org/revealingpictures/pink.html [accessed 4 September 2021]).

Pink, Visual Ethnography, 2001

Plate 10.1: The Bullfighter's Braid

Photovoice is an approach to visual ethnography that takes collaboration with research participants even further. Using this technique, the participants take photographs of their daily experiences and interpret them in terms of their own perspectives and identities, which transfers a measure of power and control away from the researcher to them. Since photovoice may be used with people from marginalized communities, those who employ it often do so with the intention of creating social change, which can be undertaken through an exhibition of the photographs. When used in this way, photovoice is a form of **participatory action research** (discussed in Chapters 1 and 9). With the power to cross cultural boundaries and language barriers, photographs can also help make findings accessible to a wide range of academic and non-academic audiences (see Box 10.7).

Holtby, Klein, Cook, & Travers (2015) used photovoice in their research on queer and trans youth in the Kitchener–Waterloo area. The researchers used the technique to explore how these young people confronted the "hostile gaze" that is often directed at people in the LGBTQ community. The 15 people in the study were given training in photography and then asked to take five to ten pictures that reflected their experiences as queer or trans youth. The participants were then invited to discuss their photos by responding to questions such as, "What is seen here?" and "How could this image be used to educate people?" One of the themes to come out of the discussion was invisibility, whereby participants were not recognized as having the gender or sexual identity that they held. This experience was particularly painful when it occurred within the LGBTQ community itself. To illustrate invisibility, one participant took a photograph of empty clothing arranged to make it appear as if a person's body were missing.

Visual research methods require researchers to "read" images while being sensitive to the context in which they were generated; the potential for multiple meanings among researchers, study participants, and others; and the potential for the researcher to influence the image and its presentation. In addition, researchers usually include non-visual research methods, such as interviews, in their investigations. This raises the question of the relative significance of words versus images in the analysis of data and the presentation of findings. Since words are the traditional medium, it's easy to slip into seeing the visual as less important, but this is not always justified. Finally, visual research methods raise certain ethical issues, such as invasion of privacy and anonymity.

Institutional ethnography

Canadian sociologist Dorothy Smith has developed an approach called **institutional ethnography** (Smith, 2005) that explores how institutional discourses (typically texts found in the workplace) relate to people's everyday experiences with institutions, and how examining institutional relationships may reveal larger systems of social control and power in a society (Devault, 2006).

Box 10.7 | Photovoice as a knowledge dissemination and social justice strategy

Ratković and Sethi (2018) make a case for using photovoice as part of an arts-based approach to knowledge dissemination. As researchers committed to social justice, they seek to bring practitioners, policy-makers, and community members into conversations about important issues such as racialization and citizenship. Sethi describes a study she conducted on Canadian immigrant and refugee women, where participants were given a camera and taught by a photographer how to take professional pictures that captured their perspectives and experiences. She then worked with participants to select photos that they would be comfortable sharing with the public. A graphic artist helped turn the images into art pieces, which were displayed at art exhibits across southwestern Ontario. For the opening exhibit at Wilfrid Laurier University's Yellow Brick Wall Gallery, "The research launch was attended by over 150 people, including the local member of parliament, the mayor's office, the local member of provincial parliament, employers, health care practitioners, academics, social workers, immigrants, refugees, religious leaders, and community members. The local media also wrote about the exhibit" (Ratković & Sethi, 2018, pp. 344–345). Using photographs as part of her approach to knowledge dissemination, Sethi was able to achieve what many researchers find difficult to accomplish with traditional text-based research outputs such as books and journal articles. Ratković and Sethi (2018, p. 345) write, "Reaching practitioners, policy-makers, and community members can lead to new understandings of citizenship and new alliances between visible minority immigrant women and the Canadian state."

Institutional relationships are analyzed in detail, with the aim of finding out how they affect the personal experiences of the individuals involved. The approach can be explicitly change oriented in that previously unrecognized opportunities to transform institutions may come to light as the research runs its course, and the researcher may even collaborate with the people studied in an effort to create institutional relationships that serve them better.

For example, Restoule and colleagues (2013) combined Anishinaabe methodology (which honours Indigenous Elders' wisdom and places a strong emphasis on representing and serving the people involved) with institutional ethnography to examine how well Indigenous students in Ontario made the transition from high school to post-secondary institutions. They first established that although the vast majority of young Indigenous people hoped for a post-secondary education, and that their parents were in favour of it as well, a much smaller proportion of Indigenous youth than non-Indigenous youth actually graduated from those institutions. The researchers found that some informants declined to identify as Indigenous in their applications, citing a lack of trust in government institutions, which itself indicated a problematic relationship between prospective Indigenous students and post-secondary bureaucracies. Participants also stated that the promotional information provided by universities did not address concerns felt by Indigenous applicants, although a majority of informants who made it to college or university said they felt welcome once they got there. In keeping with the activist orientation of institutional ethnography, a member of the research team took some of the recommendations made by Indigenous youth to a university assistant registrar for discussion. Box 10.8 provides another illustration of this type of ethnography.

Box 10.8 | Institutional ethnography

Campbell (2000) did institutional ethnographic research to investigate how people with disabilities in Victoria, British Columbia, interacted with local health-care providers. She was particularly interested in how that interaction was influenced by government regulations and policies. The health-care system in the province was in a state of transition at the time and had been subject to funding reductions associated with government deficits and debt. As is typical in this kind of research, Campbell's goal was not only to describe how the situation was perceived by the people experiencing it, but also to give them—in this case both people with disabilities and health-care providers—the means to transform the situation themselves. Both groups were trained as researchers and paid for their involvement.

The study focused on Home Support services and especially how access to those services affected the lives of disabled people. One person mentioned that because of government criteria, she was unable to get the support she needed: "I'm dog tired. And I just get the basics done. My partner is away. I've been on my own since August and it's been hard because my home care was cut off two years ago because I'm not sick enough—which is such a joke" (Campbell, 2000, p. 138). The lack of assistance put the woman's relationship with her partner in jeopardy because he had to devote what little time they could spend together to doing heavy housework for her.

In another case, a woman confined to a wheelchair suffered because she qualified for only 12 physiotherapy and massage sessions a year—the same number as a person without a disability. The institutional justification given was that all citizens had to be treated equally. Campbell makes the point that "generic" rules about health care, which essentially establish "relations of ruling" in the health-care system, are created by and for the able-bodied and thus do not serve the needs of people with disabilities (Campbell, 2000, pp. 141, 143). The texts used to implement government health policies (such as assessment forms), Campbell argues, serve to bolster the government's legitimacy in the face of challenges from dissenting parties such as the disabled, who would benefit from a more inclusive system of health-care delivery. Bringing such matters to light can be a first step in improving service provision for people with disabilities or anyone else who is ill served by an institution.

Sampling

Informants in ethnographic research are usually selected through a version of **purposive sampling** that involves searching for people who are likely to be a rich source of information on the group or setting under study. Sometimes it is obvious who these people are, as in the case of political or religious movements in which the key players and organizational insiders are well known. In other situations, it may take some digging to discover who would be a knowledgeable informant. However, once such people are identified it may be difficult or even impossible to get them to open up about the topic of the study. Ethnographers often face opposition, or at least indifference, to their research and for that reason are usually willing to listen to anyone who is prepared to divulge information or views. One way to get access to such people is through **snowball sampling** (see Chapter 7) in which a viable contact is used to identify others who may be willing to provide information on the topic of the study, who are then used to establish further contacts, and so on. Snowball sampling was a component of Taylor's (1993) strategy. Her female drug users were

> eventually obtained by a mix of "snowballing techniques" . . . and my almost continuous presence in the area. . . . Rather than ask to be

> introduced or given names of others I could contact, when I met a woman I would spend as much time with her as she would allow, participating in her daily round, and through this come to meet others in her social circle. My continued presence in the area also led other women drug users to approach me when I was alone. . . . In addition, the drug worker in the area would mention my presence and interest to women with whom he came in contact and facilitate introductions where possible. (Taylor, 1993, p. 16)

Ethnographers who take on a role closer to that of observer-as-participant rely somewhat more on formal requests for the names of other people who may have relevant information and who can be contacted.

Probability sampling is almost never used in ethnographic research and is rarely employed even in qualitative research based on interviews. In many cases, a probability sample is not feasible because it is difficult, if not impossible, to map "the population" from which a random sample may be taken. Instead, ethnographers have to ensure that they gain access to as wide a range of individuals as possible, so that many different perspectives and ranges of activity can be analyzed.

Theoretical sampling

Another type of purposive sampling is *theoretical sampling*, advocated by Strauss and Corbin (1998). In their view, because of its reliance on statistical rather than theoretical criteria, probability sampling is not appropriate to qualitative research. Theoretical sampling is an alternative strategy, used "in order to discover categories and their properties and to suggest the interrelationships into a theory. Statistical sampling is done to obtain accurate evidence on distributions of people among categories to be used in descriptions and verifications" (Glaser & Strauss, 1967, p. 62).

In theoretical sampling, the researcher simultaneously collects and analyzes the data, decides what data to collect next and where to find them, and develops a theory in the process. Data collection is influenced by the emerging theory and—unlike quantitative data collection—is an ongoing process, subject to change as the study progresses (Breckenridge & Jones, 2009). For Charmaz (2000, p. 519), theoretical sampling is a "defining property of grounded theory" and is concerned with refining ideas rather than boosting sample size.

Moreover, theoretical sampling can involve not only people but also settings and events. This can be seen in Strauss and Corbin's (1998, p. 201) definition: "Data gathering driven by concepts derived from the evolving theory and based on the concept of 'making comparisons,' whose purpose is to go to places, people, or events that will maximize opportunities to discover variations among concepts and to identify categories in terms of their properties and dimensions."

Figure 10.3 outlines the main steps in theoretical sampling. Data collection (observing, interviewing, and collecting documents) continues until the point of **theoretical saturation** is reached: "This means, until (a) no new or relevant data seem to be emerging regarding a category, (b) the category is well developed in terms of its properties and dimensions demonstrating variation, and (c) the relationships among categories are well established and validated" (Strauss & Corbin, 1998, p. 212). In the language of grounded theory, a category operates at a somewhat higher level of abstraction than a **concept** in that

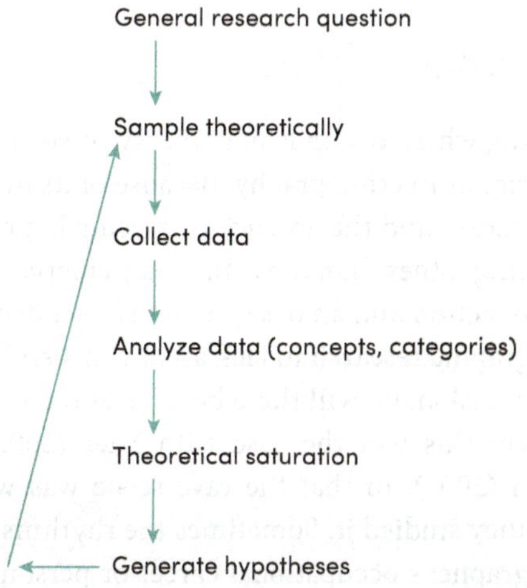

FIGURE 10.3 The process of theoretical sampling

it may group together several concepts that have common features denoted by the category.

Saturation means that previous interviews/observations have both formed the basis for the creation of a category and confirmed its importance. Thus, there is no longer any need to collect data in relation to that category. Instead, the researcher should move on and generate hypotheses out of the categories that are forming, and then collect data related to those hypotheses.

Not just people

As we pointed out in the last section, ethnographic sampling is not just about people. Time and context may also be sampled. Attending to time means that the ethnographer must make sure that people or events are observed at different times of the day and different days of the week, to avoid drawing inferences valid only for particular times (mornings, for example, or weekdays rather than weekends).

Because behaviour is influenced by contextual factors, it is also important to observe in a variety of locations. For instance, soccer hooliganism is not a full-time occupation. To understand the hooligans' culture and world view, writers like Armstrong (1993) and Giulianotti (1995) had to ensure that they interacted with their participants in a variety of contexts other than soccer stadiums, such as the pubs where they engaged in general socializing. Rosenhan (1973) had to do the same in his study of psychiatric hospitals (see Chapter 6).

The end

Knowing when to stop is not an easy or straightforward matter in ethnography. Because of its unstructured nature and the absence of specific hypotheses for testing (other than those that may emerge during data collection and analysis), there is a tendency for ethnographic research to lack an obvious end point. Only occasionally will there be a natural end to the research; this was the case with Hier (2002) and Wilson (2002), in that the rave scene was waning when they studied it. Sometimes the rhythms of the ethnographer's occupational career or personal and family life—the end of a sabbatical leave, the need to submit a doctoral thesis by a certain date, exhaustion of funding—necessitate withdrawal from the field: Taylor (1993) wrote that one factor contributing to her departure from the field was the lengthy illness of her youngest son.

Also relevant is the fact that ethnographic research can be highly stressful for many reasons: the nature of the topic, which may place the fieldworker in tense situations (as in research on crime); the marginal position of the researcher in the social setting; the constant need to maintain a front; the often prolonged absence from one's normal life. Ethnographers may simply feel that they have had enough.

An important reason for bringing fieldwork to a close is that reasonable answers to the research questions have been formulated. The ethnographer may even feel a strong sense of déjà vu toward the end of data collection if new data simply reiterate what has already been discovered. In the language of grounded theory, all the researcher's categories may become thoroughly *saturated*, although Glaser and Strauss's (1967) approach suggests that one should be certain that there are no new questions to be asked and no new comparisons to be made.

In sum, the reasons for bringing ethnographic research to a close can range from personal factors to matters of research design. Whatever the reason, disengagement has to be *managed*. For one thing, this means that promises must be kept (was a report promised as a condition of entry?). It also means that ethnographers must provide good explanations for their departure. Participants may know that the researcher is not a permanent presence in their social setting, but over a long period of time they can forget, especially if there has been genuine participation in activities within that setting; therefore, farewells may have to be arranged. It's also essential to remember the ethnographer's *ethical* commitments, such as the need to ensure that persons and settings are kept anonymous—unless, of course, there has been an agreement that the social setting can be disclosed (as often occurs in studies of religious sects and cults). Because of how involved ethnographic research can be, it's also important to consider the continuing social and emotional impact fieldwork can have on researchers and participants (see Box 10.9).

Box 10.9 | Leaving the field: There and back again

Ethnographers often wonder whether it's truly possible to leave the field. The question is not about one's physical departure, but about the shared stories, emotions, and experiences that remain well after a study has ended. The intimate familiarity ethnographers cultivate often has a residual effect on both participants and researchers. In an anthology exploring qualitative research's craft-like features (see Kleinknecht, van den Scott, & Sanders, 2018), some of the chapter authors reflect on the actualities of completing their research and leaving the field. For instance, Edwards (2018) found that having conducted a qualitative study on the relationship between feminism and heterosexuality, ongoing emotional attachments to her participants were par for the course. Given the type of in-depth, personal research she was doing, she found it natural to become invested in her participants' lives. She writes,

> To say that I have left the field would be naive as these women have played, and continue to play, an important role in my life as an academic, a feminist researcher, and a feminist-identified woman who engages in relationships with men. They are also inherently the reason I have a PhD—a simple fact of reality. So I ask you, how could I not be emotionally attached to the field? How could I truly ever leave? [. . .] If we, as researchers, are interested in unpacking the complexities and realities of various populations in order to produce the most nuanced understandings of their lived experiences, is it not our duty to ensure that we do *not* become disengaged, detached, and disembodied? (Edwards, 2018, p. 330, emphasis in original)

In the same volume, Jeffrey van den Scott, the husband of Lisa-Jo van den Scott (see Box 10.3), also questions, "Can you leave the field?" He had lived in Arviat, Nunavut, for five years before departing and then returning to spend another five years researching the role of music in Inuit culture. He found that "leaving" was not simply a matter of physical departure. Left lingering were questions about having collected enough data, doing right by his participants, and reintegrating into his home culture. He concludes, "I continue asking to what degree the field has left me" (J. van den Scott, 2018, p. 309). Similarly, looking back on over 40 years of researching Hasidic Jewish culture, Shaffir (2018) writes,

> I would make the case that even while diminishing one's ties with informants, or severing one's connections completely, the researcher never leaves the field entirely. To be sure, there are degrees of leaving. But some parts of one's experiences from the field remain—be these recollections or reminiscences—that, in some form or manner, impact upon the researcher. (Shaffir, 2018, p. 324)

Benbow and Hall (2018), who studied the lives of marginalized groups such as street-level sex workers and mothers experiencing homelessness, reached the point of emotional exhaustion. They purposely embody the stories of their participants, carrying their findings and experiences forward as part of their ongoing activism. For those undertaking similarly difficult research, they advise creating a self-care plan. Taking time for oneself, spending time with friends and family, and reaching out to supportive colleagues can help mitigate some of the enduring stressors that accompany emotionally demanding research.

Given how involved ethnographic research is, it's hard to envision this form of data collection not having lasting effects. Writing up findings, revisiting field sites, and reflecting on the stories that were shared take field researchers back to their participants' lives. So, not only is it important to consider how to secure and maintain access to a field site, it's equally important to prepare for the end of a project and its ongoing social and emotional effects.

Key Points

- The ethnographer is typically a participant observer who also uses interviews and documents.
- The ethnographer may adopt an overt or covert role, but the latter comes with serious ethical difficulties.
- The method of access to a social setting depends in part on whether it is open (public) or closed (private or restricted).
- Key informants frequently play an important role in ethnography, but care is needed to ensure that their impact on the research is not excessive.
- Field notes are important memory aids for the ethnographer.
- Visual materials such as photographs and videos have attracted considerable interest among ethnographers in recent years, not just as adjuncts to data collection but as objects of interest in their own right.
- Ethnographers must decide when to end their data collection and how to manage the ongoing social and emotional effects of their research after they leave the field.

Questions for Review (R) and Creative Application (A)

Access

R1 "Covert ethnography can make it easier to gain access to certain settings and therefore has much to recommend it." Explain how this may be true, then outline the shortcomings of covert research.

A1 Assume that you have decided to do an ethnographic study of a tech start-up company that has just arrived in your community. Explain how you could gain access to the company, how you would approach potential informants, and how you would interact with members of the company once ongoing access was achieved.

R2 What is the role of key informants in ethnographic research? Is there anything to be concerned about when using them?

A2 Assume that you are doing the ethnographic study of the start-up mentioned above and have been present in the company for several weeks, but the CEO refuses to speak to you. What could you do to ensure that your study will produce enough information to provide a meaningful analysis of the activities and culture of the start-up?

Roles for ethnographers

R3 How does it happen that some ethnographers overidentify with the people they are observing? What are some consequences of overidentification ?

A3 With regard to the ethnography of the tech start-up mentioned earlier, outline the benefits and drawbacks to approaching this research as a complete participant, a participant-as-observer, an observer-as-participant, and a complete observer.

Field notes

R4 Why are field notes important for ethnographers? What are the main types of field notes and why is it useful to distinguish between them?

A4 Assume you are doing the ethnography of the start-up mentioned earlier, and have observed that no one in the company is over the age of 25. Write an analytic memo that explains the significance of that fact.

The rise of visual ethnography

R5 How can visual materials be used in ethnography?

A5 The start-up described earlier has just found out that it has successfully negotiated a business deal with a major corporation. You take a photograph of several members of the start-up at the meeting where the deal was announced to all employees. Would the photograph provide an unproblematic image of reality? Discuss.

Sampling

R6 What is theoretical sampling? How can it be used in ethnographic research?

A6 You've decided to do an ethnographic study of a women's shelter that will be shut down in six months because of a lack of government funding. How could you use snowball sampling to gain access to informants?

The end

R7 How do ethnographers decide when it's time to conclude their data collection?

A7 Your study on the women's shelter described above (A6) is now complete. In what ways might you have become emotionally attached to your participants? What obligations do you have to them once the research is complete? What impact might your study have on future researchers' attempts to gain access to similar field sites?

Interactive Classroom Activities

1. Hold a class discussion to decide on a setting or group for which ethnographic research would be appropriate, for example, biker gang, religious organization, sports team, dating service, and so on. Divide the class into three groups:
   - Group 1 prepares a mock funding proposal to conduct a *covert* study of the site.
   - Group 2 prepares a mock funding proposal to conduct a *participant-as-observer* study of the site.
   - Group 3 prepares a mock funding proposal to conduct an *observer-as-participant* study of the site.

   Each group must do the following:

   a. Explain how its methodology would be superior to that employed by the other two groups—for example, Group 1 would explain how a covert study is superior to a participant-as-observer study and an observer-as-participant study.
   b. Discuss the ethical implications of the proposed research.
   c. Explain how access to the site could be gained.
   d. Explain what the researchers' demeanour and dress would be as they interact with people at the site.
   e. Explain how they would record the data they get, for example, with field notes, photographs, video recording, and so on.
   f. Explain how the study will make a valuable contribution to knowledge.
   g. Upon completion of these tasks, each group presents the mock proposal to the rest of the class, who are to take the role of a funding committee that will decide whether the project will be funded.
2. As homework, each person in the class is required to "hang out" at a public, safe location on campus (e.g., residence dining hall, campus café, weight room, library space, etc.) for 30 minutes as a *complete observer*. On an appointed date, each student gives a five-minute mini-presentation on his or her experience. The presentation should:

   a. highlight anything of significance that was observed; and
   b. provide suggestions as to how a more in-depth ethnographic study of the site could be conducted.

Relevant Websites

For examples of ethnographic studies, take a look at the journal ***Ethnography*** and the ***Journal of Contemporary Ethnography*** (you may have to log on to your institution's library server to access them).

http://eth.sagepub.com

http://jce.sagepub.com

Since 1984, the annual Canadian ***Qualitative Analysis Conference*** has brought ethnographers and other qualitative researchers together from around the world to discuss their research findings and methodological issues in qualitative research.

www.qualitatives.ca

The ***Ethnography Lab*** at the University of Toronto is a collaboration between anthropology faculty and students. It was established to "promote ethnographic research methods and practice inside and outside the university." The lab runs a speakers series and serves as a resource centre for ethnographers.

https://ethnographylab.ca

PhotoVoice is a charity based in the United Kingdom that assists with ethical participatory photography projects to help promote positive social change.

https://photovoice.org/

(Websites accessed 9 September 2021.)

OXFORD learning link

More resources are available on Oxford Learning Link. Visit https://learninglink.oup.com/ for:

- Student self-quiz
- Flash cards
- Audio clips
- Videos
- Activities

11 Interviewing in Qualitative Research

Chapter Overview

This chapter examines the use of interviews in qualitative research. Two types are discussed: **unstructured** and **semi-structured**. This chapter is concerned mainly with interviews with individuals, but the **focus group** method is also examined. The highlights of this chapter include:

- the differences between **structured** and qualitative interviewing;
- the main characteristics of and differences between unstructured and semi-structured interviewing;
- how to devise and use an **interview guide** for semi-structured interviewing;
- the kinds of questions that can be placed in an interview guide;
- the importance of recording and transcribing qualitative interviews;
- the potential uses and pitfalls of online interviewing;
- how focus groups should be conducted, including matters such as the number of participants, how to select them, and how direct the questioning should be;
- issues concerning the interactions between participants in focus group discussions;
- some practical difficulties with focus group sessions, such as loss of control over the proceedings and the potential for unwanted group effects; and
- the advantages and disadvantages of qualitative interviewing relative to **ethnography**.

▲ kate_sept2004/iStockphoto

Key Learning Outcomes

Here is a list of goals you should try to achieve as you read and think about the material in this chapter. After completing this chapter, you should be able to:

1. Detail the differences between structured and qualitative interviews.
2. Discuss the features of unstructured and semi-structured interviews, including how to prepare an interview guide, the different kinds of questions qualitative researchers use, and considerations for recording and transcribing interviews.
3. Explain how qualitative researchers use focus groups as a form of data collection, including how focus groups are conducted, determining an appropriate focus group size, selecting participants, asking questions and moderating group discussion, the role of group interaction, and the limitations of focus groups.
4. Describe qualitative researchers' approach to online interviewing and focus groups, as well as the advantages and disadvantages of using these two methods online versus face-to-face.
5. Compare the advantages and limitations of using qualitative interviews to those of ethnography.

Practice makes perfect, so why not hone your qualitative interviewing skills in casual, everyday conversations? It's often said that the art of conversation is dying in modern times, but if you approach every discussion you have as a qualitative interview in the making, that may change. Everyday conversation rarely has a narrowly restricted purpose, and neither does qualitative research. A good way to start a discussion is to ask other people where they grew up, or what their most memorable experiences were; then get them to expand on their answers, taking care to draw out how they felt about the experiences, what the experiences meant to them, how they affected their lives, and so on. If you're with a group of people at a party or on a long trip, you can even hold an impromptu focus group session, secretly appointing yourself the moderator. Besides being good practice, chance conversations and seemingly inconsequential interactions can spark some very good research ideas. Just remember that institutional ethics approval will be required if your casual conversations morph into actual qualitative research.

Introduction

The interview is probably the most widely used method in qualitative research. Since interviews were not discussed in detail in previous chapters, we will give them our full attention here.

Ethnography usually involves a substantial amount of qualitative interviewing, and this undoubtedly contributes to its wide use. But it is possible to conduct qualitative interviews without doing a full-blown ethnographic study. In fact, the flexibility of the qualitative interview and its relatively low cost compared to ethnography make it an attractive option for many researchers. Although interviewing, transcribing interviews, and analyzing transcripts are all very time-consuming, they don't intrude on researchers' personal lives to the degree that spending extended periods of time with research informants does.

There are two main types of qualitative interview: unstructured and semi-structured. A variety of specialized interview forms fall under those two headings and will be explored below, including focus groups, **oral history interviews**, and **life history interviews**.

Differences between structured and qualitative research interviews

Qualitative interviewing is quite different from interviewing in **quantitative research**:

- In quantitative research, the approach is highly structured to maximize **reliability** and **validity** in measuring key **concepts**. The researcher usually has a clearly specified set of research questions that the interview is designed to answer. Qualitative interviewing, on the other hand, is much less structured and tends to be more open-ended. It also allows greater freedom to modify and add research ideas once the investigation has begun.
- There is greater interest in the interviewee's perspectives and concerns in qualitative interviewing; in quantitative research, the interview is driven mainly by the research agenda of the person conducting the study.
- In qualitative interviewing, going off on a tangent is often encouraged. The interviewer may vary both the order and the wording of questions, and may even ask unplanned questions to follow up on interviewees' replies; the additional replies may provide new insight into what the interviewee sees as relevant and important. In quantitative research, departing from the **interview schedule** is usually discouraged because it diverges from the specific research plan and may affect reliability and validity.
- Qualitative interviewing tends to be flexible, responding to the direction in which interviewees take the interview and perhaps adjusting the emphases in the research as a result of the issues that emerge during the interview. For instance, in describing her approach to conducting qualitative interviews with social movement actors in Ontario, Maiolino (2019) writes, "A set of interview questions was used to guide the interview, but I also tried to be flexible and create space for interviewees to direct the discussion as it developed" (p. 170). By contrast, structured interviews are typically inflexible, because of the need to standardize the interactions with all interviewees.
- In qualitative interviewing, the researcher wants rich, detailed answers; in structured interviewing the interview is normally designed to generate specific answers that can be coded and processed quickly.
- In qualitative interviewing, it is not uncommon for the interviewee to be interviewed more than once. For example, in his research on "clubbers" (people who frequent night clubs), Malbon (1999) conducted an initial interview to put the participant's mind at ease about the research, help plan his approach to observation, and begin collecting preliminary data. In a follow-up interview, he discussed club visits, the experience of clubbing, and occasionally, wider aspects of participants' lives. In structured interviewing, unless the research is longitudinal in character, the person is usually interviewed only once.

Unstructured and semi-structured interviewing

As we have noted, there are two main types of qualitative interview:

- In an *unstructured interview* the researcher uses at most a memory aid: a small set of self-prompts to investigate certain topics. The interviewer may ask just a single question; then the interviewee is allowed to respond freely, with the interviewer pursuing points that seem worthy of follow-up. Unstructured interviewing tends to be similar in character to a conversation (see Box 11.1 for an example).
- In a *semi-structured interview* the researcher has a list of questions or fairly specific topics to be covered (an *interview guide*), but the interviewee still has a great deal of leeway in deciding how to reply (see Box 11.2 for an illustration). Questions may not follow the exact order in

Box 11.1 | Unstructured interviewing

Torelli (2019) adopted a largely unstructured interview approach when conducting field research on the "dirty work" of Canadian homeless shelter caseworkers. His introspective reflections offer insights into how qualitative interviewers must listen attentively, think on their feet, and carefully follow lines of inquiry presented to them by participants. Torelli (2019) described his strategy for interviewing caseworkers as follows:

> I perceived the interview as a social event, a process whereby, through our interactions, me as a researcher and the researched were collaborating jointly in knowledge production. . . . This interchange produced unique conversational avenues which could only be achieved naturalistically rather than with strict, albeit aloof, adherence to a structured interview guide. I therefore saw the interview process contingently: unpredictable, spontaneous conversational instances emerging out of our interaction that would have not occurred had I stuck necessarily to my interview guide and structured the interview in a determinative way. (Torelli, 2019, p. 76)

Box 11.2 | Semi-structured interviewing

Wright, Alaggia, & Krygsman (2014) used qualitative interviewing to assess the success of an after-school arts program that was offered to Canadian youth living in low-income communities. The study indicated that the program, which involved having the youth participate in theatre productions, had a number of long-term benefits for the participants that went beyond developing their theatre skills. Here are some sample interview questions, along with sample probe questions that were used to get the respondents to elaborate on their initial replies:

Interview questions	Probe questions
Did you enjoy the art program?	What activities did you like? Did you like the instructors?
Do you have many friends/get along with others your age?	Do you sometimes get into arguments with others your age? What do you do when you get into arguments?
Have you been getting along with your parents?	Do you sometimes get into arguments? About what?

the guide, and some questions not included on the list may be asked in response to what the interviewee says. Sometimes lines of thought identified by earlier interviewees are taken up and presented to later ones. Nonetheless, all the questions on the list are usually asked and similar wording is used from interviewee to interviewee. Box 11.3 illustrates how these features of qualitative interviewing are used in life history research.

In semi- and unstructured interviews, the process is designed to bring out how the *interviewees themselves* interpret and make sense of issues and events. Bell

Box 11.3 | Life history interviews

One special form of interview associated with qualitative research is the life history interview. It is often combined with **personal documents** such as diaries, photographs, and letters. Participants are invited to look back in detail across their entire life course and to report their experiences and how they understood their world. Valuable insights may be gained from a life history regardless of whether other people have had the same experiences as the person described in the work. It also has the advantage of illustrating *process*: how events unfold and interrelate in people's lives over long periods of time.

An example of the life history interview approach is provided by Lewis (1961) in his research on the Sánchez family and their experiences in a Mexican slum:

> I asked hundreds of questions of [the five members of the Sánchez family]. . . . While I used a directive approach to the interviews, I encouraged free association, and I was a good listener. I attempted to cover systematically a wide range of subjects: their earliest memories, their dreams, their hopes, fears, joys, and sufferings; their jobs; their relationship with friends, relatives, employers; their sex life; their concepts of justice, religion, and politics; their knowledge of geography and history; in short, their total view of the world. (Lewis, 1961, p. xxi)

Miller (2000) points out that interest in the life history method is reflective of the popularity of "narrative interviews" (discussed in Chapter 13) in which the person studied, instead of responding to an interviewer's questions, "tells a story." In the past this approach was associated with the study of a single life, or perhaps two, but today it is increasingly applied to several lives in a single project. M. Atkinson (2002; 2004), for example, conducted narrative interviews with women tattoo enthusiasts.

P. Atkinson (2004) observed that the duration of life story interviews varies considerably from study to study, but that it usually takes two or three sessions lasting 60 to 90 minutes each. He provided a catalogue of questions that can be asked, and divided them into the following groups (1990, pp. 43–53):

- birth and family of origin (e.g., "How would you describe your parents?")
- cultural traditions (e.g., "Was your family different from others in town?")
- social factors (e.g., "What were some of your struggles as a child?")
- education (e.g., "What are your best memories of school?")
- love and work (e.g., "How did you end up in the work you do or did?")
- inner and spiritual life (e.g., "What are the stresses of being an adult?")
- major life themes (e.g., "What were the crucial decisions in your life?")
- vision of the future (e.g., "Is your life fulfilled yet?")
- closure questions (e.g., "Have you given a fair picture of yourself?")

A variant of the life history interview is the *oral history* interview, a technique often used by historians. It is usually somewhat more specific in tone than the interviews described above in that the participants may be asked to reflect on certain historical events or eras they have lived through. The emphasis is often on how the individual's life was affected by those things. The information gathered is sometimes combined with other sources of data, such as documents.

The chief problem with the oral history interview (a problem it shares with life history interviews in general) is the possibility of bias caused by memory lapses and distortions. Sugiman (2004)

(Continued)

pointed out in her work on Japanese-Canadian women interned during the Second World War that remembering is a social and even political act, involving recalling, forgetting, transforming, and shaping of recollections. On the other hand, oral history testimonies can give a voice to groups that are typically marginalized in historical research (this is true of life history interviews in general), either because of their lack of power or because they are regarded as unimportant.

(2007), for example, wanted to understand what western Canadian separatists thought of Canadian federalism and the federal party system. Tastsoglou and Miedema (2003) sought to understand the meaning of community from the perspective of immigrant women, and Smith (2008) examined the meanings of pain for professional wrestlers. Projects like these, unlike quantitative studies, are usually not designed to test hypotheses or theories. In short, qualitative research is not just quantitative research without the numbers.

There is a growing tendency to refer to semi-structured and unstructured interviews collectively as *in-depth interviews* or *qualitative interviews*, although the semi- and unstructured types can produce very different results. The choice of one type rather than the other is affected by a variety of factors:

- Researchers who feel that using even the most rudimentary interview guide hinders genuine access to the world views of members of a social setting are likely to favour an unstructured approach. But even here the interview is rarely completely unstructured: the researcher usually has at least a general topic that is to be discussed.
- If the researcher is beginning the investigation with a fairly clear rather than a general focus, it is likely that the interviews will be semi-structured, so that they can address more specific issues.
- If more than one person is to carry out the fieldwork, semi-structured interviewing may be preferred, to ensure that interviewing styles are comparable.
- Multiple-case study research generally needs some structure to ensure cross-case comparability.

Preparing an interview guide

An interview guide is much shorter and less detailed than a structured interview schedule. In fact, it is often simply a brief list of memory prompts for areas to be covered in unstructured interviewing and a somewhat more elaborate list of issues to be addressed or questions to be asked in semi-structured interviewing. What is crucial is that the actual questioning is flexible, allowing interviewers to pursue leads offered by research participants as they begin to open up and reveal their view of the social world. Ricciardelli's (2019) approach to interviewing Canadian correctional officers about the realities of prison work is illustrative of the flexibility qualitative researchers attempt to build into their interviews and interview guides:

> A semi-structured interview guide—a list of open-ended questions I constructed—was available during interviews, but was often only used as a sort of checklist to ensure that conversational paths included select topics. . . . The conversation tended to be determined by the interviewee because my objective was to hear what was on each participant's mind, what stood out in his or her experiences, and how he or she interpreted the correctional officer role. Although I rarely directed conversation, I did at points ask interviewees for clarification or for more detail. (Ricciardelli, 2019, pp. 159–160)

In preparing for qualitative interviews, Lofland and Lofland (1995, p. 78) suggested that researchers ask themselves "Just what about this thing is puzzling me?" This question can be applied to each of the research questions generated; it can also serve as a mechanism for generating research questions. Lofland and

Lofland suggested that puzzlement may be stimulated in various ways: by recording random thoughts in different contexts (writing them down as quickly as possible); through discussions with colleagues, friends, and relatives; and, of course, by reading the existing literature on the topic. The formulation of the research question(s) should not be so specific as to close off the alternative avenues of inquiry that may arise during fieldwork. Premature closure of the research focus would be inconsistent with qualitative research's prime purpose: to explore the world view of the people being studied, rather than to test the researcher's own ideas about that world.

The interview guide should:

- establish a certain amount of order, so that questions flow reasonably well, but still allow for changes in the order of the questions and the impromptu asking of different questions;
- include questions or topics that address the research questions (without being too specific);
- use language that is comprehensible and familiar to those being studied;
- not ask leading questions—that is, questions that imply a "correct" or socially acceptable answer (for example, "Have you ever done something really stupid, like taking crack?"); and
- include prompts to remind the researcher to record basic information about the participant (name, age, gender, etc.) as well as more specific information that is relevant to the research questions (position in company, number of years employed, number of years involved in a group, etc.); such information is useful for putting people's comments into context.

There are also some practical details to attend to before the interview begins:

- Become familiar with the research setting, which in many cases will be the everyday surroundings of the interviewees. This will help to put their comments in context.
- Get a reliable recording device. Qualitative researchers (with the possible exception of ethnographers and people doing participant observation research) nearly always record and then transcribe their interviews. This is important for the detailed analysis required in qualitative research, and to ensure that the interviewees' answers are captured in their own terms. Simply taking notes makes it too easy to lose specific words and phrases.
- Make sure as far as possible that the interview takes place in a setting that is quiet (so that the quality of the recording will be as good as possible) and private (so that the interviewee won't worry about being overheard).
- Prepare for the interview by cultivating the traits of a quality interviewer suggested by Kvale (1996) (see Box 11.4).

After the interview, make notes about:

- how the interview went (obstacles, ethical issues, surprises, the interviewee's demeanour, what worked well and what can be improved upon);
- how you felt during the interview and how this may have impacted the process (relaxed, nervous, in control, sad, cheerful);
- where the interview took place and what the setting was like (noisy/quiet, many/few other people in the vicinity); and
- tentative insights gleaned about your research question and potential new lines of inquiry.

The steps required to formulate questions for an interview guide in qualitative research are presented in Figure 11.1.

Kinds of questions

The kinds of questions asked in qualitative interviews are highly variable; Kvale (1996) suggested nine. Most interviews contain virtually all of them, although those that rely on lists of topics are likely to follow a somewhat looser format. Kvale's nine types are as follows:

- *Introducing questions.* "Please tell me about when your interest in X first began"; "Have you ever . . . ?"; "Why did you go to . . .?"

Box 11.4 | Kvale's ten traits of an effective interviewer (plus three others)

Kvale (1996) proposed that a successful interviewer has ten characteristics:

- ***Knowledgeable:*** is thoroughly familiar with the topic of the interview
- ***Structuring:*** tells the interviewee the purpose of the interview; asks if the interviewee has questions
- ***Clear:*** asks simple, easy, and short questions; no jargon
- ***Gentle:*** lets people finish; gives them time to think; tolerates pauses
- ***Sensitive:*** listens attentively both to what is said and to how it is said; is empathetic
- ***Open:*** responds to what the interviewee considers important; is flexible
- ***Steering:*** knows what needs to be found out
- ***Critical:*** is prepared to challenge what is said when, for example, there is an inconsistency in the interviewee's replies
- ***Remembering:*** relates what is said to what has previously been said
- ***Interpreting:*** clarifies and extends the meaning of interviewees' statements but without imposing meaning on them

To Kvale's list of traits, please add the following three:

- ***Balanced:*** does not talk too much, which can make interviewees passive, but does not talk too little, which can cause interviewees to feel that their responses are not satisfactory
- ***Ethically sensitive:*** for example, assures the interviewee that all answers will be treated confidentially
- ***Non-judgmental:*** does not communicate (even subtly) a moral judgment about what an interviewee has said or done; negative judgments may cause people to withhold information that could be useful to the study, while positive judgments may encourage them to focus on pleasing the interviewer rather than providing authentic commentary

- *Follow-up questions.* These get the interviewee to elaborate on an answer; for example: "What do you mean by that?"; even, "Yeesss?" Kvale suggested repeating significant words in an answer to stimulate further explanation, an approach used by Davies (2000) in a study of female offenders. One of Davies's interviewees mentioned the use of foil to block detection of security tags on clothing, so she asked, "You mentioned security tags and foil?" which launched the interviewee into a detailed description of shoplifting techniques.
- *Probing questions.* These follow up what has been said through direct questioning, for example: "Can you say some more about that?"; "You said earlier that you prefer not to do X. Can you say what kinds of things have put you off it?"; "In what ways do you find X disturbing?" Box 11.2 provides more examples.
- *Specifying questions.* "What did you do then?"; "How did (name) react to what you said?"; "What effect did (event) have on you?"
- *Direct questions.* "Do you find it easy to keep smiling when serving customers?"; "Are you happy with the way you and your husband decide how money should be spent?" Such questions are perhaps best left until later in the interview, in order not to influence the direction of the interview too much.
- *Indirect questions.* Before asking an indirect question—for example, "What do most people around here think of the ways that management treats its staff?"—be sure to ask the interviewee for his or own view ("How do you feel about . . .?").

- *Structuring questions.* "Now I would like to move on to a different topic. Could you describe . . .?"
- *Silence.* A pause will give the interviewee an opportunity to reflect and amplify an answer; just don't pause for so long that the interviewee feels embarrassed.
- *Interpreting questions.* "Do you mean that your leadership role had to change from one of encouraging others to a more directive one?"; "Is it fair to say that you don't mind being friendly toward customers most of the time, but you find it more difficult when they are unpleasant or demanding?"

As this list suggests, one of the main jobs of the interviewer is listening: being attentive to what the interviewee is saying or not saying. The interviewer must be active without being intrusive—a difficult balance. This means that the interviewer can't just sit back and relax, even if the interview is being recorded. In fact, the interviewer must be attuned and responsive not just to what is said and not said,

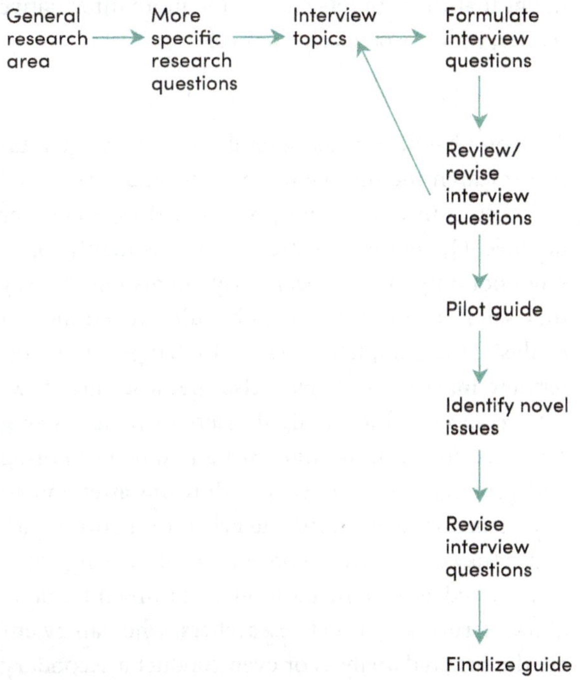

FIGURE 11.1 Formulating questions for an interview guide for social research

but also to what the interviewee is doing. This is important because body language can indicate that the interviewee is becoming uneasy with a line of questioning. An ethically sensitive interviewer does not place undue pressure on an interviewee and is prepared to cut short any line of questioning that is clearly a source of anxiety.

It's likely that the kinds of questions asked will vary in the different stages of a qualitative interview. Charmaz (2002) distinguished three types of question in this connection. Note that questions about the past and factual matters come first, then questions about feelings, and finally questions of process and summing up.

- *Initial open-ended questions.* "What events led to . . .?"; "What was your life like prior to . . .?"; "Is this organization typical of others you have worked in?"
- *Intermediate questions.* "How did you feel about . . . when you first learned about it?"; "What immediate impact did . . . have on your life?"; "What do you like most/least about working here?"
- *Ending questions.* "How have your views about . . . changed?"; "What advice would you give to someone who is undergoing a similar experience . . .?"; "If you had to do it over, would you choose to work for this organization?"

Most questions are likely to be of the intermediate kind, and some categories are likely to overlap. Nonetheless, these are useful distinctions to bear in mind.

Remember as well that interviews include different kinds of topics, such as the following:

- *Values*: of the interviewee, of the group, of the organization
- *Beliefs*: of the interviewee, of individual others, of the group
- *Behaviour*: of the interviewee, of others
- *Formal and informal roles*: of the interviewee, of others
- *Relationships*: of the interviewee, of others
- *Places and locales*

- *Emotions*: particularly of the interviewee, but also of others
- *Encounters*
- *Stories*

Try to vary the types of questions you ask (see Kvale's nine types) and, where appropriate, the topic areas (see the list above). Vague or overly general questions are usually best avoided; as Mason (2002) pointed out, they only force interviewees to puzzle over them or to ask for clarification.

Vignette questions can be used to ground interviewees' ideas and accounts of behaviour in particular situations (Barter & Renold, 1999). By presenting interviewees with concrete and realistic scenarios, the researcher can elicit a sense of how certain contexts mould behaviour. Hughes (1998) employed the technique in a study of perceptions of HIV risk among intravenous drug users. Context is important for this topic because drug users' willingness to engage in risky behaviour is influenced by situational factors. Scenarios depicting risk behaviour were presented and respondents were asked about the kinds of behaviour they felt that drug users *should* engage in (such as using prophylactics when having sex) and then about how they felt the hypothetical users *would* behave (when, for example, there was an opportunity for unprotected sex). Hughes argued that a scenario approach is particularly valuable with sensitive topics and for eliciting a range of responses to different contexts.

Using an interview guide: An example

Box 11.5 is taken from a study of visitors to Disney theme parks (Bryman, 1999). The interviewees were a man in his sixties and his wife who was two years younger. They had visited Walt Disney World, and were very enthusiastic about the visit.

The sequence begins with the interviewer asking what is considered a "direct question," in terms of the nine question types suggested by Kvale (1996). The replies are very bland and do little more than reflect the interviewees' positive feelings about their visit to Disney World. The wife acknowledges this when she says, ". . . but I need to say more than that, don't I?" Interviewees frequently know that they are expected to be expansive in their answers. This sequence occurred about halfway through the interview, so by then the interviewees were primed to recognize that more details were expected. There is a tinge of embarrassment that the answer is so brief and not illuminating. The husband's answer is more expansive but not particularly enlightening.

Then the first of two important prompts by the interviewer follows. The husband's response after the initial prompt is more interesting in that he begins to wonder whether Black people are under-represented at attractions like the American Adventure. The second prompt yields further useful reflection, this time that developing countries are under-represented in World Showcase. The couple are clearly aware that it was the prompting that led them to these reflections: "I hadn't really given this any consideration before you started asking about it." This is the whole point of prompting: to get the interviewee to think more about the topic and to provide an opportunity for a more detailed response. It isn't a leading question, since the interviewees were *not* asked whether they thought the Disney company failed to recognize the significance of Black history or ignored developing countries. There is no doubt that the prompts elicited the more informative replies, which is precisely their role.

Recording and transcription

The point has been made several times that in qualitative research the interview is usually audio-recorded and then transcribed (not just listened to) whenever possible. Qualitative researchers are frequently interested not only in what people say but also in the way they say it. If this aspect is to be fully woven into an analysis, the complete series of exchanges in an interview must be available. Also, because interviewers are supposed to be highly alert to what is being said—following up on interesting points, prompting and probing where necessary, drawing attention to any inconsistencies in the interviewee's answers—it's best if they don't have to concentrate on writing down what is said as well. In addition, recording interviews allows scrutiny by other researchers, who can evaluate the original analysis or even conduct a secondary analysis, which can help to counter accusations that the findings were influenced by the researcher's values

Box 11.5 | Part of the transcript of a semi-structured interview

Interviewer: OK. What were your views or feelings about the presentation of different cultures, as shown in, for example, Jungle Cruise or It's a Small World at the Magic Kingdom or in World Showcase at Epcot?

Wife: Well, I thought the different countries at Epcot were wonderful, but I need to say more than that, don't I?

Husband: They were very good and some were better than others, but that was down to the host countries themselves really, as I suppose each of the countries represented would have been responsible for their own part, so that's nothing to do with Disney, I wouldn't have thought. I mean some of the landmarks were hard to recognize for what they were supposed to be, but some were very well done. Britain was ok, but there was only a pub and a Welsh shop there really, whereas some of the other pavilions, as I think they were called, were good ambassadors for the countries they represented. China, for example, had an excellent 360-degree film showing parts of China and I found that very interesting.

Interviewer: Did you think there was anything lacking about the content?

Husband: Well I did notice that there weren't many Black people at World Showcase, particularly the American Adventure. Now whether we were there on an unusual day in that respect I don't know, but we saw plenty of Black Americans in the Magic Kingdom and other places, but very few if any in that World Showcase. And there was certainly little mention of Black history in the American Adventure presentation, so maybe they felt alienated by that, I don't know, but they were noticeable by their absence.

Interviewer: So did you think there were any special emphases?

Husband: Well, thinking about it now, because I hadn't really given this any consideration before you started asking about it, but thinking about it now, it was only really representative of the developed world, you know, Britain, America, Japan, world leaders many of them in technology, and there was nothing of the Third World there. Maybe that's their own fault, maybe they were asked to participate and didn't, but now that I think about it, that does come to me. What do you think, love?

Wife: Well, like you, I hadn't thought of it like that before, but I agree with you.

Source: Bryman, A. (1999). Global Disney. In P. Taylor & D. Slater (Eds.), *The American century*. Oxford: Blackwell.

or biases. Recording also makes it possible for the data to be reused in ways other than those intended by the original researcher; for example, to be analyzed using new theoretical ideas or analytic strategies.

As with just about everything in social research, there is a cost (apart from the financial cost of buying recording equipment) in that the use of a recorder can upset respondents, who may become self-conscious or alarmed at the prospect that their words will be preserved in that way. Most people will allow their interviews to be recorded, though it's not uncommon for a small number to refuse. When that happens (or when the recording device malfunctions), the interview can still proceed with the interviewer taking notes. Among those who do agree to be recorded, some will still be fearful and as a result their interviews may not be as informative as they otherwise would be.

Practical Tip | Transcribing interviews

A student doing research for a thesis may not have the resources to pay for professional transcription, and unless he or she is an accurate touch typist, transcription can take a lot of time. The usual estimate is five to six hours per hour of speech, although using transcription software along with a foot pedal for stops and starts makes the task much easier. Speech-to-text software, which transcribes spoken words directly into a text file, is also available, although it is not yet widely used and at present has certain drawbacks, especially for focus groups. The important thing is to allow sufficient time for transcription and to be realistic about how many interviews can be transcribed in the time available.

Another consideration, as we have seen, is the time required to transcribe a recorded interview. There is some debate over who should do the transcribing: the interviewer (more familiar with what was actually said) or someone else (less time-consuming) (Rafaeli, Dutton, Harquail, & Mackie-Lewis, 1997, p. 14). Furthermore, the vast amounts of text produced must then be read. Beardsworth and Keil (1992) reported that their 73 interviews on vegetarianism generated "several hundred thousand words of transcript material" (p. 262). Clearly, even though transcription has the advantage of keeping the interviewee's (and interviewer's) words intact, it does so by piling up the text to be analyzed. It's no wonder that writers like Lofland and Lofland (1995) advise researchers not to leave the analysis of qualitative data until all the interviews have been completed and transcribed. Insights may be gained by examining the content of early interviews, and it may be useful to pursue those points in greater detail in later interviews. Thus, there are good grounds for making analysis an ongoing activity. Also, to wait until all interviews have been completed may make the task of transcription seem overwhelming.

Transcription may seem a relatively unproblematic matter of converting the spoken word into written form. However, given the importance of transcripts in qualitative research, the process should not be taken lightly. Transcribers need to be trained in much the same way that interviewers are. Moreover, even experienced transcribers can make mistakes. Poland (1995) provided some fascinating examples of the errors that can result from factors such as mishearing, fatigue, or carelessness. For example, one transcript contained the following passage:

> I think unless we want to become like other countries, where people have, you know, democratic freedoms . . .

But the actual words on the audiotape were:

> I think unless we want to become like other countries, where people have no democratic freedoms . . . (1995, p. 294)

Clearly, steps need to be taken to check on the quality of transcription.

In qualitative research there is often wide variation in the time that different interviews take. For example, in Wilson's (2000) rave study, the interviews lasted between 45 minutes and four hours. Shorter interviews are not necessarily inferior, with the exception of those in which the interviewee was non-cooperative or anxious about being recorded. Indeed, when a long interview contains very little of significance, it may not be worth the time and cost of transcription. Thankfully, such occasions are relatively rare. People who have agreed to be interviewed are usually cooperative, and most loosen up once they get over their initial anxiety about the microphone. As a result, even short interviews are often quite revealing.

Flexibility in the interview

Flexibility in interviewing means more than being responsive to what interviewees say and following up on the interesting points they make. A flexible

Practical Tip | Transcribing sections of an interview

It's not always necessary to transcribe every word of an interview. Quite often you will find that large portions of a particular interview (even all of it) won't be useful, perhaps because the interviewee was reticent or because the comments made were not as relevant to the research topic as you had expected. There seems to be little point in transcribing such material. Before you begin transcribing, therefore, listen to the interviews closely once or twice, and then transcribe only the portions that seem useful or relevant. The same applies to focus group research, which is often more difficult and time-consuming to transcribe because of the number of speakers involved. The downside is that you may miss things, or certain comments may emerge as significant only later on. If that happens, you will have to go back to the recording to get the needed material.

interviewer is able to vary the order of questions and clear up inconsistencies in answers. Flexibility is also important when audio recording equipment breaks down, or when an interviewee refuses permission for recording to take place. Sometimes researchers find that their questions do not resonate with participants. Flexibility here can mean revising questions on the spot and making adjustments to the interview guide going forward. This is what Jones did in her 2018 study, with Hannem, of sexual scripts used by escort clients:

> The initial interview questions asked the participants to discuss any concerns they had about criminalization or being arrested for soliciting to purchase sex, experiences of stigmatization connected to being a client, how much of their identity and self was invested in being a client or "hobbyist," and their impressions of clients in the media. However, the first three clients arrived at their interviews prepared to tell the story of how and why they hire sex workers, and gave succinct and distracted answers to our intended line of inquiry. The first author decided to adjust the interview schedule to better suit what the clients wanted to talk about: what they felt was misunderstood by the public and researchers alike, which was, chiefly, the nuanced experiences that they had hiring sex workers. (Jones & Hannem, 2018, p. 494)

Another common problem for interviewers is knowing when to switch off their recording equipment. Often an interviewee will resume talking about the topic of interest as soon as the machine is turned off. It's usually not feasible to switch the machine back on again, so try to keep it going as long as possible. If that fails, take some notes either while the person is talking or as soon as possible after the interview. Such "unsolicited accounts" can often be the source of revealing information. This is certainly what Parker (2000) found in his study of organizations: many interviewees offered "unrecorded comments prefixed with a silent or explicit 'well, if you want to know what I really think.' . . . Needless to say, a visit to the toilet to write up as much as I could remember followed almost immediately" (p. 236).

Being reflexive about how qualitative data are co-constructed

Finally, when transcribing and later interpreting qualitative interviews, researchers should reflect on how their own interactions with participants have affected what was said, how it was said, and what was left unsaid. Qualitative interviewing is more than simply digging out pre-existing verbal gems from interviewees. The interviewee and the interviewer construct meaning together through their verbal and non-verbal symbolic interactions. Interpretations emerge out of those interactions; they are not simply "out there" in the minds of the study participants, waiting to be discovered.

Ajodhia-Andrews (2016), in her research on how six Canadian children with disabilities viewed their experiences at school, makes this co-construction of understanding explicit and even weaves it into her methodology:

> After coding and searching for emerging themes and patterns, participants and I collaboratively told, re-told, wrote, and re-wrote their narratives, negotiating which pieces of stories to include, what they thought of surfacing themes and interpretations. . . . Through this dialogue and debate participants and I co-constructed narratives together, whereby I also became part of the conversations, responding to their stories and experiences, thus shaping and re-storying their narratives. These narratives become unique to the interaction between myself and participants; if participants shared their stories and understandings with any other person/researcher, the narratives would never be conveyed and told in the same way. . . . (Ajodhia-Andrews, 2016, p. 262)

Focus groups: An introduction

Most people think of an interview as an exchange between one interviewer and one interviewee. The focus group technique, however, involves speaking with more than one (usually at least four) interviewees at the same time. Essentially it is a group interview in which the interviewees can speak to and interact with one another.

- Most focus group researchers work within a qualitative research tradition. They try to provide a fairly unstructured setting in which the person who runs the focus group, usually called the **moderator** or **facilitator**, guides the session but does not intrude. A focus group offers several advantages. One of the most important is that it allows the researcher to develop an understanding of *why* people feel the way they do. In individual interviews, participants are often asked about their reasons for holding a particular view, but a focus group allows participants to probe one another's reasons. This can be more informative and revealing than the question-followed-by-answer method of ordinary interviews. For example, an individual who has already answered a certain question may decide, after hearing others' answers, to qualify or modify that response in some way. Some people may want to voice agreement with a view they might not otherwise have thought of. These possibilities permit focus groups to elicit a wide variety of perspectives on an issue.
- In conventional one-to-one interviewing, interviewees are rarely challenged; they may say things that are inconsistent with earlier replies or that patently cannot be true, but interviewers are often reluctant to point out such deficiencies. In a focus group, participants may argue and challenge one another's views. Arguing often produces more realistic accounts of what people think, because it forces them to defend and possibly revise their views.
- A focus group offers an opportunity to study how individuals collectively make sense of a phenomenon and construct meanings of it. It is a central tenet of theoretical positions such as **symbolic interactionism** that meanings and understandings are not derived by individuals in isolation: rather, they develop out of interactions and discussions with others. In this sense, focus groups reflect the processes through which meaning is constructed in everyday life, which allows them to be more **naturalistic** than individual interviews (Wilkinson, 1998). On the other hand, it is not clear whether these new meanings persist beyond the focus group session.

Box 11.6 provides an example of focus group research conducted by Ricciardelli and Adorjan (2019), who were interested in understanding Canadian teens' views on sexting (sending sexually suggestive or explicit text messages and images to others).

Box 11.6 | Focus groups in action: Canadian teenagers and sexting

Focus groups were used by Ricciardelli and Adorjan (2019) to examine Canadian teenagers' perspectives on sexting. The focus groups were concerned with how "the attitudes and perceptions of youth related to cyber-risks involved with digital sexual expression" (p. 564). Details of the groups in this study are given in Table 11.1.

By using focus groups, Ricciardelli and Adorjan sought to better understand how teens interpret their experiences with sexting. Focus groups offered participants a platform to engage in group discussion with their peers, "illuminating social contexts and personal interpretations which are largely left out of survey-based methods" (p. 567). Male and female participants were sampled from urban Western and rural Atlantic schools. This offered the researchers an opportunity to compare the different regional contexts, but they did not find any significant differences based on location—"gender and age were the primary drivers of difference" (p. 567). The researchers mostly had participants of the same age and gender in each group, and "used a sampling stratification strategy designed to help ensure participants interacted with others that they would not perceive as threatening and with whom their experience may also resonate" (p. 567). Each session lasted an average of one hour and was audio-recorded to maintain accuracy and so that the moderators could focus on participants' discussion. A key finding of the study was the gender double-standard that exists with online sexual expression: males disproportionately send females non-consensual sexts, while females are expected to regulate their sexual expression to a much greater extent and are more likely to suffer serious stigmatization for not doing so.

Conducting focus groups

A number of practical aspects of conducting a focus group are considered below.

How many groups?

How many focus groups are needed? Table 11.1 provides some data on this question, and on some other aspects of focus groups (cf. Deacon, Pickering, Golding, & Murdock, 1999). As it suggests, there is a good deal of variation in the number of groups required for a particular study, but it generally ranges from 10 to 15.

A single group is unlikely to be sufficient, since the responses may not be typical of other groups. Nonetheless, there are good reasons for limiting the number of groups (besides saving time and resources). Once the moderator is able to anticipate fairly accurately what the next group is going to say, enough groups have participated. This notion is similar to **theoretical saturation** in grounded theory, discussed in Chapters 10 and 13.

One factor that can affect the number of groups required is whether the researcher thinks that the range of views is likely to be affected by socio-demographic factors such as age, gender, or social class. Many focus group researchers like to ensure that different demographic groups are included, which usually requires a large number of groups. In connection with Kitzinger's (1994) research on audience responses to media messages about AIDS (see Table 11.1), she wrote that a large number of groups is preferred in order to capture as many different perspectives as possible. On the other hand, conducting more groups increases the complexity of the analysis. For example, Schlesinger, Dobash, Dobash, & Weaver (1992, p. 29; see Table 11.1 and Box 11.7) reported that their 14 tape-recorded hour-long sessions produced more than 1400 pages of transcription for analysis.

Size of groups and selecting participants

How large should a single focus group be? Morgan (1998) suggested six to ten members. To control for the problem of "no-shows," researchers often find themselves over-recruiting (for example, Wilkinson, 1999, p. 188). Morgan recommended small groups when the participants are likely to have a lot to say, as often occurs when they are emotionally involved with the topic, when the topic is controversial or complex, or when exploring personal interpretations. A larger group is appropriate when the researcher wants "to hear numerous brief suggestions" (Morgan, 1998, p. 75).

For most topics there is no need to select a particular kind of participant; however, the topic should be relevant to those taking part. A wide range of people is often required, but participants may be put into separate groups on the basis of age, gender, education, ethnicity, whether they have (or have not) had a certain experience, and so on. The aim is to look for any variation in how the different groups discuss the matter at hand. For example, to examine women's responses to scenes of violence against women, Schlesinger et al. (1992) showed 14 groups (see Table 11.1 and Box 11.7) four levels of mass-media violence: incidental violence, moderate violence, marital violence, and an extremely vivid sexual assault scene. The authors concluded:

> Having a particular experience or a particular background does significantly affect the interpretation of a given text. The four programs screened are obviously open to various readings. However, on the evidence, *how* they are read is fundamentally affected by various socio-cultural factors and by lived experience. (Schlesinger et al., 1992, p. 168; emphasis in original)

A slight variation on this approach is Kitzinger's (1994) study of reactions to media representations of AIDS (see Table 11.1). Her groups were made up of people in a variety of situations. Some were what she called "general population groups" (for example, a team of civil engineers working on the same site) but others were made up of people likely to have a special interest in AIDS, such as male sex workers and intravenous drug users. Increasingly, focus group practitioners try to discern patterns of variation by putting together groups with particular attributes.

A further issue in designing a focus group is whether to select people who are unknown to each other, or to use natural groups (for example, friends, co-workers, or students in the same class). Some researchers prefer to exclude people who know each other, fearing that known status differences or pre-existing patterns of interaction would contaminate the session. Others prefer to select natural groups whenever possible. Holbrook and Jackson (1996) reported that, for their research on shopping centres, they initially tried to secure participants who were unknown to each other, but this strategy attracted no takers. They then sought out participants in various social clubs. They defended this new approach on the grounds that, because their research questions concerned shopping in relation to the construction of identity and how it relates to people's sense of place, recruiting people who knew each other would be highly appropriate. Recruiting people from natural groups is not always feasible, however, because of the difficulty of getting everyone in the group to participate. Morgan (1998) revealed another downside: because people in natural groups know one another, they may share certain assumptions that they feel no need to explain or justify. He suggested that in cases where it is important that such assumptions are made explicit, a group of strangers is a better choice.

Asking questions and level of moderator involvement

There are different questioning strategies and approaches to moderating focus group sessions. Most lie somewhere between a rather open-ended style and a more structured one. In Ricciardelli and Adorjan's (2019) research on sexting among teenagers (see Box 11.6 and Table 11.1), they began each session by asking a general, open-ended question about participants' experiences with technology. Follow-up questions pertained to concerns that were raised by participants,

TABLE 11.1 Composition of groups in focus groups research

AUTHORS	RICCIARDELLI AND ADORJAN (2019)	EADY, DOBINSON, & ROSS (2011)	FROHLICH, POTVIN, CHABOT, & CORIN (2002)	KITZINGER (1993, 1994)	LETT, HIER, & WALBY (2010)	MIRAFTAB (2000)	SCHLESINGER ET AL. (1992)
Area of research	Teenagers' perspectives on sexting	Bisexual people's experience with mental health services	A contextual understanding of pre-adolescent smoking behaviour	Audience responses to media messages about AIDS	Extent of public consultation on the introduction of street surveillance cameras, and perceptions of their effectiveness in preventing crime	Housing experiences of Kurdish and Somali refugees in Vancouver	Responses of women to watching violence against women
Number of groups	35	8	Not specified	52	4	Not specified	14
Size range of groups	2–5	3–9	Probably 12	Not specified but appears to be 3, 9, or 10	5–10	10–15	5–9
Average (mean) size of groups	3.3	Not specified	n.a.	6.75	7	n.a.	6.6
Criteria (if any) for inclusion	Age, gender, rural/urban location	Age, sexual orientation	4 groups out of 32 Quebec communities	No, but groups made up of specific groups (e.g., retirement club members, male sex workers)	People identified in promotional campaigns and justificatory arguments relating to street surveillance cameras	None, except being recent immigrant	Experience of violence, Scottish/English, ethnicity, class
Natural groups	No	No	No	Yes	Some	No	Some

Box 11.7 | Asking about violence

Stigur Már Karlsson/Heimsmyndir/iStockphoto

Semi-structured interviewing offers researchers and interviewees a degree of flexibility in shaping the course and content of an interview. What are some difficulties that researchers might face when conducting a semi-structured interview that they might not face when conducting a structured interview?

Researchers usually want to inject some structure into their focus group sessions. An example can be seen in the research conducted by Schlesinger et al. (1992; see Table 11.1) on women viewing mass media presentations of varying levels of violence against women. For a rape scene depicted in a movie, reactions were gleaned through "guiding questions" under five main headings, the first three of which had several more specific elements:

- Initially, participants were given the opportunity to discuss the film in terms of things such as its purpose, its realism, and its storyline.
- The questioning then moved on to reactions to the characters: the woman who was raped, the three rapists, the female lawyer, the male lawyers.
- Participants were then asked about their reactions to particular scenes, including the rape; the female lawyer's decision to support the case after initially not supporting it; and the victory in court.
- Participants were asked for their reactions to the inclusion of the rape scene.
- Finally, they were asked to give an assessment of the film's value, in particular whether the fact that it was American made a difference to their reactions. (The study was conducted in the UK.)

While the research by Schlesinger and colleagues examined a lot of specific topics, initial questions were designed to generate relatively open-ended reactions. Such a general approach to questioning is fairly common in focus group research. It allows the investigator to address the research questions, ensures that there is some comparability between sessions, and permits participants to raise issues that *they* see as significant.

Practical Tip | Number of focus groups

Even one focus group session takes a long time to arrange. It also takes a long time to transcribe the recordings made during the session. Thus, most students will not be able to conduct as many focus group sessions for a project or dissertation as a professional researcher would. In your report, make sure to justify the number of groups used in your research, explaining why the data are still significant even though you had to make do with a relatively small number of groups.

which often centred around privacy and sexting. Their middle-of-the-road approach to question structuring can be seen in the following question asked by one of the focus group moderators: "Do you think it's the same though for boys and girls, cuz you said boys send the pictures and they don't care, but girls obviously send them too (Rebecca and Carolyn reply affirmatively). But do you think it's a different context, like they think something different is going to come of it?" (Ricciardelli & Adorjan, 2019, p. 570). Here, the moderator focuses on the topic to be addressed but is also able to pick up on what the group says.

How involved should the moderator or facilitator be? As with question structuring, above, the most common approach is middle-of-the-road. There is a tendency to use a fairly small number of very general questions to guide a focus group session. Obviously, if the discussion goes completely off topic it may be necessary to refocus the participants' attention, but even then the moderator must be careful, because apparent digressions can often reveal something of significance. More direction is probably needed if the participants are not addressing the research questions, or if a particularly meaningful point made by one participant is not followed up by the others.

Both intervention and non-intervention carry risks. The style of questioning and moderating depends on the nature of the research topic; if it is embarrassing for some participants, for example, additional direction may be required from the moderator. Levels of interest and knowledge among the participants can make a difference as well. Limited interest or knowledge on the part of participants may require a somewhat more structured approach. If in doubt, the best advice is to err on the side of minimal intervention.

Recording and transcription

Recording is even more important with focus groups than it is in other forms of qualitative research. Writing down not only exactly what is said but who says it is too difficult. In an individual interview you may be able to ask a respondent to "hold on" while you write down a response, but this is not feasible in an interview where several people are speaking rapidly, and would almost certainly break the flow of the discussion.

Transcribing focus group sessions is also more complicated and hence more time-consuming than it is with other interview forms. Sometimes voices are hard to distinguish, making it difficult to determine who is speaking. Also, people sometimes talk over each other, which can make transcription even more problematic. Therefore, a very high-quality recording device, capable of picking up even faint voices from many directions, is a necessity. Focus group transcripts always seem to have more missing bits than transcripts from other sorts of interview, mainly because of audibility problems.

Research in the News

What does it mean to be a working-class, first-generation student in Canada?

When Proudfoot (2019) first interviewed Wolfgang Lehmann, a Professor of Sociology at Western University in London, Ontario, she recalls his research findings bringing tears to her eyes. She writes, "I never forgot his research because he was talking about me, explaining my life in ways that simultaneously made a deep sort of sense and had never occurred to me before." The research she is referring to examined what it means to come from a working-class home and be the first person in the family to attend university (a "first-generation student"). The idea of "working class" (and "social class" more generally) is a concept that social scientists and politicians alike have a hard time pinning down. Lehmann did not specify "working class" in his study's recruitment materials; rather,

(Continued)

he "described those who were the first among their parents or grandparents to attend university, and whose parents worked in fields like construction, factories or hairdressing." From this sample of students, he conducted in-depth interviews when they were in first, second, and fourth year, and then again five years after they had graduated. When asking students about their social class, they often initially felt that they were middle class. After Lehmann described some of the qualities of what it means to be working class, though, most identified as such and were somewhat surprised by the realization.

Lehmann found that working-class students encounter a variety of hurdles, such as money concerns and having to balance school and work commitments. He also discovered that his participants tended to ignore their working-class background except to highlight its advantages, such as fostering resilience, a strong work ethic, and a sense of not having things handed to them. One of Lehmann's participants stated, "A lot of the people here have a good amount of money behind them, or their parents are paying . . . and at times it's like 'Oh man, I wish it was that easy.' . . . But honestly, I like the struggle of it. I think it makes me a better person." Striving to become middle class also presents a conundrum: the conditions that working-class students credit as advantages are also what they are trying to escape. Climbing the ladder of social mobility leads to being caught between two worlds, no longer fully belonging to the working-class culture of their up-bringing, while also at times feeling like an outsider in the middle-class world they aspired to.

Group interaction in focus group sessions

Kitzinger (1994) observed that reports of focus group research frequently fail to take group interaction into account. This is surprising, given that such interaction is a distinguishing feature of focus groups. Wilkinson (1998) reviewed more than 200 focus group studies, published between 1946 and 1996, and concluded: "Focus group data is most commonly presented as if it were one-to-one interview data, with interactions between group participants rarely reported, let alone analyzed" (p. 112).

In the context of her research on the coverage of AIDS in the mass media, Kitzinger (1994) drew attention to two types of interaction in focus groups: complementary and argumentative. Complementary interaction allows collective interpretations and understandings to develop, with each participant building on the preceding remark, as in the following passage taken from Morgan and Spanish's (1985, p. 414) research on heart-attack victims:

> *No. 1*: But I think maybe what we're saying here is that there's no one cause of heart attacks, there's no one type of person, there's probably umpteen different types of heart attacks and causes coming from maybe smoking, maybe obesity, maybe stress, maybe design fault, hereditary, overwork, change in life style. Any of these things in themselves could be . . .
>
> *No. 2*: And when you start putting them in combination [unclear].
>
> *No. 3*: Yeah, you may be really magnifying each one of these particular things.
>
> *No. 2*: Yeah, and depending on how, and in each person that magnification is different. Some people can take a little stress without doing any damage, some people can take a little smoking, a little drinking, a little obesity, without doing any damage. But you take a little of each of these and put them together and you're starting to increase the chances of damage. And any one of these that takes a magnitude leap increases the chances.

This sequence brings out the emerging consensus around the question of who has heart attacks and why. However, as Kitzinger (1994) suggested, argumentative interaction in focus groups can be equally revealing. In such cases moderators can play an important role in identifying differences of opinion and exploring with participants the factors that lie behind them. Disagreement can give participants a chance to revise their opinions or to think about why they hold them. A passage from Schlesinger et al. (1992; see Table 11.1) illustrates. The group is made up of women with no experience of violence, and the debate concerns a rape scene in a film:

> *Speaker 1:* I think . . . that they could've explained it. They could easily leave [out] that rape scene.
>
> *Speaker 2:* But it's like that other film we watched. You don't realize the full impact, like, the one we were watching, the first one, until you've got the reconstruction.
>
> *Speaker 3:* Yeah, but I think with that sort of film, it would cause more damage than it would good, I mean, if someone had been raped, would you like to have [to] sit through that again?

The debate then moved on to consider the significance of the scene for men:

> *Speaker 1:* Men would sit down and think, "Well, she asked for it. She was enjoying it and look, the men around enjoyed it." (Schlesinger et al., 1992, pp. 51–52)

It seems, then, that behind the unease some of the women expressed about the rape scene was the idea that some men might enjoy it and identify with the onlookers depicted in the movie. This interpretation came out because of an earlier disagreement within the group, which allowed the women to give a fuller account of their reactions to the scene.

In sum, as Kitzinger (1994) argued, drawing attention to patterns of interaction in focus groups allows a researcher to determine how group participants view the issues at hand. The posing of questions by focus group members as well as the agreement and disagreement among them help to bring out this knowledge. The resolution of disagreements also forces participants to explain why they hold the views they do.

Methods in Motion | Applications to Canadian Society

Social capital and Indigenous education

Many scholars have expressed concern over the fact that in Canada, Indigenous people are less likely to graduate from high school than non-Indigenous individuals, and likewise that Indigenous youth have lower levels of participation in post-secondary educational institutions (e.g., Milne, 2017). To look into this issue, Milne (2016) conducted semi-structured interviews with 26 educators and 24 parents/guardians of students from off-reserve schools in southern Ontario. Twenty of the teachers identified as Indigenous, as did 20 of the parents/guardians. Lareau and Weininger's (2003) concept of "cultural capital," which maintains that certain kinds of knowledge, skills, and competence give people an advantage in negotiating how they are treated in formal institutions, served as the theoretical backdrop to the study.

The interviews revealed that the legacy of colonialism, especially the intergenerational, traumatic effects of attending residential schools, created a high level of mistrust of educational institutions on the part of Indigenous people. This was evident in a remark made by one of the Indigenous parents: "I have the worst fear of teachers, to be honest with

(Continued)

you. Even if the teacher's the same age as me, I'm nervous around them" (Milne 2016, p. 276).

Another key finding was that class differences among Indigenous participants were linked to how well they were able to pursue the educational interests of their children with school authorities. Lower-class individuals (defined as having at most a high school education and a household income of less than $30,000) encountered a great deal of difficulty in getting their children's educational needs met. They were hesitant to approach school officials about their children's progress and tended to stay away from the schools. When asked about what role she played in her children's education, one low-income parent said that she "doesn't know how to go about that kind of stuff" (Milne 2016, p. 281). Middle-class Indigenous parents (who had a post-secondary education and incomes between $30,000 and $112,335) were much better able to navigate the educational system on their children's behalf. A middle-class mother, after having a confrontation with her daughter's teacher, told him "You're fired," and insisted that the principal move the child to a different class immediately. She got her way.

Limitations of focus groups

Focus groups are particularly useful in illustrating how meaning is jointly constructed. What, then, are their chief limitations?

- The researcher probably has less control over the proceedings than in individual interviews. As we have seen, not all writers on focus groups perceive this as a problem; indeed, researchers concerned with **reflexivity** often see it as an advantage. However, the question of control raises questions about the extent to which a researcher should allow the participants to "take over" the discussion. There is clearly a delicate balance to be struck in deciding how involved moderators should be and how much a set of prompts or questions should be allowed to influence the conversation. What is not clear is the degree to which it is appropriate to surrender control, especially when there is a set of research questions to be answered.
- An unwieldy amount of data is sometimes produced. For example, Bloor, Frankland, Thomas, & Robson (2001) suggested that one focus group session can take up to eight hours to transcribe—somewhat longer than an equivalent personal interview, because of variations in voice pitch and the need to identify who says what. Also, group recordings often include inaudible comments from participants sitting too far from the microphone, and these also affect transcription.
- The data may be difficult to analyze. Developing an analysis strategy that incorporates both the themes of the discussion and the patterns of interaction is not easy.
- Focus groups are difficult to arrange. It may be hard to get people to agree to participate, and harder still to get them to show up. Very small payments, such as gift cards, are sometimes offered to induce participation, but it is still common to find that some people will not turn up.
- Group effects may be a problem. This category includes the obvious challenge of dealing with participants who either are too reticent to speak up or hog the stage. Krueger (1998) suggested that the people running the focus group should make it clear to participants that other people's views are definitely required; for example, he suggested saying something like "That's one point of view. Does anyone have another point of view?" (1998, p. 59). As for those who are reluctant to speak, Krueger recommended that they be actively encouraged to say something.

It would be interesting to know whether agreement among focus group participants is more common than disagreement; if that is the case, one reason might be group pressure to conform. It's also possible that participants are more likely to express socially acceptable views in a group setting than in individual interviews. Morgan (2002) cited a study in which group interviews with boys on the topic of relationships with girls were compared with individual interviews with boys on the same subject. Alone, the boys expressed a degree of sensitivity that was not evident in the group context, where they tended to express more macho views. This suggests that in the group setting the boys were trying to impress each other or avoid embarrassment, and were influenced by peer pressure. But this does not mean that such data are tainted: in fact, it may be the gulf between privately and publicly held views that is of interest.

- Madriz (2000) proposed that there are circumstances when individual interviews are more appropriate. One is when participants are likely to disagree profoundly with each other; another is when participants are not comfortable in one another's presence (for example, people in hierarchical relationships). Finally, because of the potential for focus groups to cause discomfort among participants (for example, when intimate details of private lives need to be revealed), an individual interview or even a questionnaire may be better.

Online interviews and focus groups

Conducting qualitative interviews and focus groups online has become increasingly common as more and more people incorporate Internet communication technologies into their everyday lives. Being aware of what topics and types of participants are best suited for online interviews and focus groups is an important consideration. While some people are comfortable with online communication, there are still many who are not. Selecting participants can also be difficult since everyone taking part must have access to the necessary hardware and software. Still, the Internet has great potential for facilitating access to groups of participants that were often difficult to reach in the past. Even if the technology is not used specifically for data collection, carefully selected websites, online forums, and social media sites can be excellent sources for recruitment.

Online qualitative interviews

Price and Puddephatt (2018) conducted qualitative research on the perspectives and experiences of Canadian open access journal editors. Because their participants were geographically dispersed, they decided to use a combination of Skype, telephone, email, and face-to-face interviews to collect their data. Of the two online communication mediums, they discovered that Skype worked better than email for establishing rapport and eliciting in-depth answers. Email participants' responses tended to be short and glib. Note the following brief sequence (Price is Taylor):

> *Taylor:* What was the hardest day or week you had as an open access journal editor?
>
> *Email respondent:* Whenever I learn a new HTML program. (Price & Puddephatt, 2018, p. 194)

Not being in a shared interactional space made it difficult for the interviewer to know how to respond.

Skype is a rich, synchronous communication medium, meaning that it allows for visual and auditory communication cues and instant interactive exchange between the interviewer and interviewee. The immediate back-and-forth flow of information creates greater opportunity for developing mutual understanding and working out misunderstandings in real-time. Hanna (2012) also reports that Internet interviews using webcam technologies such as Skype can be as effective as in-person qualitative interviews, and that they have advantages similar to telephone interviews. No travelling is needed with Skype interviews, they can be postponed and rescheduled without difficulty, and the interviewee is allowed to stay home and thus feel safe and secure. Moreover, both audio and visual aspects of the interview are easily recorded.

Skype can be a valuable interview tool, allowing for rich visual and auditory communication without the need to travel. What might be some of the drawbacks of Skype interviews?
insta_photos/Shutterstock

Price and Puddephatt (2018) suggest that while real-time communication technologies generally offer greater advantages for long distance data collection, the fit between the research question and communication medium should also be considered. For instance, asynchronous (non-real-time) communication mediums like email can be useful for exploring topics where more deliberate, careful reflection is called for. However, if there is no interactional history between the participant and researcher, Price and Puddephatt recommend using a rich, synchronous medium prior to an email interview to help establish rapport and buy-in from the participant.

Online focus groups

Mann and Stewart (2000) suggested that an online focus group should have between six and eight people. Larger groups make it difficult for some people to participate. This is especially true when solely using text-based communication technologies as it curtails input from those with limited keyboard skills. Also, moderating an online session can be more difficult with larger numbers, and as Adriaenssens and Cadman (1999) suggested, large groups can present administrative problems.

Before starting an online focus group session, moderators are advised to send out a welcome message introducing the research and laying out some of the ground rules for the discussion. There is evidence that participants respond more positively if the researchers reveal something about themselves (Curasi, 2001). This can be done in advance of the session, as was suggested by Price and Puddephatt (2018) in the case of online interviews, through the moderator's opening remarks or by creating links to a personal website.

In online focus groups, participants respond more or less immediately to whatever has just been "said," whether by the moderator or by other participants. As all are simultaneously online, text-based contributions can be responded to as soon as they appear on the screen (and with some forms of software, the contributions can be seen as they are being typed). As Mann and Stewart (2000) observed, because several participants can type in a response to something at the same time, the convention of taking turns in regular conversation is largely sidelined. Even with the benefits of visual and verbal cues in video-based focus groups, turn-taking behaviour is somewhat more difficult to read and facilitate online than it is when moderating a face-to-face focus group.

Online focus groups are unlikely to replace their face-to-face counterparts, but they are likely to be used for certain kinds of research topics and/or samples. As regards the latter, people who are dispersed or inaccessible are especially suitable for online focus group research; slow typists, for instance, are not well-suited if the focus group is run in a text-based format. As Sweet (2001) pointed out, the most appropriate topics for online research are likely to be those involving sensitive issues or Internet use itself (as in Box 11.8).

Much research on the Internet treats the technology as a given, but some studies examine how it is *interpreted* by users. Hine (2000, p. 9), for instance, presented the Internet "as a product of culture . . . shaped by the ways in which it is marketed, taught, and used." Box 11.9 summarizes the main advantages and disadvantages of conducting focus groups and individual qualitative interviews online in a text-based format compared to administering them in person. The two types of qualitative interviewing are combined because the tally of advantages and disadvantages applies more or less equally well to both of them.

Box 11.8 | An online focus group study

O'Connor and Madge (2001; 2003; see also Madge & O'Connor, 2002) employed text-based conferencing software in a virtual focus group study that examined the use of an online information website for parents. Initially, the researchers set up a Web survey on the use of the site. When respondents sent in their questionnaires, they were thanked for their participation and asked via email whether they were willing to take part in an in-depth interview. Of the 155 respondents who returned the questionnaires, 16 agreed to be interviewed and were sent the software to install on their computers. The researchers tried to ensure that each group was asked more or less the same questions. For each session, the researchers introduced themselves and asked participants to do likewise. In addition, they placed descriptions and photographs of themselves on a website to which participants were directed. An important part of the process of building rapport was the fact that both of the researchers were mothers. They found that the relative anonymity afforded by the Internet gave participants greater confidence in asking embarrassing questions, a finding that has implications for online focus groups in general. This can be seen in the following excerpt:

> *Amy:* I feel better asking BW [Babyworld] than my health visitor as they're not going to see how bad I am at housekeeping!!!
>
> *Kerry:* I feel the same. Like the HV [health visitor] is judging even though she says she isn't
>
> *Kerry:* Although my HV has been a lifeline as I suffer from PND [post-natal depression]
>
> *Amy:* Also, there are some things that are so little that you don't want to feel like you're wasting anyone's time. Asking the HV or GP might get in the way of something mroe important, whereas sending an email, the person can answer it when convenient.
>
> *Amy:* My HV is very good, but her voice does sound patronising. I'm sure she doesn't mean it, but it does get to me . . .
>
> *Kerry:* Being anon means that you don't get embarrassed asking about a little point or something personal. (O'Connor & Madge, 2001, p. 10.4)

This extract reveals a good flow without intervention by the researchers. It contains several mistakes ("mroe," "I'msure"), but they are retained to preserve the authenticity of the interaction. Another plus is that there is no need to transcribe the material because it is already in textual form. Also, the fact that participants appear to relish the anonymity of the Internet has implications for online focus groups, since participants may find it easier to ask naive questions or make potentially embarrassing comments online than in face-to-face focus groups.

Qualitative interviewing (without immersion in a social setting) versus ethnography

The aim of this section is to compare the merits and limitations of qualitative interviewing that does not involve spending extensive periods of time in a particular social setting with those of ethnography. They are probably the two most prominent methods of data collection in qualitative research, so there is some value in assessing their relative strengths.

Advantages of ethnography compared to qualitative interviewing

Seeing through others' eyes

As we noted in Chapters 1 and 9, seeing through others' eyes is one of the main purposes of qualitative research. On the face of it, ethnographers would

Box 11.9 Advantages and disadvantages of conducting focus groups and individual qualitative interviews using an online, text-based format rather than face-to-face

Advantages

- Online interviews and focus groups are much less expensive to conduct than their face-to-face equivalents, especially when conducting long distance research.
- People who would otherwise be inaccessible (for example, in another country) or reluctant to participate (for example, busy senior executives) are more easily brought into the study.
- Interviewees and focus group participants are able to read and reread their statements (and in focus groups, those of the other participants as well), thus allowing for greater reflection.
- Audio recording is not required; this eliminates both interviewee apprehension and the need for time-consuming and expensive transcription.
- Records of online interviews are more accurate because nothing has to be transcribed and problems of mishearing don't arise. This is a particular advantage with focus group discussions.
- Participants can use pseudonyms to conceal their identity, making it easier for them to discuss embarrassing issues or to divulge potentially unpopular views.
- In focus groups, shy or quiet people may find it easier to participate and overbearing participants are less likely to predominate, though variations in keyboard skills may still prevent equal participation.
- Focus group participants are less likely to be influenced by factors such as the age, ethnicity, appearance, and (if pseudonyms are used) possibly even the gender of the other participants.
- Similarly, interviewees and focus group participants are less likely to be affected by the characteristics of interviewers or moderators, and the latter are less likely to be affected by the participants' characteristics; in this way, **reactivity** is reduced.
- Online focus groups and interviews allow people to participate in an environment that is "anonymous, safe and non-threatening" (O'Connor & Madge, 2001, p. 11.2); this may be especially helpful for vulnerable groups.
- Similarly, researchers do not need to enter potentially unsafe environments to reach the people they are studying.

Disadvantages

- Online focus groups and interviews take longer than their face-to-face counterparts.
- Only people with access to online facilities and who are comfortable using them are likely to participate.
- It is more difficult for the interviewer to establish rapport with interviewees, though this is less of a problem when the topic is of particular interest to the participants.
- Probing is more difficult, though not impossible. Curasi (2001) reported some success in eliciting further information from respondents, but working online makes it easier for them to ignore or forget about such requests.
- There is less spontaneity in responding since interviewees are able to reflect on their answers more carefully than is possible in a face-to-face situation. However, this can be construed as an advantage in some respects since interviewees are likely to give more considered replies.
- There is a tendency for non-response rates to be higher in online personal interviews.
- The researcher cannot be certain that the participants are who they say they are (though this may sometimes be the case in face-to-face interviews as well).
- Online interviews and focus groups require considerable commitment from interviewees

and participants if they have to install software and remain online for extended periods of time. This is especially problematic if they have to pay for the software (though reimbursement may be possible).

- The interviewer/moderator may not be aware that the interviewee/participant is distracted by something and in such circumstances will continue to ask questions as if they have the person's full attention.
- Online connections may be lost and long breakdowns may ensue, interrupting the flow of the discussion.
- Interviewers cannot rely on body language to tell them when someone is puzzled or (in the case of focus groups) losing interest in the discussion.

Sources: Adapted from Adriaenssens & Cadman (1999); Bampton & Cowton (2002); Clapper & Massey (1996); Curasi (2001); Mann & Stewart (2000); O'Connor & Madge (2001); Sweet (2001); Tse (1999).

seem to be especially well placed to gain insight into social reality in this way, because of their prolonged immersion in the social settings they study. Ethnographers are not only in much closer contact with people for a longer period of time than interviewers are, they also participate in many of the same kinds of activity as the people they are studying. Research that relies on interviewing alone is likely to entail more fleeting contacts, although qualitative research interviews can last many hours and re-interviewing is not unusual.

Learning the local language

Becker and Geer (1957) argue that ethnographers are like social anthropologists visiting a distant land: to understand its culture, they must have a good grasp of its language. To penetrate the culture of a group, it's particularly important to be familiar with its "argot": its informal slang and special uses of words. Learning that informal language takes prolonged observation and interaction with others. See Chapter 12 for more on language analysis.

Things taken for granted

Because interviews rely primarily on the interviewees' accounts of their world, elements of that world that the interviewees take for granted may not be mentioned. For example, a street sex worker may never mention her relationship with the police, and an interviewer may never think to ask about it. By contrast, an ethnographer immersed in the street scene may learn that sex workers have to deal with police surveillance on a regular basis, and that it is an important part of their daily lives.

Deviant and hidden activities

There are certain activities that most people are reluctant to talk about in one-on-one interviews: drug-taking, violence, shoplifting, illegal commerce, hooliganism, and so on. For that reason, much of what is known about criminal and "deviant" subcultures has been gleaned from ethnography. Ethnographers have also uncovered information about workplace resistance practices (such as working-to-rule and industrial sabotage) and have observed groups that support socially unacceptable ideologies, such as white supremacists. Ethnographers are better positioned than interviewers to infiltrate the social worlds of people who are wary of talking to outsiders.

Sensitivity to context and flexibility

Extensive contact with a social setting allows the ethnographer to map the context of people's behaviour. Interacting with people in a variety of different situations makes it possible to connect behaviour and context.

Naturalistic emphasis

Ethnography can be more naturalistic because the researcher confronts members of a social setting in their natural environments. Interviewing, which tends to interrupt the normal flow of events even when it is informal, is often less naturalistic. It's no surprise that when discussing naturalism as a tradition in qualitative research, Gubrium and Holstein (1997) referred mostly to ethnography.

Advantages of qualitative interviewing in comparison to ethnography

Issues resistant to observation

Many issues are simply not open to observation, so asking people about them may be the only way to get information about them. For example, consider domestic violence. Would it be feasible for a researcher to hang around in other people's homes, waiting for the violence to unfold? Reactivity would impinge in a big way, since perpetrators would do their best to hide their violence.

Reconstruction of events and future plans

In-depth reconstruction of past events and plans for future behaviour is not possible through observation alone. Qualitative research entails reconstruction of events when interviewees are asked to think about how a series of previous activities might have created a current situation. Beardsworth and Keil (1992) used the symbolic interactionist notion of *career* to understand how people become vegetarians. In fact, most qualitative studies ask about events that occurred before the study began; for example, questions may be asked about the early family experiences of gang members, recent immigrants, or sex workers. Some call this "retrospective interviewing."

Reactive effects

Reactive effects are by no means straightforward. As with structured observation (see Chapter 6), it can be anticipated that the presence of an ethnographer will lead people to behave unnaturally (although ethnographers, like researchers using structured observation, typically find that their informants become accustomed to their presence and over time begin to behave more naturally). Ethnography also suffers from the related problem that an observer disturbs the very situation under study, sparking conversations and interactions, both with and about the observer, that otherwise would not occur.

Less intrusive in people's lives

Ethnography can be costly in that the researcher is likely to take up more of the participants' time than would be the case with interviews alone. Interviews in qualitative research can sometimes be very long, and as we have noted, re-interviewing is not uncommon. Nevertheless, the impact of undergoing an interview is probably still less than the impact of having to deal with an ethnographer on a regular basis. Ethnography can be especially intrusive in terms of time when it is conducted in organizational settings, because it disrupts the rhythm of the work day and other routine activities.

Longitudinal research easier

Interviewing can be carried out within a longitudinal research design somewhat more easily than ethnography because repeat interviews may be easier to organize than repeat visits to the ethnographer's research settings.

Ethnography can be used for longitudinal studies, but the time that ethnographers can spend away from their normal lives is usually not more than two or three years, and this limits the extent to which an ethnographic study can be longitudinal. When research is conducted on an episodic basis, however, a longer time period may be feasible. Armstrong's (1993) research on soccer hooligans, mentioned in Chapters 9 and 10, entailed six years of participant observation, but since hooliganism was not a full-time occupation for his informants, the research did not require any sustained absence from work or other personal commitments.

Greater breadth of coverage

Interviewing may allow access to a wider variety of people and situations. In ethnographic work, the researcher is invariably limited to a fairly restricted range of people, places, and incidents. An ethnographer observing a large organization, for example, is unlikely to have extensive knowledge of operations outside the area under study.

Specific focus

As we noted in Chapter 9, qualitative research sometimes begins with a specific focus; Silverman (1993) was even critical of the notion that it should be regarded as an open-ended form of research. Qualitative interviewing seems to be better suited for dealing with a specific issue, since an interview can address a particular matter in detail. Research by Bryman, Stephens, & Campo (1996) had a very specific focus: namely, conceptions of leadership among police officers. Because of its clear focus, it was more appropriate to conduct the research using semi-structured interviewing than ethnography, since issues involving leadership are unlikely to emerge naturally on a regular basis.

Overview

When Becker and Geer (1957, p. 28) proclaimed over half a century ago that the "most complete form of the sociological datum . . . is the form in which the participant observer gathers it," Trow (1957, p. 33) reprimanded them for making such a universal claim. He argued that "the problem under investigation properly dictates the methods of investigation." The latter view is very much the one taken in this book. Specific research methods are appropriate for some issues but not for others. Our discussion of the merits and limitations of ethnography versus qualitative interviews is meant to draw attention to some of the factors that researchers should take into account if given the opportunity to choose one method or the other. The points raised can also be used to evaluate existing research.

Checklist

Checklist of issues to consider in qualitative interviewing

- ☐ Have you thought about how you will present yourself in the interview, such as how you will dress?
- ☐ Do you have a clear and comprehensive way of introducing the research to your interviewees and acquiring their informed consent to participate?
- ☐ Does the interview guide clearly relate to the research questions?
- ☐ Has a pilot test been done with some appropriate respondents?
- ☐ Have the interviewers been fully trained?
- ☐ Does the interview guide contain a good mixture of question types (e.g., probing, specifying, and direct questions)?
- ☐ Do the interviews allow novel or unexpected themes and issues to arise?
- ☐ Is the language in the questions free of jargon?
- ☐ Are the questions relevant to the people being interviewed?
- ☐ Have the questions been designed to elicit in-depth responses so that interviewees are not tempted to answer simply "yes" or "no"?
- ☐ Do the questions offer a real prospect of seeing the world from the interviewees' point of view rather than imposing a frame of reference on them?
- ☐ Has the setting in which the interviews will take place been checked out? Has the recording equipment been put through a dry run? Have all aids to be used (e.g., visual aids, film clips, case studies) been pre-tested?
- ☐ Is there a plan in place if the interviewee does not turn up for the interview?

For a focus group:

- ☐ Have you planned what you will do if not all participants turn up for the session?
- ☐ Have the questions been designed to encourage group interaction and discussion?
- ☐ Is there a strategy for dealing with silences and for participants who are reluctant to speak?
- ☐ Is there a strategy for dealing with participants who speak too much and "hog" the discussion?
- ☐ Is there a strategy to follow if the discussion goes off on a tangent?

Key Points

- Interviewing in qualitative research is typically unstructured or semi-structured.
- Qualitative interviewing is meant to be flexible in order to explore the world views of research participants.
- If an interview guide is used, it should allow some flexibility in the way questions are asked.
- Qualitative interviews should be recorded and then transcribed.
- Qualitative interviews can be conducted online.
- The focus group allows the researcher to explore the joint production of meaning.
- The selection of focus group participants requires several decisions, including whether to use natural groups.
- The focus group moderator generally tries to give free rein to the discussion. However, there may be contexts in which it is necessary to ask specific questions.
- Group interaction is an important aspect of focus groups.
- The Internet offers significant opportunities for gaining access to potential focus group participants.
- Whether to use ethnography or qualitative interviews alone depends mainly on the research questions to be addressed. Still, ethnographers usually conduct some interviews in the course of their investigations.

Questions for Review (R) and Creative Application (A)

Differences between structured interviews and qualitative interviews

R1 How does qualitative interviewing differ from structured interviewing?

A1 You've decided to use qualitative interviewing to examine the way varsity athletes view their coaches. Explain how using this form of interviewing would be more advantageous than structured interviewing for this topic.

Unstructured and semi-structured interviewing

R2 What are the differences between unstructured and semi-structured interviewing?

A2 Devise a semi-structured interview guide that could be used to conduct research on what Canadians think about the Black Lives Matter movement. The guide must cover the topic of racism in Canadian society.

R3 Qualitative data may be "co-constructed" by the researcher and the interviewee. What does that mean?

A3 Invent a hypothetical scenario in which the interpretation of an event (e.g., the death of a loved one) emerges out of the interaction between a researcher and an interviewee. The scenario must include at least three exchanges between interviewer and interviewee.

R4 Why is it important to record and transcribe qualitative interviews?

A4 Imagine that you are reviewing a 50-page transcript of an interview you just did, and you realize that the interview ended up covering many issues that you had no intention of examining before the interview began. Explain how this could strengthen your research, then explain how it could be a weakness.

Introduction to focus groups

R5 What advantages can a focus group offer compared to an individual qualitative interview?

A5 Come up with three general topics that would be appropriate for focus group research, and explain how the data generated from focus groups on those topics might differ from what would be produced through individual qualitative interviews.

Conducting focus groups

R6 Are there any circumstances in which it is an advantage to select participants who know each other? Explain.

A6 You've decided to conduct a focus group using university students to explore the topic of cheating on exams. Would it be better to use students who already know each other, or students who don't? Explain.

Group interaction in focus group sessions

R7 Why is it important to examine group interaction when analyzing focus group data?

A7 "The interaction that takes place in a focus group is not more 'natural' than what transpires in a one-on-one qualitative interview." Discuss.

Qualitative research using online personal interviews

R8 What are the pros and cons of doing online personal interviews?

A8 Can online, text-based personal interviews really be personal interviews? To what extent does the absence of direct contact mean that the online interview cannot be a true interview? Explain.

Qualitative research using online focus groups

R9 Is the role of the moderator in online focus groups different from that in the face-to-face variety? Explain.

A9 Online focus groups are appropriate for research involving sensitive issues. Identify three issues that, because of their sensitive nature, would be better researched with online rather than in-person focus groups, then explain why the online technique would be more appropriate.

Qualitative interviewing alone versus ethnography

R10 Outline the advantages and disadvantages of qualitative interviewing (without immersion in a social setting) compared to ethnography.

A10 Is one method more in tune with the research needs of qualitative researchers than the other? Explain, using the topic of intimate partner violence to illustrate your answer.

Interactive Classroom Activities

1. The instructor divides the class into groups of 6–10 people. Each group is to conduct interviews using the focus group method. The group first decides on a general topic (e.g., legalization of marijuana, domestic violence, racism, prevalence of rape culture, climate change, etc.), and then produces a list of five general questions that will be posed by the moderator, who is chosen by group members from within the group. The moderator conducts the focus group interviews with the other members of the group for about 20–30 minutes. When the interviews are finished the class as a whole then reconvenes, with the instructor asking each group:
   a. whether shared meanings and conclusions emerged from their focus group discussions, and if so, to explain what they were and how they developed;
   b. whether the moderator's control of the discussion was excessive, about right, or too weak, and what the consequences of that were;
   c. to explain the advantages of the focus group method compared to one-on-one qualitative interviews for researching the topic chosen;
   d. to explain the disadvantages of the focus group method compared to one-on-one qualitative interviews for researching the topic chosen; and
   e. to explain how the focus group method may be better than structured interviews for exploring the world views of the participants on the topic chosen.

2. Each member of the class is given five minutes to think of a general topic that would be appropriate for a semi-structured, one-on-one qualitative interview (e.g., views on gay marriage, how the Internet impacts one's life, life goals and how they might be achieved, etc.). Each person then constructs a five-point interview guide that could be used in a semi-structured interview. The instructor then uses a random method to pair students up so they can take turns interviewing each other on their selected topics. Each interview is to last for a minimum of 15 minutes. When the

interviews are completed, the class as a whole reconvenes for a general discussion of:

a. difficulties in getting the interview to flow smoothly, and how those difficulties may be resolved;
b. illustrations of how topics that were not on the interview guide made their way into the interview anyway, and how that helped or hindered the investigation of the topic; and
c. the sorts of topics that could be usefully researched using semi-structured interviews, and which topics would be better pursued using ethnography or structured interviews.

Relevant Websites

A YouTube video of a ***qualitative interview*** uses the life history approach to examine the experiences of a Holocaust survivor.

www.youtube.com/watch?v=-jJ6s7ob_Dg

A YouTube video of a ***focus group*** discusses university student involvement in extracurricular activities.

https://www.youtube.com/watch?v=I5CYg08Abvw

A YouTube video demonstrates how to moderate a ***focus group***.

www.youtube.com/watch?v=xjHZsEcSqwo

A YouTube video offers tips for moderating online ***focus groups***, with comparisons to in-person ***focus groups***.

https://www.youtube.com/watch?v=KlCDgVCQRNg

A YouTube video provides basic tips on ***qualitative interviewing***.

www.youtube.com/watch?v=LPwO-vOVxD4

A YouTube video demonstrates the use of ***semi-structured interviewing*** as a ***Participatory Action Research*** method.

https://www.youtube.com/watch?v=cGQz8hZQ8fU

(Websites accessed 4 September 2021)

OXFORD learning link More resources are available on Oxford Learning Link. Visit https://learninglink.oup.com/ for:

- Student self-quiz
- Flash cards
- Audio clips
- Videos
- Activities

12 Content Analysis

Chapter Overview

Content analysis involves the examination of various documents and **texts**, which may be printed, visual, aural, or virtual. It can be **quantitative**, focused on **coding** data into predetermined categories in a systematic and easily **replicable** manner, or **qualitative**, seeking to uncover deeper meanings in the materials. Although both approaches are discussed, this chapter deals primarily with the qualitative variety. It considers:

- the kinds of research question that content analysis can answer;
- the features of documents or texts that are commonly analyzed;
- how to code (a key part of content analysis);
- **semiotics** and **hermeneutics**;
- active and passive audiences;
- **conversation analysis** and its roots in **ethnomethodology**;
- the assumptions and analytic strategies of **discourse analysis**, including **critical discourse analysis**; and
- the advantages and disadvantages of content analysis.

Key Learning Outcomes

Here is a list of goals you should try to achieve as you read and think about the material in this chapter. After completing this chapter, you should be able to:

1. Describe how content analyses can be conducted quantitatively and qualitatively and list the criteria social researchers use to assess the quality of documents to be used as data.
2. Discuss the different types of documents researchers use for conducting content analyses and compare the strengths and limitations of these data sources.

▲ selimaksan/iStockphoto

3. Describe how words, subjects and themes, and value positions are analyzed within documents.
4. Explain how content analysts code their data with or without pre-existing coding schemes.
5. Discuss the different positions in the debate about audiences actively or passively consuming messages they see and hear.
6. Compare conversation analysis and discourse analysis as distinctive approaches for studying language.
7. Identify the advantages and disadvantages of content analysis.

Rebecca and her boyfriend, Daniel, were sitting at home watching TV on a Saturday night. Neither was in a particularly good mood; both thought there must be a more exciting way to spend the weekend. "Have you ever noticed that there are way more food commercials—burgers, pizza, chicken—at night than in the daytime?" Rebecca asked. "Are there?" Daniel replied. "I know hockey games always seem to come with a lot of beer ads."

"You ever notice how the women look in those ads?" Rebecca fumed. "They're always in bathing suits or shorts, even if they're standing on a ski hill in winter. And by some miracle they all have perfect bodies." "Yeah," said Daniel. "It's a little different with the guys. A lot of them look like dorks, doing stupid things. But some guys look cool, and they're the ones who get the girls. They're better-looking and taller than the dorks." "We could probably do a study comparing men and women in beer commercials," Rebecca said, her mood beginning to lighten. "We could even throw in a comparison with detergent ads. Ever see a man selling detergent?" "You could do that," Daniel said. "You'd just have to find a way to categorize the portrayals—flattering or unflattering, active or passive, the age of the people, how attractive they are, overtly sexual or non-sexual behaviour—that kind of thing." "That wouldn't be too hard to do," Rebecca answered. "Sounds like a lot more fun than watching this stupid stuff."

Introduction

There can be similarities between quantitative and qualitative approaches to social research, and even where there are differences the two orientations can sometimes be combined or at least used in a complementary fashion. Content analysis in some ways is a blend of the two. It examines forms of communication to see what they reveal about a society, a culture, or even the relationships between individuals. Meanings and interpretations are important aspects of content analysis, but so is formal categorization of the communications, which often includes some quantification. For example, suppose you are interested in how newspapers cover crime. You come up with the following questions:

- Do certain newspapers report more crimes than others?
- How much crime is reported? Where in the paper do crime stories appear—on the front page, or inside?
- Do columnists as well as reporters write about crime?
- Are some crimes given more attention than others?
- Do more crime stories appear during the week or on weekends?
- What sorts of crime predominate in newspaper articles (crimes against the person, property crime, crimes in which society is the victim)?

Most content analysis of the media is likely to entail several research questions, generally revolving around the same five W's that are the basis of any news report: *who* (does the reporting); *what* (gets reported); *where* (does the issue get reported); *why* (does the issue get reported); and *when* (does it get reported). But researchers are also interested in what media coverage omits. For example, interviews with the family of the accused are rare; such inattention is itself notable, revealing what is and is not important to writers and publishers.

Another common theme in content analysis is change in the coverage of an issue over time. For example, Buchanan (2014) found that in the period 1894–2005 there was a significant decrease in the amount of local news featured in the *Toronto Star* and the *Ottawa Citizen*, and that both papers had increased their national news coverage over this period.

Content analyses of this kind yield a predominantly quantitative description of the characteristics of a communication. Those who perform content analysis in this way claim to be objective and systematic, clearly specifying the rules for the categorization of the material in advance. Researchers try to create transparency in the coding procedures so that personal biases intrude as little as possible. The coding rules in question may, of course, reflect the researcher's interests and concerns and therefore be a product of subjective bias to some degree, but once the rules have been formulated, it should be possible to apply them without bias.

Content analysis can be performed on unstructured information, such as transcripts of semi- and unstructured interviews, and even qualitative case studies of organizations (for example, Hodson, 1996). Until recently it was used mainly to examine printed texts and documents, but other sorts of materials may also be analyzed. If you were interested in gender roles or representations, for example, you might look at:

- differences in the degree to which men and women are sexualized on the covers of popular magazines (Hatton & Trautner, 2013);
- pictures on social media (e.g., how parents portray their children's gender on Instagram) (Choi & Lewallen, 2018);
- profiles on dating sites and apps (Wada, Hurd Clarke, & Mortenson, 2019);
- animated cartoons (Thompson & Zerbinos, 1995); and
- lyrics of popular songs (e.g., to look for changes in the representation of women) (Marcic, 2002).

Here we will call all such materials "documents," and define them as any data source that:

- can be "read" (including visual materials such as photographs); and
- was *not* produced specifically for the purpose of social research.

Documents are important because they are unobtrusive and non-**reactive**. The fact that the subjects don't know they are being studied removes a common threat to the **validity** of the data.

In discussing the different kinds of documents used in social science, Scott (1990) distinguished between personal and official documents and, within the latter group, between private and state documents. These distinctions are used in much of the discussion that follows. Scott also enumerated four criteria for assessing the quality of documents (p. 6):

- *Authenticity.* Is the evidence genuine and of unquestionable origin?
- *Credibility.* Is the evidence free from error and distortion?
- *Representativeness.* Is the evidence typical of what it is supposed to represent (for example, social life at a particular time and place)? If not, is the extent of its uniqueness known?
- *Meaning.* Is the evidence clear and comprehensible?

Note that this use of "authenticity" is different from how the term was used in Chapter 9 to assess qualitative research.

Personal documents

Diaries, letters, and autobiographies

Diaries and letters are often used by historians, but they have been given less attention by other social researchers (see Box 12.1). Whereas letters are written to communicate with other people, diarists presumably write for themselves. When written for wider consumption, diaries are difficult to distinguish from another kind of personal document: the autobiography. Used with a **life history** or **biographical method**, diaries, letters, and autobiographies (whether solicited or unsolicited) can be either primary sources of data or adjuncts to other sources such as life story interviews. However, this chapter is primarily concerned with unsolicited documents.

The distinction between biographies and autobiographies can sometimes break down. Walt Disney provides a case in point. The first biography of Disney, written by his daughter, Diane Disney Miller (1956), almost certainly included information from Mr Disney himself. Subsequent biographies were very similar, because of the tight control exercised by the Walt Disney Corporation over the primary materials in the Disney archive (letters, notes of meetings, and so on) out of which the biographies were fashioned. As a consequence, even though Walt Disney never wrote an autobiography in the conventional meaning of the term, he (and, later, his company) clearly controlled what was written about him.

In evaluating personal documents, the *authenticity* criterion is obviously important. Is the purported author of the letter or diary the real author? In the case of autobiographies, the increasing use of "ghost" writers has made this a standard question. But the same kind of problem can arise with other documents. For example, in the case of Augustus Lamb (Box 12.1), Dickinson (1993,) noted that there are "only three letters existing from Augustus himself (which one cannot be certain were written in Augustus's own hand, since the use of amanuenses was not uncommon)" (pp. 126–127). This raises the question of whether Augustus was in fact the author of the letters, especially in the light of his apparent learning difficulties.

Turning to the issue of *credibility*, Scott (1990) observed that there are at least two major concerns with respect to personal documents: their factual accuracy and whether they express the true thoughts and feelings of the writer. The case of Augustus Lamb suggests that a definitive, factually accurate account is at the very least problematic. Scott recommended a healthy skepticism regarding the sincerity with which the writer reports his or her feelings. Famous people who are aware that their letters or diaries will

Box 12.1 | Using historical personal documents: The case of Augustus Lamb

Dickinson (1993) provided an interesting account of the use of historical personal documents in the case of Augustus Lamb (1807–36), the only child of the novelist Lady Caroline Lamb and her husband, the second Viscount Melbourne, who was prime minister of the UK from 1834 to 1841. It is possible that Augustus suffered from epilepsy, though he seems to have had other medical problems as well throughout his short life. Dickinson was drawn to him because of her interest in nineteenth-century reactions to non-institutionalized people with mental disabilities. In fact, Dickinson doubted that Augustus was mentally disabled, and suggested the somewhat milder diagnosis of "learning difficulties." At the same time, she found that the people around him had difficulty coming to terms with his conditions, in large part because of the challenge of finding words to describe him that were consistent with his high social status.

The chief sources of data were "letters from family and friends; letters to, about and (rarely) from Augustus" (p. 122). Other sources included the record of the post-mortem examination conducted on his remains and extracts from the diary of his resident tutor and physician for the years 1817–21. Despite the many sources she consulted, Dickinson still could not conclude with certainty that she understood definitively what Augustus was like.

West7megan/Dreamstime.com/GetStock

What sorts of dilemmas do you face if you use historical personal documents as primary sources for research?

be of interest to others may be very careful about how much of themselves they reveal in their writings. Similarly, adolescent diary-keepers are often aware that their parents could "accidentally" read what they write. In short, what is *not* said can be of great importance. A particularly poignant illustration is Sugiman's (2004) suggestion that the reason many Japanese-Canadian women interned during the Second World War did not write down their experiences was to shield their children from that painful episode in their family histories.

Representativeness is clearly a major concern in assessing these materials. Since literacy rates were very low in the past, letters, diaries, and autobiographies were largely the preserve of a small class of wealthy, literate people. Moreover, because boys were more likely to receive an education than girls, the voices of women tended to be under-represented in documents of that kind. Some researchers also argue that in the past it was less socially acceptable for women than men to write diaries and autobiographies. Therefore, such historical documents are likely to be biased in terms of their applicability to the society as a whole.

A further problem is the selective survival of documents like letters. What proportion are damaged, lost, or thrown away? How representative are suicide notes of the thoughts and feelings of all suicide victims? It seems that only a relatively small percentage of suicide victims leave notes, and some of the notes that are written may be destroyed by the victims' relatives, especially if they contain accusations against family members.

Finally, understanding the meaning of the documents we do have is often problematic. Some pages in a letter or diary may be missing or damaged, or the writer may have used abbreviations or codes that are difficult to decipher. Also, as Scott (1990) observed, letter writers tend to leave much unsaid when they take it for granted that the people they are writing to have the same values, assumptions, and information as they do.

Researchers often have to search long and hard for new or surprising materials in diaries. However, this was not the case with the diaries of William Lyon Mackenzie King. When the King diaries were first released to the public in the 1970s, they caused a sensation (see Box 12.2).

Box 12.2 | The Mackenzie King diaries

William Lyon Mackenzie King was prime minister of Canada for 21 of the 27 years between 1921 and 1948. He was an avid diarist for most of his life, recording his thoughts and feelings about both personal issues and national and international events. The contents of the diaries suggest that he did not expect them to be made public. They reveal his political views in considerable detail, but also a side of the man that shocked many people when the transcripts were released. King believed strongly in psychic phenomena and spiritualism—he attended séances, consulted mediums, and believed that he was in communication with various deceased persons, including Franklin Delano Roosevelt and his own mother. He also believed that he could commune with his deceased dog, Pat. (To place these revelations in their proper historical context, the practice of spiritualism was quite common when King was a young man in the late nineteenth and early twentieth centuries.) Sensationalism aside, the King diaries are a valuable primary source of information for a significant portion of Canadian and world history.

Nevertheless, the publication of the King diaries does raise ethical questions. Is it a violation of privacy rights to publish or quote from someone's diary, especially if the person is deceased and cannot raise objections? King's diaries are now available online at Library and Archives Canada: https://www.bac-lac.gc.ca/eng/discover/politics-government/prime-ministers/william-lyon-mackenzie-king/Pages/diaries-william-lyon-mackenzie-king.aspx (accessed 4 September 2021).

Visual objects

There is a growing interest in the use of visual materials, especially photographs, in social research (see Box 12.3). One of the main reasons why photographs are of interest to social researchers is their potential to reveal important information about families.

As Scott (1990) observed, many family photos are taken as records of ceremonial occasions such as weddings and graduations, or of recurring events such as reunions and holidays. Scott distinguished three types of home photograph: *idealization* (a formal portrait of a wedding party or the family in its finery); *natural portrayal* (an informal snapshot capturing

Box 12.3 | Photographs in social research

Photographs can play a variety of roles in social research. They can be used in qualitative research, as well as in surveys and experiments. Three prominent roles photographs can play are the following:

- ***As illustrations.*** Photographs may be used to illustrate points and thus to enliven what might otherwise be rather dry discussions of findings. This was certainly the case with some classic reports by anthropologists.
- ***As data.*** Photographs may be data in their own right. When produced for research purposes, they essentially become part of the researcher's field notes. When based on extant photographs, they may become the main source of data about the field in which the researcher is interested, as in the work of Blaikie (2001) and Sutton (1992, see Box 12.4). Mannay (2018) points out that photographs can be particularly useful in providing data about everyday life in spaces that are often off limits for sustained observation, such as people's homes.
- ***As prompts.*** Photographs may be used as prompts to entice people to talk about what they see in them. Both researcher-created photographs and previously existing ones may be used in this way. Sometimes research participants may volunteer their own photographs. For example, Riches and Dawson (1998) found in their interviews with bereaved parents that many parents showed them pictures of their deceased children, likely the same pictures they had shown to neighbours and friends when they were first grieving their loss.

JD Moodie/Library and Archives Canada/C-001823

This photo of Niviaqsarjuk (left), Suzie (centre), and Jennie (right) was taken by Geraldine Moody at Fullerton (in what is now Nunavut) in 1904, although the names of the women depicted were unknown to Library and Archives Canada until 2002. How might photos like this one be used as data? What issues around representation or ethics might arise when Indigenous cultures are represented by people who are not community members? How might community consultation help mitigate these issues?

action as it happens, though there may be a contrived component); and *demystification* (depicting the subject in an atypical—often embarrassing—situation). Scott suggested that researchers need to be aware of these different types in order to avoid being deceived by the superficial appearance of images. One must probe beneath the surface:

> There is a great deal that photographs do not tell us about their world. Hirsch [1981, p. 42] argued, for example, that "The prim poses and solemn faces which we associate with Victorian photography conceal the reality of child labour, women factory workers, whose long hours often brought about the neglect of their infants, nannies sedating their charges with rum, and mistresses diverting middle class fathers." (Scott, 1990, p. 195)

As Scott argued, this means not only that the photograph must not be taken at face value when used as a research source, but that the viewer must have considerable knowledge of the social context in order to get its full meaning. Sutton (1992) makes a similar point in Box 12.4. In fact, we may wonder whether photographs in such situations can be of any use to a researcher. At the same time, a researcher's interpretations should not be accepted uncritically. For example, the "prim poses and solemn faces" of Victorian portraits might well "conceal" a bleak and miserable reality; but is that all? Could they not also conceal moments of human warmth or compassion? Or fun?

A particular problem for the analyst of photographs, according to Scott, is judging *representativeness*. Photos that survive the passage of time—in archives, for example—are very unlikely to be representative for the simple reason that somebody at some time decided they should be preserved. The discussion in Box 12.4 suggests that decisions about which photos to keep or post online may reflect the needs and biases of the people who make those decisions. Another problem relates to the issue of what is *not* photographed, as suggested by Sutton's idea that unhappy events at Disney theme parks may not be photographed at all. Awareness of what is not photographed can reveal the "mentality" of the person(s) behind the camera. It's clear that the question of representativeness is much more fundamental than the issue of what survives, because it points to how the selective survival of photographs may be part of a reality that family members (or others) deliberately seek to fashion. As in Sutton's example, that manufactured reality itself may then become a focus of interest for the social researcher.

Government documents

The state is a source of much information of potential significance for social researchers. It produces a great deal of quantitative statistical information. For example, Bell, Jansen, & Young (2007) used government voting records as well as census information to analyze the issue of one-party dominance in Alberta. The state is also the source of a great deal of textual material of potential interest, such as official reports. For instance, in his study of the issues surrounding synthetic bovine growth hormone, Jones (2000) used transcripts of a Canadian senate inquiry on the topic. Briefly, Monsanto, the manufacturer, lost the battle to have the hormone accepted for use; health groups claimed that it was unnecessary and, worse, that it posed a health risk both to cows and to the humans who drank their milk. Abraham (1994) used similar materials in his research on the role of self-interest and values in scientists' evaluations of the safety of medicines, specifically the drug Opren. The author described his sources as "publicly available transcripts of the testimonies of scientists, including many employed in the manufacture of *Opren*, Parliamentary debates, questions and answers in *Hansard*, and leaflets, letters, consultation papers and other documentation disposed by the [drug regulatory authority]" (Abraham, 1994, p. 720). His research showed inconsistencies in the scientists' testimonies, suggesting that self-interest can play an important role in such situations. He also used his findings to argue that the scientific ethos of "objectivity" has limited applicability in areas where self-interest may be a factor.

In terms of Scott's (1990) four criteria, such materials can certainly be seen as authentic and as

Box 12.4 | Photographs of the Magic Kingdom

Sutton (1992) noted a paradox about visitors to Disney theme parks. The Magic Kingdom is supposed to be "the happiest place on Earth," and employees ("cast members") are trained to enhance visitors' experiences. Yet it is clear that some people do not enjoy themselves while visiting. Time spent waiting in lines is a particularly common gripe for "guests" (Bryman, 1995). Nonetheless, because people expect their visit to be momentous, they take photographs that support their assumption that Disney theme parks are happy places. When they return home, they "discard photographs that remind them of unpleasant experiences and keep those that remind them of pleasant experiences" (Sutton, 1992, p. 283). In other words, positive feelings about an experience may be a post hoc reconstruction, substantially aided by the photos that are not thrown away or deleted. Thus, photographs may provide an incomplete, somewhat distorted record.

Similar observations can be made with regard to pictures posted on social media. How common is it to see Instagram photographs of people having unpleasant experiences on their holidays? With social media, the purpose of photo-assisted reconstruction seems to be expanding: Now photos may be used not only to create happy memories, but also to present a public image of oneself as a fun-loving, interesting person. Clearly, holiday photos represent more than an objective account of a vacation.

PamelaJoeMcFarlane/iStockphoto

This family seems to be enjoying their vacation, but should we conclude that their holiday was fun in every respect? How can the knowledge that a photo may not provide a complete record of an event or experience affect how we approach the use of photographs as data?

having meaning (in that they are clear and comprehensible to the researcher). However, the credibility criterion requires us to consider whether the documentary source is biased. This is exactly the point of Abraham's (1994) research: such documents can be interesting precisely because of the bias they reveal. Equally, this point suggests that caution is necessary in attempting to treat them as depictions of reality.

Official documents from private sources

Official documents available from "private sources" vary widely, but a common category is company documents. Companies (and organizations generally) produce many documents, some of which are in the public domain; the latter include annual reports, press releases, advertisements, and public relations material both in printed form and on the Web. Other documents, such as company newsletters, organizational charts, minutes of meetings, memos, correspondence (internal and external), and manuals for new recruits, may not be accessible to the public. This kind of material is often used by organizational ethnographers in their investigations, but the difficulty of gaining access to it means that many other researchers have to rely on public domain documents. Even if the researcher is an insider with the organization, certain private documents may remain inaccessible.

Private documents also need to be evaluated using Scott's four criteria. As with the materials considered in the previous section, documents deriving from private sources such as companies are likely to be authentic and meaningful (in the sense of being clear and comprehensible to the researcher). However, issues of credibility and representativeness are still likely to require scrutiny.

People who write documents generally want to convey a particular point of view. An interesting illustration is provided by Forster's (1994) study of career development issues in a major retail company. Forster analyzed company documentation as well as interviews and a questionnaire. Because he was able to interview many of the authors of the documents, "both the accuracy of the documents and their authorship could be validated by the individuals who had produced them" (p. 155). In other words, the authenticity of the documents was confirmed and apparently the credibility as well. However, Forster also said that the documents revealed divergent interpretations of key events and processes:

> One of the clearest themes to emerge was the apparently incompatible interpretations of the same events and processes among the three sub-groups within the company—senior executives, HQ personnel staff, and regional personnel managers. . . . These documents were not produced deliberately to distort or obscure events or processes being described, but their effect was to do precisely this. (p. 160)

The perspectives that members of the different groupings expressed in the documents reflected their positions in the organization. Consequently, although the authors of the documents were able to confirm their authenticity, their contents could not be regarded as "free from error and distortion," as Scott put it. In other words, the accounts that documents provide may not be completely objective. They have to be analyzed critically and compared with other sources of data. As Forster's study suggests, the different stances taken by the authors of documents can be used to develop insights into the processes and factors that lie behind their creation.

Issues of representativeness are also important. Did Forster have access to a complete set of documents? It could be that some had been destroyed, or that he was not allowed access to certain sensitive ones. This is not to say that such documents necessarily exist, but a healthy skepticism is often warranted.

Mass media outputs

Newspapers, magazines, television programs, films, and other mass media are potential sources for social scientific analysis. For example, Parnaby's (2003) study of how Toronto tried to deal with its squeegee kids examined 200 newspaper articles that appeared between 1995 and 2000. Hallgrimsdottir, Phillips, & Benoit (2006) looked at how newspapers in Victoria, BC, characterized sex-trade workers in the province, while Harding (2006; 2010) analyzed press coverage of Indigenous people and their institutions. Dumitrica and Bakardjieva (2018) examined how Canadian newspapers construct the role played by social media in civic engagement. Bhuyan, Jeyapal, Ku, Sakamoto, & Chou (2017) used documents published by Citizenship and Immigration Canada as well as articles from the *Toronto Star*, the *Globe and Mail*, and the *National Post* to investigate how the use of language in those sources is related to the development of social ideologies and the implementation of government policies on immigration. All of these studies are examples of **critical discourse analysis** (discussed later in this chapter) in that they examined the social and political implications of the materials they examined, an approach that can be taken with virtually any medium of communication.

Films, television shows, and magazines have similar potential for research. For example, when Coté and Allahar (1994) examined magazines aimed at adolescents, they concluded that these "teenzines" turned adolescents into uncritical consumers and diverted them from protesting against their lack of adult privileges.

Authenticity is sometimes difficult to ascertain in the case of mass media outputs. The authors are not always identified, as in the case of a TV news report, so it is sometimes difficult to know whether a given

Research in the News

Tracking the gender gap in Canadian online news sources

Shari Graydon's non-profit organization, Informed Opinions, aims to promote women's voices to enhance democracy. Collaborating with a group of researchers from Simon Fraser University, Graydon and her team are examining the gender gap in Canadian online news coverage (Graydon, 2019). To do so, they are harnessing the power of big data (see Chapter 8) to track, in real time, the ratio of males to females quoted online as sources by Canadian news outlets. Their digital monitoring system, the Gender Gap Tracker, "analyzes in microseconds what it used to take researchers hours to assess" (Graydon, 2019). The tool, in effect, offers an ongoing content analysis of the gender gap by news outlet. The aggregate data from October 2018 onward shows that women's voices accounted for 26 per cent of those quoted by major Canadian news outlets. Graydon (2019) points out, "For context, that's a mere four-point increase over data we collected almost three decades ago." She hopes that making the tracker publicly accessible will help promote change, but acknowledges that the tool is just one piece of the puzzle: "To make a difference, journalists need to actively seek to improve the data—and news consumers need to give them reasons to do so." The Gender Gap Tracker can be accessed online at https://gendergaptracker.informedopinions.org.

account was prepared by someone in a position to know all the facts. Credibility is frequently an issue, and as the examples used in this section show, it is often the uncovering of error or distortion that is the objective of the analysis. Representativeness may not be an issue with newspaper or magazine articles, since many publications make a point of maintaining a consistent tone or ideological bent. Finally, although the literal meaning of mass media outputs is often clear, it usually takes some reflection and theoretical analysis to appreciate the broader societal impact these forms of communication can have.

Virtual outputs and the Internet as objects of analysis

"Text" is a word that has up to this point been used sparingly in this chapter. It originally referred to a written document, but in recent years it has been applied to an increasingly wide range of phenomena including theme parks, technologies, paintings, and buildings. Contemporary writers and researchers regard such "texts" as materials that can be interpreted to produce "readings."

Websites and webpages are further examples of "texts" that can be "read." The vastness of the Internet and its accessibility make it a valuable source of documents for both quantitative and qualitative data analysis. Hier (2000), for example, examined a Toronto-based racial supremacy website and found that it allowed people access to racist ideas in a relatively anonymous way (e.g., without having to subscribe to a hard-copy newsletter). For that reason, he feared that it might be more successful in reaching ordinary citizens than non-Internet sources would be. Johnston, Sanscartier, and Johnston conducted qualitative content analyses exploring the online ratings of Canadian psychiatrists (M.S. Johnston, 2020), retail employers (Johnston, Sanscartier, & Johnston, 2019), and food service employers (Johnston, Sanscartier, & Johnston, 2018). Drawing on patient and employee reviews from the websites RateMDs.com and RateMyEmployer.ca, they make a case for how virtual spaces provide opportunities for resistance and discourse about healthcare and workplace issues that might otherwise be suppressed.

The use of images on websites can also be quite revealing. Crook and Light (2002) analyzed the photographs in 10 university prospectuses and found that although there were many photos of students apparently studying, the setting was rarely a library carrel or a dorm room. Instead, students were usually shown in "social" learning situations that allowed them to appear active and engaged, frequently out of doors. The authors argued that those less typical learning contexts were chosen because they are more seductive. In a study of Web-based family photography, Pauwels (2008) concluded that digital technology has made it easier for families to "construct fictions and fantasies" and to project their values and norms than was the case when paper-based family albums were more common.

Other forms of Internet-based communication, such as email lists, discussion groups, and chat rooms, have also been used as objects of analysis. For their study of online social support groups, Nettleton, Pleace, Burrows, Muncer, & Loader (2002) examined the interactions between people who use those sorts of virtual communications. Similarly, social media such as Facebook, Instagram, Twitter, and YouTube have been analyzed by social researchers. For instance, Lalancette and Raynauld (2019) studied Justin Trudeau's use of Instagram during his first year as prime minister. They found that his embrace of social media helped Trudeau present himself as a happily married and loving husband and father, and as a leader comfortable in both informal and formal settings. Such framing conveyed a personal image in keeping with his "sunny ways" campaign to reintroduce a positive approach to politics. O'Connor (2017) studied how Canadian police departments use Twitter to share information and interact with the public. He points out that social networking sites allow police departments to bypass the news media in getting their message directly to the public. This not only helps increase police visibility and build a sense of community with citizens, it affords departments greater control in managing their public image.

Websites and other online data sources clearly have huge potential, but it's important to keep Scott's criteria in mind. First, authenticity: anyone can set up a website, so you have no guarantee that a person offering information (such as financial advice) is an authority. Second, credibility: is the information on the site credible, or might it be distorted for some reason? For example, a site that encourages you to buy stock held by its author might exaggerate its value. Third, given the constant flux of the Internet, it's doubtful that one can ever know how representative websites on a certain topic are. New websites are continually appearing, others disappearing, still others being modified. Online searching is like trying to hit a target that is not only moving but also in a constant state of metamorphosis. In a related vein, any one search engine can provide access to only a portion of the Web; there is evidence that even the combined use of several search engines gives access to just under half of the sites that exist, and there is no way of knowing if they are a biased sample. Finally, websites are notorious for a kind of "webspeak" that makes it difficult to comprehend what is being said without some insider knowledge.

Practical Tip | Referring to Websites

It has become common practice in academic work, when referring to websites, to include the date they were consulted. This convention is closely associated with the fact that websites often disappear and frequently change, so that if subsequent researchers want to check or follow up a Web reference, they may find that the site has changed or even disappeared. Citing the date(s) the site was visited can help to relieve anxieties about citing Web sources.

Researchers basing their investigations on websites need to recognize these limitations as well as the opportunities available. Scott's suggestions invite consideration of why a website was constructed in the first place: for commercial reasons? Political reasons? In other words, you should be no less skeptical about websites than about any other kind of document. Employing both traditional printed documents and website materials will allow you to cross-validate sources.

Beyond Scott's criteria

So far, most of the biases discussed in the context of Scott's criteria have been of the personal type—someone may write a flattering if somewhat unrealistic autobiography, pictures for public display may be chosen in order to create a favourable impression, and so on. Keep in mind that there may be larger cultural and political biases involved in the creation and use of any type of text or document. Hales (2006), for example, points out that a colonialist mentality often pervades research conducted on subject or subordinated peoples. Where there is a power differential between the researcher and those who are being studied, Hales notes that one would do well to ask, "Why is the research done? How is it done? Who defines, initiates and conducts the research? On/with/for whom is the research carried out? What topics are addressed? Who benefits and how? Who interprets for whom and who represents whom?" (p. 243). Many sources of information, including much of the research in the social sciences, serves some larger if unstated political or cultural purpose. Kempf (2006), for example, in an analysis of history textbooks and Ontario Ministry of Education guidelines from 1860 to 2006, concludes that a lot of this material showed a disrespect for Indigenous perspectives and ways of knowing, and in effect provided a rationalization for the mistreatment of Indigenous Canadians.

What things need to be analyzed?

Obviously, what is to be analyzed depends on the specific research questions. In mainly quantitative studies, these elements are usually specified in advance in order to guide both the selection of the media to be assessed and the construction of the coding schedule. They usually include words, subjects and themes, and value positions, as discussed next.

Words

Determining the frequency with which certain words are used is often the first step in content analysis. Jagger (1998), for example, searched dating

Checklist

Checklist for evaluating documents

Have the following questions been answered?

- ☐ Who produced the document?
- ☐ Why was the document produced?
- ☐ Was the person or group who produced the document in a position to write authoritatively about the subject?
- ☐ Is the material genuine?
- ☐ Did the author have an axe to grind or a particular slant to promote?
- ☐ Is the document typical of its kind? If not, is it possible to establish how atypical it is and in what ways?
- ☐ Is the meaning of the document clear?
- ☐ Can the events or accounts presented in the document be corroborated?
- ☐ Are there different interpretations of the document from the one you offer? If so, what are they? Have you discounted them? If so, why?

advertisements and counted words such as "slim" and "non-smoker" to compare women and men with respect to what each deemed desirable in a date (see Box 12.5). Simple counting of particular words can reveal emphasis, style of writing or presentation, and even the overplaying of certain events. For example, Dunning, Murphy, & Williams (1988) noted a tendency for the British press to sensationalize disturbances at soccer matches by using emotive words such as "hooligans" and "louts" to refer to audience members, and terms such as "battle" to refer to a game; less dramatic terms such as "fans" or "contest" would have encouraged more neutral responses among readers.

A variation on the search for individual keywords is the search for pairings of keywords. The growing availability of the written news media online greatly facilitates this kind of search. Hier (2002) found "rave" and "drug use" to be frequently linked, which may have encouraged readers to believe that raves must be controlled. Parnaby (2003), on the other hand, noted that "squeegee kids" and "homelessness" were not paired, even though many of the "kids" were in fact homeless; as a result of this omission, he argued, the "kids" were constructed "as a social problem requiring a law and order resolution" (p. 281). The search for pairings of keywords can be a starting point for a more in-depth analysis.

Subjects and themes

A more interpretative approach is required to code text in terms of subjects and themes. At this point, the analyst is searching not just for the obvious or *manifest* content, but also for some of the underlying or *latent* content as well. This occurs if the researcher wants to probe beneath the surface to ask deeper questions about what is happening. In reports on crime, for example, is the victim blamed along with the accused? Is the occupation of the accused or the victim stated? If not, is it implied in an address or a picture? Why is it that news stories about men who have been mugged sometimes mention their marital status? In seeking to answer these sorts of questions, the quantitative aspects of content analysis can serve as a starting point for a study in which qualitative research becomes the central focus of the endeavour.

Value positions

A further level of interpretation is likely when the researcher is seeking to demonstrate that the writer of a particular text has taken a certain value position. For example, is a journalist who writes about crime sympathetic or hostile to the accused? Is all the blame put on the accused, with the implication that punishment is appropriate? Or is the focus on social conditions, with the assumption that less blame should be placed on the criminal? If there is no manifest indication of the writer's value positions, can inferences be made from the latent content?

Another way in which content analysis can reveal value positions is through the coding of ideologies, beliefs, and principles. For instance, Sturgeon and Morrissette (2010) examined suicide ideation among Manitoba farmers who called a rural crisis line. The data were gathered from forms that were filled out by the crisis line counsellors (which are similar in design to the coding manual depicted in Figure 12.2). One of the themes that emerged as codes were developed was "family salvation," which involved the belief that life is worth living if one has meaningful relationships with family members. "I just keep going because I think someday my son will need me," said one farmer (p. 199). Surprisingly, only a small proportion of farmers mentioned their spouses or life partners as the people who made their lives bearable; others such as siblings, children, and extended family members were more likely to be cited.

Coding

As the foregoing has implied, coding is a crucial part of content analysis. There are two main elements to a content analysis coding scheme: designing a coding schedule and creating a **coding manual**. To illustrate, imagine that you are interested in crime reports in a local newspaper. To simplify, assume that your study is limited to crimes where the victim is a person rather than an organization, and that it considers these variables:

1. nature of the offence(s)
2. gender of suspect
3. occupation of suspect

Box 12.5 | Finding love: Then and now

Jagger (1998) reported a content analysis of 1094 dating advertisements in four newspapers with a general readership. The sample was chosen over two four-week periods in 1996. Three research questions drove the study:

- What is "the relative significance of monetary resources and lifestyle choices as identity markers and desirable attributes for men and women"?
- How do men and women vary in the ways they choose to market themselves and describe their preferred (or ideal) partners in terms of the body?
- To what extent are "traditional stereotypes of masculinity and femininity . . . still in operation"? (p. 799)

Jagger noted the tendency for considerable percentages of both men and women to market themselves in terms of their lifestyle choices (film preferences, clubs frequented, sports activities, etc.). She also found that women were far more likely than men to stress the importance of economic and other resources in a preferred partner. There was also a somewhat greater propensity for women to market themselves in terms of physical appearance. As an aside, men were just as likely to market themselves as "slim," suggesting that certain preferences in body shape were not exclusive to one gender. More generally, her results pointed to the significance of the body in identity construction for both men and women. In a later publication, Jagger (2001) reported the findings from a qualitative content analysis of a sub-sample of the 1094 advertisements.

Much has changed in the years since Jagger did her research. Internet dating sites and apps such as Match and Tinder have eclipsed the classified newspaper advertisement as the mediums of choice for people whose in-person activities do not provide adequate opportunities to meet a romantic partner. Since space is not at a premium, digital platforms allow participants to give far more information than was the case with newspaper ads, and of course the provision of photographs means that verbal descriptions of physical appearance have become far less important than

4. age of suspect
5. gender of victim
6. occupation of victim
7. age of victim
8. depiction of victim
9. position of news item in the paper

Content analysts are normally interested in a much larger number of variables, but this simple illustration can help to get across how a coding schedule and coding manual operate.

Coding schedule

The coding schedule is a form onto which the data are entered (see Figure 12.1). Each of the columns in Figure 12.1 is a dimension (indicated by the column heading) to be coded. The blank cells on the coding form are the places in which codes are to be written. One row is used for each media item coded. The codes can then be transferred to a computer data file for analysis with a software package such as **IBM SPSS Statistics** (SPSS).

Coding manual

On the face of it, the coding schedule in Figure 12.1 seems bare, providing little information about what is to be done or where. This is where the coding manual comes in. It is a set of instructions to coders that includes all possible categories for each dimension to be coded. It provides a list of all the dimensions; the they once were. However, many sites still feature "dating profiles" in which people have a few paragraphs to describe themselves and to outline what they would like to find in a partner, and the content of these profiles is somewhat similar to the older-style ad descriptions. For example, Wada et al.'s (2019) research on older (60+) Canadians' use of the dating site Plenty of Fish focused on analyzing the "About Me" and "Interests" sections of users' profiles. They found that users emphasized an idealized image of aging in portraying themselves and what they were looking for in a partner. Being active, healthy, productive, positive, and personable were some of the standout attributes people used to characterize themselves. For instance, words such as "active," "busy," and "on the go" were chosen to describe how engaged they were with their communities.

Not surprisingly, a major concern with people who engage in online dating is the misrepresentation of personal characteristics by potential mates (Hall, Park, Song, & Cody, 2010). Most users want an in-person meeting before getting involved in a romantic relationship (Finkel, Eastwick, Karney, Reis, & Sprecher, 2012), and not without reason. Hitsch, Hortaçscu, & Ariely (2010) compared the information provided in online dating sites with American national averages, and found that both men and women on the sites claimed higher than average heights, and that women but not men indicated lower than average weights. Using self-reports of probable misrepresentation on dating sites, Hall et al. (2010) found that men were more likely than women to be deceptive about their personal assets (e.g., income), but that there was no gender difference in misrepresentation of relationship goals (e.g., interest in pursuing a serious relationship). Women were found to be more likely to misrepresent their weight, while men, contrary to expectation, were more likely to mislead about their age. Older adults often use vague language about age in their profiles (e.g., "youthful mindset and optimal health") to portray themselves as being younger than they are (Wada et al., 2019, p. 954).

different categories subsumed under each dimension; the numbers (that is, *codes*) that correspond to each category; and guidance to coders on what should be taken into account in coding a particular dimension. Figure 12.2 shows a coding manual that corresponds to the coding schedule in Figure 12.1.

Our coding manual includes the occupation of both the suspect and the victim of the crime, using a simple social-class scheme. The offences are classified according to the categories used by the police in recording crimes. (Since police statistics have been criticized for weak **reliability** and **validity**—recall Chapters 4 and 5—a comparison between police data and crime reports in local newspapers is a possible research topic.) Finer distinctions can be used, but unless you are planning to examine a large sample of

Case number	Day	Month	Nature of offence I	Gender of suspect	Occupation of suspect	Age of suspect	Gender of victim	Occupation of victim	Age of victim	Depiction of victim	Nature of offence II	Position of news item

FIGURE 12.1 Coding schedule

Nature of offence I

01. Violence against the person
02. Sexual offences
03. Robbery
04. Burglary in a dwelling
05. Burglary other than in a dwelling
06. Theft from a person
07. Theft of bicycle
08. Theft from shops
09. Theft from vehicle
10. Theft of motor vehicle
11. Other theft and handling stolen goods
12. Fraud and forgery
13. Drug offences
14. Other offences

Gender of suspect

1. Male
2. Female
3. Unknown

Occupation of suspect

01. Professionals, administrators, officials and managers in large establishments; large proprietors
02. Lower-grade professionals, administrators, and officials; higher-grade technicians; managers in small business and industrial establishments; supervisors of non-manual employees
03. Routine non-manual employees in administration and commerce
04. Personal service workers
05. Small proprietors, artisans, etc., with employees
06. Small proprietors, artisans, etc., without employees
07. Farmers and smallholders; self-employed fishermen
08. Lower-grade technicians, supervisors of manual workers
09. Skilled manual workers
10. Semi-skilled and unskilled manual workers (not in agriculture)
11. Agricultural workers
12. Other
13. Unemployed
14. Homemaker
15. Student
16. Retired
17. Unknown

Age of suspect

Record age (−1 if unknown)

Gender of victim

1. Male
2. Female
3. Unknown

Occupation of victim

Same as for occupation of suspect

If not applicable, code as 99

Age of victim

Record age (−1 if unknown)

Depiction of victim

1. Victim responsible for crime
2. Victim partly responsible for crime
3. Victim not at all responsible for crime
4. Not applicable

Nature of offence II (code if second offence mentioned in relation to the same incident; code 0 if no second offence)

Same as for Nature of offence I

Position of news item

1. Front page
2. Inside
3. Back page

FIGURE 12.2 Coding manual

news items, broader categories are preferable. Note also that the coding schedule and manual permit the recording of two offences for any incident. If there are more than two, you will have to make a judgment concerning the two most significant offences.

The coding manual is crucial because it provides a complete listing of all categories for each dimension to be coded, as well as guidance on how to interpret the dimensions. It is on the basis of these lists that a coding schedule of the kind presented in Figure 12.1 is created. Detailed rules about how to code should be formulated, because reliability, both inter-coder and intra-coder, is always a concern (see further on in this section).

Here is a news report of a fictional road-rage incident. Two male motorists, one a retired schoolteacher aged 68, the other a 26-year-old assembly-line worker, got into an argument and the worker allegedly punched the retired man, causing him to fall, hit his head, and suffer a concussion. There was no second offence. The coding of the incident would then appear as in Figure 12.3 and the data would be entered into a computer program such as SPSS.

Suppose a second article, appearing the next day, described how an unemployed 34-year-old female reportedly took an 86-year-old woman's purse and then knocked her down. The code is provided in Figure 12.4 but with a few errors. Can you spot them? Forms like these would be completed for each news item within the chosen period(s) of study.

Potential pitfalls in devising coding schemes

The potential dangers in devising a content analysis coding scheme are similar to those involved in designing **structured interview** and **observation schedules**. Points to recall include the following:

- *Mutually exclusive categories.* There should be no overlap in the categories supplied for each dimension. If the categories are not mutually exclusive, coders will not know how to code an item that fits into more than one category.
- *Exhaustive categories.* Every possible dimension should have a category.
- *Clear instructions.* Coders should be clear about what factors to take into account when assigning codes. Sometimes these have to be very elaborate. In the sort of content analysis described in the previous section, coders generally have little or no discretion in deciding how to code the units of analysis.
- *A clear unit of analysis.* For example, in the imaginary study of the reporting of crime in the local press, there is both a media item (for example, one newspaper article) and a topic to be coded (one of two offences). In practice, a researcher is interested in both but needs to keep the distinction in mind.

To enhance the quality of a coding scheme, it is advisable to conduct a pilot study to identify difficulties, such as finding there is no code to cover a particular case (not exhaustive). A pilot test will also help to reveal if one category of a dimension includes an extremely large percentage of items. When this occurs, it may be necessary to break that category down to allow for greater specificity.

As we have mentioned, the reliability of coding is a further concern. An important part of pre-testing the coding scheme is examining consistency between coders (**inter-coder reliability**) and, if time permits, **intra-coder reliability**. The process of gauging reliability is more or less the same as in **structured observation**, discussed in Chapter 6.

Case number	Day	Month	Nature of offence I	Gender of suspect	Occupation of suspect	Age of suspect	Gender of victim	Occupation of victim	Age of victim	Depiction of victim	Nature of offence II	Position of news item
001	24	11	01	1	10	26	1	16	68	2	00	2

FIGURE 12.3 Completed coding schedule

Case number	Day	Month	Nature of offence I	Gender of suspect	Occupation of suspect	Age of suspect	Gender of victim	Occupation of victim	Age of victim	Depiction of victim	Nature of offence II	Position of news item
002	25	12	06	1	13	32	2	16	86	3	01	2

FIGURE 12.4 Completed coding schedule with errors

Content analysis without a pre-existing coding scheme

Content analysis may be undertaken before any specific decisions have been made regarding how the information available for analysis will be coded. In such cases the data are searched in order to find underlying themes, making the study primarily qualitative in nature. Like other qualitative approaches, qualitative content analysis tends to be inductive, with themes emerging through an iterative process as the researcher interprets the data. Kennedy (2006), for example, in his study of the Canadian fathers' rights movement called "Fathers 4 Justice," used content analysis in conjunction with participant observation and semi-structured interviews to examine how the movement developed a collective identity. The content analysis was conducted on documents such as position papers submitted to government agencies, newsletters, pamphlets, and minutes from meetings, and was used mainly to make sense of the data gathered through participant observation and interviews. Similarly, Bell (2007) used pamphlets, speeches, newsletters, and other texts to arrive at an overall assessment of western Canadian separatism as a neo-liberal movement. The processes by which the themes are extracted in this kind of content analysis are often left implicit, although they are usually illustrated with quotations from the text in question.

Lynch and Bogen (1997) examined core sociological textbooks and found that they contained recurring themes that presented an upbeat and scientific view of the discipline—one that, in the researchers' view, was biased and value laden. Seale (2002) examined newspaper reports about people with cancer. One of the phases of his analysis entailed an "NVivo coding exercise, in which sections of text concerning themes of interest were identified and retrieved" (p. 109). He was especially interested in gender differences in the representation of sufferers, and demonstrated that stories about men were much more likely than stories about women to discuss the role that the individual's character played in dealing with the disease.

Altheide and Schneider (2013) outlined an approach they called *ethnographic content analysis* (ECA). They described this approach as differing from quantitative content analysis in that the researcher is constantly revising the themes or categories distilled from the examination of documents. As they put it:

> ECA follows a recursive and reflexive movement between concept development-sampling-data collection-data coding-data analysis-interpretation. The aim is to be systematic and analytic but not rigid. Categories and variables initially guide the study, but others are allowed and expected to emerge during the study, including an orientation toward ***constant discovery*** and ***constant comparison*** of relevant situations, settings, styles, images, meanings, and nuances (p. 26; emphases in original).

While more quantitatively oriented analysis typically entails applying predefined categories to the sources, ECA allows for greater refinement of those categories as well as generation of new ones. For example, Canadian researchers Schneider and Hannem (2019) examined how the sexual misconduct allegations against Donald Trump in the 2016 US election were framed as a political issue, which had the effect of minimizing victims' experiences. Instead of beginning with a pre-existing coding scheme, they conducted a preliminary analysis of a few potential documents to be used in their study (articles from the *Washington Post* and *New York Times*). This early reading of possible data informed their initial categories and codes to be used as part of a data collection protocol. The subsequent analysis then followed an iterative process to construct qualitative themes in the data. In addition, ECA emphasizes the context within which documents are generated. For instance, a study of newspaper reports of crime would require some understanding of news organizations and the work that journalists do (Altheide, 2004).

Semiotics

Another form of predominantly qualitative content analysis is semiotics, the *science of* ***signs***. In social research, semiotics involves analysis of the signs and symbols encountered in everyday life. It can be applied to documentary sources as well as many other kinds of data. The main terms employed in semiotics are as follows:

- The *sign* is something that stands for something else, such as a yellow traffic light; it has two components, a *signifier* and a *signified*.
- The *signifier* is the thing (here the yellow light) that points to an underlying meaning.
- The *signified* is the meaning to which the signifier points ("caution: stop if possible").
- The **denotative meaning** is the manifest or obvious meaning of a signifier and as such indicates its function (here to regulate traffic).
- A **connotative meaning** is one that can arise in conjunction with the denotative meaning (for example, "speed up to beat the coming red light").
- *Polysemy* refers to the notion that signs can be interpreted in many different ways.

Semiotics seeks to uncover the hidden meanings that reside in texts, broadly defined. Consider, by way of illustration, the curriculum vitae (CV) in academic life. The typical academic CV contains information on matters such as degrees earned; previous and current posts; administrative responsibilities and experience; teaching experience; research experience; research grants acquired; and publications. It can be seen as a system of interlocking signifiers denotatively providing a summary of the individual's experience (its sign function). At the connotative level, it is an indication of an individual's value, particularly in connection with employability. Every CV is capable of being interpreted in different ways and is therefore polysemic, but there is a shared code among academics whereby certain attributes of CVs (such as lists of publications) are seen as especially desirable and are therefore less contentious in terms of their meaning. Applicants for posts know this and design their CVs to highlight the desired qualities and downplay others, so that the CV becomes a presentation of self, as Miller and Morgan (1993) suggested.

Box 12.6 outlines a semiotic study (Gottdiener, 1997) in which the "text" was Disneyland. The chief strength of semiotics lies in its invitation to see beyond and beneath the apparent ordinariness of everyday life and its manifestations. The main difficulty with semiotic analysis is that, although it may offer a compelling exposition of some aspect of everyday life, the interpretation may be somewhat arbitrary. For example, Gottdiener's association of "Adventureland" with colonialism/imperialism might not be shared by other analysts. However, the results of a semiotic analysis may be no more arbitrary than those of any other interpretive approach. Indeed, it would be surprising not to be struck by a sense of arbitrariness in semiotics, given its emphasis on the principle of polysemy.

Hermeneutics

The hermeneutic approach has been used in understanding and interpreting the Bible, but it has also been employed in the analysis of other texts. It was influential in the formation of interpretivism as an **epistemology** (see Chapter 1) and has much in common with Weber's notion of *Verstehen*. The central idea behind hermeneutics is that the analyst of a text must seek its meanings from the perspective of its author, considering the social and historical context within which the text was produced.

Phillips and Brown's (1993) hermeneutic study of the corporate image advertisements of a Canadian synthetic crude oil company was a "formal analysis of the structural and conventional aspects of the text" (p. 1563). For them this meant examining the texts of the advertisements in terms of their constituent parts and the writing conventions they reflected. They also relied on a large database of magazine and newspaper articles relating to the company for additional documentary materials. They showed how corporate image advertisements were used to mobilize support for company activities from government and the public, and to ward off the environmental legislation that threatened them.

Readers and audiences—active or passive?

Audience reception is a prominent area of inquiry in media and cultural studies. The key question is whether audiences/readers are active interpreters of

Box 12.6 | A semiotic Disneyland

Joshuaraineyphotography/Dreamstime.com/GetStock

Visitors see this plaque as they enter Disneyland in California. How does it support Gottdiener's notion of a semiotic Disneyland?

Gottdiener (1997, pp. 108–115) proposed that Disneyland can be fruitfully explored through semiotic analysis. He concluded that its meaning is based on the contrast between the alienated daily lives of nearby Los Angeles residents and the life they experience at the theme park. He identified, through this principle, several sign systems contrasting the park with the surrounding environment: transportation, food, clothing, shelter, entertainment, social control, economics, politics, and family. The first of these sign systems—transportation—revealed a difference between the Disneyland visitor as pedestrian (walking with others in a group) and the Los Angeles resident as passenger (a car is necessary; danger on the congested freeways). A further component of his research entailed analysis of the connotations of the different "lands" that make up the park. He suggested that each land was associated with one or more signifiers of capitalism; for example:

- Frontierland: predatory capital, conquering
- Adventureland: colonialism/imperialism
- Tomorrowland: state capital for space exploration

what they see or hear. Do they passively accept the meanings that authors or designers infuse into their texts, as in the oil company advertisements just described, or do they resist those meanings and strive for independent readings? Do they arrive at a middle point that incorporates both passive and active elements? Much of the research on this issue suggests that audiences frequently come up with readings different from those intended by authors (see Fenton, Bryman, & Deacon, 1998, for a summary of some of this research).

Although the idea of the "active audience" has not gone unchallenged (see, for example, McGuigan, 1992), it is so well supported that many of the interpretations of texts offered by social scientists have been questioned. This suggests caution in reading Giulianotti's (1997) study of "fanzines" or Hier's (2002) examination of city council minutes to understand the rave issue. Would other social scientists arrive at the same interpretations? Do their interpretations match those of the original readers or audiences? The social researcher is always putting a personal "spin" on the texts analyzed. The same is true of all social science data: the conclusions derived from questionnaire or ethnographic data reflect the author's interpretations, not the complete set of possible interpretations. The point is that close scrutiny and critical thinking are always required.

Two approaches to the study of language

In this section two approaches to the study of language are examined: conversation analysis (CA) and discourse analysis (DA). While CA and DA do not exhaust the range of possibilities for studying language, they do represent two of the most prominent approaches, and each includes both quantitative and qualitative aspects. Both have developed a technical vocabulary and a set of techniques. This section outlines some of their basic elements and draws attention to their contrasting features.

Conversation analysis

The roots of CA lie in ethnomethodology, a sociological approach to communication focusing on the "practical, common-sense reasoning" that people use in their everyday lives. It includes notions of cause and effect ("if I do this, then that will happen") and the generalizations that allow people to perform everyday tasks. This process of reasoning and communication is presented as a way in which social order is created. Social order is not seen as a pre-existing force constraining individual action, but as something that is worked at and achieved by people through interaction. Garfinkel, one of the pioneers of conversation analysis, claimed that the role of sociology is not to uncover "objective" social facts as Durkheim suggested, but to see them as an accomplishment, as the eventually taken-for-granted patterns established through the activities of ordinary people going about their daily lives (Garfinkel, 1967, p. vii).

Two ideas are particularly central to ethnomethodology and find clear expression in CA: *indexicality* and reflexivity. The former suggests that the meanings of words or utterances, including pauses and sounds, depend on the context in which they are used. Reflexivity means that talk is not a "mere" representation of the social world, standing for something else, but is itself a reality. In these ways, ethnomethodology fits squarely with two aspects of qualitative research: a preference for a contextual understanding of action (see Chapter 9) and an **ontological** position associated with **constructionism** (see Chapter 1).

In the years following its introduction, ethnomethodological research sought to conduct fine-grained analyses of the sequences of interaction revealed in conversations recorded in naturally occurring contexts. As such, CA is a multifaceted approach, part theory, part method of data acquisition, part method of analysis. The predilection for the analysis of talk gleaned from naturally occurring situations suggests that CA fits well with another preoccupation among qualitative researchers: a commitment to **naturalism** (see Chapter 9).

Conversation analysts have developed a variety of ways to study talk. Psathas (1995, p. 1) described them as "rigorous, systematic procedures" that can "provide reproducible results." Such a framework brings to mind the procedures used to generate valid, reliable, and replicable findings in quantitative research. It is not surprising, therefore, that CA is sometimes described as having a **positivist** orientation. Thus, some features that are broadly in tune with qualitative research (contextual and naturalistic analysis without prior theoretical commitments) are married to traits associated with quantitative research.

However, the emphasis on context in CA is somewhat at variance with contextual understanding as it is normally thought of in qualitative research. For CA practitioners, context refers to the specific here-and-now context of immediately preceding talk, whereas for most qualitative researchers it has a much wider focus, encompassing phenomena such as the broader culture of the group within which the social action occurs, including their values, beliefs, and typical modes of behaviour. This is precisely the kind of attribution that CA practitioners seek to avoid. To import elements that are not specifically grounded in the here and now of what has just been said during a conversation is to risk imposing an understanding that is not grounded in the participants' immediate concerns. It is no wonder, therefore, that writers like Gubrium and Holstein (1997) treated CA as a separate tradition within qualitative research, whereas Silverman (1993) found it difficult to fit CA into broad descriptions of qualitative research.

Assumptions of conversation analysis

Analysts often begin practising conversational analysis when they notice something significant about the way a speaker says something, and this recognition generates interest in the function that the turn of phrase serves. To illustrate, Clayman and Gill (2004) referred to the way a child will often begin a conversation with an adult by saying "You know what, Daddy [or whoever]?" The question generally produces a "What?" reply that allows the child to find a slot in a sequence of communications, or to inaugurate such a sequence. The use of a question, rather than a declarative statement, may reflect the child's lesser power.

Once such a focus has been identified, conversation analysts typically follow certain basic assumptions. Heritage (1984; 1987) proposed three:

- *Talk is structured.* Talk comprises patterns, and participants are implicitly aware of the rules that underpin these patterns. As a result, conversation analysts do not attempt to infer the motivations of speakers from what they say, or to ascribe their talk to purely personal characteristics. Such information is unnecessary, since the conversation analyst is oriented to the underlying structures that are revealed in pauses, emphases, questions followed by answers, and so on.
- *Talk is forged contextually.* Talk must be analyzed in terms of its context and understood in terms of the talk that has preceded it.
- *Analysis is grounded in data.* Conversation analysts shun prior theoretical schemes and argue that the characteristics of talk and social order must be derived from the data.

In doing a project based on CA, it is important not to collect too much data. The real work of CA is the painstaking analysis that its underlying theoretical stance requires. It may be that just one or two portions of transcribed text will be sufficient to answer the research questions.

Transcription and attention to detail

The transcript in Box 12.7 includes some basic symbols used by conversation analysts:

We:ll A colon indicates that the sound that occurs directly before the colon is prolonged. More than one colon means further prolongation (e.g., Ye: : :s).

.hh A row of h's preceded by a dot indicate an intake of breath. If no dot is present, it means breathing out. The more h's, the longer the breath.

(0.8) A figure in parentheses indicates a period of silence, usually measured in tenths of a second. Thus, (0.8) indicates eight-tenths of a second of silence.

<u>you</u> and k<u>n</u>owing An underline indicates an emphasis in the speaker's talk.

<u>you</u>- you A hyphen means the speaker was interrupted or stopped speaking.

(.) Indicates a very slight pause.

The attention to detail in the sequence of talk in Box 12.7 is striking, but what is significant in it? Silverman (1994) drew two main inferences. First, *P* initially tries to deflect any suggestion that there may be a special reason why she needs an HIV test. As a result, the disclosure that she has been engaging in potentially risky behaviour is delayed. Second, *P*'s use of "you" depersonalizes her behaviour. Silverman argued that sequences like these show how "people receiving HIV counselling skilfully manage their talk about delicate topics" (p. 75). The hesitations are designed by patients to establish that issues like these are not the subject of normal conversation. The rather general replies to questions indicate that the speaker is not the kind of person who immediately launches into a discussion about difficult sexual matters with a stranger. As an aside, Silverman suggested that *P*'s hesitancy and depersonalization are minimal. Others stall more, lie, or totally refuse to answer (p. 76).

Some basic characteristics of conversations

There are recurring features in the way talk is organized that can be discerned in sequences of conversation. Among them are the following.

Turn-taking

One of the most basic features of everyday conversation is the fact that the participants take turns speaking. Only one speaker tends to talk at a time, the other listening, and turns are taken with minimal

Box 12.7 | Conversation analysis showing a question-and-answer adjacency pair

Silverman (1984, p. 72) provided the following extract from a conversation between an HIV counsellor (*C*) and a patient (*P*):

1. C: Can I just briefly ask why: you thought about having
2. an HIV test done:
3. *P*:.hh We:ll I mean it's something that you have these
4. I mean that you have to think about these da:ys, and
5. I just uh:m felt (0.8) you- you have had sex with
6. several people and you just don't want to go on (.)
7. not knowing.

gaps between them (Hutchby & Wooffitt, 1998, p. 47). **Turn-taking** is particularly important to conversation analysts because it points to the existence of shared codes indicating the ends of utterances. Without such codes, conversation could not proceed in an organized manner, with smooth transitions between speakers.

Of course, things sometimes go wrong, as when people speak at the same time. Silverman (1993, p. 132) described some repair mechanisms for instances in which turn-taking conventions are not followed. For example, when a turn transfer does not occur at an appropriate point (such as when someone does not respond to a question), the first speaker may speak again, perhaps reinforcing the need for the other person to speak (possibly by rephrasing the question).

The crucial point to note about such repair mechanisms is that they allow the rules of turn-taking to be maintained even after the rules have been breached.

Adjacency pairs

One feature of turn-taking is the tendency for an exchange to have two linked phases known as an **adjacency pair**; for instance, a question followed by an answer, as in Box 12.7; an invitation followed by a response (accept/decline); or a greeting followed by a returned greeting. The first phase assumes that the other part of the adjacency pair will be forthcoming—for example, that an invitation will get a response. The second phase is of interest to the conversation analyst not just because it invites a response in its own right but because compliance with the model indicates recognition of the way one is supposed to respond to the initial phase. In this way "intersubjective understandings" are continuously reinforced. This does not mean that the second phase *always* follows the first. Failure to respond appropriately—for example, when one answers a question with another question—has itself been the focus of attention for conversation analysts.

Preference organization

Some responses are clearly preferred to others. An example is when an invitation or a request is proffered: acceptance is the *preferred response* and refusal the *non-preferred response*. To illustrate, Potter (1996, p. 59) contrasted a sequence in which an offer is met with a straightforward acceptance—"thank you"—with a sequence (reproduced in Box 12.8) in which an invitation is declined.

According to Potter, *A*'s response is fairly typical of rejections, which have their own standard features. For example, *A* delays the start of his or her response and fills it with "hehh." In addition, the rejection is "softened" by *A*'s saying "I don't think I can make it" (which suggests that acceptance is still possible) and then offering an explanation for his or her failure to provide the preferred response. The key point is that the participants recognize the preference structure of this kind of adjacency pairing and that this recognition affects the response (hesitancy,

Box 12.8 | Conversation analysis in action: A non-preferred response

1. *B*: Uh if you'd care to come over and visit a little while
2. this morning I'll give you a cup of coffee.
3. *A*: hehh
4. Well
5. that's awfully sweet of you,
6. I don't think I can make it this morning. hh uhm
7. I'm running an ad in the paper and-and uh I have to
8. stay near the phone. (Atkinson & Drew, 1979, p. 58; quoted in Potter, 1996, p. 59)

acknowledgment of the invitation, explanation of failure). Acceptance of an invitation does not have to be justified, whereas refusal generally does, in order to protect the relationship between the two parties from the harm that the non-preferred response might otherwise do.

Conversational patterns can be a good subject for student research to see if different groups, such as men and women, or students and professors, exhibit varying patterns. (Keep in mind that status hierarchies can sometimes determine who the interrupters are, who defers to the interrupters, etc.) Your class could go to an eating area on campus to collect data, each student listening to different conversations. To catch body movements, video recordings can be used (Heath, 1997), so long as ethical protocols have been followed.

A final note on conversation analysis

CA considers it illegitimate to invoke cultural factors when analyzing conversations. However, some researchers see that principle as unnecessarily restrictive. In many exchanges, much of the talk is informed by the participants' shared knowledge of contexts, including cultural contexts, yet the prohibition against cultural arguments limits CA to research questions that pertain to talk itself. On the other hand, CA reduces the risk of making unwarranted speculations about what is happening in social interaction, and has contributed to our understanding of how social order is created—one of the classic concerns of social theory.

Discourse analysis

Discourse analysis incorporates aspects of CA, but is more flexible and can be applied to forms of communication other than talk. It puts less emphasis on naturally occurring talk, so the language used in research interviews can also be a legitimate subject of analysis. According to Potter (1997), DA "emphasizes the way versions of the world, of society, events and inner psychological worlds are produced in discourse" (p. 146). For continental philosophers such as Foucault (1926–84), "discourse" refers to the way a particular set of linguistic categories relating to an object frames people's understanding of that object.

For example, a certain discourse concerning mental illness can produce particular conceptions of what mentally ill persons are like, the nature of their illness, how they should be treated, and who is legitimately entitled to treat them. In this way discourse serves to justify the power of those who provide such treatment as well as the treatment regimens they prescribe. This discourse is much more than language: it is part of the social world of mental illness.

Several different approaches fall under the DA heading (Potter, 1997). The version discussed here is one associated with writers such as Potter (1997), Potter and Wetherell (1994), and Billig (1991). This version of DA exhibits two distinctive features at the level of epistemology and ontology (Potter, 1997):

- It is generally anti-realist in that it denies the existence of an external reality awaiting a definitive portrayal by the researcher. It therefore disavows the notion that researchers can arrive at accurate and objective accounts of the social world.
- It is constructionist in that it gives priority to the version of reality propounded by members of the social setting being investigated. More specifically, it recognizes that discourse analysis entails a selection from many possible interpretations of a given situation. For example, is a person who speaks to herself

dangerous or harmless? Is she more in need of treatment or social support? In the process of answering such questions, a particular reality is constructed.

Discourse is not simply a neutral device for imparting meaning. After all, there are many things that people seek to accomplish when they talk or write. DA is concerned with the strategies they employ in order to create different kinds of effect. This is illustrated in three basic questions that DA asks:

- What is this discourse doing?
- How is it constructed to make this happen?
- What resources are available to perform this activity? (Potter, 2004, p. 609)

This action orientation is revealed in a study of the first few moments of telephone calls to the helpline of the UK's National Society for the Prevention of Cruelty to Children. Through analysis of these call openings, Potter and Hepburn (2004) showed that a variety of actions are performed during the first few moments:

- The callers spell out the details of their concerns.
- The callers seek to establish, in collaboration with the "experts" on the line (the child protection officers) that the incidents they are reporting do in fact require some kind of intervention.
- The callers convey the idea that the activity they are describing is serious and that they are concerned about it, but not so concerned that the police should be contacted immediately.
- The child protection officers show a willingness to treat the reports as serious, without making judgments as to their actual truth or seriousness.

Analysis of these brief moments of conversation shows that the flow of discourse achieves a number of objectives for both parties and in that sense constitutes action. On the other hand, as Gill (1996) suggested, what is said is always a way of *not* saying something else. Either way, discourse can be seen as providing a solution to a problem (Widdicombe, 1993).

DA shares with CA a preference for locating contextual understanding in terms of the situational specifics of talk. As Potter (1997, p. 158) put it, discourse analysts prefer "to see things as things that are worked up, attended to, and made relevant in interaction rather than being external determinants." However, DA practitioners are less wedded to this principle than are conversation analysts.

Discourse analysts resist the idea of codifying their procedures and argue that such codification is probably impossible. Potter (1997) described his work as "a craft skill, more like bike riding or chicken sexing than following [a] recipe" (pp. 147–148). Gill (2000) suggested adopting a posture of "skeptical reading." This means searching for a purpose lurking behind the way things are said or presented. Gill proposed that DA can be usefully thought of in terms of four main themes, outlined in Box 12.9.

Producing facts

In this section, the emphasis is on the strategies employed to convey allegedly factual knowledge. Among them is *quantification rhetoric*: the various ways in which statements involving numbers or quantities can be made to either support or refute arguments. The interest in this issue lies partly in the importance of quantification in everyday life, but also in the tendency of many social scientists to use this strategy themselves (John, 1992). In their analysis of data such as the portions of transcript cited in Box 12.10, Potter, Wetherell, & Chitty (1991) and Potter and Wetherell (1994) show how these sorts of devices are used.

Using variation as a lever

The authors drew attention to the phrase "1 per cent of a quarter of a million" because it incorporates two different types of quantitative expression: a relative expression (a percentage) and an absolute frequency (quarter of a million). The difference is important, because it allowed the program makers to emphasize the very low cure rate (just 1 per cent) compared

Box 12.9 | Four themes in discourse analysis

Gill (2000) drew attention to four prominent themes in DA:

1. *Discourse is a topic*. In other words, discourse is a focus of inquiry itself and not just a means of gaining access to the aspects of social reality that lie behind it. This idea contrasts with the view traditionally taken by research interviewers, in which language simply reveals what people think, or serves as a mechanism for learning about their behaviour and the reasons for it.
2. *Language is constructive*. Discourse is a way of constituting a particular view of social reality. Moreover, in order to create that view, choices have to be made regarding the most appropriate way of presenting it, and these choices reflect the disposition of the person concerned.
3. *Discourse is a form of action*. As Gill put it, language is considered "a practice in its own right" p. 175). Language is a way of accomplishing acts, such as attributing blame, presenting oneself in a particular way, or getting an argument across. Moreover, a person's discourse is affected by the situation he or she is in. For instance, the reasons given for wanting a job may vary depending on whether the job seeker is talking to a prospective employer, a family member, or a friend.
4. *Discourse is rhetorically organized*. DA practitioners recognize that discourse is concerned with "establishing one version of the world in the face of competing versions" (p. 176). In other words, the version of events that a person presents is intended to persuade others.

with the very large number of cases diagnosed each year. Instead, they could have pointed to the absolute number of people who are cured (2500), but the impact would have been less dramatic. It's also worth noting that the phrase "a quarter of a million" not only exaggerates the number of new cases (adding 7000 to the actual 243,000) but also sounds significantly larger.

Reading the detail

Discourse analysts, like conversation analysts, attend to the details of discourse. For example, Potter and Wetherell (1994) suggested that the description of the three "curable cancers" as "amongst the rarest cancers" was deployed to make the point that these are atypical cancers, and that it would be unwise to generalize from them to all cancers.

Looking for rhetorical detail

Attention to rhetorical detail entails sensitivity to the way arguments are constructed. During the editing of the film, the program makers' discourse suggested they were looking for ways to present a convincing argument to show that cancer remains largely incurable in spite of the money spent on it. The program makers very consciously devised the strategy outlined in the discussion of "using variation as a lever" of playing down the numerical significance of the cancers that are amenable to treatment. Another element of their strategy was to employ a tactic that Potter et al. (1991) called a "preformulation," the discounting of a possible counterargument, as when the commentary says: "When faced with this challenge the first thing the charities point to is the small number of cancers which are now effectively curable."

Critical discourse analysis

There may be important political conflicts and social justice issues underlying the texts examined by discourse analysts. For example, the makers of the television program analyzed by Potter and colleagues in Box 12.10 infer that despite lavish funding, cancer researchers have had limited success in producing

Box 12.10 | Discourse analysis in action: Producing facts through quantification rhetoric

The study of the television program *Cancer: Your Money or Your Life* (Potter et al., 1991; Potter & Wetherell, 1994) used a variety of sources, including

- a video recording of the program;
- the observations of one of the people making the program (who acted as a participant observer while it was being made);
- drafts of the script;
- recordings of editing sessions;
- entire interviews (of people such as cancer research specialists and heads of charities) conducted for the program; and
- research interviews with some of the latter people as well as some of the people involved in making the program.

With regard to the coding process, the authors reported that they

> made a list of about a dozen keywords and phrases that related to the sequence—percentage, cure rates, death rates, 1 per cent, etc.—and then ran through each of the interview and interaction files, looking for them with a standard word-processor. . . . Whenever we got a "hit" we would read the surrounding text to see if it had relevance to our target sequence. When it did we would copy it across to an already opened coding file . . . noting the transcript page numbers at the same time. If we were not sure if the sequence was relevant we copied it anyway, for, unlike the sorts of coding that take place in traditional content analysis, the coding is not the analysis itself but a preliminary to make the task of analysis manageable. (Potter & Wetherell, 1994, p. 52)

Following is a sequence used in the research. It occurred roughly halfway through the program, following interviews with cancer scientists who had cast doubt on whether their research, much of it funded by charities, resulted in successful treatment:

> *Commentary:* The message from these scientists is clear—exactly like the public—they hope their basic research will lead to cures in the future—although at the moment they can't say how this will happen. In the meantime, their aim is to increase scientific knowledge on a broad front and they're certainly achieving this. But do their results justify them getting so much of the money that has been given to help fight cancer? When faced with this challenge the first thing the charities point to is the small number of cancers which are now effectively curable.
>
> [on screen: Dr. Nigel Kemp Cancer Research Campaign]
>
> *Kemp:* The outlook for individuals suffering from a number of types of cancer has been totally revolutionized. I mean for example—children suffering from acute leukemia—in the old days if they lived six months they were lucky—now more than half the children with it are cured. And the same applies to a number of other cancers—Hodgkin's Disease in young people and testicular tumours in young men. (Potter & Wetherell, 1994, pp. 52–53)

At this point a table showing the annual incidence of 34 types of cancer begins to scroll on the screen. The total incidence is 243,000, and the individual incidences range from placenta (20) to lung (41,400). The three forms of cancer mentioned by Kemp and their levels of incidence are highlighted in yellow: childhood leukemia (350), testis (1000), and Hodgkin's disease (1400). The program continues while the table is scrolling.

(*Continued*)

Commentary: But those three curable types are amongst the rarest cancers—they represent around 1 per cent of a quarter of a million cases of cancers diagnosed each year. Most deaths are caused by a small number of very common cancers.

Kemp: We are well aware of the fact that [pause] once people develop lung cancer or stomach cancer or cancer of the bowel sometimes—the outlook is very bad and obviously one is frustrated by the s[low], relatively slow rate of progress on the one hand but equally I think there are a lot of real opportunities and positive signs that advances can be made—even in the more intractable cancers. (Potter & Wetherell, 1994, p. 53)

Source: Excerpts from *Analyzing Qualitative Data* © 1994 Routledge. Reproduced by permission of Taylor & Francis Books UK.

cures, which one could take to mean that scarce societal resources are being misallocated. While misallocation of funds is certainly a political issue, notions of power and exploitation are not confronted directly or in any depth in their research.

Those who conduct **critical discourse analysis**, by contrast, are much more explicit in exposing the political nature of the texts they examine. The effect of power hierarchies, structural inequalities, and historical political struggles are among the issues raised by these researchers (Blommaert & Bulcaen, 2000). They also bring to their work a commitment to social change and the empowerment of the oppressed.

Harding, for instance, has examined how discourse has been used to suppress the aspirations of Indigenous peoples in Canada since the 1860s. In one study (2006), he compared Canadian newspaper coverage of Indigenous peoples' activities in the mid-nineteenth century with coverage from the late twentieth century. He concluded that although instances of overt racism in Canadian papers declined in this period, the press continued to serve dominant interests by portraying Indigenous people as a threat to White power and dominance. One way in which this occurred was through the framing of the text with a binary opposition of "us" versus "them." An article published in the 1860s stated, "To allow these [Indigenous] people all the privileges of others [with regard to homesteading] would be to throw the whole Colony [of British Columbia] into confusion. Just imagine our 80,000 Indians . . . being allowed to locate land wherever they please" (Harding, 2006, p. 213). Another binary opposition evident in press coverage was "reason" versus "emotion." Press coverage in the more recent era depicted a non-Indigenous judge presiding over an Indigenous land claims case as someone who would "rule" and offer "insight" by making his "decision" using "common sense" and a "firm" interpretation of "the rule of law" (p. 217). Indigenous individuals, however, on hearing of his ruling, are described as dealing with the death of their "dream," and as people who "argue," cry "tears," "vow to fight," and use tactics of "confrontation" (p. 217).

Similarly, G. Johnston (2020) has shown how Canadian mainstream media accounts of opioid overdose deaths often portray White youth as "innocent, normal, and victimized" while Indigenous people are characterized as "addicted and hopeless" (p. 128). She also found that mainstream reporting on White overdose deaths was nearly 30 times more common than media mentions of Indigenous deaths, even though the actual rates of Indigenous fatal and non-fatal opioid overdoses are much higher. She argues that differences in media coverage are likely to have a significant impact on public perception and understanding: "the choice not to depict Indigenous overdose deaths continues to allow many Canadians to remain ignorant of the issues facing these communities" (p. 141).

Overview

DA draws on insights from CA, particularly when analyzing strings of talk. The CA injunction to focus on the talk itself and the ways in which intersubjective meaning is arrived at in sequences of talk is also

Methods in Motion | Applications to Canadian Society

Interpreting the Highway of Tears

Morton (2016) conducted a critical discourse analysis of two billboards placed on the "Highway of Tears," a stretch of road (Highway 16) in central British Columbia that is infamous for the large number of Indigenous women who have disappeared while hitchhiking on it. The first billboard was co-sponsored by the Province of British Columbia, the regional district of Kitimat-Stikine, and the Gitxkan First Nation. The second was co-sponsored by the province and the Aboriginal Women's Action Network.

Morton analyzed the images, text, and other symbols on the billboards. The first road sign includes the words "HITCHHIKING/Is It Worth the Risk?" in large letters, with the statement, "ain't worth the risk sister" in smaller, less distinct print. The second billboard reads in part, "GIRLS DON'T HITCHHIKE/on the/Highway of Tears." Morton observes that one thing the billboards do is identify hitchhiking as a form of "contentious mobility," one which any prudent, responsible person would avoid. But nowhere on the signs are there suggestions for alternative, legitimate forms of transportation, nor is there any acknowledgment that Indigenous women often lack the resources needed to travel independently by car or public transport. Also missing from the signs, she points out, is any indication of why Indigenous women need to travel the highway in the first place, which typically includes gaining access to social services such as women's shelters, health care, and education. Morton asserts that what is and is *not* stated on the billboards are equally significant.

A key issue Morton addresses in her analysis is that the billboards in no way try to portray the social and political position Indigenous women find themselves in, and there is no attempt to set the tragedy of the Highway of Tears in its appropriate socio-historical context. Morton sees the "intersection of race, gender, mobility and violence" (2016, p. 300), all in the larger setting of European conquest and colonialism, as a more realistic interpretive frame to use when trying to remedy what happens on the Highway of Tears. But rather than taking a sociologically informed approach to the issue, the billboards imply that the disappearance of Indigenous women along this route is merely the result of reckless behaviour or misadventure.

incorporated into DA. However, DA practitioners break with their CA counterparts when they speculate on motives, which is quite evident in the critical discourse analysis discussed above. It is precisely this practice of speculating on things that are not directly discernible in the sequences of talk that conversation analysts reject, as when Schegloff (1997, p. 183) wrote of DA: "Discourse is too often made subservient to contexts not of its participants' making, but of its analysts' insistence." For their part, discourse analysts object to the restrictions that CA imposes, because those restrictions cause conversation analysts to "rarely raise their eyes from the next turn in the conversation, [which] is not an entire conversation or sizeable slice of social life but usually a tiny fragment" (Wetherell, 1998, p. 402).

Writing from a **critical realist** position, Reed (2000) argued that discourses should be examined in relation to social structures such as the power relationships that create the discourses. This approach, which is exemplified in the work of critical discourse analysts, shows how discourses work through existing structures, and expands discourse from a self-referential concept in which nothing of significance exists outside itself into a "generative mechanism." That position is perhaps closer to the classic concerns of the social sciences than the anti-realist stance taken by some CA and DA researchers.

Advantages of content analysis

Content analysis has several advantages:

- In its most quantitative form, it is a very transparent research method, making replication relatively easy. It is because of this transparency that content analysis is often said to be an "objective" method of analysis.
- It allows for longitudinal analysis. For example, a crime study can be expanded to examine changes in newspaper crime reporting over two different time periods.
- Content analysis is an unobtrusive, nonreactive method. Newspaper articles and television scripts are generally not written with the expectation that a content analysis might one day be carried out on them. On the other hand, if the object of analysis is an interview transcript or ethnography, its content may have been at least partly influenced by anticipation of such scrutiny and thus may contain some reactive error.
- Content analysis is a highly flexible method, applicable to several different kinds of unstructured information. Although it is primarily applied to mass media outputs, it has a much broader applicability.
- Content analysis can permit the study of social groups that are difficult to access. For example, much of what social scientists know about the social backgrounds of elite groups, such as company directors and top military personnel, comes from content analyses of publications such as *Who's Who* and the business pages of newspapers.

Disadvantages of content analysis

Like all research techniques, content analysis suffers from certain limitations:

- A content analysis can only be as good as the documents it explores. Recall that Scott (1990) recommended assessing documents in terms of criteria such as authenticity (the document is what it purports to be); credibility (there are no grounds for thinking that its contents have been distorted in any way); and representativeness (the specific documents examined are representative of all possible relevant documents).
- Even in quantitative content analysis, it's almost impossible to devise coding manuals that do not require some interpretation by the coder. It seems unlikely that there is ever a perfect correspondence of interpretation between different coders.
- Problems of interpretation are especially likely to arise when the aim is to identify *latent* meanings (as opposed to the more readily apparent *manifest* meanings). For example, in searching for traditional markers of masculinity and femininity (see Box 12.5), the potential for conflicting interpretations is magnified. A related distinction is sometimes made between mechanical analysis (in particular, counting certain words) and analysis that emphasizes themes in the text, which entails a higher level of abstraction and a correspondingly greater risk of measurement invalidity.
- Content analysis may not be helpful in answering "why?" questions. For example, Jagger's (1998) analysis of dating advertisements clearly showed that both men and women put less emphasis on the "attractiveness, shape and size" they desired in a partner than they did on their own appearance (p. 807; see Box 12.5). But further research would be needed to determine *why* this was the case. Similarly, Fenton et al. (1998) found that sociology was only the fourth-most common discipline explicitly referred to (after psychology, economics, and social policy) when social science research was reported in the mass media, but it was by far the most frequently *inferred* discipline (not directly mentioned, but apparently the discipline under discussion). Again, however, the reasons behind this phenomenon could only be a matter for speculation (Fenton et al., 1998).

- Some content analysis studies are accused of being atheoretical, and it's easy to see why. The emphasis on measurement in content analysis can easily lead researchers to focus on what is measurable rather than what is theoretically significant or important. However, content analysis is not necessarily atheoretical. Jagger (1998), for instance, placed her findings on dating advertisements in the context of current ideas about consumerism and the body. And Harding's (2006; 2010) content analysis of media portrayals of Canadian Indigenous people was underpinned by theoretical ideas pertaining to racism and ethnic conflict.

Key Points

- Depending on how it is done, content analysis can be mainly quantitative or qualitative in nature.
- It's important to have clear research questions and to be explicit about what is to be analyzed.
- Documents (as the term is used here) provide many different kinds of information and can take the form of personal documents, official documents from state or private sources, and output from the mass media.
- Such materials can be used for both quantitative and qualitative research.
- Documents may be in printed, visual, digital, or any other retrievable format.
- Many researchers believe that almost anything can be "read" as a "text."
- Criteria for evaluating the quality of documents include authenticity, credibility, representativeness, and meaning; some may be more relevant than others, depending on the nature of the document.
- The design of a coding schedule and preparation of a coding manual are crucial steps in content analysis. In quantitative content analysis, this is done before the materials are examined.
- Content analysis can be particularly challenging when it is used to search for latent meanings and themes.
- Semiotics and hermeneutics are qualitative approaches to content analysis.
- There is disagreement over whether readers of documents are active or passive consumers of the messages they receive.
- Both conversation analysis (CA) and discourse analysis (DA) approaches make language itself a focus of research.
- CA is a systematic approach based on the principle that talk is structured by certain rules.
- Practitioners of CA avoid making inferences about talk that are not grounded in its immediate context.
- DA shares many features with CA but comes in several different versions and can be applied to a wider variety of phenomena.
- DA sees discourse as a means of conveying meaning and generally relates meaning in talk to contextual factors.
- Critical discourse analysis situates texts in the context of larger social structures such as power hierarchies and systems of inequality.
- As with all research methods, there are advantages and disadvantages to content analysis.

Questions for Review (R) and Creative Application (A)

R1 What types of material may serve as "documents" in social research?

A1 Should there be a fifth criterion for assessing documents? If so, what should it be?

Personal documents

R2 List the different kinds of personal documents and rank them in terms of Scott's four criteria.

A2 Go online and take a look at the Mackenzie King diaries. What themes would you want to analyze if you were to do a content analysis of this information?

Official government documents

R3 How might official government documents be biased? How do these documents fare in terms of Scott's criteria?

A3 You've decided to do a content analysis of Question Period in the House of Commons, using *Hansard* as a source. Pick an issue to be analyzed, and explain what words or expressions you would search for to provide information on it.

Official documents deriving from private sources

R4 What kinds of documents may be considered private official documents? How do these documents fare in terms of Scott's criteria?

A4 You've chosen to analyze the private documents of a major oil company, but the company will only provide you with materials that have been cleared by its public relations department. Prepare a summary of what you do *not* expect to find in the documents.

Mass media outputs

R5 How might mass media outputs be biased? How do they fare in terms of Scott's criteria?

A5 You will be comparing the content provided by the print version of a major national newspaper in Canada with what it offers in its online version. How might the content differ? How might it be similar?

Manifest and latent content

R6 What is the difference between manifest and latent content? What are the implications of that distinction for content analysis?

A6 Record the first two minutes of any TV news program. Present a summary of its manifest content, and then an account of its latent content.

Coding

R7 What potential pitfalls need to be guarded against when devising coding schedules and manuals?

A7 You are planning to do a content analysis of daytime TV commercials. What themes would you examine? Explain why your themes are important.

Semiotics

R8 What is the difference between denotative and connotative meaning?

A8 Why are "used" cars sometimes referred to as "pre-owned"?

Conversation analysis

R9 Explain what each of the following means: "turn-taking," "adjacency pairs," "preference organization," "repair mechanism." How do they relate to the production of social order?

A9 Evaluate the argument that CA should examine a participant's motives.

Discourse analysis

R10 In what ways may DA be anti-realist and constructionist?

A10 You've decided to pursue a career in journalism because you believe that discourse is a form of action. Explain.

Critical discourse analysis

R11 Why do critical discourse analysts make reference to power structures, systems of inequality, and other political and sociological factors in their work?

A11 Should all researchers doing CA and DA make reference to macro political and social factors in their studies? Explain.

Advantages and disadvantages of content analysis

R12 Explain how content analysis can be used as a form of longitudinal analysis.

A12 How might the need for coders to interpret meaning undermine latent content analysis?

Interactive Classroom Activities

1. The class is divided up into small groups. Each group selects a topic of interest that has been reported in newspapers—for example, a school shooting, an act of terrorism. Each group then:

a. searches the Internet for newspaper accounts of the event, and selects three for analysis;
b. decides on at least three themes in the accounts that are noteworthy, as well as other aspects of the stories that seem relevant—for example, number of victims, type of weapons used;
c. produces both a coding schedule and a coding manual to do a content analysis of the three accounts;
d. creates a numerical summary of the three articles based on the data gathered in the coding schedule; and
e. discusses salient interpretations that arose out of the content analysis, and if possible, relates them to hypotheses or theories (either original or already established in the literature) that may follow from the content analysis.

The class as a whole then reconvenes. Each group presents the results of its analysis to the class, which is encouraged to ask questions and provide critical commentary.

2. The class is divided up into small groups. Each group searches the Internet for a five-minute clip of a movie or television drama that it considers to be worthy of analysis. Each group then:

a. decides on at least three themes in the clip that are noteworthy, as well as other aspects of it that seem relevant—for example, underlying racist assumptions, gender stereotypes, jingoism;
b. produces both a coding schedule and a coding manual to do a content analysis of the clip; the former should be created in such a way that the *number* of instances of a particular theme can be recorded;
c. creates a numerical summary of the clip based on the data gathered in the coding schedule; and
d. discusses salient interpretations that arose out of the content analysis, and if possible, relates them to hypotheses or theories (either original or already established in the literature) that may follow from the content analysis.

The class as a whole then reconvenes. Each group presents the results of its analysis to the class, which is encouraged to ask questions and provide critical commentary.

Relevant Websites

Information on ethnomethodology and conversation analysis can be found at the ***EMCA wiki page***.

http://emcawiki.net/Main_Page

The journal ***Discourse & Society*** is an international journal that features articles on discourse analysis (you may have to go through your institution's library sever to access the material).

https://journals.sagepub.com/home/das

A YouTube video describes how to do ***qualitative content analysis***.

www.youtube.com/watch?v=BhQX-zKultw

An overview of the software available to do content analysis can be found at the ***Audience Dialogue*** website.

www.audiencedialogue.net/soft-cont.html

The ***Discourse and Rhetoric Group*** at Loughborough University provides a tutorial on conversation analysis.

http://ca-tutorials.lboro.ac.uk/sitemenu.htm

(Websites accessed on 4 September 2021)

OXFORD learning link More resources are available on Oxford Learning Link. Visit **https://learninglink.oup.com/** for:

- Student self-quiz
- Flash cards
- Audio clips
- Videos
- Activities

13 Qualitative Data Analysis

Chapter Overview

Analyzing **qualitative** data from interviews, **participant observation**, **content analysis**, or any other **qualitative source** is never straightforward. For one thing, such data typically take the form of a large body of unstructured textual material. Moreover, whereas **quantitative research** has clear-cut rules for data analysis, this is not the case in qualitative research. This chapter will examine some general approaches to qualitative data management. Computer software is often used by qualitative researchers to assist with **coding**: the main feature of qualitative data analysis. This software, often referred to as computer-assisted qualitative data analysis software (CAQDAS), eliminates many, if not most, of the clerical tasks associated with the manual coding and retrieving of data. Although there is no industry leader among the different programs available for qualitative data analysis, this chapter introduces one of the most popular programs: QSR NVivo (discussed in detail in the Appendix).

This chapter will explore:

- **grounded theory** as a general strategy of qualitative data analysis; its main features, processes, and outcomes are presented along with some criticisms;
- coding as a key process in grounded theory and in qualitative data analysis more generally; there is an extended discussion of what it entails and some of its limitations;
- some of the debates about the desirability of using CAQDAS;
- the criticism that coding tends to fragment data; and
- the idea of **narrative analysis**, an approach that reduces that fragmentation.

▲ PrathanChorruangsak/iStockphoto

Key Learning Outcomes

Here is a list of goals you should try to achieve as you read and think about the material in this chapter. After completing this chapter, you should be able to:

1. Describe the general strategies of qualitative analysis, including analytic induction and, in particular, grounded theory.
2. Discuss the basic operations in qualitative data analysis.
3. Detail how coding fragments qualitative data and how computer software aids in the coding process.
4. Identify the problems inherent in coding qualitative data.
5. Explain how narrative analysis is used by qualitative researchers.

Einstein once famously said that the most incomprehensible thing about the universe is that it is comprehensible. What is it that allows us to understand how the universe works? The simple fact that it shows certain regularities or patterns. Science, including social science, is all about finding those patterns and then explaining them.

Qualitative social research may seem a long way away from Einsteinian physics, but in essence the "concepts" and "categories" that qualitative researchers look for as they navigate through vast seas of data are simply patterns. This suggests that the social world of meanings, perceptions, and feelings is not chaotic, but has a coherence to it that we can know and describe if we use the right methodology. This chapter explores how qualitative researchers make sense of the data they gather, including how some of them use it to generate theory.

Introduction

Making sense of the words contained in **field notes**, interview transcripts, or other documents presents some challenges not seen in numerical analysis, but the qualitative research process provides opportunities to pursue emergent lines of thought and interpretation that would be largely impossible in quantitative studies. One challenge of qualitative research is that it rapidly generates a large, cumbersome database. Miles (1979) described qualitative data as an "attractive nuisance"—attractive because of their richness and the insight that may be gained from them, but also a nuisance because that very richness can create analytical difficulties that are not always acknowledged.

Finding a path through a thicket of prose is not easy, especially for researchers confronting such data for the first time. "What do I do with it now?" is a common refrain. In large part this is because there are few well-established and widely accepted rules for the analysis of qualitative data. Learning the techniques of quantitative data analysis can be challenging too, but at least there are unambiguous rules for handling such data. Analytic procedures for qualitative data analysis have not reached the same degree of codification, and many feel that would be undesirable anyway (cf. Bryman & Burgess, 1994). Nevertheless, there are some broad guidelines (Okely, 1994) which we will explore. This chapter has two main sections:

- *General strategies of qualitative data analysis:* **analytic induction** and grounded theory
- *Basic operations in qualitative data analysis:* coding and narrative analysis, the latter differing in style from both grounded theory and the secondary analysis of qualitative data

General strategies of qualitative data analysis

Analytic induction

One difference between qualitative and quantitative data analysis is that, with the latter, analysis occurs after all the data have been collected. Qualitative analysis, on the other hand, is often *iterative* (as noted in Chapter 9), meaning that analysis takes place after some of the data have been collected and then the implications of that analysis shape further data collection.

Analytic induction is an example of a type of qualitative research that uses an iterative process. It begins with a rough definition of a research question, proceeds to a hypothetical answer, and then moves to data collection. What makes it unique is that analytic induction seeks universal explanations of phenomena that permit no exception. If a case inconsistent with the hypothesis is encountered, the analyst either redefines the hypothesis to exclude the deviant or negative case or reformulates the hypothesis and proceeds with further data collection. With each new deviant case they find, analysts must choose again between reformulation and redefinition. Data collection continues until no new inconsistent piece of evidence is found. It is, in effect, a special case of grounded theory, one that holds 100 per cent of the time. But it is also rare, as the requirement to be able to explain all cases means that the explanation may become too broad to be useful. While analytic induction is an extremely rigorous method of analysis, it is not favoured by many current qualitative researchers. In Canada it has been used by Whitehead and Carpenter (1999) in a qualitative study on unsafe sexual behaviour in the military. They found that the greater the social and cultural distance between sex partners, the greater the likelihood of condom use.

One further problem with analytic induction is that (unlike grounded theory) it does not provide useful guidelines on the number of cases required before the absence of negative cases can be assumed and the validity of the hypothetical explanation (whether reformulated or not) can be confirmed.

Grounded theory

Grounded theory is defined as "theory that was derived from data, systematically gathered and analyzed through the research process" (Strauss & Corbin, 1998, p. 12). Its two central features are its development of theory out of data, and an iterative or recursive approach in which data collection and analysis proceed in tandem, repeatedly referring back to each other.

Grounded theory is by far the most widely used framework for analyzing qualitative data. Yet there is considerable controversy about what it entails (Charmaz, 2000). For example, it is vague on the difference between **concepts** and categories. As we will see later in this chapter, it seems that the former term is increasingly being replaced by the latter, and this inconsistent use of key terms is not helpful either to practitioners of the craft or to people trying to understand the overall process.

Against such a background, defining grounded theory is not easy. As well, grounded theory cannot be described here in all its facets; we will simply outline its main features.

The basic features of grounded theory

Some of the basic features of grounded theory have been introduced in earlier chapters:

- *Coding*: the key process in grounded theory, whereby data are broken down into component parts and given names. It begins soon after the initial collection of data. According to Charmaz (2000): "Unlike quantitative research that requires data to fit into *preconceived* standardized codes, the researcher's interpretations of data shape his or her emergent codes in grounded theory" (p. 515, emphasis in original).
- *Constant comparison*: continuous comparison of new and existing data within a particular concept or category. Glaser and Strauss (1967) advised writing a *memo* (see page 320) on each concept/category after a few phenomena have been coded. Comparison also entails sensitivity to differences between emerging concepts/categories.
- ***Theoretical saturation:*** the point at which there is nothing to be gained by further reviewing of old data or collection of new information to see how it fits with emerging concepts or categories; new data are no longer illuminating.

Coding in grounded theory

Coding in grounded theory entails reviewing transcripts and/or field notes and giving labels (names) to items that seem to share a similar theme, to be of potential theoretical significance, and/or to be particularly salient within the social worlds under investigation. As Charmaz (1983) put it, "Codes . . . serve as shorthand devices to *label*, *separate*, *compile*, and *organize* data" (p. 186; emphases in original). This coding process differs from the coding used in the analysis of quantitative data (e.g., social **survey** data) in two ways. First, whereas quantitative analysis often involves testing a *pre-existing* theory, grounded theory uses coding as an important first step in the *generation* of theory. Second, whereas in quantitative analysis coding is more or less a way of managing data that have already been at least broadly categorized, in grounded theory (and other approaches to qualitative data analysis), coding is more tentative and fluid. The data are treated as potential indicators of concepts/categories, and the indicators are repeatedly compared to see which concepts/categories they fit with best. Ad hoc compromises may have to be made when more than one researcher is doing the coding (Tastsoglou & Miedema, 2003).

Strauss and Corbin (1990) distinguished three types of coding:

- *Open coding*: "the process of breaking down, examining, comparing, conceptualizing, and categorizing data" (p. 61); this process stays very close to the data and yields the concepts that are later grouped together to form categories. Thus, concepts such as anger, jealousy, or affection could form the category "emotion."
- *Axial coding*: "a set of procedures whereby data are put back together in new ways after open coding, by making connections between categories" (p. 96). This is done by linking codes to contexts, consequences, patterns of interaction, and apparent causes. Thus, the category of emotion, above, could be linked to the contexts in which it is expressed: for example, contexts of hardship or loss.
- *Selective coding*: "the procedure of selecting the core category, systematically relating it to other categories, validating those relationships, and filling in categories that need further refinement and development" (p. 116). A core category is the focus around which other categories are integrated—what Strauss and Corbin called the storyline that frames the account. In the case of hardship and loss, the core category might be "adaptation."

The three types of coding are really different levels of the same process, each relating to a different point in the process of elaborating concepts and categories. Not all grounded theory practitioners operate with this threefold distinction; the notion of axial coding has been especially controversial because it is sometimes perceived as closing off the coding process too quickly. Charmaz (2004) preferred to distinguish between open or initial coding and selective or focused coding. The former tends to be very detailed and may produce as much as one code per line of text. It is crucial at this stage of the research to be open-minded and to generate as many new ideas, and hence codes, as necessary to organize the data. Selective or focused coding emphasizes the codes that (a) appear most frequently and (b) seem most revealing. Combining the initial codes generates new codes. The data are then re-explored and re-evaluated in terms of the selected codes. Pidgeon and Henwood (2004) provided a useful example in their study of 60 mother–daughter relationships:

> The initial coding led to the development of a long and varied, but highly unwieldy, list of instances under the label "Relational Closeness." ... [A] closer reading and comparison of the individual instances indicated a much more mixed view of the emotional intensity of the relationships, ranging from a welcome but painful sense of gratitude and debt to a stance of hypersensitivity and a desire to flee from a relationship which involved "confinement" or "smothering." ... [T]his subdivision was retained and coded through their respective labels "Closeness" and "Overcloseness." (Pidgeon & Henwood, 2004, p. 638)

Research in the News

Natural disasters and mental health

Jason Jeandron/Shutterstock

Flooded streets in downtown Fredericton.

Julia Woodhall-Melnik, an assistant professor of sociology at the University of New Brunswick, St John, has been studying how the extensive flooding in southern New Brunswick in 2018 and 2019 impacted residents' mental health (Bissett, 2019; CBC News, 2019; Fraser 2019). Woodhall-Melnik points out, "Housing loss in general can lead to fatigue, depression, anxiety, grief, sleep disturbances and the development of post-traumatic stress disorder" (Bissett, 2019). She hopes that her research will shed light on how to reduce the impact of these types of events and determine what is needed to help people recover.

In the spring of 2019, Woodhall-Melnik conducted focus groups with over two dozen residents and interviewed 10 people involved in the official response to the 2018 flood. Her research considered the effect of informal supports like neighbours and family, and formal supports such as first responders and the provincial government. She found that people had a strong bond to their property and community. They wanted to stay after recovering from the flood, but they were worried about courting disaster. Some were optimistic that the flood was a once-in-a-lifetime, while others were concerned about more flooding in 2019. People's stress and anxiety varied, with the uncertainty about another potential disaster leading some to despair. Working alongside neighbours and banding together in responding to the flood through such things as sandbagging was found to help residents cope with the situation. When the area experienced more flooding in 2019, it provided Woodhall-Melnik with an opportunity to study the impact of a multi-year disaster. In her follow-up research she plans to also examine how the experience has influenced residents' views on climate change.

Overall, then, the process of coding begins with the data themselves and then gradually moves to more selective and abstract ways of conceptualizing the phenomenon of interest.

Outcomes of grounded theory

The following are the products of different phases of grounded theory.

- *Concepts*: the "building blocks of theory" (Strauss & Corbin, 1998, p. 101), the discrete phenomena produced through *open coding*
- *Categories*: at a higher level of abstraction, subsume two or more concepts. An especially crucial category may become a *core category* (see Box 13.1).
- *Properties*: attributes or aspects of a category
- *Hypotheses*: initial hunches about relationships between concepts
- *Theory*: "a set of well-developed categories . . . that are systematically interrelated through statements of relationship to form a theoretical framework that explains some relevant social . . . or other phenomenon" (Strauss & Corbin,

Box 13.1 | Categories in grounded theory

Whiting, Parker, & Houghtaling (2014) used grounded theory to explore how male perpetrators of intimate partner violence (IPV) perceived their actions. The researchers suggest that examining the perpetrator's point of view is important in order to fully understand IPV and develop effective therapies and interventions.

Qualitative interviews with 13 men were conducted, with three research questions guiding the analysis: How do men who have been violent describe their relationship in terms of abuse? What do men believe contributes to the violence? How do they feel about the violence in their relationship? Prior to open coding, the data were examined to identify "significant statements" or "meaning units." Open coding was then performed by labelling the selected statements with descriptors. Following that, axial coding was done to group the data into "identifiable categories that tied together" (Whiting et al., 2014, p. 279).

Although it was not uncommon for perpetrators to try to justify or rationalize their violent behaviour, one of the categories that emerged was "remorse." One interviewee stated, "I have always been upset by the abusive behaviours," while another said, "I was in the wrong forever [*sic*] putting my hands on her" (Whiting et al., 2014, p. 282). The authors mention that a finding of perpetrator remorse is rare in studies of IPV, possibly because researchers do not want to appear to be softening or excusing violence. They take the position that violence is inexcusable and make their views on that issue quite clear in the article, and also point out that the offenders' remorse may simply be an attempt at manipulation. Nonetheless, the researchers make the case that counsellors and other professionals should take the remorse expressed by perpetrators as a starting point to help them develop empathy for their victims and to reflect on how IPV goes against their values and self-image. Doing so may reduce the tendency to rationalize IPV and could ultimately result in less physical abuse.

> 1998, p. 22). In grounded theory there are two levels of theory: *substantive* and *formal*. A substantive theory pertains to a certain *empirical* instance of a phenomenon such as racial prejudice in a hospital setting (see Box 14.1). A formal theory is at a higher level of abstraction and has applicability to several substantive areas, such as prejudice generally or in a variety of spheres. The generation of formal theory requires data collection in different settings.

The various elements are portrayed in Figure 13.1. Any diagram is only an approximation, but this is particularly true in this instance, partly because there are different approaches to grounded theory and partly because it is difficult to convey diagrammatically the iterative nature of grounded theory—in particular, the recursive relationship between data collection and analysis (indicated by arrows pointing in both directions). The figure implies the following:

- The researcher begins with a general research question (step 1).
- Relevant people and/or incidents are **theoretically sampled** (step 2).
- Relevant data are collected (step 3).
- Data are coded (step 4), which may, at the level of open coding, generate concepts (step 4a).
- There is a constant movement backward and forward among the first four steps, so that early coding suggests a need for new data, which leads to theoretical sampling, and so on.
- Through constant comparison of indicators and concepts (step 5) categories are generated (step 5a). It's crucial to ensure a fit between indicators and concepts.

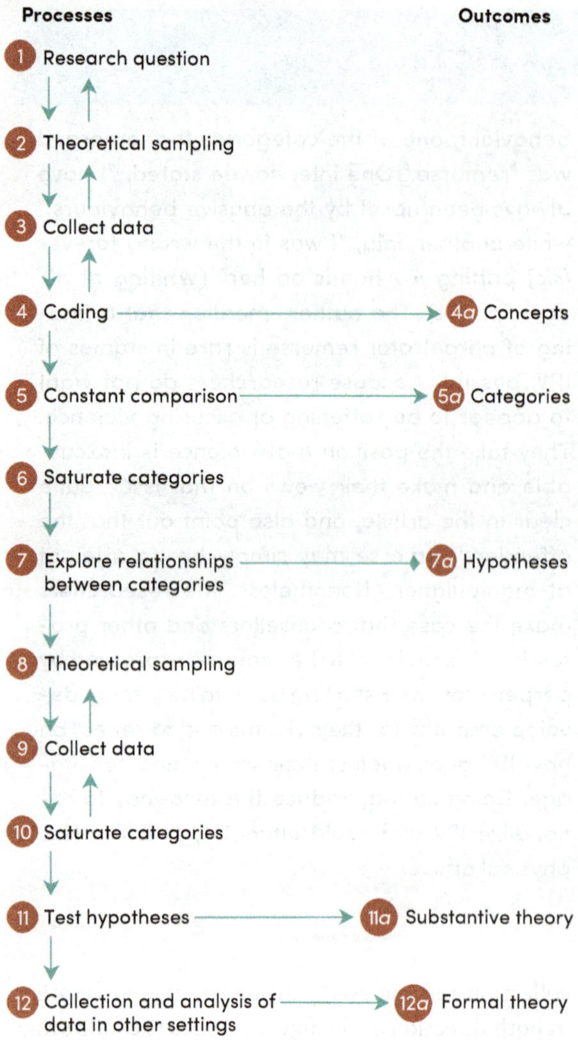

FIGURE 13.1 Processes and outcomes in grounded theory

- Categories become saturated in the course of the coding process (step 6).
- Relationships between categories are explored (step 7) in such a way that hypotheses about connections between categories emerge (step 7a).
- Further data are collected via theoretical sampling (steps 8 and 9).
- The collection of data is likely to be governed by the theoretical saturation principle (step 10) and the testing of the emerging hypotheses (step 11), which leads to specification of substantive theory (step 11a). See Box 13.2 for an illustration.
- The substantive theory may eventually be explored using grounded theory processes in a different setting from the one in which it was generated (step 12). In this way a formal theory (step 12a)—relating to more abstract categories not specifically examined in the research—can be generated.

Note that Step 12 is relatively uncommon, because researchers using the grounded theory approach typically concentrate on one particular setting.

Sometimes researchers who use grounded theory procedures produce surprising findings, as Box 13.3 shows. When you read grounded theory studies, keep in mind that some authors will claim to have used the "grounded theory" approach when in fact they have not used it at all (Charmaz, 2000) or have used just one or two features of it (Locke, 1996). Concepts and categories are at the heart of the grounded theory approach, but coding, theoretical sampling, and theoretical saturation are also key features. Again, Box 13.2 provides an illustration.

Memos

An important aid to grounded theory research is the *memo*: an analytical note that researchers write for themselves or colleagues about a code, category, or other ideas they might have about their data. Memo-writing occurs throughout the research process and assists researchers in developing their tentative analytical hunches. Charmaz (2006) advises researchers to write memos in whatever way advances their thinking and research. Memos can be very useful in helping researchers to crystallize their ideas and keep track of their thoughts on various topics; they also help to shape the researchers' reflections on broader issues.

Reflecting on their separate research projects on Canadian first responders' use of emergency technologies and the meanings Inuit attach to their living spaces, Sanders and van den Scott (2018) describe memo-writing as an integral part of how they made sense of their data. They kept notebooks with them throughout the research process so they could record "any thoughts, questions, insights, and concerns that might arise" (p. 280). During their coding,

Box 13.2 | Grounded theory in action

Charmaz (1997) used grounded theory to examine the identity dilemmas of men with chronic but not terminal illnesses. She outlined clearly the chief steps in her analysis, which were:

- interviews with men and a small number of women;
- exploring the interview transcripts for gender differences;
- searching for themes in the men's interviews and published personal accounts such as autobiographies. An example was the theme of "accommodation to uncertainty," as the men found ways of dealing with the unpredictable paths of their illnesses;
- building "analytic categories from men's definitions of and taken-for-granted assumptions about their situations" (p. 39). Of particular significance in Charmaz's work is the idea of "identity dilemmas": the ways in which men approach and possibly resolve the assault on their traditionally masculine self-images. She showed that men often use strategies to re-establish earlier selves in order to preserve their identities, at least in their own eyes;
- further interviews designed to refine the categories;
- rereading personal accounts of chronic illness with a particular focus on gender;
- reading a new group of personal accounts; and
- making "comparisons with women on selected key points" (Charmaz, 1997, p. 39).

Charmaz proposed a substantive theory that helped to explain the importance of notions of masculinity in maintaining an identity for chronically ill men.

memo-writing helped them to contemplate connections between their codes and make links between theories and ideas from the literature. It also assisted them in moving their abstract coding to a more theoretical level, and helped them identify areas where clarification and more data collection were necessary. For a further illustration of the use of memos, see Box 13.4.

Criticisms of grounded theory

Grounded theory has limitations:

- Some question whether researchers can fully suspend their awareness of existing theories or concepts until the late stages of analysis when their theories are supposed to emerge. Most social researchers are sensitive to the conceptual armoury of their disciplines and it seems unlikely that this awareness can be put aside. In fact, few people today believe that theory-neutral observation is possible. It is generally agreed that what is "seen," even in research, is conditioned by what is already known about the social world under study (in terms of both social scientific concepts and general, everyday ones). Many writers consider it an advantage to build on the work of others.
- In practical terms, the time required to transcribe recordings of interviews, for example, can make it difficult for a researcher with a tight deadline to carry out a genuine grounded theory analysis, given the constant interplay of data collection and conceptualization that it requires.
- It isn't clear that the grounded theory method necessarily results in *theory*. It offers a rigorous approach to the generation of concepts and categories, but it is often difficult to see what theory, in the sense of an *explanation* of something, is put forward. Moreover, although lip-service is frequently paid to the idea of generating formal theory, most grounded theories pertain only to the specific social phenomenon under investigation—not to a broader range of phenomena.

Box 13.3 | Some counterintuitive results arising from a grounded theory approach

One of the key insights of qualitative research is that people often interpret their situations in ways that an outsider might not expect. Take the example of women with eating disorders. You might think that they would definitely want to change their eating habits, but Whitehead (2010) found that that is not always the case. Instead, she found that some women suffering from anorexia nervosa and bulimia do not want to change that aspect of their lives, and in fact may seek to develop a collective identity with women in similar situations by interacting with them on pro-eating disorder (Pro-ED) websites. These sites are controversial in that they do not present eating disorders in a negative light or recommend that sufferers seek treatment, but instead foster a sense of solidarity and companionship for people who already have the condition and who do not want to change. Some openly revel in their situation, such as one woman who wrote that "Ana [anorexia] loves me, She may use me, But she won't forget me. I am not her victim, I am one of her lovers. Every day I pray to be loved above the rest" (Whitehead, 2010, p. 617).

The research involved the author regularly visiting pro-ED websites and closely monitoring the postings made there. Since the research was not conducted in person, Whitehead was not able to get information on the demographic characteristics of the participants and she makes no mention of their nationality. Like many other virtual interactions, the ones she observed were probably not limited to people from a single country, although much of what she describes is applicable to Canadian society.

Taking a grounded theory approach to the issue, Whitehead identified five practices that contributed to the development of a collective identity: encouraging surreptitious eating behaviours by sharing stories about how they had hidden their bulimia from their partners or family members; focusing on domestic tasks such as cooking (for example, sharing recipes for dishes that are delicious but not calorific and that are easily purged); encouraging the idea that beauty, in particular thinness, is essential to self-worth; promoting friendships among people with eating disorders and even casting the disorder as a friend; and drawing inspiration from celebrity women who have battled eating disorders or who are simply thin and beautiful. One of the author's main conclusions is that these practices are "gendered" in the sense that they reinforce and reproduce dominant norms and stereotypes about what it means to be a woman.

- Grounded theory tends to invite researchers to code their data into discrete chunks. However, some commentators believe that this kind of fragmentation results in a loss of context and narrative flow (Coffey & Atkinson, 1996); we will return to this point later in this chapter.

That said, and even though many studies do not use it consistently, grounded theory is probably the most influential overall strategy in use today for qualitative data analysis. Many of its core elements, from coding and memos to the very idea of allowing theory to emerge from data, have also been very influential. It is striking that the use of computer software has implicitly promoted grounded theory, because the software programs have in many cases been written with its processes in mind (Lonkila, 1995).

Basic operations in qualitative data analysis

Coding (or *indexing*) is the starting point for most forms of qualitative data analysis. The principles involved have been well developed by writers

Box 13.4 | A memo

In their research into the bus industry, Bryman, Gillingwater, and McGuinness (1996) noticed that managers frequently mentioned that their companies still followed officially discontinued rules and practices. Managers often suggested that "inherited" characteristics were holding them back in their efforts to adapt to a new competitive environment. "Inheritance" is what Strauss (1987) called an *in vivo code*: one derived from the language of people in the social context under study, as opposed to a *sociologically constructed code*, which is a label created by the researcher. The following memo outlines the concept of inheritance, provides some illustrative quotations, and suggests some properties of the concept.

Memo for inheritance

> *Inheritance:* Many of our interviewees suggest that they have inherited certain company traits and traditions that they themselves would not have chosen. The key point about this inheritance is that our interviewees see it as hindering their ability to respond to a changing environment.

Inherited features might include:

- expensive and often inappropriate fleets of vehicles and depots;
- the survival of attitudes and behaviour patterns, particularly among bus drivers, that are seen as inappropriate to the new environment (for example, lack of concern for customer service) and that hinder service innovation; and
- high wages from the earlier era, which make it possible for competitors who pay their drivers lower wages to enter the market and charge less for their services.

Sample comments:

> "I suppose another major weakness is that we are very tied by conditions and practices we've inherited." (Commercial Director, Company G)
>
> "We have what we've inherited and we now have a massive surplus of double decks [i.e., too many buses of the wrong size]. ... We have to go on operating those." (Managing Director, Company B)
>
> Managing Director of Company E said the company had inherited staff steeped in old attitudes: "We don't have a staff where the message is 'the customer is number one.'"

concerned with grounded theory and other perspectives. Among the issues they consider in developing codes (cf. Lofland & Lofland, 1995) are the following:

- Of what general category is this datum an instance?
- What does this datum represent?
- What is this datum about?
- What question does this datum suggest?
- What sort of answer to that question does this datum imply?
- What is happening here?
- What are people doing?
- What do people say they are doing?
- What kind of event is going on?

Steps and considerations in coding

Following are some guidelines for coding:

- *Code as soon as possible (that is, as data are being collected), as grounded theory suggests.* This may sharpen an understanding of the data and help with theoretical sampling.

It can also help to alleviate the feeling of being swamped by the data. At the very least, begin transcribing recorded interviews at a relatively early stage.

- *Read through the initial set of transcripts, field notes, documents, and so on, without taking any notes or considering any interpretations.* Only when you have finished should you consider jotting down a few general notes about what seems especially interesting, important, or significant.
- *Do it again.* Read through the data again, but this time make marginal notes about significant remarks or observations—as many as possible. Initially, they will be very basic: perhaps keywords used by respondents or themes in the data. Now you are *coding*: generating terms that will help in interpreting the data.
- *Don't worry about generating too many codes—at least in the early stages of analysis.* Some will be fruitful, others not. The important thing is to be as inventive and imaginative as possible; tidying up can be done later. Remember that any one datum can, and often should, be coded in more than one way. An outburst of anger, for example, can be seen as an emotion, a cause of stress, or the beginning of a new level of integration. As a first stage, Charmaz (2004) recommended "line by line coding," in which virtually every line in the transcript (or other data source) has a code attached to it: this way, the qualitative researcher does not lose contact with the data and the perspectives and interpretations of those being studied. Although the line-by-line approach almost always results in a proliferation of codes, this should not be alarming. What qualitative researchers need to do is ask what these codes have in common so that they can be combined into higher-order and more abstract codes.
- *Review the codes, possibly in relation to the transcripts.* Are two or more words or phrases being used to describe the same phenomenon? If so, remove one of them. Do some of the codes relate to concepts and categories in the existing literature? If so, would it make sense to use the existing terms? Are there connections between the codes? Is there evidence that respondents believe one thing tends to be associated with or caused by something else?
- *Consider more general theoretical ideas in relation to codes and data.* Now you can start generating some general theoretical ideas about the data. Try to outline connections between concepts and any developing categories. Consider in more detail how they relate to the existing literature. Develop hypotheses about the linkages you perceive and go back to the data to see if they can be confirmed.
- *Finally, keep coding in perspective.* It's only one part (albeit an important part) of the analysis: a mechanism for thinking about the meaning of the data *and* for reducing the data to a manageable size. The larger task of interpretation awaits, including forging interconnections between codes, reflecting on the overall importance of the findings for the research literature, and pondering the significance of the coded material for the lives of the people who are the subjects of the research.

Turning data into fragments

The coding of materials such as interview transcripts typically entails writing marginal notes on them and gradually refining those notes into codes and then cutting and pasting (sometimes in the literal sense, with scissors and glue). It entails cutting transcripts into chunks of data (and of course carefully identifying the origins of each chunk with, for example, name, position in organization, date) for later data retrieval. Although word-processing programs can be used for this task, CAQDAS has become popular.

CAQDAS has been a growth area in terms of both the proliferation of programs and the numbers of people using them. Most of the best-known programs allow analysts to code text and later retrieve it, tasks that were once done manually. For example, the software can search for all chunks of text relating to a code, and then cut and paste them together. Human input is still crucial, however. CAQDAS cannot help with decisions about the codes, or the coding of textual materials, or the interpretation of

Methods in Motion | Applications to Canadian Society

Using grounded theory to make sense of mothers' experiences with food insecurity in Nova Scotia

Lesley Frank (2020), an associate professor of sociology at Acadia University, conducted a qualitative study on infant food insecurity in Nova Scotia. The questions that guided her research included: "What is the relationship between household food insecurity and infant feeding practice?" and "What role, if any, does Canadian public policy play in this relationship?" (Frank, 2020, p. 121). By seeking answers to these questions, her book, *Out of Milk: Infant Food Insecurity in a Rich Nation* (2020), addresses the breastfeeding paradox: why mothers who can least afford to feed their infants formula are the ones who use it the most. The experience of food insecurity and poverty was at the heart of the issue.

In the first phase of Frank's research, she conducted 20 in-depth interviews with low-income mothers of infant children. To assist with her inductive analysis, Frank used NVivo as part of the coding process. She started by conducting line-by-line coding of participants' responses. The codes were not predetermined; instead, she allowed them to emerge from the data as she worked toward developing grounded theory. After completing her open coding, she sought to reduce the number of broad categories by making connections between the codes. She then re-coded her data through the lens of this new set of categories. During the last step of her analysis, she grouped the themes into three broad categories: "breastfeeding as a food security measure, breastfeeding as an insecure food system, and infant food insecurity related to formula feeding" (Frank, 2020, p. 127). Together, the categories that emerged out of Frank's analysis offer a typology of infant feeding practices for mothers' experiencing food insecurity. The impact of public policy on mothers' lives was also studied and became a subtheme of each of the three overarching themes identified by Frank.

Frank learned that relying exclusively on breastfeeding is largely unsustainable for low-income mothers. Some of the mothers in her study described wanting to breastfeed because it was seen as healthier and less expensive than formula, necessary for parent-child bonding, or because it was in keeping with cultural traditions; however, many mothers found breastfeeding challenging, and some found it impossible given the stress of living in poverty. Mary, one of the mothers in Frank's study, put it this way:

> I don't know if what I was producing was really enough, nutrient wise, if it was—How would you put it?—healthy enough for him, giving him what he needed. Plus, in order to be able to produce milk, the mother needs to be food secure and you don't have that all the time, and the situation could change for you on the drop of a dime.

Frank discovered that infant feeding practices have to do with more than what happens at the individual level. If the problem was to be understood, she realized that her analysis needed to also take into account how public policy and community supports intertwine with people's everyday lives. She writes, "Building infant food security means enhancing [. . .] practical institutional and community supports to form an integral component of health and social services for families. Doing so will help us to fulfil our collective responsibility for the welfare of children and the social reproduction of society" (p. 119).

findings. As with quantitative data analysis software such as **IBM SPSS Statistics** (SPSS), someone must still choose the variables to be analyzed and the analytic techniques to be used, and then make sense of the results. Each form of software requires creativity. CAQDAS differs from SPSS largely in terms of the type of data that can be used with it.

There is no CAQDAS industry leader, but NVivo is a package that most researchers would at least know by name. Earlier versions of the software became very popular in the 1990s. The Appendix outlines how to use NVivo for qualitative data analysis.

To use or not to use CAQDAS? With a very small data set, it is probably not worth the time and trouble required to become familiar with new software. Catterall and Maclaran (1997) have argued that CAQDAS is not very suitable for focus group data because the code and retrieve function tends to hide the communication process typical of focus groups. On the other hand, learning new software will give you skills that you may need in the future. CAQDAS is likely to be too expensive for personal purchase, though there are student and educational discounts. Demonstration copies of some of the main packages can be downloaded from the distributors' websites.

There is no one correct approach to coding data. As we suggested earlier, grounded theory conceives of different types of code. Coffey and Atkinson (1996) pointed to three different levels of coding, applied below to a passage from an interview that first appeared in Box 11.5 (p. 259).

- First there is a very basic coding, which, in the case of the Box 11.5 material could be liking or disliking the visit to a Disney theme park. However, such a coding scheme is unlikely to provide anything more than a superficial analysis.
- A second level involves a deeper awareness of the content of what is said and is organized around the focus of the research. An example might be countries "well-represented" and "missing" at Disney World.
- A third level moves slightly away from what the respondent says to explore broader analytic themes. The responses in the Box 11.5 transcript were coded in terms of characteristics such as enthusiasm ("uncritical enthusiasm"), attitudes toward the Disney Corporation ("not critical of Disney"); comments made about typical visitors ("visitors' ethnicity"); and the nature of critical comments ("aesthetic critique," "ethnicity critique," "nationality critique"). Interestingly, the passage also reveals the potential for a code employed by Coffey and Atkinson (1996, pp. 43–45): the use of a "contrastive rhetoric" (making a point about one thing by comparing it to something else). This feature occurred when the husband made a point about the representation of British culture, which he regarded as poor compared to that of China.

As Coffey and Atkinson (1996) observed, following Strauss and Corbin's account (1990) of grounded theory, codes should not be thought of purely as mechanisms for the fragmentation and retrieval of text. They can do more than simply manage the data gathered. For example, examination of the interconnections between codes may reveal that some are dimensions of a broader phenomenon. For example, "ethnicity critique" came to be seen as a dimension of "ideology critique," along with "class critique" and "gender critique." In this way, a map of the more general or formal properties of the concepts under development can be started.

Problems with coding

One of the most common criticisms of coding qualitative data is the risk of losing the context of what is said. (For a general critique of qualitative data analysis packages see Box 13.5.) By plucking chunks of text out of the context in which they appear, such as a particular interview transcript, the social setting can be lost. A second criticism of coding is that it results in fragmentation of the data, causing the narrative flow to be lost (Coffey & Atkinson, 1996). Sensitivity to this issue has been heightened since the late 1980s by a growing interest in narrative analysis (see later in this chapter). Riessman (1993) became concerned about fragmentation when

Box 13.5 | Lack of agreement about the utility of CAQDAS

Whereas the use of computer software is almost universal in quantitative data analysis, among qualitative data analysts it is sometimes avoided, for several reasons.

- Some writers worry that because qualitative data analysis packages make it so easy to quantify coded text, qualitative research will become subject to the reliability and validity criteria of quantitative research (Hesse-Biber, 1995).
- Others feel that CAQDAS reinforces and even exaggerates the tendency toward a fragmentation of the textual materials (Weaver & Atkinson, 1995), destroying the natural flow of interview transcripts and field notes. Awareness of context is crucial to many qualitative researchers, and they are concerned by the prospect that this awareness may be pushed to the sidelines. Stanley and Temple (1995) suggested that most of the coding and retrieval features needed for qualitative data analysis, such as search, cut, and paste, already exist in word-processing software. Using Microsoft Word, for example, would save not only money but also the time required to learn new software.
- Coffey, Holbrook, & Atkinson (1996) argued that the style of qualitative data analysis in most CAQDAS presumes a methodology—based on coding and retrieving text—that owes a great deal to grounded theory. In their view, the emergence of grounded theory as a new standard is inconsistent with a key strength of qualitative research: its flexibility.

On the other hand, several writers have extolled the virtues of such packages:

- CAQDAS, like NVivo, invites thought about "trees" of interrelated ideas—a useful feature in that it encourages the analyst to consider possible connections between concepts.
- Quantitative researchers often criticize the tendency toward "anecdotalism" found in much qualitative research—that is, the tendency to use quotations from interview transcripts or field notes with little sense of how representative they might be. CAQDAS makes it possible to count the frequency with which a particular form of behaviour occurs or a particular viewpoint is expressed in interviews.
- CAQDAS enhances the transparency of qualitative data analysis. How qualitative data were analyzed is often unclear in published reports (Bryman & Burgess, 1994). CAQDAS may force researchers to be more explicit and reflective about the process of analysis, and may indirectly encourage replication, a feature often lacking in qualitative analysis.
- When working with large amounts of qualitative data ("big qual") on multi-person international research teams, technological advances in CAQDAS, like cloud-based storage, can assist with data management and collaboration (Brower, Bertrand Jones, Osborne-Lampkin, Hu, & Park-Gaghan, 2019).

coding themes in her structured interview study on divorce and gender:

> Some [interviewees] developed long accounts of what had happened in their marriages to justify their divorces. I did not realize these were narratives until I struggled to code them. Applying traditional qualitative methods, I searched the texts for common thematic elements. But some individuals knotted together several themes into long accounts that had coherence and sequence, defying easy categorization. I found myself not wanting to fragment the long accounts into distinct thematic categories. (p. vi)

Riessman's account is interesting because it suggests several possibilities: that the coding method can fragment the data; that some forms of data may be unsuitable for coding; and that researchers can produce narrative analysis, since what she provided in this passage is precisely a narrative. Interest in narrative analysis has grown and in large part this trend parallels the rebirth of interest in the **life history** approach (see Box 11.3). Nonetheless, coding is unlikely to become less prominent, for several reasons: it is widely accepted in the research community; not all analysts are interested in research questions that lend themselves to narratives; grounded theory and the techniques associated with it are very influential; and the use of computer software for qualitative data analysis frequently invites a coding approach.

Regardless of analytical strategy, it is unacceptable to simply say: "This is what my participants said and did; isn't that incredibly interesting?" Interpretation and theorizing are necessary. Many researchers worry that focusing on those tasks may prevent them from doing justice to what they have seen and heard, or lead them to contaminate their subjects' words and behaviour. Those are real risks, but they must be balanced against the fact that findings acquire significance in an intellectual community only when they have been subject to reflection. The researcher has to do more than simply take notes or record answers.

Narrative analysis

The term "narrative analysis" covers a wide variety of approaches based on the search for and analysis of stories that people tell to understand their lives and the world around them. It has become particularly prominent in connection with the life history or biographical approach. However, as Box 13.6 shows, narrative analysis is not exclusively concerned with telling life histories. As Roberts (2002) observed, the term is often used to refer both to the research approach itself and to the accounts that it examines—the stories that people tell about their lives and other events. In general, narrative analysis entails sensitivity to the connections between people's accounts of past, present, and future events and states of affairs; to people's sense of their place in those events and situations; to the stories they generate about them; and to the significance of context for the unfolding of events and people's sense of their roles in them. The way people forge connections between events and the sense they make of those connections are the raw material of narrative analysis. Riessman (2004b) helpfully distinguished four models of narrative analysis:

- *Thematic analysis* examines what is said rather than how it is said.
- *Structural analysis* emphasizes the way a story is told. Issues of content do not disappear, but attention is focused on the use of narrative mechanisms to increase the persuasiveness of a story.
- *Interactional analysis* looks at the dialogue between the teller of a story and the listener. The co-construction of meaning by the two parties is especially prominent, although content and form are also taken into account.
- *Performative analysis* analyzes narrative as a performance and explores the use of words and gestures to get a story across. This model of narrative analysis also examines audience responses to the narrative.

With narrative analysis, attention shifts from "What happened?" to "How do people make sense of what happened?" Proponents of narrative analysis argue that most approaches to the collection and analysis of data ignore the fact that people perceive their lives in terms of continuity and process, and that efforts to understand social life that do not take that fact into account may misunderstand the perspective of those being studied. Narrative analysis is obviously suitable for life history research, but its applications can be much broader. For example, it can also be applied to accounts of shorter episodes and their interconnections.

Some researchers apply narrative analysis to interviews. In her account of her "click moment" as a narrative researcher, Riessman (1993) described how she applied narrative analysis to conventional interview transcript material, and then began to uncover the stories her interviewees were telling her. In this case,

Box 13.6 | Tattoo narratives

grandriver/iStockphoto

How can narratives be used to analyze a social trend such as the increasing popularity of tattoos for women?

As part of a three-year participant observation study of tattooing, Atkinson (2002, 2004) elicited tattoo narratives from the women he interviewed. The great increase in the numbers of women getting tattoos has clearly challenged the standard "masculinity" explanations of male tattooing. Drawing on feminist theories about bodies, he found that these women are not misfits, and that they use tattoos to signify their "established" or "outsider" constructions of femininity. Ideas about femininity, including conformity to and resistance against cultural norms, are crucial in explaining women's tattooing.

Riessman was applying a narrative approach to materials gathered in a conventional way for conventional purposes. Other researchers start out with the intention of conducting a narrative analysis and deliberately ask people to recount stories (for example, Miller, 2000). While stories can emerge in response to questions not designed to elicit a narrative, certain kinds of question are especially likely to produce them. Riessman (2004a) suggested that prompts such as "Tell me what happened" followed by "And then what happened?" are much more likely to elicit a narrative account than "When did X happen?" While some narrative researchers prefer to start people off by asking them to tell their story of an event, Riessman argued that it is usually necessary to keep asking follow-up questions to stimulate the flow of details and impressions. For example, in her study of divorce, she often asked: "Can you remember a time when . . . ?" and then followed it up with "What happened that makes you remember that particular moment in your marriage?"

Coffey and Atkinson (1996) argued that a narrative should be examined in terms of the functions that it serves for the teller. The aim of narrative interviews is to elicit interviewees' reconstructed accounts of connections between events and links between events and contexts. Miller (2000) proposed that narrative interviews in life story or biographical research are far less concerned with eliciting facts than with drawing out interviewees' reflections and interpretations, as revealed in their accounts of their lives or families.

Narrative analysis, then, is an approach to the analysis of qualitative data that examines the stories that people use to explain events. It can be applied to data that have been acquired through a variety of research methods (notably semi-structured and unstructured interviewing and participant observation), but it has also become an interviewing approach in its own right. Also, there is growing recognition of ethnography as a narrative designed to tell a story about a way of life (Falconi & Graber, 2019).

Narrative analysis has been criticized. Bury (2001), while noting the increased interest in *illness narratives* (accounts of illnesses people have experienced), argued that there has been a tendency for narrative researchers to treat such stories uncritically. For example, he suggested that the frequent references in illness narratives to coping with and "normalizing" illness may often represent attempts to convince the audience (whether the interviewer or the reader of the narrative) of the subject's competence; in other words, such accounts may be motivated more by the desire to be seen as a fully functioning member of society than by the desire to give a realistic account of coming to terms with a medical condition. However, as Bury recognized, the social conditions that prompt such narratives and the forms the narratives take are themselves revealing. In drawing attention to the motives behind illness narratives, he was not seeking to undermine narrative analysis but to show how the range of issues addressed in this form of research can be expanded.

Key Points

- The collection of qualitative data frequently results in the accumulation of a large volume of information.
- Qualitative data analysis is not governed by codified rules to the same extent that quantitative data analysis is.
- There are different approaches to qualitative data analysis; grounded theory is probably the most prominent.
- Coding is a key process in most qualitative data analysis strategies, but it may have the effect of fragmenting and decontextualizing information.
- Narrative analysis emphasizes the stories that people tell in the course of interactions with a qualitative researcher; it has become a strategy for producing and analyzing qualitative data in its own right.

Questions for Review (R) and Creative Application (A)

General strategies of qualitative data analysis

R1 What are the main components of analytic induction?

A1 Why is analytic induction a rarely used approach?

R2 What are the main features of grounded theory? What are the different types of coding used in grounded theory?

A2 You are conducting grounded theory research on divorced couples, using data derived from qualitative interviews. What concepts might emerge when you begin open coding?

R3 What is theoretical sampling?

A3 Charmaz (2000) wrote that theoretical sampling "represents a defining property of grounded theory" (p. 519). Why do you think she feels this way?

R4 What are some of the main criticisms of grounded theory?

A4 How realistic is the assumption in grounded theory that a researcher can begin to collect data without being influenced by existing theories and concepts? Explain.

Basic operations in qualitative data analysis

R5 What are the main steps in coding?

A5 Is narrative analysis the answer to the problem of data fragmentation that results from coding? Explain.

Narrative analysis

R6 Explain how the emphasis on stories in narrative analysis represents a distinctive approach to the production and analysis of qualitative data.

A6 Come up with a research question pertaining to gender roles that can be answered using narrative analysis.

Interactive Classroom Activities

1. Each student in the class is paired up with another student. For 20 minutes, one student in the pair conducts a qualitative interview with the other on the topic of what the interviewee hopes to be doing with his or her life in 10 years' time, why they have chosen those goals, how they hope to achieve their goals, and so on. The interviewer takes field notes the whole time.

When the 20 minutes are up the roles are reversed: the interviewer becomes the interviewee. Once the second interview is completed, each person in the class is asked to:

a. conduct "open coding" of their field notes, identifying "concepts" and "categories" where possible;
b. write at least one "analytic memo" that describes noteworthy themes that have emerged in their data;
c. put the concepts and categories together to form a tentative hypothesis or interpretative framework;
d. identify topics that would benefit from further questioning or investigation.

Each student then re-interviews their interviewee for 20 minutes. When both interviews have been completed, students conduct open, axial, or selective coding, as appropriate, on all the data they have gathered. They then revisit their original hypotheses or interpretive framework, and revise as needed. When the process is complete students are asked to share with the rest of the class the concepts, constructs, hypotheses, and interpretive frameworks they have developed. Then the instructor facilitates an open discussion of the strengths and weaknesses of the grounded theory approach to qualitative research.

2. Each student in the class is paired up with another student. For 20 minutes, one student conducts a qualitative interview with the other using the "narrative analysis" technique. The topic to be addressed is the interviewee's most memorable childhood or adolescent experience, and how that experienced shaped their lives over time. Students are reminded that their goal as interviewers is to get the interviewees to "tell their stories"—i.e., to provide narratives that illustrate how their lives have been a *process* rather than a series of disconnected events and experiences. When the 20 minutes are up the students reverse roles, with the interviewer becoming the interviewee. Once the second set of interviews has been completed, the instructor asks students to share any difficulties they encountered in conducting the interviews, in particular any issues they had in establishing and sustaining the flow of the narrative. The class is also asked for suggestions as to how such difficulties could be overcome. The instructor then leads a general class discussion on the strengths and weaknesses of the narrative analysis approach to qualitative research compared to the grounded theory method.

Relevant Websites

A wealth of information is available at the website of the ***Grounded Theory Institute***.

www.groundedtheory.com

In this YouTube video, Kathy Charmaz provides an overview of the ***grounded theory*** method, describes its historical emergence, and defines constructivist grounded theory.

https://www.youtube.com/watch?v=Es-PHU52qEE

These YouTube videos discuss ***grounded theory***, including coding and constant comparison.

www.youtube.com/watch?v=4SZDTp3_New

www.youtube.com/watch?NR=1&v=gn7Pr8M_Gu8

www.youtube.com/watch?v=vi5B7Zo0_OE&NR=1

If you'd like to experiment with NVivo software, trial downloads are available at the ***NVivo*** website.

https://www.qsrinternational.com/nvivo-qualitative-data-analysis-software/try-nvivo

(Websites accessed 4 September 2021)

OXFORD learning link

More resources are available on Oxford Learning Link. Visit **https://learninglink.oup.com/** for:

- Student self-quiz
- Flash cards
- Audio clips
- Videos
- Activities

PART IV

Bringing It All Together: Revisioning Quantitative and Qualitative Research, and Some Practical Advice

This section of the book expands on the comparison between quantitative and qualitative approaches to research that were touched on in earlier chapters. Chapter 14 invites readers to consider the distinction between those two approaches in greater depth, and makes the point that some of the differences between them alluded to previously may not be as fundamental as one might think. The aim here is not to deny the distinction, but to show that in addition to differences, there are some similarities between the two. The final chapter of the book, Chapter 15, offers practical advice on completing a small-scale research project, including some tips on writing up social research. These two chapters return to issues raised in earlier sections of the book, probing them more extensively and making connections between them.

14 Bridging the Quantitative/ Qualitative Divide

Chapter Overview

This chapter is concerned with how far the **quantitative/qualitative** distinction should be taken. Although there are many differences between the two research strategies, there is also much that unites them, as we will see when we discuss how they can be combined. This chapter explores:

- aspects of qualitative research that can contain elements of the natural science model;
- aspects of quantitative research that can contain elements of **interpretivism**;
- the idea that research methods are more independent of **epistemological** and **ontological** assumptions than is sometimes supposed;
- ways in which the quantitative/qualitative contrast may break down;
- studies in which qualitative research is used to analyze quantitative research and vice versa;
- the use of quantification in qualitative research;
- arguments against the combination of quantitative and qualitative research;
- two versions of the debate on combining quantitative and qualitative research, one concentrating on methods of research and the other on epistemological issues;
- different ways in which **multi-strategy research** has been carried out; and
- the claim that multi-strategy research is not inherently superior to research employing just one research strategy.

▲ SeanZeroThree/iStockphoto

Key Learning Outcomes

Here is a list of goals you should try to achieve as you read and think about the material in this chapter. After completing this chapter, you should be able to:

1. Describe how qualitative research exhibits some of the features of the natural science model.
2. Discuss how quantitative research can be used to study meaning.
3. Explain how quantitative research can contribute to constructionist research and how the tenets of constructionism can help inform our understanding of quantitative data.
4. Identify how research methods are not always guided by epistemological and ontological considerations.
5. Summarize the ways in which quantitative and qualitative approaches are not as divergent as they are often portrayed.
6. Describe how a qualitative approach can be applied to quantitative research and vice versa.
7. Detail how quantification is used in qualitative research.
8. Discuss different approaches to multi-strategy research, criticisms against combining methods, and reasons why a multi-strategy approach is not necessarily a better approach than using a single method.

Philosophers of science sometimes use the term "consilience" to refer to the notion that there is a unity or compatibility between all branches of knowledge. The word came into wide usage after biologist E.O. Wilson published *Consilience: The Unity of Knowledge* (1998), in which he argued that the natural sciences, the social sciences, and even the humanities may one day have a unity of form and purpose that will allow for a more thorough and profound understanding of natural and social phenomena. This chapter is written in a similar spirit, seeking to show that quantitative and qualitative research strategies have a great deal in common and can complement each other. It makes the case that both are required to gain knowledge of the social world.

As you progress through your academic career, you may be tempted to take a dismissive attitude toward approaches and methodologies that are different from your own. Try to resist that temptation: giving in to it can lead to needless tensions and rivalries between researchers and can ultimately be quite destructive. Drawing on the insights of multiple perspectives is much more conducive to good research and produces a deeper level of understanding.

Introduction

Given the emphasis we have placed on the distinction between quantitative and qualitative research, it might seem strange at this stage to suggest that the differences between them are sometimes exaggerated. The dichotomy has been maintained to this point for two simple reasons:

- There *are* differences between quantitative and qualitative research strategies.
- Contrasting the two *is* a useful way of organizing research methods and approaches to data analysis.

As we have seen in earlier chapters, certain epistemological and ontological positions may be associated with particular research methods: for example, a natural science epistemology is often paired with social survey research, and an interpretivist epistemology with qualitative interviewing. However, the connections posited in Chapter 1 between epistemology and ontology, on the one hand, and research method, on the other, are best thought of as tendencies rather than definitive connections. The use of a **structured interview** or self-completion **questionnaire** does not *necessarily* imply an exclusive commitment to a natural science model; nor does **ethnographic** research *necessarily* mean an interpretivist epistemology.

Research methods are much more free-floating than is sometimes supposed. A method of data collection like **participant observation** can be employed in such a way that it is in tune with **constructionism**, but it can also be used in a way that reveals an **objectivist** orientation. Also, it's easy to underestimate the importance of practical considerations in determining how social research is carried out. It's not impossible to conduct a study of drug dealers by using questionnaires, but for practical reasons such a strategy is unlikely to succeed. The rest of this chapter will demonstrate why the distinction between quantitative and qualitative research should not be overstated.

It is of course possible to combine the two approaches so that their various strengths can be capitalized on and their weaknesses compensated for. Indeed, the number of studies that combine different strategies has been increasing since the early 1980s. However, not all research methodologists would agree that such integration is either feasible or desirable. In discussing the combination of quantitative and qualitative strategies, this chapter looks at three main issues:

- the arguments against integrating quantitative and qualitative methods
- the different ways in which quantitative and qualitative strategies have been combined
- whether a combined research strategy is necessarily superior to one relying on a single approach

This chapter uses the term *multi-strategy research* for work that integrates quantitative and qualitative approaches (sometimes referred to as *mixed methods* research; Timans, Wouters, & Heilbron, 2019). This term does not refer to the use of several quantitative methods in a single study, or the integration of two or more qualitative methods—for example, combining structured interviewing with **structured observation**, or ethnography with **semi-structured interviewing**. In the current discussion, "multi-strategy research" refers only to studies that combine qualitative and quantitative methods in the same project.

The natural science model and qualitative research

One of the chief difficulties in linking issues of epistemology and ontology with research methods is the frequent characterization of the natural sciences as inherently **positivist** in orientation. But the term "positivism" is often used in a polemical way, usually as an unhelpful criticism of another's work. Moreover, qualitative research itself frequently exhibits features associated with a natural science model. This tendency is revealed in several ways:

- ***Empiricist*** *overtones.* Although empiricism (see Chapter 1) is typically associated with quantitative research, many qualitative researchers place a similar emphasis on the importance of direct, sensory contact with social reality. They frequently stress the importance of direct experience with social settings, and advocate understanding social reality via that contact. The very idea that theory should be grounded in data is central to empiricism. It's not surprising, therefore, that some writers claim to detect "covert positivism" in qualitative research.

  Another example of empiricist overtones can be seen in the idea that social reality must be studied from the vantage point of the research participants. The fact that ethnographers rely on extended contact to gain access to the perspectives of the people they observe implies acceptance of the empirical notion that meaning is accessible to the senses. The empiricism of qualitative research is perhaps most notable in **conversation analysis** (examined in Chapter 12), an approach that starts with precise transcriptions of speech and applies rules of analysis to them. The analyst is actively discouraged from speculating about intention or context; in other words, the empiricist notion that one should not stray too far from the data is strictly upheld.

- *A specific problem focus*. Qualitative research *can* investigate quite specific, tightly defined research questions of the kind normally associated with the natural science model.
- ***Hypothesis** and theory testing*. Following from the last point, qualitative researchers typically test hypotheses or theories generated in the course of conducting their research, as in **analytic induction** or **grounded theory**. This is well within the bounds of a natural science model, even if the natural sciences tend to be **deductive**. Also, there is no reason why hypothesis or theory testing in qualitative social research cannot be done with previously specified hypotheses or theories. In fact, this has been done on many occasions. For example, Wilson's (2002) qualitative study of raves used theory as a departure point. The research by Festinger, Riecken, & Schachter (1956) on a doomsday cult used the qualitative technique of participant observation to test a theory about how people respond when a belief they zealously endorse—in this case, the imminent end of the world—is disconfirmed. The authors argued that it is possible to imagine a number of conditions that, if met, would lead group members to embrace their belief even *more* fervently after its disconfirmation. They thought that the cult would provide an ideal opportunity for testing their theory. The researchers (and hired observers) pretended to be converts and gained entry to the group in order to make first-hand observations. The theory was substantiated when cult members decided that their faith had saved the world and began proselytizing—an activity they had not engaged in before.
- ***Realism***. Critical realist ethnography (Porter, 1993; Barron, 2013; see Box 14.1) illustrates how ethnographic studies can be based on epistemological and ontological positions that have considerable affinity with those found in the natural sciences. It also relates to the previous point in providing a further illustration of hypothesis testing in qualitative research.

Box 14.1 | Critical realist ethnography

Critical realism (Bhaskar, 1975; 1979; 1986) presents a view of reality that in many ways is in keeping with the ontological approaches taken in the natural sciences, despite important differences (Gorski, 2013). Critical realist ethnography, for example, maintains that the social world has a form and structure that exists independently of our perception of it and which affects human consciousness and behaviours in complex ways. This sort of ethnography is also based on the idea that the descriptions and explanations presented by social researchers are inherently provisional and fallible, and as such should be subject to empirical scrutiny, and on the notion that researchers should seek to uncover causal tendencies to explain their subject matter.

These sorts of positivist-friendly assumptions are evident in the work of Porter (1993; 2002), who took a critical realist stance in his ethnographic study of racism in a large Irish hospital where he spent three months as a staff nurse. He found that racism was expressed in the form of remarks made behind the backs of members of racial minorities. However, it did not intrude into

(Continued)

work relationships, because more weight was given to achievements and performance (such as qualifications and medical skills) than to "race" when judging members of professions. In terms of critical realism, one possible structural mechanism (racism) was countered by the operation of another structural mechanism (professional ideology). Only on rare occasions did racial tension surface.

Similarly, Barron (2013) used the critical realist paradigm in his ethnographic study of ethnic identity among white British and Pakistani-British children. He concluded that his previous ethnographic work on the topic, although insightful, could have been improved by acquiring a broader range of empirical data, a practice that has important parallels in the natural sciences.

In addition, some qualitative researchers include explicitly quantitative elements in their research. Miller (2000), for example, engaging in what he called *neo-positivism*, made theoretically based predictions about people's lives using the **life history** method. Another illustration is Charmaz's (2000) suggestion that in spite of the differences that developed between Glaser (1992) and Strauss (for example, Strauss & Corbin, 1998)—who were major proponents of grounded theory—both maintained that an objective, external reality exists (the position taken in the natural sciences). Each posited a social world beyond the researcher and maintained that it was the job of the social investigator to reveal its nature and functioning.

Quantitative research and interpretivism

Qualitative research would seem to have a near-monopoly on the ability to study meaning. But is it really the case that only qualitative research makes it possible to see the social world through the eyes of the people studied? That contention seems at odds with the widespread study of *attitudes* using structured interviews and questionnaires. For example, there is a huge literature on political attitudes, and many indexes and scales have been designed to measure them (see Bell, Kandler, & Riemann, 2018; Robinson, Shaver, & Wrightsman, 1999). The widespread inclusion of questions about attitudes in social surveys suggests that quantitative researchers are interested in matters of meaning too.

It may be objected that survey questions do not really tap issues of meaning because they are based on categories devised by the designers of the interview schedule or questionnaire and not by the participants themselves. Two points are relevant here. First, the notion that qualitative research is better at gaining access to the point of view of those being studied is generally *assumed rather than demonstrated.* Qualitative researchers frequently claim to have tapped into participants' world views because of their extensive participation in the daily life of the people who are the focus of their study, the length of time they spend in the setting under investigation, or the lengthy and intensive interviews they conduct. However, the explicit demonstration that interpretative understanding has been accomplished—for example, through respondent validation (see Chapter 9)—is rarely undertaken. Second, if the design of attitude questions is based on prior questioning that seeks to bring out the range of possible attitudinal positions on an issue, attitudinal questions can certainly provide access to meaning.

Also, the practice in much survey research of asking respondents the reasons for their actions implies that quantitative researchers are frequently concerned with uncovering meaning. For example, in the research on delinquency in Box 1.2, the boys were asked to give the reasons for their actions in their own words and then to choose the sociological theories that came closest to explaining them. Examples such as these point to the possibility that the gulf between quantitative and qualitative research is not as wide as is sometimes supposed.

Quantitative research and constructionism

We noted in Chapter 1 that a keynote in qualitative analysis is constructionism: how people build up images or representations of the social world. **Qualitative content analysis** plays an important role in developing an understanding of how people construct their visions of reality, in the same way that **discourse analysis** (Chapter 12) does using materials such as newspaper reports and television programs.

Lantz and Booth's (1998) research on the social construction of breast cancer provides an example. As Box 1.5 makes clear, much of their understanding of the representation of breast cancer came from a qualitative content analysis, but they conducted a quantitative content analysis as well. The latter showed that 80 per cent of the women in the photographs attached to breast cancer articles were under age 50, and that 85 per cent of the anecdotes and case stories related to women in this age group. This emphasis on younger women helped to create the impression that they were the most at risk. But in reality, fewer than 20 per cent of new cases of breast cancer were in women under 50, and the mean age at diagnosis was 65. This inconsistency allowed Lantz and Booth to uncover how the media drew a connection between youthful lifestyles (working outside the home, postponing parenthood, greater sexuality) and breast cancer—a connection consistent with the articles' "blame the victim" theme. The quantitative content analysis of articles on breast cancer played an important part in revealing the social construction of beliefs about the disease. More generally, this example shows how quantitative research can contribute to constructionist research.

It is also important to remember that quantitative data are not formulated in a social vacuum: statistics themselves are social constructions (see Box 14.2).

Box 14.2 | The Social Construction of Numbers and COVID-19

From a constructionist standpoint, interpreting statistics can benefit from understanding how claims about numbers are socially constructed. Best (2020) writes, "Teaching numeracy cannot be understood only as a mathematical project that can ignore the way numbers are brought into being" (p. 13). He suggests that those interested in using numbers to make sense of social problems should take into account the following constructionist observations: (1) facts are social constructions; (2) measuring involves making decisions; (3) counting is not straightforward; (4) all comparisons involve choices; and, (5) social patterns shape numbers. To illustrate his five propositions, Best (2020) considers how numbers are used to make sense of the COVID-19 pandemic:

1. *Facts are social constructions:* "Facts are products of particular social groupings at particular times and in particular places. . . . Labelling something a fact always occurs within a particular social context" (p. 3). Best is not arguing that all claims are equally true. Instead, he is pointing out that one group might treat something as true, while another might not—each has different standards for evaluating claims and determining which are factual. Just because one group deems something to be a fact, and brings numbers to bear to support their contention, does not mean that another group will agree and the debate will disappear.
2. *Measuring involves making decisions:* "A long series of choices shapes whatever is being counted and how the counting occurs. When we talk about the resulting numbers as facts (e.g., equating the crime rate with the amount of crime), we ignore the very real processes by which those numbers are socially constructed, and the inevitable flaws and limitations in the results" (p. 4). For instance, COVID-19 infection and fatality rate estimates have

(Continued)

significant variations between countries, partially owing to different decisions made about the measurement process and the social contexts from which the numbers are drawn.

3. *Counting is not straightforward:* "Any time we count anything, we are inevitably forced to choose—to decide what to count and how to go about counting" (p. 6). In the case of COVID-19, this leads to both an under- and over-counting of cases. As an example, an American who might be sick with COVID-19, but who does not have health insurance coverage, is typically less likely to seek treatment and be counted compared to someone who does have coverage.
4. *All comparisons involve choices:* "It is often hard to know what to make of a number. Is it large or small? Ordinarily, placing a figure in some interpretive context requires making some sort of comparison" (p. 8). With COVID-19, this has involved making statistical comparisons to data from other epidemics, other geographical areas, and other causes of death.
5. *Social patterns shape numbers:* Social factors influence the data in terms of the direction a problem takes and how it is understood. For example, Best indicates that about a month after COVID-19 was declared a pandemic, commentators began drawing attention to how the disease was disproportionately impacting ethnic minority groups. It was not a matter of inter-group biological differences, though: ethnicity was being used as a proxy for social class. Best suggests that for different reasons, such as the messiness of measuring social class, advocates drawing attention to ethnic inequalities, and Americans' greater receptivity toward making racial over class distinctions, ethnicity became the initial governing narrative.

Research methods and epistemological and ontological considerations

That each research method does not carry with it a full cluster of epistemological and ontological commitments can be seen in studies on social research itself. For example, Platt's (1986) historical research on American sociology suggested that the alleged connection between conservative functionalist theory (which is often associated with positivism) and survey research is greatly exaggerated. Her research indicated that "the two originated independently, and that leading functionalists had no special propensity to use surveys and leading surveyors no special propensity for functionalism" (p. 527). Moreover, Platt's (1996) general conclusion on the use of research methods in American sociology between 1920 and 1960 is very revealing:

> Research methods may on the level of theory, when theory is consciously involved at all, reflect intellectual … *post hoc* justifications rather than … carefully chosen fundamental assumptions. Frequently methodological choices are steered by considerations of a practical nature … and are just slogans and aspirations. … (p. 275)

Again, even when there are discernible links between research methods and assumptions about knowledge, the connections are not absolute.

Further evidence of the autonomy of research methods is the fact that both quantitative and qualitative approaches may be employed in a single piece of research, a point that will be illustrated later in this chapter.

Problems with the quantitative/qualitative contrast

The contrasts between quantitative and qualitative research drawn in Chapter 9 suggest a sharp distinction between the two (see, in particular, Table 9.1). Here is a more nuanced view.

Behaviour versus meaning

A distinction is sometimes drawn between a quantitative focus on behaviour and a qualitative focus on meaning. Yet, as noted, quantitative research frequently seeks to study meanings in the form of attitudes. In recent decades the social sciences in general have increasingly recognized the importance of examining not only what people do, but also how they think and make sense of the world. The "cognitive revolution" in psychology has made people's thoughts and feelings the topic of extensive research. The use of rational choice theory and game theory in economics, political science, and sociology reflects a similar emphasis on examining how people think and make choices. Many different perspectives in the social sciences now acknowledge the importance of meanings and interpretations in understanding social phenomena.

Looking at the other side of the divide, qualitative researchers frequently, if not invariably, examine *behaviour*, although they also pay close attention to the context in which it occurs. Qualitative researchers often seek to interpret people's behaviour in terms of the norms, values, and culture of the group or community in question. In other words, quantitative and qualitative researchers alike are typically interested both in what people do and in what they think, even if they go about their investigations in different ways. The degree to which quantitative and qualitative research reflect the "behaviour versus meaning" distinction should not be overstated.

Theories and concepts tested in research versus those emerging from the data

A related point concerns the characterization of quantitative research as driven by theory testing. **Experimental** investigations probably fit this model well, but survey-based studies are often more exploratory in nature. Although **concepts** have to be measured, specific hypotheses are frequently not identified in advance. Surveys ask so many questions, and there are so many possible correlations and ways of organizing the findings, that hypotheses are often not formulated until *after* the data collection has taken place. The analysis of quantitative survey data is often more exploratory than is generally appreciated and consequently offers many opportunities for generating theories.

The common depiction of quantitative research as an exercise in theory testing also fails to take into account how often its findings can result in new theoretical departures and contributions. Reflecting on his career in survey research, Glock (1988, pp. 45–46) provided the following example from his study of American church involvement. Having found that women, older persons, the poor, and those without families were more religiously active than people not in those categories, he suggested that such people might have more time than others to become involved. Alternatively (or in addition), these religiously active people might be compensating for some kind of deprivation relative to their counterparts—a conflict view that Marx would have appreciated. Since the existing data did not allow him to rule out either explanation, he collected *new* data to test them: in this way his original quantitative data led to new research ideas. Quantitative research commonly follows this path.

Numbers versus words

Even the most basic distinction between quantitative and qualitative research—numbers versus words—is problematic. Qualitative researchers will sometimes undertake to quantify a limited amount of their data in an effort to determine the generality of the phenomena they are describing. After observing doctor–patient interactions in public and private oncology clinics, for example, Silverman (1985) quantified some of his data to show that patients in private clinics have more influence over what goes on in the consultations. Still, Silverman warned that such quantification should reflect the research participants' own ways of understanding their social world.

It has often been noted that qualitative researchers engage in "quasi-quantification" when they use terms such as "many," "often," and "some" (see page 344). The only difference in studies like Silverman's is that the researcher makes such estimates of frequency more precise.

Artificial versus natural

The distinction between artificial and natural is similarly open to criticism. It is often assumed that because much quantitative research employs research instruments (such as questionnaires) that offer only limited and indirect indicators of people's lives, its account of the social world is artificial. Qualitative research tends to be considered more **naturalistic** in that it focuses on observing people in their natural settings, behaving as they normally do. This would seem to be particularly true of ethnographic research, since the participant observer studies people in their normal social worlds and contexts, as they go about their everyday activities. However, when qualitative research is based on interviews, the "natural" label is less applicable. Interviews still have to be arranged and interviewees have to be taken away from activities they would otherwise be engaged in, even when the interviewing style is of the more conversational kind. Furthermore, little is known about interviewees' reactions to and feelings about being interviewed.

Phoenix (1994) reported on the responses of interviewees to in-depth interviews in connection with two studies: one focusing on mothers under the age of 20 and the other on the social identities of young people. Although many of the participants seemed to enjoy being interviewed, they were clearly conscious of the fact that they had been engaged in interviews rather than conversations. This was revealed in some of their replies. For example, Phoenix reported one young Black woman as saying that she had liked the interview, adding: "I had the chance to explain how I feel about certain things and I don't really get the opportunity to do that much" (p. 61). Another interviewee said it was a "good interview" and added: "I have never talked so much about myself for a long time, too busy talking about kids and their problems" (p. 61). While such qualitative interviews are clearly valuable in allowing the perspectives of people whose voices are normally silent to surface, they don't fit the definition of "naturalistic" used by critics of quantitative social science. Thus, it would be incorrect to assume that artificiality is a problem only in quantitative research.

As we noted in Chapter 11, focus group research is often described as more natural than qualitative interviewing because it resembles the way people discuss issues in real life. Natural groups (people already known to each other) are often used to emphasize this element. Whether focus group participants see their interaction as "natural" is unclear, however. In particular, since the participants are often paid strangers who have travelled some distance to discuss topics they rarely if ever talk about, it's clear that this sort of research may not be as natural as some have assumed.

In participant observation, the researcher can be a source of interference, making the research situation less natural than it might appear. It's difficult to estimate how much impact **reactivity** has on the research findings in such cases, but once again the naturalism of such studies is questionable. When the ethnographer also engages in interviewing (as opposed to casual conversation), the naturalistic quality is definitely compromised, although the research will probably be somewhat less artificial than it would be if quantitative methods were used.

These observations cast doubt on the rigidity of the quantitative/qualitative distinction. Once again, this is not to suggest that the usual contrasts are unhelpful: only that they should not be exaggerated. Quantitative and qualitative research strategies are not absolutely divergent.

Mutual analysis

The divisions between quantitative and qualitative research are also undermined when one approach is used to analyze research conducted using the other.

A qualitative approach to quantitative research

There has been growing interest in using some of the methods associated with qualitative research to examine quantitative research. In part, this trend reflects qualitative researchers' growing interest in ethnography. The qualitative study of quantitative research is part of this trend because it reveals that the written account of research constitutes not only the formal presentation of findings but an attempt to persuade readers of the credibility of those findings. This is true of the natural sciences as well; research by Gilbert and Mulkay (1984) showed that scientists, when writing up their findings, took pains to demonstrate that proper procedures were followed. They also learned from interviewing scientists that the research process was influenced by the scientists' personal biographies.

One way in which a qualitative approach has been applied to quantitative studies is through what Gephart (1988) called *ethnostatistics*: "the study of the construction, interpretation, and display of statistics in quantitative social research" (p. 9). For example, Gephart showed that the use of statistics in itself can be regarded as a rhetorical device, because quantification makes social research look more like natural science—an association that tends to give it greater legitimacy and credibility. This is just one example of the way qualitative research can shed light on the nature of quantitative research.

A quantitative approach to qualitative research

When Hodson (1996) conducted a content analysis of workplace ethnographies (discussed below), he essentially applied a quantitative content analysis to qualitative research. This type of research, sometimes called *meta-ethnography*, may have potential in other areas of social research where ethnography has been a popular method, such as the study of social movements, religious sects, and cults. Hodson's approach was one solution to the problem of comparing ethnographic studies in a given area. However, he largely ignored contextual factors in order to explore relationships between variables abstracted from the studies.

Among the key issues in a study of this kind is the selection of works suitable for analysis. Hodson chose to analyze just books, excluding articles because they usually contain only a limited amount of information. To qualify for selection, a book had to meet three criteria: "(a) the book had to be based on ethnographic methods of observation over a period of at least 6 months, (b) the observations had to be in a single organization, and (c) the book had to focus on at least one clearly identified group of workers" (Hodson, 1999, p. 22). The application of these criteria resulted in the exclusion of 279 out of the 365 books he had considered. A second crucial issue was the coding of the studies. Hodson stressed the importance of knowing the subject area, adopting clear coding rules, and pilot testing the coding schedule. In addition, he recommended checking the **reliability** of coding by having 10 per cent of the documents coded by two people. The process was time-consuming; each book took at least 40 hours to code.

Among the many attractions of this approach is the fact that it allowed a single researcher to investigate a varied set of organizations and provided more in-depth data than is typically gathered by quantitative researchers. It also allowed for the testing of hypotheses derived from established theories: for example, the "technological implications" approach, which sees technology as having an impact on the experience of work (Hodson, 1996). However, the loss of social context is likely to make Hodson's approach unattractive to many qualitative researchers.

Of particular significance is Hodson's remark that "the fundamental contribution of the systematic analysis of documentary accounts is that it creates an analytic link between the in-depth accounts of professional observers and the statistical methods of quantitative researchers" (Hodson, 1999, p. 68). In other words, the application of quantitative methods to qualitative research may provide a meeting ground for the two research strategies.

Quantification in qualitative research

As we noted in Chapter 9, perhaps the most basic difference between quantitative and qualitative research is the "numbers versus words" distinction. Yet most qualitative research does contain some quantification. Three observations are worth making about quantification in the analysis and writing up of qualitative data.

Thematic analysis

Chapter 13 noted that qualitative data analysis often takes the form of a search for themes in transcripts or field notes. The choice of themes to look for is often determined by how frequently certain incidents, words, phrases, and so on recur. This process may also account for the prominence given to some themes over others. In other words, a kind of implicit quantification probably influences both the identification of themes and the elevation of some themes over others.

Quasi-quantification in qualitative research

As we have noted, qualitative researchers engage in "quasi-quantification" when they use terms such as "many," "frequently," "rarely," and "some," which by definition are based on the relative frequency of the phenomenon of interest. As expressions of quantity, however, these terms are imprecise, and it's often difficult to tell why they are being used at all. When quantification is needed to support a point, it may be better to use actual numbers.

Combatting anecdotalism through limited quantification

Qualitative research is sometimes criticized for the anecdotal nature of its data, which leaves the reader with no way of assessing their generalizability. Brief sequences of conversation, snippets from interview transcripts, and accounts of encounters between people say little or nothing about the prevalence of the phenomena that such evidence is supposed to indicate. There is also the related risk that the researcher may attribute undue significance to a particularly striking statement or unexpected activity.

At least partly in response to these problems, qualitative researchers sometimes undertake a limited quantification of their data. Gabriel (1998) collected 377 stories about organizational culture in the course of 126 interviews in five organizations. He identified different types of stories and noted the frequency of each type. For instance, there were 108 comic stories (usually a mechanism for the disparagement of others); 82 epic stories (survival against the odds); 53 tragic stories (undeserved misfortune); and 40 gripes (personal injustices). The stories could have been presented as anecdotes, but simple counting conveyed a clear sense of their relative prevalence. As a further example, Aurini, Missaghian, & Pizarro Milian (2020) used quantification to a limited degree in their qualitative study of how Canadian upper-middle-class parents structure and rationalize their children's after-school activities. Tables of frequencies and percentages were used to summarize their data on children's extracurricular activities and their parents' rationales for selecting those activities. This approach allowed the researchers to offer a big-picture overview of parental choices, which was then followed up by a deeper look at the data by presenting excerpts from interviews conducted with the participants.

Using actual numbers can counter the criticism that qualitative data are too anecdotal and do nothing to indicate the *extent* to which certain beliefs or behaviours occur. The precision of numbers also makes them superior to the estimates of frequency that must be inferred from quasi-quantification terms such as "some" or "many."

The use of "layering" has been presented as another way of addressing concerns about anecdotalism (McAleese & Kilty, 2019). Layering involves bringing together statements and stories from participants in multiple research projects and considering which narratives are supported. Given that qualitative researchers often work with a small number of cases, layering can lend credibility to researchers' findings by demonstrating that a pattern holds across a series of studies. Layering is similar to replication in quantitative research, but with layering, qualitative researchers seek to validate the narrative even though the research methods may differ from study to study. McAleese and Kilty (2019) argue that "By layering stories from different people in different contexts over time, qualitative research can solidify a particular narrative, which may then be considered a more valid and reliable one" (p. 836). Although findings from small qualitative studies can be credible and trustworthy in their own right, layering helps to address the critique that qualitative findings are "just anecdotal."

We may see greater use of quantification in qualitative research in the future as a result of the growing use of software programs for qualitative data analysis. Most of the major software programs make it possible to produce simple counts for the use of a particular word or the incidence of a coded theme. In many cases, they can also produce simple cross-tabulations—for example, showing which sex uses the passive voice more often. Software programs also assist with managing large amounts of qualitative data, which makes layering as an analytical approach more feasible.

Multi-strategy research

The ways in which quantitative and qualitative research can complement each other can be seen most clearly in multi-strategy research, which by definition involves combining the two modes of investigation. However, there are two basic arguments against this sort of research.

Arguments against multi-strategy research

Arguments against multi-strategy research tend to be based on the following assumptions:

- Particular research methods are associated with particular epistemological and ontological positions.
- Quantitative and qualitative research strategies are inherently incompatible on epistemological and ontological grounds.

These two positions are briefly reviewed below.

The embedded methods argument

Advocates of the first position, outlined earlier in this chapter, argue that every research method is firmly rooted in a particular set of epistemological and ontological commitments. According to this view, a decision to employ (for example) participant observation is not simply a choice about data collection but a commitment to an epistemological position that is consistent with interpretivism and incompatible with positivism or a natural science model in general.

This view has led some writers to argue that multi-strategy research is not feasible. An ethnographer

Research in the News

COVID-19 and intimate partner violence

Early in the COVID-19 pandemic, women's shelters in Manitoba reported an increased demand for their services (Hoye, 2020). Researchers suspect that more time spent at home during the pandemic with a violent partner is creating greater risks of victimization among abuse survivors. To better understand this issue, Kendra Nixon, an associate professor in the Faculty of Social Work at the University of Manitoba, and Nadine Henriquez, an assistant professor in the Faculty of Health Studies at Brandon University, will be interviewing abuse survivors and service providers. Nixon believes that there are several pandemic-related factors putting survivors at greater risk. For example, women may be concerned about leaving their home for a shelter and potentially exposing themselves and their children to the coronavirus. Also, women who have lost employment during the pandemic may not have the financial means to leave an abusive partner. Nixon and Henriquez's research will include participants from both rural and urban areas and different ethnic groups, as well as refugees and immigrants. Partnering with the Manitoba government's family violence prevention program, the researchers hope their findings will improve services and help inform policy decisions. Nixon points out, "It's important, now that we have this opportunity, that we look at the research, that we look at the risk so we can develop better policies and practices should a future pandemic or a future surge of COVID-19 surface" (Hoye, 2020).

may collect questionnaire data about a slice of social life not amenable to participant observation, but this does not represent an integration of quantitative and qualitative research because the epistemological positions of the two methods are irreconcilable. The chief difficulty with this kind of argument is that the idea of research methods carrying fixed epistemological and ontological implications is very difficult to sustain.

The paradigm argument

The paradigm argument is closely related to the previous one. It conceives of quantitative and qualitative research as **paradigms**. A paradigm is a set of beliefs and assumptions about how the world works and how knowledge of it is to be gained. Kuhn (1970) popularized the term in his portrayal of natural science as going through periods of revolution, whereby "normal" science (science carried out in terms of the prevailing paradigm) is increasingly challenged by new findings inconsistent with the assumptions and established findings of the discipline. The increasing frequency of such anomalies eventually sparks a crisis, which in turn sparks a revolution. The period of revolution comes to an end when a new paradigm gains acceptance and a period of the new "normal" science sets in. An important feature of paradigms is that they are incommensurable: inconsistent with each other because of their divergent assumptions and methods. Disciplines in which no paradigm has emerged as pre-eminent, such as sociology and other social sciences, are deemed "pre-paradigmatic."

The paradigm argument maintains that quantitative and qualitative research approaches are based on incompatible paradigms in which epistemological assumptions, values, and methods are inextricably intertwined (Morgan, 1998). Therefore, when researchers combine participant observation with a questionnaire, they are not really combining quantitative and qualitative research, since the paradigms are incompatible: the integration is only superficial and within a single paradigm.

The problem with the paradigm argument, as with the embedded methods claim, is that it rests on a connection between method and epistemology that has not been demonstrated. Moreover, although Kuhn (1970) argued that paradigms are incommensurable, it is by no means clear that quantitative research and qualitative research are fully separate paradigms. As we have suggested throughout this chapter, there are areas of overlap and commonality between them.

Two positions in the debate over quantitative and qualitative research

There are two opposing arguments regarding the question of whether quantitative and qualitative research can be combined.

- An *epistemological argument*, as in the embedded methods and paradigm positions discussed above, sees quantitative and qualitative research as grounded in incompatible epistemological principles (and ontological ones too, though these tend to be given less attention). According to this version, multi-strategy research is not possible in principle.
- A *technical argument* perceives research methods as independent of any specific epistemological position. According to this view, a research method from one research strategy can be pressed into the service of another: quantitative and qualitative methods can be fused. This is the position taken by most researchers whose work is mentioned in the next section.

The technical argument views the two research strategies as compatible, and multi-strategy research as both feasible and desirable. It is in that spirit that we will now consider the ways in which quantitative and qualitative research can be combined.

Approaches to multi-strategy research

Hammersley (1996) proposed three approaches to multi-strategy research:

- ***Triangulation***: the use of quantitative research to corroborate qualitative research findings or vice versa

- *Facilitation*: the use of one research strategy to aid research using another
- *Complementarity*: the use of two different research strategies so that diverse aspects of an investigation can be combined

The logic of triangulation

Triangulation entails using more than one method in the study of social phenomena. The term has been used somewhat more broadly by Denzin (1970, p. 310) to refer to an approach that uses "multiple observers, theoretical perspectives, sources of data, and methodologies," but the emphasis has tended to be on methods of investigation and sources of data. One of the reasons Webb, Campbell, Schwartz, & Sechrest (1966) called for greater use of **unobtrusive methods** is their potential for triangulation (see Box 6.5). Triangulation can operate within and across research strategies. It was originally conceptualized by Webb et al. (1966) as a way of developing additional measures, resulting in greater confidence in findings, and was strongly associated with a quantitative research strategy. However, triangulation can also take place within qualitative research. In fact, ethnographers often check their observations with interview questions to look for possible misunderstandings. Bloor (1997) reported that he tackled the process of death certification in two ways: interviewing clinicians responsible for certifying causes of deaths, and asking the same people to complete dummy death certificates based on case summaries he had prepared. Increasingly, triangulation refers to the cross-checking of findings from both quantitative and qualitative research (Deacon, Bryman, & Fenton, 1998).

An illustration of a triangulation approach is Hughes et al.'s (1997) study of the consumption of "designer drinks" (fortified wines and strong white ciders) by young people. The authors used two main research methods:

- *Qualitative method*: eight focus groups with 56 children and young adults, with each discussion lasting around two hours
- *Quantitative method*: a survey administered in two parts to a multi-stage cluster sample of 824 12- to 17-year-olds. The first part was an interview and the second was a questionnaire designed to elicit more sensitive information.

The results achieved with the two research strategies were mutually reinforcing. The qualitative findings showed age differences in attitudes toward designer drinks and other types of alcohol: the youngest people (12- and 13-year-olds) tended to adopt a generally experimental approach; the 14-and 15-year-olds thought of drinking as a way of having fun and losing inhibitions, and felt that designer drinks met their needs well; the oldest group (16- and 17-year-olds) were mainly concerned with appearing mature and establishing relationships with the other sex, and tended to think of designer drinks as targeted at immature younger drinkers. These connections with age were confirmed by the quantitative evidence, which also corroborated the suggestion from the qualitative evidence that the consumption of designer drinks was largely associated with a desire to get drunk.

In this study the use of triangulation appears to have been planned, but this need not always be the case. Researchers may start out using different research strategies for different purposes but in the process discover that they have generated quantitative and qualitative findings on related issues, and that they can treat their overlapping results as a triangulation exercise.

Whether triangulation is planned or unplanned, there is always the possibility that the two sets of findings will not corroborate one another. In the event that the results are inconsistent, the solution is *not* to arbitrarily decide which set of findings is correct. Usually, further research is required to resolve the matter.

Deacon and colleagues (1998) used several quantitative and qualitative research methods to gather information, without intending to conduct a triangulation exercise. But analysis of their data revealed an inconsistency: the quantitative data suggested a broad consensus between journalists and social scientists on the reporting of social scientific research in the media, but the qualitative findings suggested some conflict of approaches and values between the two groups.

Instead of favouring one set of findings over the other, the researchers re-examined the data and found that social scientists tended to answer questions about media coverage of their work differently, depending on the research instrument. In response to survey questions, they typically expressed relief that the coverage was not as bad as they had expected, whereas in interviews they tended to emphasize "war stories" of wounding encounters with the media. In general, then, the questionnaires showed social scientists to be relatively pleased with the reporting of their research, but their replies were more negative when they were encouraged to reflect on specific problems in the past.

Another example of triangulation can be found in Fenton, Bryman, & Deacon's (1998) study of the same topic. It employed both quantitative and qualitative methods:

1. content analysis of news and current affairs coverage (local and national newspapers, TV, and radio)
2. mailed questionnaires soliciting social scientists' views about media coverage and their own practices (674 replies)
3. mailed questionnaires soliciting the views of social scientists identified in the content analysis as having received media coverage (123 replies)
4. semi-structured interviews with 20 of the latter
5. semi-structured interviews with 34 journalists identified in the content analysis
6. semi-structured interviews with 27 representatives of funding bodies and government
7. observing journalists' movements and activities at three conferences
8. focus group analysis of audience reception of media coverage (13 focus groups)

Qualitative research facilitates quantitative research

Here are two ways in which qualitative research can serve as a guide for quantitative research:

- *By suggesting hypotheses.* Because of its tendency toward unstructured, open-ended methods of data collection, qualitative research is often a source of hypotheses that can be tested using a quantitative strategy. An example is Phelan's (1987) research in which she conducted qualitative interviews and conversations with people attending a treatment program for families dealing with incest. After a considerable amount of qualitative data had been collected, Phelan became aware of differences between biological fathers and stepfathers in how they interpreted their incestuous acts, and in the frequency with which certain behaviours occurred. Quantifiable data were collected through interviews with family counsellors that supported her hypothesis that "the process of incest in structurally different families may vary" (Phelan, 1987, p. 39). Similarly, Bell's (2007) study of western Canadian separatism started out as a qualitative investigation involving attendance at separatist events and hanging out with separatists. Analysis of these data led to the hypothesis that support for separatism was associated with a neo-liberal ideology and a partisan dislike for the ruling federal Liberal Party, a view that was later substantiated in a multiple regression analysis using survey data.
- *By aiding measurement.* The in-depth knowledge of social contexts acquired through qualitative research can be used to inform the design of survey questions for structured interviewing and self-completion questionnaires. Johnson and colleagues (2003) used data from unstructured interviews to develop highly structured questions for later interviews with adolescent smokers. Walklate (2000) explained that for her research on fear of crime and safety issues in high-crime areas, a survey using traditional questions about victimization was used. However, the questions were amended to reflect the local context following six months of interviews, ethnography, and examination of local newspapers. Similarly, the survey questions that Bell (2007) used in his study of western Canadian separatism were prompted in part by his experiences in gathering qualitative data.

Quantitative research facilitates qualitative research

One way in which quantitative research can prepare the ground for qualitative work is through the selection of people to be interviewed. This can occur in several ways. In the case of Fenton et al.'s (1998) research on the reporting of social science research in the mass media, discussed above, a media content analysis (method 1) was used as a source of data. However, it also served as a means of identifying journalists who had reported relevant research (method 5). In addition, replies to questions in the general survey of social scientists (method 2) were used to help identify two groups of social scientists, those with high and those with low levels of media coverage of their research, who were then interviewed with a semi-structured approach (method 4). Similarly, Jamieson (2000) administered a questionnaire to a sample of young men on their criminal activity. On the basis of their replies, qualitative interviews were conducted with equal numbers of young men in each of three categories: those who had never committed a criminal offence; those who had offended but not recently; and persistent offenders.

Filling in the gaps

When the researcher cannot rely on either a quantitative or a qualitative method alone, a multi-strategy approach can be used to fill in the gaps. For example, ethnographers may employ structured interviewing or self-completion questionnaires if not everything they need to know is accessible through direct observation, or if they have difficulty gaining access to certain groups of people.

Morgan (1998) suggested a two-step approach to planning multi-strategy research:

- *The priority decision.* Will the principal data-gathering tool be qualitative or quantitative?
- *The sequence decision.* Should the "complementary" method be used first, as a preliminary to the principal method, or second, as a follow-up?

These decisions yield four possible types of research design (see Figure 14.1).

		Priority	
		Quantitative	*Qualitative*
Sequence	*Preliminary*	M1	M2
	Follow-up	M3	M4

FIGURE 14.1 Morgan's classification of approaches to multi-strategy research

One difficulty with using Morgan's typology is that it may be difficult to know whether quantitative or qualitative research had priority, and which one came first in the sequence. Sometimes research uses both strategies and several methods, but no single one is dominant.

Static and process features

Together, the characteristics listed in Table 9.1 suggest that quantitative research presents a static picture of social life, while qualitative research presents a more dynamic picture, emphasizing process. In some contexts "static" may be considered a negative term, but in this case it's positive. In fact, it is the regularities revealed by quantitative research that allow for the analysis of process. A multi-strategy research approach makes it possible to combine the two. An illustration is provided by MacKinnon and Luke's (2002) study of cultural change from 1981 to 1995. Their main method of data collection was survey research, but to complete the picture they also examined census and public opinion data, as well as newspaper articles on historical events. They found that levels of homophobia and anti-Semitism decreased over that period, but that sympathy for Indigenous people also declined. They cautioned that their small sample (70) and what were essentially "good guesses" meant that their conclusions, "like the interpretations of an ethnographer [were] subject to alternative interpretations by others" (MacKinnon & Luke, 2002, p. 332).

Researcher and participant perspectives

Sometimes researchers want to gather two kinds of data: qualitative data that show the general perspectives of the people they are studying, and quantitative data on specific issues. For example, Milkman (1997) was interested in the meaning of industrial work: in particular, whether factory conditions had changed since the 1950s, when they were portrayed very negatively. To find out, she employed semi-structured interviews and focus groups with General Motors production workers. She was also interested in a "buyout" plan that the company's management introduced in the mid-1980s after it had initiated a variety of changes to work practices. The plan offered workers the opportunity to give up their jobs for a substantial cash payment. In 1988 and again in 1991, Milkman carried out a questionnaire survey of workers who had accepted the company's buyout offer. The surveys inquired about the reasons for taking the buyout, how those taking it had fared since leaving General Motors, how they felt about their current employment, and differences among social groups (in particular ethnic groups) in current earnings relative to those at General Motors.

The problem of generality

As we noted above, there is a tendency in qualitative research to present findings without evidence indicating how typical they are, or how the group under study compares with some larger population. Partly to counter this problem, Tastsoglou and Miedema (2003) used quantitative national data on women's volunteer work to compare their admittedly non-random sample of immigrant women with the Canadian population; they found that the immigrant women actually volunteered more than the national average.

Qualitative research may help to interpret the relationship between variables

A frequent problem for quantitative researchers is how to explain relationships between variables. One strategy is to look for an intervening variable: one that is influenced by the **independent variable** but in turn has an effect on the **dependent variable**. For example, in a relationship between ethnicity and occupation, education may be an intervening variable:

ethnicity → education → occupation

This sequence implies that the variable ethnicity has an impact on education (for example, ethnic groups differ in their levels of education), which in turn has implications for the jobs that people in different ethnic groups attain. Qualitative work could examine how different ethnic groups perceive education, which could lead to a fuller understanding of education as an intervening variable. It could also provide leads to a different theoretical perspective on the general topic of ethnicity, education, and occupation.

Another illustration is provided by Barnard and Frischer's (1995) research on HIV-related risk behaviour among drug injectors. Structured interviews with 503 injectors revealed that "females report[ed] significantly higher levels of needle sharing, sexual activity, and AIDS awareness than their male counterparts," and that "women . . . co-habiting with sexual partners who [were] themselves injectors, [were] particularly likely to report high levels of risk behaviour and also AIDS awareness" (p. 357). What produced this relationship between gender, risk behaviour, and cohabitation? Semi-structured interviews with 73 injectors suggested that the relationship between these variables could be explained "by the tendency for women to be in sexual relationships with men who themselves inject and with whom they are unlikely to use condoms" (p. 360). Here qualitative data were used to shed light on relationships among variables derived from quantitative research.

Studying different aspects of a phenomenon

There is a tendency to think of quantitative research as best suited to the investigation of "macro" phenomena (such as social mobility and social stratification) and qualitative research as more appropriate for "micro" issues (such as interactions between wait staff and their customers). The macro/micro distinction can also be discerned in Table 9.1. In the example outlined in Box 14.3, Wajcman and Martin (2002) used a quantitative method in the form of a questionnaire survey to explore the career patterns of male and female managers. However, they also carried out qualitative, semi-structured interviews to explore how managers *made sense* of their career patterns in terms of their identity. Thus, the choice of methods was determined by the research question.

Box 14.3 Combining survey research and qualitative interviewing in a study of managers

Weekend Images Inc/iStockphoto

Why do the findings from structured interviews sometimes differ from those derived from semi-structured or unstructured interviews?

Wajcman and Martin (2002) used a questionnaire to survey male and female managers (470 in total) in six Australian companies and conducted semi-structured interviews with 136 managers in each company. The survey evidence showed that male and female managers were generally more similar than different in terms of career orientations and attitudes: contrary to what many had anticipated, women's career experiences and orientations were *not* found to be distinctive. They then examined the qualitative interviews for narratives of identity and found that both male and female managers depicted their careers in "market" terms (they responded to the requirements of the managerial labour market by developing their skills and experience). But whereas for men narratives of career meshed seamlessly with narratives of domestic life, for women there was a disjuncture. Female managers found it harder to reconcile managerial identities with domestic ones and more often had to opt for one or the other. In this way, choices about career and family were still gendered. This example illustrates how a multi-strategy approach can work to reveal much more than could have been gleaned through the use of one method alone.

The use of multi-strategy research to study different aspects of a phenomenon can also be seen in the family obligations studies conducted by Finch (1985) and Mason (1994). Focusing on the distribution within families of the obligation to care for relatives, this research had two main data collection elements: a survey of a sample of nearly 1000 people by structured interview, and semi-structured interviewing with 88 people. A major component of the survey interviewing was the use of the vignette technique described in Box 5.4. Mason described the purpose of integrating quantitative and qualitative research as follows:

> From the beginning … we were using the two parts of our study to ask different sets of questions about family obligations. Not only were we employing different methods to generate different types of data, but we also anticipated that these would tell us about different aspects of family obligations. … [O]ur view was that an understanding of kin obligations *in practice* would require an analysis of the relationship between the two data sets and the social processes they expressed. (Mason, 1994, pp. 90–91)

What were the two sets of research questions to which Mason referred? The survey was designed to elicit information about "'the proper thing to do' for relatives in a variety of circumstances" (Mason, 1994, p. 90). Through the semi-structured interviews, Mason tried "to discover what people actually did in practice for their own relatives, and also the processes by which they came to do it and make sense of it: did a sense of obligation or responsibility have a role in the process? How did people in practice work out what to do for their kin, or ask of their kin?" (p. 90).

Box 14.4 | Qualitative and quantitative methods combined to study children's knowledge of learning difficulties

Nowicki, Brown, & Stepien (2014) combined qualitative and quantitative approaches in a study that examined how children aged 9–11 viewed the causes of classroom learning difficulties. The study was conducted at five schools in a medium-sized Ontario city where students with learning issues were fully integrated with other students in the classroom. The researchers employed the technique of concept mapping, which combines qualitative interviewing with cluster analysis, a statistical procedure. The qualitative interviewing of individual students formed the first phase of the study, with the focal question being "Why do some children have learning difficulties?" After editing for redundancy and clarity, this produced 42 unique statements, or a mean of 1.2 responses per student. This result was in keeping with previous qualitative research that indicated that children at this age have a very limited store of "explicit" knowledge of learning difficulties, which refers to knowledge that can be verbalized on one's own.

But the researchers also tested the children's "implicit" knowledge of the topic, a type of understanding that often cannot be verbalized but may manifest itself in recognition tasks. To do this the students were given cards on which were written each of the 42 statements. They were asked to place the cards in groups based on similarity, and to produce labels for each group they had created. The cluster analysis showed that five distinct clusters of statements could be identified, and that the clusters were meaningful, coherent categories that indicated a surprising level of understanding of learning difficulties. The clusters had the themes fate, family stress, neurological problems, information processing difficulties, and issues related to motivation and instruction. It turned out that the students were more astute in identifying a diverse range of possible causes of learning difficulties when given a list of statements produced by their peers than they were in verbalizing the causes on their own. This study illustrates how combining qualitative and quantitative methods may produce more informative results than employing just one of those approaches.

In multi-strategy research, then, the different methods may be geared to addressing different kinds of research questions. The study on the reporting of social science research in the British mass media by Fenton et al. (1998), discussed earlier, is a further example of a project that used quantitative and qualitative research to answer different types of questions:

- *Questions about coverage.* For example: How much coverage is there of social science research? What gets covered? Where? (method 1).
- *Questions about the production of media coverage.* For example: What kinds of attributes do journalists look for when deciding whether to write an item on social science research? (methods 5 and 7).
- *Questions about social scientists' attitudes to media reports of research.* This includes reporting of research in general (method 2) and of their own research (methods 3 and 4). Method 4 was designed to allow the findings reached through method 3 to be elaborated and more fully understood.
- *Questions about reception.* For example: How do readers/viewers interpret media reporting of social science research? (method 8).
- *Questions about the communication environment.* For example: What are the policies of universities, government departments, and funding bodies concerning the media reporting of research? (method 6).

This form of multi-strategy research entails making decisions about which kinds of research question are best answered using a quantitative method and which by a qualitative method. (Box 14.4 provides another example.) It also requires that researchers think about how best to interweave the different elements, especially since, as was suggested in the context of the discussion about triangulation, the outcomes of mixed method research are not always predictable.

Like unplanned triangulation, this category of multi-strategy research is more or less impossible to plan in advance. Essentially, it offers quantitative researchers an alternative to either revising their hypotheses or filing the inconsistent results away (and probably never looking at them again).

Moving beyond Triangulation

Building on Hammersley's (1996) idea of *facilitation*, University of Toronto sociologists Childress, Calonga, & Schneiderhan (2020) propose using what they term *propulsive facilitation* for conducting multi-strategy research. They point out that while this approach is not new, their goal is to reinforce the value of facilitation in fostering new insights. The idea of "propulsion" captures both (a) the movement across different findings and methods as the research progresses, and (b) the difficulty of getting the research started, but once underway keeping it in motion becomes easier.

Propulsive facilitation entails beginning with the research method best suited for answering one's research question. As the data begin to shed light on the question, new questions often arise that are best answered through a different form of data collection. This, in turn, might lead to other questions arising that are studied using additional methods. With each successive step in the process the researcher is propelled in new directions, producing iterative questions that require different research techniques to answer them. For example, Childress et al.'s (2020) research on Nelson Mandela's presidential memoirs began with archival research. In answering their initial question, a new one arose which was best answered through an ethnography of the archive itself. The data they collected for that led them to study a different set of archival materials. This, in turn, produced further research questions that were well-suited for study through interviews.

Childress et al. (2020) make a case for the value of propulsive facilitation in moving researchers beyond triangulation. They state that "It is worth acknowledging that when methodological triangulation is evoked, findings almost always seem to triangulate" (p. 370). While triangulation seeks to confirm findings using different methods, propulsive facilitation is characterized by ongoing methodological adaptation and flexibility: research discoveries raise new questions which may "present an occasion to apply a new or alternative method which is better equipped to making sense of the unexpected datum or phenomena one is presented with along the way" (p. 380). Instead of directing one's research energies to confirming what is already known through application of the first method, Childress et al. (2020) propose redirecting our research energies toward thinking iteratively about the application of our research methods.

Reflections on multi-strategy research

There can be little doubt that multi-strategy research is becoming more common (Timans, Wouters, & Heilbron, 2019), although research that incorporates only one approach remains the norm, especially in disciplines such as sociology, psychology, and political science. One factor that is relevant to the growth in the popularity of multi-strategy methods is a growing willingness to see research methods simply as techniques of data collection, unencumbered by epistemological and ontological baggage. For example, research on audience reception of media and cultural texts had traditionally relied mainly on qualitative methods (in particular, focus groups), but lingering unease regarding the reliability and generalizability of their findings led some researchers to recommend using quantitative research methods in tandem with qualitative methods (for example, Schrøder, 1999).

However, multi-strategy research is not necessarily superior to one-method or one-strategy research. Four points must be borne in mind:

- Multi-strategy research must be competently designed and conducted: otherwise its findings will be suspect, no matter how many methods are employed.
- Multi-strategy research must be appropriate for the research questions asked. There is no point in collecting additional kinds of data on the assumption that "more is better."
- Multiple methods are likely to take considerably more time and financial resources than research using just one approach, and spreading resources too thinly can dilute the effectiveness of the research.
- Not all researchers have the skills and training required to carry out both quantitative and qualitative research, and their "trained incapacities" may prevent them from integrating the different forms of research.

Compared to studies involving a single research method, conducting multi-strategy research is often more complex and "messy" (Sanscartier, 2020). Sanscartier (2020) explains that mixed methods researchers encounter two broad types of "messiness:" "empirical mess" and "design-related mess." Empirical mess occurs when quantitative and qualitative methods produce conflicting findings. Design-related mess is the result of researchers needing to make ad hoc design adjustments to respond to the challenges presented by diverse and fluid research contexts. To navigate the messiness of multi-strategy research, Sanscartier recommends developing a "craft attitude," which he describes as follows:

> a disposition (not a paradigm, method, or design type) towards the mixed methods research process that (a) is comfortable with uncertainty, (b) favors non-linearity and recursiveness in research design, and (c) treats research as an exercise in storytelling, about both the research object and our engagement with that object. (p. 53)

Adjusting to the messiness of multi-strategy research requires researchers to be open to the mess, to be prepared to improvise and remain flexible with their methods, to be reflexive about their approach, and to be transparent when sharing accounts of the decisions made in conducting their research (Sanscartier, 2020).

Multi-strategy research is not a panacea. It may provide a better understanding of a phenomenon than if just one method is used. It may enhance confidence in the findings, and it may even improve the chances of access to research settings. Milkman (1997, p. 192), for example, suggested in her research on a General Motors factory that her promise of "hard," quantitative data facilitated her entry to the plant even though she had no experience with this method. But the general point remains: multi-strategy research, while offering great potential in many instances, is subject to constraints similar to those in research relying on a single strategy.

Methods in Motion | Applications to Canadian Society

Combining quantitative and qualitative research to understand poverty and mental health among bisexuals

Although bisexuals form the largest sexual minority group, there is relatively little research on the experiences of bisexual people. Ross and colleagues (2016) sought to rectify this by using a multi-strategy approach to examine the empirical relationships between bisexuality, poverty, and mental health among a sample of 302 adult bisexuals living in Ontario.

The research grew out of an awareness that previous studies had shown that low socioeconomic status was associated with higher risk of negative mental health outcomes, and that people with a minority sexual orientation (gays, lesbians, and bisexuals) tended to have lower incomes than heterosexuals, although some data indicated that non-heterosexual women earned more on average than heterosexual women. Previous research also found that bisexuals were more likely to live in poverty than lesbians or gays, and had more health problems than people with other sexual orientations. Earlier studies also indicated that bisexuals experienced discrimination in the form of homophobia, heterosexism, biphobia, and monosexism, with the latter two forms of prejudice coming not only from heterosexual individuals but also from lesbian and gay people.

Ross et al. gathered quantitative data with an online survey that measured whether participants had incomes below the Low Income Cut-Off (LICO), a widely used indicator of poverty. The survey also included measures of mental health issues such as depression, anxiety, post-traumatic stress disorder (PTSD), and suicidality. Variables measuring "outness" (how open a person with a minority sexual orientation is about their sexual identity) and perceived discrimination were included on the survey as well. In addition, information was collected on the participants' demographic characteristics such as their age, sex assigned at birth, gender identity, and racial/ethnic/cultural identity.

After the quantitative data were collected, Ross and her co-researchers acquired a qualitative perspective on the matter by conducting semi-structured interviews with a subset of the survey participants. The interviews were designed to provide a social context for the quantitative results, and to explore possible theoretical connections between poverty, bisexuality, and mental health.

In the quantitative part of the study, Ross and her associates found that a sizable proportion (25.7 per cent) of all study participants lived below the LICO poverty line, and that poverty was associated with depression and PTSD. Bisexuals living in poverty also experienced more discrimination, and after demographic controls were introduced they were more likely to be open about their sexual orientation.

The qualitative data analysis gave rise to four models of the pathways by which poverty and bisexuality may intersect with mental health. One male participant described being gang raped at age 15, which led to a "lost decade" of substance abuse and risky sexual behaviours at a stage in his life that might otherwise have been devoted to advancing his education and developing his job credentials. This and other accounts of early life experiences were used by the researchers to produce a model in which bisexuality and poverty impact adolescent development, which in turn affects both mental health and subsequent poverty. Other participants discussed how biphobic or homophobic discrimination resulted in job loss, promotion denials, or lack of hiring, which led the authors to develop a theoretical model in which bisexuality affects employment experiences and earning potential, which then influences mental health in a reciprocal way. Other models explored how bisexuality and poverty may impede access to social support and mental health services, which can contribute to poor mental health.

This study provides a good example of how quantitative and qualitative approaches can complement each other, and how a combination of the two may be used to generate empirically based theories that can be the subject of further research.

Key Points

- It's important not to exaggerate the differences between quantitative and qualitative research.
- Connections between epistemology and ontology on the one hand, and research methods on the other, are not fixed or absolute.
- Qualitative research can exhibit features normally associated with a natural science model.
- Quantitative research can incorporate an interpretivist stance.
- The artificial/natural contrast used to distinguish quantitative and qualitative research is often exaggerated.
- A quantitative research approach can be used to analyze qualitative data, and qualitative research methods can be used to analyze the rhetoric of quantitative researchers.
- Some qualitative researchers employ quantification in their work.
- Although the practice of multi-strategy research has increased, not all writers support it.
- The view that there are epistemological and ontological impediments to the combination of quantitative and qualitative research is a barrier to multi-strategy research.
- There are several different ways of combining quantitative and qualitative research; some can be planned in advance, others cannot.

Questions for Review (R) and Creative Application (A)

The natural science model and qualitative research

R1 Under what circumstances can some qualitative research use a natural science model?

A1 A qualitative researcher finds that many of the homeless people she encounters in her fieldwork have addiction issues. How might she use that finding to launch a quantitative study?

Quantitative research and interpretivism

R2 Under what circumstances can some quantitative research exhibit characteristics of interpretivism?

A2 A quantitative researcher finds that 25 per cent of the people aged 18–25 in a national sample have no intention of voting in the next federal election, while the figure for people aged 65 and over is only 10 per cent. Explain this difference, making reference to how people at different ages may perceive the political process differently. If you were to write up your answer in a research report, would it be appropriate to describe it as qualitative in nature? Explain.

Quantitative research and constructionism

R3 Under what circumstances can some quantitative research be constructivist?

A3 You do a quantitative content analysis that examines the portrayal of women in detergent commercials. How might your study be constructivist in nature?

Research methods and epistemological and ontological considerations

R4 How closely tied are research methods to epistemological and ontological positions? Explain.

A4 You decide to do a secondary analysis of quantitative data taken from the General Social Survey, Victimization Study. You have no preconceived theoretical position when you begin, but decide to see if there is any association between gender and fear of crime. How does your approach deviate from a strictly positivist orientation to research?

Problems with the quantitative/qualitative contrast

R5 Outline some of the ways in which the quantitative/qualitative contrast is not as hard and fast as is often supposed.

A5 Explain how grounded theory methods could be used to develop a theory of the relationship between body shaming and the use of social media, then describe how this sort of research can be thought of as a form of theory testing.

The mutual analysis of quantitative and qualitative research

R6 How might a researcher take a qualitative approach to quantitative research?

A6 What are some implications of Gilbert and Mulkay's (1984) work (on how scientists write up their findings) for the qualitative analysis of quantitative research?

R7 What is ethnostatistics and why is it used?

A7 How can ethnostatistics inform the debate about whether quantitative and qualitative research are based on incompatible paradigms?

R8 What is a meta-ethnography?

A8 Assess the significance of Hodson's (1996; 1999) research on workplace ethnographies. How can it be used to evaluate the embedded methods argument?

Quantification in qualitative research

R9 What is meant by quantification in qualitative research?

A9 Should there be more quantification in qualitative studies? What are some drawbacks to increased quantification in qualitative research? Explain your answer to these questions as they would pertain to a qualitative content analysis of a local gay pride parade.

The argument against multi-strategy research

R10 What is multi-strategy research?

A10 What are the strengths and weaknesses of the embedded methods and paradigm arguments against multi-strategy research that combines quantitative survey approaches with qualitative interviewing?

Opposing arguments about combining quantitative and qualitative research

R11 What are the epistemological and technical arguments regarding the prospect of combining quantitative and qualitative research? What are their implications for multi-strategy research?

A11 Explain how multi-strategy research could be carried out on the topic of white-collar crime.

Approaches to multi-strategy research

R12 What are the chief ways in which quantitative and qualitative research have been combined?

A12 Traditionally, qualitative research is depicted as having a preparatory role in relation to quantitative research. To what extent do the different forms of multi-strategy research reflect this view? How can quantitative studies of conservative political attitudes be a precursor to qualitative research?

Reflections on multi-strategy research

R13 Why has multi-strategy research become more prominent?

A13 Is multi-strategy research necessarily superior to single-strategy research? Describe a specific, hypothetical instance in which it would be superior, and one in which it would not.

Interactive Classroom Activities

1. The instructor divides the class into small groups. Each group:
   a. selects a general topic that could be researched using quantitative methods—e.g., variables that predict people's participation in political activities;
   b. develops a theory or hypothesis pertaining to their general topic—for example, young people are less likely to participate (vote, run as a candidate, etc.) in national elections than older people, and this occurs because of a sense of alienation from conventional political parties and any other organization that has a pronounced power hierarchy;
   c. produces an outline of how the research could be conducted, including sample selection, wording for key survey questions (if applicable), description of statistical techniques that could be employed (e.g., correlation, cross-tabulation, regression), and so on;
   d. discusses how qualitative methods could be incorporated into the research at each step in the process—for example, by holding focus groups with young people to explore how

they feel about politics and their participation in it; acquiring and analyzing qualitative data to develop testable hypotheses on the topic; using the qualitative data to create survey questions; or doing qualitative research to make sense of quantitative findings; and

e. considers the following question: "Does quantitative research differ from qualitative research in fundamental, irreconcilable ways? Explain."

The class as a whole then reconvenes. Each group presents a summary of its discussions to the class, which is invited to ask questions and provide critical commentary on each group's presentation.

2. The instructor divides the class into small groups. Each group:
   a. selects a general topic that could be researched using qualitative methods—for example, how people with eating disorders view themselves and their relationships with food;
   b. produces an outline of how the research could be conducted, including the recruitment of informants; questions that could be explored in qualitative interviews (if applicable); commentary on whether ethnographic research would be appropriate; a consideration of how narrative analysis might be used; and so on;
   c. discusses how quantitative methods could be incorporated into the research at each step in the process—for example, by coding qualitative data; addressing the issue of how prevalent certain eating disorders are among particular social groups or in the larger society; examining whether people with eating disorders share certain psychological traits or demographic characteristics; or generating hypotheses that could be tested using quantitative methods; and
   d. considers the following question: "Does qualitative research differ from quantitative research in fundamental, irreconcilable ways? Explain."

   The class as a whole then reconvenes. Each group presents a summary of its discussions to the class, which is invited to ask questions and provide critical commentary on each group's presentation.

3. A class debate is held to evaluate the following statement: "Quantitative research differs from qualitative research in fundamental, irreconcilable ways." The instructor divides the class into three groups. The first group must present arguments supporting the statement, the second must oppose it, and the third can chose to either support or oppose the statement. At the conclusion of the debate a class vote is held to determine which group presented the most convincing case.

Relevant Websites

In this YouTube video, one of this book's authors (the late ***Professor Alan Bryman***) discusses multi-strategy research in the social sciences.

www.youtube.com/watch?v=L8Usq_TPfko&list=PLoem9zOwhTaD3dpk1aCp4eOBzFgmOQ6DC

Using examples about holocaust survivors and baseball, in this YouTube video ***Professor John W. Creswell*** speaks about the value of combining qualitative and quantitative methods in telling a more complete story.

https://www.youtube.com/watch?v=l5e7kVzMIfs

For examples of multi-strategy research, see the ***Journal of Mixed Methods Research*** (to access the journal you may have to go through your institution's library server).

https://journals.sagepub.com/home/mmr

(Websites accessed on 4 September 2021)

OXFORD learning link More resources are available on Oxford Learning Link. Visit **https://learninglink.oup.com/** for:

- Student self-quiz
- Flash cards
- Audio clips
- Videos
- Activities

15 Conducting a Research Project

Chapter Overview

The goal of this chapter is to guide you through a small-scale research project from beginning to end. The guidance offered goes beyond the discussions presented in previous chapters in that it focuses on the practical aspects of doing research. A wide variety of issues is explored, including:

- generating research questions;
- time management when doing research;
- dealing with the existing literature on your subject; and
- writing up social research.

Key Learning Outcomes

Here is a list of goals you should try to achieve as you read and think about the material in this chapter. After completing this chapter, you should be able to:

1. Identify several ways of generating research questions.
2. Produce a plan for managing your time effectively while completing a research project.
3. Search the existing literature on your topic, and integrate relevant material into your project in various ways and at different stages of your research.
4. Develop a strategy for writing up your project in an informative and engaging way.

When one of the authors of this book was a graduate student and had his first meeting with his dissertation advisor, the advisor listened to his research proposal, offered a few suggestions, and then said, somewhat acerbically, "Just *do* it!" (This was years before that phrase became a marketing slogan.)

Those three words contain a lot of wisdom. It's easy to overthink things and waste time worrying

▲ Hemis/Alamy Stock Photo

that your plans aren't worthwhile or that you're not up to the task. Just assume that with proper guidance and a lot of hard work, you'll be just fine. But you must *follow through* with concrete actions, every day. Dreaming is not enough.

Don't wait for the perfect time to start. There is no such thing. Imagine you're at work and your boss has given you an unbreakable deadline. You'll find that once you get absorbed in the task, your inspiration and motivation will pick up even if they were minimal when you began. It also helps if you think of your research project as a series of small jobs rather than one monumental undertaking.

The same goes for the writing. Try to write something related to the project—*anything*—every day. And for your first draft, allow yourself to be sloppy. Don't worry about finding the perfect word or crafting the perfect sentence or ensuring that the logic flows flawlessly. Those issues can be dealt with later, at the editing stage. When Michael Jackson was asked about his method for writing songs, he replied, "Don't get in the way of the music." That advice applies to completing a research project too: don't get in the way of the ideas. Just let them flow. Write first and evaluate later. Just do it.

Introduction

This chapter provides advice for those readers carrying out their own small-scale research projects. Previous chapters have provided helpful information about the methodological and conceptual choices available and how to implement them. Here we offer some hands-on advice on how to generate research ideas and take them through the various stages of development to produce a successful project of your own, such as an honours thesis or a course assignment. The advice is tailored for students engaged in empirical research, that is, studies in which they either collect new data or analyze existing data. Although the discussion is mainly geared toward undergraduate projects, students in graduate programs will also find the observations helpful.

Know what is expected by your institution

Quite often a course instructor will have specific guidelines and requirements for class projects. Look them over carefully and follow them. People doing undergraduate theses and students in graduate school should be aware that their institution or department may have specific requirements concerning things like binding and page margins, as well as the format for referencing, the inclusion of an abstract, the structure of the presentation, plagiarism, and deadlines.

Identifying research questions

Most students want to conduct research in areas of personal interest. This is not a bad thing; as we noted in Chapter 1, many professional social researchers want to do the same thing (see also Lofland & Lofland, 1995, pp. 11–14). However, even open-ended qualitative research must begin with the formulation of research questions. Although Chapter 10 referred to some studies that were not driven by specific research questions, open-ended research is risky. It can lead to the collection of data that will never be used, and to serious problems in data organization and analysis. The lack of focus can also cause the project to take too long or even to be abandoned. So, unless your supervisor or instructor advises you to the contrary, you need to formulate some research questions that are not completely open-ended. What is it about your area of interest that you want to know? Figure 15.1 illustrates some steps that can be taken to select research questions. If you need ideas for research, talk things over with your advisor or course instructor, or take a look at the list of sources for research questions provided in Box 15.1.

Research area

Example:
People's willingness or unwillingness to abide by pandemic health protocols (mask wearing, social distancing, avoiding large gatherings, etc.)
The meanings and interpretations people attach to abiding by or rejecting pandemic health protocols

⇓

Select aspect of research area

Examples:
Social causes of the variations in people's willingness to abide by pandemic protocols
How meanings and interpretations pertaining to pandemic protocols develop and become integrated into more comprehensive views of the self and society

⇓

Possible research questions

Examples:
Do political orientation, age, gender identification, socio-economic status, education, or ethnic background affect people's willingness to abide by pandemic health protocols? If so, which of these factors has the greatest impact, and why? What are the theoretical and public policy implications of these issues?
How do people feel about those who do not follow pandemic health protocols? Do people's views on this matter emerge and develop through discourse with others who are similarly socially situated? If so, how does that process unfold? How do people's perceptions of the protocols relate to their larger views of themselves and society? What are the theoretical and public policy implications of these issues?

⇓

Modification of selected research questions

Research questions may be revised and refined as the research proceeds.

FIGURE 15.1 Steps in selecting research questions

Interacting with a supervisor

Most institutions will assign a student writing a thesis or dissertation to a supervisor or advisor. However, the kind and amount of assistance you can expect varies greatly. Of course, students also vary in what they ask of their advisors. Our advice here is simple: use supervisors or advisors to the fullest extent allowable and give due consideration to their suggestions. Such people are usually well versed in the research process and can provide help and feedback at all stages of the project, subject to your institution's strictures in this regard. If they criticize your research questions, interview schedule, early drafts, or whatever, try to respond positively. Criticism isn't a personal attack. Such comments are usually accompanied by the reasons for them and some suggestions for revision. Be thankful for the opportunity to address problems *before* your work is formally examined. Supervisors have to go through the same process themselves whenever they apply for a research grant or submit an article or book for peer review.

Students who get stuck or fall behind in their work will sometimes avoid their supervisors. But the longer they wait, the harder it is to ask for help. Then, because the work has been put off, it has to be rushed at the end, and in some cases is never completed. Try to avoid this situation by confronting any difficulties head-on and getting advice on how to deal with them as soon as possible.

Undergraduate students doing course projects should follow the same basic advice. Consult your course instructor if you run into difficulties, and the sooner the better. Even if there are no apparent problems, it's always worthwhile to discuss your research with your instructor, who may pick up on issues that you have missed.

Box 15.1 | Marx's (not Karl) sources of research questions

5./15 WEST/iStockphoto

What types of research questions could emerge from a close investigation of new media technologies and social networking websites?

Marx (1997) suggested the following possible sources of research questions:

- intellectual puzzles and contradictions
- the existing literature
- replication
- a feeling that a certain theoretical perspective or notable piece of work is misguided (in this case you would explore the reasons for the shortcomings)
- a social problem in need of a social scientific (for example, sociological) explanation
- "gaps between official versions of reality and the facts on the ground" (1997, p. 113). Examine the standard explanations offered by governments, the media, or social researchers for social phenomena such as poverty, substance abuse, international conflict, or anything else of interest. Are those explanations consistent with what you know or have experienced? If not, develop some research questions pertaining to the phenomenon in question, including questions about the validity of the conventional wisdom on the topic.
- the counterintuitive; for example, cases in which social scientific truths seem to fly in the face of common sense, as they did when a doomsday cult began to proselytize rather than slink away in embarrassment when "doomsday" passed and life carried on as usual (Festinger, Riecken, & Schachter, 1956)
- "empirical examples that trigger amazement" (1997, p. 114); for example, atypical events, cases that contradict widely accepted theories, and so on
- new methods and theories—in what settings and with what people might they be applied?
- "new social and technical developments and social trends" (1997, p. 114)

Managing time and resources: Start thinking early about the research area

Students are usually asked to start thinking about a potential research topic well before they are expected to start work on the project. That thinking is worth doing, because all research is constrained by time. Two pieces of advice are relevant here:

- Work out a timetable, preferably with your supervisor or instructor, detailing the different stages of the research (including the literature review and the writing up). The timetable should specify the different stages and the specific dates for starting and finishing them (see Figure 15.2 for an example of a quantitative research outline). Some stages are likely to be ongoing—for example, searching the literature for references (see below)—but that should not delay the development of a timetable.

Issue(s) to be researched

⇓

Review literature/theories relating to topic/area

⇓

Formulate research question(s)

⇓

Consider whether a social survey is appropriate (if not, consider an alternative research design)

⇓

Consider what kind of population is appropriate

⇓

Consider what kind of sample design is appropriate

⇓

Determine whether there is a sampling frame available

⇓

Decide sample size

⇓

Decide on mode of administration (face-to-face, telephone, postal, email, web)

⇓

Develop questions (and devise answer alternatives for closed questions)

⇓

Review questions and assess face validity

⇓

Complete ethics protocols

⇓

Pilot study to test the questions

⇓

Revise questions

⇓

Finalize questionnaire/schedule

⇓

Sample from population

⇓

Administer questionnaire/schedule to sample

⇓

Follow up non-respondents at least once

⇓

Transform completed questionnaires/schedules into computer readable data (coding)

⇓

Enter data into statistical analysis program such as SPSS

⇓

Analyze data

⇓

Interpret findings

⇓

Consider implications of findings for research questions, existing theories, future research, and the discipline as a whole.

FIGURE 15.2 Steps in conducting a social survey study

- Find out what resources, if any, are available for carrying out your research. For example, can your institution help with the cost of printing, postage, stationery, and so on? Can it lend you hardware to record and transcribe interviews? Does it have the necessary software, such as **IBM SPSS Statistics (SPSS)** or **NVivo**? This kind of information will help you decide whether your research design and methods are financially feasible and practical. The fictional "gym study" in Chapter 8 is an example of a project feasible within the kind of time frame usually allocated to undergraduate projects. However, it would require resources for printing covering letters and questionnaires for participants who are unable to respond electronically; postage both for sending the questionnaires out to them and for follow-up letters; and return postage for the questionnaires. In addition, quantitative data analysis would require software such as SPSS.

Searching the existing literature

Online bibliographical databases (accessible through most university libraries) are an invaluable source of references. The best one for sociology students is probably *Sociological Abstracts*; databases for other disciplines are available as well. They normally allow searches by keyword (topic), author, title, journal, and other descriptors. The focus is easily narrowed by specifying language, year, and type of presentation. For example, "English, post-2015, scholarly journal articles only" can be searched and listed from latest to earliest. The "scholarly journal articles only" restriction removes papers presented at meetings but not published in journals, and also excludes dissertations, which are too hard for most students to access in any event. Searches can be conducted using keywords in different combinations with the Boolean operators "and," "or," and "not." Thus, a search for material on "sexism and universities" will produce articles that deal with both topics in the same piece. Choosing "sexism or universities" will produce those articles plus articles on each one alone. That is probably not a good choice—it's too broad. "Universities and sexism or prejudice" is better because it expands the first option above to cover university prejudice in addition to university sexism. Finally, "not" restricts the search. "Sexism not universities" will find articles about sexism in places other than universities. You can experiment with the use of keywords and Boolean options; if you don't find what you need, ask a librarian for help.

Following these procedures will produce a list of journal articles in which the keyword(s) appears, with full citation details and an abstract, and sometimes a link to a full-text download. Other databases are more specialized: examples include the *Canadian Periodicals Index Quarterly* (*CPI.Q*) (formerly the *Canadian Periodical Index*), the *LGBT Life with Full Text*, *Family & Society Studies Worldwide*, and *Contemporary Women's Issues*. Mark the records you want and email them to yourself for a permanent record. The bibliographies in the articles you find can provide additional sources to examine.

Two particularly interesting tools are the *Social Sciences Citation Index* (accessible through the *Web of Science*) and *Google Scholar*, which look forward from the original article to later ones that cite it, revealing what others have thought of it. Perhaps some who cited the article were critical; perhaps others accepted or expanded on it. In this way a history of the research in the area of interest can be built up. To many professors, these indexes provide measures of how often they have been cited. To those granting tenure and raises, it can be a crude indicator of merit, following the logic of "more citations, better researcher."

The library catalogue is an obvious tool for finding books, even those held at other universities. Again, ask a librarian if you run into difficulty. However, since books are often dated, checked out, or too specialized for student papers, the above sources may be preferable. The rule of thumb is similar to the idea of theoretical saturation in qualitative research: stop searching when the same items keep appearing.

Why review the existing literature? The most obvious reason is to find out what is already known about your area of interest, in order to avoid "reinventing the wheel." In addition, the process of reviewing the literature will help you revise and refine your research questions. Beyond this, the existing literature on your topic will help you develop an argument regarding the significance of your research and where it will lead. The metaphor of a *story* is sometimes used in this context (see below). A competent review of the literature will help to establish your credibility as someone knowledgeable in your chosen area.

As you explore the existing literature, look for answers to the following questions:

- What is already known about this area?
- What concepts and theories are relevant?
- What research methods and strategies have been employed in studying this area?
- Are there any significant controversies?
- Are there any inconsistencies in the findings relating to this area?
- Are there any unanswered research questions?

While reading, take good notes, and be sure to record full citations for all the materials you consult. It's infuriating to find that you've forgotten some detail, such as the volume number of an article, when you come to assemble your bibliography. Also keep in mind that your written review of the literature should be critical as well as descriptive. How does a particular article relate to others you have read? Does it contradict them? Are there any apparent strengths or deficiencies—for example, in the methods used or the conclusions drawn? What theoretical ideas influenced the author(s)?

In some areas of research you will find huge numbers of references. Try to identify the major ones and work outward from there. Move on to the next stage of the research at the point you identified in your timetable (see above). This is not to say that your literature search will cease: only that you need to force yourself to move on. Ask your supervisor or instructor for advice on whether you need to extend your search of the literature.

Preparing for research

In choosing a methodology you need to consider its ethical implications and what you will do to prevent any potential ethical violations. Keep in mind the various ethical issues discussed in Chapter 3 and flagged throughout this book.

Don't begin collecting data until you have clearly identified your research questions, and design your data collection instruments with those questions in mind. If at all possible, conduct a small pilot study to see how well your research instruments work. You will also need to think about access to research sites. If the research requires entry to a closed setting such as an organization, you need to get permission at the earliest opportunity. This usually takes so long that many advisors do not recommend using closed settings for student research. You also need to consider how you will go about gaining access to people. This issue leads you into sampling considerations, such as the following:

- Whom do you need to study in order to answer the research questions?
- Is an adequate sampling frame available?
- What kind of sampling strategy is feasible—probability, quota, theoretical, convenience?

Practical Tip | Reasons for writing a literature review

The following are reasons for writing a literature review:

1. to find out what is already known in a research area, and what remains to be researched
2. to learn from other researchers' mistakes and omissions
3. to learn about different theoretical and methodological approaches to the research area
4. to get help in developing an analytic framework
5. to find additional variables to include in the research
6. to search for further research questions
7. to view examples of how findings can be interpreted
8. to compare and contrast your findings with those of other researchers
9. it's expected

Writing up research

Once the data gathering and analysis have been completed, the findings must be conveyed to an audience. This is an important matter because regardless of how well your research is conducted, readers have to be convinced that your findings are valid and worth knowing about, and that requires good writing.

As with other skills, the best way to become proficient at writing up social research is to do it as often as you can. And be patient with yourself—even the best writers edit and revise their work many times over before they consider it finished. It's also helpful to get a knowledgeable person to read what you've written and offer advice.

There are structural and technical requirements that vary depending on the type of research you've done, but it's equally important to pay attention to the quality of your writing as *writing*. Writing, even the formal variety, shouldn't be thought of as drudgery: consider it an art to be cultivated. Among other things, try to bring your enthusiasm for your topic to the page. If your exuberance has waned by the time you start writing, think about how your project relates to some larger societal or theoretical issue, and keep that in mind as you write.

Here are few more suggestions:

inbj/123RF, vm/iStockphoto

Even formal writing should showcase your enthusiasm for your topic. What strategies could you use to maintain your interest in your research project?

Start early

There are good reasons for beginning the writing process early on. It forces you to think about issues such as how best to present and justify the research questions, and how to structure the discussion of the literature cited. A second reason is entirely practical: many people find it difficult to get started and tend (often unwittingly) to use procrastination strategies. But putting off the inevitable almost always results in rushed, last-minute writing. Writing under that kind of pressure is not ideal, to say the least. How you present your findings and conclusions is a crucial aspect of the research process, and if you fail to produce a convincing account of your findings because of time pressures, you will not do your work justice.

Get feedback

Try to get as much feedback on your writing as possible, and respond positively to whatever comments you receive. Your supervisor or instructor is likely to be the main source of feedback; show as many drafts of your work as regulations allow, leaving plenty of time for a response. You will not be the only student seeking advice, and if comments are rushed, they may not be particularly helpful. You can also ask others in your program or class to read your drafts and comment on them, and they may ask you to do the same. Their comments may be very useful, but those from your supervisor or instructor are likely to be the most valuable.

Avoid sexist, racist, and other prejudicial language

Remember that writing should be free of sexist, racist, and other prejudicial language.

Structure your writing

A 10,000- to 15,000-word research project entailing data collection is typically structured as follows.

Box 15.2 | Safety in research

In 2002, a 19-year-old sociology student was supposed to interview a homeless person in Manchester, UK. Because of safety concerns, her advisor recommended that she take a friend with her and conduct the interview in a public place. When she did not return, she was reported missing (Barkham & Jenkins, 2002). Four days later she showed up in Dublin, where she claimed to have fled after the man robbed her; however, it was later suggested that her disappearance might have been sparked by a family argument.

Whether or not her story was true, there is an important lesson in it: social research can place you in potentially dangerous circumstances. Avoid situations where personal harm is a real possibility. Just as you should ensure that no harm comes to research participants, individuals conducting research should not place themselves in unsafe situations. The advice given by the student's advisor—to take someone with you and conduct the interview in a public place—is sensible. Keep your cellphone nearby and switched on. Establish a routine whereby you keep in regular contact with friends or family members. Even in seemingly safe conditions, a researcher can be faced with a sudden outburst of abuse or threatening behaviour; you can't always predict how people will react to a particular trigger, such as an interview question. If there are signs that trouble is imminent (for example, through body language), calmly withdraw from the situation. Further guidelines on these issues can be found in Craig (2004).

Sometimes researchers may be unaware of possible hazards. Lankshear (2000), for instance, found out only after her study had begun that her research in a hospital laboratory could expose her to dangerous pathogens. Be sure to do a thorough risk assessment of the research environment before you undertake your project.

Finally, once you've assessed the risk and are convinced that you will not be placing yourself in harm's way, it may be necessary to persuade your instructor, advisor, or research ethics board (REB) that your safety will not be compromised. Small, Maher, & Kerr (2014), who did ethnographic research with people in Vancouver who inject themselves with illegal drugs, were told by their REB that they had to consult with local police about safety issues and provide police with the names of the ethnographers who would be observing the drug users. The researchers had to go to great lengths to convince the REB that proper precautions would be taken and that they would not be in danger, and that involving the police in their safety would make it very difficult to recruit participants and ensure the confidentiality of the results. Eventually the board relented and the study went ahead as planned, but only after a prolonged review process.

Title page

Your institution or class may have specific requirements for the title page. Typically, it should include your name, your instructor's name, the course, and the date, as well as the title of the paper.

Acknowledgments

You may want to acknowledge the help of people such as gatekeepers who gave you access to an organization and those who read your drafts and provided you with feedback or advice, including your supervisor.

Table of contents (if applicable)

Your institution or class may have recommendations or prescriptions about the form the Table of Contents should take.

An abstract

An abstract is a brief (less than one page) summary of your work. Not all institutions or instructors ask for this component, so find out if it is required. Most journal articles include abstracts; draw on them for ideas and models.

Introduction

The purpose of the Introduction is to explain what you are writing about and why it is important. It should also:

- describe in general terms the theoretical perspective you have chosen to take (where applicable);
- explain your choice; and
- outline your research questions (remember that in qualitative studies, research questions are often more open-ended than is the case with quantitative work).

The opening sentence is often the most difficult of all. Becker (1986) strongly advised against "vacuous" opening sentences on the model of "This study deals with the problem of careers." This kind of sentence "is evasive, pointing to something without saying anything, or anything much, about it. *What* about careers?" (Becker, 1986, p. 51). To those concerned that too much detail might give away the plot, he countered that it is much better to give readers a quick and clear indication of what is going to be presented.

Literature review

As we have seen, the Literature Review section provides an overview of the main ideas and research done in your area of interest. However, your review should do more than simply summarize the relevant literature.

- Remember that, whenever appropriate, your approach should be critical.
- You should use your review of the literature to show why your research questions are important. For example, suppose that the basis for your research questions is the idea that although a lot of research has been done on *X* (a general topic or area, such as food insecurity), little research has been done on *Y* (an aspect of *X*, like food insecurity in rural areas). In that case the literature review is where you should justify this assertion. Alternatively, it may be that there are two competing positions

Practical Tip | Non-sexist writing

One of the biggest challenges (though by no means the only one) when trying to write in an inclusive way is how to avoid those awkward "she/he" and "his/her" formulations. One solution is to write in the plural where possible. For example:

> I wanted to give each respondent the opportunity to complete the questionnaire at a time and location that was convenient for him or her.

This sentence, although grammatically correct, can be rephrased as:

> I wanted to give all respondents the opportunity to complete their questionnaires at times and locations that were convenient for them.

"They" and "them" are also acceptable as singular pronouns, and some people prefer to be addressed that way. In such cases their wishes should be respected.

with regard to *Y* and you are going to investigate to see which one provides a better understanding. In the literature review, you should outline the differences between the competing positions. The literature review, then, locates your own research within a tradition of related research.

- Bear in mind that you will return to points made in the review when you present your findings and write up the conclusions.
- Don't try to get everything you've read into the literature review. Forcing it all in (because of the effort you've put into finding and reading the material) will not help. The literature review is there to assist you in developing an argument, and if you stuff it with material of passing relevance you will undermine your ability to get your argument across.
- Recall that reading the relevant literature should continue more or less throughout the research process. This means that a literature review written before the data collection begins is provisional. If you find that you want to revise your initial review, go ahead.
- Additional reflections on producing a literature review are presented in Box 15.3. They were derived from a review of qualitative studies of organizations, but they also apply to quantitative research.

Research methods

The term "research methods" is a kind of catch-all for several things that need to be outlined: research design; sampling approach; how access was achieved (if relevant); specific procedures used (for example, in the case of an online questionnaire, whether and how non-respondents were contacted for follow-up); and, where relevant, the nature of the questionnaire, interview schedule, participant observation, observation schedule, or coding frame. Although copies of these usually appear in an appendix, you should comment on matters such as your style of questioning or observation and why you asked the questions you did. Other issues to be discussed in this section may include procedures for note taking and data analysis. When discussing each of these matters, you should describe and defend the choices you made: for example, why you decided to use an online questionnaire rather than a structured interview, or why you chose a particular population for sampling.

Results

In the Results section you present the gist of your findings. If you will be including a separate Discussion section, the results should generally be presented with little or no commentary on how they relate to the claims made in the literature. If there is no Discussion section to follow, you need to include some reflections on the significance of your findings for your research questions and for the literature. Bear the following points in mind:

- If you are presenting tables, graphs, and so on, you need to comment on each one; otherwise, readers will be left wondering why they were included. Don't just summarize what a table shows: direct the reader to the parts of it that are especially striking from the point of view of your research questions. Ask yourself what story you want the table to convey; then relay that story to your readers.
- Whichever approach you choose, remember not to include *all* your results. You should present and discuss only those findings that relate directly to your research questions. Omitting some of your findings can be painful, but it's necessary to ensure that the thread of your argument is not lost. This is especially true in the case of qualitative research. As one experienced qualitative researcher put it: "The major problem we face in qualitative inquiry is not to get data, but to get rid of it!" (Wolcott, 1990, p. 18). If you don't leave out some of your results, you will not only obscure your argument but run the risk that your account of your findings will appear too descriptive and lack an analytical edge. This is why it's essential to use your research questions as a focus and to orient your presentation of the findings to them.

Box 15.3 | Presenting qualitative research literature

In their examination of journal articles reporting qualitative research on organizations, Golden-Biddle & Locke (1993) argued that good articles in this area develop a story; that is, a clear and compelling framework around which the writing is structured (see also Golden-Biddle, 1997). This idea is very much in tune with Wolcott's (1990, p. 18) advice on writing up qualitative research: "determine the basic story you are going to tell." Golden-Biddle & Locke suggest that establishing how your research relates to the existing literature on the topic is an important component of storytelling. They identified two things that are done to effectively review the literature and convey the relevance and significance of your research:

- ***Constructing inter-textual coherence.*** The author shows how existing contributions to the literature relate both to each other and to the research that will be reported. Golden-Biddle & Locke distinguished three approaches to the coherence question:
  - ***Synthesized coherence.*** The author pieces together theory and research previously regarded as unconnected.
  - ***Progressive coherence.*** The author traces the building of consensus in a particular area of knowledge.
  - ***Non-coherence.*** The author emphasizes disagreements in the contributions to a certain research program.

Each of these strategies is designed to leave room for the writer to make their own contribution to the field.

- ***Problematizing the situation.*** The literature is then criticized by identifying a problem, for example:
  - ***Incomplete.*** There is a gap in the existing literature.
  - ***Inadequate.*** The existing literature has ignored useful ways of looking at the phenomenon; alternative perspectives or frameworks are then introduced.

According to Golden-Biddle & Locke, the authors they studied used their accounts of the literature in various ways:

- They demonstrated their knowledge and competence by referring to prominent writings in the field.
- They developed their review of the literature in such a way as to highlight the contribution they would make in the article.
- They explained how the gaps or problems they identified in the literature corresponded to their research questions.

The idea of writing up research as storytelling serves as a useful reminder that reviewing the literature, which is part of the story, should link seamlessly with the rest of the article.

Discussion

If you are including a Discussion section, it should address the implications of the findings for your research questions. If you have specified hypotheses, the discussion should revolve around whether or not they were supported. If they were not, you might speculate about the reasons. Was the sample too small? Did you forget a key variable? In this section you can also bring out the main theoretical contributions of your research and explore their implications.

Conclusion

The main guidelines for the Conclusion are as follows:

- A conclusion is not the same as a summary. However, it is frequently useful to briefly recapitulate your main arguments at the beginning of the Conclusion section. Once that is done, hammer home to readers the significance of your research.

Checklist

Checklist of issues to consider for writing up research

- ☐ Is there a good correspondence between the title of the project and its contents?
- ☐ Have you clearly specified your research questions?
- ☐ Have you clearly linked the literature cited to your research questions?
- ☐ Is your discussion of the literature critical and not just a summary of what you have read?
- ☐ Have you clearly outlined your research design and research methods? Make sure you have explained:
    - why you chose a particular research design or method;
    - why you implemented your research design in the way you did (for example, how the interview questions relate to the research questions, or why you observed people in particular situations);
    - how you selected your research participants;
    - whether you experienced any problems with cooperation (for example, response rates);
    - if your research required access to an organization, how and on what basis the agreement was achieved;
    - any difficulties encountered in implementing your research;
    - the steps taken to ensure that the research was ethical; and
    - how the data were analyzed.
- ☐ Have you presented your data in such a way that they clearly relate to your research questions?
- ☐ Are your interpretations of the data fully supported with tables, figures, or segments from transcripts?
- ☐ Is every table and/or figure properly labelled with a title and number?
- ☐ Is every table and/or figure commented on in the text?
- ☐ Does the discussion of the findings relate to the research questions?
- ☐ Does that discussion show how the findings shed light on the literature presented?
- ☐ Do the conclusions clearly establish what your research contributes to the literature?
- ☐ Have you explained the limitations of your study?
- ☐ Do your conclusions consist solely of a summary of findings? If so, rewrite them, explaining their significance.
- ☐ Do the conclusions provide clear answers to your research questions?
- ☐ Have you broken up the text in each chapter or section with appropriate subheadings?
- ☐ Have you provided signposts so that readers know what to expect next, and why it is there?
- ☐ Does the writing avoid sexist, racist, and other prejudicial language?
- ☐ Have you checked to ensure that the text does not make excessive use of jargon?
- ☐ Have you included all the necessary appendices (for example, interview schedule, letters requesting access, communications with research participants)?
- ☐ Does the list of references include all the items referred to in your text?
- ☐ Does the format of the references follow precisely the style required by your institution or instructor?
- ☐ Have you met all requirements regarding matters such as word count (so that the paper is neither too long nor too short) and inclusion of an abstract and table of contents?
- ☐ Have you ensured that you do not quote excessively when presenting the literature?
- ☐ Have you fully acknowledged the work of others, so that you cannot be accused of plagiarism?

- ☐ Have you acknowledged, preferably in an Acknowledgments section, the help of others where appropriate (for example, your supervisor, people who helped with interviews, people who read drafts)?
- ☐ Finally, have you checked to make sure that your tenses, margins, pagination, and capitalization are consistent? Many forms may be acceptable, but all must be used consistently.

- This is the place to draw attention to any limitations of your work that cannot be rectified without unduly expanding the scope of the research.
- You may also suggest avenues for further research.

Two things to avoid are (a) engaging in speculations that either take you too far from your data or cannot be substantiated by the data, and (b) discussing issues or ideas that have not already been introduced.

Appendices

Researchers often have some material that would help readers assess their work, but is too detailed or technical to include in the main text. Such material—questionnaires, coding frames, observation schedules, letters sent to those sampled, letters to and from gatekeepers, and so on—can be included in appendices.

References

Be sure to include all the sources cited in the text. Follow the format suggested by your department or instructor. The format is usually an author-date system such as the one used in this book.

Finally

Remember to fulfill any obligations you have incurred, such as supplying a copy of your report to those who have been promised one. Maintain the confidentiality of the information given and the anonymity of informants and other research participants by securing—and later, as appropriate, destroying—the primary data.

Interactive Classroom Activities

1. The instructor reviews the various aspects of a good research question. The class is then divided into small groups. Each group is to select a topic of interest—for example, sexual assault on Canadian university campuses. The group then carefully constructs a research question or set of research questions based on the topic. Once completed, each group takes turns putting its questions on the classroom screen or board for class discussion and critical comment. The class is asked a series of evaluative questions such as: Is the question(s) clear? Could anything be done to improve the question(s)? Should additional questions be asked?
2. The instructor, or better yet a reference librarian, provides a detailed description of the procedures for using the databases available via the institution's library system. The steps taken can be shown on the classroom screen.
3. In situations where students have ready access to the Internet, each student uses library databases to find five articles that address the research question(s) his or her group came up with in exercise 1. Once completed, the groups then reconvene so students can compare the articles they found with those selected by the other members of their group.

Relevant Websites

Databases such as *Sociological Abstracts*, *PsycINFO*, *Worldwide Political Science Abstracts*, *Social Work Abstracts*, the *Canadian Periodicals Index Quarterly* (*CPI.Q*), *LGBT Life with Full Text*, *Family & Society Studies Worldwide*, *Contemporary Women's Issues*, and the *Social Sciences Citation Index* (through the *Web of Knowledge*) are all accessible online. To use them, log on to your institution's library server and call them up from there. *Google Scholar* can be accessed directly.

This YouTube video from the *University of Maryland* discusses the fundamentals of doing a literature review.

www.youtube.com/watch?v=2IUZWZX4OGI&feature=related

In this YouTube video, *Jared Wright* walks you through the steps that need to be taken to write a sociological research paper.

www.youtube.com/watch?v=n-5xlA71aRQ

In this YouTube video, *David Taylor* discusses how to choose and narrow down a research topic.

www.youtube.com/watch?v=jSHXb83Xtsk

This *Social Sciences and Humanities Research Council of Canada* site discusses best practices to promote equity, diversity, and inclusion in research.

https://www.sshrc-crsh.gc.ca/funding-financement/nfrf-fnfr/edi-eng.aspx

(Websites accessed 4 September 2021)

OXFORD learning link

More resources are available on Oxford Learning Link. Visit https://learninglink.oup.com/ for:

- Student self-quiz
- Flash cards
- Audio clips
- Videos
- Activities

APPENDIX
Using IBM SPSS Statistics and NVivo Software

Chapters 8 and 13 described a number of methods for analyzing quantitative and qualitative data. This appendix illustrates how to perform those analyses using IBM SPSS Statistics (SPSS) and NVivo software.*

Quantitative data analysis using SPSS

The gym survey described in Chapter 8 will be used to illustrate how SPSS software is used. Learning new software requires some perseverance, but is well worth the effort. It would take far longer to perform the calculations by hand (even on the small gym survey sample of 90) than to learn the software. With more advanced techniques and larger samples, the time saved is even more substantial. Imagine calculating the mean age of 2500 people by hand!

Getting started in SPSS

Introduction

SPSS is the software most widely used for this kind of analysis, probably because it is relatively straightforward. It has been in existence since the mid-1960s and over the years has undergone many revisions, particularly since the arrival of personal computers. The version used in preparing this section is IBM SPSS Statistics 25.

SPSS operations and other on-screen terms are presented in **bold** (e.g., **Analyze**). The names given to variables are in ***bold italics*** (e.g., ***gender*** or ***reasons***). Labels (longer versions of names; see pp. 377–78) given to variables or values are in bold but are not italicized (e.g., **reasons for visiting** or **male**). A right-pointing arrow (→) means "left-click once with the mouse" to make selections. Box A.1 presents a list of basic operations in SPSS.

If you have SPSS software loaded onto the hard disk of the computer you are using, click on the SPSS icon on the Desktop screen or find the program using the Start button in the bottom left-hand corner of the screen. If you don't have SPSS software on your computer, it may be available from a special server provided by your university.

After SPSS loads, an opening dialogue box with a number of options may appear. If so, for the purposes of this exercise disable it: → **Close**. This will give you the SPSS **Data Editor**, made up of two components: **Data View** and **Variable View**. Move between these two by selecting the appropriate button at the bottom left of the screen. The **Data View** provides a spreadsheet grid into which data are entered (see Plate A.1). The columns represent *variables*—in our example, information about the characteristics of each person in the gym study sample, such as ***gender*** and ***age***. Until data are entered, each column simply has **var** as its heading. The rows represent *cases*, which can be people (as in this example) or other units of analysis. Each block in the grid is referred to as a **cell**. Note that when the data are entered in the SPSS spreadsheet, they will look different: for example, 1 becomes 1.00 (this can be adjusted if necessary).

Box A.1 | Basic operations in SPSS

- IBM SPSS Statistics **Data Editor**. This is the mode in which data may be entered and subsequently edited and defined. It is made up of two screens: **Data View** and **Variable View**. Move between these two views by selecting the appropriate button at the bottom left of the screen.
- **Data View**. This is the spreadsheet into which the data are entered. It appears when SPSS is started.
- **Variable View**. Another spreadsheet, this one displays information about each of the variables (such as the variable name, the variable labels, and value labels) and allows that information to be changed (see below).
- IBM SPSS Statistics **Viewer**. After a statistical analysis or the production of a graph (sometimes called a "chart" in SPSS), the output is deposited here. The output window superimposes itself over the Data Editor after an analysis has been performed or a graph has been generated.
- **Variable Name**. This is the name given to a variable (for example, ***gender***). Until they are given names, variables are referred to as var00001, var00002, and so on. Once a variable is given a name, the name appears in the column for that variable in the Data View window. It is generated from the Variable View.
- **Variable Label**. This is a label attached to a particular variable, and is optional. It is usually longer than the variable name and therefore more explanatory. Spaces can be used (for example, **reasons for visiting**). The label appears in any output generated and comes from the Variable View.
- **Value Label**. This is a label attached to the code used when entering the data. Thus, for var00001, the label **male** can be attached to 1 and the label **female** to 2. In output, such as a frequency table or chart, the labels for each value appear, making the interpretation of output easier than if the code were used. It is generated from the Variable View.
- **Missing Values**. If data for a particular variable are missing, you must specify how missing values are coded so that the computer can omit them from the calculations. Missing values are generated from the Variable View.
- **Analyze**. This is the button on the menu bar along the top of the Data Editor from which (via a drop-down menu) the method of analysis is selected. Note that whenever a menu item appears with a right-pointing arrowhead after it, a further sub-menu is available.
- **Graphs**. This is the button (at the top of the Data Editor) used to get access to the **Chart Builder** (via a drop-down menu), which can be used to create various graphs and charts.
- **Chart Builder**. This feature is used to make charts and graphs. A very useful tutorial is available from the **Data Editor** by clicking **Help → Topics**. Use the search engine to find **Tutorial → Creating and editing charts**.
- **Chart Editor**. This is used to make various changes to graphs. To activate it, double-click anywhere in the graph. A small Chart Editor window appears along with a version of the main graph and stays until the Chart Editor is exited.

Entering data in the Data View

To input the data given in Box 8.2 into the **Data View**, make sure that the top left-hand cell in the grid is highlighted (Plate A.1). If it is not, simply click once in that cell. Then type the appropriate number in that cell—that is, 1. This number goes directly into that cell and into the box beneath the toolbar. Although you can use the mouse, many people find it easier to use the arrow keys on their keyboard to move from cell to cell. If you make a mistake, simply click once in the cell in question, type in the correct value, and hit the Enter key. The last piece of data goes into the bottom right-hand cell of what will be a perfect rectangle of data. Plate A.2 shows the **Data View** with the data from the gym survey entered (though only part of the data set is visible). The first row of data contains the coded answers (provided by the first respondent) from the completed questionnaire in Box 8.1.

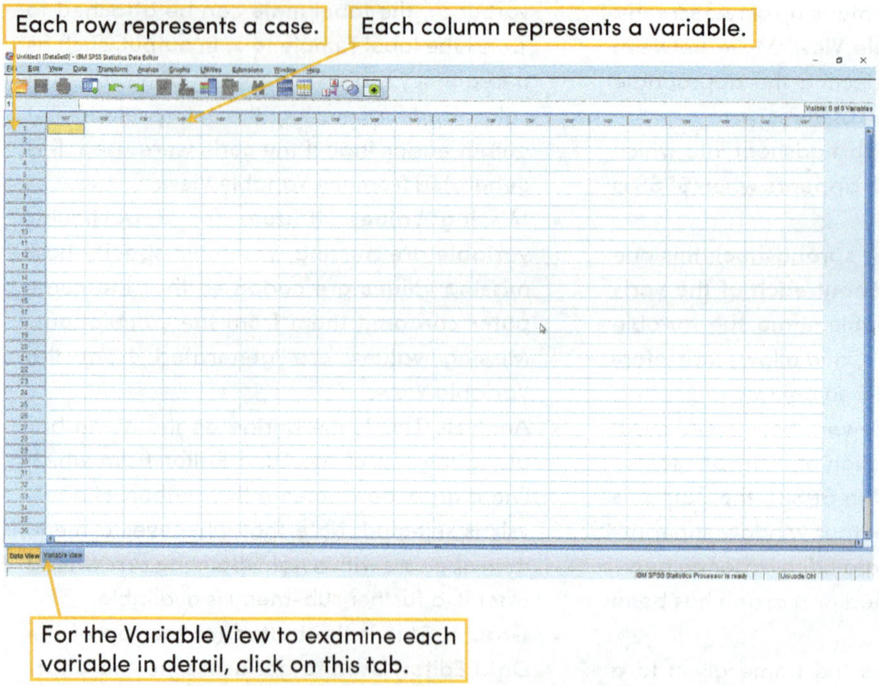

PLATE A.1 The SPSS Data Editor **Data View**

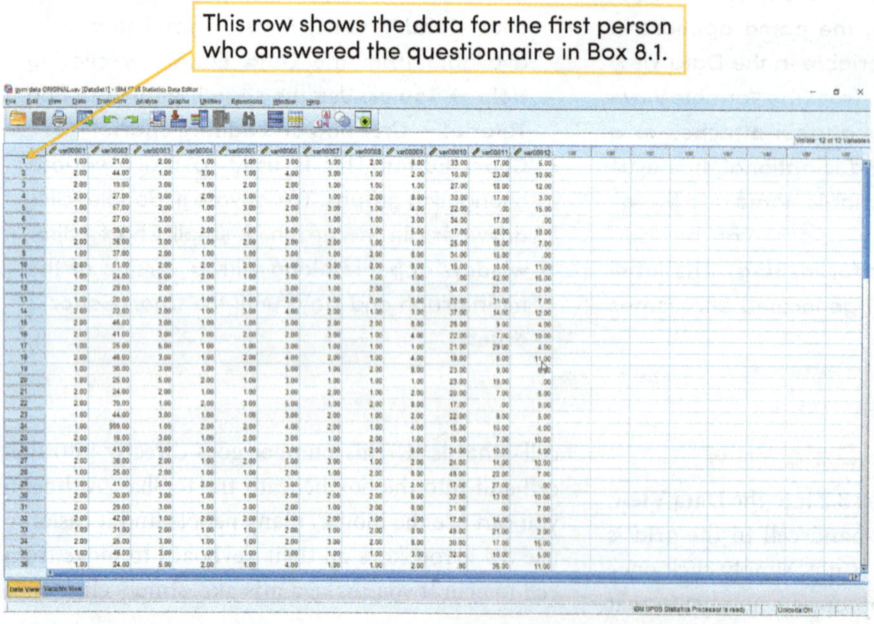

PLATE A.2 The **Data View** with the "gym study" data entered

To proceed further, SPSS works in the following typical sequence for selecting variables and analyzing data.

1. Make a selection from the menu bar at the top of the screen, for example, → **Analyze**.
2. From the menu that will appear, make a selection, for example, → **Descriptive Statistics**.
3. This will bring up another menu where you will specify which statistics you want, for example, **Frequencies**.
4. This will bring up a *dialogue box* in which you provide further information, such as the variables to be analyzed.
5. Very often, further information is needed; → a button that brings up a *sub-dialogue box*.
6. Provide the information in the sub-dialogue box and then go back to the dialogue box. Sometimes, a further sub-dialogue box is required before you can return to the dialogue box.

When you have finished going through the entire procedure, → **OK**. The toolbar beneath the menu bar allows shortcut access to certain SPSS operations.

Defining variables: Variable names, missing values, variable labels, and value labels

Once you have finished entering the data, prepare the variables. The following steps explain how this is done:

1. → **Variable View** tab at the bottom left of the **Data Editor** [opens the window shown in Plate A.3]
2. To name a variable, click on the current variable name (for example, **var00003**) and type a name for it (for example, ***reasons***). This name, which cannot include spaces, is the identification needed for instructing the computer to perform an analysis with this variable. It can be anything you like, but you should choose a name that indicates what the variable is measuring.
3. To give the variable a more detailed designation, known in SPSS as a **variable label**, → the cell in the **Label** column for this variable. Then type in the label (for example, **reasons for visiting**). This label will appear on your output, just as a designer label appears on a piece of clothing. If no variable label is specified, the variable name will be used for the output.

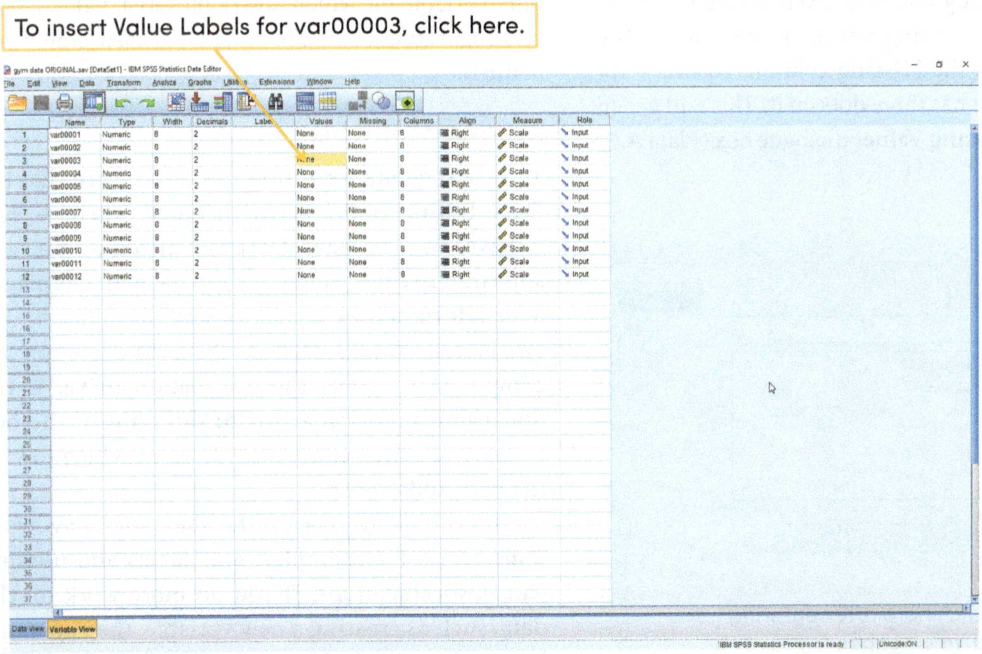

PLATE A.3 The Data Editor **Variable View**

4. Provide "value labels" for the values of the variables, where appropriate. The procedure generally applies to variables that are not interval/ratio (the interval/ratio level of measurement is called "scale" in SPSS terminology). Scale variables do not need value labels unless you are grouping them in some way. To assign value labels, → in the cell in the **Values** column for the variable in question. A small button with three dots on it appears. → the button. The **Value Labels** dialogue box appears (Plate A.4). → the box to the right of **Value** and begin to define the value labels. To do this, enter the value (for example, 1) in the area to the right of **Value** and then type in the value label (for example, **relaxation**) in the area to the right of **Label**. Then → **Add**. Do this for each value. When finished, → **OK**. A variable name for question one on the questionnaire could be ***gender***; the variable label "gender of respondent;" and the value labels, 1, "male" and 2, "female." The computer reads only numbers (male is 1; female, 2) so the value labels are optional, but if you omit them the output will tell you about 1s and 2s instead of males and females.
5. Designate missing values. In the case of ***reasons***, missing data are given a value of 0. To assign the missing value, → the cell for this variable in the **Missing** column. Again, → the button that has three dots on it. This will generate the **Missing Values** dialogue box (Plate A.5).

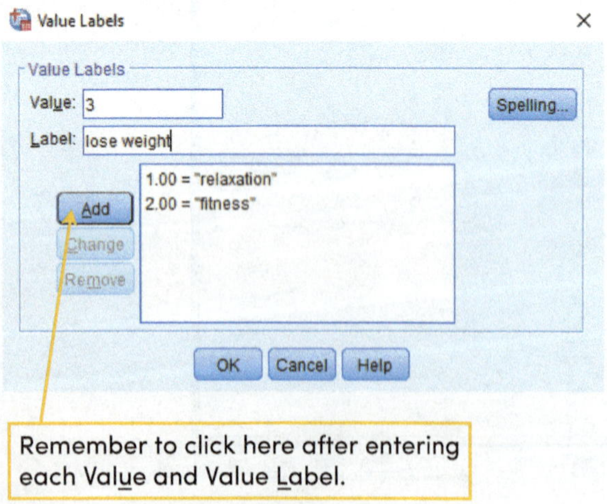

PLATE A.4 The **Value Labels** Dialogue Box

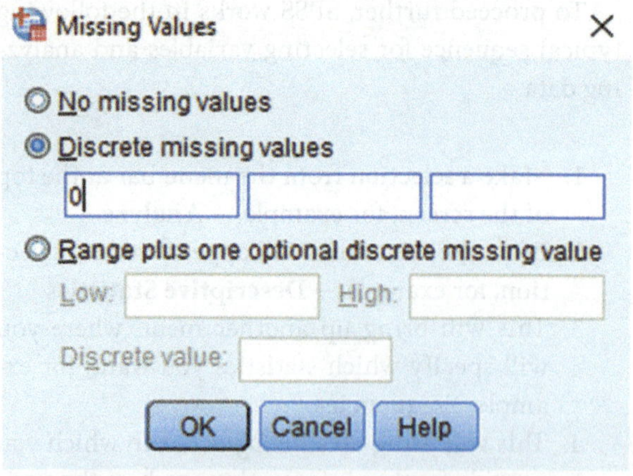

PLATE A.5 The **Missing Values** Dialogue Box

In the **Missing Values** dialogue box, enter the missing value (0) below **Discrete missing values** and then → **OK**.

6. Designate the level of measurement of the variable. ***Reasons*** is a nominal variable. To enter this information, → the cell for this variable in the **Measure** column. A drop-down menu will appear; → **Nominal**.

To simplify the following presentation, ***reasons*** is the only variable for which a variable label, value labels, missing values, and the level of measurement are defined.

Saving the data

To save the data for future use, make sure that the **Data Editor** is the active window. Then, → **File** → **Save As**. The **Save Data As** dialogue box will appear. It needs a name for the data, which is placed after **File name** and a place to save the data—for example, onto a USB drive or the hard drive of your computer. To select the destination drive, → the downward pointing arrow to the right of the box by **Look in**. Then choose the drive on which to save the data and → **Save**.

This procedure saves the data *and* any work done on it—for example, value labels and missing values specifications. If you do more work on the data, such as creating a new variable, the data must be saved again or the new work will be lost. SPSS gives you a choice of renaming the data—in which case there will be two data files (one with the original data and one with the revised data)—or keeping the same name. In the latter case the original file is lost but its name is retained and applied to the modified file.

Retrieving data

To retrieve a data file, → **File** → **Open** → **Data . . . .** The **Open Data** dialogue box will appear. Go to the location in which the data are deposited to retrieve the file containing the data, and then → **Open**.

Computing a new variable

The total amount of time a respondent spent in the gym is made up of three variables: ***cardmins***, ***weimins***, and ***othmins*** (questions 10, 11, and 12 respectively in Box 8.1, referring to cardiovascular equipment, weights, and other activities). Adding them up gives the total number of minutes spent on various activities in the gym, and a new variable, ***totalmin***, can be created for that purpose. To do this, take the following steps:

1. → **Transform** → **Compute Variable . . .** [opens the **Compute Variable** dialogue box shown in Plate A.6]
2. Under **Target Variable**, type ***totalmin***
3. Under **Function group**, → **Statistical**; under **Functions and Special Variables**, → **Sum**; then → the button with an upward-pointing arrowhead to send it into the box under **Numeric Expression**
4. From the list of variables at the left, → ***cardmins*** → adjacent button [puts ***cardmins*** in box after **SUM**]; → ***weimins*** → button [puts ***weimins*** in box after ***cardmins***]; → ***othmins*** → button [puts

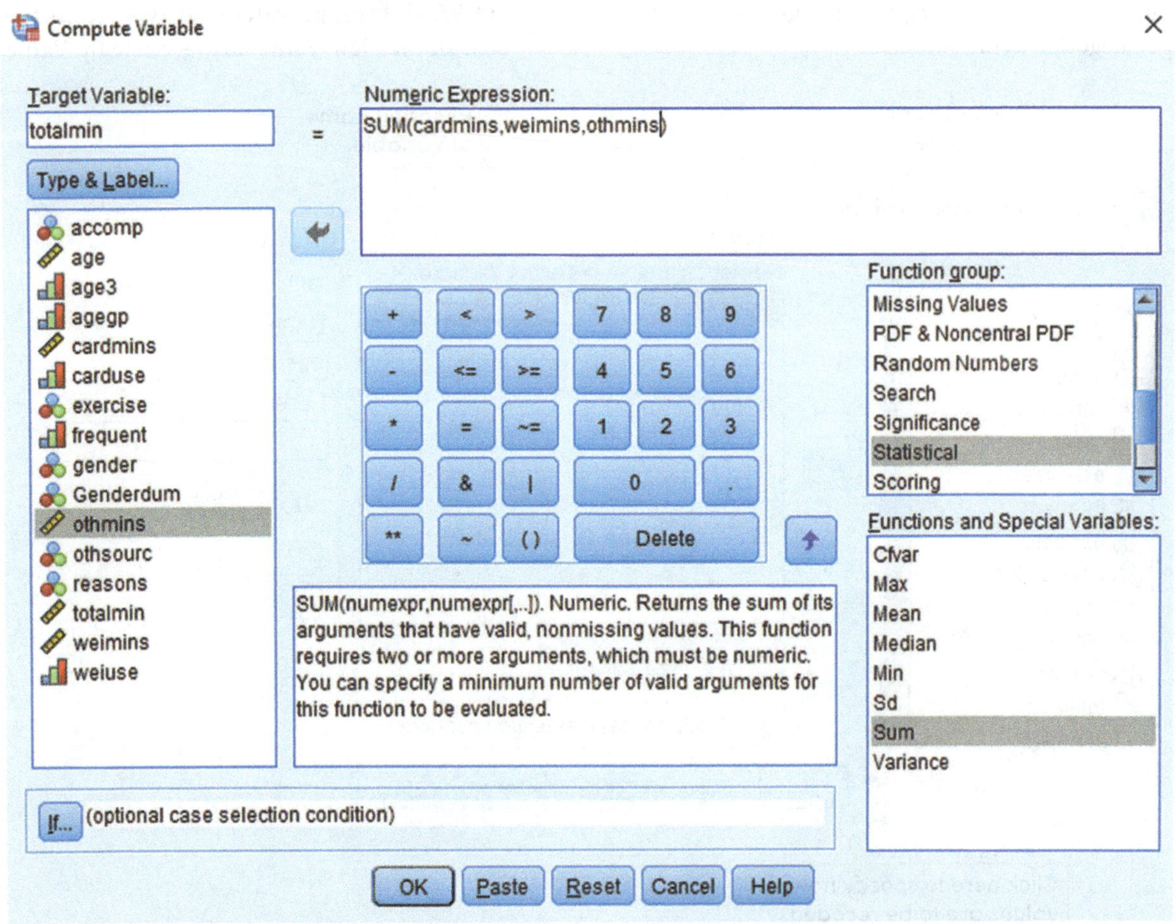

PLATE A.6 The **Compute Variable** Dialogue Box

othmins in box after ***weimins***]; be sure to put commas (but not spaces) between the variable names, and to delete any "?" that remain in the **Numeric Expression** box

5. → **OK**

The new variable ***totalmin*** is created and appears in the **Data Editor**.

Recoding variables

Sometimes you will need to recode variables—for example, to group scores together, as was done to produce Table 8.3 for an interval/ratio variable (var00002, now given the variable name ***age***). SPSS offers two choices: change ***age***, or keep ***age*** as it is and create a new variable. The latter option is appropriate here, because you may need the data for ***age*** in its original form for some other analysis. We will preserve the original variable and create a new one, ***agegp***, for age groups, with five age categories, as in Table 8.3.

1. → **Transform** → **Recode into Different Variables** [opens the **Recode into Different Variables** dialogue box shown in Plate A.7]
2. → ***age*** → adjacent button [puts ***age*** in the **Numeric Variable → Output Variable** box]; → box beneath **Output Variable Name** and type ***agegp*** → **Change** [puts ***agegp*** in the **Numeric Variable → Output Variable** box]; → **Old and New Values . . .** [opens the **Recode into Different Variables: Old and New Values** sub-dialogue box shown in Plate A.8]
3. If there are missing values for a variable (as in this case), in the **Old Value** box, → the circle by **System- or user-missing**, and in the **New Value** box, → **System-missing**, then → **Add**
4. In the **Old Value** box, → circle by **Range: LOWEST through value** and type 20 in the box. In the **New Value** box, → circle by **Value**

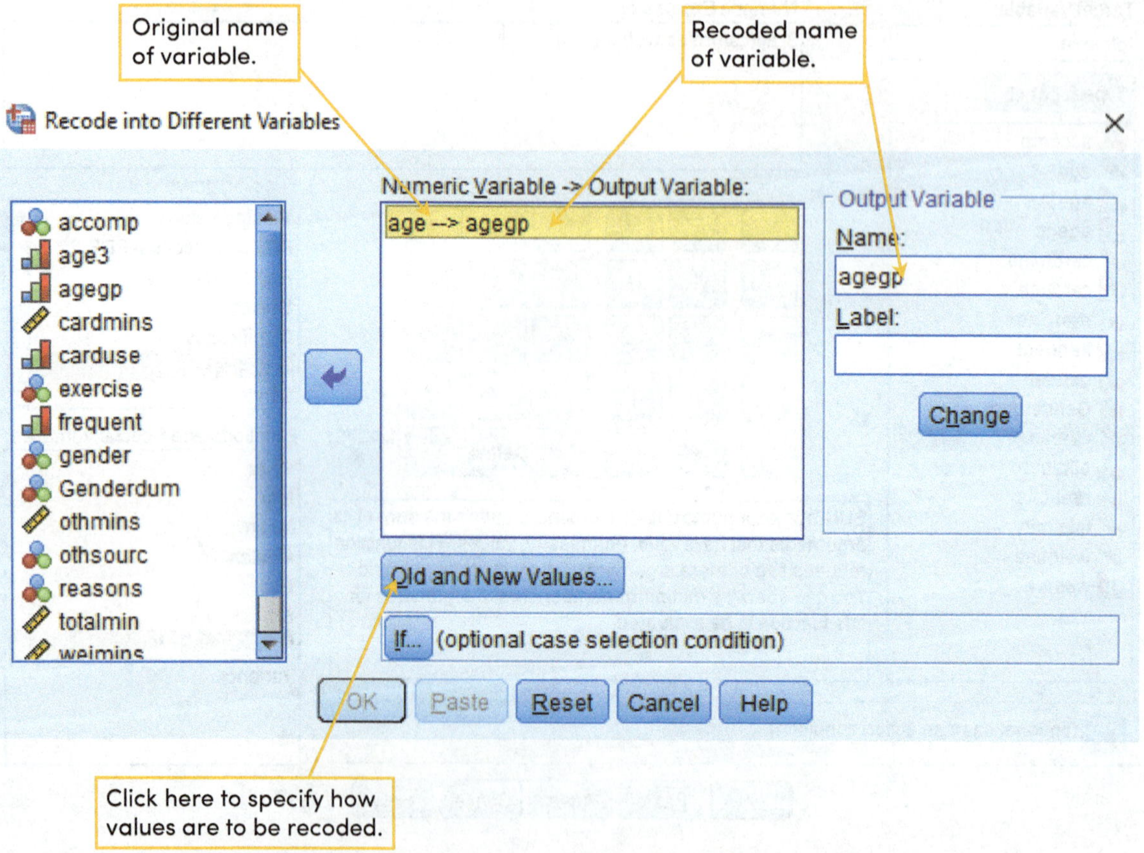

PLATE A.7 The **Recode into Different Variables** Dialogue Box and type 1; → **Add** [the new value appears in the Old → New box]

5. In the **Old Value** box, → first circle by **Range** and type 21, and in the box after **through** type 30. In the **New Value** box, → circle by **Value** and type 2; → **Add**
6. In the **Old Value** box, → first circle by **Range** and type 31 and in the box after **through** type 40. In the **New Value** box, → circle by **Value** and type 3; → **Add**
7. In the **Old Value** box, → first circle by **Range** and type 41, and in the box after **through** type 50. In the **New Value** box, → circle by **Value** and type 4; → **Add**
8. In the **Old Value** box, → circle by **Range: value through HIGHEST** and type 51 in the box. In the **New Value** box, → circle by **Value** and type 5; → **Add** → **Continue** [closes the **Recode into Different Variables: Old and New Values** sub-dialogue box shown in Plate A.8 and returns to the **Recode into Different Variables** dialogue box shown in Plate A.7]
9. → **OK**

The new variable ***agegp*** is created and appears in the **Data View**. To generate value labels for the five age bands and a variable label, repeat the approach described above for those procedures.

Using SPSS for data analysis

Generating a frequency table

To produce a frequency table like the one in Table 8.2:

1. → **Analyze** → **Descriptive Statistics** → **Frequencies . . .** [opens the **Frequencies** dialogue box shown in Plate A.9]
2. → ***reasons*** → adjacent button [puts *reasons* into **Variable(s)** box]
3. → **OK**
4. The table then appears in the IBM SPSS Statistics **Viewer** (see Plate A.10)

Note that in the **Frequencies** dialogue box, the variable name appears. If you would prefer to work with variable labels (which provide more information on

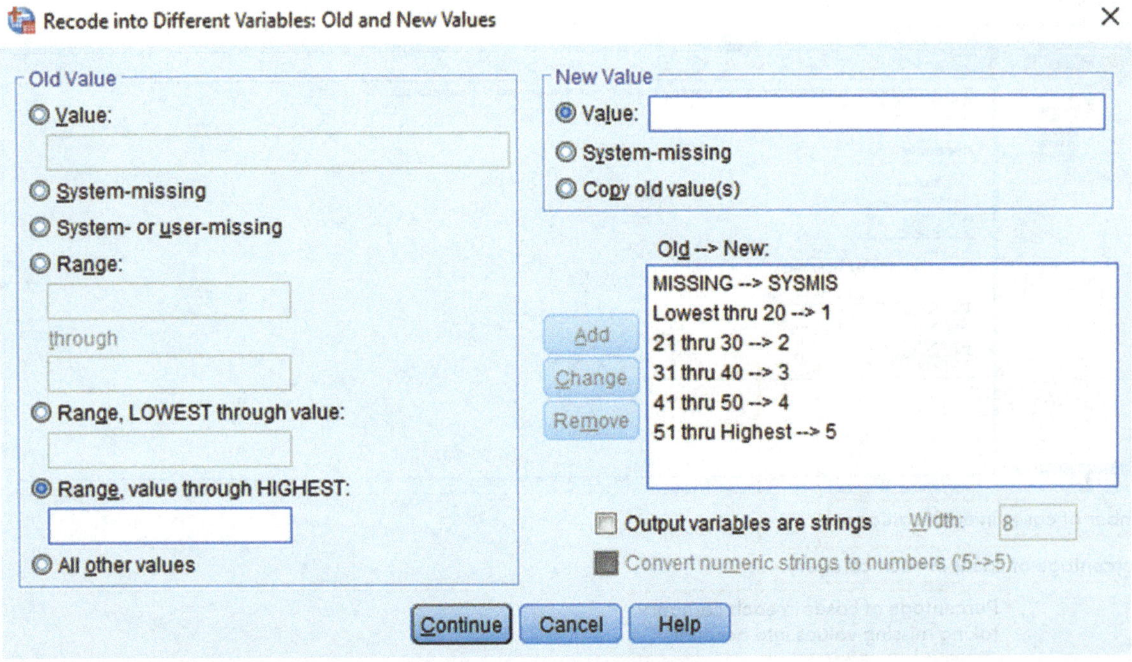

PLATE A.8 The **Recode into Different Variables: Old and New Values** Sub-Dialogue Box

what the variable measures), go into the **Data Editor**, → **Edit** → **Options** → **General**, and in the top left-hand corner you can select variable labels to be used. Similarly, if you prefer that the variables be arranged in alphabetical order, you can specify that there.

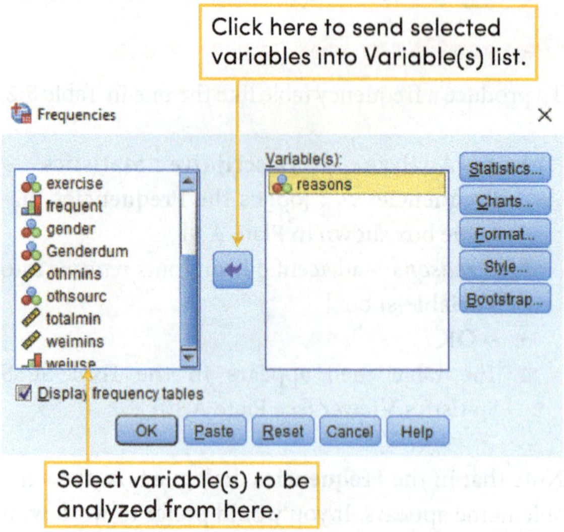

PLATE A.9 The **Frequencies** dialogue box

Generating a bar chart

To produce a bar chart like the one in Figure 8.2:

1. → **Graphs** → **Chart Builder** → **Define Variable Properties** [opens the **Define Variable Properties** dialogue box shown in Plate A.11]
2. → ***reasons*** → adjacent button [puts ***reasons*** in the **Variables to Scan** box]
3. → **Continue** [opens the **Define Variable Properties** sub-dialogue box shown in Plate A.12]. This allows you to edit properties such as variable labels, value labels, and so on before creating a graph, or to enter that information if you have not already done so. We've already entered all the information needed, so exit this box.
4. → **Graphs** → **Chart Builder** → **OK** [opens the **Chart Builder** dialogue box shown in Plate A.13]
5. → **Gallery** → **Bar**, and drag the type of bar chart you want into the "canvas," the large area above the Gallery
6. Drag ***reasons*** into the ***X-Axis?*** box at the bottom of the canvas
7. → **OK**

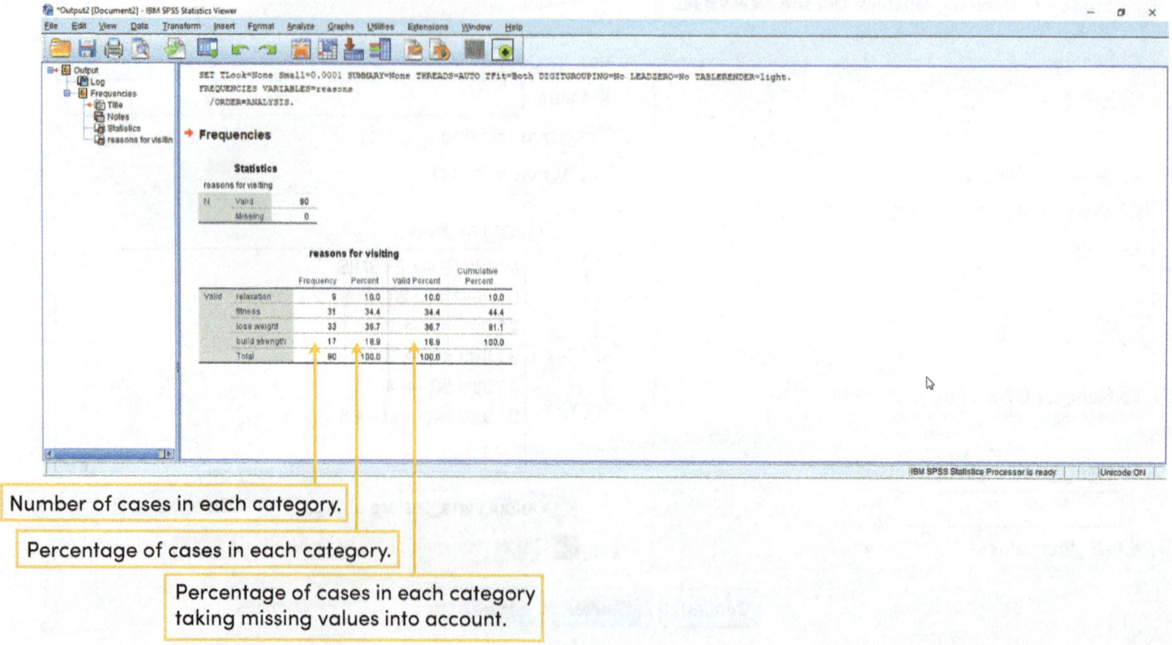

PLATE A.10 The IBM SPSS Statistics **Viewer**

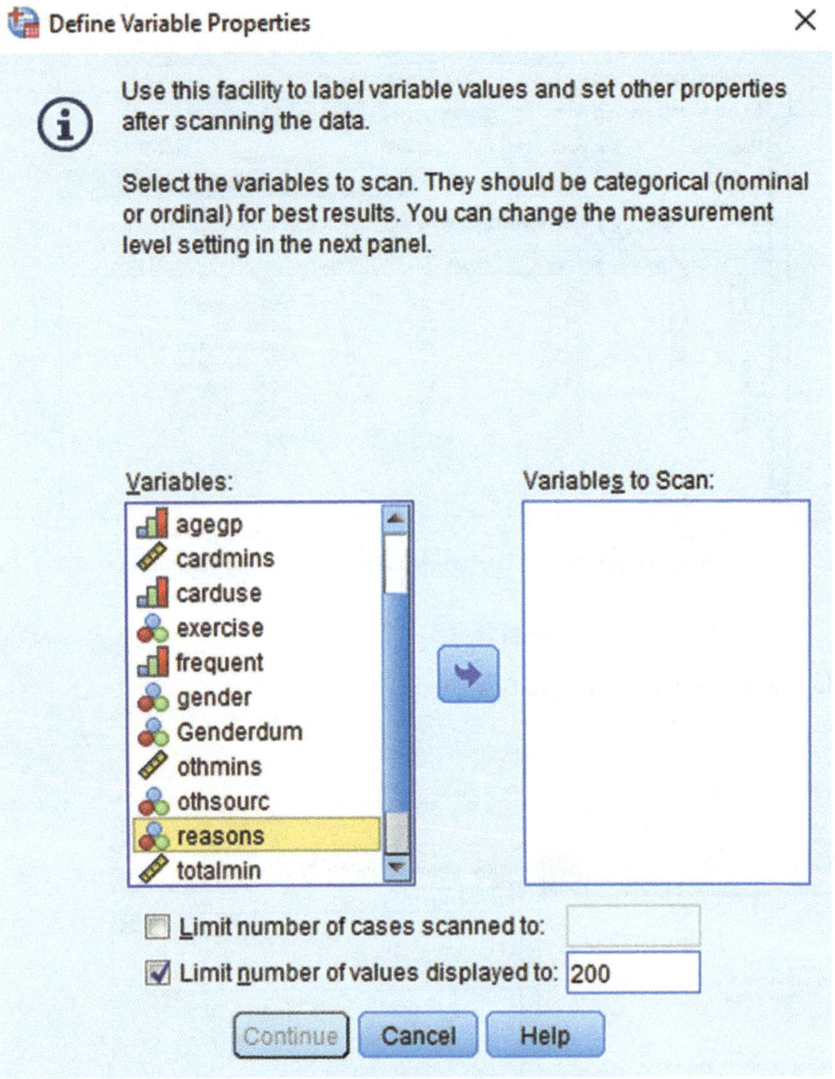

PLATE A.11 The **Define Variable Properties** Dialogue Box

As mentioned earlier, for some useful details on this procedure, do the tutorial available in the **Data Editor** at **Help** → **Topics**. Use the search engine to find **Tutorial** → **Creating and editing charts.**

Generating a pie chart

To produce a pie chart like the one in Figure 8.3:

1. → **Graphs** → **Chart Builder** → **OK** [opens the **Chart Builder** dialogue box]
2. → **Gallery** → **Pie/Polar**, and drag the pie chart into the "canvas," the large area above the Gallery
3. Drag ***reasons*** into the **Slice by?** drop zone at the bottom of the canvas
4. → **OK**
5. *Double-click* anywhere in the chart to bring up the **Chart Editor** (Plate A.14)
6. → **Elements** → **Show Data Labels**. This will place the percentage in each category in the appropriate slice of the pie (see Plate A.15).

This pie chart is in colour, but if you only have access to a monochrome printer, you can change the colours into patterns. Get into the **Chart Editor**, which

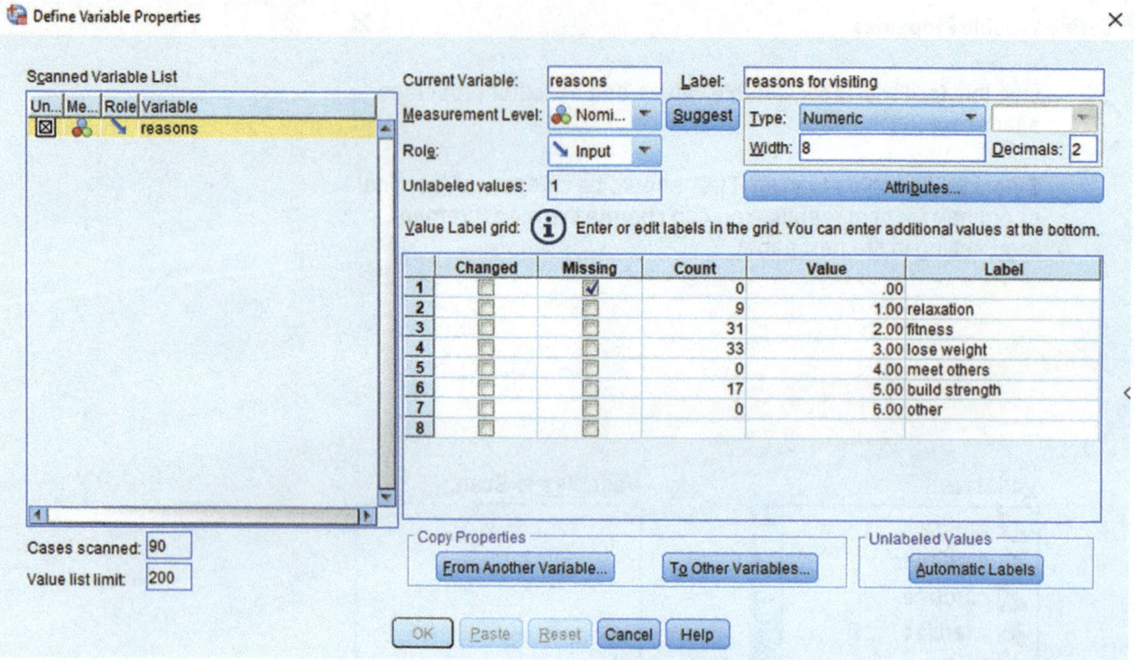

PLATE A.12 The **Define Variable Properties** Sub-Dialogue Box

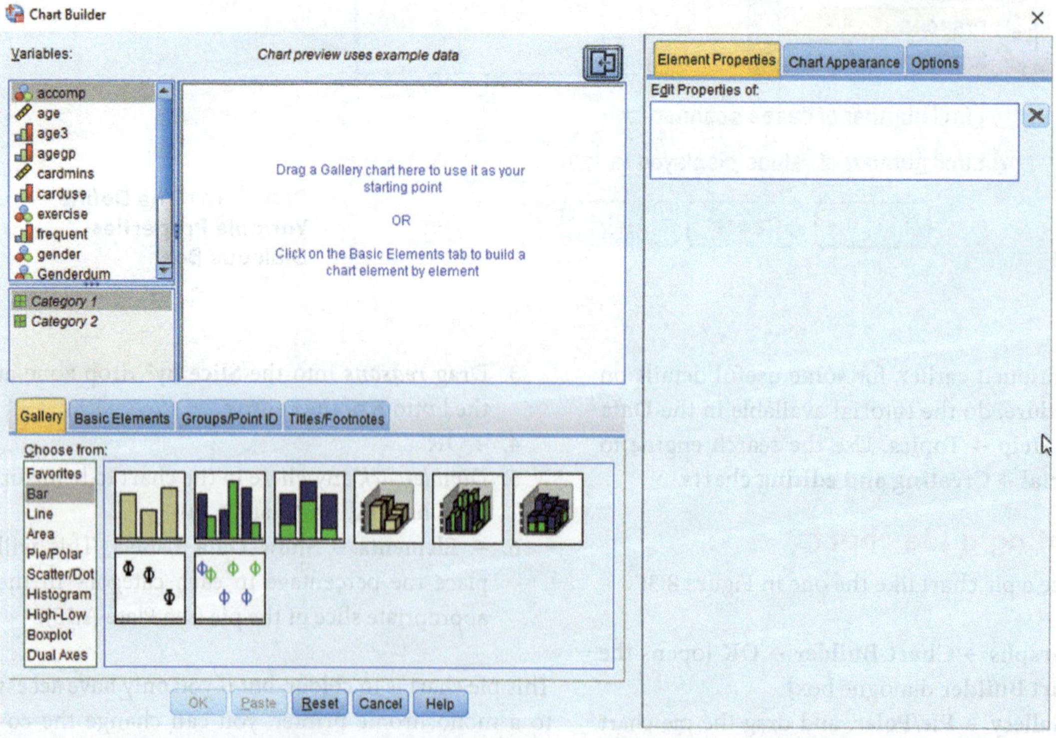

PLATE A.13 The **Chart Builder** Dialogue Box

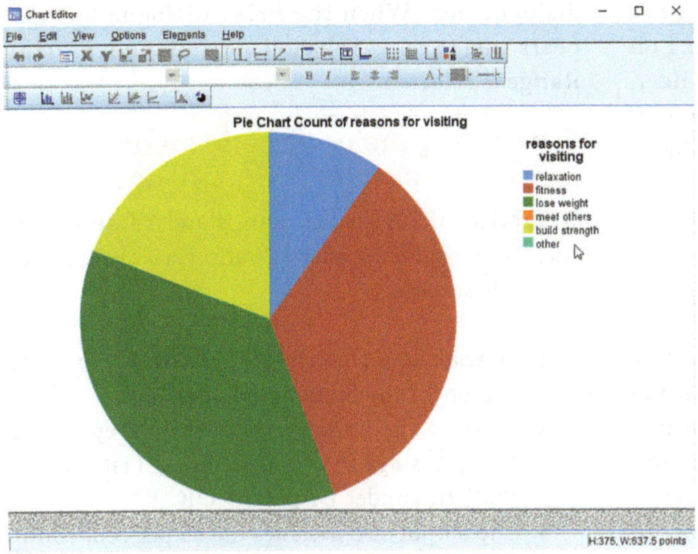

PLATE A.14 The **Chart Editor**

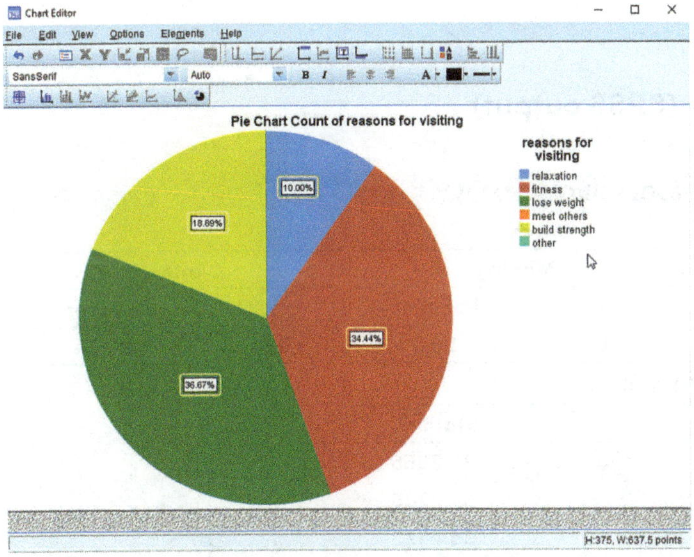

PLATE A.15 The **Chart Editor** Showing Pie Chart Percentages

enables editing of all figures: → **Edit** → **Properties** → **Variables**. By **reasons for visiting** (the variable label) → **Style: Colour**, and → **Style: Pattern** → **Apply**. Use the same procedure for all charts.

Generating a histogram

Producing the histogram in Figure 8.4 is just as simple, except that it requires you to define the ages to be grouped together. The general procedure for doing this is → **Graphs** → **Chart Builder** → **OK** → **Gallery** → **Histogram**, and drag the histogram into the "canvas." Then, → **Element Properties** → **Statistic: Histogram** → **Set Parameters**. However, since we have already recoded age into the categories we want, you can use the newly created ***agegp*** variable. Although technically it is an ordinal variable, to create a histogram it is necessary to define *agegp* as a scale (interval/ratio) variable by right-clicking on it in the **Variables** list while in the **Chart Builder**. Drag *agegp* into the ***X*-Axis?** drop zone at the bottom of the canvas; → **OK**. Other ways of presenting interval/ratio data, such as measures of central tendency and dispersion, will be discussed below.

Printing output

To print all the output in the IBM SPSS Statistics **Viewer**, make sure that the **Viewer** is the active window and then → **File** → **Print . . . .** When the **Print** dialogue box appears, → **OK**. To print just some of the output, hold down the Ctrl button on the keyboard and click once on the parts of the output you want to print. The easiest way to do this is to select the elements from the output summary in the left-hand segment of the **Viewer** shown in Plate A.10. Then bring up the **Print** dialogue box. When the **Print** dialogue box appears, make sure **Selected output** under **Print Range** is selected.

Generating the arithmetic mean, median, standard deviation, and range

To produce the mean, median, standard deviation, and the range for an interval/ratio variable like *age*, follow these steps:

1. → **Analyze** → **Descriptive Statistics** → **Explore . . .** [opens the **Explore** dialogue box]
2. → *age* → the button to the left of **Dependent List** [puts *age* in the **Dependent List** box]; → **Statistics** under **Display**; → **OK**
3. The output also includes the 95 per cent confidence interval for the mean, which is based on the standard error of the mean. The output is in Table A.1.

TABLE A.1 Explore output for age (SPSS output)

EXPLORE

CASE PROCESSING SUMMARY

	Cases					
	Valid		Missing		Total	
	N	Per cent	N	Per cent	N	Per cent
AGE	89	98.9%	1	1.1%	90	100.0%

DESCRIPTIVES

			Statistic	Std. Error
AGE	Mean		33.5955	.9420
	95% Confidence Interval for mean	Lower bound	31.7235	
		Upper bound	35.4675	
	5% Trimmed mean		33.3159	
	Median		31.0000	
	Variance		78.971	
	Std. deviation		8.8866	
	Minimum		18.00	
	Maximum		57.00	
	Range		39.00	
	Interquartile range		14.0000	
	Skewness		.446	.255
	Kurtosis		2.645	.506

Generating a contingency table

To generate a contingency table like Table 8.4, follow this procedure:

1. → **Analyze** → **Descriptive Statistics** → **Crosstabs . . .** [opens the **Crosstabs** dialogue box shown in Plate A.16]
2. → ***reasons*** → button by **Row(s)** [***reasons*** appears in the **Row(s)** box]; → ***gender*** → button by **Column(s)** [***gender*** appears in the **Column(s)** box]; → **Cells** [opens the **Crosstabs: Cell Display** sub-dialogue box shown in Plate A.17]
3. Make sure **Observed** in the **Counts** box is selected. Make sure **Column** under **Percentages** is selected. If either of these was not selected, simply → at the relevant point. → **Continue** [closes the **Crosstabs: Cell Display** sub-dialogue box and returns to the **Crosstabs** dialogue box shown in Plate A.16]
4. → **Statistics . . .** [opens the **Crosstabs: Statistics** sub-dialogue box shown in Plate A.18]. For example, suppose Cramér's *V* is needed (because of having two nominal variables). → **Chi-square** → **Phi and Cramér's *V*** → **Continue** [closes the **Crosstabs: Statistics** sub-dialogue box and returns to the **Crosstabs** dialogue box shown in Plate A.16]
5. → **OK**

The resulting output is in Table A.2. Cramér's *V* is just one of the available statistics.

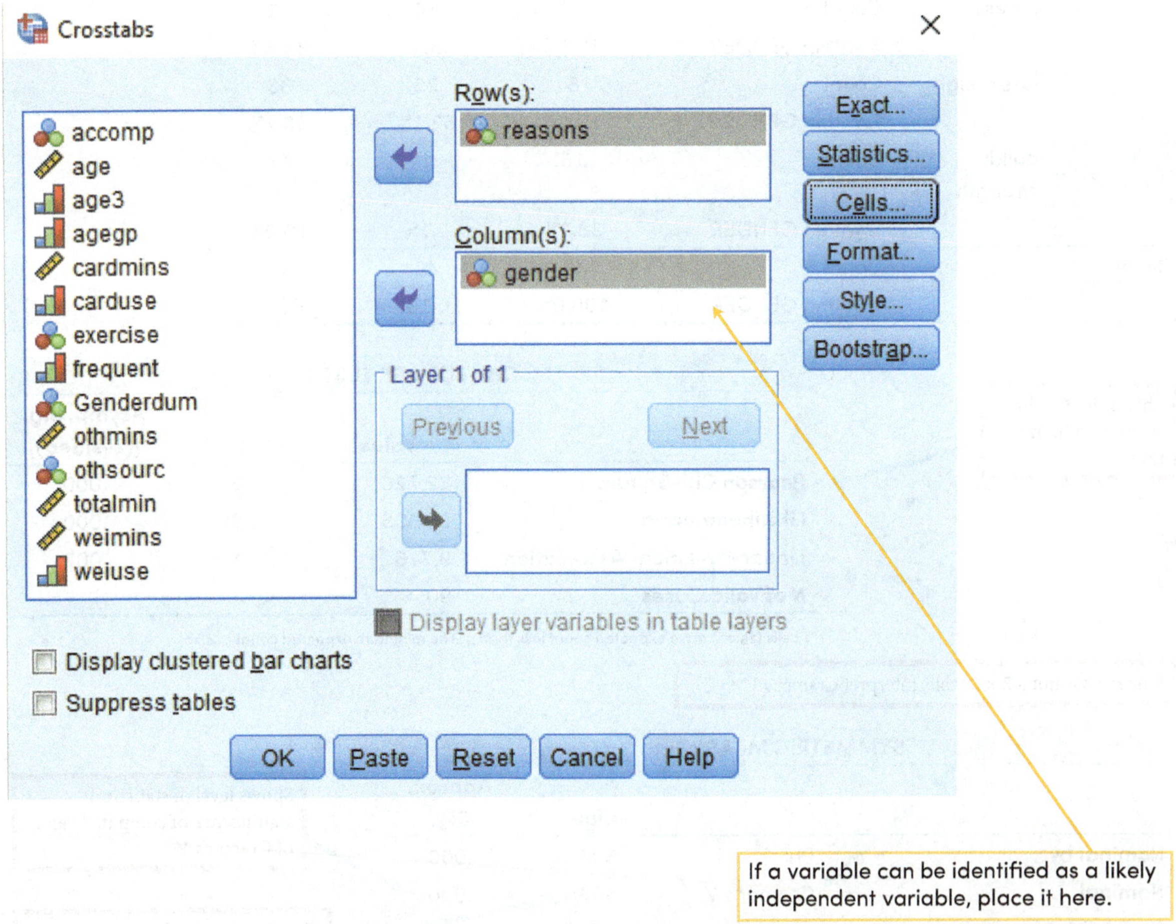

PLATE A.16 The **Crosstabs** Dialogue Box

TABLE A.2 Contingency table for reasons for visiting by gender (SPSS output)

CROSSTABS

CASE PROCESSING SUMMARY

	Cases					
	Valid		Missing		Total	
			Case Processing			
	N	**Per cent**	**Summary**	**Per cent**	***N***	**Per cent**
reasons for visiting * GENDER	90	100.0%	0	.0%	90	100.0%

REASONS FOR VISITING * GENDER CROSSTABULATION

			GENDER		
			male	**female**	**Total**
reasons for visiting	relaxation	Count	3	6	9
		% within GENDER	7.1%	12.5%	10.0%
	fitness	Count	15	16	31
		% within GENDER	35.7%	33.3%	34.4%
	lose weight	Count	8	25	33
		% within GENDER	19.0%	52.1%	36.7%
	build strength	Count	16	1	17
		% within GENDER	38.1%	2.1%	18.9%
Total		Count	42	48	90
		% within GENDER	100.0%	100.0%	100.0%

This is the χ^2 value referred to in the text

CHI-SQUARE TESTS

	Value	df	Asymp. Sig. [(2-sided)]
Pearson Chi-Square	22.726[a]	3	.000
Likelihood Ratio	25.805	3	.000
Linear-by-Linear Association	9.716	1	.002
***N* of Valid Cases**	90		

[a]2 cells (25.0%) have expected count less than 5. The minimum expected count is 4.20.

Since this is not a 2 × 2 table, interpret Cramér's *V*

SYMMETRIC MEASURES

		Value	Approx. Sig.
Nominal by Nominal	Phi	.503	.000
	Cramér's *V*	.503	.000
***N* of Valid Cases**		90	

Shows level of statistical significance of computed value of Cramér's *V*

Shows strength of relationship

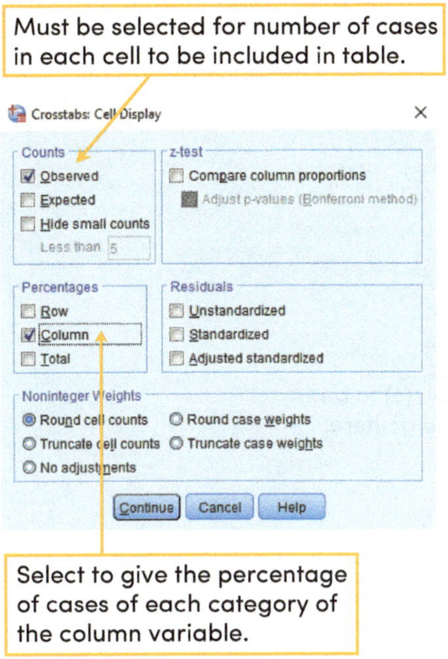

PLATE A.17 The **Crosstabs: Cell Display** Sub-Dialogue Box

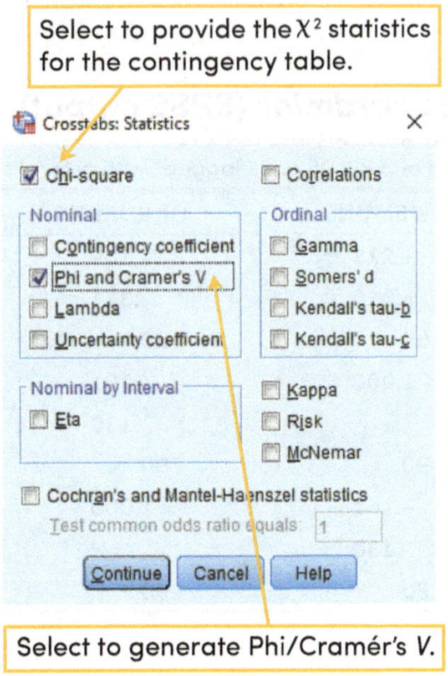

PLATE A.18 The **Crosstabs: Statistics** Sub-Dialogue Box

Generating scatter diagrams

The production of scatter diagrams, known as *scatterplots* in SPSS, is illustrated in the relationship between ***age*** and ***cardmins***. If one variable can be identified as likely to be the independent variable, it is by convention placed on the *X*-axis (the horizontal axis). Since ***age*** is bound to be the independent variable, follow these steps:

1. → **Graphs** → **Chart Builder** → **OK** → **Gallery** → **Scatter/Dot**
2. Drag the Simple Scatter diagram into the canvas
3. Drag *age* into the *X*-**Axis?** box at the bottom of the canvas
4. Drag *cardmins* into the *Y*-**Axis?** box at the left side of the canvas
4. → **OK**

Generating Pearson's *r*

To produce Pearson's *r*, in particular the correlation between ***age***, ***weimins***, and ***cardmins*** shown in Table 8.5, follow these steps:

1. → **Analyze** → **Correlate** → **Bivariate . . .** [opens the **Bivariate Correlations** dialogue box shown in Plate A.19]
2. → ***age*** → button → ***weimins*** → button → ***cardmins*** → button [***age***, ***weimins***, and ***cardmins*** should now be in the **Variables** box]; → **Pearson** (if not already selected) → **OK**

The resulting output is shown in Table A.3.

To produce Kendall's tau-b, follow the same procedures, but instead of selecting **Pearson**, → **Kendall's tau-b**. Spearman's rho is another option.

Comparing means

To produce a table like Table 8.6, follow these steps:

1. → **Analyze** → **Compare Means** → **Means . . .** [opens the **Means** dialogue box shown in Plate A.20]
2. → ***cardmins*** → button to the left of **Dependent List** → ***reasons*** → button to the left of **Independent List** → **Options** [opens the **Means: Options** sub-dialogue box]
3. → **Anova table and eta** under **Statistics for First Layer** → **Continue** [closes the **Means: Options** sub-dialogue box and returns to the **Means** dialogue box shown in Plate A.20]; → **OK**

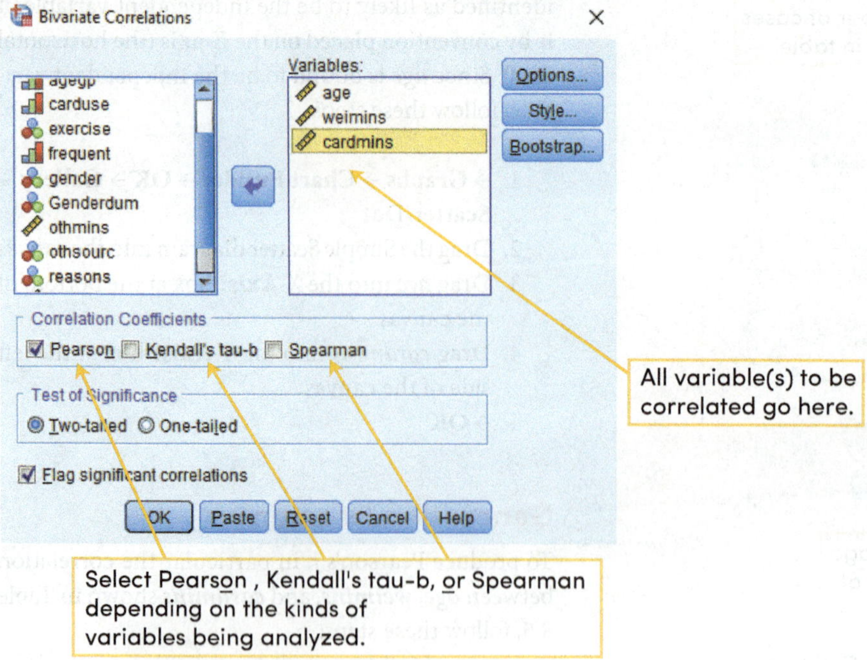

PLATE A.19 **Bivariate Correlations** Dialogue Box

TABLE A.3 Correlations output for *age*, *weimins*, and *cardmins* (SPSS output)

CORRELATIONS		AGE	WEIMINS	CARDMINS
AGE	Pearson Correlation	1.000	-.273 **	-.109
	Sig. (2-tailed)	.	.010	.311
	N	89	89	89
WEIMINS	Pearson Correlation	-.273 **	1.000	-.161
	Sig. (2-tailed)	.010	.	.130
	N	89	90	90
CARDMINS	Pearson Correlation	-.109	-.161	1.000
	Sig. (2-tailed)	.311	.130	.
	N	89	90	90

**Correlation is significant at the 0.01 level (2-tailed).

Correlations of p < 0.05 are "flagged" with asterisks

Shows strength of relationship as indicated by Pearson's *r*

Shows number of cases, less any cases for which there are missing data for either or both variables

Shows level of statistical significance of computed value of Pearson's *r*

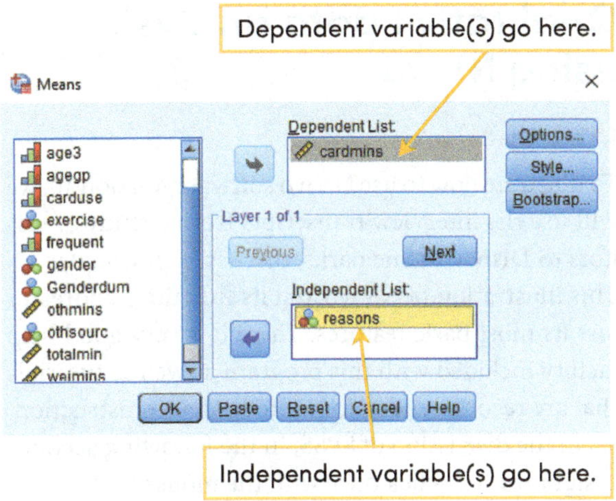

PLATE A.20 The **Means** Dialogue Box

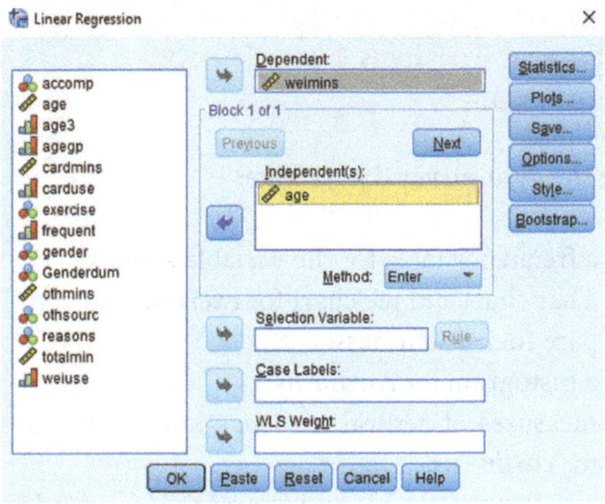

PLATE A.21 The **Linear Regression** Dialogue Box

Generating a contingency table with three variables

To create a table like Table 8.9, do as follows:

1. → **Analyze** → **Descriptive Statistics** → **Crosstabs . . .** [opens the **Crosstabs** dialogue box shown in Plate A.16]
2. → ***othsourc*** → button by **Row(s)** [*othsourc* appears in the **Row(s)** box]
3. → ***age3*** (assume this is the name given to a newly created variable with ***age*** recoded into the three categories listed in Table 8.9); → button by **Column(s)** [*age3* appears in the **Column(s)** box]; → ***gender*** → button in **Layer 1 of 1** box [***gender*** appears in the box under **Layer 1 of 1**]; → **Cells** [opens the **Crosstabs: Cell Display** sub-dialogue box shown in Plate A.17]
4. Make sure **Observed** in the **Counts** box has been selected. Make sure **Column** under **Percentages** has been selected. If either has not, simply click at the relevant point. → **Continue** [closes the **Crosstabs: Cell Display** sub-dialogue box and returns to the **Crosstabs** dialogue box shown in Plate A.16]
5. → **OK**

The resulting table looks somewhat different from Table 8.9 in that ***gender*** appears as a row rather than as a column variable.

Regression

To perform a bivariate regression in SPSS:

1. → **Analyze** → **Regression** → **Linear** [opens the **Linear Regression** dialogue box shown in Plate A.21]
2. → ***weimins*** → button to the left of the **Dependent** box
3. → ***age*** → button to the left of the **Independent(s)** box
4. → **OK**. The output appears in Table 8.10.

To perform multiple regression, simply add additional independent variables to the model. Once you are in the **Linear Regression** dialogue box (described above and shown in Plate A.21), just click on whatever variable you would like to add, then click the arrow button to put the variable in the **Independent(s)** box along with ***age***.

Questions for Review

Getting started in SPSS

- Outline the differences between variable names, variable labels, and value labels.
- In what circumstances is it appropriate to recode a variable?
- In what circumstances is it appropriate to create a new variable?

Exercises: Data analysis with SPSS (see Table 8.1 to identify the variables)

Using the gym survey data, create:

- a frequency table for the variable ***exercise***;
- a bar chart and pie chart for ***exercise*** and compare their usefulness;
- a histogram for ***cardmins***;
- measures of central tendency and dispersion for ***cardmins***;
- a contingency table and Cramér's *V* for ***gender*** and ***exercise***;
- a scatter diagram for ***age*** and ***cardmins***;
- Pearson's *r* for ***age*** and ***cardmins***;
- Kendall's tau-b for ***carduse*** and ***weiuse***; and
- a difference of means analysis for ***reasons*** and ***totalmin***.

Qualitative data analysis using NVivo

Introduction

To illustrate how to use NVivo software, version 10, we will use the interview transcripts from a study of visitors to Disney theme parks, discussed in Chapter 13. This illustration of NVivo and its functions addresses just its most basic features. There is a very good help facility included with this program as well as tutorials that are recommended for more in-depth instruction. As in the discussion of SPSS, in the following account → signifies "left-click once with the mouse."

Getting started with NVivo

On opening NVivo, you will be presented with a welcome screen (Plate A.22). This screen shows any existing NVivo projects and is the springboard for

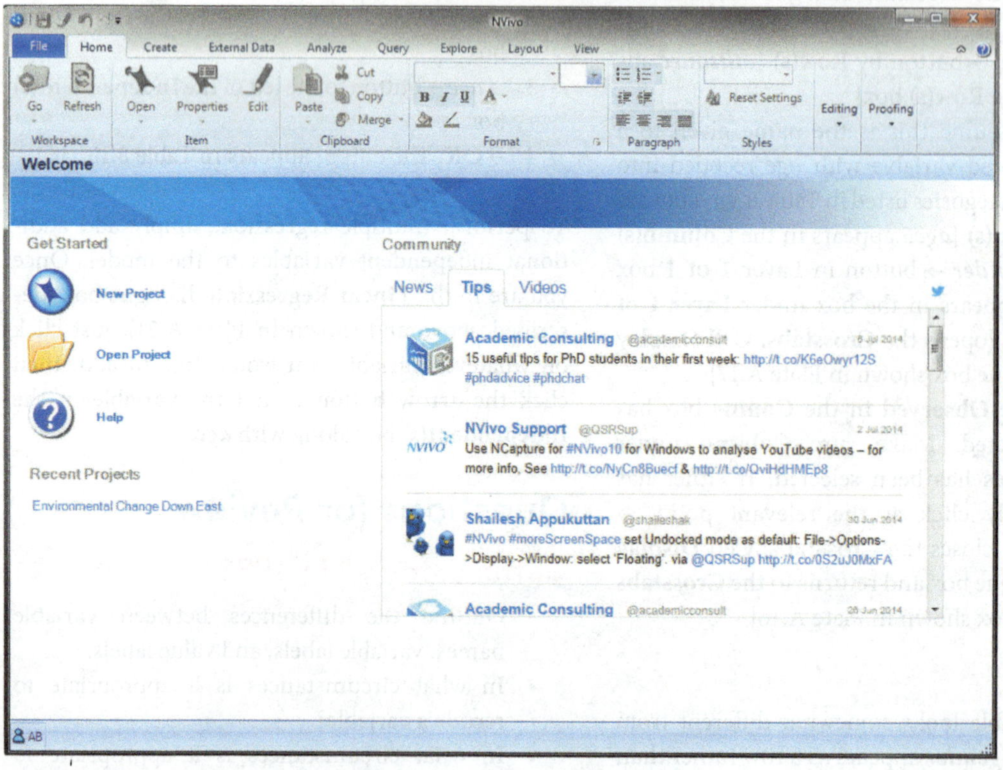

PLATE A.22 The Opening Screen

either opening one of the existing projects or starting a new one. If you are starting a new project, as in the example that follows, → **File** → **New Project**. The **New Project** dialogue box appears and you are asked to provide a **Title** for your project. For this exercise, the title "Disney Project" was chosen. You are also asked to give a **Description** of the project, although this is an optional feature. When you have done this, → **OK**.

You then need to import the documents you want to code. In this case, they will be interview transcripts from the project on visitors to Disney theme parks, referred to in Box 11.5 and Chapter 13. Other kinds of documents can be imported such as fieldwork notes. NVivo 10 can accept documents in both rich text (.rtf) and Word (.doc, .docx) formats. To import the documents (see Plate A.23), → **Internals** (below **Sources** at the top of the **Navigation view**) → **External Data** on the ribbon (see Plate A.24 for a description of how to find the ribbon and other key areas of the screen) → **Documents** button on the find bar [opens the **Import Internals** dialogue box] → **Browse** to locate the documents that are to be imported. → the documents to be imported (you can hold down the Ctrl key to select several documents; if you want to select all of them, hold down the Ctrl key and tap the A key); → **Open**. The documents

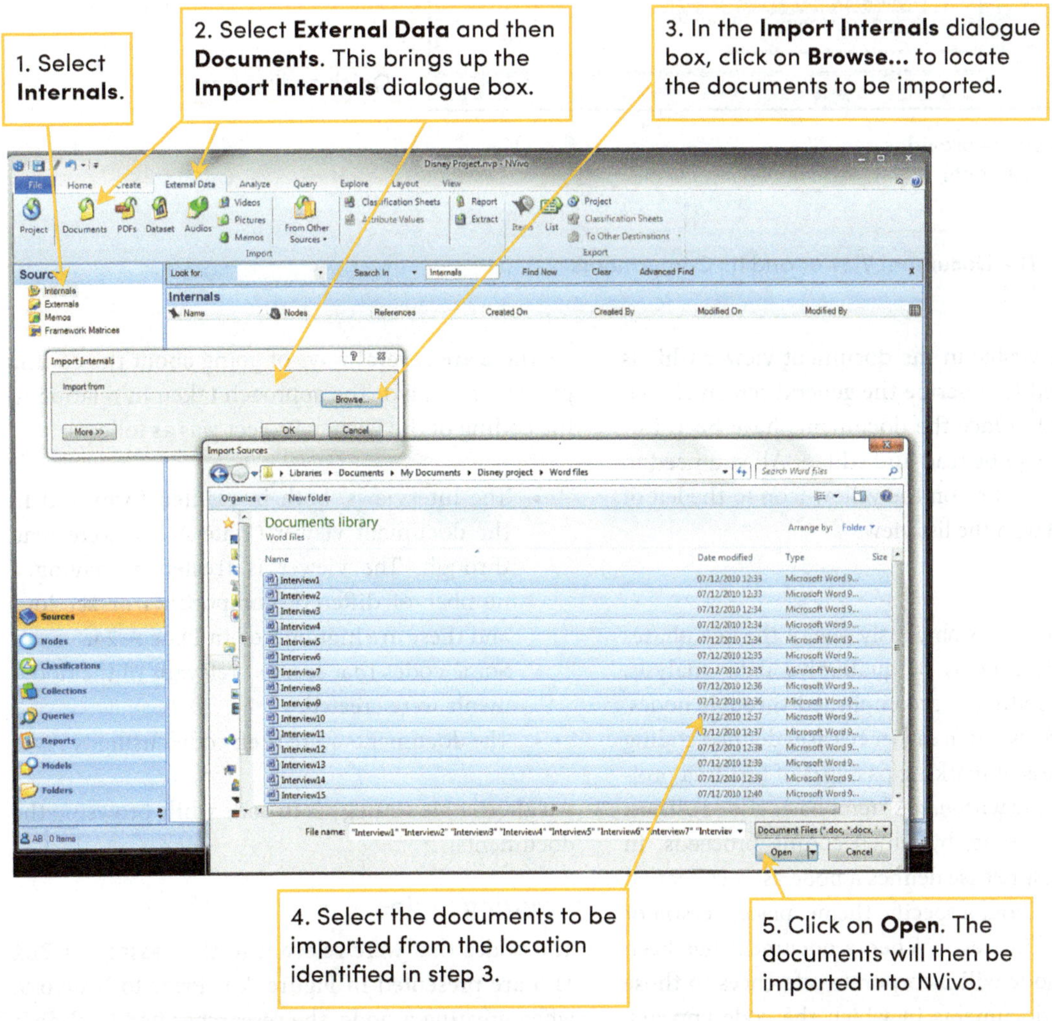

PLATE A.23 Stages in Importing Documents into NVivo

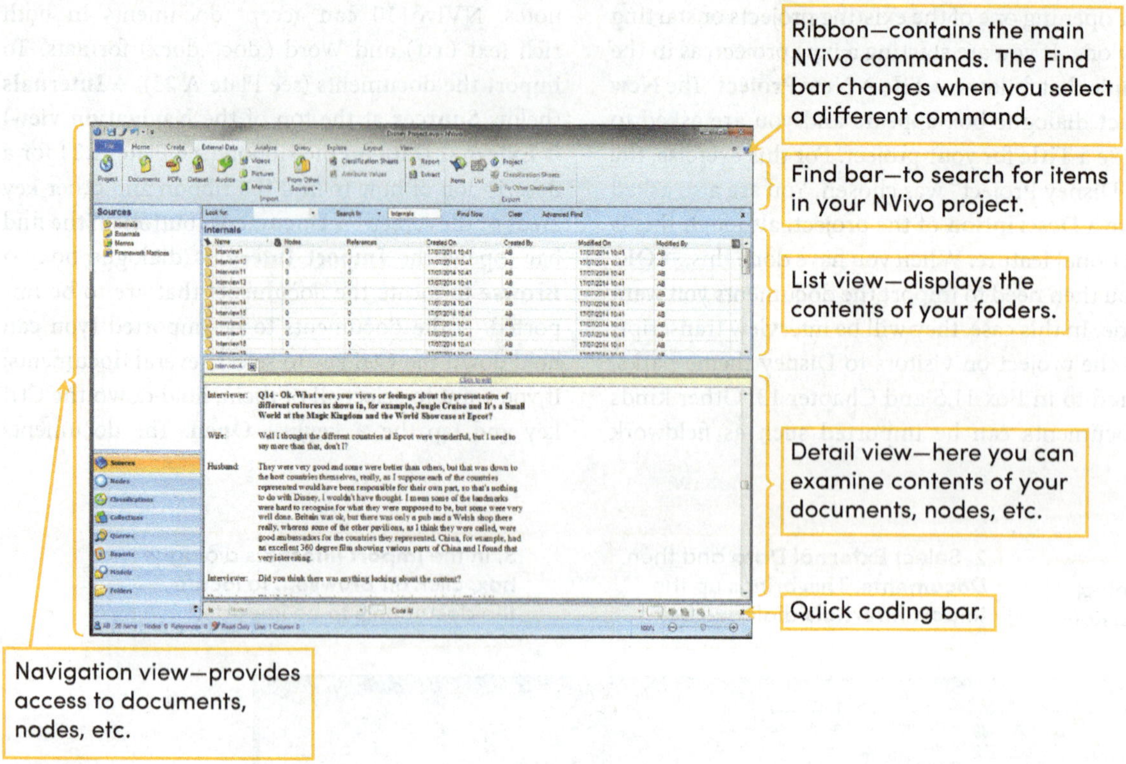

PLATE A.24 The Document Viewer and Its Components

will then be visible in the document viewer (this is the term used to describe the general screen shown in Plate A.24). Once the documents have been imported, they can be read and edited. All you need to do is to double-click on the yellow icon to the left of each interview in the list view.

Coding

Coding your data is obviously one of the key phases in the whole process of qualitative data analysis. For NVivo, coding is accomplished through nodes. NVivo's help system in earlier releases defined coding as "the process of marking passages of text in a project's documents with *nodes*" (emphasis added). Thus, nodes are the route by which coding proceeds. In turn, the latest release defines a node as "a collection of references about a specific theme, place, person or other area of interest." When a document has been coded, the node will incorporate references to those portions of documents in which the code appears. Once established, nodes can be changed or deleted.

There are several ways of going about the coding process in NVivo. The approach taken in relation to the coding of the Disney Project was as follows:

- The interviews, both in printed form and in the document viewer (Plate A.24), were read through. The viewer is treated as having a number of different components or sections and these are highlighted in Plate A.24.
- Some codes that seemed relevant to the documents were created.
- The documents were then coded using NVivo.

An alternative strategy is to code while browsing the documents.

Creating nodes

The nodes that were relevant to the passage in Box 11.5 are presented in Figure A.1. Prior to NVivo 9, when creating a node, the researcher had to choose either a free node or a tree node. The latter is a node that is organized in a hierarchy of connected nodes, whereas free nodes were not organized in this way. This distinction has been dropped in versions after NVivo 9, and the software assumes that a tree node is being created. Two points are crucial to note here for users of earlier releases of the software. First, the tendency now is not to refer to "tree nodes" but to treat them as hierarchically organized nodes. Second, free nodes (that is, nodes that are not hierarchically organized) can still be created; they are simply nodes without "children" (to use the latest NVivo terminology).

Notice that there are three groups of *hierarchically organized nodes* and two *non-hierarchically organized nodes* in Figure A.1. The nodes can be created in the following way.

Creating non-hierarchically organized nodes

This sequence of steps demonstrates how to create the non-hierarchically organized node ***Not critical of Disney***.

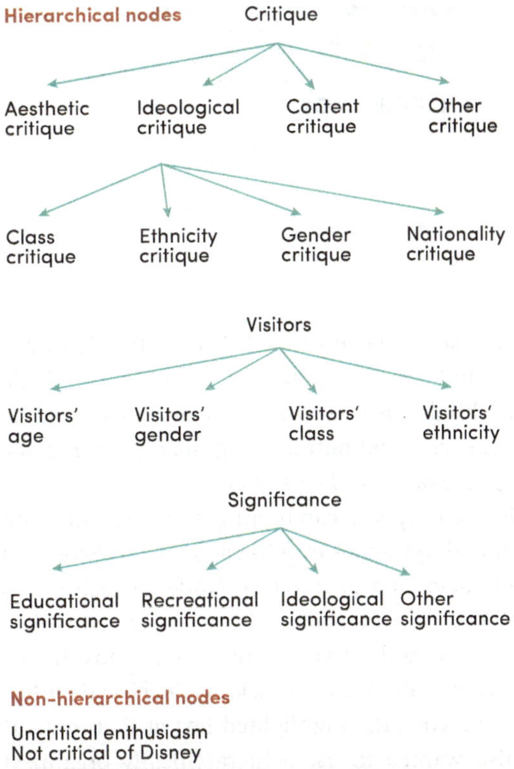

FIGURE A.1 Nodes used in the Disney Project

1. In the document viewer → **Create** in the ribbon
2. → **Node** in the find bar [opens the **New Node** dialogue box shown in Plate A.25]
3. Enter the node **Name** (***Not critical of Disney***) and a **Description** (the latter is optional)
4. → **OK**

Creating hierarchically organized nodes

To create a hierarchically organized node, the initial process is exactly the same as with a non-hierarchically organized node. The following example will show how to create the hierarchically organized node ***Class critique***, which is a child of the hierarchically organized node ***Ideological critique***, which is itself a child of the hierarchically organized node ***Critique*** (see Figure A.1). The following steps will generate this node.

1. In the document viewer → **Create** in the ribbon
2. →**Node** in the find bar [opens the **New Node** dialogue box shown in Plate A.26]
3. Enter the node **Name** (***Critique***) and a **Description** (the latter is optional)
4. →**OK**
5. →***Critique*** in the list of nodes in the list viewer
6. →**Node** in the find bar [opens the **New Node** dialogue box shown in Plate A.26]
7 Enter the node **Name** (***Ideological critique***) and a **Description** (the latter is optional). This node will form a child of the hierarchically organized node (make sure that in **Hierarchical name** it reads **Nodes\\Critique**, as this will mean it is a child of **Critique**). See Plate A.26.
8. → ***Ideological critique*** in the list of nodes in the list viewer
9. → **Node** in the find bar [opens the **New Node** dialogue box shown in Plate A.26]
10. Enter the node **Name** (***Class critique***) and a **Description** (the latter is optional). This node will form a child of the hierarchically organized node (make sure that in **Hierarchical name** it reads **Nodes\\Critique\Ideological critique**, as this will mean it is a child of **Ideological critique,** which is itself a child of **Critique**). See Plate A.26.
11. → **OK**

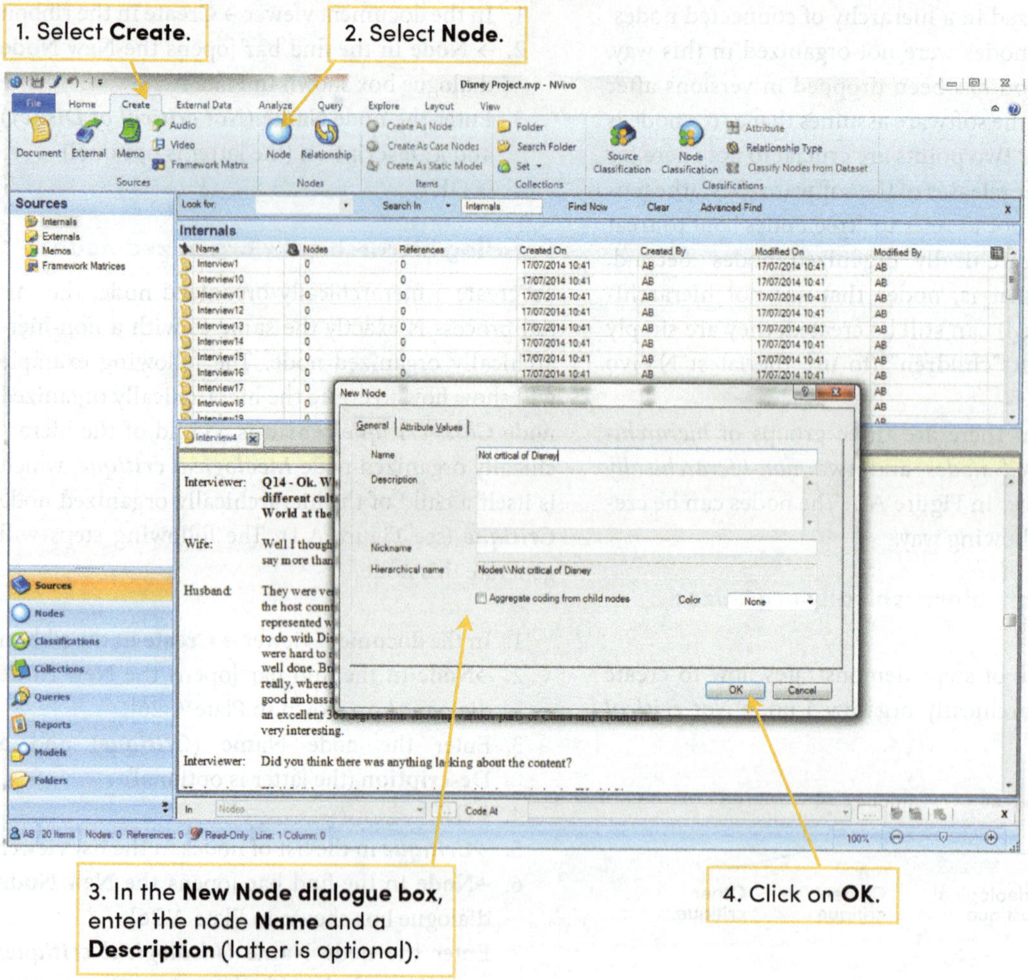

PLATE A.25 Stages in Creating a Non-Hierarchically Organized Node

Applying nodes in the coding process

Coding is carried out by applying nodes to segments of text. Once you have set up some nodes (remember that you can add and alter them at any time), you can look at a document in the viewer and highlight the area of the document that you want to code; then right-click on the mouse while holding the cursor over the highlighted text. If the node that you want to use has not been created yet, highlight the text you want to code, right-click on the highlighted text, and then → **Code Selection** → **Code Selection at New Node . . .** . This opens the **New Node** dialogue box. You can then create a new node in the manner outlined in the previous sections. If the code you want to use has been created, NVivo 10 allows you to drag and drop text into it (see Plate A.27). To do this, highlight the text to be coded and then, holding down the left-hand button, drag the text over to the appropriate node in the list view.

Alternatively, you can highlight the text you want to code and right-click over it. Then → **Code Selection** → **Code Selection at Existing Nodes**, which opens the **Select Project Items** dialogue box (see Plate A.28). → the node(s) you want to use. Thus, in the example in Plate A.28, the tick by ***Uncritical enthusiasm*** will code the highlighted text at that node. If you also wanted to use a hierarchically organized node, you would need to find the appropriate parent

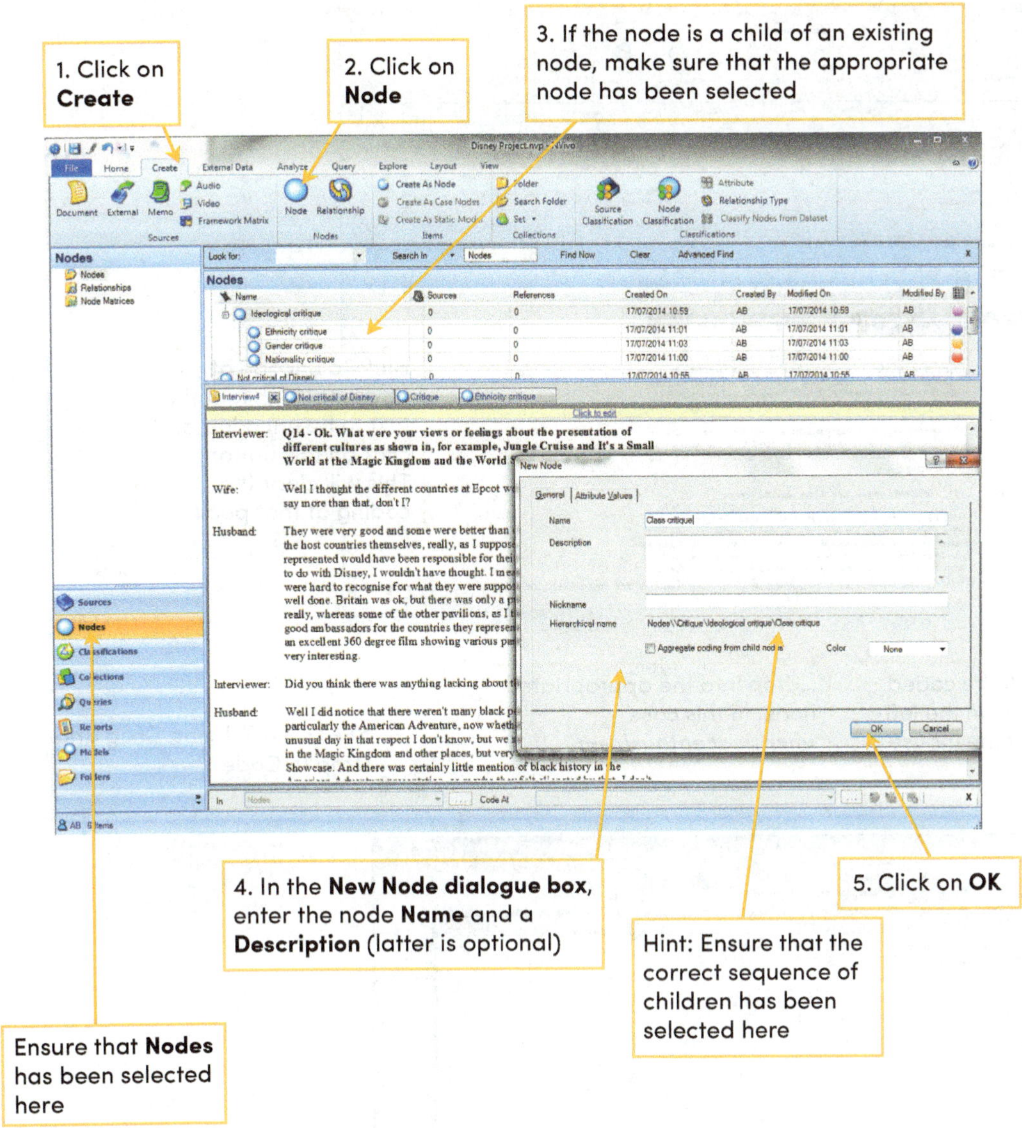

PLATE A.26 Stages in Creating a Hierarchically Organized Node

in the list of nodes within the list view and then → the plus sign to the left of it. To *uncode* at any point, simply highlight the passage to be uncoded, and → the button with a red cross in it in the quick coding bar (see Plate A.24). Alternatively, you can right-click on the highlighted text and → **Uncode**.

Coding stripes

It's very helpful to be able to see the areas of text that have been coded and the nodes applied to them. To this end NVivo has a useful aid called *coding stripes*. Selecting this feature allows you to see multi-coloured stripes that represent portions of coded text and the nodes that have been used. Overlapping codes do not represent any problem at all.

To activate this feature, → **View** in the ribbon and then → **Coding Stripes** in the find bar → **Nodes Recently Coding**. Plate A.29 shows these stripes. We can see that some segments have been coded at two or more nodes (for example, ***Visitors' ethnicity*** and ***Ethnicity critique***). All the nodes that have been used are clearly displayed.

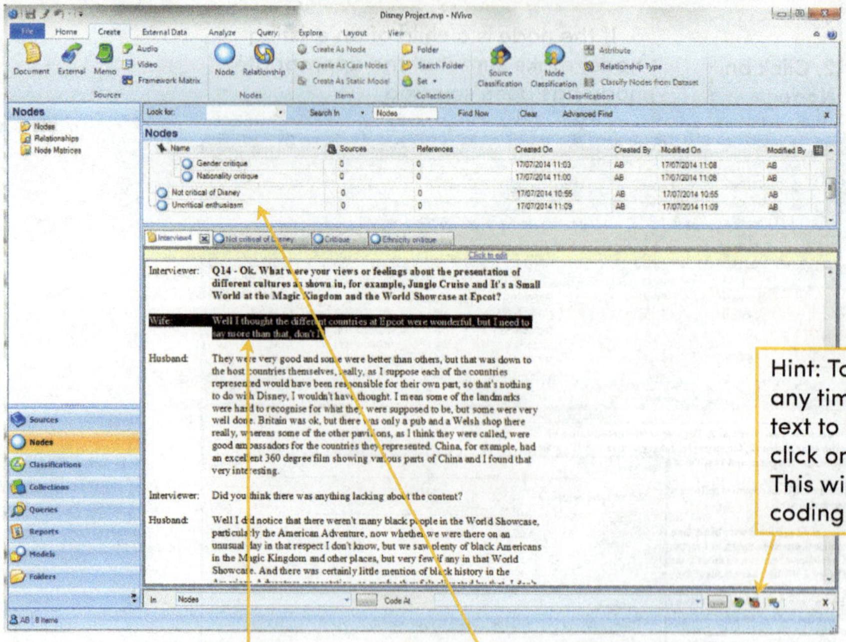

PLATE A.27 Using Drag and Drop to Code

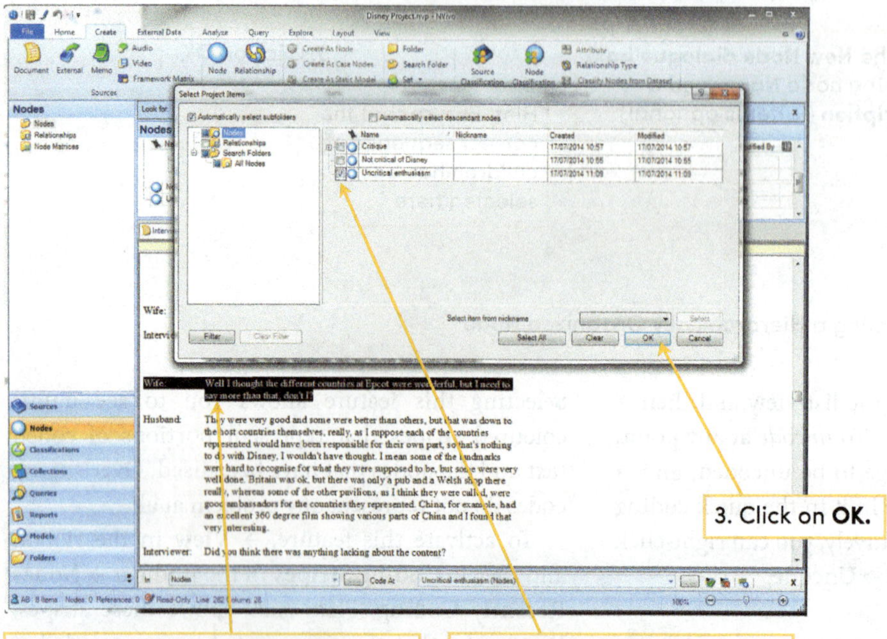

PLATE A.28 Coding in NVivo

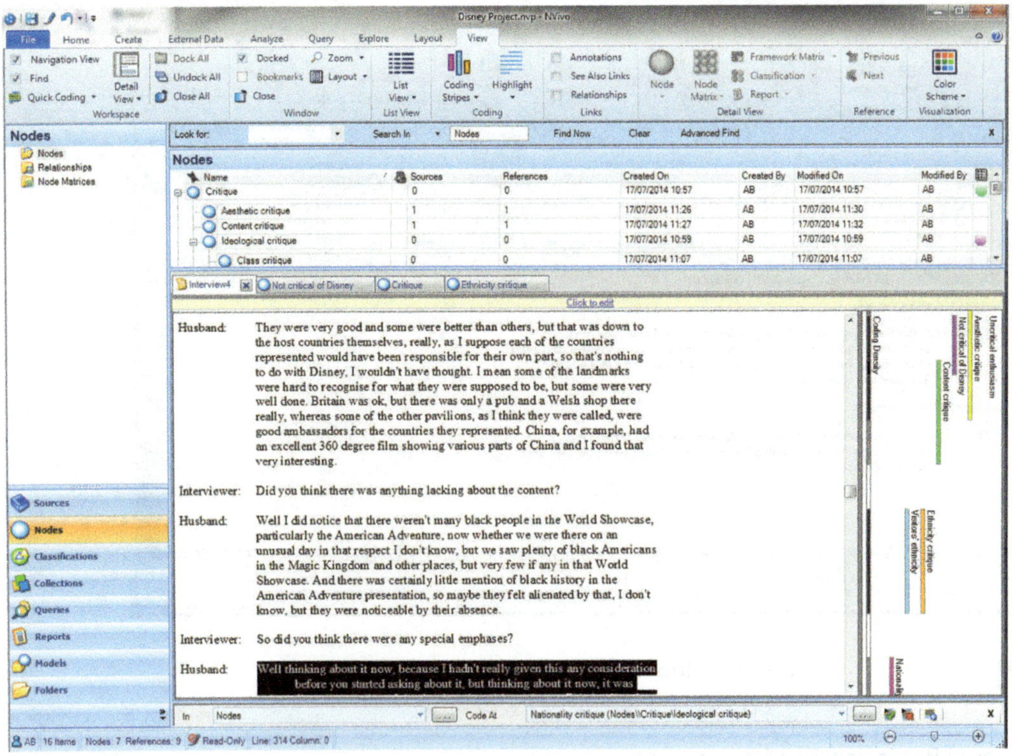

PLATE A.29 Coding Stripes

Searching text

Once you have coded your data, however preliminary that coding may be, at some point you will want to conduct a search of your data. For instance, suppose that you want to retrieve all occurrences of a particular node. NVivo allows you to trawl rapidly through all your documents and find all the text that was coded at a particular node. This is very easy to do in NVivo 10.

To search for occurrences of a single node

These steps describe how to conduct a search for sequences of text that have been coded in terms of the node ***Ethnicity critique***. The stages are outlined in Plate A.30.

1. In the document viewer → **Nodes** in the navigation view. This will bring up your list of nodes in the list view.
2. If you cannot find the parents of ***Ethnicity critique***, → on the little box with a plus sign (+) to the left of ***Critique*** [this brings up a list of all branches of the node ***Critique***]
3. → on the + to the left of ***Ideological critique*** [this brings up a list of all branches of the node ***Ideological critique***]
4. Double-click on ***Ethnicity critique***
5. All instances of coded text at the node ***Ethnicity critique*** will appear at the bottom of the screen, as in Plate A.30.

To search for the intersection of two nodes

This section is concerned with searching for sequences of text that have been coded at two nodes: ***Aesthetic critique*** and ***Not critical of Disney***. This type of search is known as a Boolean search. It will locate text coded in terms of the two nodes together (that is, where they intersect), *not* text coded in terms of each of the two nodes. The steps are as follows:

1. In the document viewer, → **Queries** in the navigation view
2. → **Query** tab in the ribbon

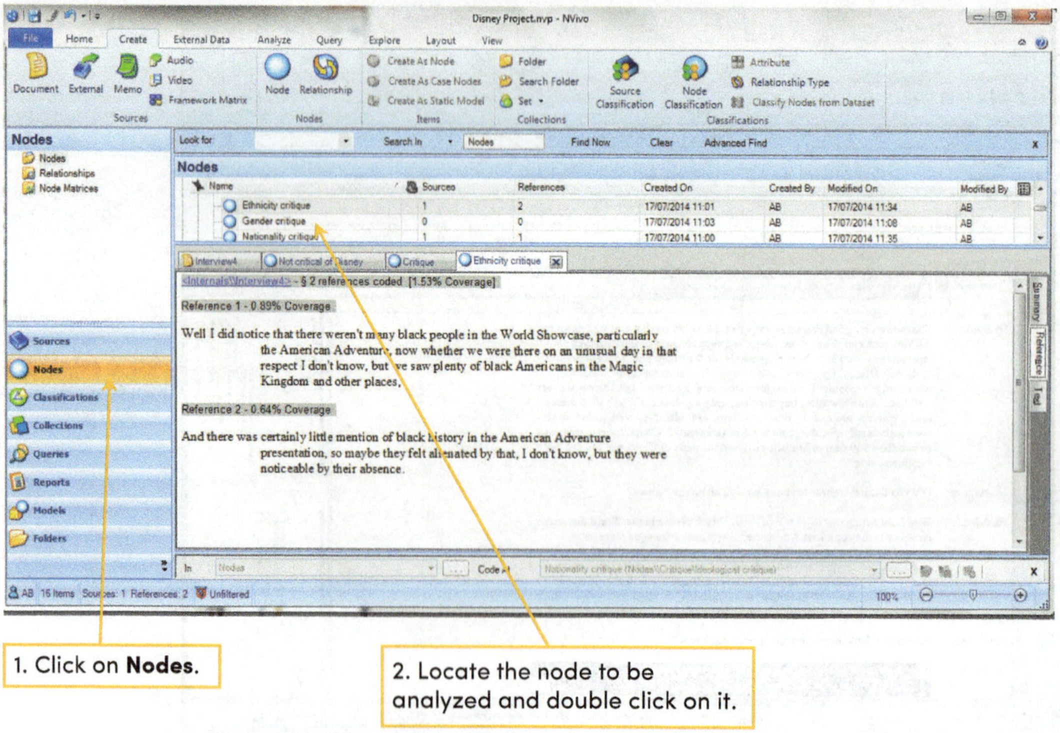

PLATE A.30 Stages in Retrieving Text from a Node

3. → **Coding . . .** from the menu of options [opens the **Coding Query** dialogue box shown in Plate A.31]
4. → **Coding Criteria** tab
5. → **Advanced** tab
6. In the **Define more criteria** panel, → **Coded at** from the drop-down menu
7. → **Select**. You then need to choose the two nodes to be analyzed from the **Select Project Items** dialogue box.
8. Once the nodes have been selected, → **OK** which returns you to the **Coding Query** dialogue box → **Add to List**
9. Make sure **AND** has been selected immediately below **Define more criteria**
10. → **Run**

To search for specific text

NVivo can also perform searches for specific words or phrases, often referred to as "strings" in computer jargon. For example, to search for **magic kingdom**, you would:

1. → **Home** on the ribbon
2. → **Find . . .** [opens the **Find Content** dialogue box shown in Plate A.32]
3. Type **magic kingdom** to the right of **Text**.
4. To the right of **Look in**, make sure **Text** has been selected.
5. → **Find Next**

Text searching can be useful for the identification of possible *in vivo* codes (introduced in Chapter 13). You would then need to go back to the documents to create nodes to allow you to code in terms of any *in vivo* codes.

Output

To find the results of coding at a particular node, → the **Nodes** button in the bottom left. This will bring up your node structure. Find the node that you are interested in and simply double-click on it. This will bring up all text coded at that node along with information about which interview(s) the text comes from.

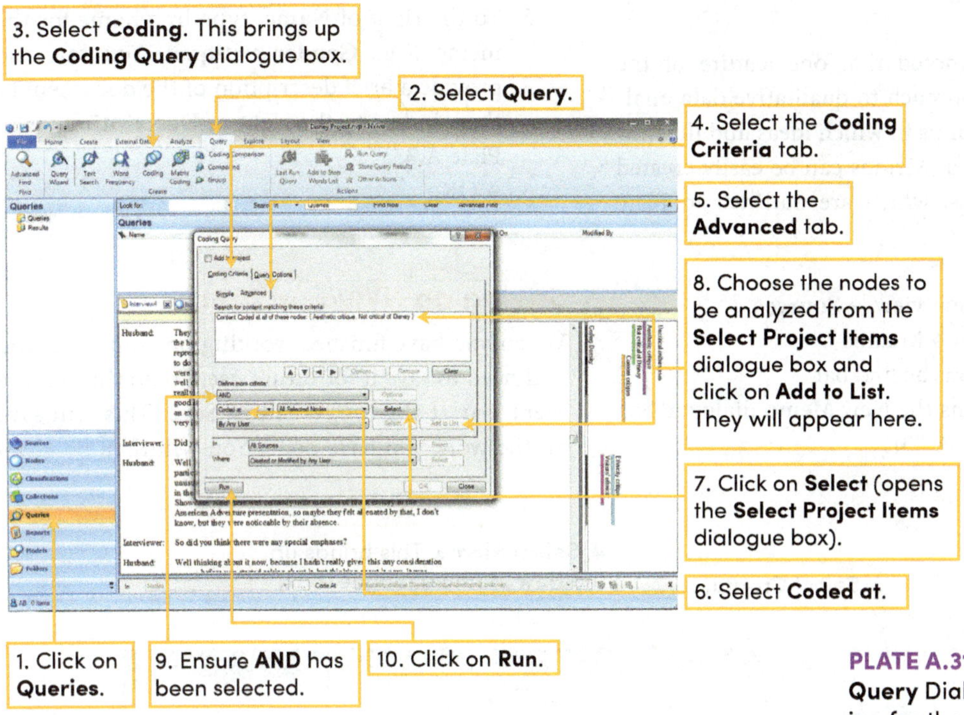

PLATE A.31 The **Coding Query** Dialogue Box (searching for the intersection of two nodes).

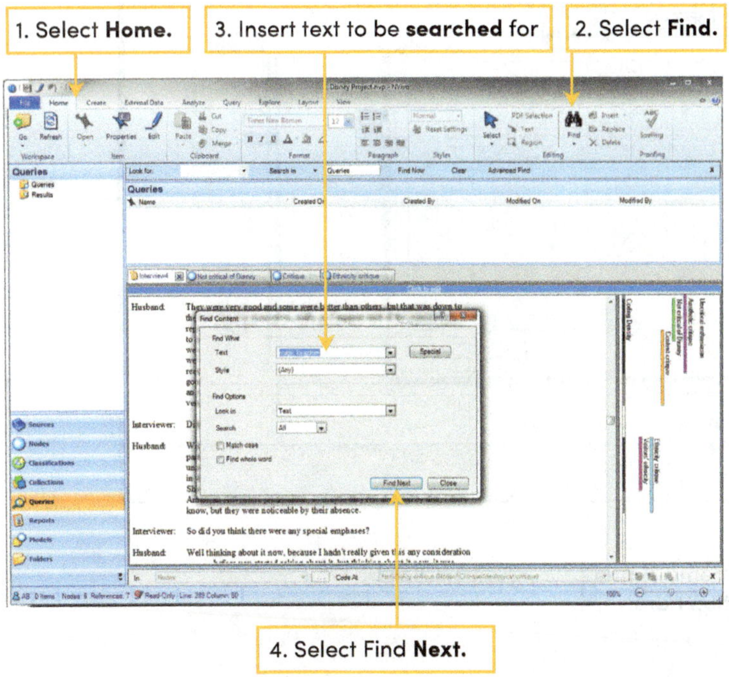

PLATE A.32 The **Find Content** Dialogue Box

Memos

In Chapter 13 we noted that one feature of the grounded theory approach to qualitative data analysis is the use of memos in which ideas and illustrations might be stored. Memos can be easily created in NVivo. The steps, which are outlined in Plate A.33, are as follows:

1. In the navigation view, → **Sources**
2. Under **Sources** → **Memos**
3. → **Create** tab on the find bar
4. → **Memo** [opens the **New Memo** dialogue box shown in Plate A.33]
5. To the right of **Name**, type in a name for the memo (e.g., **Gender critique**). You can also provide a brief description of the document in the window to the right of **Description**, as in Plate A.33.
6. → **OK**

Saving an NVivo project

When you have finished working on your data, you will need to save it for future use. To do this, on the menu bar at the top, → **File** → **Save**. This will save all the work you have done. You will then be given

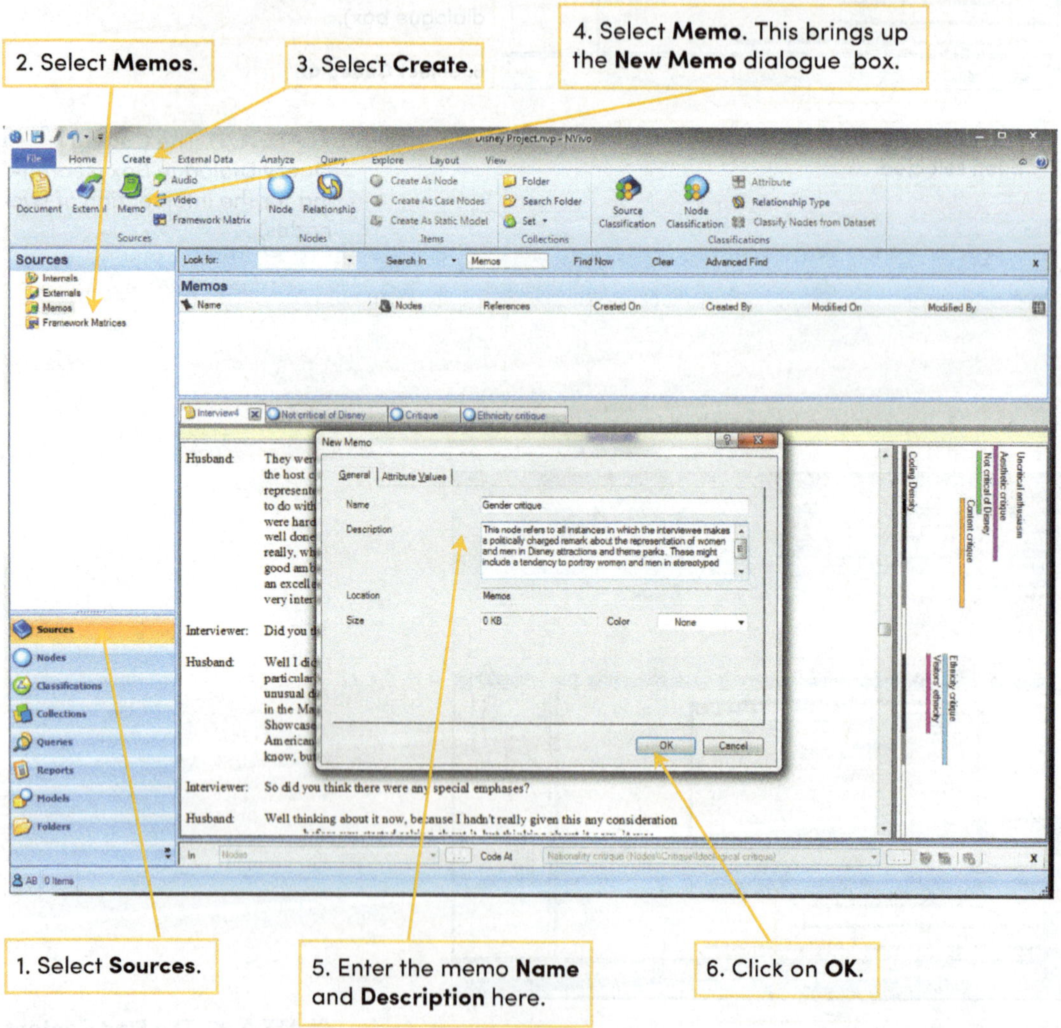

PLATE A.33 Stages in Creating a Memo

the opportunity to exit NVivo or to create or open a project without worrying about losing all your hard work. You might also consider backing up the project.

Opening an existing NVivo project

To retrieve a project you have created, at the Welcome screen, → **File** → **Open**. This opens the **Open Project** dialogue box. Search for and then select the project you want to work on. Then → **Open**. Alternatively, simply click on the project you want to retrieve on the opening screen.

You can also open a NUD*IST project, or one designed using an earlier release of NVivo, by selecting the appropriate project type from the drop-down menu to the right of **File name**.

Final thoughts

As with SPSS, space limitations allow us to introduce only the most basic features of the NVivo software. In so doing, we hope to have given readers unfamiliar with CAQDAS a sample of how the system works. No doubt some will decide that they prefer the tried-and-tested scissors-and-paste approach. On the other hand, the software warrants serious consideration because of its power and flexibility.

For useful online help with NVivo, see the Online QDA website and the CAQDAS Networking Project website at:

http://onlineqda.hud.ac.uk
www.surrey.ac.uk/computer-assisted-qualitative-data-analysis
(Websites accessed 4 September 2021)

Questions for review

Learning NVivo

- What is a node?
- What is the difference between a hierarchically organized node and a node that has not been hierarchically organized?
- What is *in vivo* coding?
- Do nodes have to be set up in advance?
- In NVivo, what is the difference between a document and a memo?
- How do you go about searching for a single node and the intersection of two nodes?
- Why might it be useful to display coding stripes?
- How do you search for specific text?

Glossary

Terms in *italic* type are defined elsewhere in the Glossary.

action research Same as participatory action research.

adjacency pair Two kinds of talk activity that are linked together, such as an invitation and a response.

analytic induction An approach to the analysis of qualitative data in which the collection of data continues and the hypothesis is modified until no cases inconsistent with it are found.

arithmetic mean What everyday language refers to as the "average": the sum of all the scores divided by the number of scores. Also known simply as the **mean**.

biographical method See *life history method*.

bivariate analysis Examination of the relationship between two variables, as in *contingency tables*; *correlation*.

CAQDAS An abbreviation of "computer-assisted (or computer-aided) qualitative data analysis software."

case study A *research design* that entails detailed and intensive analysis of either a single case or (for comparative purposes) a small number of cases.

causality A connection between *variables* in which one variable changes as a result of a change in another, as opposed to a mere *correlation* between them.

cells The areas in a table where the rows and columns intersect and data are inserted.

census A count of an entire *population*; by contrast, a *sample* counts only some units of a population.

chi-square test Chi-square (χ^2) is a test of *statistical significance* used to establish confidence that a finding displayed in a *contingency table* can be generalized from a *probability sample* to the *population* from which it is drawn.

closed, closed-ended question A question in an *interview schedule* or *questionnaire* that presents the respondent with a fixed set of possible answers to choose from; also called a **fixed-choice question**.

cluster sampling A procedure in which the researcher first samples sets of cases ("clusters") and then samples units within them, usually using a *probability sampling* method.

code, coding In *quantitative research*, codes are the tags used to assign the data on each *variable* to a category of the variable in question. Numbers are usually assigned to each category to allow easier computer processing. In *qualitative research*, coding is the process in which data are broken down into component parts, which are then assigned names.

coding frame or coding manual A list of the codes to be used in the analysis of a particular set of data. For answers to a structured interview schedule or questionnaire, the coding frame delineates the categories used for each *open question*. With *closed questions*, the coding frame is essentially incorporated into the fixed answers from which respondents must choose; hence the term "pre-coded question."

concept A general or abstract idea; a category that serves to organize observations and ideas about some aspect of the social world.

concurrent validity A type of validity that is tested by relating a measure to an existing criterion or a different indicator of the concept to see if one predicts the other; one of the main forms of *measurement validity*.

connotation A term used in *semiotics* to refer to the meanings of a *sign* associated with the social context within which it operates: a sign's connotations are supplementary to its *denotation* and less immediately apparent.

constant An attribute on which cases do not differ; compare with *variable*.

constructionism, constructionist An *ontological* position (the antithesis of *objectivism*) according to which social phenomena and their meanings are continually being created by social actors; also known as **constructivism**.

construct validity (1) Same as *measurement validity*; (2) a type of measurement validity that is established by determining whether the concepts being measured relate empirically in a manner that would be predicted by relevant theories.

content analysis An approach to the analysis of documents and texts that seeks to quantify content in terms of predetermined categories in a systematic and replicable manner. The term is sometimes used in connection with qualitative research as well; see *qualitative content analysis*.

contingency table A table made up of rows and columns that shows the *relationship* between two *variables*. Usually, at least one of the variables is a *nominal variable* or *ordinal variable*. Each *cell* in the table shows the number or (more often) the percentage of cases for that specific combination of the two variables.

control group See *experiment*.

convenience sample A sample that is selected because of its availability to the researcher; a form of *non-probability sample*.

conversation analysis The fine-grained analysis of talk (recorded in naturally occurring situations and then transcribed) to uncover the underlying structures in interaction that make social order possible. Conversation analysis is grounded in *ethnomethodology*.

correlation An approach to the analysis of relationships between *interval/ratio variables* and/or *ordinal variables* that seeks to assess the strength and direction of the relationship between the variables concerned. *Pearson's r* and *Spearman's rho* are both correlational measures. The corresponding term **measure of association** is often used with *nominal variables*.

covert research A term frequently used in connection with *ethnographic* research in which the researcher does not reveal their true identity and/or intentions. Such research may violate the ethical principle of *informed consent*.

Cramér's V A statistical measure used to assess the strength of the relationship between two *nominal variables*.

critical discourse analysis A type of *content analysis* that brings issues such as power hierarchies, structural inequalities, and historical political struggles to bear on the analyses of texts.

critical realism A *realist* epistemology according to which the study of the social world should be concerned with the identification of social structures in order to change them and thereby counteract inequalities and injustices. Unlike positivism, which is an *empiricist* epistemology, critical realism maintains that the structures may not be directly perceivable.

cross-sectional design A *research design* in which data are collected at a single point in time.

deduction, deductive An approach to inquiry that begins with the statement of a theory from which hypotheses may be derived and tested; compare with *inductive*.

denotation A term used in *semiotics* to refer to the principal and most manifest meaning of a *sign*; compare with *connotation*.

dependent variable A *variable* that is caused (or assumed to be caused) by an *independent variable*.

diary A written memoir. Three types of diary are discussed in this book: personal diaries that are spontaneously produced and can be analyzed as *personal documents*; diaries written at the behest of a researcher; and diaries written by researchers to log their activities and reflections.

dichotomous variable A variable with just two categories.

dimension An aspect of a *concept*.

discourse analysis An approach to the analysis of talk and other forms of communication that emphasizes the way language can create versions of reality.

dispersion The degree of variation in a set of scores. Commonly used measures of dispersion include the *range* and the *standard deviation*.

ecological fallacy The error of assuming that inferences about individuals can be made from data on the characteristics of groups.

empiricism An approach to the study of reality according to which only knowledge gained by observation through the senses is acceptable.

epistemology, epistemological A branch of philosophy concerned with what constitutes knowledge and how knowledge is to be acquired; see *positivism*, *realism*, and *interpretivism*.

eta A test of the strength of the *relationship* between two *variables*. The *independent variable* is usually a *nominal variable* while the *dependent variable* must be an *interval variable* or *ratio variable*.

ethnography, ethnographer, ethnographic Like *participant observation*, a research method in which the researcher is immersed in a social setting for an extended period of time, observing behaviour, asking questions, and analyzing what is said in conversations both between participants and with the fieldworker. As a term, "ethnography" is more inclusive than "participant observation," which emphasizes the observational component. Written accounts of ethnographic research are often referred to as **ethnographies**.

ethnomethodology A sociological perspective concerned with the way social order is established and maintained through talk and interaction; the intellectual foundation of *conversation analysis*.

evaluation research Research that concentrates on the evaluation of real-life interventions, such as policy changes.

experiment A *research design* that rules out alternative explanations of findings deriving from it (in other words, that possesses *internal validity*) because it involves (a) both an experimental group, which is exposed to a treatment, and a control group, which is not, and (b) *random assignment* to the two groups.

experimental group See *experiment*.

external validity A type of validity that is achieved if the results of a study can be generalized beyond the specific research context in which they were generated.

face validity A type of validity that is achieved if, on inspection, an *indicator* appears to measure the *concept* in question.

facilitator See *moderator*.

factor analysis A statistical technique used for large numbers of *indicators* to establish whether there is a tendency for groups of them to be interrelated. It is often used with *multiple-indicator measures* to see if they cluster into one or more groups (factors).

field experiment A study in which the researcher directly intervenes in and/or manipulates a natural setting to observe what happens as a consequence.

field notes A detailed *ethnographic* account of events, conversations, and behaviour, and the researcher's initial reflections on them.

focus group A form of group interview in which there are several participants (in addition to the *moderator/facilitator*), there is an emphasis in the questioning on a particular topic or related topics, and interaction within the group and the joint construction of meaning is observed.

frequency table A table that displays the number and/or percentage of units (for example, people) in different categories of a variable.

gatekeeper A non-researcher who controls researchers' access to a research setting.

generalization, generalizability To **generalize** a research finding is to apply it to people or groups who were not in the study.

grounded theory An approach to the analysis of qualitative data in which the goal is to use the data to generate theory; the data collection and analysis proceed in an iterative (recursive) fashion.

hermeneutics An approach to the interpretation of texts that emphasizes the need to understand them from the perspective of their authors.

hypothesis An informed speculation, which is set up to be tested, about the possible relationship between two or more variables.

IBM SPSS Statistics software A computer program that facilitates the management and analysis of quantitative data.

idiographic An approach to understanding that seeks specific, unique knowledge about a person or group, typically concerning interpretations or meanings held by the persons studied.

independent variable A *variable* that has (or is assumed to have) a *causal* impact on a *dependent variable*.

index See *scale*.

indicator Something employed to measure a *concept*; it may refer to any measure, but sometimes it means an indirect measure used when no direct measure is available.

induction, inductive, inductivist An approach to inquiry that begins with the collection of data, which are then used to develop theories, hypotheses, and concepts; compare with *deductive*.

informed consent The principle that prospective participants in social research should be given as much information as they need to make a sound decision about whether to participate in a study; a key principle in social research ethics.

institutional ethnography A type of *ethnography* that explores how institutional discourses (typically workplace texts) relate to people's everyday experiences with institutions, and how institutional relationships intersect with larger systems of social control and power in a society.

interaction See *statistical interaction*.

inter-coder reliability The degree to which two or more individuals agree on the *coding* of an item; a frequent concern in the *coding* of answers to *open questions* in research based on *questionnaires* or *structured interviews*.

internal reliability or internal consistency The degree to which the items that make up a *scale* or *index* are consistent or correlated.

internal validity A type of validity that is achieved if there is sufficient evidence that a *causal* relationship exists between two or more variables.

interpretivism, interpretivist An *epistemological* position that requires the social scientist to grasp the subjective meanings that people attach to their actions and behaviours.

intersubjectivity A condition in which two or more observers of the same phenomenon are in agreement as to what they have observed. *Empiricists* assume that intersubjectivity is possible insofar as knowledge is based on data acquired through the senses.

interval variable A *variable* for which the intervals between the categories are identical and quantifiable.

intervening variable A *variable* that is affected by another variable and in turn has a *causal* impact on a third. Taking an intervening variable into account often facilitates the understanding of the relationship between two variables. An intervening variable is the "Y" in "X→Y→Z."

interview guide A brief list of memory prompts regarding areas to be covered in *unstructured* and *semi-structured interviewing*.

interview schedule A collection of questions designed to be asked by an interviewer; always used in a *structured interview*.

intra-coder reliability The degree to which an individual coder is consistent over time in the *coding* of an item; likely to be an issue in the coding of answers to *open questions* in research based on *questionnaires* or *structured interviews*.

Kendall's tau-b A test of the strength of the *relationship* between two *ordinal variables*.

key informant Someone who offers the researcher, usually an *ethnographer*, particularly perceptive information about the social setting, important events, and individuals.

life history interview An *unstructured interview* that is similar to an *oral history interview*, but designed to gather information on the entire biography of a respondent.

life history method A method (often referred to as the *biographical method*) that emphasizes the inner experience of individuals and its connections with larger societal events throughout the life course. It usually entails *life history interviews* and the use of *personal documents* as data.

Likert item, Likert scale A widely used format in which respondents are typically asked their degree of agreement with a series of attitude statements that together form a *multiple-indicator* measure. The scale is designed to measure the intensity of respondents' feelings about an issue.

longitudinal research A *research design* in which data are collected on at least two separate occasions.

mean See *arithmetic mean*.

measure of central tendency A measure that summarizes the magnitude of a set of scores; examples include the *arithmetic mean*, *median*, and *mode*.

measure of dispersion A measure (such as the *range* or *standard deviation*) that summarizes the amount of variation in a set of scores.

measurement validity The degree to which a measure of a concept actually measures what it is supposed to measure; see also *face validity* and *concurrent validity*.

median The mid-point in a set of scores that is arranged in order.

member validation See *respondent validation*.

missing data Data that are not available, for example, when a respondent in social survey research does not answer a question. These are referred to as "missing values" in *IBM SPSS Statistics software*.

mode The score that occurs most frequently in a set of scores.

moderated relationship A *relationship* between two *variables* is said to be "moderated" when the effect of the *independent variable* varies at different levels of a second independent variable (also known as a *statistical interaction*).

moderator The person who guides the questioning of a *focus group*, also called a *facilitator*.

multiple-indicator measure A measure that uses more than one *indicator*.

multi-strategy research Research that combines *quantitative* and *qualitative* approaches.

multivariate analysis The examination of relationships among three or more *variables*.

narrative analysis An approach focused on the search for and analysis of stories that people use to understand their lives and the world around them.

naturalism, naturalistic A style of research designed to minimize disturbance to the natural or everyday social world.

negative relationship A *relationship* between two *variables* in which one decreases as the other increases.

nominal variable A *variable* comprised of categories that cannot be ranked; also known as a **categorical variable.**

nomothetic An approach to explanation that utilizes general laws and principles, which are said to apply to some population beyond the people studied.

non-probability sample A sample selected using a non-random sampling method. Essentially, this means that some units in the population are more likely than others to be selected.

non-response Occurs if someone in a sample refuses to participate in the study, cannot be contacted, or for some other reason does not supply the required data.

null hypothesis A *hypothesis* of no relationship between two variables; the hypothesis that the researcher hopes to disprove.

NVivo See *QSR NVivo*.

objectivism, objectivist An *ontological* position according to which social phenomena have an existence independent of social actors or their perceptions; compare with *constructionism*.

observation schedule A device used in *structured observation* that specifies the categories of behaviour that are to be observed and gives instructions on how behaviour should be allocated to those categories.

official statistics Data compiled by (or on behalf of) state agencies in the course of conducting their business.

ontology, ontological A branch of philosophy concerned with the nature of reality: for example, whether social entities can and should be considered objective entities with a reality external to specific social actors, or as social constructions built up through the perceptions and actions of these actors. See *objectivism* and *constructionism*.

open, open-ended question In an *interview schedule* or *questionnaire*, a format that does not present the respondent with a set of possible answers to choose from; compare with *closed question*.

operationalization The way in which a *concept* is measured empirically; for example, one could operationalize the concept "level of education" with a survey item that asks people to indicate their highest level of education by choosing from categories such as "some elementary," "high school," "university graduate," etc.; see also *operational definition*.

operational definition A definition that spells out the operations that are to be performed to measure a *concept*.

oral history interview A largely *unstructured interview* in which respondents are asked to recall and reflect on events they have experienced.

ordinal variable A variable whose categories can be rank-ordered, but the distances between the categories are not equal or known across the range.

outlier An extreme value (either very high or very low) in a distribution of scores. If a *variable* has an outlier, it will distort both the *arithmetic mean* and the *range*.

paradigm A cluster of beliefs and assumptions, often unstated, that influence views on what should be studied, how research should be done, and how results should be interpreted.

participant observation Research in which fieldworkers are immersed in a social setting for an extended period of time, observing behaviour, asking questions, and analyzing what is said in conversations both between the people under study and with the researcher. It usually includes interviewing *key informants* and studying documents. In this book, "participant observation" refers to the observational aspect of *ethnography*.

participatory action research Research in which local people affected by a particular social problem collaborate as equals with professional researchers and government officials to generate knowledge pertinent to the problem and to take action to ameliorate it.

Pearson's *r* A measure of the strength and direction of the *relationship* between two *interval/ratio variables*.

personal documents Documents not written for an official purpose that provide first-person accounts of the writer's life and events within it. Examples include *diaries*, letters, and autobiographies.

population All cases or people covered by a theory or explanation; the universe of units from which a *sample* is selected.

positive relationship A *relationship* between two *variables* whereby both move in the same direction, either increasing or decreasing simultaneously.

positivism, positivist An *epistemological* position that advocates using the methods of the natural sciences in the study of social reality.

postal questionnaire A *questionnaire* that is sent out and returned by regular (non-electronic) mail.

postmodernism A position that questions the notion of a pre-existing external reality that dispassionate social scientists can simply uncover, and argues that no single account of social reality can be authoritative. Postmodernists prefer qualitative methods.

pre-coded question Another name for a *closed question*; used because a numerical *code* has been pre-assigned to each of the predetermined answers (hence there is no need for a *coding frame*).

probability sample A sample, selected at random, in which each unit in the population has a known chance of being selected.

purposive sampling A form of non-probability sampling in which cases are selected on the basis of their ability to provide information relevant to the topic of the study.

QSR NVivo A *CAQDAS* package that derives from but goes beyond NUD*IST (Non-numerical Unstructured Data Indexing Searching and Theorizing).

qualitative content analysis An approach to constructing the meaning of documents and text that allows categories to emerge out of data analysis and recognizes the significance of the context in which items appear.

qualitative research Inquiry that uses mainly words, images, and other non-numerical symbols as data and involves little or no quantification. As a research strategy it tends to be *inductivist*, *constructivist*, and *interpretivist*, but qualitative researchers do not always subscribe to all three features; compare with *quantitative research*.

quantitative research Inquiry using quantitative data-gathering techniques and statistical analysis. As a research strategy it tends to be *deductivist* and *objectivist* and to incorporate a natural science model of the research process (in particular, one influenced by *positivism*), but quantitative researchers do not always subscribe to all three features; compare with *qualitative research*.

quasi-experiment A *research design* that resembles an *experiment* but does not meet all the requirements and therefore does not exhibit complete *internal validity*.

questionnaire A collection of written questions or response items that the respondent completes without the aid of an interviewer.

quota sample A type of *non-probability sample* that matches the proportions of people in different categories in the *population*.

random assignment The random allocation of research participants to either the experimental or the control group(s) in an *experiment*.

random sampling The form of sampling in which all units of a *population* have the same chance of being selected.

range The difference between the maximum and the minimum score in a set of scores associated with an *interval* or *ratio variable*.

ratio variable An *interval variable* with a true zero point.

reactivity, reactive effect The effect on research participants of knowing that they are being studied, which may result in atypical or inauthentic behaviour.

realism, realist An *epistemological* position according to which reality is independent of the senses but is to some degree accessible to the researcher's tools and theoretical speculations. See also *critical realism*.

reflexive, reflexivity Terms used to refer to social researchers' awareness of the implications that their methods, values, biases, decisions, and mere presence in the situations they investigate have for the knowledge they generate.

relationship An association between two *variables* whereby the variation in one variable coincides with variation in another variable.

reliability The degree to which a measure of a *concept* is stable or consistent.

replication, replicability The degree to which a study can be repeated using the same methods.

representative sample A sample that is similar to the *population* in all important respects.

research design The term used in this book to refer to a framework for the collection and analysis of data. The choice of research design reflects the goals that the researcher hopes to achieve (for example, *generalization*, establishing *causality*, or producing empathetic understanding).

respondent validation A process whereby researchers provide the people on whom they conducted research with an account of their findings and request their feedback on it; sometimes called **member validation**.

response set A term for the tendency for some people, when responding to *multiple-indicator* measures, to respond to every item in the same way, suggesting that their answers are motivated by something other than their actual feelings. Three of the most common response-set effects are "acquiescence," "social desirability," and "laziness or boredom."

sample The segment or subset of the *population* selected for research. The selection may be based on either *probability* or *non-probability sampling*.

sampling error Differences between the characteristics of a *random sample* and the *population* from which it is selected.

sampling frame A listing of units in the *population* from which a *sample* is to be selected.

scale A term that can be used interchangeably with **index** when referring to a *multiple-indicator measure* of a *variable* in which the scores a research participant provides for each component *indicator* are combined to produce a composite score for that person. A *scale* can also refer to a single-item measure of a *variable*.

secondary analysis The analysis of data (*quantitative* or *qualitative*) by researchers other than those responsible for their collection, often for purposes that the latter may not have envisaged.

semiotics An approach to the analysis of documents and other materials that emphasizes the importance of *signs* and symbols, seeking out their deeper meaning and exploring their intended effects.

semi-structured interview A type of interview in which the interviewer has a series of questions in the general form of an *interview guide* and is able to vary the sequence of questions. The questions are typically more general than those specified by a *structured interview* schedule, and the interviewer usually has some latitude to ask further questions in response to replies that appear significant.

sensitizing concept A *concept* that is not fixed in advance (as with an *operational definition*) but rather is treated as a guide that suggests what may be relevant or important in an investigation.

sign A term used in *semiotics*. Each sign has two parts: the signifier (manifestation of a sign) and the signified (the deeper meaning to which the signifier refers).

simple random sample A *sample* in which each unit selected from the *population*, and each combination of units, has an equal probability of being included.

snowball sample A *non-probability sample* in which the researcher makes initial contact with a small group of people connected to the research topic and then uses them to establish contact with others.

social desirability bias Distortion of data caused by respondents' efforts to construct accounts that conform to a socially acceptable model of behaviour.

Spearman's rho [ρ] A measure of the strength and direction of the *relationship* between two *ordinal variables*.

spurious relationship A *relationship* in which two *variables* are *correlated* but not *causally* related. It is produced by the impact of a common third variable on each of the two variables. When the third variable is controlled, the relationship disappears.

standard deviation A measure of how widely the scores that make up a set are dispersed around the *arithmetic mean*.

standard error of the mean An estimate of the degree to which a *sample mean* is likely to differ from the *population mean*.

statistical interaction Occurs if the effect of one independent variable varies at different levels of a second independent variable.

statistical significance (test of) A test (such as the *chi-square* test) that allows analysts to estimate the probability that the results of a study of a randomly selected *sample* are generalizable to the *population* from which the sample was drawn. Note that statistical significance has nothing to do with substantive significance or importance. Using a test of statistical significance to generalize from a sample to a population is known as **statistical inference.**

stratified random sample A *sample* in which units are *randomly sampled* from a *population* that has been previously divided into sub-groups (strata).

structured interview One in which all respondents are asked exactly the same questions in the same order with the aid of a formal *interview schedule*.

structured observation Often called **systematic observation**, this is a research method in which the researchers follow explicitly formulated rules regarding not only what they should look for, but when and where, and how they should record what they have observed.

survey research A *research design* in which data are collected from respondents, mainly by *questionnaire* or *structured interview*; typically, the data are then examined to detect *relationships* among *variables*.

symbolic interactionism A theoretical perspective in which social interaction is understood to be based on the meanings that actors attach to their actions and the contexts in which they occur.

systematic sample A *probability sampling* method in which units are selected from a *sampling frame* at fixed intervals (for example, every fifth unit).

text A written document or, in more recent years, anything (from paintings to buildings to theme parks) that may be "read" and analyzed for its symbolic value.

theoretical sampling A term used mainly in the context of *grounded theory* to refer to sampling carried out in such a way that emerging theoretical considerations guide the collection of data and/or the selection of cases (usually research participants). This process is supposed to continue until a point of *theoretical saturation* is reached.

theoretical saturation In *grounded theory*, the point where emerging *concepts* have been fully explored and no new insights are being generated. See also *theoretical sampling*.

thick description A term coined by Geertz (1973; see Chapter 9) to refer to detailed accounts of a social setting or people's experiences that can form the basis for general statements about a culture and its significance in peoples' lives.

transcription, transcript The verbatim written record of a taped *interview* or *focus group* session.

triangulation The use of more than one method or source of data so that findings may be cross-checked.

trustworthiness A general criterion (composed of four more specific criteria) used by some writers in assessing the quality of *qualitative research*.

turn-taking In *conversation analysis*, the idea that taking turns to speak is a rule that helps to maintain order in everyday conversation.

univariate analysis The analysis of one *variable* at a time.

unobtrusive measures, unobtrusive methods, unobtrusive observations Measures that do not cause *reactivity* because they do not make research participants aware that they are being studied.

unstructured interview An interview in which the interviewer is free to explore any topic, although an *interview guide* is often used. The questioning is usually informal and the content, phrasing, and sequencing of questions may vary from one interview to the next.

validity A research criterion concerned with the integrity of the conclusions generated by a particular study. There are several types of validity: see, in particular, *measurement validity*, *internal validity*, and *external validity*. When used on its own, *validity* is usually taken to refer to *measurement validity*.

variable An attribute or characteristic that may vary over time or from case to case. See also *dependent variable* and *independent variable*; compare with *constant*.

vignette technique A method in which people are presented with "vignettes" (hypothetical scenarios) and then asked how they would respond if they faced the circumstances depicted in the scenarios.

References

Preface

World Bank. (2018). Nearly half the world lives on less than $5.50 a day. https://www.worldbank.org/en/news/press-release/2018/10/17/nearly-half-the-world-lives-on-less-than-550-a-day

Chapter 1

Beagan, B. (2001). Micro inequities and everyday inequalities: "Race," gender, sexuality and class in medical school. *Canadian Journal of Sociology, 26*, 583–610.

Bell, E. (2007). Separatism and quasi-separatism in Alberta. *Prairie Forum, 32*, 335–55.

Bikos, L. (2017, 17 May). It's not just the RCMP: Police culture is toxic. *Globe and Mail*. https://www.theglobeandmail.com/opinion/its-not-just-the-rcmp-police-culture-is-toxic/article35014971/

Blumer, H. (1962). Society as symbolic interaction. In A. Rose (Ed.), *Human Behavior and Social Processes*. London: Routledge & Kegan Paul.

Charpentier, M., & Quéniart, A. (2017). Aging experiences of older immigrant women in Québec (Canada): From deskilling to liberation. *Journal of Women & Aging, 29*, 437–47.

Collins, R. (1994). *Four sociological traditions* (Rev. ed.). New York: Oxford University Press.

Creswell, J. (2013). *Qualitative inquiry and research design: Choosing among five approaches* (3rd ed.). Los Angeles: SAGE.

Debbink, G., & Ornelas, A. (1997). Cows for *Campesinos*. In S.E. Smith & D.G. Willms (Eds.), *Nurtured by knowledge: Learning to do participatory action research*. New York and Ottawa: Apex Press and International Development Research Centre.

Demaiter, E.I., & Adams, T.L. (2009). "I really didn't have any problems with the male–female thing until . . . ": Successful women's experiences in IT organizations. *Canadian Journal of Sociology, 43*, 31–53.

Dinovitzer, R., Hagan, J., & Parker, P. (2003). Choice and circumstance: Social capital and planful competence in the attainments of immigrant youth. *Canadian Journal of Sociology, 28*, 463–88.

Duncan, L. (2010). Money and membership: Effects of neighbourhood poverty, income inequality and individual income on voluntary association membership in Canada. *Canadian Journal of Sociology, 35*, 573–93.

Durkheim, E. (1938). *The rules of sociological method*. S. Solavay & J. Mueller (Trans.). New York: Free Press.

Durkheim, E. (1952). *Suicide: A study in sociology*. J. Spaulding & G. Simpson (Trans.). London: Routledge & Kegan Paul. (Original work published 1897)

Ellis, B.H., Lincoln, A.K., Abdi, S.M., Nimmons, E.A., Issa, O., & Decker, S.H. (2020). "We all have stories": Black Muslim immigrants' experience with the police. *Race and Justice, 10* (3), 341–62. https://doi.org/10.1177/2153368718754638

Foster, J. (1995). Informal social control and community crime prevention. *British Journal of Criminology, 35*, 563–83.

Frisby, W., Crawford, S., & Dorer, T. (1997). Reflections on participatory action research: The case of low-income women accessing local physical activity services. *Journal of Sport Management, 11*, 8–28.

Giddens, A. (1984). *The constitution of society*. Cambridge, UK: Polity.

Goffman, E. (1963). *Stigma: Notes on the management of spoiled identity*. Harmondsworth, UK: Penguin.

Hallgrimsdottir, H., Phillips, R., & Benoit, C. (2006). Fallen women and rescued girls: Social stigma and media narratives of the sex industry in Victoria, B.C., from 1980 to 2005. *Canadian Review of Sociology and Anthropology, 43*, 265–80.

Hay, D. (2014). An investigation into the swiftness and intensity of recent secularization in Canada: Was Berger right? *Sociology of Religion, 75*, 136–62.

Hier, S. (2002). Raves, risks and the ecstasy panic: A case study in the subversive nature of moral regulation. *Canadian Journal of Sociology, 27*, 33–57.

Hochschild, A. (1983). *The managed heart*. Berkeley and Los Angeles: University of California Press.

Hughes, G. (2000). Understanding the politics of criminological research. In V. Jupp, P. Davies, & P. Francis (Eds.), *Doing criminological research*. London: SAGE.

Kandler, C., Bell, E., & Riemann, R. (2016). The structure and sources of Right-Wing Authoritarianism and Social Dominance Orientation. *European Journal of Personality, 30*, 406–20.

Lantz, P., & Booth, K. (1998). The social construction of the breast cancer epidemic. *Social Sci. and Medicine, 46*, 907–18.

Layder, D. (1993). *New strategies in social research*. Cambridge, UK: Polity.

Lewin, K. (1946). Action research and minority problems. *Journal of Social Issues, 2*, 34–46.

Lofland, J., & Lofland, L. (1995). *Analyzing social settings: A guide to qualitative observation and analysis* (3rd ed.). Belmont, CA: Wadsworth.

Lyon, K., & Frohard-Dourlent, H. (2015). Let's talk about the institution: Same-sex common-law partners negotiating marriage equality and relationship legitimacy. *Canadian Review of Sociology, 52*, 402–28.

Maiolino, E. (2015). Political pugilists: Recuperative gender strategies in Canadian electoral politics. *Canadian Review of Sociology, 52*, 115–33.

Marx, K. (1998). *The German ideology including theses on Feuerbach and Introduction to the critique of political economy*. Amherst, NY: Prometheus Books. (Original work published 1845)

McKeganey, N., & Barnard, M. (1996). *Sex work on the streets*. Buckingham, UK: Open University Press.

Merton, R. (1938). Social structure and anomie. *American Sociological Review, 3*, 672–82.

Merton, R. (1967). *On theoretical sociology*. New York: Free Press.

Mies, M. (1993). Towards a methodology for feminist research. In M. Hammersley (Ed.), *Social research: Philosophy, politics and practice*. London: SAGE.

Milgram, S. (1963). A behavioural study of obedience. *Journal of Abnormal and Social Psychology, 67*, 371–78.

Morgan, R. (2000). The politics of criminological research. In R. King & E. Wincup (Eds.), *Doing research on crime and justice*. Oxford: Oxford University Press.

Nagra, B., & Maurutto, P. (2016). Crossing borders and managing racialized identities: Experiences of security and surveillance among young Canadian Muslims. *Canadian Journal of Sociology, 41*, 165–94.

Neves, B.B., Waycott, J., & Malta, S. (2018). Old and afraid of new communication technologies? Reconceptualizing and contesting the "age-based digital divide." *Journal of Sociology, 54*, 236–48.

Nietzsche, F. (1968). *The will to power*. W. Kaufmann & R. J. Hollingdale (Trans.). New York: Vintage Books. (Original work published 1883)

Neuman, W.L. (2003). *Social research methods*. Toronto: Pearson Canada.

Orwell, G. (1933). *Down and out in Paris and London*. Toronto: Harcourt.

Peltier, C. (2018). An application of two-eyed seeing: Indigenous research methods with participatory action research. *International Journal of Qualitative Methods, 17*, 1–12.

Pew Research Center. (2019). 5 facts about religion in Canada. https://www.pewresearch.org/fact-tank/2019/07/01/5-facts-about-religion-in-canada/

Potter, J. (1996). *Representing reality: Discourse, rhetoric and social construction*. London: SAGE.

Pratt, A., & Valverde, M. (2002). From deserving victims to "masters of confusion": Redefining refugees in the 1900s. *Canadian Journal of Sociology, 27*, 135–62.

Ring, K. (1967). Experimental social psychology: Some sober questions about some frivolous values. *Journal of Experimental Social Psychology, 3*, 113–23.

Schutz, A. (1962). *Collected papers I: The problem of social reality*. The Hague: Martinus Nijhof.

Smith, D. (2004). Women's perspective as a radical critique of sociology. In S. Harding (Ed.), *The feminist standpoint theory reader: Intellectual and political controversies*. New York: Routledge.

Smith, D. (2005). *Institutional ethnography: A sociology for people*. Walnut Creek, CA: AltaMira Press.

Smith, S.E. (1997). Deepening participatory-action research. In S.E. Smith & D.G. Willms (Eds.), *Nurtured by knowledge: Learning to do participatory-action research*. New York and Ottawa: Apex Press and International Development Research Centre.

Statistics Canada. (2013). *Cycle 27: Giving, volunteering and participating*. General Social Survey.

Statistics Canada. (2017). *Marital status and opposite- and same-sex status by sex for persons aged 15 and over living in private households for both sexes, total, presence and age of children, 2016 counts, Canada, provinces and territories, 2016 Census—100% data*. Families, Households and Marital Status Highlight Tables. http://www12.statcan.gc.ca/census-recensement/2016/dp-pd/hlt-fst/fam/Table.cfm?Lang=E&T=11&Geo=00&SP=1&view=1&sex=1&presence=1

Strauss, A., Schatzman, L., Ehrich, D., Bucher, R., & Sabshin, M. (1973). The hospital and its negotiated order. In G. Salaman & K. Thompson (Eds.), *People and organizations*. London: Longman.

Sugiman, P. (2004). Memories of the internment: Narrating Japanese-Canadian women's life stories. *Canadian Journal of Sociology, 29*, 359–88.

Tastsoglou, E., & Miedema, B. (2003). Immigrant women and community development in the Canadian Maritimes: Outsiders within? *Canadian Journal of Sociology, 28*, 203–34.

Teevan, J., & Dryburgh, H. (2000). First person accounts and sociological explanations of delinquency. *Canadian Review of Sociology and Anthropology, 37*, 77–93.

Turnbull, P. (1973). *The mountain people*. London: Cape.

Weber, M. (1947). *The theory of social and economic organization*. A.M. Henderson & T. Parsons (trans.). New York: Free Press.

Wilson, B. (2002). The Canadian rave scene and five theses on youth resistance. *Canadian Journal of Sociology, 27*, 373–412.

Wolcott, H. (2008). *Ethnography: A way of seeing* (2nd ed.). Toronto: AltaMira Press.

Chapter 2

Alford, J.R., Funk, C.L., & Hibbing, J.R. (2005). Are political orientations genetically transmitted? *American Political Science Review, 99*, 153–67.

Baer, D., Curtis, J., & Grabb, E. (2001). Has voluntary association membership declined? Cross-national analyses for fifteen countries. *Canadian Review of Sociology, 38*, 249–74.

Bahr, H., Caplow, T., & Chadwick, B. (1983). Middletown III: Problems of replication, longitudinal measurement, and triangulation. *Annual Review of Sociology, 9*, 243–64.

Beardsworth, A., & Keil, T. (1992). The vegetarian option: Varieties, conversions, motives and careers. *Sociological Review, 40*, 253–93.

Bell, E., Aitken Schermer, J., & Vernon, P.A. (2009). The origins of political attitudes and behaviours: An analysis using twins. *Canadian Journal of Political Science, 42*, 855–79.

Bell, E., Jansen, H., & Young, L. (2007). Sustaining a dynasty in Alberta: The 2004 provincial election. *Canadian Political Science Review, 1*, 27–49.

Bell, E., & Kandler, C. (2017). The genetic and the sociological: Exploring the possibility of consilience. *Sociology, 51*, 880–96.

Bell, E., Kandler, C., & Riemann, R. (2018). Genetic and environmental influences on socio-political attitudes: addressing some gaps in the new paradigm. *Politics and the Life Sciences, 37*, 236–49.

Berthoud, R. (2000). Introduction: The dynamics of social change. In R. Berthoud & J. Gershuny (Eds.), *Seven years in the lives of British families: Evidence on the dynamics of social change from the British Household Panel Survey*. Bristol: Policy Press.

Blaxter, M. (1990). *Health and lifestyles*. London: Routledge.

Bowen, R. (2015). Squaring up: Experiences of transition from off-street sex work to square work and duality—concurrent involvement in both—in Vancouver, BC. *Canadian Review of Sociology, 52*, 429–49.

Brannigan, A. (2004). *The rise and fall of social psychology: The use and misuse of the experimental method.* Hawthorne, NY: Aldine de Gruyter.

Canadian Government News. (2020, June 8). Will the pandemic change the world of work? U of T researcher Scott Schieman aims to find out.

Carroll, L. (2009). *Alice's adventures in Wonderland.* Toronto: Penguin Group. (Original work published 1865)

Charlton, T., Coles, D., Panting, C., & Hannan, A. (1999). Behaviour of nursery class children before and after the availability of broadcast television: A naturalistic study of two cohorts in a remote community. *Journal of Social Behavior and Personality, 14*, 315–24.

Charlton, T., Gunter, B., & Coles, D. (1998). Broadcast television as a cause of aggression? Recent findings from a naturalistic study. *Emotional and Behavioural Difficulties, 3*, 5–13.

Chowdhury, F.D. (2018). Immigration through marriage: A case study of Bangladeshis in Toronto. *Journal of Muslim Minority Affairs, 38*, 280–300.

Clairborn, W. (1969). Expectancy effects in the classroom: A failure to replicate. *Journal of Educational Psychology, 60*, 377–83.

Cook, T., & Campbell, D. (1979). *Quasi-experimentation: Design and analysis for field settings.* Boston: Houghton Mifflin.

Demers, A. (1996). Effect of support groups on family caregivers to the frail elderly. *Canadian Journal on Aging, 15*, 129–44.

Dinovitzer, R., Hagan, J., & Parker, P. (2003). Choice and circumstance: Social capital and planful competence in the attainments of immigrant youth. *Canadian Journal of Sociology, 28*, 463–88.

Dobash, R.E., & Dobash, R.P. (2000). Evaluating criminal justice interventions for domestic violence. *Crime & Delinquency, 46*, 252–70.

Dyer, W., & Wilkins, A. (1991). Better stories, not better constructs, to generate better theory: A rejoinder to Eisenhardt. *Academy of Management Review, 16*, 613–19.

Festinger, L., Riecken, H., & Schachter, S. (1956). *When prophecy fails.* New York: Harper & Row.

Fisher, R., & Ma, Y. (2014). The price of being beautiful: Negative effects of attractiveness on empathy for children in need. *Journal of Consumer Research*, 41. doi:10.1086/676967

Foran, C. (2010). *Mordecai: The life and times.* Toronto: Knopf Canada.

Goyder, J., Guppy, N., & Thompson, M. (2003). The allocation of male and female occupational prestige in an Ontario urban area: A quarter-century replication. *Canadian Review of Sociology and Anthropology, 40*, 417–39.

Greene, J. (2000). Understanding social programs through evaluation. In N. Denzin & Y. Lincoln (Eds.), *Handbook of Qualitative Research* (2nd ed.). Thousand Oaks, CA: SAGE.

Hanson, R.K., Broom, I., & Stephenson, M. (2004). Evaluating community sex offender treatment programs: A 12-year follow-up of 724 offenders. *Canadian Journal of Sociology, 36*, 87–96.

Houghton, E. (1998). Sex is good for you. *Guardian*, 92, 14–15.

Huey, L. (2003). Explaining Odlin Road: Insecurity and exclusivity. *Canadian Journal of Sociology, 28*, 367–86.

Hughes, E. (1943). *French Canada in transition.* Chicago: University of Chicago Press.

Kerr, D. (2004). Family transformations and the well-being of children: Recent evidence from Canadian longitudinal data. *Journal of Comparative Family Studies, 35*, 73–90.

Kerr, D., & Michalski, J. (2007). Family structure and children's hyperactivity problems: A longitudinal analysis. *Canadian Journal of Sociology, 32*, 85–112.

Knopik, V.S., Neiderhiser, J.M., DeFries, J.C., & Plomin, R. (2017). *Behavioural genetics* (7th ed.). New York: Worth.

Knott, C. (2016). Contentious mobilities and cheap(er) labour: Temporary foreign workers in a New Brunswick seafood processing community. *Canadian Journal of Sociology, 41*, 375–97.

Laplante, B. (2006). The rise of cohabitation in Quebec: Power of religion and power over religion. *Canadian Journal of Sociology, 31*, 1–24.

Lewis, O. (1961). *The children of Sánchez.* New York: Vintage.

Lipset, S. (1990). *Continental divide: The values and institutions of the United States and Canada.* New York: Routledge.

Lynd, R., & Lynd, H. (1929). *Middletown: A study in contemporary American culture.* New York: Harcourt Brace.

Lynd, R., & Lynd, H. (1937). *Middletown in transition: A study in cultural conflicts.* New York: Harcourt Brace.

Mead, M. (1928). *Coming of age in Samoa.* New York: Morrow.

Menard, S. (1991). *Longitudinal research.* Newbury Park, CA: SAGE.

Michaud, S. (2001). The National Longitudinal Study of Children and Youth—Overview and changes after three cycles. *Canadian Studies in Population, 28*, 391–405.

Nemni, M., & Nemni, M. (2006). *Young Trudeau: Son of Quebec, father of Canada, 1919–1944.* W. Johnson (Trans.). Toronto: Douglas Gibson Books.

Pawson, R., & Tilley, N. (1997). *Realistic evaluation.* London: SAGE.

Phinney, A., Moody, E., & Small, J. (2014). The effect of a community-engaged arts program on older adults' well-being. *Canadian Journal on Aging, 33*, 336–45.

Pratt, A., & Valverde, M. (2002). From deserving victims to "masters of confusion": Redefining refugees in the 1900s. *Canadian Journal of Sociology, 27*, 135–62.

Radley, A., & Chamberlain, K. (2001). Health psychology and the study of the case: From method to analytic concern. *Social Science and Medicine, 53*, 321–32.

Rinehart, J. (1996). *The tyranny of work* (3rd ed.). Toronto: Harcourt Brace.

Rosenthal, R., & Jacobson, L. (1968). *Pygmalion in the classroom: Teacher expectation and pupils' intellectual development.* New York: Holt, Rinehart & Winston.

Rosnow, R.L., & Rosenthal, R. (1997). *People studying people: Artefacts and ethics in behavioral research.* New York: W.H. Freeman.

Russell, R., & Tyler, M. (2002). Thank heaven for little girls: "Girl Heaven" and the commercial context of feminine childhood. *Sociology, 36*, 619–37.

Sanderson, S.K. (2001). *The evolution of human sociality: A Darwinian conflict perspective.* Lanham, MD: Rowman & Littlefield.

Scriven, M. (1991). *Evaluation thesaurus* (4th ed.). Newbury Park, CA: SAGE.

Seabrook, J., & Avison, W. (2015). Family structure and children's socioeconomic attainment: A Canadian sample. *Canadian Review of Sociology, 52*, 66–88.

Shalla, V. (2002). Jettisoned by design? The truncated employment relationship of customer sales and service agents under airline restructuring. *Canadian Journal of Sociology, 27*, 1–32.

Shepherd, R.P., & Graham, K.A.H. (2020). Evaluation in Indigenous contexts: An introduction to practice. *Canadian Journal of Program Evaluation, 34.3*, 391–99.

Smith, N., Lister, R., & Middleton, S. (2004). Longitudinal qualitative research. In S. Becker & A. Bryman (Eds.), *Understanding research for social policy and practice: Themes, methods, and approaches*. Bristol: Policy Press.

Stake, R.E. (1995). *The art of case study research*. Thousand Oaks, CA: SAGE.

Statistics Canada. (2010). *Detailed information for 2008–2009 (Cycle 8)*. National Longitudinal Survey of Children and Youth (NLSCY). http://www23.statcan.gc.ca/imdb/p2SV.pl?Function=getSurvey&SDDS=4450

Tilley, N. (2000). Doing realistic evaluation of criminal justice. In V. Jupp, P. Davies, & P. Francis (Eds.), *Doing criminological research*. London: SAGE.

Truth and Reconciliation Commission of Canada. (2015). *Honouring the truth, reconciling for the future: Summary of the final report of the Truth and Reconciliation Commission of Canada*. http://caid.ca/TRCFinExeSum2015.pdf

Walsh, M., Hickey, C., & Duffy, J. (1999). Influence of item content and stereotype situation on gender differences in mathematical problem solving. *Sex Roles, 41*, 219–40.

Walters, D. (2004). A comparison of the labour market outcomes of postsecondary graduates of various levels and fields over a four-cohort period. *Canadian Journal of Sociology, 29*, 1–27.

White, J. (1990). *Hospital strike*. Toronto: Thompson.

Wilson, B. (2002). The Canadian rave scene and five theses on youth resistance. *Canadian Journal of Sociology, 27*, 373–4412.

Yin, R. (1984). *Case study research: Design and methods*. Beverly Hills, CA: SAGE.

Young, N., & Dugas, E. (2012). Comparing climate change coverage in Canadian English- and French-language print media: Environmental values, media cultures, and the narration of global warming. *Canadian Journal of Sociology, 37*, 25–54.

Chapter 3

Aronson, E. (1992). *The social animal* (6th ed.). New York: W.H. Freeman and Company.

Bailey, K.D. (1994). *Methods of social research* (4th ed.). Toronto: Maxwell Macmillan Canada.

Beagan, B. (2001). Micro inequities and everyday inequalities: "Race," gender, sexuality and class in medical school. *Canadian Journal of Sociology, 26*, 583–610.

Blair, G., Imai, K., & Zhou, Y.Y. (2015). Design and analysis of the randomized response technique. *Journal of the American Statistical Association*, 110, 1304–19.

Blum, B. (2018, June 7). The lifespan of a lie: The most famous psychology study of all time was a sham. Why can't we escape the Stanford Prison Experiment? *Medium GEN*.

Canadian Institutes of Health Research, Natural Sciences and Engineering Research Council of Canada, and Social Sciences and Humanities Research Council (2018). *Tri-council policy statement: Ethical conduct for research involving humans*. Her Majesty the Queen in Right of Canada.

Canadian Institutes of Health Research, Natural Sciences and Engineering Research Council of Canada, and Social Sciences and Humanities Research Council of Canada (1998, with 2000, 2002, 2005 amendments). *Tri-council policy statement: Ethical conduct for research involving humans*. Public Works and Government Services Canada.

Castonguay, P. (2017, June 7). Quebec ruling reaffirms research data confidentiality. *University Affairs*. https://www.universityaffairs.ca/news/news-article/quebec-ruling-reaffirms-research-data-confidentiality/

Charbonneau, L. (2005, June 6). Ethics boards harming survey research, says York professor. *University Affairs*. http://www.universityaffairs.ca/ethics-boards-harming-survey-research-says-york-professor.aspx

Desroches, F. (1990). Tearoom trade: A research update. *Qualitative Sociology, 13*, 39–61.

Le Devoir. (2016, November 3). L'affaire Maillé, ou l'avenir de la confidentialité dans la recherche scientifique. https://www.ledevoir.com/opinion/libre-opinion/483756/l-affaire-maille-ou-l-avenir-de-la-confidentialite-dans-la-recherche-scientifique

Dinovitzer, R., Hagan, J., & Parker, P. (2003). Choice and circumstance: Social capital and planful competence in the attainments of immigrant youth. *Canadian Journal of Sociology, 28*, 463–88.

Festinger, L., Riecken, H., & Schachter, S. (1956). *When prophecy fails*. New York: Harper & Row.

Gans, H.J. (1962). *The urban villagers*. New York: Free Press.

Goode, E. (1996). The ethics of deception in social research: A case study. *Qualitative Sociology, 19*, 11–33.

Haney, C., Banks, C., & Zimbardo, P. (1973, September). A study of prisoners and guards in a simulated prison. *Naval Research Reviews*, 1–17.

Homan, R. (1991). *The ethics of social research*. London: Longman.

Homan, R., & Bulmer, M. (1982). On the merits of covert methods: A dialogue. In M. Bulmer (Ed.), *Social research ethics*. London: Macmillan.

Humphreys, L. (1970). *Tearoom trade: Impersonal sex in public places*. Chicago: Aldine.

Kimmel, A. (1988). *Ethics and values in applied social research*. Newbury Park, CA: SAGE.

Kondro, W. (2016, November 22). Canadian researcher in legal battle to keep her interviews confidential. *Sciencemag.org*. http://www.sciencemag.org/news/2016/11/canadian-researcher-legal-battle-keep-her-interviews-confidential

Le Texier, T. (2019). Debunking the Standford prison experiment. *American Psychologist, 74*, 823–39.

Milgram, S. (1963). A behavioural study of obedience. *Journal of Abnormal and Social Psychology, 67*, 371–78.

Mosby, I. (2013). Administering colonial science: Nutrition research and human biomedical experimentation in Aboriginal communities and residential schools, 1942–1952. *Histoire sociale/Social History, 46*, 145–72.

O'Connell Davidson, J., & Layder, D. (1994). *Methods, sex, and madness*. London: Routledge.

Perry, G. (2012). *Behind the shock machine: The untold story of the notorious Milgram psychology experiments.* New York: New Press.

Punch, M. (1994). Politics and ethics in qualitative research. In N. Denzin & Y. Lincoln (Eds.), *Handbook of Qualitative Research.* Thousand Oaks, CA: SAGE.

Rosenthal, R., & Jacobson, L. (1968). *Pygmalion in the classroom: Teacher expectation and pupils' intellectual development.* New York: Holt, Rinehart & Winston.

Small, W., Maher, L., & Kerr, T. (2014). Institutional ethical review and ethnographic research involving injection drug users: A case study. *Social Science & Medicine*, 104, 157–62.

Totten, M. (2001). Legal, ethical, and clinical implications of doing fieldwork with youth gang members who engage in serious violence. *Journal of Gang Research, 8*, 35–49.

van den Hoonaard, W.C. (2001). Is research-ethics review a moral panic? *Canadian Review of Sociology and Anthropology, 38*, 19–36.

van den Hoonaard, W.C., & Connolly, A. (2006). Anthropological research in light of research-ethics review: Canadian master's theses, 1995–2004. *Journal of Empirical Research on Human Research Ethics, 1*, 59–69.

van den Hoonaard, W.C., & Tolich, M. (2014). The New Brunswick Declaration of Research Ethics: A simple and radical perspective. *Canadian Journal of Sociology, 39*, 87–97.

Van Maanen, J. (1991). The smile factory: Work at Disneyland. In P. Frost, L. Moore, et al. (Eds.), *Reframing organizational culture.* Newbury Park, CA: Sage.

Vidich, A., & Bensman, J. (1968). *Small town in mass society.* Princeton, NJ: Princeton University Press.

Von Hoffman, N. (1970, January 30). *The sociological snoopers. Washington Post.*

Zimbardo, P. (1971). *The psychological power and pathology of imprisonment.* Statement prepared for the U.S. House of Representatives Committee on the Judiciary, Subcommittee No. 3: Hearings on Prison Reform, San Francisco.

Appendix to Part I

Orwell, G. (2004). *Why I write.* London: Penguin. (Original work published 1946)

Chapter 4

Beardsworth, A., Bryman, A., Ford, J., & Keil, T. (n.d.). *"The dark figure" in statistics of unemployment and vacancies: Some sociological implications.* Discussion paper, Department of Social Sciences, Loughborough University.

Bell, E., Aitken Schermer, J., & Vernon, P.A. (2009). The origins of political attitudes and behaviours: An analysis using twins. *Canadian Journal of Political Science, 42*, 855–79.

Berthoud, R. (2000). A measure of changing health. In R. Berthoud & J. Gershuny (Eds.), *Seven years in the lives of British families: Evidence on the dynamics of social change from the British Household Panel Survey.* Bristol: Policy Press.

Blumer, H. (1956). Sociological analysis and the "variable." *American Sociological Review, 21*, 683–90.

Bourdieu, P. (1987). The historical genesis of a pure aesthetic. *Journal of Aesthetics and Art Criticism, 46* (Analytic Aesthetics), 201–10.

Brannigan, A. (2004). *The rise and fall of social psychology: The use and misuse of the experimental method.* Hawthorne, NY: Aldine de Gruyter.

Bridgman, P. (1927). *The logic of modern physics.* New York: Macmillan.

Bryman, A., & Cramer, D. (2001). *Quantitative data analysis with SPSS release 10 for Windows: A guide for social scientists.* London: Routledge.

Bulmer, M. (1984). Facts, concepts, theories and problems. In M. Bulmer (Ed.), *Social research methods.* London: Macmillan.

Cicourel, A. (1964). *Method and measurement in sociology.* New York: Free Press.

Cicourel, A. (1982). Interviews, surveys, and the problem of ecological validity. *American Sociologist, 17*, 11–20.

Cramer, D. (1998). *Fundamental statistics for social research.* London: Routledge.

Deng, J., Walker, G., & Swinnerton, G. (2006). A comparison of environmental values and attitudes between Chinese in Canada and Anglo-Canadians. *Environment and Behavior, 38*, 22–47.

Edin, K., & Kefalas, M. (2005). *Promises I can keep: Why poor women put motherhood before marriage.* Berkeley: University of California Press.

Foddy, W. (1993). *Constructing questions for interviews and questionnaires: Theory and practice in social research.* Cambridge: Cambridge University Press.

Frazer, R., & Wiersma, U. (2001). Prejudice vs. discrimination in the employment interview: We may hire equally, but our memories harbour prejudice. *Human Relations, 54*, 173–91.

Gabor, T., Hung, K., Mihorean, S., & St-Onge, C. (2002). Canadian homicide rates: A comparison of two data sets. *Canadian Journal of Criminology, 44*, 351–63.

Gazso-Windlej, A., & McMullin, J. (2003). Doing domestic labour: Strategizing in a gendered domain. *Canadian Journal of Sociology, 28*, 341–66.

George, U., & Chaze, F. (2014). Discrimination at work: Comparing the experiences of foreign-trained and locally-trained engineers in Canada. *Canadian Ethic Studies, 46*, 1–21.

Goyder, J., Guppy, N., & Thompson, M. (2003). The allocation of male and female occupational prestige in an Ontario urban area: A quarter-century replication. *Canadian Review of Sociology and Anthropology, 40*, 417–39.

Guppy, L., & Siltanen, J. (1977). A comparison of the allocation of male and female occupational prestige. *Canadian Review of Sociology and Anthropology, 14*, 320–30.

Hay, D. (2014). An investigation into the swiftness and intensity of recent secularization in Canada: Was Berger right? *Sociology of Religion, 75*, 136–62.

Kennedy, E., Krogman, N., & Krahn, H. (2013). Sustainable consumption and the importance of neighbourhood: A central city/suburb comparison. *Canadian Journal of Sociology, 38*, 359–83.

LaPiere, R.T. (1934). Attitudes vs. actions. *Social Forces, 13*, 230–37.

Logie, C.H, Lys, C.L., Okumu, M. & Fujioka, J. (2019). Exploring factors associated with condom use self-efficacy and condom use among Northern and Indigenous adolescent peer leaders in Northern Canada. *Vulnerable Children and Youth Studies, 14*, 50–62.

Murphy, L., & Fedoroff, J. (2013). Sexual offenders' views of Canadian sex offender registries: A survey of a clinical sample. *Canadian Journal of Behavioural Science*, *45*, 238–49.

Reiner, R. (2000). Crime and control in Britain. *Sociology*, *34*, 71–94.

Ricciardelli, R., & Clow, K. (2009). Men, appearance, and cosmetic surgery: The role of self-esteem and comfort with the body. *Canadian Journal of Sociology*, *34*, 105–34.

Ritchie, S. (2020). *Science fictions: How fraud, bias, negligence, and hype undermine the search for truth*. New York: Henry Holt and Company.

Saba, R. (2020, July 22). New study confirms COVID-19 rates and deaths far more prevalent at for-profit long-term care homes than non-profits. *Toronto Star*. https://www.thestar.com/business/2020/07/22/new-study-confirms-covid-19-cases-and-deaths-far-more-prevalent-at-for-profit-long-term-care-homes-than-non-profits.html

Schieman, S., & Narisada, A. (2014). In control or fatalistically ruled? The sense of mastery among working Canadians. *Canadian Review of Sociology*, *51*, 343–74.

Schuman, H., & Presser, S. (1981). *Questions and answers in attitude surveys: Experiments on question form, wording, and context*. San Diego, CA: Academic Press.

Silverman, R., Sacco, V., & Teevan, J. (2000). *Crime in Canadian society*. Toronto: Harcourt Canada.

Sobel, N. (2015). A typology of the changing narratives of Canadian citizens through time. *Canadian Ethnic Studies*, *47*, 11–39.

Stall, N.M., Jones, A., Brown, K.A., Rochon, P.A., & Costa, A.P. (2020). For-profit long-term care homes and the risk of COVID-19 outbreaks and resident deaths. *Canadian Medical Association Journal*, early-released July 22. https://doi.org/10.1503/cmaj.201197

Sutton, R.I., & Rafaeli, A. (1992). How we untangled the relationship between displayed emotion and organizational sales: A tale of bickering and optimism. In P. Frost & R. Stablein (Eds.), *Doing exemplary research*. Newbury Park, CA: SAGE.

Teevan, J., & Dryburgh, H. (2000). First person accounts and sociological explanations of delinquency. *Canadian Review of Sociology and Anthropology*, *37*, 77–93.

Chapter 5

Ames, M., Rawana, J., Gentile, P., & Morgan, A. (2015). The protective role of optimism and self-esteem on depressive symptom pathways among Canadian Aboriginal youth. *Journal of Youth and Adolescence*, *44*, 142–54.

Anderson, C., & McGregor, M. (2020). National identity, attentiveness and the two sides of partisanship: the case of the 2015 Canadian federal election. *National Identities*, *22*, 347–66 .doi:10.1080/14608944.2019.1634036

Anderson, K., Sebaldt, R., Lohfeld, L., Burgess, K., Donald, F., & Kaczorowski, J. (2006). Views of family physicians in southwestern Ontario on preventive care services and performance incentives. *Family Practice*, *23*, 469–71.

Andrews, K., Smith, L., Henzi, D., & Demps, E. (2007). Faculty and student perceptions of academic integrity at U.S. and Canadian dental schools. *Journal of Dental Education*, *71*, 1027–39.

Bampton, R., & Cowton, C.J. (2002). The e-interview. *Forum: Qualitative Social Research*, *3*. http://www.qualitative-research.net/index.php/fqs/article/view/848

Beagan, B. (2001). Micro inequities and everyday inequalities: "Race," gender, sexuality and class in medical school. *Canadian Journal of Sociology*, *26*, 583–610.

Beardsworth, A., & Keil, T. (1997). *Sociology on the menu: An invitation to the study of food and society*. London: Routledge.

Beardsworth, A., Keil, T., Goode, J., Haslam, C., & Lancashire, E. (2002). Women, men and food: The significance of gender for nutritional attitudes and choices. *British Food Journal*, 104, 470–91.

Bell, E., Aitken Schermer, J., & Vernon, P.A. (2009). The origins of political attitudes and behaviours: An analysis using twins. *Canadian Journal of Political Science*, *42*, 855–79.

Bell, E., & Kandler, C. (2017). The genetic and the sociological: Exploring the possibility of consilience. *Sociology*, *51*, 880–96.

Beran, T., Hughes, G., & Lupart, J. (2008). A model of achievement and bullying: Analyses of the Canadian National Longitudinal Survey of Children and Youth data. *Educational Research*, *50*, 25–39.

Blauner, R. (1964). *Alienation and freedom: The factory worker and his industry*. Chicago: University of Chicago Press.

Boivin, R., & Leclerc, C. (2016). Domestic violence reported to the police: Correlates of victims' reporting behavior and support to legal proceedings. *Violence and Victims*, *31*, 402–15.

Bottomore, T.B., & Rubel, M. (1963). *Karl Marx: Selected writings in sociology and social philosophy*. Harmondsworth, UK: Penguin.

Brannigan, A., Gemmell, W., Pevalin, D., & Wade, T. (2002). Self-control and social control in childhood misconduct and aggression: The role of family structure and hyperactivity. *Canadian Journal of Criminology*, *44*, 119–42.

Cobanoglu, C., Ward, B., & Moreo, P.J. (2001). A comparison of mail, fax and web-based survey methods. *International Journal of Market Research*, *43*, 441–52.

Coleman, C., & Moynihan, J. (1996). *Understanding crime data: Haunted by the dark figure*. Buckingham: Open University Press.

Comeau, J., Duncan, L., Georgiades, K., Wang, L., & Boyle, M.H. (2020). Social assistance and trajectories of child mental health problems in Canada: evidence from the National Longitudinal Survey of Children and Youth. *Canadian Journal of Public Health*. https://doi.org/10.17269/s41997-020-00299-1

Corti, L. (1993). Using diaries in social research. *Social Research Update*, *2*.

Crook, C., & Light, P. (2002). Virtual society and the cultural practice of study. In S. Woolgar (Ed.), *Virtual society? Technology, cyberbole, reality*. Oxford: Oxford University Press.

Curasi, C. (2001) A critical exploration of face-to-face interviewing vs. computer-mediated interviewing. *International Journal of Market Research*, *43*, 361–75.

Dale, A., Arber, S., & Proctor, M. (1988). *Doing secondary analysis*. London: Unwin Hyman.

Durkheim, E. (1952). *Suicide: A study in sociology*. J. Spaulding & G. Simpson (Trans.). London: Routledge & Kegan Paul. (Original work published 1897)

Elliott, H. (1997). The use of diaries in sociological research on health experience. *Sociological Research Online, 2.* http://www.socresonline.org.uk/socresonline/2/2/7.html

Finch, J. (1987). The vignette technique in survey research. *Sociology, 21,* 105–14.

Fournier, P., Cutler, F., Soroka, S., & Stolle, D. (2015). *The 2015 Canadian Election Study.* https://ces-eec.arts.ubc.ca/english-section/surveys

Fowler, F. (1993). *Survey research methods* (2nd ed.). Newbury Park, CA: SAGE.

Frey, J. (2004). Telephone surveys. In M. Lewis-Beck, A. Bryman, & T. Liao (Eds.), *The SAGE. Encyclopedia of social science research methods.* Thousand Oaks, CA: SAGE.

Friedenreich, C.M, Barberio, A.M., Pader, J., Poirier, A.E., Ruan, Y., Grevers, X . . . Brenner, D.R., on behalf of the ComPARe Study Team. (2019). Estimates of the current and future burden of cancer attributable to lack of physical activity in Canada. *Preventative Medicine, 122,* 65–72.

Gidengil, E., Everitt, J., Blais, A., Fournier, P., & Nevitte, N. (2006). *Gender and vote choice in the 2006 Canadian election.* Paper prepared for the Annual Meeting of the American Political Science Association, Philadelphia.

Glavin, P., Bierman, A., & Schieman, S. (2019, November 23). Gig workers report feeling lonely and powerless. *The Province.* https://theprovince.com/opinion/op-ed/opinion-gig-workers-report-feeling-lonely-and-powerless

Goodyear-Grant, E., & Croskill, J. (2011). Gender affinity effects in vote choice in Westminster systems: Assessing "flexible" voters in Canada. *Politics and Gender, 7,* 223–50.

Goyder, J., Guppy, N., & Thompson, M. (2003). The allocation of male and female occupational prestige in an Ontario urban area: A quarter-century replication. *Canadian Review of Sociology and Anthropology, 40,* 417–39.

Grabb, E., & Curtis, J. (2004). *Regions apart: The four societies of Canada and the U.S.* Don Mills, ON: Oxford University Press.

Hay, D. (2014). An investigation into the swiftness and intensity of recent secularization in Canada: Was Berger right? *Sociology of Religion, 75,* 136–62.

Hessler, R., Downing, J., Beltz, C., Pelliccio, A., Powell, M., & Vale, W. (2003). Qualitative research on adolescent risk using e-mail: A methodological assessment. *Qualitative Sociology, 26,* 111–24.

Historica Canada. (2020, June 26). While half of Canadians know their country contributed to eradicating polio, most don't know the face on their $10 bill. https://www.historicacanada.ca/content/polls/while-half-canadians-know-their-country-contributed-eradicating-polio-most-dont-know

Holbrook, A., Green, M., & Krosnick, J. (2003). Telephone versus face-to-face interviewing of national probability samples with long questionnaires: Comparisons of respondent satisficing and social desirability response bias. *Public Opinion Quarterly, 67,* 79–125.

Kelley, J., & De Graaf, N. (1997). National context, parental socialization, and religious belief: Results from 15 nations. *American Sociological Review, 62,* 639–59.

Kent, R., & Lee, M. (1999). Using the Internet for market research: A study of private trading on the Internet. *Journal of the Market Research Society, 41,* 377–85.

Kerr, D. (2004). Family transformations and the well-being of children: Recent evidence from Canadian longitudinal data. *Journal of Comparative Family Studies, 35,* 73–90.

Kevins, A., & Soroka, S. (2018). Growing apart? Partisan sorting in Canada, 1992–2015. *Canadian Journal of Political Science, 51,* 103–33.

Kingsbury, M., & Coplan, R. (2012). Mothers' gender-role attitudes and their responses to young children's hypothetical display of shy and aggressive behaviours. *Sex Roles, 66,* 506–17.

Krosnick, J., Holbrook, A., Berent, M., Carson, R.T., Hanemann, W.M., Kopp, R.J . . . Conaway (2002). The impact of "no opinion" response options on data quality: Non-attitude reduction or an invitation to satisfice? *Public Opinion Quarterly, 66,* 371–403.

Laurenceau, J.-P., & Bolger, N. (2005). Using diary methods to study marital and family processes. *Journal of Family Psychology, 19,* 86–97.

Légaré, J., Décarie, Y., & Bélanger, A. (2014). Using microsimulation to reassess aging trends in Canada. *Canadian Journal on Aging, 33,* 208–19.

Li, P. (2003). Initial earnings and catch-up capacity of immigrants. *Canadian Public Policy, 29,* 319–37.

Mann, C., & Stewart, F. (2000). *Internet communication and qualitative research: A handbook for researching online.* London: SAGE.

Marin, A., & Hayes, S. (2017). The occupational context of mismatch: Measuring the link between occupations and areas of study to better understand job-worker match. *Canadian Journal of Sociology, 42,* 1–22.

Mata, F., & Pendakur, R. (2017). Of intake and outcomes: Wage trajectories of immigrant classes in Canada. *Journal of International Migration and Integration, 18,* 829–44.

Mayhew, P. (2000). Researching the state of crime. In R. King & E. Wincup (Eds.), *Doing research on crime and justice.* Oxford: Oxford University Press.

O'Connor, H., & Madge, C. (2001). Cyber-mothers: Online synchronous interviewing using conferencing software. *Sociological Research Online, 5.* www.socresonline.org.uk/5/4/o'connor.html.

O'Connor, H., & Madge, C. (2003). "Focus groups in cyberspace": Using the Internet for qualitative research. *Qualitative Market Research, 6,* 133–43.

O'Sullivan, L., Udell, W., & Patel, V. (2006). Young urban adults' heterosexual risk encounters and perceived risk and safety: A structured diary study. *Journal of Sex Research, 43,* 343–51.

Pahl, J. (1990). Household spending, personal spending and the control of money in marriage. *Sociology, 24,* 119–38.

Robinson, J., & Lee, C. (2014). Society's (virtually) time-free transition into the digital age. *Social Indicators Research, 117,* 939–65.

Robinson, J., Shaver, P., & Wrightsman, L. (1999). *Measures of political attitudes.* Toronto: Academic Press.

Schaeffer, D., & Dillman, D. (1998). Development of a standard e-mail methodology. *Public Opinion Quarterly, 62,* 378–97.

Schuman, H., & Presser, S. (1981). *Questions and answers in attitude surveys: Experiments on question form, wording, and context.* San Diego, CA: Academic Press.

Shafer, K., & Renick, A.J. (2020). Depressive symptoms and father involvement in Canada: Evidence from a national study. *Canadian Review of Sociology, 57,* 197–222.

Sheehan, K. and Hoy, M. (1999). Using e-mail to survey Internet users in the United States: Methodology and assessment.

Journal of Computer-Mediated Communication, 4. www.ascusc.org/jcmc/vol4/issue3/sheehan.html

Shuy, R.W. (2002). In-person versus telephone interviewing. In J.F. Gubrium & J.A. Holstein (Eds.), *Handbook of interview research: Context and method.* Thousand Oaks, CA: SAGE.

Sinclair, M., O'Toole, J., Malawaraarachchi, M., & Leder, K. (2012). Comparison of response rates and cost-effectiveness for a community-based survey: postal, Internet and telephone modes with generic or personalized recruitment approaches. *BMC Medical Research Methodology, 12,* 1–8.

Smith, D.J., & McVie, S. (2003). Theory and method in the Edinburgh Study of Youth Transitions and Crime. *British Journal of Criminology, 43,* 169–95.

Statistics Canada. (2019). *The General Social Survey: An overview, 2019.* https://www150.statcan.gc.ca/n1/pub/89f0115x/89f0115x2019001-eng.htm

Sudman, S., & Bradburn, N. (1982). *Asking questions: A practical guide to questionnaire design.* San Francisco: Jossey-Bass.

Sullivan, O. (1996). Time co-ordination, the domestic division of labour and affective relations: Time use and the enjoyment of activities within couples. *Sociology, 30,* 79–100.

Tourangeau, R., & Smith, T.W. (1996). Asking sensitive questions: The impact of data collection mode, question format, and question context. *Public Opinion Quarterly, 60,* 275–304.

Tse, A. (1998). Comparing the response rate, response speed and response quality of two methods of sending questionnaires: E-mail vs. mail. *Journal of the Market Research Society, 40,* 353–61.

Walklate, S. (2000). Researching victims. In R. King & E. Wincup (Eds.), *Doing research on crime and justice.* Oxford: Oxford University Press.

Walters, D. (2004). A comparison of the labour market outcomes of postsecondary graduates of various levels and fields over a four-cohort period. *Canadian Journal of Sociology, 29,* 1–27.

Wright, K.B. (2005). Researching Internet-based populations: Advantages and disadvantages of online survey research, online questionnaire authoring software packages, and web survey services. *Journal of Computer-Mediated Communication, 10.* https://doi.org/10.1111/j.1083-6101.2005.tb00259.x

Chapter 6

Bales, R. (1951). *Interaction process analysis.* Cambridge, MA: Addison-Wesley.

Bell, E. (2007). Separatism and quasi-separatism in Alberta. *Prairie Forum, 32,* 335–55.

Cahalan, S. (2019). *The Great Pretender.* New York and Boston: Grand Central.

Charlton, T., Gunter, B., & Coles, D. (1998). Broadcast television as a cause of aggression? Recent findings from a naturalistic study. *Emotional and Behavioural Difficulties, 3,* 5–13.

Galton, M., Simon, B., & Croll, P. (1980). *Inside the primary classroom.* London: Routledge & Kegan Paul.

Katz, J., Kuffel, S., & Coblentz, A. (2002). Are there gender differences in sustaining dating violence? *Journal of Family Violence, 17,* 247–71.

LaPiere, R.T. (1934). Attitudes vs. actions. *Social Forces, 13,* 230–37.

McCall, M.J. (1984). Structured field observation. *Annual Review of Sociology, 10,* 263–82.

Normand, S., Schneider, B., Lee, M., Maisonneuve, M., Chupetlovska-Anastasova, A., Kuehn, S., & Robaey, P. (2013). Continuities and changes in the friendships of children with and without ADHD: A longitudinal, observational study. *Journal of Abnormal Child Psychology, 41,* 1161–75.

Perrucci, R., Belshaw, R., DeMerritt, A., Frazier, B., Jones, J., Kimbrough, J., … Williams, B. (2000). The two faces of racialized space at a predominantly white university. *International Journal of Contemporary Sociology, 37,* 230–44.

Roethlisberger, F., & Dickson, W. (1939). *Management and the worker.* Cambridge, MA: Harvard University Press.

Rosenhan, D.L. (1973). On being sane in insane places. *Science, 179,* 350–58.

Schulenberg, J.L. (2014). Systematic social observation of police decision-making: The process, logistics, and challenges in a Canadian context. *Quality and Quantity, 48,* 297–315.

Webb, E.J., Campbell, D.T., Schwartz, R.D., & Sechrest, L. (1966). *Unobtrusive measures: Non-reactive measures in the social sciences.* Chicago: Rand McNally.

Weber, B. (2020, March 31). Experts study how coronavirus pandemic affects trust in officials, ourselves. *CBC News.* https://www.cbc.ca/news/canada/edmonton/alberta-covid-coronavirus-public-trust-research-1.5515929

Weber, M. (1947). *The theory of social and economic organization.* A.M. Henderson & T. Parsons (Trans.). New York: Free Press.

Whyte, W.F. (1955). *Street corner society* (2nd ed.). Chicago: University of Chicago Press.

Chapter 7

Beagan, B. (2001). Micro inequities and everyday inequalities: "Race," gender, sexuality and class in medical school. *Canadian Journal of Sociology, 26,* 583–610.

Becker, H. (1963). *Outsiders: Studies in the sociology of deviance.* New York: Free Press.

Bowen, R. (2015). Squaring up: Experiences of transition from off-street sex work to square work and duality—concurrent involvement in both—in Vancouver, BC. *Canadian Review of Sociology, 52,* 429–49.

Bryman, A. (1995). *Disney and his worlds.* London: Routledge.

Bryman, A. (1999). Global Disney. In P. Taylor & D. Slater (Eds.), *The American century.* Oxford: Blackwell.

Buchanan, C. (2014). A more national representation of place in Canadian daily newspapers. *Canadian Geographer, 58,* 517–30.

Collins, R.E. (2014). "Beauty and bullets": A content analysis of female offenders and victims in four Canadian newspapers. *Journal of Sociology, 52,* 296–310.

Czaja, R., & Blair, J. (1996). *Designing surveys: A guide to decisions and procedures.* Thousand Oaks, CA: SAGE.

Dinovitzer, R., Hagan, J., & Parker, P. (2003). Choice and circumstance: Social capital and planful competence in the attainments of immigrant youth. *Canadian Journal of Sociology, 28,* 463–88.

Dumitrica, D., & Bakardjieva, M. (2018). The personalization of engagement: The symbolic construction of social media and grassroots mobilization in Canadian newspapers. *Media, Culture & Society, 40,* 817–37.

Finch, J., & Hayes, L. (1994). Inheritance, death and the concept of the home. *Sociology, 28,* 417–33.

Fowler, F. (1993). *Survey research methods* (2nd ed.). Newbury Park, CA: SAGE.

Frey, J. (2004). Telephone surveys. In M. Lewis-Beck, A. Bryman, & T. Liao (Eds.), *The SAGE encyclopedia of social science research methods*. Thousand Oaks, CA: SAGE.

Johnson, T., & Wislar, J. (2012). Response rates and nonresponse errors in surveys. *Journal of the American Medical Association*, 307, 1805–06.

Kennedy, E., Krogman, N, & Krahn, H. (2013). Sustainable consumption and the importance of neighbourhood: A central city/suburb comparison. *Canadian Journal of Sociology, 38*, 359–83.

MacKinnon, N., & Luke, A. (2002). Changes in identity attitudes as reflections of social and cultural change. *Canadian Journal of Sociology, 27*, 299–338.

Mairs, K., & Bullock, S. (2013). Sexual-risk behaviour and HIV testing among Canadian snowbirds who winter in Florida. *Canadian Journal on Aging, 32*, 145–58.

Mangione, T.W. (1995). *Mail surveys: Improving the quality*. Thousand Oaks, CA: SAGE.

Schieman, S., & Narisada, A. (2014). In control or fatalistically ruled? The sense of mastery among working Canadians. *Can. Review of Sociology, 51*, 343–74.

Shuy, R.W. (2002). In-person versus telephone interviewing. In J.F. Gubrium & J.A. Holstein (Eds.), *Handbook of interview research: Context and method*. Thousand Oaks, CA: SAGE.

Smith, T.W. (1995). Trends in non-response rates. *International Journal of Public Opinion Research, 7*, 157–71.

Taniguchi, K. (2020, July 10). Majority view racism as provincial problem: poll. *Winnipeg Free Press*. https://www.winnipegfreepress.com/local/majority-of-manitobans-support-anti-racism-demonstrations-survey-571712532.html

Tastsoglou, E., & Miedema, B. (2003). Immigrant women and community development in the Canadian Maritimes: Outsiders within? *Canadian Journal of Sociology, 28*, 203–34.

Teitler, J., Reichman, N., & Sprachman, S. (2003). Costs and benefits of improving response rates for a hard-to-reach population. *Public Opinion Quarterly, 67*, 126–38.

Whalen, H., & Schmidt, G. (2016). The women who remain behind: challenges in the LDC lifestyle. *Rural Society, 25*, 1–14.

Wiens, K., Bhattarai, A., Pedram, P., Dores, A., Williams, J., Bulloch, A., & Patten, S. (2020). A growing need for youth mental health services in Canada: Examining trends in youth mental health from 2011 to 2018. *Epidemiology and Psychiatric Sciences 29*, e115, 1–9. https://doi.org/10.1017/S204579602000028

Chapter 8

Anderssen, E. (2014, October 2). Big data is watching you. Has online spying gone too far? *The Globe and Mail*. https://www.theglobeandmail.com/life/relationships/big-data-is-watching-you-has-online-spying-gone-too-far/article20894498/?page=all

Agresti, A., & Finlay, B. (2009). *Statistical methods for the social sciences*. Upper Saddle River, NJ: Prentice Hall.

Bryman, A., & Cramer, D. (2001). *Quantitative data analysis with SPSS release 10 for Windows: A guide for social scientists*. London: Routledge.

Cao, L. (2014). Aboriginal people and confidence in the police. *Canadian Journal of Criminology and Criminal Justice, 56*, 499–525.

Jones, A.M. (2020, April 11). Phone data reveals who is staying home during COVID-19. *CTV News*. https://www.ctvnews.ca/health/coronavirus/phone-data-reveals-who-is-staying-home-during-covid-19-1.4892194

Noack, A.M. (2018). *Social statistics in action: A Canadian introduction*. Don Mills: Oxford University Press.

Rippeyoung, P. (2013). Can breastfeeding solve inequality? The relative mediating impact of breastfeeding and home environment on poverty gaps in Canadian child cognitive skills. *Canadian Journal of Sociology, 38*, 65–85.

Rojek, C. (1995). *Decentring leisure: Rethinking leisure theory*. London: SAGE.

Sutton, R.I., & Rafaeli, A. (1988). Untangling the relationship between displayed emotions and organizational sales: The case of convenience stores. *Academy of Management Journal, 31*, 461–87.

Chapter 9

Abramovich, A. (2016). Preventing, reducing and ending LGBTQ2S youth homelessness: The need for targeted strategies. *Social Inclusion, 4*, 86–96.

Armstrong, G. (1993). Like that Desmond Morris? In D. Hobbs & T. May (Eds.), *Interpreting the field: Accounts of ethnography*. Oxford: Clarendon Press.

Becker, H.S. (1998). *Tricks of the trade: How to think about your research while doing it*. Chicago: University of Chicago Press.

Belk, R., Sherry, J., & Wallendorf, M. (1988). A naturalistic inquiry into buyer and seller behaviour at a swap meet. *Journal of Consumer Research, 14*, 449–70.

Bell, E. (2007). Separatism and quasi-separatism in Alberta. *Prairie Forum, 32*, 335–55.

Bloor, M. (1997). Addressing social problems through qualitative research. In D. Silverman (Ed.), *Qualitative research: Theory, method and practice*. London: SAGE.

Blumer, H. (1931). Science without concepts. *American Journal of Sociology, 36*, 515–33.

Blumer, H. (1954). What is wrong with social theory? *American Sociological Review, 19*, 3–10.

Blumer, H. (1969). *Symbolic interactionism: Perspective and method*. Berkeley: University of California Press.

Bochner, A., & Ellis, C. (2003). An introduction to the arts and narrative research: Art as inquiry. *Qualitative Inquiry, 9*, 506–14.

Branker, R. (2017). Labour market discrimination: The lived experiences of English-speaking Caribbean immigrants in Toronto. *Journal of International Migration & Integration, 18*, 203–22.

Bryman, A. (1994). The Mead/Freeman controversy: Some implications for qualitative researchers. In R. Burgess (Ed.), *Studies in Qualitative Methodology* (Vol. 4). Greenwich, CT: JAI Press.

Burman, M., Batchelor, S., & Brown, J. (2001). Researching girls and violence: Facing the dilemmas of fieldwork. *British Journal of Criminology, 41*, 443–59.

Charmaz, K. (2003). Grounded theory: Objectivist and constructivist methods. In N.K. Denzin & Y.S. Lincoln (Eds.), *Strategies for qualitative inquiry* (2nd ed.). Thousand Oaks, CA: SAGE.

Charmaz, K. (2008). A future for symbolic interactionism. *Studies in Symbolic Interaction, 32*, 51–59.

Coloma, R., & Pino, F. (2016). "There's hardly anything left": Poverty and the economic insecurity of elderly Filipinos in Toronto. *Canadian Ethnic Studies, 48*, 71–97.

Dolson, M.S. (2018). The role of unpredictability in ethnographic fieldwork. In S.W. Kleinknecht, L.K. van den Scott, & C.B. Sanders (Eds.), *The craft of qualitative research: A handbook*. Toronto: Canadian Scholars.

Finlay, L. (2006). "Rigour," "ethical integrity" or "artistry"? Reflexively reviewing criteria for evaluating qualitative research. *British Journal of Occupational Therapy, 69*, 319–26.

Gans, H.J. (1962). *The urban villagers*. New York: Free Press.

Geertz, C. (1973). Thick description: Toward an interpretive theory of culture. In *The Interpretation of Cultures*. New York: Basic Books.

Golafshani, N. (2003). Understanding reliability and validity in qualitative research. *The Qualitative Report, 8*, 597–606.

Green, A.I. (2010). Queer unions: Same-sex spouses marrying tradition and innovation. *Canadian Journal of Sociology, 35*, 399–436.

Guba, E., & Lincoln, Y. (1994). Competing paradigms in qualitative research. In N. Denzin & Y. Lincoln (Eds.), *Handbook of qualitative research*. Thousand Oaks, CA: SAGE.

Hallgrimsdottir, H., Phillips, R., & Benoit, C. (2006). Fallen women and rescued girls: Social stigma and media narratives of the sex industry in Victoria, B.C., from 1980 to 2005. *Canadian Review of Sociology and Anthropology, 43*, 265–80.

Hammersley, M. (1992). Deconstructing the qualitative–quantitative divide. In *What's wrong with ethnography?* London: Routledge.

Hochschild, A. (1983). *The managed heart*. Berkeley and Los Angeles: University of California Press.

Karabanow, J. (2002). Open for business: Exploring the life stages of two Canadian street youth shelters. *Journal of Sociology and Social Welfare, 29*, 99–116.

Kleinknecht, S. (2011). The hacker spirit: An interactionist analysis of the hacker ideology. In E. Ksenych (Ed.), *Exploring deviance in Canada*. Toronto: Oxford University Press.

Lassiter, L.E. (2005). *The Chicago guide to collaborative ethnography*. Chicago: University of Chicago Press.

Leidner, R. (1993). *Fast food, fast talk: Service work and the routinization of everyday life*. Berkeley and Los Angeles: University of California Press.

Lewis, O. (1961). *The children of Sánchez*. New York: Vintage.

Lincoln, Y., & Guba, E. (1985). *Naturalistic inquiry*. Beverly Hills, CA: SAGE.

Lofland, J., & Lofland, L. (1995). *Analyzing social settings: A guide to qualitative observation and analysis*. (3rd ed.). Belmont, CA: Wadsworth.

Lyon, K., & Frohard-Dourlent, H. (2015). Let's talk about the institution: Same-sex common-law partners negotiating marriage equality and relationship legitimacy. *Canadian Review of Sociology, 52*, 402–28.

Mason, J. (2002). *Qualitative researching* (2nd ed.). London: SAGE.

McDonough, P., & Polzer, J. (2012). Habitus, hysteresis, and organizational change in the public sector. *Canadian Journal of Sociology, 37*, 357–79.

Pettigrew, A. (1997). What is a processual analysis? *Scandinavian Journal of Management, 13*, 337–48.

Prus, R. (1997). *Subcultural mosaics and intersubjective realities: An ethnographic agenda for pragmatizing the social sciences*. New York: SUNY Press.

Renzetti, E. (2017, January 6). Women killed by their spouses are not casualties in someone else's story. *The Globe and Mail*. https://www.theglobe andmail.com/opinion/women-killed-by-their-spouses-are-not-casualties-in-someone-elses-story/article33535098

Santin, M., & Kelly, B. (2017). The managed heart revisited: Exploring the effect of institutional norms on the emotional labor of flight attendants post 9/11. *Journal of Contemporary Ethnography, 46*, 519–43.

Shaffir, W., & Kleinknecht, S. (2005). Death at the polls: Experiencing and coping with political defeat. *Journal of Contemporary Ethnography, 34*, 707–38.

Sharma, S., Reimer-Kirkham, S., & Meyerhoff, H. (2011). Filmmaking with Aboriginal youth for type 2 diabetes prevention. *Pimatisiwin: A Journal of Aboriginal and Indigenous Community Health, 9*, 423–40.

Shelden, D., Angell, M., Stoner, J., & Roseland, B. (2010). School principals' influence on trust: Perspectives of mothers of children with disabilities. *Journal of Educational Research, 103*, 159–70.

Silverman, D. (1993). *Interpreting qualitative data: Methods for analysing qualitative data*. London: SAGE.

Skeggs, B. (1994). Situating the production of feminist ethnography. In M. Maynard & J. Purvis (Eds.), *Researching women's lives from a feminist perspective*. London: Taylor & Francis.

Skeggs, B. (1997). *Formations of class and gender*. London: SAGE.

Whyte, W.F. (1955). *Street corner society* (2nd ed.). Chicago: University of Chicago Press.

Williams, M. (2000). Interpretivism and generalization. *Sociology, 34*, 209–24.

Chapter 10

Armstrong, G. (1993). Like that Desmond Morris? In D. Hobbs & T. May (Eds.), *Interpreting the field: accounts of ethnography*. Oxford: Clarendon Press.

Atkinson, P. (1981). *The clinical experience*. Farnborough, UK: Gower.

Becker, H. (1970). Practitioners of vice and crime. In R. Habenstein (Ed.), *Pathways to data*. Chicago: Aldine.

Bell, E. (2007). Separatism and quasi-separatism in Alberta. *Prairie Forum, 32*, 335–55.

Benbow, S., & Hall, J. (2018). Negotiating tensions in exiting the field of critical qualitative research. In S.W. Kleinknecht, L.K. van den Scott, & C.B. Sanders (Eds.), *The craft of qualitative research: A handbook*. Toronto: Canadian Scholars.

Breckenridge, J., & Jones, D. (2009). Demystifying theoretical sampling in grounded theory research. *Grounded Theory Review, 8*, 113–26.

Browne, A.J. (2007). Clinical encounters between nurses and First Nations women in a western Canadian hospital. *Social Science & Medicine, 64*, 2165–76.

Campbell, M. (2000). Research on health care experiences of people with disabilities: Exploring the social organization of service delivery. *Canadian Journal of Sociology, 1*, 131–54.

Charmaz, K. (2000). Grounded theory: Objectivist and constructivist methods. In N. Denzin & Y. Lincoln (Eds.), *Handbook of qualitative research* (2nd ed.). Thousand Oaks, CA: SAGE.

Coffey, A. (1999). *The ethnographic self: Fieldwork and the representation of reality*. London: SAGE.

Devault, M. (2006). Introduction: What is institutional ethnography? *Social Problems*, 53, 294–98.

Ditton, J. (1977). *Part-time crime: An ethnography of fiddling and pilferage*. London: Macmillan.

Edwards, N. (2018). On (still) being emotionally attached to the field. In S.W. Kleinknecht, L.K. van den Scott, & C.B. Sanders (Eds.), *The craft of qualitative research: A handbook*. Toronto: Canadian Scholars.

Fine, G. (1996). Justifying work: Occupational rhetorics as resources in kitchen restaurants. *Administrative Science Quarterly, 41*, 90–115.

Gans, H.J. (1968). The participant-observer as human being: Observations on the personal aspects of field work. In H. Becker (Ed.), *Institutions and the person: Papers presented to Everett C. Hughes*. Chicago: Aldine.

Gerson, K., & Horowitz, R. (2002). Observation and interviewing: Options and choices. In T. May (Ed.), *Qualitative research in action*. London: SAGE.

Giulianotti, R. (1995). Participant observation and research into football hooliganism: Reflections on the problems of entrée and everyday risks. *Sociology of Sport Journal, 12*, 1–20.

Glaser, B., & Strauss, A. (1967). *The discovery of grounded theory: Strategies for qualitative research*. Chicago: Aldine.

Glucksmann, M. (1994). The work of knowledge and the knowledge of women's work. In M. Maynard & J. Purvis (Eds.), *Researching women's lives from a feminist perspective*. London: Taylor & Francis.

Goffman, E. (1956). *The presentation of self in everyday life*. New York: Doubleday.

Gold, R. (1958). Roles in sociological fieldwork. *Social Forces, 36*, 217–23.

Hallett, R., & Barber, K. (2014). Ethnographic research in a cyber era. *Journal of Contemporary Ethnography, 43*, 306–30.

Hammersley, M., & Atkinson, P. (1995). *Ethnography: Principles in practice* (2nd ed.). London: Routledge.

Hessler, R., Downing, J., Beltz, C., Pelliccio, A., Powell, M., & Vale, W. (2003). Qualitative research on adolescent risk using e-mail: A methodological assessment. *Qualitative Sociology, 26*, 111–24.

Hier, S. (2002). Raves, risks and the ecstasy panic: A case study in the subversive nature of moral regulation. *Canadian Journal of Sociology, 27*, 33–57.

Hobbs, D. (1988). *Doing the business: Entrepreneurship, the working class and detectives in the east end of London*. Oxford: Oxford University Press.

Holtby, A., Klein, K., Cook, K., & Travers, R. (2015). To be seen or not to be seen: Photovoice, queer and trans youth, and the dilemma of representation. *Action Research, 13*, 317–35.

Humphreys, L. (1970). *Tearoom trade: Impersonal sex in public places*. Chicago: Aldine.

Karabanow, J. (2002). Open for business: Exploring the life stages of two Canadian street youth shelters. *Journal of Sociology and Social Welfare, 29*, 99–116.

Kleinknecht, S.W., van den Scott, L.K., & Sanders, C.B. (Eds.). (2018). *The craft of qualitative research: A handbook*. Toronto: Canadian Scholars.

Lauder, M. (2003). Covert participant observation of a deviant community: Justifying the use of deception. *Journal of Contemporary Religion*, 18, 185–96.

Lee-Treweek, G. (2000). The insight of emotional danger: Research experiences in a home for the elderly. In G. Lee-Treweek & S. Linkogle (Eds.), *Danger in the field: Risk and ethics in social research*. London: Routledge.

Leidner, R. (1993). *Fast food, fast talk: Service work and the routinization of everyday life*. Berkeley and Los Angeles: University of California Press.

Lofland, J., & Lofland, L. (1995). *Analyzing social settings: A guide to qualitative observation and analysis* (3rd ed.). Belmont, CA: Wadsworth.

Norris, C. (1993). Some ethical considerations on fieldwork with the police. In D. Hobbs & T. May (Eds.), *Interpreting the field: Accounts of ethnography*. Oxford: Clarendon Press.

Pink, S. (2001). *Visual ethnography*. London: SAGE.

Plana, V. (2019, December 4). UBC professor to debunk unwritten rules, behaviour of public transit riders. *Daily Hive*. https://dailyhive.com/vancouver/ubc-amy-hanser-rules-behaviour-bus-riders

Ranasinghe, P. (2017). *Helter shelter: Security, legality and an ethic of care in an emergency shelter*. Toronto: University of Toronto Press.

Ratković, S., & Sethi, B. (2018). Dissemination and social justice. In S.W. Kleinknecht, L.K. van den Scott, & C.B. Sanders (Eds.), *The craft of qualitative research: A handbook*. Toronto: Canadian Scholars.

Restoule, J., Mashford-Pringle, A., Chacaby, M, Smillie, C., Brunette, C., & Russel, G. (2013). Supporting successful transitions to post-secondary education for Indigenous Students: Lessons from an institutional ethnography in Ontario, Canada. *International Indigenous Policy Journal, 4*, 1–10.

Rosenhan, D.L. (1973). On being sane in insane places. *Science, 179*, 350–58.

Sanjek, R. (1990). A vocabulary for fieldnotes. In R. Sanjek (Ed.), *Fieldnotes: The making of anthropology*. Ithaca, NY: Cornell University Press.

Santin, M., & Kelly, B. (2017). The managed heart revisited: Exploring the effect of institutional norms on the emotional labor of flight attendants post 9/11. *Journal of Contemporary Ethnography, 46*, 519–43.

Sarsby, J. (1984). The fieldwork experience. In R. Ellen (Ed.), *Ethnographic research: A guide to general conduct*. London: Academic Press.

Schulenberg, J.L. (2014). Systematic social observation of police decision-making: The process, logistics, and challenges in a Canadian context. *Quality and Quantity, 48*, 297–315.

Shaffir, W. (2018). Leaving the field trajectories: Researching Hasidic Jews. In S.W. Kleinknecht, L.K. van den Scott, & C.B. Sanders (Eds.), *The craft of qualitative research: A handbook*. Toronto: Canadian Scholars.

Smith, D. (2005). *Institutional ethnography: A sociology for people*. Walnut Creek, CA: AltaMira Press.

Strauss, A., & Corbin, J. (1990). *Basics of qualitative research: Grounded theory procedures and techniques.* Newbury Park, CA: SAGE.

Strauss, A., & Corbin, J. (1998). *Basics of qualitative research: Techniques and procedures for developing grounded theory.* Thousand Oaks, CA: SAGE.

Taylor, A. (1993). *Women drug users: An ethnography of an injecting community.* Oxford: Clarendon Press.

Totten, M. (2001). Legal, ethical, and clinical implications of doing fieldwork with youth gang members who engage in serious violence. *Journal of Gang Research, 8,* 35–49.

van den Scott, J. (2018). Leaving the field/Can you leave the field? In S.W. Kleinknecht, L.K. van den Scott, & C.B. Sanders (Eds.), *The craft of qualitative research: A handbook.* Toronto: Canadian Scholars.

van den Scott, L.K. (2018). Role transitions in the field and reflexivity: From friend to researcher. (In special issue: Emotion and the researcher: Sites, subjectivities and relationships). *Studies in Qualitative Methodology, 16,* 19–32.

Van Maanen, J. (1991). Playing back the tape: Early days in the field. In W. Shaffir & R. Stebbins (Eds.), *Experiencing fieldwork: An inside view of qualitative research.* Newbury Park, CA: SAGE.

Whyte, W.F. (1955). *Street corner society* (2nd ed.). Chicago: University of Chicago Press.

Wilson, B. (2002). The Canadian rave scene and five theses on youth resistance. *Canadian Journal of Sociology, 27,* 373–412.

Winlow, S., Hobbs, D., Lister, S., & Hadfield, P. (2001). Get ready to duck: Bouncers and the realities of ethnographic research on violent groups. *British Journal of Criminology, 41,* 536–48.

Wolcott, H. (1990). *Writing up qualitative research.* Newbury Park, CA: SAGE.

Wolf, D. (1991). High risk methodology: Reflections on leaving an outlaw society. In W. Shaffir & R. Stebbins (Eds.), *Experiencing fieldwork: An inside view of qualitative research.* Newbury Park, CA: SAGE.

Chapter 11

Adriaenssens, C., & Cadman, L. (1999). An adaptation of moderated e-mail focus groups to assess the potential of a new online (Internet) financial services offer in the UK. *Journal of the Market Research Society, 41,* 417–24.

Ajodhia-Andrews, A. (2016). Reflexively conducting research with ethnically diverse children with disabilities. *The Qualitative Report, 21,* 252–87.

Armstrong, G. (1993). Like that Desmond Morris? In D. Hobbs & T. May (Eds.), *Interpreting the field: Accounts of ethnography.* Oxford: Clarendon Press.

Atkinson, M. (2002). Pretty in ink: Conformity, resistance and negotiation in women's tattooing. *Sex Roles, 47,* 219–35.

Atkinson, M. (2004). Tattooing and civilizing processes. *Canadian Review of Sociology and Anthropology, 41,* 125–46.

Atkinson, P. (1990). *The ethnographic imagination: Textual constructions of society.* London: Routledge.

Atkinson, P. (2004). Life story interview. In M. Lewis-Beck, A. Bryman, & T. Liao (Eds.), *The SAGE. encyclopedia of social science research methods.* Thousand Oaks, CA: SAGE.

Bampton, R., & Cowton, C.J. (2002). The e-interview. *Forum: Qualitative Social Research, 3.* http://www.qualitative-research.net/index.php/fqs/article/view/848

Barter, C., & Renold, E. (1999). The use of vignettes in qualitative research. *Social Research Update,* 25.

Beardsworth, A., & Keil, T. (1992). The vegetarian option: Varieties, conversions, motives and careers. *Sociological Review, 40,* 253–93.

Becker, H., & Geer, B. (1957). Participant observation and interviewing: A comparison. *Human Organization, 16,* 28–32.

Bell, E. (2007). Separatism and quasi-separatism in Alberta. *Prairie Forum, 32,* 335–55.

Bloor, M., Frankland, S., Thomas, M., & Robson, K. (2001). *Focus groups in social research.* London: SAGE.

Bryman, A. (1999). Global Disney. In P. Taylor & D. Slater (Eds.), *The American century.* Oxford: Blackwell.

Bryman, A., Stephens, M., & Campo, C. (1996). The importance of context: Qualitative research and the study of leadership. *Leadership Quarterly, 7,* 353–70.

Charmaz, K. (2002). Qualitative interviewing and grounded theory analysis. In J. Gubrium & J. Holstein (Eds.), *Handbook of interview research: Context and method.* Thousand Oaks, CA: SAGE.

Clapper, D., & Massey, A. (1996). Electronic focus groups: A framework for exploration. *Information and Management, 30,* 43–50.

Curasi, C. (2001). A critical exploration of face-to-face interviewing vs. computer-mediated interviewing. *International Journal of Market Research, 43,* 361–75.

Davies, P. (2000). Doing interviews with female offenders. In V. Jupp, P. Davies, & P. Francis (Eds.), *Doing criminological research.* London: SAGE.

Deacon, D., Pickering, M., Golding, P., & Murdock, G. (1999). *Researching communications: A practical guide to methods in media and cultural analysis.* London: Arnold.

Eady, A., Dobinson, C., & Ross, L. (2011). Bisexual people's experiences with mental health services: A qualitative investigation. *Community Mental Health Journal, 47,* 378–89.

Frohlich, K., Potvin, L., Chabot, P., & Corin, E. (2002). A theoretical and empirical analysis of context: Neighbourhoods, smoking, and youth. *Social Science and Medicine, 54,* 1401–17.

Gubrium, J., & Holstein, J. (1997). *The new language of qualitative method.* New York: Oxford University Press.

Hanna, Paul. (2012). Using Internet technologies (such as Skype) as a research medium: A research note. *Qualitative Research, 12,* 239–42.

Hine, V. (2000). *Virtual ethnography.* London: SAGE.

Holbrook, B., & Jackson, B. (1996). Shopping around: Focus group research in North London. *Area, 28,* 136–42.

Hughes, R. (1998). Considering the vignette technique and its application to a study of drug injecting and HIV risk and safer behaviour. *Sociology of Health and Illness, 20,* 381–400.

Jones, Z., & Hannem, S. (2018). Escort clients' sexual scripts and constructions of intimacy in commodified sexual relationships. *Symbolic Interaction,* 41, 488–512.

Kitzinger, J. (1993). Understanding AIDS: Researching audience perceptions of acquired immune deficiency syndrome.

In J. Eldridge (Ed.), *Getting the message: News, truth and power.* London: Routledge.
Kitzinger, J. (1994). The methodology of focus groups: The importance of interaction between research participants. *Sociology of Health and Illness, 16*, 103–21.
Krueger, R. (1998). *Moderating focus groups.* Thousand Oaks, CA: SAGE.
Kvale, S. (1996). *Interviews: An introduction to qualitative research interviewing.* Thousand Oaks, CA: SAGE.
Lareau, A., & Weininger, E. (2003). Cultural capital in educational research: A critical assessment. *Theory and Society, 32*, 185–96.
Lett, D., Hier, S.P., & Walby, K. (2010). CCTV surveillance and the civic conversation: A study in public sociology. *Canadian Journal of Sociology, 35*, 437–62.
Lewis, O. (1961). *The children of Sánchez.* New York: Vintage.
Lofland, J., & Lofland, L. (1995). *Analyzing social settings: A guide to qualitative observation and analysis* (3rd ed.). Belmont, CA: Wadsworth.
Madge, C., & O'Connor, H. (2002). On-line with e-mums: Exploring the Internet as a medium of research. *Area, 34*, 92–102.
Madriz, M. (2000). Focus groups in feminist research. In N. Denzin & Y. Lincoln (Eds.), *Handbook of qualitative research* (2nd ed.). Thousand Oaks, CA: SAGE.
Maiolino, E. (2019). Words and deeds: Social movement actors' assessments of allied politicians. In J.M. Everitt & A. Wagner (Eds.), *Gendered mediation: Identity and image making in Canadian politics.* Vancouver: UBC Press.
Malbon, B. (1999). *Clubbing: Dancing, ecstasy and vitality.* London: Routledge.
Mann, C., & Stewart, F. (2000). *Internet communication and qualitative research: A handbook for researching online.* London: SAGE.
Mason, J. (2002). Qualitative interviewing: Asking, listening, interpreting. In T. May (Ed.), *Qualitative Research in Action.* London: SAGE.
Miller, R.L. (2000). *Researching life stories and family histories.* London: SAGE.
Milne, E. (2016). "I have the worst fear of teachers": Moments of inclusion and exclusion in family/school relationships among Indigenous families in southern Ontario. *Canadian Review of Sociology, 53*, 270–89.
Milne, E. (2017). Implementing Indigenous education policy directives in Ontario public schools: Experiences, challenges and successful practices. *International Indigenous Policy Journal, 8*, 1–20.
Miraftab, F. (2000). Sheltering refugees: The housing experience of refugees in Metropolitan Vancouver, Canada. *Canadian Journal of Urban Research, 9*, 42–63.
Morgan, D. (1998). *Planning focus groups.* Thousand Oaks, CA: SAGE.
Morgan, D. (2002). Focus group interviewing. In J. Gubrium & J. Holstein (Eds.), *Handbook of interview research: Context and method.* Thousand Oaks, CA: SAGE.
Morgan, D., & Spanish, M. (1985). Social interaction and the cognitive organization of health-relevant behaviour. *Sociology of Health and Illness, 7*, 401–22.
O'Connor, H., & Madge, C. (2001). Cyber-mothers: Online synchronous interviewing using conferencing software. *Sociological Research Online, 5.* www.socresonline.org.uk/5/4/o'connor.html.
O'Connor, H., & Madge, C. (2003). "Focus groups in cyberspace": Using the Internet for qualitative research. *Qualitative Market Research, 6*, 133–43.
Parker, M. (2000). *Organizational culture and identity.* London: SAGE.
Poland, B.D. (1995). Transcription quality as an aspect of rigor in qualitative research. *Qualitative Inquiry, 1*, 290–310.
Price, T., & Puddephatt, A. (2018). "Opening access" to open access editors: Communication technologies in long distance interviewing. In S.W. Kleinknecht, L.K. van den Scott, & C.B. Sanders (Eds.), *The craft of qualitative research: A handbook.* Toronto: Canadian Scholars.
Proudfoot, S. (2019, July 16). What does it mean to be working class in Canada? *Maclean's.* https://www.macleans.ca/society/what-does-it-mean-to-be-working-class-in-canada/
Rafaeli, A., Dutton, J., Harquail, C.V., & Mackie-Lewis, S. (1997). Navigating by attire: The use of dress by female administrative employees. *Academy of Management Journal, 40*, 9–45.
Ricciardelli, R. (2019). *Also serving time: Canada's provincial and territorial correctional officers.* Toronto: University of Toronto Press.
Ricciardelli, R., & Adorjan, M. (2019). "If a girl's photo gets sent around, that's a way bigger deal than if a guy's photo gets sent around": Gender, sexting, and the teenage years. *Journal of Gender Studies*, 28, 563–77.
Schlesinger, P., Dobash, R.E., Dobash, R.P., & Weaver, C. (1992). *Women viewing violence.* London: British Film Institute.
Silverman, D. (1993). *Interpreting qualitative data: Methods for analysing qualitative data.* London: SAGE.
Smith, R. (2008). Pain in the act: The meanings of pain among professional wrestlers. *Qualitative Sociology, 31*, 129–48.
Sugiman, P. (2004). Memories of the internment: Narrating Japanese-Canadian women's life stories. *Canadian Journal of Sociology, 29*, 359–88.
Sweet, C. (2001). Designing and conducting virtual focus groups. *Qualitative Market Research, 4*, 130–35.
Tastsoglou, E., & Miedema, B. (2003). Immigrant women and community development in the Canadian Maritimes: Outsiders within? *Canadian Journal of Sociology, 28*, 203–34.
Torelli, J. (2019). On entering the field: Notes from a neophyte researcher. *Qualitative Sociology Review*, 15, 64–92.
Trow, M. (1957). Comment on "Participant Observation and Interviewing: A Comparison." *Human Organization, 16*, 33–35.
Tse, A. (1999). Conducting electronic focus group discussions among Chinese respondents. *Journal of the Market Research Society, 41*, 407–15.
Wilkinson, S. (1998). Focus groups in feminist research: Power, interaction, and the co-production of meaning. *Women's Studies International Forum, 21*, 111–25.
Wilkinson, S. (1999). Focus group methodology: A review. *International Journal of Social Research Methodology, 1*, 181–203.
Wilson, B. (2002). The Canadian rave scene and five theses on youth resistance. *Canadian Journal of Sociology, 27*, 373–412.

Wright, R., Alaggia, R., & Krygsman, A. (2014). Five-year follow-up study of the qualitative experiences of youth in an after-school arts program in low-income communities. *Journal of Social Science Research, 40*, 137–46.

Chapter 12

Abraham, J. (1994). Bias in science and medical knowledge: The Opren controversy. *Sociology, 28*, 717–36.

Altheide, D.L. (2004). Ethnographic content analysis. In M. Lewis-Beck, A. Bryman, & T. Liao (Eds.), *The SAGE. encyclopedia of social science research methods*. Thousand Oaks, CA: SAGE.

Altheide, D.L., & Schneider, C.J. (2013). *Qualitative media analysis* (2nd ed.). Thousand Oaks, CA: SAGE.

Atkinson, J.M., & Drew, P. (1979). *Order in court: The organization of verbal interaction in judicial settings*. London: Macmillan.

Bell, E. (2007). Separatism and quasi-separatism in Alberta. *Prairie Forum, 32*, 335–55.

Bell, E., Jansen, H., & Young, L. (2007). Sustaining a dynasty in Alberta: The 2004 provincial election. *Canadian Political Science Review, 1*, 27–49.

Bhuyan, R., Jeyapal, D., Ku, J., Sakamoto, I., & Chou, E. (2017). Branding "Canadian experience" in immigration policy: Nation building in a neoliberal era. *Journal of International Migration & Integration, 18*, 47–62.

Billig, M. (1991). *Ideology and opinions: Studies in rhetorical psychology*. Cambridge: Cambridge University Press.

Blaikie, A. (2001). Photographs in the cultural account: Contested narratives and collective memory in the Scottish islands. *Sociological Review, 49*, 345–67.

Blommaert, J., & Bulcaen, C. (2000). Critical Discourse Analysis. *Annual Review of Anthropology, 29*, 447–66.

Bryman, A. (1995). *Disney and his worlds*. London: Routledge.

Buchanan, C. (2014). A more national representation of place in Canadian daily newspapers. *Canadian Geographer, 58*, 517–30.

Choi, G.Y. & Lewallen, J. (2018). "Say Instagram, kids!": Examining sharenting and children's digital representations on Instagram. *Howard Journal of Communications*, 29, 144–64.

Clayman, S., & Gill, V.T. (2004). Conversation analysis. In M. Hardy & A. Bryman (Eds.), *Handbook of data analysis. London*: SAGE.

Coté, J., & Allahar, A. (1994). *Generation on hold: Coming of age in the late twentieth century*. Toronto: Stoddart.

Crook, C., & Light, P. (2002). Virtual society and the cultural practice of study. In S. Woolgar (Ed.), *Virtual society? Technology, cyberbole, reality*. Oxford: Oxford University Press.

Dickinson, H. (1993). Accounting for Augustus Lamb: Theoretical and methodological issues in biography and historical sociology. *Sociology, 27*, 121–32.

Disney Miller, D. (1956). *The story of Walt Disney*. New York: Dell.

Dumitrica, D., & Bakardjieva, M. (2018). The personalization of engagement: The symbolic construction of social media and grassroots mobilization in Canadian newspapers. *Media, Culture & Society*, 40, 817–37.

Dunning, E., Murphy, P., & Williams, J. (1988). *The roots of football hooliganism: An historical and sociological study*. London: Routledge.

Fenton, N., Bryman, A., & Deacon, D. (1998). *Mediating social science*. London: SAGE.

Finkel, E., Eastwick, P., Karney, B., Reis, H., & Sprecher, S. (2012). Online dating: A critical analysis from the perspective of psychological science. *Psychological Science in the Public Interest, 13*, 3–66.

Forster, N. (1994). The analysis of company documentation. In C. Cassell & G. Symon (Eds.), *Qualitative methods in organizational research*. London: SAGE.

Garfinkel, H. (1967). *Studies in ethnomethodology*. Englewood Cliffs, NJ: Prentice Hall.

Gill, R. (1996). Discourse analysis: Practical implementation. In J. Richardson (Ed.), *Handbook of qualitative research methods for psychology and the social sciences*. Leicester: BPS Books.

Gill, R. (2000). Discourse analysis. In M. Bauer & G. Gaskell (Eds.), *Qualitative researching with text, image and sound*. London: SAGE.

Giulianotti, R. (1997). Enlightening the North: Aberdeen fanzines and local football identity. In G. Armstrong & R. Giulianotti (Eds.), *Entering the field: New perspectives on world football*. Oxford: Berg.

Gottdiener, M. (1997). *The theming of America: Dreams, visions and commercial spaces*. Boulder, CO: Westview Press.

Graydon, S. (2019, February 8). Graydon: In numbers there is strength—how big data can help close the gender gap in Canadian journalism. *Ottawa Citizen*. https://ottawacitizen.com/opinion/columnists/graydon-in-numbers-there-is-strength-how-big-data-can-help-close-the-gender-gap-in-canadian-journalism

Gubrium, J., & Holstein, J. (1997). *The new language of qualitative method*. New York: Oxford University Press.

Hales, J. (2006). An anti-colonial critique of research methodology. In G. Dei & A. Kempf (Eds.), *Anti-colonialism and education: The politics of resistance*. Rotterdam: Sense.

Hall, J., Park, N., Song, H., & Cody, M. (2010). Strategic misrepresentation in online dating: The effects of gender, self-monitoring, and personality traits. *Journal of Social and Personal Relationships, 27*, 117–35.

Hallgrimsdottir, H., Phillips, R., & Benoit, C. (2006). Fallen women and rescued girls: Social stigma and media narratives of the sex industry in Victoria, B.C., from 1980 to 2005. *Canadian Review of Sociology and Anthropology, 43*, 265–80.

Harding, R. (2006). Historical representations of Aboriginal people in the Canadian news media. *Discourse & Society, 17*, 205–35.

Harding, R. (2010). The demonization of Aboriginal child welfare authorities in the news. *Canadian Journal of Communication, 35*, 85–108.

Hatton, E., & Trautner, M. (2013). Images of powerful women in the age of "choice feminism." *Journal of Gender Studies, 22*, 65–78.

Heath, C. (1997). The analysis of activities in face to face interaction using video. In D. Silverman (Ed.), *Qualitative research: Theory, method and practice*. London: SAGE.

Heritage, J. (1984). *Garfinkel and ethnomethodology*. Cambridge, UK: Polity.

Heritage, J. (1987). Ethnomethodology. In A. Giddens & J. Turner (Eds.), *Social theory today*. Cambridge, UK: Polity.

Hier, S. (2000). The contemporary structure of Canadian racial supremacism; Networks, strategies, and new technologies. *Canadian Journal of Sociology, 25*, 471–94.

Hier, S. (2002). Raves, risks and the ecstasy panic: A case study in the subversive nature of moral regulation. *Canadian Journal of Sociology, 27*, 33–57.

Hirsch, J. (1981). *Family photographs*. New York: Oxford University Press.

Hitsch, G., Hortaçscu, A., & Ariely, D. (2010). Matching and scoring in online dating. *American Economic Review, 100*, 130–63.

Hodson, R. (1996). Dignity in the workplace under participative management. *American Sociological Review, 61*, 719–38.

Hutchby, I., & Wooffitt, R. (1998). *Conversation analysis*. Cambridge, UK: Polity.

Jagger, E. (1998). Marketing the self, buying an other: Dating in a post modern, consumer society. *Sociology, 32*, 795–814.

Jagger, E. (2001). Marketing Molly and Melville: Dating in a post-modern, consumer society. *Sociology, 35*, 39–57.

John, I.D. (1992). Statistics as rhetoric in psychology. *Australian Psychologist, 27*, 144–49.

Johnston, G. (2020). The kids are all white: Examining race and representation in news media coverage of opioid overdose deaths in Canada. *Sociological Inquiry*, 90, 123–46.

Johnston, G., Sanscartier, M.D., Johnston, M.S. (2019). Retail therapy: Making meaning out of menial labour. *Journal of Sociology*, 55, 446–62.

Johnston, M.S. (2020). "He sees patients as lesser people": Exploring mental health service users' critiques and appraisals of psychiatrists in Canada. *Disability & Society*, 35, 258–79.

Johnston, M.S., Sanscartier, M.D., & Johnston, G. (2018). Dirty work, dirty resistance: Digital warfare in the era of precarious labor. *Canadian Review of Sociology*, 55, 278–97.

Jones, K. (2000). Constructing rBST in Canada: Biotechnology, instability, and the management of nature. *Canadian Journal of Sociology, 25*, 311–41.

Kempf, A. (2006). Anti-colonial historiography: Interrogating colonial education. In G. Dei & A. Kempf (Eds.), *Anti-colonialism and education: The politics of resistance*. Rotterdam: Sense.

Kennedy, R. (2006). Researching the intersection between collective identity and conceptions of post-separation and divorced fatherhood: A case study fathers for justice, fathers for just us, or fathers are us. *Qualitative Sociology Review, 2*, 75–97.

Lalancette, M., & Raynauld, V. (2019). The power of political image: Justin Trudeau, Instagram, and celebrity politics. *American Behavioral Scientist*, 63, 888–924.

Lynch, M., & Bogen, D. (1997). Sociology's asociological "core": An examination of textbook sociology in the light of the sociology of scientific knowledge. *American Sociological Review, 62*, 481–93.

Mannay, D. (2018). Ethnography in inaccessible fields: Drawing on visual approaches to understand the private sphere of the home. In S.W. Kleinknecht, L.K. van den Scott, & C.B. Sanders (Eds.), *The craft of qualitative research: A handbook*. Toronto: Canadian Scholars.

Marcic, D. (2002). *Respect: Women and popular music*. New York: Texere.

McGuigan, J. (1992). *Cultural populism*. London: Routledge.

Miller, N., & Morgan, D. (1993). Called to account: The CV as an autobiographical practice. *Sociology, 27*, 133–43.

Morton, K. (2016). Hitchhiking and missing and murdered Indigenous women: A critical discourse analysis of billboards on the Highway of Tears. *Canadian Journal of Sociology, 41*, 299–326.

Nettleton, S., Pleace, N., Burrows, R., Muncer, S., & Loader, B. (2002). The reality of virtual social support. In S. Woolgar (Ed.), *Virtual society? Technology, cyberbole, reality*. Oxford: Oxford University Press.

O'Connor, C.D. (2017). The police on Twitter: image management, community building, and implications for policing in Canada. *Policing and Society*, 27, 899–912.

Parnaby, P. (2003). Disaster through dirty windshields: Law, order and Toronto's squeegee kids. *Canadian Journal of Sociology, 28*, 281–307.

Pauwels, L. (2008). A private visual practice going public? Social functions and sociological research opportunities of web-based family photography. *Visual Studies, 23*, 34–49.

Phillips, N., & Brown, J. (1993). Analyzing communications in and around organizations: A critical hermeneutic approach. *Academy of Management Journal, 36*, 1547–76.

Potter, J. (1996). *Representing reality: Discourse, rhetoric and social construction*. London: SAGE.

Potter, J. (1997). Discourse analysis as a way of analysing naturally occurring talk. In D. Silverman (Ed.), *Qualitative research: Theory, method and practice*. London: SAGE.

Potter, J. (2004). Discourse analysis. In M. Hardy & A. Bryman (Eds.), *Handbook of data analysis*. London: SAGE.

Potter, J., & Hepburn, A. (2004). The analysis of NSPCC call openings. In S. Becker & A. Bryman (Eds.), *Understanding research for social policy and practice: Themes, methods, and approaches*. Bristol: Policy Press.

Potter, J., & Wetherell, M. (1994). Analyzing discourse. In A. Bryman & R. Burgess (Eds.), *Analyzing qualitative data*. London: Routledge.

Potter, J., Wetherell, M., & Chitty, A. (1991). Quantification rhetoric—Cancer on television. *Discourse and Society, 2*, 333–65.

Psathas, G. (1995). *Conversation analysis: The study of talk-in-interaction*. Thousand Oaks, CA: SAGE.

Reed, M. (2000). The limits of discourse analysis in organizational analysis. *Organization, 7*, 524–30.

Riches, G., & Dawson, P. (1998). Lost children, living memories: The role of photographs in processes of grief and adjustment among bereaved parents. *Death Studies, 22*, 121–40.

Schegloff, E. (1997). Whose text? Whose context? *Discourse and Society, 8*, 165–87.

Schneider, C., & Hannem, S. (2019). Politicization of sexual misconduct as symbolic annihilation: An analysis of news media coverage of the 2016 "rape election." *Sexuality & Culture, 23*, 737–758.

Scott, J. (1990). *A matter of record*. Cambridge, UK: Polity.

Seale, C. (2002). Cancer heroics: A study of news reports with particular reference to gender. *Sociology, 36*, 107–26.

Silverman, D. (1984). Going private: Ceremonial forms in a private oncology clinic. *Sociology, 18*, 191–204.

Silverman, D. (1993). *Interpreting qualitative data: Methods for analysing qualitative data*. London: SAGE.

Silverman, D. (1994). Analysing naturally occurring data on AIDS counselling: Some methodological and practical issues. In M. Boulton (Ed.), *Challenge and innovation: Methodological advances in social research on HIV/AIDS*. London: Taylor & Francis.

Sturgeon, R., & Morrissette, P. (2010). A qualitative analysis of suicide ideation among Manitoba farmers. *Canadian Journal of Counselling, 44*, 191–207.

Sugiman, P. (2004). Memories of the internment: Narrating Japanese-Canadian women's life stories. *Canadian Journal of Sociology, 29*, 359–88.

Sutton, R.I. (1992). Feelings about a Disneyland visit: Photography and the reconstruction of bygone emotions. *Journal of Management Inquiry, 1*, 278–87.

Thompson, T., & Zerbinos, E. (1995). Gender roles in animated cartoons: Has the picture changed in 20 years? *Sex Roles, 32*, 651–73.

Wada, M., Hurd Clarke, L., & Mortenson, W.B. (2019). "I am busy independent woman who has sense of humor, caring about others": Older adults' self-representations in online dating profiles. *Ageing & Society*, 39, 951–76.

Wetherell, M. (1998). Positioning and interpretative repertoires: Conversation analysis and post-structuralism in dialogue. *Discourse and Society, 9*, 387–412.

Widdicombe, S. (1993). Autobiography and change: Rhetoric and authenticity of "gothic" style. In E. Burman & I. Parker (Eds.), *Discourse analytic research: Readings and repertoires of text*. London: Routledge.

Chapter 13

Atkinson, M. (2002). Pretty in ink: Conformity, resistance and negotiation in women's tattooing. *Sex Roles, 47*, 219–35.

Atkinson, M. (2004). Tattooing and civilizing processes. *Canadian Review of Sociology and Anthropology, 41*, 125–46.

Bissett, K. (2019, April 29). Study of 2018 New Brunswick flooding looks at ways of easing mental health toll. *National Post*. https://nationalpost.com/pmn/news-pmn/canada-news-pmn/study-of-2018-new-brunswick-flooding-looks-at-ways-of-easing-mental-health-toll

Brower, R.L., Bertrand Jones, T., Osborne-Lampkin, L., Hu, S., & Park-Gaghan, T.J. (2019). Big qual: Defining and debating qualitative inquiry for large data sets. *International Journal of Qualitative Methods*, 18, 1–10.

Bryman, A., & Burgess, R. (1994). Reflections on qualitative data analysis. In A. Bryman & R. Burgess (Eds.), *Analyzing qualitative data*. London: Routledge.

Bryman, A., Gillingwater, D., & McGuinness, I. (1996). Industry culture and strategic response: The case of the British bus industry. *Studies in Cultures, Organizations and Societies, 2*, 191–208.

Bury, M. (2001). Illness narratives: Fact or fiction? *Sociology of Health and Illness, 23*, 263–85.

Catterall, M., & Maclaran, P. (1997). Focus group data and qualitative analysis programs: Coding the moving picture as well as snapshots. *Sociological Research Online, 2*. www.socresonline.org.uk/socresonline/2/1/6.html

CBC News. (2019, June 10). *Have back-to-back floods changed views on climate change? UNB prof launches study*. https://www.cbc.ca/news/canada/new-brunswick/new-brunswick-flood-climate-change-research-woodhall-melnik-1.5168912

Charmaz, K. (1983). The grounded theory method: An explication and interpretation. In R. Emerson (Ed.), *Contemporary field research: A collection of readings*. Boston: Little, Brown.

Charmaz, K. (1997). Identity dilemmas of chronically ill men. In A. Strauss & J. Corbin (Eds.), *Grounded theory in practice*. Thousand Oaks, CA: SAGE.

Charmaz, K. (2000). Grounded theory: Objectivist and constructivist methods. In N. Denzin & Y. Lincoln (Eds.), *Handbook of qualitative research* (2nd ed.). Thousand Oaks, CA: SAGE.

Charmaz, K. (2004). Grounded theory. In M. Lewis-Beck, A. Bryman, & T. Liao (Eds.), *The SAGE. encyclopedia of social science research methods*. Thousand Oaks, CA: SAGE.

Charmaz, K. (2006). *Constructing grounded theory: A practical guide through qualitative analysis*. Thousand Oaks, CA: SAGE.

Coffey, A., & Atkinson, P. (1996). *Making sense of qualitative data: Complementary research strategies*. Thousand Oaks, CA: SAGE.

Coffey, A., Holbrook, B., & Atkinson, P. (1996). Qualitative data analysis: Technologies and representations. *Sociological Research Online, 2*. www.socres online.org.uk/socresonline/1/1/4.html

Falconi, E.A., & Graber, K.E. (Eds.). (2019). *Storytelling as narrative practice: Ethnographic approaches to the tales we tell*. Boston: Brill.

Frank, L. (2020). *Out of milk: Infant food insecurity in a rich nation*. Vancouver: UBC Press.

Fraser, E. (2019, May 2). Stress of floodwaters can take toll on mental health. *CBC News*. https://www.cbc.ca/news/canada/new-brunswick/mental-illness-flooding-stress-st-john-river-1.5119636

Glaser, B., & Strauss, A. (1967). *The discovery of grounded theory: Strategies for qualitative research*. Chicago: Aldine.

Hesse-Biber, S. (1995). Unleashing Frankenstein's monster? The use of computers in qualitative research. *Studies in Qualitative Methodology, 5*, 25–41.

Locke, K. (1996). Rewriting The discovery of grounded theory after 25 years? *Journal of Management Inquiry, 5*, 239–45.

Lofland, J., & Lofland, L. (1995). *Analyzing social settings: A guide to qualitative observation and analysis* (3rd ed.). Belmont, CA: Wadsworth.

Lonkila, M. (1995). Grounded theory as an emergent paradigm for computer-assisted qualitative data analysis. In U. Kelle (Ed.), *Computer-aided qualitative data analysis*. London: SAGE.

Miles, M.B. (1979). Qualitative data as an attractive nuisance. *Administrative Science Quarterly, 24*, 590–601.

Miller, R.L. (2000). *Researching life stories and family histories*. London: SAGE.

Okely, J. (1994). Thinking through fieldwork. In A. Bryman & R. Burgess (Eds.), *Analyzing qualitative data*. London: Routledge.

Pidgeon, N., & Henwood, K. (2004). Grounded theory. In M. Hardy & A. Bryman (Eds.), *Handbook of data analysis*. London: SAGE.

Riessman, C.K. (1993). *Narrative analysis*. Newbury Park, CA: SAGE.

Riessman, C.K. (2004a). Narrative interviewing. In M. Lewis-Beck, A. Bryman, & T. Liao (Eds.), *The SAGE. encyclopedia of social science research methods*. Thousand Oaks, CA: SAGE.

Riessman, C.K. (2004b). Narrative analysis. In M. Lewis-Beck, A. Bryman, & T. Liao (Eds.), *The SAGE. encyclopedia of social science research methods*. Thousand Oaks, CA: SAGE.

Roberts, B. (2002). *Biographical research*. Buckingham, UK: Open University Press.

Sanders, C.B., & van den Scott, L.K. (2018). Analyzing materiality. In S.W. Kleinknecht, L.K. van den Scott, & C.B. Sanders (Eds.), *The craft of qualitative research: A handbook*. Toronto: Canadian Scholars.

Stanley, L., & Temple, B. (1995). Doing the business? Evaluating software packages to aid the analysis of qualitative data sets. *Studies in Qualitative Methodology, 5*, 169–97.

Strauss, A. (1987). *Qualitative analysis for social scientists*. New York: Cambridge University Press.

Strauss, A., & Corbin, J. (1990). *Basics of qualitative research: Grounded theory procedures and techniques*. Newbury Park, CA: SAGE.

Strauss, A., & Corbin, J. (1998). *Basics of qualitative research: Techniques and procedures for developing grounded theory*. Thousand Oaks, CA: SAGE.

Tastsoglou, E., & Miedema, B. (2003). Immigrant women and community development in the Canadian Maritimes: Outsiders within? *Canadian Journal of Sociology, 28*, 203–34.

Weaver, A., & Atkinson, P. (1995). *Microcomputing and qualitative data analysis*. Aldershot, UK: Avebury.

Whitehead, K. (2010). "Hunger hurts but starving works": A case study of gendered practices in the online pro-eating-disorder community. *Canadian Journal of Sociology, 35*, 595–626.

Whitehead, P., & Carpenter, D. (1999). Explaining unsafe sexual behaviour: Cultural definitions and health in the military. *Culture, Health, and Sexuality, 1*, 303–15.

Whiting, J., Parker, T., & Houghtaling, A. (2014). Explanations of a violent relationship: The male perpetrator's perspective. *Journal of Family Violence, 29*, 277–86.

Chapter 14

Aurini, J., Missaghian, R., & Pizarro Milian, R. (2020). Educational status hierarchies, after-school activities, and parenting logics: Lessons from Canada. *Sociology of Education*, 93, 173–89.

Barnard, M., & Frischer, M. (1995). Combining quantitative and qualitative approaches: Researching HIV-related risk behaviours among drug injectors. *Addiction Research, 2*, 351–62.

Barron, I. (2013). The potential and challenges of critical realist ethnography. *International Journal of Research and Method in Education, 36*, 117–30.

Bell, E. (2007). Separatism and quasi-separatism in Alberta. *Prairie Forum, 32*, 335–55.

Bell, E., Kandler, C., & Riemann, R. (2018). Genetic and environmental influences on socio-political attitudes: Addressing some gaps in the new paradigm. *Politics and the Life Sciences*, 37, 236–49.

Best, J. (2020). COVID-19 and numeracy: How about them numbers?. *Numeracy, 13*, Article 4.

Bhaskar, R. (1975). *A realist theory of science*. London: Verso.

Bhaskar, R. (1979). *The possibility of naturalism: A philosophical critique of the contemporary human science*. Atlantic Highlands, NJ: Humanities Press.

Bhaskar, R. (1986). *Scientific realism and human emancipation*. Abingdon, UK: Routledge.

Bloor, M. (1997). Addressing social problems through qualitative research. In D. Silverman (Ed.), *Qualitative research: Theory, method and practice*. London: SAGE.

Charmaz, K. (2000). Grounded theory: Objectivist and constructivist methods. In N. Denzin & Y. Lincoln (Eds.), *Handbook of Qualitative Research* (2nd ed.). Thousand Oaks, CA: SAGE.

Childress, C., Calonga, A., & Schneiderhan, E. (2020). Beyond triangulation: Reconstructing Mandela's writing life through propulsive facilitation at the archive. *Qualitative Sociology*, 43, 367–84.

Deacon, D., Bryman, A., & Fenton, N. (1998). Collision or collusion? A discussion of the unplanned triangulation of quantitative and qualitative research methods. *International Journal of Social Research Methodology, 1*, 47–63.

Denzin, N. (1970). *The research act in sociology*. Chicago: Aldine.

Fenton, N., Bryman, A., & Deacon, D. (1998). *Mediating social science*. London: SAGE.

Festinger, L., Riecken, H., & Schachter, S. (1956). *When prophecy fails*. New York: Harper & Row.

Finch, J. (1985). "It's great to have someone to talk to": The ethics and politics of interviewing women. In C. Bell & H. Roberts (Eds.), *Social researching: Politics, problems, practice*. London: Routledge & Kegan Paul.

Gabriel, Y. (1998). The use of stories. In G. Symon & C. Cassell (Eds.), *Qualitative methods and analysis in organizational research*. London: SAGE.

Gephart, R. (1988). *Ethnostatistics: Qualitative foundations for quantitative research*. Newbury Park, CA: SAGE.

Gilbert, G., & Mulkay, M. (1984). *Opening Pandora's box: A sociological analysis of scientists' discourse*. Cambridge: Cambridge University Press.

Glaser, B. (1992). *Basics of grounded theory analysis*. Mill Valley, CA: Sociology Press.

Glock, C. (1988). Reflections on doing survey research. In H. O'Gorman (Ed.), *Surveying social life*. Middletown, CT: Wesleyan University Press.

Gorski, P. (2013). What is critical realism? And why should you care? *Contemporary Sociology, 42*, 658–70.

Hammersley, M. (1996). The relationship between qualitative and quantitative research: Paradigm loyalty versus methodological eclecticism. In J. Richardson (Ed.), *Handbook of research methods for psychology and the social sciences*. Leicester, UK: BPS Books.

Hodson, R. (1996). Dignity in the workplace under participative management. *American Sociological Review, 61*, 719–38.

Hodson, R. (1999). *Analyzing documentary accounts*. Thousand Oaks, CA: SAGE.

Hoye, B. (2020, September 23). Domestic violence research to shed light on heightened risks facing survivors amid pandemic. *CBC News*. https://www.cbc.ca/news/canada/manitoba/intimate-partner-violence-pandemic-manitoba-research-1.5735289

Hughes, K., MacKintosh, A.M., Hastings, G., Wheeler, C., Watson, J., & Inglis, J. (1997). Young people, alcohol, and designer drinks: A quantitative and qualitative study. *British Medical Journal, 314*, 414–18.

Jamieson, J. (2000). Negotiating danger in fieldwork on crime: A researcher's tale. In G. Lee-Treweek & S. Linkogle (Eds.), *Danger in the field: Risk and ethics in social research*. London: Routledge.

Johnson, J., Bottorff, J., Moffat, B., Ratner, P., Shoveller, J., & Lovato, C. (2003). Tobacco dependence: Adolescents' perspectives on the need to smoke. *Social Science and Medicine, 56*, 1481–92.

Kuhn, T. (1970). *The structure of scientific revolutions* (2nd ed.). Chicago: University of Chicago Press.

Lantz, P., & Booth, K. (1998). The social construction of the breast cancer epidemic. *Social Science and Medicine, 46*, 907–18.

MacKinnon, N., & Luke, A. (2002). Changes in identity attitudes as reflections of social and cultural change. *Canadian Journal of Sociology, 27*, 299–338.

Mason, J. (1994). Linking qualitative and quantitative data analysis. In A. Bryman & R. Burgess (Eds.), *Analyzing qualitative data*. London: Routledge.

McAleese, S., & Kilty, J.M. (2019). Stories matter: Reaffirming the value of qualitative research. *The Qualitative Report*, 24, 822–45.

Milkman, R. (1997). *Farewell to the factory: Auto workers in the late twentieth century*. Los Angeles: University of California Press.

Miller, R.L. (2000). *Researching life stories and family histories*. London: SAGE.

Morgan, D. (1998). Practical strategies for combining qualitative and quantitative methods: applications for health research. *Qualitative Health Research, 8*, 362–76.

Nowicki, E., Brown, J., & Stepien, M. (2014). Children's structured conceptualizations of their beliefs on the causes of learning difficulties. *Journal of Mixed Methods Research, 8*, 69–82.

Phelan, P. (1987). Comparability of qualitative and quantitative methods: Studying child sexual abuse in America. *Education and Urban Society, 20*, 35–41.

Phoenix, A. (1994). Practising feminist research: The intersection of gender and "race" in the research process. In M. Maynard & J. Purvis (Eds.), *Researching women's lives from a feminist perspective*. London: Taylor & Francis.

Platt, J. (1986). Functionalism and the survey: The relation of theory and method. *Sociological Review, 34*, 501–36.

Platt, J. (1996). *A history of sociological research methods in America 1920–1960*. Cambridge: Cambridge University Press.

Porter, S. (1993). Critical realist ethnography: The case of racism and professionalism in a medical setting. *Sociology, 27*, 591–609.

Porter, S. (2002). Critical realist ethnography. In T. May (Ed.), *Qualitative research in action*. London: SAGE.

Robinson, J., Shaver, P., & Wrightsman, L. (1999). *Measures of political attitudes*. Toronto: Academic Press.

Ross, L., O'Gorman, L., MacLeod, M., Bauer, G., MacKay, J., & Robinson, M. (2016). Bisexuality, poverty and mental health: A mixed methods analysis. *Social Science & Medicine, 156*, 64–72.

Sanscartier, M.D. (2020). The craft attitude: Navigating mess in mixed methods research. *Journal of Mixed Methods Research*, 14, 47–62.

Schrøder, K.C. (1999). The best of both worlds? Media audience research between rival paradigms. In P. Alasuutari (Ed.), *Rethinking the media audience*. London: SAGE.

Silverman, D. (1985). *Qualitative methodology and sociology: Describing the social world*. Aldershot, UK: Gower.

Strauss, A., & Corbin, J. (1998). *Basics of qualitative research: Techniques and procedures for developing grounded theory*. Thousand Oaks, CA: SAGE.

Tastsoglou, E., & Miedema, B. (2003). Immigrant women and community development in the Canadian Maritimes: Outsiders within? *Canadian Journal of Sociology, 28*, 203–34.

Timans, R., Wouters, P., & Heilbron, J. (2019). Mixed methods research: What it is and what it could be. *Theory and Society*, 48, 193–216.

Wajcman, J., & Martin, B. (2002). Narratives of identity in modern management. *Sociology, 36*, 985–1002.

Walklate, S. (2000). Researching victims. In R. King & E. Wincup (Eds.), *Doing research on crime and justice*. Oxford: Oxford University Press.

Webb, E.J., Campbell, D.T., Schwartz, R.D., & Sechrest, L. (1966). *Unobtrusive measures: Non-reactive measures in the social sciences*. Chicago: Rand McNally.

Wilson, B. (2002). The Canadian rave scene and five theses on youth resistance. *Canadian Journal of Sociology, 27*, 373–412.

Wilson, E.O. (1998). *Consilience: The unity of knowledge*. New York: Knopf.

Chapter 15

Barkham, P., & Jenkins, R. (2002, December 13). Fears for fresher who vanished on mission to talk to the homeless. *The Times* [London].

Becker, H. (1986). *Writing for social scientists: How to start and finish your thesis, book, or article*. Chicago: University of Chicago Press.

Craig, G. (2004). Managing safety in policy research. In S. Becker & A. Bryman (Eds.), *Understanding research for social policy and practice: Themes, methods, and approaches*. Bristol: Policy Press.

Festinger, L., Riecken, H., & Schachter, S. (1956). *When prophecy fails*. New York: Harper & Row.

Golden-Biddle, K. (1997). *Composing qualitative research*. Thousand Oaks, CA: SAGE.

Golden-Biddle, K., & Locke, K. (1993). Appealing work: An investigation of how ethnographic texts convince. *Organization Science, 4*, 595–616.

Lankshear, G. (2000). Bacteria and babies: A personal reflection on researcher's risk in a hospital. In G. Lee-Treweek & S. Linkogle (Eds.), *Danger in the field: Risk and ethics in social research*. London: Routledge.

Lofland, J., & Lofland, L. (1995). *Analyzing social settings: A guide to qualitative observation and analysis* (3rd ed.). Belmont, CA: Wadsworth.

Marx, G.T. (1997). Of methods and manners for aspiring sociologists: 37 moral imperatives. *American Sociologist, 28*, 102–25.

Small, W., Maher, L., & Kerr, T. (2014). Institutional ethical review and ethnographic research involving injection drug users: A case study. *Social Science & Medicine*, 104, 157–62.

Wolcott, H. (1990). *Writing up qualitative research*. Newbury Park, CA: SAGE.

Index